Robert Thorne

Fugitive Facts

An Epitome of General Information

Robert Thorne

Fugitive Facts
An Epitome of General Information

ISBN/EAN: 9783337064068

Printed in Europe, USA, Canada, Australia, Japan

Cover: Foto ©Suzi / pixelio.de

More available books at **www.hansebooks.com**

AN EPITOME OF

GENERAL INFORMATION

*Obtained in Large Part from Sources not Generally Accessible,
and Covering more than One Thousand Topics of General Interest and Frequent Inquiry.*

EDITED BY

ROBERT THORNE, M. A.

NEW YORK:
A. L. BURT, PUBLISHER.

1889.

PREFACE.

THERE ARE many subjects constantly arising in conversation and in general reading upon which many have vague ideas and elusive reminiscences of former knowledge, but upon which few can give any accurate or definite information. If a large encyclopedia is consulted, these particular subjects are often not to be found, or else are treated so exhaustively and scientifically that the average reader finds it tedious and difficult, if not impossible, to ascertain the few essential facts that are desired. The following pages comprise a collection of short articles on just such topics, ranging naturally from the most frivolous to the most serious and scientific, but selected with much care, in order to include those of most general interest and frequent inquiry. Suggestions for many of them have been obtained from the queries in the correspondence departments of periodicals and newspapers. The volume is strictly popular and not intended for scientific reference; but all statements are supported by the best authorities, and in each case the effort and aim have been to state in clear and concise language just the kind and amount of information which are usually sought. The matter has been drawn from a great number of sources, many of them being quite inaccessible to the community at large. Thus, in its purpose and scope, the book is quite unlike any other now in the hands of the public, and suggests a certain sphere of usefulness and convenience which the editor trusts that it will fill.

THE EDITOR.

A DICTIONARY

OF

RARE AND CURIOUS INFORMATION.

Absinthe is a spirit flavored with the pounded leaves and flowering tops of wormwood, together with angelica-root, sweet-flag root, star-anise, and other aromatics. The aromatics are macerated for about eight days in alcohol and then distilled, the result being an emerald-colored liquor. The best absinthe is made in Switzerland, the chief seat of the manufacture being in the canton of Neufchatel. It is chiefly used in France and the United States. The evil effects of drinking this liquor are very apparent; frequent intoxication, or moderate but steady tippling, utterly deranges the digestive system, weakens the frame, induces horrible dreams and hallucinations, and may end in paralysis or in idiocy.

Achromatic Lens is so called because it transmits light without dividing it into colors. The white ray of light is made up of a number of colored rays, which have different degrees of refrangibility. When the direct ray is refracted it divides itself into the colored rays, which deviate in various degrees from the straight line of the simple ray and do not all focus at the same point, thus surrounding the object viewed with a halo of various colors. For many years it was thought that the defect could not be remedied, but the necessary improvement was invented about 1750 by John Dollond. He made a double lens of flint and crown-glass. These two kinds of glass differ as to their power of dispersing colors; so by using a convex lens of crown-glass, with a concave one of flint-glass, an almost colorless image was obtained.

Adam and Eve.—To the Scriptural account of the creation and fall of Adam and Eve the later Jewish writers in the Talmud have made many additions. According to them the stature of Adam, when first created, reached to the heavens, while the splendor of his countenance surpassed that of the sun. The very angels stood in awe of him, and all creatures hastened to worship him. Then the Lord, in order to show the angels his power, caused a sleep to fall upon Adam, and removed a portion of every limb. He thus lost his vast stature, but remained perfect and complete. His first wife was Lilith, the mother of demons; but she fled from him, and afterward Eve was created for him. At the marriage of Adam and Eve angels were present, some playing on musical instruments, others serving up delicious viands, while the sun, moon and stars danced together. The happiness of the human pair excited envy among the angels, and the seraph Sammael tempted them, and succeeded in leading them to their fall from innocence. According to the Koran, all the angels paid homage to Adam excepting Eblis, who, on account of his refusal, was expelled from Paradise. To gratify his revenge, Eblis seduced Adam and Eve, and they were separated. Adam was penitent, and lived in a tent on the site of the Temple of Mecca, where he was instructed in the divine commandments by the Archangel Gabriel. After two hundred years of separation, he again found Eve on Mount Arafat.

Adobe Houses are dwellings peculiar to Central and South America, Mexico and Texas, made of unburnt brick. They are usually one story high, and their durability is much greater than would be expected, as there are a number now in existence which have been standing for considerably more than a century. The composition of the bricks is loamy earth, containing about two-thirds fine sand and one-third clayey dust. This is mixed with water and pressed into the required size in molds, and then taken from the molds and placed on edge on the ground and left to harden in the sun. The adobes are laid with mortar, the same as an ordinary brick, and at the completion of every two feet of the structure an interval of two weeks is allowed for drying, and a similar space of time between the completion of the walls and the putting on of the roof.

Æolian Harp was the invention, it is believed, of Athanasius Kircher, who lived in the seventeenth century, and it is so called from Æolus, the god or ruler of the winds. It is a simple musical instrument, the sounds of which are produced by the vibrations of strings moved by wind. It may be composed of a rectangular box made of thin boards, five or six inches deep and about the same width, and of a length sufficient to extend across the window it is to be set at, so that the breeze coming in can sweep over it. At the top of each end of the box a strip of wood is glued, about a half-inch in height; the strings are then stretched lengthwise across the top of the box, and may be tuned in unison by means of pegs constructed to control their tension, as in the case of a violin. The sounds produced by the rising and falling wind, in passing over the strings, are of a drowsy and lulling character, and have been beautifully described by the poet Thomson as supplying the most suitable kind of music for the *Castle of Indolence.*

Aerial Navigation.—Pilatre des Rosiers made the first balloon ascension at Paris November 21, 1783. His balloon was inflated with heated air. December 1, 1783, an ascension was made by M. Charles, a Professor of Natural Philosophy, at Paris, and at about the same time successful ascensions were also made by Messrs. Rittenhouse and Hopkins, of Philadelphia, hydrogen gas being used in these instances for inflating purposes. The valve at the top of the balloon, and the hoop attached to the balloon with netting, by which is suspended the car, are the inventions of M.

Charles. In 1785 a successful passage of the English Channel was made by M. Blanchard, the first professional aeronaut, and an American traveler named Dr. Jeffries. The use of ropes for the purpose of steadying balloons was first adopted by M. Gay-Lussac, in 1803. From 1852 to 1884 French, German and American aeronauts labored with degrees of success to improve the method of construction and to invent a means for the propulsion of balloons, and in the latter year Captains Renard and Krebs produced an airship which was considered the crowning effort in this line of invention. This ship was a cigar-shaped balloon, carrying a platform, on which the steering and propelling apparatus was placed. The balloon was made of strong silk and covered with a light netting of cords. It was 197 feet long and 39 feet in diameter. To the netting was suspended the platform, 131 feet long and 10 feet broad, on the front of which was fixed the propeller, a screw of light, wooden frame-work and air-tight cloth. The rudder was at the rear of the platform. The propeller was driven by electricity, generated by a dynamo, which was in turn driven by stored electricity. The first ascension of this ship fully satisfied the most sanguine expectations of its builders. It was driven seven miles and back in the space of forty minutes, and obeyed fully every movement of the rudder. During the siege of Paris, in the Franco-German war of 1870–'71, ballooning was extensively used by the besieged for communication with the outer world, and also by the besiegers for military purposes, and since that date military ballooning has become an important subject of study and experiment by soldiers.

Æsthetics is a term invented about the middle of the last century by Baumgarten, a Professor of Philosophy in the University of Frankfort-on-the-Oder, to denote the science of the Beautiful, particularly of art, as the most perfect manifestation of the Beautiful. Notwithstanding the fact that the Beautiful was a favorite subject of contemplation among the ancients, Baumgarten is held to be the first who considered the subject from the true scientific point of view, and therefore entitled to be called the founder of the philosophy of art. All sensuous apprehension, not in one form or manifestation only, but in every possible form or manifestation, was included in his view of the subject, and this conception he expressed by the word Æsthetics, from the Greek *aistha-nomai*, I feel—indicating not absolute nor subjective knowledge of things, but such as is conditioned subjectively by the play of our sensibilities. Beauty was, with Baumgarten, the result of the highest and purest æsthetic perception, to the realization of which the finer portion of our nature aspires, and to trace which, through the whole sphere of art, was the work of æsthetic philosophy.

Age of Animals.—The exact age attained by animals other than those domesticated it is of course impossible to ascertain. It is believed, however, among East Indians, that the elephant lives about 300 years, and instances are on record of the animals having been kept in captivity as long as 130 years, their ages being unknown when they were first taken from the forest. Camels live from 40 to 50 years; horses average from 20 to 30, oxen about 20, sheep 8 or 9, and dogs from 12 to 14 years. The age of a whale is ascertained by the size and number of the laminæ of certain organs in the mouth, formed of a horny substance commonly called whalebone. These laminæ increase yearly, and if the mode of computation be correct, it is known that whales have attained to the age of 400 years. Some species of birds attain a great age. The swan has been known to live 100 years, and it is recorded that the raven has exceeded that age. Parrots have been known to live 80 years. Pheasants and domestic poultry rarely exceed 12 or 15 years. Among fishes and animals that live in the water great age is often attained. The carp has been known to live 200 years. Common river trout have been confined in a well 30 and even 50 years; and a pike was caught in 1497 in a lake near Heilbronn, in Swabia, with a brass ring attached to it recording that it was placed in the lake in the year 1230.

Ages, The.—The term "Age" is used in mythology to designate various epochs in the civilization of the human race. According to Ovid there were four such Ages, but Hesiod indicates five. The Golden Age, synchronous with the reign of Saturn, was a period of innocence and happiness, of patriarchal simplicity, when the earth yielded its fruits spontaneously, and when spring had no end. The Silver Age, under the rule of Jupiter, was a lawless or voluptuous time, when the seasons were divided, when agriculture assumed the form of a craft, and when men began to hold property in land. The Brazen Age was during the reign of Neptune, and was an epoch of war and violence. The era of Mars was the Heroic Age (omitted by Ovid), and it was filled with adventures, and was also warlike. The Golden Age of Roman literature is reckoned from the time of Livius Andronicus, about 250 years before Christ, to the time of Augustus Cæsar's death, A. D. 14. In English literature we have the Elizabethan Age, when so many eminent scholars and writers lived. Hesiod believed himself to be living in the Iron or Plutonian Age, when justice and piety were no longer upon the earth. This idea of a succession of Ages is so natural that it has inwrought itself into the religious convictions of almost all nations. It is sanctioned by Scripture, for it is symbolically adopted in the Apocalypse to a certain extent; it also manifests itself in the sacred books of the Indians. Modern Philosophy, at least in Germany and France, has also attempted to divide human history into definite Ages or periods. Fichte numbers five, of which he conceives that we are the third; Hegel and Auguste Comte reckon three, placing us in the last.

Agnosticism.—According to Herbert Spencer, a celebrated teacher of that school, agnosticism is the belief that the existence of a personal Deity can be neither proved nor disproved, because of the necessary limits of the human mind, or because of the insufficiency of the evidence furnished by psychical or physical data to warrant a positive conclusion. The words "agnosticism" and "agnostic" are derived from the Greek, signifying simply "not to know."

Agriculture, Department of.—Previous to February, 1889, the Department of Agriculture was simply a bureau. Shortly before it adjourned, the Fiftieth Congress passed a bill making the bureau a Department and the Commissioner of Agriculture a Secretary and a member of the Cabinet. Norman J. Colman, who had been commissioner of the bureau from 1885, was made Secretary of the Department by President Cleveland, and held the position until the advent of the new administration in March, when Jeremiah M. Rusk succeeded by appointment to the position. The duty of the Secretary of Agriculture consists mainly in procuring information concerning agriculture and in compiling agricultural statistics, and publishing the same at intervals in pamphlet form for distribution through the country. He has also the supervision of the purchase and distribution of rare seeds and plants; and the conduct of experiment-farms established by Congress is largely under his direction. Another important duty of the department is the investigation of the diseases of animals and the enforcement of laws against the sale of diseased stock. The salary of the Secretary is the same as that of the other Cabinet officers, *i. e.*, $8,000 per annum.

Alabama Claims were demands made upon Great Britain by the United States for damages caused by the destruction of her shipping by the privateers in the service of the Southern Confederacy which were built, or armed and equipped in and sailed from British ports. The vessel which committed the most depredations upon the United States shipping was the Alabama, which gave its name to the claims. Commissioners appointed by the two Governments, after thirty-four meetings, agreed upon the Treaty of Washington, proclaimed in force July 4, 1871, by which the claims were referred to a Tribunal of Arbitration, to be composed of one arbitrator named by the King of Italy, one by the Emperor of Brazil, one by the President of Switzerland, one by the Queen of Great Britain, and one by the President of the United States. The appointees were, respectively, Count Federigo Sclopis, of Salerano; Baron Itajuba; M. Jaques Staempfli; Sir Alexander Cockburn, Lord Chief Justice; and Charles Francis Adams, Esq. J. C. Bancroft Davis represented the United States as agent, presenting their case to the Tribunal; Lord Tenterden represented England in the same capacity. Their ultimate decision, September 14, 1872, signed by all except Sir Alexander Cockburn, who filed a long, dissenting opinion, was an award of $15,500,000, in gold, to be paid by Great Britain to the United States. The Tribunal sat in Geneva, and hence this is commonly called the Geneva Award. It was paid by Great Britain in 1874.

Alaska was purchased by the United States from Russia in 1867 for $7,200,000 in gold, and was formally taken possession of October 9th of the same year by General Rousseau on behalf of the United States at New Archangel, on the Island of Sitka. With the islands, it comprises 580,107 square miles, or nearly one-sixth of the entire area of the United States previous to this purchase. The land abounds in fur-bearing animals; the seas yield fur-bearing seals and others, and fish in immense quantities. Among other important resources of the Territory are lumber and minerals of all kinds. The southwestern part is covered for thousands of miles with dense forests of yellow cedar, white spruce, and balsam fir. Among the valuable minerals, coal has been found at different places along the coast; petroleum, lead, iron and graphite at various points; copper, marble and sulphur in great abundance; also gold and silver and valuable stones, such as amethysts, garnets, agates, and carnelians. The climate of the Territory is very severe in the inland districts, but mild along the coast. At Fort Yukon the thermometer sinks as low as seventy degrees below zero in the winter; the summers are short and hot, the winters long and cold. In Southern Alaska the winter climate is the average winter climate of Kentucky, and the summer climate about that of Minnesota. The capital of Alaska is Sitka, and the Territory is governed by a Governor and other necessary officers appointed by the authorities at Washington. The trade of seal-hunting is entirely in the hands of the Alaska Commercial Company, who in 1870 secured, by Act of Congress, a monopoly of this business for twenty years. They are not allowed, however, to kill the animals except during certain months in the year, nor more than a specified number annually.

Albigenses.—About the beginning of the thirteenth century various sects of heretics abounded in the south of France, and to these was applied the name Albigenses. The name arose from the circumstance that the district of Albigeois in Languedoc—now in the department of Tarn, of which Albi is the capital—was the first point against which the crusade of Pope Innocent III, 1209, was directed. The immediate pretense of the crusade was the murder of the papal legate and inquisitor, Peter of Castelnau, who had been commissioned to extirpate heresy in the dominions of Count Raymond VI of Toulouse; but its real object was to deprive the Count of his lands, as he had become an object of hatred from his toleration of the heretics. It was in vain that he had submitted to the most humiliating penance and flagellation from the hands of the legate Milo, and had purchased the papal absolution by great sacrifices. The expedition took by storm Beziers, the capital of Raymond's nephew Roger, and massacred 20,000 of the inhabitants, Catholics as well as heretics. Simon, Count of Montfort, who conducted the crusade under the legates, proceeded in the same relentless way with other places in the territories of Raymond and his allies. The conquered lands were given to Simon de Montfort, and by him were eventually ceded to Louis VIII. Raymond VI and Raymond VII disputed the possession of the land by the King, and after thousands had perished on both sides a peace was concluded in 1229, at which Raymond VII purchased relief from the ban of the Church by immense sums of money, gave up Narbonne and several lordships to Louis IX, and had to make his son-in-law, the brother of Louis, heir of his other possessions. The heretics were handed over to the proselyting zeal of the Order of Dominicans and the bloody tribunals of the Inquisition, and both used their utmost power to bring the recusant Albigenses to the stake. From the middle of the thirteenth century the name of the Albigenses gradually disappears.

Alexandrian Codex is an important manuscript of the Sacred Scriptures written in Greek. It is written on parchment, in finely-formed uncial letters, and is without accents, marks of aspiration, or spaces between the words. Its probable date is the latter half of the sixth century. With the exception of a few gaps it contains the whole Bible in Greek, along with the Epistles of Clemens Romanus. This celebrated manuscript, which is now in the British Museum, belonged, as early as 1098, to the library of the Patriarch of Alexandria. In 1628 it was sent as a present to Charles I of England by Cyrillus Lucaris, Patriarch of Constantinople, who declared that he got it from Egypt; and that it was written there appears from internal and external evidence.

Alexandrian Library contained in the time of Cleopatra about 700,000 volumes or rolls, and was founded at the suggestion of Demetrius Phalereus, a fugitive from Athens in the reign of Ptolemy Soter. The greater portion of this remarkable collection was destroyed during the Alexandrine war. This loss, however, was repaired by Marc Antony, who presented to Cleopatra the library taken at the siege of Pergamos. From this time until about the year 391 A. D. the library increased in size and reputation, and contained treasures of learning in all known tongues. At the burning of the Temple of Jupiter Serapis by the Christians under Theodosius the Great, about that year, a portion of the library was destroyed, and when the Arabs, under Caliph Omar, took the city in 640 A. D., the destruction of the remainder was completed.

Alexandrines.—The name Alexandrines is most probably derived from an old French poem on Alexander the Great, belonging to the twelfth or thirteenth century, and signifies rhyming verses consisting each of twelve syllables of six measures. This measure was first used in the poem referred to. The Alexandrine has become the regular epic or heroic verse of the French, among whom each line is divided in the middle into two hemistichs, the sixth syllable always ending a word. The only considerable English poem written wholly in Alexandrines is Drayton's *Polyolbion*.

Alhambra, The, is the name given to the fortress which forms a sort of acropolis or citadel to the city of Granada, and in which stood the palace of the ancient Moorish Kings of Granada. The name is a corruption of the Arabic, *Kal-at-al hamra*, "the red castle." It is surrounded by a strong wall, more than a mile in circuit, and studded with towers. The towers on the north wall, which is defended by Nature, were used as residences connected with the palace. One of them contains the famous "Hall of the Ambassadors." The remains of the Moorish palace are called by the Spaniards the Casa Real. It was begun by Ibn-al-Ahmar, and completed by his successors, 1248–1348. The portions still standing are ranged around two oblong courts, one called the "Court of the Fish-pond," and the other the "Court of the Lions." The Moorish palace, though severely plain upon the exterior, is exquisitely beautiful within. It has floors of the choicest marbles, "fretted ceilings, partitions colored and gilt, and filigree stuccoes of vail-like transparency." Slender columns support the galleries, and gracefully-bending palm-leaves of marble form the arches, while beautiful fountains are scattered here and there. Beside the halls, courts, reception-rooms, and sleeping-apartments, the building contains a whispering-gallery, a labyrinth, and vaulted sepulchers. After the expulsion of the Moors from Spain their conquerors took pleasure in defacing and destroying their works of art, and the Alhambra was remodeled and partly blocked up. In 1812 the French blew up a portion of it, and in 1821 it was shaken by an earthquake. Attempts have been made from time to time to restore it, but the small amount of the money which has been contributed has rendered all such efforts practically futile.

All-Fools'-Day.—The origin of the custom of April fooling cannot be traced with any degree of certainty. In the literature of the last century there are found many references to it, and yet beyond that it is scarcely possible to go. One suggestion is that the custom of playing tricks on the first day of April was derived from some ancient pagan custom, such as the Huli festival among the Hindus, or the Roman Feast of the Fools. One fact, however, we do know, and that is that the practice prevails in many countries, under various names, which would seem to indicate that it dates away back to the early history of the race. [See *April.*]

Amazons.—According to ancient writers the Amazons were a nation of female warriors, who allowed no men to live among them, but marched to battle under command of their Queen. They held occasional intercourse with the men of the neighboring states. If boys were born to them, they either sent them to their fathers or killed them. But the girls were brought up for war, and their right breasts were burned off that they might not be prevented from bending the bow. From this custom they received the name of Amazons, which is "breastless." Three nations of Amazons have been mentioned by the ancients: 1. The Asiatic Amazons, from whom the others branched off. These dwelt on the shores of the Black Sea and among the mountains of the Caucasus, especially in the neighborhood of modern Trebizond, on the river Thermodon (now Termeh). They are said to have at one time subdued the whole of Asia, and to have built Smyrna, Ephesus, Cumæ, and other cities. Their Queen, Hippolyte, or according to others Antiope, was killed by Hercules, as the ninth of the labors imposed on him by Eurystheus consisted in taking from her the shoulder-belt bestowed on her by Mars. On one of their expeditions the Amazons came to Attica, in the time of Theseus. They also marched under command of their Queen, Penthesilea, to assist Priam against the Greeks. 2. The Scythian Amazons, who, in aftertimes, married among the neighboring Scythians and withdrew farther into Sarmatia. 3. The African Amazons, who, under command of their Queen, Myrina, subdued the Gorgans and Atlantes, marched through Egypt and Arabia, and founded their capital on the Lake Tritonis, but were then annihilated by Hercules. At this same time, too, the Lake Tritonis disappeared as such, and became part of the ocean, the intervening land having been swallowed up.

Amber is a pale yellow, sometimes reddish or brownish, substance, analogous to the vegetable resins, and is in all probability, derived from an extinct coniferous tree, although now appearing, like coal, in connection with beds of which it is usually found, as a product of the mineral kingdom. It is sometimes transparent, and sometimes almost opaque. It formerly had a high reputation as a medicine, but the virtues ascribed to it were purely imaginary. Amber is employed in the arts for the manufacture of many ornamental articles, and for the preparation of a kind of varnish. It was obtained by the ancients from the coasts of the Baltic Sea, where it is still found, especially between Konigsberg and Memel, in greater abundance than anywhere else in the world. It sometimes incloses insects of species which no longer exist. Leaves have also been found inclosed in it. Specimens which contain insects or leaves are very highly valued. According to an ancient fable, amber is the tears of the sisters of Phaethon, who, after his death, were changed into poplars. Pieces of amber have occasionally been found of twelve or thirteen pounds weight, but such pieces are extremely rare. Great quantities are consumed in Mohammedan worship at Mecca, and it is in great demand throughout the east. The beauty and hardness of amber have caused it to be long esteemed by smokers for mouth-pieces of pipes and tubes for cigar-holders. In Turkey as much as $1,500 has been given for a single mouth-piece. It is particularly esteemed by the Turks, in the belief that no infectious disease can be communicated through it. The value of amber differs greatly according to its tint and opacity. The bright-yellow transparent amber is least valuable. Dark, nearly opaque yellow has a much higher value; and the best of all is the opaque lemon-colored. It is said that one of the most esteemed talismans or amulets belonging to the Shah of Persia is a cube of amber reported to have fallen from heaven in Mohammed's time

Amen is a Hebrew word signifying "Yes," "Truly." In Jewish synagogues the amen is pronounced by the congregation at the conclusion of the benediction. Among the early Christians the prayer offered by the presbyter was concluded by the word amen, uttered by the congregation. Justin Martyr is the earliest of the fathers who alludes to the use of the response. According to Tertullian, none but the faithful were permitted to join in the response. A somewhat noisy and irreverent practice prevailed in the celebration of the Lord's Supper until the sixth century, after which it was discontinued. "Upon the reception both of the bread and of the wine, each person uttered a loud 'amen;' and at the close of the consecration by the priest, all joined in shouting a loud 'amen.'" The same custom was observed at baptism, when the sponsors and witnesses responded vehemently. In the Greek Church the amen was pronounced after the name of each person of the Trinity; and at the close of the baptismal formula the people responded. At the conclusion of prayer it signifies (according to the English Church Catechism) *so be it;* after the repetition of the Creed, *so it is.*

American Clocks and Watches.—The first attempt to manufacture watches or clocks on a large scale in America was made by Eli Terry, a Connecticut Yankee, who invented wooden wheels for clocks in 1792. In 1837 Chauncey Jerome, of Massachusetts, first applied machinery to the making of metal-wheeled clocks, and as a result drove the wooden-wheeled clocks out of the market. The manufacture of watches by machinery, which has since become such an important business, was begun at Roxbury, Mass., in 1850, and was continued there until 1854, when the works were removed to Waltham.

American Coinage, Early.—The earliest coinage that can be called American, in the sense of Anglo-American, was ordered by the original Virginia Company only five years after the founding of Jamestown. The coin was minted at Somers Island, now known as the Bermudas. For a long while the standard currency of Virginia was tobacco, as in many of the early settlements of the Northwest it was beaver skins, and other pelts reckoned as worth such a fraction of a beaver skin or so many beaver skins. In 1645 the Assembly of the Virginia Colony, after a preamble reciting that "It had maturely weighed and considered how advantageous a quoine would be to this colony, and the great wants and miseries which do daily happen unto it by the sole dependency upon tobacco," provided for the issue of copper coins of the denomination of twopence, threepence, sixpence and ninepence; but this law was never carried into effect, so that the first colonial coinage of America was that struck off by Massachusetts under the order of the General Court of that colony, passed May 27, 1652, creating a "mint house" at Boston, and providing for the mintage of "twelvepence, sixpence and threepence pieces, which shall be for forme flatt, and stamped on the one side with N. E., and on the other side with xiid., vid., and iiid., according to the value of each pence." In 1662 from this same mint appeared the famous "pine-tree shillings," which were twopenny pieces, having a pine-tree on one side. This mint was maintained for thirty-four years. In the reign of William and Mary copper coins were struck in England for New England and Carolina. Lord Baltimore had silver shillings, sixpences and fourpences made in England to supply the demand of his province in Maryland. Vermont and Connecticut established mints in 1785 for the issue of copper coin. New Jersey followed a year later. But Congress had the establishment of a mint for the confederated States under advisement, and in this same year agreed upon a plan submitted by Thomas Jefferson, and the act went into operation on a small scale in 1787. After the adoption of the Constitution of the United States in 1789 all the State mints were closed, as the Constitution specifically places the sole power of coining money in the Federal Government.

American Commanders.—Since 1775 the American army has been under the command of the following generals : Major-General George Washington, July 15, 1775, to December 23, 1783; Major-General Henry Knox, December 23, 1783, to June 20, 1784; Lieutenant-Colonel Josiah Harmer, General-in-Chief by brevet, September, 1788, to March, 1791; Major-General Arthur St. Clair, March 4, 1791, to March, 1792; Major-General Anthony Wayne, April 11, 1792, to December 15, 1796; Major-General James Williamson, December 15, 1796, to July, 1798; Lieutenant-General George Washington, July 3, 1798, to December 14, 1799; Major-General James Wilkinson, June, 1800, to January, 1812; Major-General Henry Dearborn, January 27, 1812, to June, 1815; Major-General Jacob Brown, June, 1815, to February 24, 1828; Major-General Alexander Macomb, May 24, 1828, to June, 1841; Major-General Winfield Scott (brevet Lieutenant-General), June, 1841, to November 1, 1861; Major-General George B. McClellan, November 1, 1861, to March 11, 1862; Major-General Henry W. Halleck, July 11, 1862, to March 12, 1864; Lieutenant-General Ulysses S. Grant, March 12, 1864, to July 25, 1866, and as General to March 4, 1869; General Wm. T. Sherman, March 4, 1869, to November 1, 1883; Lieutenant-General Philip H. Sheridan, November 1, 1883, to August, 1888; Major-General John M. Schofield, August, 1888.

American Flags.—It is related that the flag which was raised at Cambridge, January 2, 1776, by Washington, was composed of thirteen red and white stripes, with the crosses of St. George and St. Andrew emblazoned on the blue canton in place of the stars. This flag was also carried by the fleet under command of Commander Esek Hopkins when it sailed from the Delaware Capes February 17, 1776. In the following year, June 14, 1777, the Continental Congress passed a resolution "That the flag of the United States be thirteen stripes, alternate red and white; that the Union be thirteen stars, white on a blue field, representing a

new constellation." How or by whom the idea of the star was
first suggested is uncertain, although there are some who ascribe
it to John Adams, while others claim the entire flag was borrowed
from the coat of arms of the Washington family. In this flag the
stars were arranged in a circle, although no form was officially
prescribed. It is supposed that the first display of the National
flag at a military post was at Fort Schuyler, on the site of the
village of Rome, Oneida County, N. Y. The fort was besieged
early in the month of August, 1777, and the garrison were without a flag. So they made one according to the prescription of
Congress by cutting up sheets to form the white stripes, bits of
scarlet cloth for the red stripes, and the blue ground for the stars
was composed of portions of a cloth cloak belonging to Captain
Abraham Swarthout, of Dutchess County, N. Y., and the flag was
unfurled August 3, 1777. Paul Jones, as commander of the Ranger,
to which he was appointed June 14, 1777, claimed that he was
the first to display the Stars and Stripes on a naval vessel. It is
probable that the flag was first unfurled in battle on the banks of
the Brandywine, September 11, 1777, the first battle after its
adoption. It first appeared over a foreign stronghold June 28,
1778, when Captain Rathbone, of the American sloop of war
Providence, captured Fort Nassau, New Providence, Bahama
Islands. John Singleton Copley, the American painter, claimed
to be the first to display the flag in Great Britain. On the day
when George III acknowledged the independence of the United
States (December 5, 1782), he painted the flag in the background
of a portrait of Elkanah Watson. To Captain Mooers, of the
whaling ship Bedford, of Nantucket, is doubtless due the honor
of first displaying the Stars and Stripes in a port of Great Britain.
He arrived in the Downs with it flying at the fore, February 3,
1783. When Vermont and Kentucky were added to the Union of
States the flag was altered, the number of stripes and stars being
increased from thirteen to fifteen. In 1818 a new flag, having
thirteen stripes and a star for every State, twenty at that time,
was devised by Captain Samuel C. Reed, and this has remained
the form of the United States flag.

Americanisms.—The great body of Americanisms, or words and
phrases which have a meaning peculiar to America, consists in
giving an unusual sense to existing words, as *clever* in the sense
of amiable, and *smart* for clever; *wagon* for a very light kind of
carriage; *bookstore* for book-seller's shop; *wilted* for withered;
creek for a small river. The number of absolutely new words introduced into the English language in America is remarkably
small. As an instance may be mentioned *caucus*, for a secret political assembly. This is a corruption of *calk-house*, a calker's shed
in Boston, where the patriots before the Revolution had usually
held their meetings. The several divisions of the United States
have their characteristic Americanisms. In the New England
States *ugly* is used for ill-natured, and *guess* for a great variety of

things—to think, presume, suppose, etc. This use of *guess* is confined to New England; the inhabitants of New York and the Middle States employ *expect* in the same way, while those of the Southern States *reckon*, and those of the Western States *calculate*. Several words current in the Middle States are of Dutch origin, as *loafer* for a vagabond, from the Dutch *loopen*, to run; and *boss* for a head workman or employer. The verb *to fix* is made to do duty all over the country for expressing every conceivable kind of action. The well-known phrase *go-ahead* is a coinage of the West; and *posted up* in a subject, for well informed, is one of a class of metaphors indicative of the prominence of mercantile pursuits. As the Americans of Anglo-Saxon origin do not exceed one-third of the whole population of the United States, it seems wonderful that the English language should have held its ground so well, that it should not have been completely corrupted, or even in some places extruded by other tongues.

American Mine, Oldest.—The first recorded account of the discovery of coal in the United States is contained in Hennepin's narrative of his explorations in the West between 1673 and 1680, when he saw the coal outcrop in the bluffs of the Illinois River not far from Ottawa and La Salle. In New Mexico and Arizona there are silver mines which were operated by the Toltecs and Aztecs years before the Spanish invasion. So there are copper mines in the Lake Superior region in which the tools and mining marks of ancient miners of prehistoric times were found by the pioneers of the present American mining companies. Where the first colonists of Virginia got the ship-load of " fool's gold " which they sent back to England, to the great disgust of the London Company, is not certainly known; but it is known that at the same time, in 1608, they shipped a quantity of iron from James-town which yielded seventeen tons of metal—the first pig-iron ever made from American ore. In North and South Carolina and Georgia there are diggings, now overgrown with forests, which are supposed to have been excavated by the followers of De Soto and his immediate successors between 1539 and 1600. The oldest mining enterprise of the United States, still active, is generally conceded to be the mine La Motte, in the lead district of Eastern Missouri, which was opened about 1720 under Renault, of Law's notorious Mississippi Company. It was named after La Motte, the mineralogist of the expedition, and has been worked at intervals ever since it was opened.

America's Cup, The, was originally called the Queen's Cup, and was given by the Royal Yacht Squadron in May, 1851, for a race around the Isle of Wight. The schooner-yacht America, of which Commodore J. C. Stevens, of the New York Yacht Club, was the principal owner, won the trophy August 22, 1851. The cup then came to this country and has since remained here, although contests were held for it in 1870, 1871, 1876, 1881, 1885, 1886 and 1887. In 1857 the cup was presented to the New York Yacht Club, by its owners, as a perpetual challenge cup. In appearance it is rather in the shape of a vase with a handle, or a pitcher, than a cup. It stands two feet high and weighs at least 100 ounces. Around its broadest part are medallions variously inscribed. The first inscription is as follows: "One hundred guinea cup, won August 22, 1851, at Cowes, England, by yacht America, at the Royal Yacht Squadron regatta, open to all nations, beating"—and then follow the names of all the vessels that took part in the race of 1851. On the next medallion is engraved: "Schooner; 170 tons; Commodore John C. Stevens; built by George Steers; New York, 1851." The other spaces contain records of the results of the various races for the cup. In the race for the cup in 1870 the New York Yacht Club's schooner Magic beat the Cambria, the representative of several English yacht clubs. In 1871, New York Yacht Club's schooners Columbia and Sappho beat the English schooner Livonia. In this race the Columbia was disabled after the third race, and the series was finished by the Sappho. In 1876, New York Yacht Club's schooner Madeleine beat the Canadian schooner Countess of Dufferin. In 1881, New York Yacht Club's sloop Mischief beat the Canadian sloop Atalanta. In 1885, Eastern Yacht Club's sloop Puritan beat the cutter Genesta, representing the Royal Yacht Squadron. In 1886, Eastern Yacht Club's Mayflower beat the cutter Galatea, representing the Royal Northern Yacht Club. In 1887 the sloop Volunteer, representing the Eastern and New York Yacht Clubs, beat the cutter Thistle, representing the Royal Clyde Yacht Club.

Amulet is any object worn as a charm. It is often a stone, or piece of metal, with an inscription or some figure engraved on it, and is generally suspended from the neck, and worn as a preventive against sickness, witchcraft, etc. Its origin, like its name, seems to be Oriental. The ancient Egyptians had their amulets, sometimes forming necklaces. Among the Greeks such a protective charm was called *phylacterion;* among the Romans, *amuletum*. From the heathen, the use of amulets passed into the Christian Church, the inscription on them being *ichthus* (the Greek word for a fish), because it contained the initials of the Greek words for Jesus Christ, Son of God, Saviour. Amulets soon became so common among Christians that in the fourth century the clergy were interdicted from making and selling them on the pain of deprivation of holy orders, and in 721 the wearing of amulets was solemnly condemned by the Church. Among amulets in repute in the middle ages were the coins attributed to St. Helena, the mother of Constantine. These and other coins marked with a cross were thought specially efficacious against epilepsy, and are generally found perforated, for the purpose of being worn suspended from the neck.

Anagram is the transposition of the letters of a word, phrase or short sentence so as to form a new word or sentence, and is from the Greek *ana*, backward, and *gramma*, writing. The Cabalists attached great importance to anagrams, believing in some relation of them to the character or destiny of the persons from whose names they were formed. Plato entertained a similar notion, and the later Platonists rivaled the Cabalists in ascribing to them mysterious virtues. The best anagrams are such as have, in the new order of letters, some signification appropriate to that from which they are formed. It was a great triumph of the mediæval anagramist to find in Pilate's question, *Quid est veritas?* (What is truth?) its own answer, *Est vir qui adest* (It is the man who is here). D'Israeli, in his "Curiosities of Literature," has a chapter on anagrams. Among the great many considered by him worthy of record are the following: The mistress of Charles IX of France was named Marie Touchet; this became *Il charme tout* (I charm every one), which is historically just. The flatterers of James I of England proved his right to the British monarchy as the descendant of King Arthur from his name, Charles James Stuart, which becomes *claims Arthur's seat.* The author, in dedicating a book to the same monarch, finds that in James Stuart he has *a just master.* On a visit to King's Newton Hall, in Derbyshire, Charles II is said to have left written on one of the windows *Cras ero lux* (To-morrow I shall be light), which is the anagram of Carolus Rex.

Ancient Year, The.—The Jewish year had two commencements. The religious year began with the month Abib (April), the civil year with Tissi (October). The year was solar. There were two seasons—summer and winter. The months were lunar, of thirty days each, and twelve in number, although a thirteenth was sometimes necessarily intercalated. It was called "Ve-adar." The ancient Egyptians, Chaldeans, Persians, Syrians, Phœnicians and Carthaginians each began their year at the autumnal equinox, or about September 22d. The beginning of the year among the Greeks, until 432 years before Christ, when Meton introduced the cycle called after him, was at the winter solstice, or about December 22d, and afterward at the summer solstice, about June 22d. The Roman year from the time of Numa began at the winter solstice. It was not probably the original intention of Cæsar to change this time, and his motive for delaying it several ways till January 1st was doubtless the desire to make the first of the year of the reformed calendar begin with the day of the new moon. In England, from the fourteenth century till the change of style in 1752, the legal and ecclesiastical year began March 25th, although it was not uncommon to reckon it from January 1st.

Angon.—A barbed spear, used by many early natives. The Franks, in the seventh century, employed angons both for thrusting and hurling. The staves were armed with iron, so as to leave but little of the wood uncovered. The head had two barbs. When hurled or thrust at an opponent, the head of the angon became fixed in the flesh by means of the barbs. This form of spear was mostly adopted by the Anglo-Saxon and other Teutonic nations.

Animal Worship.—Among primitive peoples, all animals are supposed to be endowed with souls which in many cases have formerly animated human beings. Hence a likeness is often recognized between an animal and some deceased friend, and the animal is addressed as the person would have been, and honored with a kind of worship. Many tribes call themselves by the name of, and even derive their pedigree from, some animal. Its cries become the omens of the tribe; and thus originate the divination and augury of more civilized nations. In the modern world the most civilized people among whom animal-worship vigorously survives lie within the range of Brahmanism. Here the sacred cow is not merely to be spared; she is as a deity worshiped and bowed to daily by the pious Hindu. Siva is incarnate in Hanuman, the monkey-god. The divine king of birds, Garuda, is Vishnu's vehicle, and the forms of fish and boar and tortoise assumed in the avatar legends of Vishnu. Perhaps no worship has prevailed more widely than that of the serpent. It had its place in Egypt and among the Hebrews; in Greece and Rome; among the Celts and Scandinavians in Europe; in Persia and India; in China and Thibet; in Mexico and Peru; in Africa, where it still flourishes as the state religion in Dahomey; in Java and Ceylon; among the Fijians and elsewhere in Oceanica; and even within the limits of Christianity we find the sect of the Ophites, who continued or renewed snake-worship, blended curiously with purer rites.

Apocrypha, The.—In the earliest Churches the word Apocrypha was applied with very different significations to a variety of writings; sometimes it was given those whose authorship and original form were unknown; sometimes to writings containing a hidden meaning; sometimes to those whose public use was not thought advisable. In this last signification it has been customary, since the time of Jerome, to apply the term to a number of writings which the Septuagint had circulated among the Christians, and which were sometimes considered as an appendage to the Old Testament, and sometimes as a portion of it. At the Council of Laodicea, 360 A. D., the Greek Church rejected all books except those in the present Protestant canon. In 474 Pope Gelasius convened a council of seventy bishops, which confirmed the opinion of Pope Innocent I, recognizing the Apocryphal books as sacred, and rejecting some of the doubtful books of the New Testament. The Council of Trent, 1545-'63, finally settled the question for the Roman Catholic Church, accepting the Apocrypha as a part of the sacred canon. The Protestant Churches reject their use in public worship. It was customary at one time to bind up the Apocrypha between the authorized versions of the Old and New Testaments, though this has now ceased, and, as a consequence, this curious, interesting and instructive part of Jewish literature is now known only to scholars.

Apollo Belvedere, one of the most perfect statues ever created by the sculptor's art—possibly the greatest existing work of antiquity. Its origin and date are unknown, being variously attributed to Agasias, Praxiteles and Calamis. It was found in 1503 in the ruins of ancient Antium (now Porto d'Anzo), and subsequently placed in the Belvedere of the Vatican (whence the name) by Pope Julius II, who had purchased it before his accession to the papacy. The French removed it in 1797, but replaced it after 1815. When found, the right hand and part of the arm and the left hand were wanting; they were restored by Angelo de Montorsoli, a pupil of Michael Angelo. The statue represents the god at the moment of his victory over the Python, and is of heroic size and nude. The left arm is extended, still holding the bow, while the right hand, which has just left the string, is near the hip. The figure is muscular and poised with exquisite grace. It shows the very perfection of manly beauty.

Apostles, Deaths of.—It is generally believed that only one of Christ's Apostles, John, escaped martyrdom. Matthew is supposed to have been slain with a sword in Ethiopia. James, son of Zebedee, was beheaded at Jerusalem. James, the brother of our Lord, was thrown from a pinnacle of the Temple and then beaten to death with a fuller's club. Philip was hanged up against a pillar at Hieropolis, a city of Phrygia. Bartholomew was flayed alive at Albanapolis, in Armenia. Andrew suffered martyrdom on a cross at Patræ, in Achaia. Thomas was run through the body with a lance at Coromandel, in the East Indies. Thaddeus was shot to death with arrows. Simon Zelotes was crucified in Persia. Peter was crucified, head downward it is said, during the Neronian persecution. Matthias was first stoned and then beheaded, and Paul was beheaded at Rome by the tyrant Nero. Judas Iscariot, after the betrayal of our Lord, hung himself.

Apostles, Emblems of.—The artists of early times having no knowledge of the features of the Apostles, used some signs to designate them which might always be recognized. For this purpose, frequently, a symbol of the holy man's martyrdom was used. The emblem of St. Peter, a large key or keys, is readily explained as referring to the words of Christ to Peter (Matt. xvi, 19): "And I will give unto thee the keys of the kingdom of heaven." A book is also used in some portraits of St. Peter, but with probably no more significance than to indicate his calling as a teacher of the Holy Word. The emblem of St. Paul was a sword and a book—the latter to indicate his calling as a teacher, the former to remind the beholder that he was beheaded with the sword. That of St. Andrew was a cross like the letter X, because he was crucified on one of this shape; that of St. James the Great a sword, in token of his beheading, or sometimes a pilgrim's staff, as he was a great traveler, and is thought to have journeyed all over Southern Europe. St. John has the emblem of a caldron, in remembrance of the fact that he is said to have been once thrown into a caldron of boiling oil, but miraculously escaped injury; he has also sometimes a dragon, or an eagle, by which the imagery of the Book of Revelation is probably indicated. Why St. Philip should have a spear and a cross, when he suffered death by hanging, it is hard to say; but such are his emblems. St. Bartholomew, having been flayed alive, is represented with a flaying-knife and with his skin hanging over his arm. St. Matthew usually has a carpenter's square, in reference to the occupation of Christ as a man, perhaps; sometimes he has a spear, to indicate martyrdom, though he is believed to have been slain with a sword. St. Thomas bears a dart, as having perished by being run through with a lance; St. James the Less a club, with which he was beaten to death; St. Matthias an ax, with which he was beheaded; St. Simon's emblem is a saw, which must be a general emblem of martyrdom or point to some legend now forgotten, as it is known that that saint suffered death by crucifixion.

April.—The Romans gave this month the name of *Aprilis*, from *Aperire*, to open, because it was the season when the buds began to open; by the Anglo-Saxons it was called Ooster, or Easter-month; and by the Dutch Grass-month. The custom of sending one on a bootless errand on the first day of this month is perhaps a travesty of the sending hither and thither of the Saviour from Annas to Caiaphas, and from Pilate to Herod, because during the middle ages this scene in Christ's life was made the subject of a miracle-play at Easter. It is possible, however, that it may be the relic of some old heathen festival. The custom, whatever be its origin, of playing tricks on the first day of this month is universal throughout Europe. It is also somewhat curious that the Hindus practice precisely similar tricks on the 31st of March, when they hold what is called the Huli festival.

Apse.—The origin of the peculiar semicircular recess called the Apse, placed at the east end of the choir of an Anglo-Saxon or Anglo-Norman church, is curious. It is well known that the heathen structure from which the early Christians borrowed the form of their churches was not the temple but the basilica [see *Basilica*], or public hall, which served at once for a market-place and a court of justice. The basilica, for the most part, was a parallelogram, at one of the shorter sides of which, opposite to the entrance, there was a raised platform destined for the accommodation of the persons engaged in and connected with the distribution of justice. This portion of the building was the prototype of the rounded choir to which the name of Apse was given, and which is still to be seen in so many of the Rhenish churches. For the praetor's chair which was placed in the center of this semicircular space, the altar was substituted; and the steps which led to the seat from which he dispensed justice were destined henceforth to lead to the spot where the Fountain of all justice should be worshiped.

Archimedes, Principle of.—Archimedes, the most celebrated of ancient mathematicians, was born at Syracuse about 287 B. C.

He is said to have been a kinsman of King Hiero, though he does not seem to have held any public office, but devoted himself entirely to science. He is the only one of the ancients who contributed anything satisfactory on the theory of mechanics and on hydrostatics. He first established the truth that a body plunged in a fluid loses exactly as much of its weight as is equal to the weight of the fluid displaced by it. This is one of the most important principles in the science of hydrostatics, and is called by his name. It was by this law that he determined how much alloy the goldsmith, whom Hiero had commissioned to make a crown of pure gold, had fraudulently mixed with the metal. The solution of the problem had suggested itself to him as he was entering the bath, and he is reported to have been so overjoyed as to hasten home without waiting to dress, exclaiming, "I have found it! I have found it!" Among the numerous inventions ascribed to Archimedes is that of the endless screw, and the cochlea, or water-screw, in which the water is made in a manner to ascend by its own gravity.

Architectural Ruins, Oldest.—The oldest ruins in the world are probably the rock-cut temples at Ipsambul or Abousambul, in Nubia, on the left bank of the Nile. The largest temple contains fourteen apartments hewn out of solid rock. The first and largest of these is 57 feet long and 52 feet broad, and is supported by two rows of massive square pillars, four in each row, and 30 feet high. To each of these pillars is attached a standing colossus, or human figure, of enormous proportions, reaching to the roof, overlaid with a kind of stucco and painted with gaudy colors, apparently as brilliant now, after the lapse of over 4,000 years, as when first laid on. In front of this temple are seated four still larger human figures, two of them being 65 feet in height—presumed to represent Rameses the Great, more frequently termed Sesostris, whose marvelous military exploits are depicted in drawings and paintings on the temple walls. Reproductions of two of these colossal figures on the scale of the original, and also a fac-simile on a small scale of the temple itself, were made for exhibition in the Crystal Palace in Sydenham, England.

Arctic Dwellings.—The winter huts or igloos of the Eskimos are usually a half or more underground, and finished above ground with stones, bones, turf and moss, and finally with ice and snow. Sometimes they are constructed of blocks of ice and compact snow, with transparent ice windows. The igloo is reached by a long, tunnel-like entrance, and is unventilated. The ordinary means of lighting and warming these huts is a large basin of oil, furnished with a moss wick. These basins are scolloped from soapstone or similar material. The oil is the product of the whale, seal, or other fish, or of the white bear, but usually the former.

Argol is a crude variety of cream of tartar which forms a crust in the interior of wine-vats and wine-bottles. Originally, it exists in the juice of the grape, and is soluble therein; but during the fermentation of the juice, and as it passes into wine, much alcohol is developed, which, remaining in the fermenting liquor, causes the precipitation of argol. It is generally of a reddish tint, obtained from the color of the grapes, but sometimes is of a grayish-white color where it has been deposited during the fermentation of the juice of the colorless grape. Some wines, when they are bottled, are not fully ripe, and more alcohol being thereafter developed, a further precipitation of argol takes place as a crust in the bottles, and hence the meaning of the term *crusted port*. The red or white argol is denominated in commerce crude tartar, and its principal uses are in the preparation of cream of tartar and tartaric acid.

Argonauts, The, were heroes of Greek antiquity, who were so named from their ship Argo. They accompanied Jason in his search for the Golden Fleece, which, after many perilous adventures, was obtained. [See *Golden Fleece.*] The fabled crew of the Argo included all the famous heroes of Greek legend, as Hercules, Castor and Pollux, sons of Jupiter; Peleus and Telamon, grandsons of that god; Theseus, Polyphemus, Atalanta, Idmon, the seer, the son of Apollo; Mopsus, also a prophet; Orpheus, the son of the muse, Calliope; and many others. The entire number was fifty. On the voyage to Colchis, where the Golden Fleece was, Hercules and Polyphemus were left behind at Mysia. Hylas, a youth beloved by Hercules, having gone for water, was seized and kept by the nymphs of the spring into which he dipped his urn. Polyphemus, hearing his call, went with drawn sword to his aid, supposing him to have fallen into the hands of robbers. Meeting Hercules, he told him what had happened, and both proceeded in quest of the youth. Meantime the Argo put to sea and left them behind. Polyphemus settled in Mysia and built the city of Kios, and Hercules returned to Argos.

Ark of the Covenant.—Previous to the destruction of the Temple of Solomon by the Babylonians the Ark of the Covenant was contained therein, but what became of it after that time is unknown. It is believed by some to have been taken away or destroyed by Nebuchadnezzar, while certain of the Jews believe that it was concealed from the spoilers, and account it among the hidden things which will be revealed by the Messiah. That the old Ark was not contained in the second Temple all Jewish writers agree; and the absence of the Ark is one of the important particulars in which this Temple was held to be inferior to that of Solomon. It is held by some writers, however, that the Jews could not properly carry on their worship without an Ark, hence that a new one must have been made and placed in the Temple if the original Ark was not recovered. The silence of Ezra, Nehemiah, the Maccabees and Josephus, who repeatedly mention all the other sacred utensils but never name the Ark, would, nevertheless, seem conclusive on this subject.

Army Officers, Salaries of.—The salaries of officers of the United States army are as follows: General, $13,500 per annum;

Lieutenant-General, $11,000; Major-General, $7,500; Brigadier-General, $5,500; Colonel, $3,500; Lieutenant-Colonel, $3,000; Major, $2,500; Captain, mounted, $2,000; Captain, not mounted, $1,800; Regimental Adjutant, $1,800; Regimental Quartermaster, $1,800; First Lieutenant, mounted, $1,600; First Lieutenant, not mounted, $1,500; Second Lieutenant, mounted, $1,500; Second Lieutenant, not mounted, $1,400; Chaplain, $1,500.

Arquebus.—A hand-gun bearing some comparison to the modern musket. The earliest form of this gun was fired by applying a match by hand to the touch-hole; but about 1476 a contrivance suggested by the trigger of the arbalost or cross-bow was added, by which the burning match could be applied with more quickness and certainty. In 1485, when the corps known as the Yeomen of the Guard was formed, it was armed with this weapon. The arquebus was further improved by the Germans, who gave a hooked form to the butt, which elevated the barrel and thus enabled a person to take a moderately accurate aim. Under this form the arquebus obtained the name of haquebut. Soldiers armed with these two kinds of weapon were designated arquebusiers and harquebutters. The former were common in the English army in the time of Richard III, the latter in that of Henry VIII.

Arundel Marbles are a collection of ancient sculptures consisting of 37 statues, 128 busts and 250 inscribed stones, which were found on the Island of Paros about 1610. They were collected by Mr. W. Pefty, purchased by Lord Arundel, and given by his grandson, Henry Howard—afterward Duke of Norfolk—to the University of Oxford in 1667. These sculptures contain inscriptions in the Greek tongue. In their perfect state they evidently contained a chronological table of the principal events of Grecian history from the time of Cecrops, 1582 B. C., to the Archonship of Diogenes, 264 B. C. The chronicle of the last ninety years of this period, however, is lost, and the portion still extant is much corroded and defaced.

Asbestos is a fibrous, white, gray or green mineral not fusible. The variety called *rock-cork* very much resembles cork, is soft and easily cut, and so light as to float on water. *Rock-leather* and *rock-wood* are varieties somewhat similar to *rock-cork*, but not so light. The finest fibrous variety, with easily separable fibers, is called *amainthus*, because cloth made of it was cleansed by passing it through fire. This cloth was used by the ancients to enwrap dead bodies placed on the funeral-pile, so as to preserve the ashes of the body unmixed. It was also woven by them into handkerchiefs and towels. Of late years it has been considerably used as fire-proof roofing, flooring, and packing in safes, journal-boxes and around steam pipes. Paper has also been made of it; but though, at red heat, the paper remains uninjured, the writing disappears. It is said that Charlemagne had a table-cloth of asbestos, which, for the amusement of his guests, he was wont to throw into the fire at the close of the meal. The finest specimens of this mineral come from Corsica and Savoy, though some are found in the Alps, Pyrenees and Ural Mountains, and in North America and New South Wales; while commoner varieties, such as the *rock-cork* and *rock-wood*, are found in Lanarkshire, Tyrol, Dauphiny, and parts of Scotland.

Ash-Wednesday is so called from the custom of strewing ashes on the head as a sign of penitence which prevailed in the Roman Catholic Church. It was instituted probably by Gregory the Great, 590–604, and was sanctioned by later Popes. The ashes were consecrated on the altar before mass, sprinkled with holy water and signed three times with the cross, while the priest recited the words, *Memento quod cinis es, et in cinerem reverteris!* (Remember that thou art dust, and must return to dust.) They were then strewed on the heads of the officiating priests, the clergy and the assembled people. The ashes were said to be those of the palms consecrated on the preceding Palm-Sunday. Ash-Wednesday is not observed in the Protestant Church in Germany.

Assassins, The, were a branch of the secret sect of the Ismaelites. The secret doctrine of these Ismaelites, who had their headquarters in Cairo, declared the descendants of Ismael, the last of the seven so-called Imaums, to be alone entitled to the caliphate, and gave an allegorical interpretation to the precepts of Islam which led, as their adversaries asserted, to considering all positive religions equally right and all actions morally indifferent. The founder of the Assassins, Hassan-ben-Sabbah el Homairi, was of Persian descent, and imbued with the free-thinking tendencies of his country. He had, about the middle of the eleventh century, studied at Nishpur, under the celebrated Morrasek, and had subsequently obtained from Ismaelite *dais*, or religious leaders, a partial insight into their secret doctrines and a partial consecration to the rank of dai; but on betaking himself to the central lodge at Cairo he quarreled with the heads of the sect and was doomed to banishment. He succeeded, however, in making his escape from the ship, and reached the Syrian coast, after which he returned to Persia, everywhere collecting adherents. In 1090 Hassan conquered the fortress of Alamut, in the Persian district of Rudbar, and continued to increase in strength, intimidating princes and governors by a series of secret murders, and gaining possession of several fortified castles with their surrounding territories. The head of the Assassins was called the Sheikh-al-jebal, the Prince, or the Old Man of the Mountain. His vice-regents were the three Dai-al-Kebir, or grand-priors. Next came the Dais and Refiks, which last were not initiated, like the former, into every stage of the secret doctrines. To the uninitiated belonged, first of all, the Fedavies, the devoted, a band of resolute youths, the ever-ready and blindly-obedient executioners of the Old Man of the Mountain. Before he assigned to them their bloody tasks he used to have them thrown into a state of ecstasy by the intoxicating influence of hashish, which circumstance led to the order being called Hashishim, or hemp-eaters. The word was changed by Europeans into Assassins, and transplanted into the languages of the west with the signification of murderers. Several princes secretly paid tribute to the Old Man of the Mountain, and the Assassins held their power until 1256, when the Mongolian Prince Hulagu burst with his hordes upon the hillforts of Persia, held by the Assassins, and captured and destroyed them. In 1352 a body of Assassins reappeared in Syria, and in fact they are still reported to exist as a heretical sect both there and in Persia.

Associated Press was organized about thirty years ago by the following New York City papers: *Herald, Tribune, World, Times, Sun, Evening Express* and *Journal of Commerce*, for the purpose of facilitating the collection of news. The general agent of the Association is located in New York, and associate agents in Chicago, Washington, Cincinnati and other news centers. There is also a complete reportorial staff, and the news collected is used not only by the syndicate of papers, but is transmitted by telegraph to others in almost every city in the country who have secured the privilege by purchase.

Atalanta was the daughter of Jasus and Clymene, and was celebrated as a huntress. According to ancient legends she was exposed, while an infant, on Mount Parthenios by her father, who had wished a son. There she was found near the entrance of a cave by hunters, who brought her up and eventually restored her to her parents. She slew the centaurs Rhœcus and Hylæus, and sailed with the Argonauts on their search for the Golden Fleece. She had many suitors, and being the swiftest of mortals, offered to become the wife of him who should outstrip her, the penalty of defeat being death. She was conquered by a trick of one Meilanion, whom she was compelled to marry. He obtained from Venus a gift of three golden apples, which he successively dropped in the race, and Atalanta was so charmed by their beauty that she could not refrain from stopping to gather them, and so lost the race.

Athens, Walls of.—The city of Athens, in Greece, embraced three parts—the Acropolis, or central hill, on which were the magnificent temples of the Erechtheum and the Parthenon; the Astey, or upper town, which really included the Acropolis; and the port towns Piræus, Munychia, and Phalerum. The Astey was surrounded by walls, and three similar walls—the two long walls and the Phaleric wall—connected it with the port towns. The wall around the Astey measured sixty stadia; that around Piræus and Munychia the same. The length of each of the long walls was forty stadia, and of the Phaleric wall thirty-five stadia. The height of these walls was probably between fifty and sixty feet. The stadia was about 606 3-4 feet.

Atlantic Cables.—In July, 1866, the first permanent Atlantic cable was laid from Valentia Bay, Ireland, to Trinity Bay, N. F., and in September of the same year a cable which had been lost in 1865 was recovered and its laying completed, thus giving two lines between the two points. These lines were known as the Anglo-American Cable, and were managed by a company of the same name. The French Atlantic Telegraph Company was formed in 1868, and it laid a line from Brest, France, to Roxbury, Mass., the following year. In the summer of 1873 the fourth Atlantic telegraph cable was laid from Valentia, Ireland, to Heart's Content, Trinity Bay, N. F., and the Brazilian telegraph cable was laid from Rio de Janeiro, Brazil, to a bay on the coast of Portugal a few months later. The Direct United States Cable Company was formed, and laid a line from Ballenskillings Bay, Ireland, to Rye, N. H., via Nova Scotia, in 1874. The same year a sixth line across the Atlantic was laid from Ireland to Newfoundland, and in 1880 another French line was laid from Brest to St. Pierre, an island in the Gulf of St. Lawrence. In 1884-'85, the companies owning all these lines having previously formed a combination to keep up rates, a competing company was formed by James Gordon Bennett and Mr. Mackay, who laid two lines from Ireland to Nova Scotia, and also a connecting line from Ireland to France. The difficulty with these submarine cables at first was to send through them a current of sufficient power to record the message. The method adopted is as follows: Two keys, which when depressed transmit respectively positive and negative currents, are employed at the sending-station in connection with the battery. The current of the battery does not pass directly into the cable, but into a condenser, which passes it into the submarine line. This greatly increases the force of the current used, and serves to cut off interfering earth-currents. The receiving-instrument first employed was a reflecting galvanometer. Upon the magnet of this instrument is carried a small curved mirror. About two feet in front of it is placed a lamp behind a frame in which is a vertical slit, while above it is a screen. The light from this lamp, passing through the slit, falls on the surface of the mirror, which throws it back upon the screen. The flash of light, moving from right to left with the motion of the needle, indicates the message sent. This method, however, has been of late years almost entirely superseded by an invention called the syphon galvanometer. In this the movements of the needle are recorded by means of ink spurted from a fine glass syphon-tube. This tube is attached to a coil suspended between two fixed magnets, which swing to right or left as the pulsations of the needle pass through it. The possibility of laying an electric cable in the Atlantic from Europe was suggested by Professor Morse as far back as 1843, but it was not until 1854 that Mr. Cyrus W. Field discussed the means of practically realizing the idea, and it is to his energy that the successful completion of this great work is due.

Atlantis was a celebrated island supposed to have existed at a very early period in the Atlantic Ocean, and to have been eventually sunk beneath its waves. Plato is the first to give an account of it, and he obtained his information from the priests of Egypt. In the Atlantic Ocean, he said, over against the Pillars of Hercules, lay an island larger than Asia and Africa taken together, and in its vicinity were other islands, from which there was a passage to a large continent lying beyond. The Mediterranean, compared with the ocean in which these islands were situated, resembled a mere harbor with a narrow entrance. Nine thousand years before the time of Plato this Island of Atlantis was both thickly settled and very powerful. Its sway extended over Africa as far as Egypt, and over Europe as far as the Tyrrhenian Sea. The further progress of its conquests, however, was checked by the Athenians, who, partly with the other Greeks, partly by themselves, succeeded in defeating these powerful invaders, the natives of Atlantis. After this, a violent earthquake, which lasted for the space of a day and a night, and was accompanied with inundations of the sea, caused the islands to sink, and for a long period subsequent to this the sea in this quarter was impassable by reason of the slime and shoals. This was the story of Plato. The description of Atlantis, as handed down to us by ancient writers, though a mere picture of the imagination, will serve to show the opinion entertained on this subject—the ideal condition of the hu man race—by the poetic minds of antiquity. The Isle of Atlantis was one of the finest and most productive countries in the uni verse. It produced abundance of wine, grain, and the most ex quisite fruits. Here were seen wide-spread forests, extensive pleasure-grounds, mines of various metals, hot and mineral springs; in a word, whatever could contribute to the necessities or comforts of life. Here commerce flourished under a most excellent system of government. The island, divided into ten kingdoms, was governed by as many kings, all descendants of Neptune, and who lived in perfect harmony with each other, though severally independent. Atlantis had numerous and splendid cities, together with a large number of rich and populous villages. Its harbors beheld the product of almost every country wafted to them, and they were strengthened with fortifications and supplied with arsenals containing everything calculated for the construction and equipment of navies. Neptune was not only the progenitor and legislator, but also the principal divinity of the people. He had a temple a stadium in length, and ornamented with gold, silver, orichalchum and ivory. Among various statues with which it was adorned was seen that of the god himself, which was of gold, and so high that it touched the ceiling. He was represented as standing in a chariot and holding the reins of his winged steed.

Attar of Roses is a volatile oil of soft consistency, is nearly colorless, and is obtained from rose-water by setting it out during the night in large open vessels, and early in the morning skimming off the essential oil which floats at the top. The India and Persia roses are chiefly used in its manufacture, and it is stated that 10,000 bushes with 100,000 roses will yield only 180 grains of attar. It is a delicious perfume, and is exported to European countries in small vials, and is exceedingly costly. The word "attar" is traced to the Arabic "itr," which means perfume.

August.—The sixth month in the Roman year, which began with March, was originally styled *Sextilis*, and received its present name from the Emperor Augustus on account of several of the most fortunate events of his life having occurred during this month.

Aurora Borealis.—Since the discovery of electricity, and especially electro-magnetism, all speculation on the nature of the aurora has taken in that force as a principal element, and modern experiments have been especially turned to securing proof of the electric nature of the auroral display. The theory advanced by M. de la Rive, a Genoese scientist, and which is generally accepted, is, that the aurora is caused by the recomposition of the positive and negative electricity, always to be found in the upper and lower strata of air respectively. Miniature auroras have been produced by electricity by M. De la Rive, and also by a M. Lenstrom. In M. Lenstrom's experiments, which were made in Finland in 1882, the peak of a mountain was surrounded with a coil of copper wire, pointed at intervals with tin nibs. This wire was charged with electricity, and a yellow light was produced on the tin points, in which the spectroscope analysis revealed the greenish-yellow ray that characterizes the aurora borealis. The aurora was supposed to be of supernatural origin by the ancients.

Aztecs.—The Aztec nation, according to tradition, was one of the seven tribes of the Nahuatlecas who are represented as emerging from seven caverns in the region called Aztlan. Each of these tribes are supposed to have wandered away from their companions after a confusion of tongues. The traditional Aztlan has given rise to much conjecture to those who would locate it by metes and bounds. Some have advanced the theory that Asia was the birthplace of the Nahuatlecas, and that the paintings in existence in Mexico, all of which picture the passage over a body of water in canoes or upon rafts, represent the migration of these people from that continent to America. Others claim that they came from the north of Mexico. Wherever they may have originally come from, which at best can be but a matter of conjecture, the Aztecs founded the city of Tenochtitlan, or Mexico, in 1325, and on the arrival of the Spaniards in 1519 their empire was found to extend from ocean to ocean. The women shared in all the occupations of the men, and were taught, like them, the arts of reading, writing, ciphering, singing, dancing, etc., and even initiated in the secrets of astronomy and astrology. The temples of their chief god, the frightful Huitzilopochtli, were most splendid and imposing, and in every city of the empire his altars were drenched with the blood of human sacrifice. The god, as described by Cortes, had a broad face, wide mouth and terrible eyes, and was covered with gold, pearls and precious stones, and was girt about with golden serpents. On his neck were the faces of men wrought in silver and their hearts in gold. Near him stood braziers with incense, and on the braziers there were real hearts of men. It is said that the victims who were sacrificed to this god numbered at least 20,000 each year. They were borne in triumphal processions, and to the sound of music, to the summits of the great temples, where the priests, in sight of assembled crowds, bound them to the sacrificial stones, and opening their breasts, tore from them their bleeding hearts, which were either laid before the image of the god or else eaten by the worshipers, after having been carefully cut up and mixed with maize. In addition to Huitzilopochtli they had twelve other chief gods and two hundred inferior divinities, each of whom had his sacred day and festival. At the time of the conquest of the country by the Spaniards the throne was occupied by Montezuma, who had been told by the oracles that great changes were impending over the empire, and that the fall of his race was at hand. Therefore, when news of the arrival on the coast of the Spanish expedition was brought to him he was overcome with terror, and endeavored to propitiate the dreaded strangers by sending an embassy, with valuable gifts, to meet them. The conquest of the country was accomplished with a mere handful of men.

Babel, Tower of.—The distinction of being a remnant of the Tower of Babel has been claimed for three different masses, but the majority of opinions are in favor of the Birs Nimrud in Babylonia, the ruins of this temple appearing to more nearly correspond with the conceived notion of that structure. It is of an oblong form, the total circumference being 762 yards. At the eastern side it is cloven by a deep furrow, and is not more than 50 or 60 feet high; but on the western side it rises in a conical figure to the elevation of 198 feet; and on its summit is a solid pile of brick 37 feet high by 28 in breadth, diminishing in thickness to the top, which is broken and irregular, and rent by a large fissure extending through a third of its height. The fire-burnt bricks of which it is built have inscriptions on them; and so excellent is the cement, which appears to be lime-mortar, that it is nearly impossible to extract a whole brick. The other parts of the summit of the hill are occupied by immense fragments of brick-work of no determinate figure, tumbled together, and converted into solid vitrified masses, as if they had undergone the action of the fiercest fire or had been blown up with gunpowder. These ruins stand on a prodigious mound, the whole of which is itself in ruins, channeled by the weather, and strewed with fragments of black stone, sandstone and marble. Taken in connection with the ancient tradition that the Tower of Babel was rent and overthrown by fire from heaven, this is a curious circumstance.

Babylon.—According to Herodotus, the ancient city of Babylon stood on a broad plain, and was an exact square 120 stadia (equal to fourteen miles) each way, so that the entire circuit of the city was 480 stadia. It was surrounded by a broad and deep moat, full of water, behind which rose a wall 50 royal cubits (equal to 93 1-3 feet) in width and 200 in height. On the top, along the edges of the wall, were constructed buildings of a single chamber facing one another, leaving between them room for a four-horse chariot to turn. In the circuit of the walls were a hundred gates, all of brass, with brazen lintels and side-posts. Subsequent writers reduce the circuit of the city to 360 stadia, and the height of the wall to from 60 to 70 feet. The other walls ran along the banks of the Euphrates, and the quays with which it was lined each contained twenty-five gates, which answered to the number of the streets they led into. The most remarkable edifice in the city was the Temple of Bel, a pyramid of 8 square stadia, the basement stage being over 200 yards each way. On the summit were a golden image of Bel 40 feet high, two other statues of gold, a golden table 40 feet long and 15 broad, and many other colossal objects of the same precious metal. At the base was a second shrine, with a table and images and altars. A similar temple stood at Borsippa, the suburb of Babylon; and it is believed that the ancient Babel of the Bible was also at Borsippa, a little below the later Babylon. The city came prominently into notice about 747 B. C., but its great importance dates from the fall of Nineveh, when Nabopolassar made it the capital of the Chaldean empire, and began the series of fortifications and public works completed by his son, Nebuchadnezzar. It was several times dismantled, and when Alexander the Great took possession of it, was a comparative ruin. Much of the material from which it was built was used by his successors to build Seleucia. That city in its turn fell into decay, and from its material several other cities were built, among them Bagdad. Since 1847 it has been established beyond reasonable doubt that the village Hilleh is located on the site of ancient Babylon.

Bachelors.—At some period of its history the legislation of almost all countries has imposed penalties on unmarried men or bachelors on the principle that every citizen is bound to rear up children to the state. The Hebrews regarded marriage as a duty, and interpreted strictly the command, "Be fruitful and multiply." By the laws of Lycurgus criminal proceedings were authorized in Sparta not only against those who did not marry, but also against those who married so late in life as to render the procreation of healthy children unlikely. The laws of Solon also treated celibacy as a crime. From an early period penalties and disabilities were imposed on unmarried men and women in Rome; and by the laws called *Lex Julia et Papia Pappæa* no unmarried person could take a legacy, whether a portion or the whole of the possessions of a deceased person, unless he got married within a prescribed time from the testator's death. Childless married persons, from the ages of twenty-five to sixty in males, and twenty to fifty in females, according to one of the provisions of this law forfeited one-half of any inheritance or legacy which might be bequeathed to them. There are numerous instances of additional or higher taxes being imposed on bachelors and spinsters in Great Britain, but probably more with a view to the revenue than with any other object.

Bacteria is the name given to certain forms found in animal and vegetable fluids because of their shape, and is derived from a Greek word meaning a club. They are mere points of organized matter, and constitute the lowest form of organic life. They are found in the sap of plants, in the blood of man and of the lower animals, and are abundant in eggs. They bear an important part in healthy as well as morbid processes, in the ripening of fruit as well as decay. They also exist in suspension in the air, and the festering of an open sore is occasioned by the entrance of bacteria from the surrounding air. They also act as powerful organic ferments in the transformation of starch into sugar, of sugar-cane into glucose, etc.

Bad Lands, The, or "Mauvaises Terres," as the old French fur-traders called them, are in Dakota, Wyoming and Northwestern Nebraska, between the north fork of the Platte and the south fork of the Cheyenne River, and cover an area of about 60,000 square miles. They are described as one of the most wonderful regions in the world. Geologists hold that during the miocene period a vast fresh-water lake covered this portion of the American continent. As these lakes drained off, after the subsidence of the plains further east, the original lake-beds were worn into canyons that wind in every conceivable direction. Here and there abrupt, almost perpendicular portions of the ancient beds remain in all imaginable forms, some resembling the ruins of abandoned cities. Towers, spires, cathedrals, obelisks, pyramids and monuments of various shapes appear on every side. Dr. Hayden, the earliest explorer of this region, says: "Not unfrequently the rising or setting sun will light up these grand old ruins with a wild, strange beauty, reminding one of a city illuminated in the night, as seen from some high point. The harder layers project from the sides of the canyons with such regularity that they appear like seats of some vast, weird amphitheater." These lands are entirely unsuited for agriculture, and with rare exceptions are of little value for grazing. They are, however, one of the richest treasuries of fossil remains to be found anywhere. The soft, clayey deposits are in some places literally filled with the bones of extinct species of the horse, rhinoceros, elephant, hog, camel, a deer that strongly resembled a hog, saber-toothed lions, and other marvelous creatures.

Bagnes.—In 1748 the punishment of the galleys was abolished in France, and in its place were established convict prisons known by the name of Bagnes, from the Italian *bagno*, literally a bath—a name supposed to have originated in the fact that the slave prisons at Constantinople contained baths, or because they stood near the baths of the Seraglio. The prisoners were employed during the day at hard labor in arsenals and other public works. The labor of the convicts was turned to profitable account, and various handicrafts were taught, under the direction of overseers. Small wages could be earned by the industrious and clever, and a gradual relaxation of restraint was granted for good behavior. This form of prison was suppressed in 1852 by the Imperial Government, and deportation to Guiana was substituted therefor.

Baiæ.—In ancient times a favorite sea-side resort of the Roman nobles. It was situated on the coast of Campania, ten miles west of Naples, where the present Castle of Baja stands. The town was noted for the beauty of its situation and the excellence of its mineral springs. The ruins, still standing on the desolate coast or rising from the sea, are now the only evidences of the former magnificence of the town. Julius Cæsar, Piso, Pompey, Marius, Julia Mammæa, and others, had country-houses at Baiæ. Seneca warned every one who desired to maintain dominion over his passions to avoid this watering-place. It was considered by the stricter moralists of those times as the abode of voluptuousness and luxury, and a den of vice. The ruins of three supposed temples—one of Venus, one of Mercury and one of Diana Lucifera—as well as the remains of a few *thermæ*, or warm baths, still remain. The harbor, one of the largest belonging to the Romans, is now much destroyed. The surrounding country is covered with the ruins of Roman villas, sepulchral monuments, and other buildings.

Bakshish.—In certain Eastern countries, as Turkey, Egypt, Asia Minor or Syria, the smallest service that is rendered to a traveler must be paid for with bakshish, or, in other words, with a present or gratuity. Ambassadors to the Supreme Porte, on obtaining an audience from the Sultan or the high dignitaries, are obliged by the prompt gift of a bakshish to avoid a peremptory demand for it on the part of the door-keepers and other servants. By degrees bakshish has been fixed by custom at a certain sum, but that is demanded loudly and even insolently.

Balm of Gilead, which is alluded to in the Old Testament as being extremely precious, and which is spoken of by Strabo, Pliny and other ancient writers as being a cure for almost every disease, is a liquid, resinous substance of high fragrance, and enjoys a very high reputation in the east. It is generally believed to be taken from a species of *Balsamodendron*—a small tree growing in Arabia and Abyssinia, and known as *Balsam Gileadense.* The finest balsam, called Opobalsam, or Balm of Mecca, is obtained by incisions, is at first turbid and white, but finally becomes a golden-yellow color, and of a consistence like honey. Inferior kinds are obtained by boiling the fruit and the wood.

Balmoral Castle is the autumnal residence of Queen Victoria, and is situated in a beautiful dell in Braemar, the southwest district of Aberdeenshire, on a natural platform that slopes gently down from the base of Craigengowan to the margin of the river Dee in front. The castle commands a magnificent prospect on all sides. In 1848 Prince Albert purchased the reversion of a thirty-eight-year lease from the representatives of Sir Robert Gordon, who had held it under the Earl of Fife, and in 1852 he acquired the fee-simple of the estate from the Fife trustees for a sum of £32,000. The old castle not being sufficiently commodious for the royal family, Prince Albert erected a new one at his own expense, in what is called the Scottish baronial style of architecture. The castle consists of two separate blocks of buildings, united by wings, and a massive tower, 35 feet square, rising to the height of 80 feet, surmounted by a turret 20 feet high. At a distance the castle, which is built of granite, has a strong and imposing appearance, looking almost as if it had been hewn out of one huge rock of that material. The estate now includes Birkhall, Knock Castle ruins, Loch Muick, and "Dark Lochnagar," celebrated by Byron, and contains about 10,000 acres, in addition to 30,000 acres of hill ground which have been converted into a deer-forest.

Banco, a commercial term meaning the standard money in which a bank keeps its accounts, as distinguished from the current money of the place. The distinction was more necessary when the currency consisted, as it often did, of clipped, worn and foreign coins. These the early banks (Venice, Amsterdam, etc.) received at their intrinsic worth and credited the depositor with their bank value. The term was chiefly applied to the money in which the Hamburg Bank kept its accounts before the adoption of the new universal coinage of the German Empire. It was not represented by any coinage. Sweden had a peculiar bank money, eight dollars banco being equal to three dollars specie. Genoa had at one time a bank standard; and the present current money, being different from that, is still called "fuori banco" outside the bank.

Bank of England, The, was projected by William Paterson, and was incorporated July 27, 1694. At first the charter of the bank was for eleven years only, but in consequence of the great services of the institution to the Government it has been several times renewed. It is governed by a Board of Directors consisting of twenty-four persons, a Governor and a Deputy Governor. The offices of Governor and Deputy Governor are given in rotation; the Deputy Governor always succeeds the Governor, and usually the oldest director who has not been in office becomes Deputy Governor. The Governor and Deputy Governor change every two years. The elder members of the Board—that is, those who have passed the chair, or, in other words, served as Governor—form a standing committee of indefinite powers (no precise description has ever been given of them), and this committee is called the Committee of Treasury. Some of the directors retire annually, but by

courtesy it is always the young ones; those who have served as
Governor always remain.   In the English sense, no banker has a
chance of becoming a bank director.   The mass of the directors
are merchants of experience, who have information as to the present course of trade, and as to the character and wealth of merchants, which is invaluable to the bank.   It is usually about
twenty years from the time of a man's first election that he arrives,
as it is called, at the chair; accordingly, bank directors, when first
chosen by the Board, are comparatively young men.   The management of the entire public debt of Great Britain is in the hands
of the bank, for which it receives a compensation which has from
time to time varied in amount, according to circumstances.

Banks, Origin of.—Banks existed in China, Babylon, Greece,
Rome and other nations long before the Christian era, but the earliest records of European banks now in existence are those of the
Bank of Venice, founded A. D. 1171; the Bank of Barcelona in 1401,
the Bank of Geneva in 1407, and the Bank of Amsterdam in 1609.
The oldest bank-notes of which we have any record were issued in
China as far back as 2657 B. C.   The popular name of this paper
currency was "flying money" or "convenient money," and it was
in form similar to that of American bank-bills, except in the addition of mottoes, such as "Produce all you can; spend with econo-
my."   They bore the name of the bank, number of the note, value,
place of issue, date, and signature of the proper bank officers.
The value was in some cases expressed in figures, in words, and in
pictorial representations showing coins or ingots equal in amount
to the face value of the paper.   They bore also a notice of the
penalties of counterfeiting.   A specimen of these notes, issued in
1399 B. C., is on exhibition in the Asiatic Museum, St. Petersburg,
It is printed in blue ink on paper made from the fiber of the mul-
berry-tree.   In the Metropolitan Museum of Art, New York, there
are Babylonian tablets of banking transactions dating back to the
reign of Nebuchadnezzar.   The earliest of these tablets belong to
the year 601 B. C.   The earliest known Babylonian banking-house
is said to be that of Egibi & Co., a house that seems to have acted
as a sort of imperial banking institution in Babylon from the time
of Sennacherib (about 700 B. C.) down to the reign of Darius, 516
B. C., having been traced through five generations.   Records of
this house, on clay tablets found in an earthen jar in the neighborhood of Hilleh, near Babylon, may be seen in the British
Museum.

Barber's Pole.—The spiral red stripe on a barber's pole is said
to symbolize the winding of a ribbon or bandage around the arm of
a patient upon whom the barber had operated in the capacity of
surgeon.   In former times, when the operation of bleeding was extensively practiced, blood-letting formed a part of the duties of a
barber.

Barbican, a watch-tower before the gate of a castle or fortified
town.   In ancient times the barbican formed an important por-

tion of any defensive work, as from it an enemy could be descried at a great distance. There are a few perfect barbicans remaining in England, as at Alnwick and Warwick; but the best examples of it, as of other parts of the fortifications of the middle ages, are probably to be seen in the town of Carcassone. The street called Barbican, in London, near Aldersgate Street, marks the site of such a work in front of one of the gates of the old city.

Barilla is an impure carbonate of soda, used in the manufacture of soap and of glass, and for other purposes in the arts. It is procured from plants which grow in salt-marshes or other places near the sea. It is obtained by burning the plants much in the same way that sea-weeds are burned upon the coasts of Scotland to procure kelp. The greatest quantities of barilla are produced in Spain and the Balearic Islands, but the Canary Islands, Italy and France also contribute a part. The Spanish barilla is the most esteemed, especially that produced near Alicante. The manufacture of barilla has of late years greatly declined, from the fact that soda can now be made artificially from common salt.

Bashi-Bazouks are wild, turbulent troopers in the service of the Sultan. They are mostly Asiatics, and during the Russo-Turkish war in 1854 had many encounters with the Russians. They fight for pay and plunder, and are greatly dreaded by villagers. In 1855 it was determined by the British Government to take into their pay a Turkish contingent to aid in the operations of the war, and for this purpose an Indian officer was placed in charge of a corps of Bashi-Bazouks; but it was found utterly impossible to reduce them to discipline. Their ferocity was exhibited in the Servian war, but most relentlessly in the massacre of Batak, where, in May, 1876, under Achmet Agha, they slew over 1,000 defenseless Bulgarians in a church in which they had sought refuge.

Basilica was originally a hall in which the laws were administered by the king. Among the Romans it attained its chief importance, and was used not only as a court of justice, but also as a market and meeting-place for the transaction of general business. The earliest form of the basilica was a structure open to the air, surrounded by a peristyle of columns. Eventually an external wall was substituted for the columns; they, if continued at all, being used only as a decoration, and confined generally to the vestibules. The idea of the Christian church was suggested by this form of basilica. [See *Apse.*] Some twenty of these structures are known to have existed in Rome; and later every provincial town, even those of small extent, had each its basilica, as that of Pompeii, which is now the most perfect example, still testifies. The most frequented part of the city was always selected for its site. Some of these buildings were of vast size, as is evidenced by the fact that they furnished seats for the jurymen, who often numbered as many as 180, in addition to the accommodations required by the prætor, the suitors, and their advocates. In the middle ages the term basilica was also applied to the large structures erected over the tombs of persons of distinction, probably from their resemblance to small churches; thus the tomb of Edward the Confessor, in Westminster, is called a basilica. In Italy, and particularly in Rome, many of the churches are still called basiliche.

Basilisk.—According to ancient and mediæval writers the basilisk was a terrible creature. The ancients, Galen and Pliny, describe it as a serpent. In the middle ages it was generally represented as more of a lizard in appearance, but provided with eight instead of four feet. It appears to have been at last pretty completely identified with the cockatrice, which was believed to be generated in a very wonderful manner, being produced from an egg laid by an extremely old cock and hatched by a toad; for which reason we sometimes find the basilisk figured with something like a cock's head. The basilisk was the king of dragons and serpents, all of which left their prey to it whenever it approached. It inhabited the deserts of Africa, and, indeed, could only inhabit a desert, for its breath burned up all vegetation, the flesh fell from the bones of any animal with which it came in contact, and its very look was fatal to life; but a brave man could venture into a cautious contest with it by the use of a mirror, which reflected back its deadly glance upon itself. The basilisk occupies an important place in some of the legends of the saints, and Pope Leo IV is said to have delivered Rome from a basilisk whose breath caused a deadly pestilence.

Basques are a simple, brave and independent people, who from earliest times have inhabited both slopes of the Pyrenees Mountains. Their early history is unknown, but they are supposed to be the descendants of the ancient Iberi, who once occupied the whole of the peninsula. The Basques are a robust and active race, of darker complexion than the Spaniards, and their women are beautiful and skilled in all outdoor work. Their dwellings are scattered over all the heights of the Pyrenees, and they have but few cities or villages. They number about 800,000, somewhat less than a fourth of this number living on the French side of the mountains and the others on the Spanish side. They have been, through the different ages, nominally under the control of the Carthaginians, the Romans, the Goths, the Saracens, the French and the Spanish; but they have never really been conquered, nor have their peculiar characteristics been in any way changed. Their language, which is different from and older than other languages of Europe, is preserved among them in its pristine purity. Politically they are divided into districts, each of which chooses annually an alcalde, who is both a civil and a military officer and a member of the Supreme Junta, which meets every year for deliberation on matters of general interest. Until 1876 the Basques retained a separate constitution guaranteeing them many political and fiscal privileges not possessed by the rest of Spain; but on the suppression of the Carlist insurrection, which had all along its strongholds in the Basque Provinces and in Navarre, the old immunities were abolished. The Basques were known to the Romans as the Cantabri.

Bastile.—The famous French prison known by this name was originally the Castle of Paris, and was built by order of Charles V, between 1370 and 1383, as a defense against the English. When it came to be used as a State prison it was provided with vast bulwarks and ditches. The Bastile had four towers, of five stories each, on each of its larger sides, and it was partly in these towers and partly in underground cellars that the prisons were situated. It was capable of containing seventy to eighty prisoners, a number frequently reached during the reigns of Louis XIV and Louis XV, the majority of them being persons of the higher ranks. The Bastile was destroyed by a mob on the 15th of July, 1789, and the Governor and a number of his officers were killed. On its site now stands the Column of July, erected in memory of the patriots of 1789 and 1830.

Batrachomyomachia.—A serio-comic poem in Greek, describing a battle between frogs and mice. The authorship has been ascribed to Homer, with whose works it has been generally printed. It is a parody of the *Iliad*, in which the military preparations and contests of frogs and mice, with single combats, intervention of the gods and other Homeric circumstances are described with much humor.

Bayeaux Tapestry, The, is a web of canvas or linen cloth upon which is embroidered, in woolen threads of various colors, a representation of the invasion and conquest of England by the Normans. The canvas is 214 feet long by 20 inches broad, and is preserved in the public library at Bayeaux. Tradition asserts that it is the work of Matilda, wife of William the Conqueror, and it is believed that if she did not actually stitch the whole of it with her own hands, she at least took part in it, and directed the execution of it by her maids, and afterward presented it to the Cathedral of Bayeaux as a token of her appreciation of the effective assistance which its bishop, Odo, rendered her husband at the battle of Hastings. Some antiquarians contend that it was not the work of Queen Matilda (the wife of the Conqueror), who died in 1083, but of the Empress Matilda (the daughter of Henry I), who died in 1167. The tapestry contains, beside the figures of 505 quadrupeds, birds, sphinxes, etc., the figures of 623 men, 202 horses, 55 dogs, 37 buildings, 41 ships and boats, and 49 trees—in all, 1,512 figures. It is divided into 72 distinct compartments, each representing one particular historical occurrence, and bearing an explanatory Latin inscription. A tree is usually chosen to divide the principal events from each other. This pictorial history—for so it may be called—gives an exact and minute portraiture of the manners and customs of the times; and it has been remarked that the arms and habits of the Normans are identical with those of the Danes as they appear in the miniature paintings of a manuscript of the time of King Cnut in the British Museum.

Bay, Symbolism of.—The leaves of the bay-tree, by which name are known a number of trees and shrubs, have from early times been associated with popular superstitions and usages. They have adorned houses and churches at Christmas along with evergreens; and sprigs of bay, as well as laurel, have been worn in the hat or wreathed around the head in token of rejoicing or of some meritorious deed. The withering of bay-trees was reckoned an omen of death, according to Shakespeare. Thus, Richard II: "'Tis thought the King is dead; we will not stay. The bay-trees in our country all are withered." "Parkinson's Garden of Flowers," published in 1629, says: "The bay-leaves are necessary both for evil uses and for physic, both for the sick and for the sound, both for the living and the dead. It serveth to adorn the house of God as well as man; to crowne or enriche, as with a garland, the heads of the living; and to strike and deck forth the bodies of the dead; so that from the cradel to the grave we still have need of it."

Beating the Bounds is an expression used in England to designate periodical surveys, which are made for the preservation of the ancient boundaries of parishes. The clergyman of the parish, with the parochial officers and other parishioners, followed by the boys of the parish school headed by their master, go in procession, on Holy Thursday or Ascension Day, to the different parish boundaries, which boundaries the boys strike with peeled willow wands that they bear in their hands; hence the expression "beating the bounds." In olden times the beating was not, however, always confined to the boundaries; but when it was desired to preserve evidence of particular boundaries, the boys themselves, or one of them, was beaten, and received a stated fee for the castigation out of the parish funds. It was thought that the impression made on the boy's memory by the whipping was calculated to have a beneficial effect on the preservation of his evidence.

Beer, Origin of.—The Germans, Gauls and Bretons manufactured beer from barley and wheat as far back as there are any written records regarding them. Tacitus tells us that beer was a common beverage of the Germans when he wrote, in the first century. We learn from Pliny that "The people of Spain, in particular, brew this liquor so well that it will keep a long time." He describes it as made from corn and water. The earliest of Greek writers speak of wine made from barley, and of the art of making it as derived from the Egyptians. It is believed that Archilocus, the Parian poet, who lived about 700 B. C., referred to beer-drinking when he depicted the follies and vicious indulgences of his time In the ancient writings of China reference is made to a fermented drink called "sam-shoo," made from rice. When it was first invented is unknown, but it was probably long before the Christian Era.

Behistun, Sacred Rock of.—The Persian King, Darius Hystaspis, about 500 B. C. ordered a number of inscriptions to be made on a rock called Mount Bagistanus, which stood near the town of Behistun, or Baghistan. The lines are in three languages—Persian, Babylonic and Scythic—and are on the face of the rock three hundred feet from the ground. The inscriptions give the genealogy of Darius for eight generations, and recount the provinces of his empire and his various achievements. The monarch is also pictorially represented armed with a bow, his foot upon the prostrate figure of a man, while nine rebels chained together by the neck stand humbly before him. The rock upon which these inscriptions were made rises to a height of 1,700 feet on one side, and is now known as the Sacred Rock of Behistun.

Bellerophon.—According to Greek legend Bellerophon was the son of Glaucus and grandson of Sisyphus, and was endowed by the gods with great manly vigor and beauty. Anthea, the wife of Prœtus, King of Argos, became enamored of him; but the virtuous youth rejecting all her advances, hate occupied the place of love in the bosom of the disappointed queen, and she accused him to Prœtus of an attempt on her honor. This induced the king to send Bellerophon to Iobates, King of Lycia, with a sealed message. After being entertained at the court nine days he delivered the letter, which contained a request that Iobates would cause the youth to be slain. As Bellerophon was his guest, this Iobates was reluctant to do, and he consequently imposed upon the youth the seemingly impossible task of slaying the formidable Chimæra. Bellerophon, mounted on the winged steed Pegasus, given him by Pallas, ascended into the air and succeeded in slaying the monster with his arrows. He was then sent by King Iobates against the Amazons, whom he defeated. On his way home he destroyed an ambuscade of Lycians which Iobates had set for his destruction. The king now perceiving him to be of the race of the gods, kept him in Lycia, giving him his daughter and half the royal dignity, and the people bestowed upon him an ample *temenus* of arable and plantation land. Bellerophon at last attempted, by means of Pegasus, to ascend to heaven; but Jupiter, incensed at his boldness, sent an insect to sting the steed, which flung its rider to the earth, where he wandered in solitude and melancholy until his death.

Benedick.—A term commonly used in allusion to a married man, taken from Benedick, a young lord of Padua, who in Shakespeare's "Much Ado About Nothing" marries Beatrice after a courtship of wit and raillery. It is now generally written Benedict.

Benedict, Saint, was born at Nursia, in Umbria, Italy, in 480 A. D., of a rich and respected family. At an early age he became dissatisfied with the instruction which he was receiving at school, and believing that only in the holy science of solitary meditation could a safe refuge from the sins of the times be found, he retired to a deserted country lying on a lake. Here, in a cavern (which afterward received the name of the Holy Grotto), he dwelt for three years, until his fame spread over the country, and multitudes came to see him. He was now appointed abbot of a neighboring monastery, but soon left it, as the morals of the half-wild monks were not severe enough for his taste. He drew crowds of wanderers about him, and wealthy Romans also placed their sons under his care, anxious that they should be trained for a spiritual life. He was thus enabled to found twelve cloisters, over each of which he placed a superior. Along with a few followers he founded a monastery on Monte Cassino, near Naples, afterward one of the richest and most famous in Italy. Here he extirpated the lingering relics of paganism, and had his celebrated interview with Totila, King of the Goths, to whom he spoke frankly and sharply on his errors. The monasteries which were founded by Benedict were simply religious colleges, intended to develop a high spiritual character which might beneficially influence the world. Saint Benedict was the founder of monasticism in the west. He died March 21, 543.

Benedictines, as the order of monks were called who followed the rule of St. Benedict, are regarded as the main agents in the spread of Christianity, civilization and learning in the west. At one time the order is said to have had as many as 37,000 monasteries, and counted among their branches the great Order of Clugny, founded about 910; the still greater Order of the Cistercians, founded in the following century; the congregations of Monte Cassino in 1408, of St. Vanne in 1600, and of St. Maur on the Loire in 1627. All the Benedictine houses in France were affiliated to this last congregation. Among the monks of St. Maur were many noted scholars, and the services they rendered to literature it would be difficult to overestimate. At the Revolution in 1792 the Benedictines were suppressed in France and their splendid conventual buildings were destroyed, but the order was revived later. Most of the richest abbeys and all the cathedral priories (excepting Carlisle) in England belonged to the Benedictines, and they had numerous monasteries in Scotland. The Benedictines gained great distinctions in both Italy and Germany—in the former as literati, jurists and physicians, and in the latter as promoters of education and as the founders of mediæval scholasticism. As early as 1354 this order could boast of having numbered among its followers 24 popes, 200 cardinals, 7,000 archbishops, 15,000 bishops, 1,560 canonized saints, and 5,000 holy persons judged worthy of canonization, besides 20 empresses, 47 kings, above 50 queens, 20 sons of emperors, 48 sons of kings, 100 princesses, and an immense number of the nobility. In the fifteenth century the order had 15,107 monasteries, of which only 5,000 were left after the Reformation, and there are now not more than 800. They were commonly styled the "Black Monks" from their dress, a long black gown with a cowl or hood of the same, and a scapulary. The rule of St. Benedict was much less severe than that which the eastern ascetics followed. Beside implicit obedience to their superiors, the Benedictines were to shun laughter, to hold no private property, to live sparely, to exercise hospitality, and, above all, to be industrious.

Benefit of Clergy.—Until the reign of Henry VI all members of the clerical order were almost totally exempted from the jurisdiction and authority of the secular magistrate in respect of crimes and offenses. This was called "Benefit of the Clergy." If a priest or "clerk" happened to be imprisoned by the secular arm on a criminal charge, he was, on the demand of the bishop, instantly delivered up without any further inquisition—not to be let loose upon the community, it is true, but to be detained by the ordinary till he had either purged himself from the offense, or, having failed to do so, had been degraded. In the reign mentioned this was so far altered that the prisoner had first to be arraigned, but could arrest judgment by plea, declining the jurisdiction either before or after conviction. At first the test of admission to this singular privilege was the clerical dress and tonsure; but in course of time all who could read—a mark of great learning in those days —whether of the clergy or laity, were allowed the privilege. Laymen, however, could only claim it once, and upon doing so were burned on the hand and discharged. He was then tried by the bishop and usually acquitted, even though he had been previously convicted either by his country or his own confession. By this acquittal the offender was restored to his liberty, his credit and his property—in short, in the eye of the law he became a new and innocent person. The test of reading was applied as follows: On conviction, the felon demanded his clergy, whereupon a book (commonly a Psalter) was put into his hand, which he was required to read, when the judge demanded of the bishop's commissary, *Legit ut clericus?* If the answer was simply *legit*, the prisoner was burned on the hand and discharged; but if it was *non legit*, he suffered the punishment due to his offense. During the reign of Queen Anne the benefit of clergy was extended to all persons convicted of clergyable offenses, whether they could read or not, but it was discretionary with the judge whether a fine or imprisonment was inflicted. The benefit of clergy was totally abolished during the reign of George IV.

Beowulf is an Anglo-Saxon epic poem descriptive of legendary events referring to the Teutonic races in about the middle of the fifth century. The manuscript of the poem which is in the Cottonian Library consists of two portions, written at different times and by different hands, and is manifestly a copy executed probably about the beginning of the eighth century from an older and far completer version of the poem. It is one of the greatest literary and philological curiosities, and one of the most remarkable historical monuments in existence. Much learned labor has been bestowed upon this strange relic. The following is a brief outline of the story; Beowulf is introduced to us preparing for a piratical adventure. Then the scene changes, and the Palace of Hrothgar rises before us. Here the Danish King has assembled his warriors, and holds a feast unconscious of his deadly peril. Grendel, a mighty hunter of the marshes, malignant and cruel, hears the sounds of revelry, and stealing into the palace after dark, when the feast is over, he seizes and destroys thirty of the sleeping *thegns.* Twelve years pass before the outrage is avenged. Beowulf has heard of the crimes of the monster and comes with his Geats (Jutes) to inflict punishment. The inevitable feast follows his arrival, and that night, when the shadows of darkness have fallen, Grendel comes swiftly to the palace from the misty moors and assails Beowulf. A fierce struggle ensues, but the monster is baffled and obliged to flee. Next day a second feast is held in honor of the hero's success, and that night the mother of the monster secretly enters and destroys one of the king's dearest *thegns.* Beowulf undertakes to avenge him, and with the help of a magic sword, which came into his grasp, he first slays the mother and then destroys Grendel. Beowulf then returns home, and eventually succeeds to the throne on the death of his kinsman, Higelac.

Berbers are tribes inhabiting the mountainous regions of Barbary and the northern portions of the Great Desert. They were originally a branch of the Semitic stock, and notwithstanding the fact that in consequence of having been conquered in succession by the Phœnicians, Romans, Vandals and Arabs they have become to some extent a mixed race, they still retain, in great part, their distinctive peculiarities. It is estimated that there are between three and four million of these people. They are of medium stature, sparely but strongly built, and their complexion varies from a red to a yellow brown. They live in clay huts and tents, but in the larger villages they have stone houses. They practice agriculture, and have herds of sheep and cattle. They work the mines of iron and lead in the Atlas Mountains, and they manufacture rude agricultural implements, as well as swords, guns and gunpowder. They formerly professed Christianity, but are now followers of Mohammed. In disposition they are cruel, suspicious and implacable, and are usually at war among themselves or with their neighbors. The name by which they call themselves, and which was known to the Greeks and Romans, is Amazigh, or Mazigh, Mazys, Amoshagh, Imoshagh, etc., according to the locality, and whether singular or plural. They formed the larger portion of the population inhabiting the southern coast of the Mediterranean from Egypt to the Atlantic Ocean till the eleventh century; but on the great Arab immigrations, which then took place, they were driven to the Atlas Mountains and to the desert regions, where they now live.

Berchta.—According to German mythology, Berchta was the name given in the south of Germany and Switzerland to a spiritual being who was apparently the same as the Hulda of North

Germany. Originally she represented one of the kindly and benign aspects of the unseen powers, but eventually she became an object of terror and a bugbear to frighten children. The last day of the year is ascribed sacred to her, and as she has the oversight of spinners, she destroys any flax that she finds left on the distaff on that day. Oatmeal gruel or pottage and fish is the prescribed fare with which her festival is kept. If she catches any person eating other food on that day she cuts them up, fills their paunches with chopped straw and other such agreeable stuffing, and then sews up the wound with a plowshare for a needle and an iron chain for a thread. She is also in some places the queen of crickets. She is represented as having an immensely large foot and an iron nose. It is probable that the numerous stories of the " White Lady " who appears in noble houses at night, rocks and nurses the children and acts as the guardian angel of the race have their origin in the ancient heathen goddess Berchta. Berchta is the original form of the name Bertha, and is from the same root as the English name *bright*, and means " shining," " white."

Bible, English Translations of.—Between the eighth and tenth centuries portions of the Bible were translated into Anglo-Saxon by Aldhelm, Egbert, Bede, and others. In 1290 an English version of the Psalms was made. Wycliffe's version of the New Testament was finished in 1380, and a little later he completed the Old. The seven penitential Psalms were apparently printed in 1505. Before 1526 William Tyndale had completed an English translation of the New Testament. In the beginning of that year they were secretly conveyed to England from the Continent, where the translation had been made, where they were bought up and burned. The excellence of his translation is evidenced by the fact that in our present version a very large portion of the New Testament is taken *verbatim* from Tyndale's translation. In 1535 the first English version of the whole Bible was published by Miles Coverdale, a friend of Tyndale's, and was dedicated to Henry VIII. Between that year and 1557 several versions of the Bible were printed, but they were in the greater part revisions of Tyndale's previous work. The Geneva Bible, or, as best known, the Breeches Bible, appeared in 1557. It was translated by several English divines who had fled to Geneva to escape from the persecutions of Bloody Mary, and received the name of Breeches Bible on account of the rendering of Genesis iii. 7: " Then the eyes of both of them were opened, and they knew that they were naked, and they sewed fig-tree leaves together and made themselves *breeches.*" The Bishops' Bible was published in London in 1568. The text of this was compared with the original by eight bishops and seven other scholars of reputation, who appended their initials to their respective tasks. In 1582 appeared, at Rheims, in France, an English version of the New Testament prepared by several Roman Catholic exiles, and in 1609-'10 a similar version of the Old Testament at Douay. They form the standard English Scriptures of the Roman Catholics, being generally known as the Douay Bible. In July, 1604, King James appointed fifty-four scholars to prepare a new version of the Bible. Only forty-seven accepted the appointment, and the result of their labors was the publication in 1610 of the version known as "King James' Bible," which has been in common use from that time to this, slightly modified by the revision prepared by the most learned English and American scholars a few years ago.

Billings, Josh, the *nom de plume* of Henry W. Shaw, who was born in Lanesborough, Mass., in the year 1818. He first became known as a humorous writer and lecturer in 1863, and since that time his comic sketches have been extensively published in the journals of the United States and England.

Black Death is believed to have been an aggravated outburst of the Oriental plague, which from the earliest records of history has periodically appeared in Asia and Northern Africa. It appeared in great virulence in 1348–'49, and was brought from the Orient to Constantinople, and then appeared in Sicily and several coast towns of Italy. It shortly broke out at Avignon, advanced then to Southern France, Spain, and Northern Italy. Passing through France, and visiting but not yet ravaging Germany, it made its way to England, cutting down its first victims at Dorset in August, 1348. Thence it traveled slowly, reaching London early in the winter. Soon it embraced the entire kingdom, penetrating to every rural hamlet, so that England became a mere pest-house. The utter powerlessness of medical skill before the disease was owing partly to the physicians' ignorance of its nature, and largely to the effect of the spirit of terror which hung like a pall over men's minds. The havoc wrought by the disease in England was terrible, as it is believed that at least 2,500,000 souls perished. The ravages of the pestilence over the rest of the world was no less great. Germany is said to have lost 1,244,434 victims; Italy, over half the population. On a moderate calculation it may be estimated that there perished in Europe during the first appearance of the black death fully 25,000,000 human beings. To add to the horrors of that dreadful time a fearful persecution was visited upon the Jews, who were accused of having caused the pestilence by poisoning the public wells, and they were killed by fire and torture wherever found. The chief symptoms of the disease are described as "spitting, in some cases actual vomiting, of blood, the breaking out of inflammatory boils in parts or over the whole of the body, and the appearance of those dark blotches upon the skin" which suggested its most startling name. The prevalence and severity of the pestilence at this time is ascribed to the disturbed conditions of the elements that preceded it, as for a number of years Asia and Europe had suffered from mighty earthquakes, furious tornadoes, violent floods, and clouds of locusts darkening the air and poisoning it with their corrupting bodies.

Black Forest.—A noted wooded mountain chain, situated in Baden and Wurtemberg. Two of its passes, the Kniebis and the Halle, acquired considerable celebrity during the wars of the French Revolution. The first, situated on the borders between Baden and Wurtemberg, at the source of the Murg, was taken by the French in 1796 and in 1797. The Halle is known in connection with Moreau's retreat in 1796. The Black Forest attains its greatest elevation in the bare and round-topped Feldberg, which rises near the source of the Wiesen. The great mass called the Kaiserstuhl (Emperor's chair), situated near Breisach, is quite isolated. Among its numerous valleys the Murgthal is the most famous for its natural beauties. Summer rye, oats and potatoes are cultivated in some parts of the Black Forest, but it is with difficulty, and the rearing of cattle is prosecuted with much greater success. The manufacture of wooden clocks and other kinds of time-pieces and music-boxes is an important industry of the inhabitants. The Black Forest is rich in mineral waters, as the baths of Baden-Baden and Wildbad.

Black Friday.—The term "Black Friday" was first used in England, and was applied to the Friday on which the news reached London that Charles Edward, the young Pretender, had arrived at Derby. This created a terrible panic. On May 11, 1866, the term was again used in London, when the failure of Overend, Gurney & Co., on the previous day, was followed by a wide-spread financial ruin. In September, 1869, occurred the celebrated Black Friday in the United States. The cause of the panic was the attempt made by Jay Gould and others to create a corner in the gold market by buying all the gold in the banks of New York City, amounting to $15,000,000. For several days the value of gold rose steadily, and the speculators aimed to carry it from 144 to 200. On the Friday following (September 24th) the whole city was in a ferment, the banks were rapidly selling, gold was at 162 1-2 and still rising. Men became insane, and everywhere the wildest excitement raged, for it seemed probable that the business houses must be closed from ignorance of the prices to be charged for goods. But in the midst of the panic it was reported that Secretary Boutwell of the United States Treasury had thrown $4,000,000 in gold on the market, and at once gold fell and the excitement ceased. It is estimated that the profits of Gould and his partners were at least $11,000,000.

Blackmail.—In the beginning of the eighteenth century the Scottish Highlands, and part of the Lowlands bordering on the Highlands, were in an extremely barbarous state, enjoying but an imperfect protection under the law. Theft and robbery were not then regarded as they are now; to carry off the cattle of a neighbor was perhaps only wreaking out an old family feud or clan dispute. In these circumstances a class of men rose up who proposed to take upon themselves the duty of protecting the property of individuals on the payment by them of a percentage on their rents, generally four per cent. This was known as blackmail. Notwithstanding the fact that the men engaged in this business were nearly all of them of good Highland families, there was only too good reason to suspect that they encouraged and profited by robberies, in order to make the blackmail a necessity. About 1730 the celebrated Rob Roy was a notable levier of blackmail in the southern Highlands. The levier of the import held himself bound to pay an equivalent for all cattle which were lost by the payers of blackmail which he was unable to recover. Blackmail ceased to be heard of after the breaking out of the rebellion under the young Pretender in 1745, and the word was gradually identified with the blackmail of modern society.

Blind, Education of the.—The main end to be sought in the education of the blind is to fit them to compete in as many ways as possible with the more fortunate who can see, and take them out of their despondency and give them a worthy object to accomplish in life. The first institution for the blind was founded in Memmingen by Weef VI in 1178, the second in Paris by St. Louis in 1260, and the first for the employment of the adult blind in Edinburgh by Dr. Johnson in 1793. The work in a school for the blind is about equal to the ordinary high-school course. Pupils are classified as in other schools; but persons who become blind at the age of twenty, for instance, must begin with the alphabet, as little children do. Writing is taught by tracing with a pencil letters sunk into a stiff card. This manner of writing can be read by seeing-persons only. The point systems—Braille's and Waite's—are generally used by blind persons to communicate with each other. In the Illinois Institution for the Blind the use of the typewriter is being taught, and it is said that some excellent work has already been done by the pupils. In the study of music the notes are read to the pupil, who writes them down in the Braille or Waite systems, and then studies them at the instrument until they are memorized. In most schools books in raised print are used. The first book of this character was printed in Paris in 1698 by M. Valentine Hauy.

Blood, Circulation of.—The true theory regarding the circulation of blood was discovered by the celebrated English physiologist, William Harvey, about 1616. He received his diploma as Doctor of Medicine from the University of Padua in 1602, and in 1615 was made Lecturer at the College of Physicians in London, an appointment which he held for forty years. It is generally supposed that he expounded his views regarding blood circulation in his first course of lectures. He died at London June 3, 1657.

Bloody Statute was six articles having for their object the compelling of all the subjects of the Crown to a uniform profession of certain doctrines. It was passed January 7, 1541, in the thirty-third year of the reign of Henry VIII, and at first was enforced with great severity; but it was somewhat mitigated in 1544, and was finally repealed in 1549. The doctrines were: 1.

The real presence of Christ in the Eucharist and Transubstantiation. 2. The sufficiency of communion in one kind only. 3. The unlawfulness of the marriage of priests. 4. The obligation of vows of chastity. 5. The propriety of retaining private masses. 6. The expediency and necessity of auricular confession. The penalties attached to the act exceeded in severity almost every precedent, at least in England, and were particularly severe against impugners of the first article, death being the prescribed penalty.

Bluebeard, Story of, was written during the reign of Louis XIV by a Frenchman named Perrault, and was probably suggested by the deeds of Giles de Laval, better known as Marshal de Retz. This bloodthirsty character was born in 1396, and subsequently served under the Duke of Bretagne and Charles VII with distinction, and was one of the trusted captains of Joan of Arc. In 1432 he was reputed the richest man in France, but quickly squandered his fortune. It is said that soon after this event, through the influence of an alchemist named Prelati, Giles pledged all but his soul to the devil in exchange for wealth equal to that which he had spent. At all events, his career from that time became that of a demon. Young women, girls of tender age, and even little children were inveigled into his strongly-guarded castles and never seen alive again. It is related that the children were dangled at ropes' ends, pricked with needles, and otherwise tortured until dead, and their heads were afterward used as ornaments for his mantels and bed-posts. After he had carried on this career of crime for about eight years he was arrested, confessed, and burned at the stake about December 22, 1440. The remains of fifty-four of his victims were identified.

Blue-Books, a name popularly applied to the reports and other papers printed by the English Parliament, because they are usually covered with blue covers. The practice of printing, and to some extent publishing, the proceedings of the House of Commons began in the year 1681, when dispute ran high on the question of excluding the Duke of York from the succession to the throne.

Blue Laws on Smoking.—The Massachusetts laws against the use of tobacco were at one time exceeding stringent. In October, 1632, a law was passed to the effect that "It is ordered, that noe person shall take any tobacco publiquely, under paine of punishment; also that every one shall pay 1d. for every time hee is convicted of taking tobacco in any place, and that any Assistant shall have power to receive evidence and give order for levyeing of it, as also to give order for the levyeing of the officer's charge. This order to begin the 10th of November next." In September, 1634, another law on the same article was passed. It read: "Victualers, or keepers of an Ordinary, shall not suffer any tobacco to be taken in their howses, under the penalty of 5s. for every offence, to be payde by the victuler, and 12d. by the party that takes it. Further it is ordered, that noe person shall take tobacco publiquely, under penalty of 2s. 6d., nor privately, in his own house, or in the howse of another, before strangers, and that two or more shall not take it togeather, anywhere, under the aforesaid penalty for every offence." In November, 1637, the record reads: "All former laws against tobacco are repealed, and tobacco is sett at liberty;" but in September, 1638, "the (General) Court, finding that since the repealing of the former laws against tobacco, the same is more abused than before, it hath therefore ordered, that no man shall take any tobacco in the fields, except in his journey, or at meale times, under paine of 12d. for every offence; nor shall take any tobacco in (or so near) any dwelling house, barne, corne or hay rick, as may likely indanger the fireing thereof, upon paine of 10s. for every offence; nor shall take any tobacco in any inne or common victualing house except in a private roome thereat, which if they do, then such person is fourthwith to forbeare, upon paine of 12s. 6d. for every offence. Noe man shall kindle fyre by gunpowder, for takeing tobacco, except in his journey, upon paine of 12d. for every offence."

Blue Stockings.—The term "blue stocking" originated in England about a century ago. Its invention is traced to the days of Doctor Johnson, and was applied then as now to ladies who cultivated learned conversations, and found enjoyment in the discussion of questions which had been monopolized by men. It is said by Dr. John Doran, who in his work, "A Lady of the Last Century," gave an account of Mrs. Montague and the "blue stockings" of her time, that in 1757 it was quite the thing for ladies to form evening assemblies, when they might participate in talk with literary and ingenious men. One of the best known and most popular members of one of these societies was said to have been a Mr. Stillingfleet, who always wore blue stockings, and when at any time he happened to be absent from these gatherings it was usually remarked that "we can do nothing without blue stockings;" and by degrees the term "blue stockings" was applied to all clubs of the kind described, and eventually to the ladies who attended their meetings.

Boiling-Point.—By the boiling-point is meant that temperature at which any particular liquid will boil, boiling being a passing into vapor with ebullition. It varies for different substances, but is always the same for a given substance if the pressure and other conditions are unchanged. The ordinary pressure is that of the atmosphere at the sea-level, viz., about fifteen pounds to the square inch. If the pressure is reduced, as by going up on a high mountain, or by experimenting in a partial vacuum, the boiling-point will be much lowered; and, on the other hand, increased pressure will raise it. In every case it indicates that amount of heat-energy which is necessary in order to overcome the cohesive force of the liquid and the pressure on its surface in order that the molecules may pass off as vapor. While a liquid is boiling the temperature remains constant, the heat which is continually supplied being used up in converting new particles of the liquid into vapor, doing *internal work* by overcoming the cohesion of the molecules. The presence of salt in water raises its boiling-point, and when it passes off in vapor the salt is left behind. The material of the containing-vessel also has an effect upon the boiling-point. Under fixed conditions, sulphurous acid boils at 13.10 degrees, Fahr.; ether, 96.3; carbon bisulphide, 118.5; wood-spirit, 151.3; ethylic (ordinary) alcohol, 173; water, 212; sulphuric acid, 620; mercury, 662.

Bonnet.—The English bonnet, which was superseded in the early part of the sixteenth century by the hat, was made of cloth, silk or velvet, less or more ornamented, according to the taste or means of the wearer. In Scotland, however, bonnets were universally worn for a century or two later, and they still are, to a certain extent, a national characteristic. The bonnet worn by the Lowland Scottish peasantry was of a broad, round, and flat shape, overshadowing the face and neck, and of a dark-blue color, excepting a red tuft like a cherry on the top. It was made of thick milled woolen, and with reasonable care would last a man his whole life. From having been worn, till comparatively late times, by small rural proprietors—such as owners of a cottage and an acre or two of land—it gave to these local notabilities the distinctive appellation of Bonnet Lairds. The bonnets worn by the Highlanders were made of the same fabric, but rise to a point in front and are without any rim. From time immemorial these various kinds of Scots bonnets have been manufactured at Stewarton, a small town in Ayrshire. Formerly the Stewarton bonnet-makers formed a corporation, which, like other old guilds, was governed by regulations conceived in a narrow and often amusingly absurd spirit; one of the rules of the fraternity, however, can be spoken of only with commendation, for it enforced a certain weight of material in each bonnet, as well as durability in the color.

Boomerang is an instrument of war or of the chase used by the aborigines of Australia. It is of hard wood, of a bent form; the shape is parabolic. It is about two and a half inches broad, a third of an inch thick, and two feet long, the extremities being rounded. The method of using this remarkable weapon is very peculiar. It is taken by one end, with the bulged side downward, and thrown forward as if to hit some object twenty-five yards in advance. Instead of continuing to go directly forward, as would naturally be expected, it slowly ascends in the air, whirling round and round, and describing a curved line till it reaches a considerable height, when it begins to retrograde, and finally sweeps over the head of the projector and falls behind him. This surprising motion is produced by the reaction of the air upon a missile of this peculiar shape. The boomerang is one of the ancient instruments of war of the natives of Australia. They are said to be very dexterous in hitting birds with it—the birds being, of course, behind them, and perhaps not aware that they are objects of attack.

Bore.—When a river expands gradually toward a very wide mouth, and is subject to high tides, the spring flood-tide drives an immense volume of water from the sea into the river, the water accumulates in the estuary more rapidly than it can flow up into the river, and thus there is gradually formed a kind of watery ridge stretching across the estuary, and rushing up toward the river with great violence. This is called a bore. It is many feet in height in some cases, and contends against the descending river with frightful noise. The most celebrated bores are those of the Ganges, Brahmaputra and Indus, and the phenomenon is also observable in several rivers of Great Britain.

Boreas, the North wind, regarded in the Grecian mythology as a deity. According to the poets he was the son of Astræus and Aurora. He loved Orithyia, the daughter of Erechtheus, King of Athens, and carried her off to Thrace, where she bore him the winged youths, Zetes and Calais, and two daughters, Chione and Cleopatra. The Athenians ascribed the destruction of the fleet of Xerxes by a storm to the partiality of Boreas for the country of Orithyia, and built a temple to him after that event. Boreas is also said by Homer to have turned himself into a horse, out of love for the mares of Erichthonius, and to have begotten on them twelve foals remarkable for their fleetness. The rape of Orithyia was represented on the ark of Cypselos, where Boreas, instead of feet, has the tails of serpents.

Boston Mob.—A mob of several thousand people endeavored on October 21, 1835, to break up a meeting of the Female Anti-Slavery Society in Boston. The cause of this hostile demonstration was primarily owing to the fact that it was expected that an address would be delivered by a Mr. George Thompson, who was very unpopular—first, because he was an Abolitionist; second, because he was an Englishman; and third, because he was said to use very strong language, even advocating the rising of the slaves against their masters. Thompson, however, had left Boston the day previous to the meeting in order to prevent just what occurred. Notwithstanding the fact that the rioters were informed by the mayor that Thompson was not in the hall, the excitement continued so great that the ladies were forced to retire. The mob then turned their attention to William Lloyd Garrison, who had intended to address the meeting, but who had, by the solicitation of the ladies who feared for his personal safety, retired to the office of the *Liberator*, next door. When the excitement was at its height Garrison escaped from his office through a rear window and made his way into the upper part of a carpenter shop near by, where an effort was made to conceal him. He had, however, been seen by the mob, and soon several ruffians broke into the room and seized him, with the evident intention of hurling him from the window, but abandoned that idea in favor of dragging him through the streets by a rope. Before this could be put in practice, fortunately he was rescued by two powerful men, and eventually reached the mayor's office in the City Hall uninjured, but with his clothing literally torn into shreds. From there he was removed for safety to a jail, and the following day left Boston for a time.

Botanic Gardens.—In 1309, A. D., the first approach to a Botanic Garden was made in the garden of Matthæus Sylvaticus, at Salerno; botanic science, however, being merely subservient to medicine, and it was not until 1533 that the first true botanic garden was formed. This was made for Gaspar de Gabrieli, a wealthy Tuscan noble at Padua, and was followed by similar gardens at Pisa, Florence, Bologna and Rome, the first public garden being that at Pisa. In 1545 a public garden was established at Padua by decree of the Republic of Venice. In 1580 the Elector of Saxony established a public botanic garden at Leipsic, which was soon followed by others. There was no botanic garden in France till Louis XIII established the *Jardin des Plantes* at Paris, which was completed in 1634. The first public botanic garden was established in England at Oxford by the Earl of Danby, although numerous private gardens had existed in England for the greater part of a century. The botanic garden at Edinburgh, the first in Scotland, was founded about 1680. The botanic garden at Kew occupies a high place among British national institutions, and possesses one of the richest collections of plants in the world. The gardens connected with the imperial palace at Schonbrunn, in Austria, and that of Berlin, are the greatest in Germany. The *Jardin des Plantes* in Paris undoubtedly may be regarded as holding the first place on the continent of Europe, both with reference to the strictly scientific study of botany and to the care bestowed upon the introduction and diffusion of useful or beautiful plants from all parts of the world. In the United States the botanic gardens of New York and Philadelphia are the most worthy of notice.

Bottle Chart.—In 1843 a chart of bottle-voyages in the Atlantic was constructed by Lieutenant Beecher, an English naval officer, with the idea that by such means the determination of currents might be illustrated. The time which elapses between the launching of the bottle from the ship and the finding of it on shore or the picking of it up by some other ship has varied from a few days to sixteen years, while the straight-line distance between the two points has varied from a few miles to 5,000 miles. The chart is marked by several hundred straight lines, each drawn from the latitude and longitude of immersion to the latitude and longitude of the finding.

Boy Bishop.—In most Catholic countries the custom of electing a boy bishop on St. Nicholas' Day prevailed from an early period. He was chosen from the children of the church or cathedral choir, or from the pupils of the grammar-school, and his authority lasted to Holy Innocents' Day (December 28th). He was arrayed in episcopal vestments, and, attended by a crowd of subordinates in priestly dress, went about with songs and dances from house to house blessing the people. He and his fellows performed all the ceremonies of the church with the exception of the mass. In portions of England the boy bishop had the power of disposing of such prebends as happened to fall vacant during the days of his episcopacy, and if he died during his office the funeral honors of a bishop, with a monument, were granted him. The custom was finally abolished in England at about the close of the reign of Queen Elizabeth.

Boycott and Boycotting.—The origin of the term "Boycotting" was as follows: A Captain Boycott was the agent of a landowner in Ireland. His policy proved to be distasteful and offensive to the tenants, and such was their feeling in the matter that they asked the landlord to remove him. This was refused, and in retaliation the tenants and their friends refused to work for or under Boycott. They would not harvest his crops, and they made an agreement among themselves that none of them or theirs should assist or work for him in the harvest. His crops were endangered, when relief arrived in the person of certain Ulster men, who, under the protection of troops, harvested the crops of Boycott. The defensive league of the tenantry was much more powerful and effective than might be supposed from the single instance of the combination referred to above. The ramifications of their compact were very numerous and extensive. For example, if any one had dealings with Boycott or those who represented him, then no one was to have any dealings with that person. If a man worked for Boycott he was looked upon by his old friends and neighbors as a stranger—no one would sell to or buy of him, no one was to know him. The effect of this agreement when carried to this extent was just what its authors proposed, and "Boycotting" has become a very forcible phrase.

Bread-Fruit-Tree is a native of the islands of the Pacific Ocean and of the Indian Archipelago, and grows to a height of from forty to fifty feet. It has large, pinnatifid leaves, frequently twelve to eighteen inches long, dark green and glossy. The fruit of the bread-tree, which in shape and size resembles a muskmelon, supplies the principal part of the food of the inhabitants of these islands. It is attached to the small branches of the tree by a small, thick stalk, and hangs either singly or in clusters of two or three together. It contains a somewhat fibrous pulp, which, when ripe, becomes juicy and yellow, but has then a rotten taste. At an earlier stage, when it is gathered for use, the pulp is white and mealy and of a consistence resembling new bread. The common method of preparing this fruit for eating is to cut it into three or four pieces, and then take out the core, then to place heated stones in the bottom of a hole dug in the ground, to cover them with green leaves, and upon these to place a layer of the fruit, then stones, leaves and fruit alternately, till the hole is nearly filled, when leaves and earth to the depth of several inches are spread over all. In rather more than half an hour the bread-fruit is ready for eating. It has little taste, and more resembles the plantain than bread made of wheat flour. The inner bark of the bread-fruit-trees supplies a considerable part of the clothing of the islanders, and its timber and its milky juice are employed for economical purposes.

Breviary.—The books in which the offices used at the seven Canonical Hours were contained were formerly distinct, but out of these separate books the Breviary was compiled, about the eleventh century, by Pope Gregory VII, the lessons, anthems, hymns and responses for the different days of the year being all arranged in their proper places in the same volume with the psalter, prayers, etc. The Breviary is in Latin, portions of it being sometimes translated for the use of the unlearned. It is necessarily a very bulky volume, when complete, and although some of the legends of the saints and martyrs may be of doubtful authenticity, yet it is a mine of interesting and devotional reading. The Roman Church enjoins, under pain of excommunication, all religious persons, *i. e.* all persons, male or female, who have taken vows in any religious order, to repeat, either in public or private, the services of the Canonical Hours as contained in the Breviary.

Bride, Throwing Shoe After.—The custom of throwing a shoe after a departing bride and groom originated so far back in the dim and mystical past that the memory of man stretcheth not back to its beginning. It is by some thought to typify an assault, and is a lingering trace of the custom among savage nations of carrying away the bride by violence. Others claim that it has a likeness to a Jewish custom mentioned in the Bible. Thus, in Ruth, when the kinsman of Boaz gave up his claim to the inheritance of Ruth, and to Ruth also, he indicated his assent by plucking off his shoe and giving it to Boaz. Also, we read in Deuteronomy that when the brother of a dead man refused to marry his widow she asserted her independence of him by "loosing his shoe."

Bridge of Sighs is the bridge connecting the palace of the Doge with the State prison in Venice. It was so called because prisoners once having crossed it from the Judgment Hall were never seen again, and it was supposed that many of them were dropped through a trap-door into the dark and deep waters of the Canal flowing beneath.

Bridges of the World, Notable.—The Brooklyn Bridge, which connects the cities of New York and Brooklyn, was commenced, under the direction of J. Roebling, in 1870, and completed in 1883. It is 3,475 feet long and 135 feet high, and cost nearly $15,000,000. The Cantalever Bridge, over the Niagara, is built almost entirely of steel. Its length is 910 feet, and it cost to build $900,000.

The Niagara Suspension Bridge is 821 feet long, 245 feet above water, and its strength is estimated at 1,200 tons. It cost $400,000. The bridge at Havre de Grace over the Susquehanna River is 3,271 feet long. The Britannia crosses the Menai Strait, Wales, at an elevation of 103 feet above high water. It is of wrought iron, 1,511 feet long, and cost $3,008,000. The new London Bridge is constructed of granite. It was commenced in 1824, and completed in about seven years, at a cost of $7,291,000. The old London Bridge was the first stone bridge. It was commenced in 1176 and completed in 1209. Its founder, Peter of Colechurch, was buried in the crypt of the chapel erected on the center pier. Coalbrookdale Bridge, England, was the first cast-iron bridge. It was built over the Severn in 1779. The bridge at Burton, over the Trent, was formerly the longest bridge in England, being 1,545 feet. It was built in the twelfth century, but is now partly removed. The Rialto, at Venice, is a single marble arch 98 1-2 feet long. It was built in 1591 from the designs, it is said, of Michael Angelo. The Bridge of Sighs, at Venice, over which condemned prisoners were transported from the Hall of Judgment to the place of execution, was built in 1589. The bridge of the Holy Trinity, at Florence, was built in 1569. It is 322 feet long, constructed of white marble, and stands unrivaled as a work of art. The St. Louis Bridge over the Mississippi is 1,524 feet long, exclusive of approaches. There are three arched spans of cast steel, the center arch being 520 feet, with a rise of 47 1-2 feet, and the side spans 502 feet each, with a rise of 46 feet. The width on top between the rails is 50 feet. The Rush Street Bridge, Chicago, Ill., was erected in 1884 at a cost of $132,000. It is the largest general traffic drawbridge in the world. Its roadway will accommodate four teams abreast, and its footways are seven feet wide. It is swung by steam and lighted by electric light. The Cleveland, Ohio, viaduct is 3,211 feet in length and 64 feet wide, 42 feet of which is roadway; the drawbridge is 332 feet in length, 46 feet wide, and is 68 feet above the ordinary stage of water.

Buccaneers.—From the middle of the sixteenth to the end of the seventeenth century an association of piratical adventurers maintained themselves in the Caribbean Sea, at first by systematic reprisal on the Spaniards, later by indiscriminate piracy, who were known as buccaneers. Their simple code of laws bound them to a common participation in the necessaries of life; and every man had his comrade, who stood by him when alive, and succeeded to his property after his death. The principal center of their wild and predatory life was for some time the Island of Tortuga, near St. Domingo. Among the " great captains " whose names figure most prominently in the records of buccaneering were the Frenchman Montbars, surnamed by the terrible title of " The Exterminator;" his countryman, Peter of Dieppe, surnamed " The Great;" Michael de Busco and Van Horn. Pre-eminent, however, among them all was the Welshman, Henry Morgan, who organized fleets and armies, took strong fortresses and rich cities, and displayed throughout the bold genius of a born commander. He it was that led the way for the buccaneers to the Southern Ocean by his daring march in 1670 across the Isthmus of Panama to the city of that name, which he took and plundered after a desperate battle. He was knighted by Charles II, and became Deputy-Governor of Jamaica. The war between France and England after the accession of William III dissolved the ancient alliance which had existed between the French and English buccaneers, and after the accession of the Bourbon, Philip V, to the Spanish throne, they finally disappeared. The last great event in their history was the capture of Carthagena in 1697, when the booty was enormous.

Bucentaur was a galley about 100 feet long by 21 feet in extreme breadth; on the lower deck were 32 banks or rows of oars, manned by 168 rowers, and on an upper deck were accommodations for the illustrious visitors who occasionally came on board. The vessel was employed only once a year, when the Doge of Venice " married the Adriatic." At this ceremony a magnificent water procession was formed with the Doge and the chief notables in the Bucentaur, and other distinguished persons in gondolas and feluccas. When the vessels arrived at the mouth of one of the channels opening into the Adriatic the Doge dropped a ring into the water, using the words, " We wed thee with this ring, in token of our true and perpetual sovereignty." This singular ceremony arose out of an honor or privilege conferred by the Pope on the Doge in 1177, consequent on a splendid victory gained by the Venetians over the Emperor Frederick Barbarossa, and was celebrated on Ascension-Day.

Buddhism.—The religion known as Buddhism is one of the oldest existing religions, and traces its origin back to Siddhartha or Buddha, a Hindoo prince. In Hindustan, the land of its birth, it has now little hold, except among the Nepaulese and some other northern tribes, but it bears full sway in Ceylon and over the whole eastern Peninsula. It divides the adherence of the Chinese with the system of Confucius. It prevails also in Japan and north of the Himalayas. It is the religion of Thibet, and of the Mongolian population of Central Asia. Its adherents are estimated at 340,000,000. According to the Buddhist Belief, when a man dies he is immediately born again, or appears in a new shape; and that shape may, according to his merit or demerit, be any of the innumerable orders of being composing the Buddhist universe from a clod to a divinity. If his demerit would not be sufficiently punished by a degraded earthly existence—in the form, for instance, of a woman or a slave, of a persecuted or a disgusting animal, of a plant, or even of a piece of inorganic matter—he will be born in some one of the 136 Buddhist hells situated in the interior of the earth. These places of punishment have a regular gradation in the intensity of the suffering and in the length of time the sufferers live, the least term of life being 10,000,000 years, the longest term being almost beyond the powers of even Indian notation to express. A meritorious life, on the other hand, secures the next birth either in an exalted and happy position on earth or as a blessed spirit, or even divinity, in one of the many heavens in which the least duration of life is about 10,000,000,000 years. But however long the life, whether of misery or bliss, it has an end, and at its close the individual must be born again, and may again be either happy or miserable. The Buddha himself is said to have gone through every conceivable form of existence on the earth, in the air and in the water, in hell and in heaven, and to have filled every condition in human life; and a great part of the Buddhist legendary literature is taken up in narrating his exploits when he lived as an elephant, as a bird, as a stag, and so on. A second Buddhist doctrine is embodied in the "Four Sublime Verities." The first asserts that pain exists; the second that the cause of pain is desire or attachment; the third that pain can be ended by *nirvana;* and the fourth shows the way that leads to nirvana, from simple faith to complete regeneration. Theoretically this religion has no priests, nor clergy nor public religious rites. Every man is his own priest and confessor, and the monks are ascetics only for their own advancement in holy living; but in fact Buddhist countries swarm with priests or religious teachers, so reputed. The central object in a Buddhist temple, corresponding to the altar in a Roman Catholic church, is an image of the Buddha, or a dagoba or shrine containing his relics. Here flowers, fruit and incense are daily offered, and processions are made, with singing of hymns. Of the relics of the Buddha, the most famous are the *teeth* that are preserved with intense veneration in various places. The quantities of flowers used as offerings are prodigious. A royal devotee in Ceylon, in the fifteenth century, offered on one occasion 6,480,320 flowers at the shrine of the tooth, and at one temple it was provided that there should be offered "every day 100,000 flowers, and each day a different flower."

Bulls and Bears are terms used to designate two opposing factions engaged in speculation, the one endeavoring to raise the values, and the other to depress them. The "bulls" magnify every circumstance favorable to the appreciation of the stocks or other mediums of speculation they hold or have agreed to take at a given time, while those who have contracted to deliver the same, or who for any reason wish to buy, do all in their power to depreciate them, and are therefore nicknamed "bears." The origin of the terms is probably the natural proclivities of the animals—the bulls to toss things into the air, and the bears to squeeze any enemy with which they may come in contact.

Bundesrath and Reichstag.—The Federal Council of Germany, or Bundesrath, as it is called, combines the functions of a legislative assembly with those of an executive body, and is presided over by the Emperor, who has power to appoint the Chancellor as acting chairman and controller of the business of the Council. It consists of fifty-nine delegates from the several states, appointed by the legislative assemblies, who are supposed to act directly on the instructions of their respective governments, each delegation casting its vote as a unit. The Reichstag, or Imperial Diet, has the usual power of a chamber of deputies, but it has no power to force a change of ministry. Its actual work is confined to checking the arbitrary powers of the Bundesrath. The members of the Reichstag are elected for three years in the ratio of one representative for every 10,000 inhabitants; but states having less than that number of inhabitants can still have a representative. Every citizen of twenty-five years may vote for members of the Reichstag, and any voter may be a candidate for election, provided he has been a resident of the state for one year.

Bunker Hill Monument.—The corner-stone of this monument was laid on the fiftieth anniversary of the battle of Bunker Hill, June 17, 1825, by Lafayette, and the oration was pronounced by Daniel Webster. It is a square shaft of Quincy granite, 221 feet high, 31 feet square at the base and 15 feet at the top. Inside the shaft is a round hollow cone, 7 feet wide at the bottom and 4 feet 2 inches at the top, encircled by a winding staircase containing 224 stone steps, which leads to a chamber 11 feet in diameter immediately under the apex. The chamber has four windows, and contains two cannons, named Hancock and Adams respectively, which were used in the war. The monument was completed and was dedicated June 17, 1843.

Burial Customs.—The modes of burying the dead differ widely among various peoples. Among some the dead are buried lying, others sitting—as is the case with several of the Indian tribes, among whom, it is related, warriors or leaders in the nations have been buried upon their favorite war-horses. This was the manner of burial of the famous Indian chief Blackbird, of the once powerful Omahas. There is a remarkable agreement of custom, however, in the practice of placing the body east and west. It is held by some writers that this custom is due to solar symbolism, and the head is placed to the east or to the west according as the dead are thought of in connection with the sunrise, the reputed home of the Deity, or the sunset, the reputed home of the dead. There are, however, some tribes that lay their dead north and south, and others bury men with the face to the north and women with the face to the south; while among some of the African tribes, if one happens to die away from his home, he is buried facing his native village.

Business Terms, Vocabulary of.—[See Appendix.]

Byzantine Empire was the Roman Empire of the East. The name was derived from Byzantium, the ancient name of Constantinople, the capital of the empire. As a separate power it began its existence in 395 A. D., when Theodosius the Great died, bequeathing the Empire of Rome to his two sons, who divided it—Arcadius taking the eastern half, with his capital at Constantinople. It was a rich and powerful sovereignty, and continued to exist for over ten centuries. During the last few centuries it was gradually but surely declining before the Turks and Saracens, and ended with the Mohammedan conquest of Constantinople in 1453. It was also called the Greek Empire, and was the home and head of the Greek Church.

Cache is the name given by parties of travelers on the Western prairies of the United States to places for concealing provisions and other articles. The making of a cache is a matter of much labor and ingenuity. A hole is dug to a depth of perhaps six or eight feet, and several feet broad, and then, the articles being interred, the surface is replaced with the greatest care. The excavated earth is also carefully removed, so as to leave no trace whatever of the excavation. The situation of the cache, however, is known to the party by some landmark. Similar depositories are constructed by Arctic explorers.

Cadmus was the son of Agenor, King of Phœnicia, by Telephassa, and was sent by his father, along with his brothers Phœnix and Cilix, in quest of their sister Europa, who had been carried off by Jupiter, and they were ordered not to return until they had found her. The brothers were accompanied by their mother and by Thasus, a son of Neptune. Their search was to no purpose—they could get no intelligence of their sister; and, fearing the indignation of their father, they resolved to settle in various countries. Phœnix thereupon established himself in Phœnicia, Cilix in Cilicia, and Cadmus and his mother went to Thrace, where Thasus founded a town, also named after himself. After the death of his mother Cadmus went to Delphi, to inquire of the oracle respecting Europa. The god desired him to cease from troubling himself about her, but to follow a cow as his guide, and to build a city where she should lie down. On leaving the temple he went through Phocis, and, meeting a cow belonging to the herds of Pelagon, he followed her. She went through Bœotia till she came to where Thebes afterward stood, and there lay down. Wishing to sacrifice her to Minerva, Cadmus sent his companions to fetch water from the fountain of Mars; but the font was guarded by a serpent, who killed the greater part of them. Cadmus then engaged and destroyed the serpent. By the direction of Minerva he sowed its teeth, and immediately a crop of armed men sprung up, who slew each other quarreling or through ignorance. For killing the sacred serpent Cadmus was obliged to spend a year in servitude to Mars. At the expiration of that time Minerva herself prepared for him a palace, and Jupiter gave him Harmonia, the daughter of Mars and Venus, in marriage. Cadmus and Harmonia were eventually changed into serpents and sent by Jupiter to the Elysian plain, or, as some writers say, were conveyed thither in a chariot drawn by serpents. Greek tradition ascribed to him the first introduction of the alphabet, derived from Phœnicia, and consisting, then, of six-teen letters. He is also credited with the discovery of brass, or the introduction of its use.

Cairns are piles of stones, and were erected doubtless for various purposes. From old records it would appear that they were often raised to distinguish the marches or boundaries of lands. A cairn near Balmoral, on the Highland Dee, is said to have been erected as a mustering-place for the men of Strathdee, who took its name, *Cairn-na-cuimhne*, or Cairn of Remembrance, for their war-cry. In later times, places where great crimes had been committed were marked by cairns. Thus Mushet's Cairn in the Queen's Park, at Edinburgh, shows the spot where a wife was murdered by her husband, under circumstances of peculiar atrocity, in 1720. The great purpose of cairns, however, was sepulchral, as is shown by the human remains found in so many of them. These bones are generally calcined or half-burned, and inclosed either in what are called *cists*—small, rude coffins of unhewn stone—or in urns of earthenware, which, again, are in many cases protected by stone cists. Along with the bones are often found flint arrow-heads, flint ax-heads, stone hammers, stone rings, glass beads, implements of bone, bones of horses and oxen, spear-heads and other weapons of bronze. Many cairns are of considerable size. Of the three large cairns at Clava, on the banks of the Nairn River, near the battle-field of Culloden, one was found to contain a gallery, about two feet wide, leading from the south side of the cairn to a circular chamber in the center, about fifteen feet in diameter, built of unhewn and uncemented stones, each course overlapping the other so as to meet at the top in a sort of rude dome, which has received the name of the "beehive-house." The Boss Cairn on the moor of Dranandon, in the parish of Minnigaff, had two galleries crossing each other, each 80 feet long, 4 feet wide, and 3 feet high. Of all the chambered cairns, however, the most remarkable is that at New Grange, on the banks of the Boyne, near Drogheda, in Ireland. It is 400 paces in circumference and about 80 feet high, and is supposed to contain 180,000 tons of stone. In 1699 it was described by Edward Llhwyd, the Welsh antiquary, as "a mount or barrow, of very considerable height, encompassed with vast stones, pitched on end, around the bottom of it, and having another, lesser, standing on the top." This last pillar has disappeared. Of the outer ring of pillars ten still remain. The opening to this cairn was accidentally discovered about the year 1699. The gallery, of which it is the external entrance, communicates with a dome-roofed chamber or cave nearly in the center of the mound. This gallery, which measures in length about 50 feet, is at its entrance 4 feet high, and in breadth about 3 feet. Toward the interior its size gradually increases; and its height, where it forms the chamber, is 18 feet. The chamber is cruciform, the head and arms of the cross being formed by three recesses, each containing a basin of granite. The sides of these recesses are composed of immense blocks of stone, several of which bear a great variety of carving, supposed by some to be symbolical. The length of the passage and chamber from north to south is 75 feet, and the breadth of the chamber from east to west is 20 feet. Of the urns or basins in the recesses, that to the east is the most remarkable. It is formed of a block of granite, and appears to have been set upon, or rather within, another of somewhat larger dimensions.

Calico-Printing.—The art of calico-printing was introduced into Europe about the seventeenth century, although it is believed to have been known in India and Egypt as early as the first or second centuries. In this early period the printing was done by means of blocks on which the designs to be transferred to the cloth had been engraved in relief. These were dipped into dye-stuff, and then pressed upon the material by hand. Later, presses for this block-printing were invented, and the use of several was introduced so engraved as to fill up each other's vacancies, and thus several colors were put into the pattern. About 1770 copper-plate printing was invented in England. By this method the design was cut into plates, the color filled into the sunken parts of the engraving, and the cloths were printed by being pressed upon it. This invention finally led to the introduction of cylinder-printing, the method now in use. The cylinders are of copper, and the design is engraved upon their surface. A separate cylinder is required for each color or shade of color to be used in printing the cloth, and in fine and intricate designs as many as twenty cylinders are sometimes used. These are set in a strong frame against the face of a large central drum made of iron and covered with woollen cloth in several folds, between which and the cylinders the calico is printed as it passes. The color is spread upon the cylinders, as they revolve, by contact with another roller, which dips into a trough containing the coloring-matter properly thickened. This roller is made of an absorbent, elastic material, similar to the roller used in inking a printing-press. Each cylinder thus receives its proper color, and imparts it, in revolving, to the calico pressed between its face and that of the fixed drum. A sharp blade of metal pressing against the copper cylinder removes all superfluous color from its surface, so that only the design cut in the metal is imprinted in clear outline upon the cloth. The employment of a number of rollers to make one design is attended with much difficulty, as in passing under them the cloth is in much danger of being displaced and the regularity of the print destroyed. As the cloth leaves the printing-machine it is drawn over rollers through a hot-air chamber, by which it is thoroughly dried, and the colors become fully set.

Calumet.—The Calumet is a tobacco-pipe having a stem of reed about two-and-a-half feet long, decorated with locks of women's hair and feathers, and a large bowl of soft red sandstone. It is the peace-pipe of the American Indians, and plays an important part in the conclusion of treaties. After the treaty has been signed, the Indians fill the calumet with tobacco and present it to the representatives of the party with whom they have been entering into alliance, themselves smoking out of it afterward. The presentation of it to strangers is a mark of hospitality, and to refuse it would be considered an act of hostility.

Cambridge, University of, is situated at the town of Cambridge, forty-eight miles north-east of London. The first regular society of students was that of Peter-House, founded in 1257. The history of the University, however, may be said to date from the opening of the twelfth century, but until the year mentioned there were no public halls or hostels, each student living in his own hired lodging. About 1257 the students began to live together in hostels, under the rule of a principal. These hostels were named after the saints to whom they were dedicated, the churches which they adjoined, or the persons who formerly built or possessed them. In the year 1280 there were as many as 34, and some of them contained from 20 to 40 masters of arts, and a proportionate number of younger students. These hostels were the beginning of what may be called the college system, which distinguishes the sister universities of Oxford and Cambridge from those of Edinburgh, London and the Continent. All the royal and religious foundations, with one exception, which now constitute the University were endowed between the latter part of the thirteenth and the close of the sixteenth century. The governing body of the University is the senate; but, before being submitted to it, all university laws must be approved by the council, a body elected by the resident members of the senate. After the chancellor and high-steward, the chief executive power is vested in the vice-chancellor, who is elected annually from the heads of colleges. There are three terms in this University—the Michaelmas or October term, the Lent term, and the Easter term. To take an ordinary B. A. degree a student must reside nine terms. The M. A. degree follows, without examination, about four years after. There are four classes of students—Fellow-Commoners and Noblemen, Pensioners, Sizars and Subsizars, and the more distinguished who are elected Scholars on the foundation of this college. The pensioners are the great body of students, are not on the foundation, and pay for their own commons, viz., dinners in halls, etc., and for their rooms. The sizars are poorer students, selected, however, by examination, who receive free commons and certain money payments, and are admitted at lower charges than the pensioners, but wear the same dress, and are no longer subject to the performance of menial offices, as they once were. The scholars are elected, by examination, from the pensioners and sizars. They are on the foundation of the college, from which they receive certain emoluments. The fellows are subsequently elected from the scholars and the students who have distinguished themselves in the Tripos examinations. The University has forty professors, in

addition to readers, demonstrators and assistants. The tutor of
the college is understood to be *in loco parentis* to his pupils, the
dean has the oversight of "religion and morals," and instruction
is given by college lecturers. The great prizes at the University
are the Fellowships, of which there are about 400. The following
is a list of the colleges and their founders: St. Peter's College or
Peter-House, founded by Hugh de Balsham, Bishop of Ely, 1257;
Clare College, founded under the name of University Hall by
Richard Baden in 1326, was burned in 1338, and rebuilt and en-
dowed by Elizabeth, Countess of Clare; Pembroke College, found-
ed by the Countess of Pembroke, 1347; Gonville and Caius College,
founded by Edward Gonville in 1348; Trinity Hall, founded by
William Bateman, Bishop of Norwich, 1350; Corpus Christi or
Benedict College, founded by the guilds of Corpus Christi and the
Blessed Virgin, 1351; King's College, founded by Henry VI, 1441;
Queen's College, founded by Margaret of Anjou, wife of Henry
VI, 1446; St. Catherine's College or Hall, founded by Robert
Wodelarke, Provost of King's College, 1473; Jesus College, found-
ed by John Alcock, Bishop of Ely, 1496; Christ College, founded
by the Countess of Richmond, 1505; St. John's College, founded
the by Countess of Richmond, 1511; Magdalene College, founded by
Thomas, Baron Audley, of Walden, 1519; Trinity College, founded
by Henry VIII, 1546; Emmanuel College, founded by Sir Walter
Mildmay, 1584; Sidney Sussex College, founded by Lady Frances
Sidney, 1598; Downing College, founded by Sir George Downing,
1800.

Camp-Meeting, Origin of.—In 1799 the first camp-meeting
ever held in the United States took place on the banks of the Red
River in Kentucky. Two brothers named McGee, one a Methodist
and one a Presbyterian, were on a religious tour from Tennessee
to a place called in those days the "Barrens." They stopped at
a settlement to attend a sacramental occasion with a Presbyterian
minister—the Rev. Mr. McGreedy, by name. John McGee, the
Methodist, preached, on invitation, and his services are described
as having been marked "with great liberty and power." McGee's
brother and the Rev. Mr. Hoge followed with sermons, and their
effects were remarkable, as they produced "tears of contrition
and shouts of joy." The several Presbyterian ministers—the Rev.
Messrs. McGreedy, Hoge and Rankins—left the house, but the
McGee's were too powerfully affected to depart. John was expected to preach again, but when the time came he arose and
informed the people that the overflowing nature of his feelings
would not allow of his preaching, and he exhorted them to surrender their hearts to God. The excitement is said to have been
indescribable. The reports of these wonderful services were
heard by the people in the country around, and many rushed to
the place to see the preachers and witness the religious exercises.
The meeting-house was overflowed, and an altar was erected
to the Lord in the forest. This added new interest to the move-

ment, and people assembled from far and near, with provisions and other necessaries for camping out, and remained several days, living in tents. For the time denominational divisions seemed to be forgotten, and the services were conducted by Presbyterians, Methodists and Baptists. The results were so wonderful that another meeting of the same sort was suggested, and was held on the Muddy River, and still another was held on what was called the Ridge, both having been attended by great crowds, who came for many miles around. These services were continued and extended, with similar results, the Presbyterians and Methodists directing and conducting them. It is stated that at one of these meetings in Kentucky there were present at least 20,000 people. The Presbyterians gradually retired from the field, while the Methodists carried the meetings to all parts of the country. Since then other denominations have adopted them, and they have continued with more or less efficacy to the present time.

Canals, Great.—The Imperial Canal of China, which is the largest canal in the world, is over 1,000 miles in length. The longest canal in Europe is the canal of Languedoc, which connects the Atlantic with the Mediterranean. It was completed in 1881 and is 148 miles long. The largest ship-canal in Europe is the great North Holland Canal, completed in 1825. It is only fifty-one miles in length, but is very deep and wide. The Suez Canal is eighty-eight miles in length, but only sixty-six are actual canal. There are a number of canals of notable length in the United States, as the Wabash and Erie Canal, 374 miles long; the Erie Canal, 350 1-2 miles long; the Ohio Canal, 332 miles long, and the Miami and Erie Canal, 291 miles long.

Candles.—It was not until the fourteenth century that candles having any resemblance to those now in use were manufactured Previous to that time our English ancestors soaked splints of wood in fat or oil to obtain their light. The candles used by the Greeks and Romans were rude torches made by dipping strips of papyrus or rushes into pitch and then coating them with wax. These candles were also in use in Europe during the middle ages, and were very large and heavy. A dipped candle made from tallow was introduced in England in the fourteenth century, and wax-candles were also made at the same time. These latter were very costly, and were considered great luxuries. In 1484 a company for the manufacture of wax-candles was incorporated in London. Mold candles are said to be the invention of the Sieur Le Brez, of Paris.

Cannel-Coal is a bituminous coal which burns with a bright flame, and is mined in large quantities in Great Britain. At one time cannel-coal was used as a substitute for candles, owing to the fact that it can be cut into blocks or strips and burns with a clear, yellow flame. The name cannel-coal is a corruption of candle-coal. In Scotland it is known by the name of parrot-coal, from the crackling or chattering noise it makes when burned.

Canopy.—The original meaning of the word "canopy" was probably a mosquito-curtain. Herodotus tells us that the fishermen on the Nile were in the habit of suspending the net with which they had fished during the day on an upright pole, from which it was expanded into the form of a tent, and served to protect them from the attacks of insects during the night. Horace and others of the ancient writers mention gnat-curtains (canopea). Subsequently the same term came to be used for the projecting coverings and hangings of a bed without reference to their original use, and latterly for any projecting covering of a similar form, to whatever use it might be adapted, or of whatever material it might be formed. "Canopy" is thus used to signify the covering which is borne over the heads of kings and other persons of distinction, and still more frequently over the Holy Sacrament and the image of Christ in processions in Roman Catholic countries.

Cape Cod Ship-Canal.—From the time of the Revolutionary War up to 1880 the project of a ship-canal across Cape Cod was repeatedly brought forward. Several surveys were made, both under the authority of the Federal Government and of the Commonwealth of Massachusetts, but nothing was done until the latter year, when an association of Boston and New York capitalists purchased a strip across the isthmus 1,000 feet in width, and began to make arrangements for the cutting. From one cause or another work was not actually commenced, however, until some time during during 1886. The canal is to cut through Cape Cod at its narrowest part, connecting Buzzard's Bay, the deepest indentation on the southern New England coast, with the arm of Cape Cod Bay, called Barnstable Bay, which hollows the opposite shore. The route here seems to have been marked out by Nature, as two shallow water-courses made a depression for over seven-eighths of the way across the peninsula at this narrow part. The length of the canal will be somewhat less than eight miles, and it will shorten the distance by water from Boston to New York over ninety miles, and the saving in time will be eight hours, beside the great advantage in escaping the dangerous coast at the point of the cape. The material to be removed from this water-way is generally easy of excavation, so it is thought there will be few delays in its construction. The canal will be 23 feet deep at low water and 200 feet wide, and the cost will be between $5,000,000 and $6,000,000. There has been spent already $800,000. The estimated tonnage around the cape yearly is 15,000,000 tons, and the canal company will get ten cents a ton, or a revenue of $1,500,000.

Captain Kidd was born in Scotland, and took to the sea when a mere boy. In 1695 a company composed of leading gentlemen in Great Britain and in the Colonies was formed to make a business of privateering and reap the profits, which were known to be immense. The Adventure, a galley of 287 tons, quite a large vessel for those days, was purchased, and the command given to Kidd, who sailed with two commissions, one of which empowered him to act against the French, and the other to cruise against pirates. Besides these commissions under the Great Seal, he had the ordinary letters of marque from the Commissioners of the Admiralty. The King was to have one-tenth of all the booty, and the rest was to be divided between the shareholders and Kidd in certain specified proportions. A portion was to be appropriated to the crew, who were to receive no regular pay. Kidd left Plymouth April 23, 1696, captured a French fishing vessel off Newfoundland, and in July reached New York, where he remained until September, when he sailed for Madagascar, then one of the strongholds of the buccaneers. In January of the following year he arrived at the island, and in 1698 reports were abroad in England that he had raised the black flag, and orders were dispatched to the effect that he be apprehended should he come within reach. April, 1699, found him in the West Indies, whither he had gone in a vessel called the Quidah Merchant. This he secured in a lagoon in the Island of Saona, near Hayti, and re-embarked in a small sloop named the San Antonio for the Colonies of America. He sailed up Long Island Sound to Oyster Bay, after making a landing in Delaware Bay, and there took aboard a New York lawyer named James Emott, whom he afterward sent to Boston to the Earl of Bellamont, who had become Governor of the Colonies. Emott was Kidd's advance agent, sent forward to ascertain how the privateersman would be received. While the lawyer was absent on this mission Kidd buried some bales of goods and treasure on Gardiner's Island. To the inquiries of the New York lawyer Bellamont made evasive answers, and then later induced Kidd to proceed to Boston, where he landed July 1, 1699. Five days later, Kidd, who was examined by the Council, was sent to England, where he was given something of the form of a trial. He was permitted to have no counsel, was not allowed to send for papers or witnesses, and was, of course, found guilty of piracy and of the murder of one of his crew, and was hanged at Execution Dock with nine of his associates. Bellamont fitted out another vessel to go in search of the Quidah Merchant, but news came before the search began that the latter had been stripped and burned by the men left with it by Kidd. The treasure which was secured on Gardiner's Island, with what was found with Kidd on the San Antonio, amounted to $70,000.

Carat is the designation of the weight commonly used for weighing precious stones, and particularly diamonds, and is also the term which designates the proportion of pure gold contained in any alloy of gold with other metals. The name seems to have come through the Arabic *girrat*, from the Greek *bezation*, the fruit of the carob or locust-tree, used also as a weight. The carat used for weighing diamonds has a fixed weight, equal to 3 1-6 troy grains, and is divided into quarters, eighths, sixteenths, thirty-seconds and sixty-fourths. In determining the fineness of gold the troy pound, ounce, or any other weight, is divided into twenty-four parts, and each part is called a carat, twenty-four carats being considered the standard of purity ; hence an eighteen-carat gold ring is a ring containing eighteen parts in twenty-four of pure gold.

Cardiff Giant, The.—This stupendous fraud was conceived in the fertile brain of one George Hull, a tobacconist of Binghamton, N. Y. He secured a gypsum slab in Iowa, and had it cut into the form of a huge man by a stone-cutter of Chicago. To simulate the appearance of great age the figure was rubbed with sand and water, then bathed in writing-fluid, and also in sulphuric acid. The image was then boxed, taken to the vicinity of Binghamton, N. Y., and secretly buried in a spot where it was conveniently found a year later, and heralded as the most marvelous discovery of archæological history—a petrified specimen of prehistoric man. People flocked to see the curiosity by thousands and tens of thousands; and, palpable as the fraud was, numbers of very intelligent persons, even among those whose names were known in the scientific world, were hoaxed. It is due to the intelligence of these spectators to say that few gave any credence to the absurd idea that this monster was a petrifaction, but hundreds who ought to have known better believed it to be a very ancient statue. After this hoax was exposed, Hull, not satisfied with the large gains which the credulity of his fellow-men had afforded him through it, got up another. This was a smaller figure, made of a composition of ground stone, pulverized bones, clay, plaster, blood and dried eggs, and baked in a kiln. This was advertised as the "Colorado Stone Man," Colorado being then the "wonder State" of the Union. But when it was brought out the public had not recovered from the mortification induced by the "Cardiff Giant," and bit but warily at the bait of the second humbug. Its originators, therefore, were disappointed in their hopes of great gains.

Carolina Constitution.—In 1669 Lord Shaftesbury, one of the proprietaries of the Carolina colony, had a constitution prepared by the philosopher John Locke for the government of that colony, by means of which an endeavor was made to establish in America what can only be called a feudal empire—with what success, however, can be readily imagined. The constitution contained 120 articles. The eight proprietaries who held the grant of the Carolina colonies were to combine the dignity and power of a Governor and an upper house of the Legislature. Their position and rule were to be hereditary, and their number was never to be increased or diminished; for in the case of the death of a member without heirs his survivors elected a successor. The territory contained in the grant was divided into counties, each containing 480,000 acres, and this was again divided into five equal parts, of which one remained the inalienable property of the proprietaries, and another formed the inalienable and indivisible estate of the nobility, of which, according to the constitution, there were two orders—one earl and two barons for each county. The remaining three-fifths were reserved for the people, and might be held by lords of the manor who were not hereditary legislators. The members of the nobility might neither be increased nor diminished, election supplying all places left vacant for want of heirs. All political rights were dependent upon hereditary wealth. The cultivators of the soil were each to be allowed the use of ten acres at a fixed rent, but were not to be allowed to purchase land or exercise the right of suffrage. They were adscripts to the soil, were under the jurisdiction of their lord, without right of appeal to the courts, and from generation to generation were forbidden to hold land or acquire any political power. The eight proprietaries constituted the highest court, or court of appeals, over which the oldest one of their number presided, with the title of Palatine. There were seven other courts, each presided over by one of the seven other proprietaries, with the respective titles of Admiral, Chamberlain, Chancellor, Constable, Chief Justice, High Steward, and Treasurer, and each had six counselors, all appointed for life, of whom four at least were to be nobles. The supervision of everything in the colonies was vested in these courts, and altogether they formed what was called a grand council, who exercised the exclusive right of proposing laws. These laws, however, were to be submitted for approval or rejection to the Parliament, which was composed of all the proprietaries, the nobles, and four representatives of the lords of the manor from each county. The proprietaries, in their capacity as an upper house, could, however, veto the acts of Parliament. Slavery was tolerated, and masters were given absolute power and authority over their slaves. Each county was to have four local courts, whence appeals could be made to the court of the Chief Justice, and no lawyer was to be allowed to plead for money or reward in any court. The religion was to be that of the Church of England. Of course all attempts to foist such a scheme of government on the few scattered Huguenots, who formed the population, met with deserved failure, and after twenty years was abandoned.

Carrier-Pigeons.—That pigeons have been used for a great many years for the transmission of messages is well known, but with what nation the custom originated it is impossible to discover. The Romans used the birds for this purpose, they were in use among the Asiatics, and we have the assertion of the poet Tasso for believing that they were employed during the siege of Jerusalem in 1099; and it is a historical fact that they were used during the crusade of St. Louis, in 1250. Their most remarkable use in modern times was during the siege of Paris, in 1870. In Turkey they have been more generally used than in any other country, and it is said that there the art of training them is carried to its highest perfection. Pigeons intended for this use are taken, when they have acquired full strength of wing, in a covered basket to a distance of about half a mile from their home, and then set at liberty and thrown into the air. If they return home they are then taken to greater distances, progressively increased from forty to fifty miles. When the bird is able to accomplish this flight he may be trusted to fly any distance, overland, within the limits of physical power. It is the general plan to keep the birds in a dark room for some hours before they are used. They are then fed sparingly, but are given all the water they can drink. The paper on which the message is written is tied around the upper part of the bird's leg, or to one of the large feathers of the tail, so as not to impede its flight. The feet are washed in vinegar to keep them from getting too dry, so that the bird will not be tempted to descend to water and thus possibly ruin the message. The rate of flight is from twenty to thirty miles an hour, though the bird has been known to pass over great distances much more rapidly. When thrown up in the air, the pigeon at first flies round and round, as though for the purpose of sighting some landmark that it knows. When this is discovered, it flies toward it, and thence onward to its home.

Casting Plate-Glass.—The whole operation of casting a plate of glass occupies but a very short time. The casting-tables, the most important pieces of apparatus in plate-glass works, are 19 feet long, 14 feet wide, and 7 inches thick. Each is provided with an iron roller 30 inches in diameter and 15 feet long. Strips of iron on each side of the table afford a bearing for the rollers and determine the thickness of the plate of glass to be cast. The rough plate is commonly 9-16ths of an inch in thickness. After polishing, it is reduced to 6-16ths or 7-16ths. The casting-tables are mounted on wheels, and run on a track that reaches every furnace and annealing-oven in the building. The table having been wheeled as near as possible to the melting-furnace, the pot of molten glass is lifted by means of a crane and its contents quickly poured on the table. The heavy iron roller is then passed from end to end, spreading the glass into a layer of uniform thickness. The cold metal of the table cools the glass rapidly. As soon as possible the door of the annealing-oven is opened and the plate of glass introduced. The floor of the oven is on the same level as the casting-table so the transfer can be conveniently and quickly made. When, after several days, the glass is taken out of the oven, its surface is found to be decidedly rough and uneven. A small quantity is used in this condition for skylights and other purposes where strength is required without transparency. It is known as rough-plate. The greater part of the glass, however, is ground, smoothed and polished before it leaves the establishment. Few industries offer such fine scenic displays as the pouring of the molten glass.

Castor and Pollux were twin brothers, the latter the son of Leda and Jupiter, the former of Leda and Tyndarus. They took part in all the great undertakings of the heroes of their time, were at the Calydonian hunt, accompanied Hercules against the

Amazons, sailed in the Argo, and aided Peleus to storm Iolcos. Pollux was the most distinguished pugilist, Castor the most experienced charioteer of his day. Castor was killed by his cousin Idas. Pollux was inconsolable for the loss of his brother; and Jupiter, on his prayer, gave him his choice of being taken up himself to Olympus, and sharing the honors of Mars and Minerva, or of dividing them with his brother, and for them to live day and day alternately in Heaven and in Hades. Pollux chose the latter, and divided his immortality with Castor. The two principal stars in the constellation of Gemini were named after the twin brothers.

Catacombs.—Those in Paris were originally quarries which had existed under the city from the earliest time. In 1774 the Council of State issued a decree for clearing the Cemetery of the Innocents, and for removing its contents, as well as those of other grave-yards, into these quarries. These quarries—or catacombs, as they were called—were consecrated with great solemnity on April 7, 1786, and the work of removal from the cemeteries was immediately begun. The bones were brought at night in funeral-cars, covered with a pall, and followed by priests chanting the service of the dead. At first the bones were heaped up without any kind of order except that those from each cemetery were kept separate; but in 1810 a regular system of arranging them was commenced, and the skulls and bones were built up along the wall. From the main entrance to the catacombs, which is near the Barriers d'Enfer, a flight of ninety steps descends, at whose foot galleries are seen branching in various directions. Some yards distant is a vestibule of octagonal form, which opens into a long gallery lined with bones from floor to roof. The arm, leg and thigh-bones are in front, closely and regularly piled, and their uniformity is relieved by three rows of skulls at equal distances. This gallery conducts to several rooms resembling chapels, lined with bones variously arranged. One is called the " Tomb of the Revolution," another the " Tomb of Victims"—the latter containing the relics of those who perished in the early period of the Revolution and in the " massacre of September." It is estimated that the remains of fully 3,000,000 human beings lie in this receptacle. Owing to the unsafe condition of the roof, admission to the catacombs has been forbidden for years. Of the other catacombs in existence, the most celebrated are those on the Via Appia, at a short distance from Rome, where, it is believed, the early Christians were in the habit of retiring in order to celebrate their new worship in times of persecution. These catacombs consist of long, narrow galleries, usually about eight feet high and five feet wide, which twist and turn in all directions, very much resembling mines, and at irregular intervals into wide and lofty vaulted chambers. The graves, where are buried many of the saints and martyrs of the primitive church, were constructed by hollowing out a portion of the rock at the side of the gallery large enough to contain the body. The catacombs at Naples, cut into the Capo di Monte, resemble those at Rome, and evidently were used for the same purpose, being in many parts literally covered with Christian symbols. In one of the large vaulted chambers there are paintings which have retained a freshness which is wonderful. Similar catacombs have been found at Palermo and Syracuse, and in Greece, Asia Minor, Syria, Persia, Egypt, and in Peru and other parts of South America.

Cat Out of the Bag, Letting the.—This saying probably has its origin in the trick of substituting a cat for a young pig in the days when it was customary for the country-folks in England to carry the latter animals to market in bags. These bags, in old phraseology, were known as "pokes." If any one was foolish enough to buy an animal without looking at it he was said to have bought "a pig in a poke," but if he opened the sack the cat would jump out and the trick was discovered.

Cecrops, the first king of Attica, figures in Greek mythology as an Autochthon—half-man and half-dragon. Tradition declares him to be the founder of marriage, the author of the political division of Attica into twelve states, and the introducer of agriculture, of navigation and of commerce. He is also said to have civilized the religious rites of the people.

Celebrated Paintings.—It is generally agreed by art critics that Michael Angelo and Raphael stand at the head of the line of master painters. Conspicuous among the great paintings of the former are "The Last Judgment," "The Conversion of St. Paul," and "The Crucifixion of St. Peter;" and among those of the latter, "The Dispute Concerning the Sacrament," the "Madonna de Foligno," and the "Madonna del Pisce, or Virgin of the Fish." The "Last Judgment" is a large fresco-painting, sixty feet high by thirty feet wide, occupying the wall opposite the entrance of the Sistine Chapel, in the Vatican Palace at Rome. Over 300 figures are represented in "the most violent attitudes and most admired disorder." "The Conversion of St. Paul" is another large fresco-painting in the Vatican. "The Crucifixion of Peter," also in the Vatican, is one of the last from the hands of Angelo. "The Dispute Concerning the Sacrament" is a fresco representing, above, a convocation of the saints about the Almighty, the Saviour and the Virgin, enveloped in heavenly glory, while beneath, the ceremony of the Consecration of the Sacrament is depicted. This is found in the Camera della Segnatura of the Vatican. "The Madonna de Foligno," in the Vatican gallery, derives its name from the City of Foligno, which is represented in the background. The "Madonna del Pisce," now in the gallery at Madrid, Spain, represents the Virgin and Child enthroned, with St. Jerome on one side, and on the other an archangel with the young Tobit, who carries a fish, from which circumstance the name is derived. "The Madonna di San Sisto" is considered by many critics the best of Raphael's works. It is located in the gallery of Dresden, Germany, and represents the Madonna standing upon the clouds surrounded with glory, holding in her arms the eternal son. Saint Sixtus and Saint Barbara kneel at the sides. It was originally painted on wood, but has been transferred to canvas. The painting of "The Last Supper," by Leonardo da Vinci, is recognized as one of the masterpieces. It was originally painted by order of the Duke of Milan on the walls of the refectory in the Dominican convent of the Madonna della Grazie. Rubens' paintings of the "Descent from the Cross" and "Elevation of the Cross," at Antwerp, rank high as masterpieces. The "Adoration of the Trinity" by Albert Durer, at Vienna, and his two pictures containing life-size figures of Peter and John, Mark and Paul, presented to the Council of Nuremberg, Germany, are also very famous. The two pictures of Mary Magdalen are also among the most famous in the world—"La Bussendi Magdalina" by Corregio, now in the Dresden Gallery, and one by Guido Reni. [See also *Venus, Pictures and Statues of.*]

Celibacy in the Roman Catholic Church.—Previous to the close of the fourth century there was no law nor uniformity of opinion regarding the celibacy of the Romish priests. About this time, however, Pope Siricius forbade priests to marry, and those who had married previous to ordination were commanded to put away their wives. Children born to a clergyman after ordination were declared by the Emperor Justinian to be illegitimate and incapable of inheritance. This doctrine was opposed by the Eastern Church, and in 692 it was condemned as heretical by the Council of Constantinople, and the marriage of priests has, therefore, always been sanctioned by the Orthodox Greek Church. Notwithstanding the action taken by the Romish Church, it was several centuries before celibacy was firmly established, and this was not accomplished until Pope Gregory VII, in the face of violent opposition in all countries, deposed all married priests and excommunicated all laymen who upheld them in the exercise of their spiritual functions. This decree was carried out with the utmost rigor, and brought about the result which the Church had been aiming at for centuries, and which still continues to be the canonical law.

Celluloid is made from the cellulose contained in cotton cloth or raw cotton. The cotton is treated to a weak solution of nitric acid. This has the effect of making a pulp of cotton very much like paper pulp. After the acid has acted the pulp is treated to a copious water-bath that in a large measure washes out the acid. Then it goes through a partial drying process, and a large quantity of camphor-gum is mixed with it, and it is rolled into sheets ready for the drying-room, where it is dried on hot cylinders, the same as paper is dried. It can be softened by steam, but hardens again when it is dry. Celluloid, when ready for market, burns as readily as ordinary sealing-wax.

Celts, Records of.—Of the separation of the Celts from the other Aryans or Indo-Europeans, and their early migrations to

Western Europe, no record has come down. In parts of Wales, as in the southeastern counties of Munster, Ireland, there are, it is true, inscriptions, consisting of long and short lines, known as Ogamic characters, on certain rude stone monuments, but their antiquity is not well determined. The only key of any importance to the origin of the Celts is their spoken language, reduced to writing after the introduction of Christianity, which plainly marks them as an offshoot of the Aryan family. The descriptions left by the Romans of the aborigines of Britain at the time of the Roman Conquest represent them as fierce, cruel barbarians. Neither "Cæsar's Commentaries" nor the writings of Tacitus and other historians of the period of the Roman domination convey evidence that the Britains had any knowledge of letters until the Greek and Roman characters were taught them; neither do these historians preserve any oral traditions of the British bards or Druids calculated to shed much light upon the early history of the Celtic race.

Centaurs.—A Thessalian race fabled to have been half-men and half-horses. According to Pindar, the offspring of Ixion and the cloud was a son named Centaurus, who, when grown up, wandered about the foot of Mount Pelion, where he united with the Magnesian mares, who brought forth the Centaurs, a race partaking of the form of both parents. The common account makes the Centaurs to have been the immediate offspring of Ixion and the cloud. By his wife Dia, Ixion had a son named Pirithous, who married Hippodamia, daughter of Adrastus, King of Argos. The chiefs of his own tribe, the Lapithæ, were all invited to the wedding, as were also the Centaurs. At the feast, Eurytion, one of the Centaurs, becoming intoxicated with the wine, attempted to offer violence to the bride. The other Centaurs followed his example, and a dreadful conflict arose, in which several of them were slain. They were finally driven from Pelion and obliged to retire to other regions. The most celebrated of the Centaurs was Chiron, the son of Saturn by the nymph Philyra.

Century-Plant is a species of cactus which matures at different ages in different climates. In tropical countries it attains its perfect state in about ten years, while in colder climates it often requires from seventy years to a full century to reach its maturity. When the plant has matured it sends up a stem which grows to the height of from 24 to 36 feet, out of which grow numerous branches, forming a perfect cylindrical pyramid, and each is crowned with a cluster of greenish-yellow flowers, which continue in perfect bloom for several months. After flowering the plant always dies to the ground, but the root continues to live and send up new shoots. The century-plant, or *Agave Americana*, its botanical name, grows through all the central part of the American continent from Mexico to Chili. It is called the maguey in South America and the mezcal in Mexico. From the leaf-fibers of the plant a coarse flax is made. The dried flower-stems make a thatch which is perfectly impervious to rain. From its sap is obtained a fermented liquor known as pulque, which is an agreeable but intoxicating drink. From the center of the stem, split longitudinally, a substitue for a hone or razor-strop is obtained; and an extract of the leaves is made into soap-balls, which are largely used in Mexico for washing purposes.

Chancellor, Lord.—The existence of the office of Lord Chancellor in England, as in the other states of Europe, is to be ascribed to the influence of the constitution of the Roman Empire which was exercised in no small degree by the Romish Church, "ever emulous of imperial state." The name is probably derived from *cancellarius*, so termed from his high function of *canceling* the King's letters-patent when granted contrary to law. The Chancellor is the confidential adviser of the Sovereign in state affairs, and always has the custody of the great seal. He is a Privy Councilor by his office, and a member of the Cabinet, and as such retires on a change of Ministry. He is also Prolocutor or Speaker of the House of Lords by prescription. An important branch of his patronage arises out of his having been originally an ecclesiastic, as he still continues to be the patron of all the Crown livings of the value of £20 per annum or under, and visitor of all hospitals and colleges of the King's foundation. In this capacity he presided over the King's chapel, and hence came to be styled the Keeper of the King's Conscience. As representing the paternal character of the Sovereign, the Chancellor is the general guardian of all infants, idiots and lunatics, and has general supervision of all charitable uses in the kingdom. In addition to all his other functions he had a vast and important jurisdiction in a judicial capacity, being the Supreme Judge of the Court of Chancery. He had the appointment of all justices of the peace throughout the kingdom, but this privilege he generally exercised on the recommendations of the Lord Lieutenants. He also generally appointed all the judges of the Superior Courts except the two Chief Justices, who were nominated by the Prime Minister of the day. His judicial duties and functions have been much modified and decreased by the Acts of 1871-'73 and '81, by which the entire judiciary of England has been remodeled.

Chancery, Court of.—The Court of the Chancellor, the name being hence derived. It at first included an *ordinary* court of law and an *extraordinary* court of equity. The latter becoming of such vast importance and power, the term "chancery" came to be used as synonymous with "equity." The jurisdiction of this court included all those causes and actions which, by the technical rules, the narrow forms and the inadequate remedies in the courts of law, were excluded from those courts. It sought to ascertain and mete out to all parties concerned perfect justice without being hampered and restricted by any forms and technicalities, a maxim of the court being, "He who asks equity must do equity." The equity system still exists in England, and has been introduced into this country along with the Common Law, all our courts now having concurrent jurisdiction in law and equity.

Charges d'Affaires, Salaries of.—The salaries of the Charges d'Affaires of the United States are as follows: Paraguay and Uruguay, $5,000. The Charge d'Affaires at San Domingo is also accredited to Hayti as Minister Resident, and receives remuneration only for the latter office.

Charivari is a French term used to designate a wild tumult and uproar, produced by the beating of pans, kettles and dishes, mingled with whistlings, bawlings, etc., and are gotten up for the purpose of expressing a general dislike for the person against whom it is directed. During the middle ages a charivari was raised against persons contracting second marriages, especially widows. The participators in it, who were masked, accompanied their hubbub by the singing of satirical and indecent verse, which they continued till the wedding-couple had purchased their peace by ransom. In certain country districts of the United States a relic of the charivari is still in vogue, known under various local appellations, as "hornings," etc., in which the newly-married couple are treated to a serenade of fish-horns, drums, guns, bells, etc., but not always indicating dislike or disapprobation. This continues until the groom makes his appearance and entertains his self-invited guests.

Chartreuse, the well-known *liqueur*, derives its name from a monastery where its manufacture is a main industry of the inmates. This is La Grande Chartreuse, situated in a wild and rugged but picturesque part of France, in the Department of Isere. It is the residence of the General of the Carthusian Order, and hence various other monasteries of this order in France and Italy are called by the same name. The *liqueur* is distilled from aromatic herbs.

Charybdis.—[See *Scylla and Charybdis.*]

Chess, Origin of.—Although the origin of chess is enshrouded in considerable mystery, there is but little doubt that its birthplace was in India, and that it is an offspring of a game called Chaturanga, which is mentioned in Oriental literature as in use fully 2,000 years before the Christian era. From India chess spread into Persia, and thence into Arabia, and ultimately the Arabs took it to Spain and the rest of Western Europe. The game was in all probability invented for the purpose of illustrating the art of war. The Arab legend upon this point is that it was devised for the instruction of a young despot by his father, a learned Brahman, to teach him that a king, notwithstanding his power, was dependent for safety upon his subjects. The Greek historians credit the invention of the game to Palamedes, who, they claim, devised it to beguile the tedium of the siege of Troy during the Trojan war.

Chevy Chase is the name of perhaps the most popular of British ballads, and the event which it means to commemorate appears to have been the battle of Otterburn in August, 1388. There are two versions of this ballad. The first is very ancient, and was originally published by Thomas Hearne, an English antiquary who lived from 1678 to 1735. He reprinted "Chevy Chase" from the manuscript copy in the Ashmolean collection at Oxford, which was written by Rychard Sheale, of Tamworth, who was a reciter of ballads and stories. The authorship of Sheale, however, is questioned, the general belief being that he was simply a preserver of the story. The second version is a modernized one, supposed to be of the Elizabethan period. It is much inferior to the original, but at the same time is a fine ballad.

Chief Justices of the United States.—The office of Chief Justice of the United States has been held since 1789 by John Jay, John Rutledge, Oliver Ellsworth, John Marshall, Roger B. Taney, Salmon P. Chase, Morrison R. Waite and Melville W. Fuller, the present incumbent.

Children's Crusade.—In the summer of 1212 two immense armies of children were gathered at Cologne, in Germany, and at Vendome, in France, summoned thither by two boy-prophets, Stephen of Cloys (France) and Nicholas of Cologne (Germany), both about twelve years of age. These boy-prophets believed, or pretended to believe, that they were inspired by heaven, and the crusade which they preached was not a crusade of blood against the Saracens, but a crusade of prayer. The children were to march to the sea, which would open, as it once did for the Israelites, to permit them to pass over into Palestine dry-shod. There they were to convert the leaders of Islam and baptize the heathen. The excitement aroused by this preaching spread so among the children that within short intervals of each other two unarmed hosts of German children, drawn from all classes, and nearly all under twelve years of age, left Cologne to march over the sea to the Holy Land. The first was led by the famous Nicholas, and the second by a boy whose name is not known. Their combined numbers are believed to have been 40,000. At about the same time an army of French children to the number of about 30,000 left Vendome under Stephen. The mortality among the German children in their passage across the Alps was frightful. Nearly 30,000 succumbed to exposure, fatigue and hunger. Of the French army, 10,000 died before it reached Marseilles. The army under Nicholas was broken up at Genoa when it was found that the sea did not open to let them pass, and some of the children were returned to their homes by the humane Genoese; but others pressed on to Pisa and obtained passage by ship to the Holy Land. A part of the children under the unknown leader were shipped to Palestine from Brindisi, and about 5,000 of the French children were shipped from Marseilles, and all who survived the voyages were sold as slaves to the Turks. Of the 70,000 children who joined this crusade, it is probable that less than 20,000 were ever heard of afterward by their parents.

Chillon, Castle of, is a celebrated castle and fortress of Switzerland, in the canton of Vaud, six miles southeast of Vevay. It is situated at the east end of the Lake of Geneva, on an isolated rock, almost entirely surrounded by deep water, and is connected with the shore by a wooden bridge. The castle is said to have been built by Amadeus IV, of Savoy, in 1238, and it long served as a state prison. It is built of white stone, but though large is not of very imposing appearance, as its foundations only rise a few feet above the water. The lake here is 800 feet deep. Over one of the entrances to the castle the Bernese inscribed, in 1643, in the German language, the words "The Lord God save those who come in and go out." In the gloomy dungeons are still to be seen the stone pillars, with strong iron rings attached, to which the unhappy prisoners were fettered. Chillon is famous as the prison of Bonnivard, the prior of St. Victor, who, having by his efforts to free the Genevese rendered himself obnoxious to the Duke of Savoy, was carried off by emissaries of that potentate, and confined here for six years, at the end of which time the castle was forced to surrender to the Bernese and Genevese, when Bonnivard secured his liberty. Since 1738 the castle has been employed as a magazine for military stores. Chillon has been immortalized by Byron's poem, "Prisoner of Chillon," referring to the Bonnivard mentioned above.

China, Great Wall of, was begun 214 years before Christ, its purpose being to protect China from the incursions of the northern tribes, and was completed in about ten years. The wall, as it can be seen now, begins at a coast-town known as Shanhai K'wan, and runs along the shore for several miles, terminating on the beach near a long reef. From this point its course is west, trending a little to the north till it strikes the Yellow River. This is the best-built part of the wall. Beyond, it goes nearly west till it strikes the Yellow River again, and then goes in a northwestern direction to its termination near Kraya K'wan. The entire length of the wall is 1,255 miles in a straight line, but its turnings and doublings increase it to fully 1,500 miles. The eastern part is composed of earth and pebbles faced with large bricks, weighing from forty to sixty pounds each, supported on a coping of stone. The wall here is 20 feet thick at the base and 15 feet at the top, and varies from 15 to 30 feet in height. There are brick towers at intervals, some of them more than 40 feet high; but these are not built on the wall—they are independent structures. Beyond the Yellow River the wall is mostly a mere mound of earth and gravel, with occasional towers of brick or gateways of stone. At Kalgan portions of it are made of porphyry and other stones piled up in a pyramidal form between the brick towers. The wall is most visited at Nan-Kan, in the Ku-yung Pass, a remarkable *thermopylæ* fifteen miles in length which leads from the plain at Peking up to the first terrace above it, and at one time was guarded by five additional walls and gates, now all in ruins.

China, Porcelain Tower of, was situated in Nankin, and was nineteen years in building, being completed in 1430. In 1856 the

Taiping rebels blew it up and carried away the materials of which it was composed, fearing that the magic influence of its bells and lamps would work against the success of their cause. It was of octagonal form, 260 feet high, in nine stories, each having a cornice and a gallery without. The outer face of this unique structure was covered with slabs of porcelain of various colors, principally green, red, yellow and white. At every one of its nine stories the projecting roof of the gallery was covered with green tiles, and a bell was suspended from each corner. There were 152 bells in all, which gave sweet sounds when there was a brisk wind. One hundred and twenty-eight lamps were hung on the outside. On the top was a pinnacle in the shape of a pine-apple, surmounted by a gilded ball. A spiral staircase led to the summit. It was constructed for a gift to the Empress, and was kept in repair by the Government. In 1801 it was struck by lightning and its three upper stories were broken or thrown down, but the injury was repaired. It was destroyed in 1856, as related above.

Chinese Burial Customs.—Immediately upon the decease of a person in China a priest is called, whose prayers are supposed to free the departed spirit from the necessity of going to hell, and to secure his admittance to Paradise. The body is arrayed in the most splendid garments that the family can afford. In one hand is placed a fan, and in the other a prayer written on a piece of paper, which is a letter of recommendation to open the gates of Heaven. The coffin is a very solid, substantial case. The corpse, when put in it, is laid in a bed of lime or cotton, or covered with quicklime, and the edges of the lid are closed with mortar in the groove so that no smell escapes. The nature of the site for burial is regarded as having an important influence on the prosperity of the living, the people fearing ill-luck, disease and accident if the dead are not satisfied with the site of their graves. The selection of propitious sites is made by geomancers, a class of quacks who pretend to supernatural wisdom. When the day of burial arrives, which is—if a satisfactory place for the tomb has been found—the nearest lucky day to the third seventh day after death, the friends assemble at the house. An offering of cooked provisions is laid out near the coffin. This is intended to occupy the attention of the spirit of the dead, which is supposed to linger near the body, or any other vagrant spirits that may be hovering around, and keep them from doing any mischief or harm to the living. All mourners are dressed entirely in white, and they assemble about the coffin and in turn prostrate themselves before it, a band of music playing meanwhile. The procession is then formed, the coffin going first, borne on an unwieldly bier carried by sixty-four men, or even more. A man goes before the procession and scatters paper money to buy the good-will of any stray, tricky spirits that may be prowling about. Immediately after the coffin, in a separate sedan, is borne the ancestral tablet of the deceased with the offering of food. Different figures, banners and tablets are also carried, according to the means and rank of the family. When the grave is reached the coffin is let down, and lime is abundantly mixed with the earth thrown in upon it. Crackers are then fired, libations are poured out, prayers are recited, and finally paper molds of houses, clothes, horses, money, and everything that the dead man can possibly want in the land of shadows, are burned. The origin of this latter custom is unquestionably the idea that everything that had been enjoyed or used in this life would be desired in the other. The ancient custom was to burn a man's household belongings, to kill upon his grave his favorite horse, hound or bird, and sometimes his chosen servant, that their shadows might go with him into the life beyond. After the funeral the elaborate dishes that have been borne to the grave are carried back, and the mourners feast upon them. Bodies are in some instances kept in or about the house for many years, and incense is burned before them morning and evening. Usually this occurs when the means of the family will not permit of the elaborate funeral which custom requires.

Chinese Edible Dog.—The kind of dog used as an article of food in China, and reared in order to be so used, being esteemed as a great delicacy, is a small dog of greyhound-like form, with somewhat terrier-like head, and muzzle more elongated than in terriers. It is fleet and active, gentle and affectionate. The skin is almost destitute of hair; but there is a variety having a crest of long hair on the head, and a large tuft of hair at the tip of the slender and otherwise naked tail.

Chinese Immigration Law.—According to the law passed by both houses of Congress and approved by the President in 1882, and amended in May, 1884, Chinese laborers are forbidden to come to the United States for ten years, or until May, 1894. The law further declares that any master of any vessel who shall knowingly land any Chinese laborer shall be deemed guilty of a misdemeanor, and for every Chinese brought shall be fined a sum not exceeding $500, and may also be imprisoned for one year. Chinese persons who are not laborers desiring to visit this country are obliged to bring with them from the Chinese Government (or any other Government of which they may at the time be subjects) certificates of identification, giving their names in full, description, statement of business, place of residence, etc., the certificates to be also indorsed by the American diplomatic representative in the country where issued, and the forgery or substitution of any name for the correct one in such certificates shall render the perpetrator thereof liable to a fine of $1,000 and an imprisonment of five years. A master of any vessel bringing into a United States port any such Chinese persons, not laborers, is required to give a list of them to the Collector of Customs of the port. Any master of a vessel who violates any of these provisions against admitting the Chinese forfeits his vessel to the Government, and any person aiding or abetting a Chinaman not lawfully entitled to visit this country to land here renders himself liable to a fine of $1,000 and one year's imprisonment. Further, any Chinese person found traveling in the United States without a proper certificate shall be removed to the country from whence he came at the cost of the United States, any person who may have been instrumental in bringing such Chinese to the United States being liable for all the expenses of his removal; and all peace officers of the several States and Territories are invested with the powers of a United States marshal for the purpose of carrying the law into effect. The only Chinese persons exempted from the action of this law are diplomatic officers traveling on the business of their Government, their retinue of servants, and Chinamen who arrived within ninety days after the passage of the act. The law also requires Chinese already established in the country to take out certificates, if they leave the United States, in order to prove their identity in the event of return.

Christian Association, Young Men's.—Associations of young men for Christian work have existed in Great Britain and Ireland for upward of two centuries, and also in Germany and Switzerland. In 1710 it is recorded that Cotton Mather addressed kindred societies in New England which were known as "Young Men Associated." In 1849 the societies which had been established in Germany took a wider scope, and from these associations grew the German associations of the present day. The English Young Men's Christian Association commenced in a meeting of clerks organized by George Williams in a mercantile establishment in London in 1844. The example of the British metropolis was speedily followed by the various cities of Great Britain founding associations, and in December, 1851, America caught the enthusiasm of the movement and formed an association in Montreal modeled after the one in London. Then Boston undertook the formation of one for itself, and their growth and influence since that time have been simply wonderful. They now flourish in every Protestant Christian country; and in almost every place where a colony of Christians are gathered, these associations are to be found.

Christian Era.—For a long period there was no fixed time from which dates were reckoned. Then followed the custom of dating from some event of national importance; as, for example, the Romans for centuries dated from the founding of the Eternal City, and the Greeks from the first Olympic games. When Christianity became predominant in the civilized world, writers began to date from various epochs in the history of the Saviour. About the middle of the sixth century Dionysius Exiguus, a Roman churchman of Scythian birth, introduced the method of dating from the birth of Christ, which, according to his computation, took place in the fourth year of the 194th Olympiad, or the 753d from the founding of Rome. It is generally admitted, however, that he placed this event about four years too late.

Christmas - Day.—December 25th was not celebrated as the birthday of Christ until A. D. 337, when St. Cyril, Bishop of Jerusalem, obtained authority from Pope Julian I to appoint a commission to determine, if possible, the exact day of Christ's nativity. This resulted in the Eastern and Western divisions of the Christian Church accepting December 25th as the date. Previous to this time Christmas had been a movable feast. By the Eastern branches of the Church it was celebrated in April or May, while days in January or other months were observed in the Western part of Europe.

Church-Bells.—From a remote antiquity cymbals and hand-bells have been used in religious ceremonies. In Egypt, it is certain that the feast of Osiris was announced by ringing bells. Aaron and other Jewish high-priests wore golden bells attached to their vestments, and in Athens the priests of Cybele used bells in their rites. The introduction of bells into Christian churches is usually ascribed to Paulinus, Bishop of Nola, in Campania, A. D. 400. Their use in churches and monasteries soon spread through Christendom. They were introduced into France about 550, and Benedict, Abbot of Wearmouth, brought one from Italy for his church about 680. Pope Sabinian A. D. 600 ordained that every hour should be announced by the sound of a bell, that the people might be warned of the approach of the hours of devotion. Bells came into use in the East in the ninth century, and in Switzerland and Germany in the eleventh century. Most of the bells first used in western Christendom seem to have been hand-bells. Several examples, some of them as old as the sixth century, are still preserved in Ireland, Scotland and Wales. They are made of thin plates of hammered iron, bent into a four-sided form, fastened with rivets, and brazed or bronzed. Perhaps the most remarkable is that which is said to have belonged to St. Patrick, called the *Clog-an-cad hachta Phatraic*, or " The Bell of Patrick's Will." It is six inches high, five inches broad and four inches deep, and is kept in a case or shrine of brass enriched with gems and with gold and silver filigree, and made (as an inscription in Irish shows) between the years 1091 and 1105. The bell itself is believed to be mentioned in the "Annals of Ulster" as early as the year 552. The four-sided bell of St. Gall, an Irish missionary, who died about 646, is still shown in the monastery of the city which bears his name in Switzerland. It was not until the fifteenth century that bells reached any really considerable dimensions.

Church of England.—Up to the time of the Reformation, ecclesiastical affairs would be more properly described as the history of the Church in England, as from that period the Church of England dates her existence. From the eighth to the sixteenth century the English Church was subject to Rome; but for the last two hundred years the seed sown by Wycliffe had been bearing fruit and preparing the people for a final separation, the immediate occasion for which was found in the royal caprice of Henry VIII. From 1066 to 1356 there was a constant struggle between the civil and ecclesiastical powers. Then came Wycliffe's translation of the Bible into English and his continued war against some of the leading doctrines of the Romish Church, which led to the formation of a new sect called Lollards [see *Lollards*], holding views similar to those of the present Church. Despite persecutions the new doctrines spread and had many adherents. The Reformation is ordinarily assigned to the reign of Henry VIII, the two most important acts being passed in 1532 and 1534; but the main feature of these acts was the declaration of the independence of the Church in England and the supremacy of the King over that Church. They had cast off the bondage of Rome, but in doctrine the Churches were still in accord; and it was not until thirty years afterward—1563, in the reign of Queen Elizabeth—that the Thirty-Nine Articles of Faith were finally reviewed and adopted and the Protestant Church of England finally and fully established. In 1801, by the "Act of Union," the Episcopal Churches in England and Ireland were united; but the latter Church was disestablished and disendowed in 1869. The Episcopal Church in Scotland is not, politically speaking, in union with that of England; but an Act of Parliament, passed in 1864, has taken away many restrictions imposed on Scottish Episcopalians after the battle of Culloden, and clergy ordained by Scotch bishops may now, under some slight restrictions, be presented to benefices in England.

Cincinnati, Society of, was founded by the officers of the American Revolutionary army in May, 1783. Membership is restricted to the eldest male descendant of an original member. The objects of the society at its inception was "to perpetuate their friendship, and to raise a fund for relieving the widows and orphans of those who had fallen during the war." There were originally thirteen State societies and one composed of French officers who had served in the Revolutionary War. Owing to the fact that the society was attacked as opposed to republican equality it was quietly abolished in several of the States, and there now remain only seven State societies, viz.: Massachusetts, Rhode Island, New York, New Jersey, Pennsylvania, Maryland and South Carolina. The Society of the Cincinnati in France has effected a preliminary reorganization, and is about to be re-established. General Washington was the first President-General and General Hamilton the second. Ex-Secretary Hamilton Fish is the ninth.

Circe, a fabulous sorceress, is described by Homer as "fair-haired, a clever goddess, possessing human speech." Round her palace in Æca were numbers of human beings, whom she had changed into the shapes of wolves and lions by her drugs and spells. She changed twenty-two of the companions of Ulysses into swine; but that hero, having obtained from Mercury the herb *moly*, went boldly to the palace of the sorceress, remained uninjured by her drugs and charms, and induced her to disenchant his comrades. He remained with her for a year, and when he departed she instructed him how to avoid the dangers which he would encounter on his homeward voyage.

Circus, Modern.—The origin of the modern circus dates back to about 1770, when Philip Astley, a discharged English soldier, gave exhibitions of horsemanship in an improvised ring at Lambeth, England. His success was so great that he shortly after built a rude circus on a piece of ground near Westminster Bridge, on the site of the present building there, which has borne his name for more than a century. Only the seats of this first structure were roofed over, the performers' ring being in the open air. He now hired several performers; and his wife, who entered with ardor into his work, went into the ring—the first female equestrian known. So popular did this circus become that he was in a few years able to build a large and handsome amphitheater, which was opened to the public in 1780. It was burned three times—in 1794, in 1803, and in 1842—each time being immediately rebuilt. The present structure, which is still known as "Astley's," is one of the finest of the kind in the world.

Civil Service Rules, U. S.—There are three branches of the public service classified under the Civil Service Act. 1. Offices classified in the Departments at Washington are designated as "The Classified Departmental Service." 2. Those classified under any collector or naval officer, surveyor or appraiser in any customs district, are designated as "The Classified Customs Service." 3. Those classified under any postmaster are designated as "The Classified Postal Service." The Classified Departmental Service embraces all places in the Departments at Washington excepting messengers, laborers, workmen and watchmen (not including any person designated as a skilled laborer or workman); and no person so employed can, without examination under the rules, be assigned to clerical duty, and also excepting those appointed by and with the advice and consent of the Senate. The Classified Customs Service embraces the customs districts where the officials are as many as fifty, including the places giving $900 a year, and all those giving a larger salary where the appointee is not subject to confirmation by the Senate. The Classified Postal Service embraces the post-offices where the officials are as many as fifty, including all places above the grade of a laborer. For places in the Classified Service, where technical additional qualifications are needed, special examinations are held. In the Departmental Service they are held for the State Department, the Pension, Patent and Signal Offices, Geological and Coast Survey, and others. Applicants for examination must be citizens of the United States of the proper age. No person habitually using intoxicating liquors can be appointed. No discrimination is made on account of sex, color, or political or religious opinions. The limitations of age are: For Departmental Service, not under twenty years; in the Customs Service, not under twenty-one years, except clerks or messengers, who must be not under twenty years; and in the Postal Service, not under eighteen years, except messengers, stampers, and other junior assistants, who must not be under sixteen nor over forty-five years, and carriers, who must not be under twenty-one nor over forty. The applicants to enter the services designated are examined as to their relative capacity and fitness. The general or clerk examinations are used only in the Customs and Departmental Services for clerkships of $1,000 and upward, requiring no peculiar information or skill. It is limited to the following subjects: First, orthography, penmanship and copying; second, arithmetic-fundamental rules, fractions and percentage; third, interest, discount, and elements of book-keeping and of accounts; fourth, elements of the English language, letter-writing, and the proper construction of sentences; fifth, elements of the geography, history, and government of the United States. For places in which a lower degree of education suffices, as for employes in post-offices and those below the grade of clerks in custom-houses and in the Departments at Washington, the third and parts of the fourth and fifth subjects are omitted in the examination. No one is certified for appointment whose standing upon a just grading in the general or limited examination is less than seventy per centum of complete proficiency, except that applicants claiming military or naval preference need obtain but sixty-five. The law also prescribes competitive examinations to test the fitness of persons in the service for promotion therein. Every appointment is made for a probationary period of six months, at the end of which time, if the conduct and capacity of the person appointed have been found satisfactory, the appointment is made absolute. The following are excepted from examination for appointment: Confidential clerks of heads of Departments or offices, cashiers of collectors and postmasters, superintendents of money-order divisions in post-offices, custodians of money for whose fidelity another officer is under bond, disbursing officers who give bonds, persons in the secret service, deputy collectors, and superintendents and chiefs of divisions or bureaus, and a few others. Every one seeking to be examined must first file an application-blank. The blank for the Departmental Service should be requested directly of the Civil Service Commission at Washington. The blank for the Customs or Postal Service must be requested in writing of the Customs or Postal Board of Examiners at the office where service is sought. These papers should be returned to the officers from whom they were obtained.

Civil War, Casualties of.—According to the report of the Provost-Marshal General, the casualties in the Union army from the beginning of the Civil War to August 1, 1865, were as follows: Killed—volunteer officers, white, 3,357; volunteer enlisted men, white, 54,350; officers of colored troops, 124; enlisted men, colored, 1,790; regulars, 1,355; total, 60,976. Died of wounds—volunteer officers, 1,595; volunteer enlisted men, 32,095; officers of colored troops, 46; enlisted men, colored, 1,037; regulars, 1,174; total, 35,947. Died of disease—volunteer officers, 2,141; volunteer enlisted men, 152,013; officers of colored troops, 90; enlisted men, colored, 26,211; regulars, 3,009; total, 183,464. Discharged for disability—volunteer officers, 3,058; volunteer enlisted men, 209,102; officers of colored troops, 166; enlisted men, colored, 6,889; regulars, 5,091; total, 224,306. The report of the Adjutant-General of the army about five years later—October 25, 1870—puts the total of deaths at 303,504, while the Surgeon-General of the army reports the number at 282,955. The Adjutant-General reports the total number killed in battle as 44,238; the Surgeon-General reports 35,408. The former reports the number who died of disease at 149,043; the latter, 186,216. The Quartermaster-General reports the total number of graves under his supervision as 315,555, only 172,309 of which have been identified. According to the only data at hand, the total Confederate losses in action are estimated as follows: Killed, 51,525; wounded, 227,871. In the Union navy there were 4,030 killed and wounded in action, 2,532 died of disease, and 2,070 died of other casualties.

Cleanliness Next to Godliness.—It is generally supposed that this phrase is of Bible origin, but such however is not the fact. In Chambers' "Book of Days," volume II, page 206, in an article on "Rowland Hill," the following is attributed to that noted preacher: "Good Mr. Whitefield used to say, 'Cleanliness is next to Godliness.'"

Clearing-House.—The clearing-house is an institution founded not merely upon the idea of saving time and trouble in the use of the precious metals, but also of circulating-notes. The Clearing-House of London, which was the first of the kind, originated among the bankers of that city, whose transactions in the checks, bills and drafts drawn upon each other became so large as to call for the daily, and even hourly, use of vast sums in bank-notes by all of them. Appreciating how readily the debts and credits respectively due or held by them might be set off, one against the other, they formed the Clearing-House, where, up to four o'clock each day, all drafts, bills, etc., upon each individual member were taken. This system of the London Clearing-House has, however, been much extended and improved. Clearing-houses exist in New York, Philadelphia, Boston, Chicago and other cities of the United States. A description of the system in use in Philadelphia will in the main answer for all. The clearings are made each morning at 8:30, just before which hour a messenger and a clerk from each bank are at the Clearing-House. The clerks take their seats at a series of desks arranged in the form of a half-oval. The messenger brings with him from his bank a sealed package for each other bank, containing all checks or drafts on such banks. The name of the bank sending and that of the bank to which it is sent is printed on each package, and the amount sent is written thereon. The messengers take their places near the desks of their respective banks, and they have with them tabular statements of the amount sent to each bank, and the aggregate. These are exhibited to the respective clerks and noted by them on the blank forms. At 8:30 o'clock precisely the manager calls to order and gives the word, when all the messengers move forward from left to right of the clerks, handing in to those clerks the packages addressed to their respective banks, and taking receipts for them on their statements. The several clerks then pass around a memoradum of the debts, credits and balances, each of his respective bank. When these memoranda have made the circuit, each clerk has on his statement the debts, credits and balances, whether debtor or creditor, of each bank. If these debits and credits, or debtor and creditor-balances, are found to balance, the clerks now leave the Clearing-House. If not, they remain until the error or errors are discovered. The balances due by the several banks are paid into the Clearing-House that day by 11:30 o'clock A. M., and are receivable by the creditor bank by 12:30 P. M. Each bank is obliged daily to furnish to the Clearing-House a statement of its condition at the end of the business on that day, and tables are daily furnished to the several banks of all the banks in the Clearing-House.

Clepsydra.—An instrument of great antiquity employed to measure time by the efflux of water through a small orifice. They are frequently mentioned in ancient literature, the Greeks and Romans using them to measure the time allowed for speeches in the courts of justice. Later they were introduced throughout Europe, and their use prevailed until after the invention of pendulum clocks. The earliest and simplest form was a transparent graduated vase with a small orifice, the height of the water on the scale indicating the time. Later, efforts were made to secure uniformity in the flow by maintaining the fluid at a constant level; and during the eighteenth century one of the most difficult problems engaging the attention of mathematicians was the determination of the exact effect upon the flow occasioned by the shape and height of the vase. Bernoulli solved the problem, and received a prize for it from the French Academy of Sciences.

Cloves, Oil of, or, as it is called scientifically, eugenol, is a concentrated, oily extract made from cloves, and is used as an antiseptic in dentistry, for which purpose it is said to be superior to any other substance ever used. It is found to thoroughly disinfect a decaying tooth, to arrest the progress of ulcers; and thus, while not properly an anæsthetic, it serves the same purpose in the allaying of pain.

Coal Production, Southern.—The increase in the coal production of the Southern States during 1888, as compared with the preceding years, was very heavy, though the output during 1889 will probably far exceed that of 1888, as there is a steady growth in the number of mines in operation. From the report of the United States Geological Survey, the output in each Southern State for the years 1887 and 1888 was as follows: Maryland, 1887, 3,278,023 tons; 1888, 3,479,470 tons. Virginia, 1887, 825,263 tons; 1888, 1,073,000 tons. West Virginia, 1887, 4,836,820 tons; 1888,

5,498,800 tons. Georgia, 1887, 313,715 tons; 1888. 230,000 tons. Alabama, 1887, 1,900,000 tons; 1888, 2,900,000 tons. Tennessee, 1887, 1,900,000 tons; 1888, 1,967,000 tons. Arkansas, 1887, 150,000 tons; 1888, 193,000 tons. Texas, 1887, 75,000 tons; 1888, 90,000 tons. Kentucky, 1887, 1,933,185 tons; 1888, 2,570,000 tons. Total, 1887, 15,212,006 tons; 1888, 18,001,-270 tons. In 1880 the South produced 6,049,471 tons of coal, and in 1882 only 6,569,316 tons; so that in six years the output of Southern coal-mines has advanced from 6,500,000 tons to upward of 18,000,000 tons, and before the end of 1890 the South will be producing at the rate of 25,000,000 tons or more a year. Or, in other words, between the taking of the census of 1880 and that of 1890 the output of Southern coal-mines will have more than quadrupled.

Coal Used by Steamers.—The consumption of coal by steamers has been materially decreased since the introduction of what is known as the compound engine. Previous to that time a vessel of the best type of engineering skill—for instance the Scotia, of the Cunard line, floated in 1862, having a midship section of 841 square feet—consumed 160 tons of coal per day, or 1,600 tons on the passage between New York and Liverpool. The City of Brussels, a screw-steamer of the Inman line, floated in 1869, and having a midship section of 909 square feet, consumed 95 tons per day; while the Spain, a screw-steamer of the National line, launched in 1871, with compound machinery, and the longest vessel on the Atlantic, having a length of 425 feet 6 inches on the load-line, beam-mold 43 feet, draft, loaded, 24 feet 9 inches, made the passage in September consuming only 53 tons per day, or 530 tons on the run. All these three vessels had the same average of speed. There are still later instances where but forty tons of coal per day were used. One of the most forcible illustrations of the success of compound engines is contained in the record of the voyage of the steamer Burgos, which left England in 1885 for China with a cargo weighing 5,600,000 pounds. From Plymouth to Alexandria the consumption of coal was 282,240 pounds, the distance being 3,380 miles; the consumption per mile was, therefore, only 83.5 pounds, and the consumption per ton of cargo per mile 0 028 pounds; in other words, half an ounce of coal propelled one ton of cargo a mile. The Burgos was not, it must be remembered, one of the first-class steamers, trimly built, with especial reference to making good speed, but a large vessel constructed particularly for the conveyance of bulky cargoes.

Cobden Club, The, is a British association which takes its name from Richard Cobden, the great English statesman and economist, who was born in 1804 and died in 1865. Cobden was an advocate of free trade, and among the leading objects of the Cobden Club is the spread of free-trade doctrines.

Cockatrice.—One of the fabulous monsters, a belief in the existence of which prevailed among the ancients and during the middle ages. It was sometimes distinguished from and sometimes identified with the basilisk. [See *Basilisk*.] For protection against it, travelers in Africa are said to have carried with them a cock, the crowing of which caused it instantly to expire.

Coffee, Use of.—How long coffee has been in use in Arabia, its native country, is unknown. It was first introduced into Egypt in the sixteenth century. The first coffee-house in Europe was established in Constantinople in 1551. It was introduced into Western Europe by Leonard Rauwolf, a German physician and traveler, and coffee-houses shortly after sprung up in all the chief cities. The first one in London was opened by a Greek in Newman's Court, Cornhill, in 1652. The first one in France was opened in Marseilles in 1671, and the first one in Paris in 1672.

Coins, Foreign, Values of.—The values of foreign coins in United States money are as follows: Austria—florin, value 40.6 cents; Belgium—franc, value 19.3 cents; Bolivia—boliviano, value 82.3 cents; Brazil—milreis of 1,000 reis, value 54.5 cents; Central America—peso, value 83.6 cents; Chili—peso, value, 91.2 cents; Denmark—crown, value 26.8 cents; Ecuador—peso, value 82.3 cents; Egypt—pound of 100 piasters, value $4.86 1-2; France—franc, value 19.3 cents; Great Britain—pound sterling; value $4.86 1-2; Greece—drachma, value 19.3 cents; German Empire—mark, value 23.8 cents; India, rupee, value 39.7 cents; Italy—lira, value 19.3 cents; Japan—yen, value 99.7 cents; Liberia—dollar, value 100 cents; Mexico—dollar or peso, value 89.4 cents; Netherlands—florin, value 40.2 cents; Norway—crown, value 26.8 cents; Peru—sol, value 83.6 cents; Portugal—milreis of 1,000 reis, value $1.08; Russia—ruble of 100 copecks, value 66.9 cents; Sandwich Islands—dollar, value 100 cents; Spain—peseta of 100 centimes, value 19.3 cents; Sweden—crown, value 26.8 cents; Switzerland—franc, value 19.3 cents; Tripoli, mahbub (20 piasters), value 74.3 cents; Turkey—piaster, value 4.4 cents; United States of Colombia—peso, value 83.6 cents.

Colosseum, The.—The Flavian amphitheater at Rome, known as the Colosseum, was begun by the Emperor Vespasian, and was finished by the Emperor Titus, A. D. 80. It covers about five acres of ground, and contained seats for 87,000 persons and standing-room for 15,000 more. It was in the form of an oval, the longer diameter being 612 feet and the shorter diameter 515 feet, and the height of the walls from 160 to 180 feet. The arena where the gladiators fought and the deadly conflicts with wild beasts took place was 281 by 178 feet. The exterior consists of three rows of columns, Doric, Ionic and Corinthian, and above, a row of Corinthian pilasters. Between the columns there are arches which form open galleries throughout the whole building, and between each alternate pilaster of the upper tier there is a window. There were four tiers or stories of seats, corresponding to the four external stories. The first of these is supposed to have contained twenty-four rows of seats, and the second sixteen. These were separated by a lofty wall from the third story, which is supposed to have contained the populace. Statues, sculptures, figures of chariots, metal shields and other embellishments adorned the niches and salient points. On the occasion of the dedication of the Colosseum by Titus, 5,000 wild beasts were slain in the arena, the games having lasted for nearly 100 days. There were means by which, when the combats were ended, the immense arena could be filled with water for the exhibition of sea-fights. During the various persecutions of the early Christians many of these were thrown to the wild beasts in this amphitheater. One of the first of these was St. Ignatius, who was torn to pieces by lions. In the sixth century, when Christianity gained the ascendancy, the Church put an end the use of the Colosseum. It still stood entire in the eighth century, but subsequently large quantities of the marble was used in the construction of public and private buildings. It was consecrated as a monument to the martyrs who had suffered within its walls by Pope Benedict XIV, who erected crosses and oratorios within it, and so put an end to the process of destruction.

Colossus of Memnon.—The celebrated vocal statue of Memnon, on the plain of Thebes, was originally sixty feet high, and is of a coarse, hard gritstone or breccia. The peculiar characteristic of this statue was its giving out at various times a sound resembling the breaking of a harp-string or a metallic ring. Considerable difference of opinion has prevailed as to the reason of this sound, which has been heard in modern times, it being ascribed to the artifice of the priests, who struck the sonorous stone of which the statue is composed, the passage of light draughts of air through the cracks, or the sudden expansion of aqueous particles under the influence of the sun's rays. This remarkable quality of the statue is first mentioned by Strabo, who visited it in company with Ælius Gallus, about 18 B. C.; and upward of 100 inscriptions of Greek and Roman visitors, incised upon its legs, record the visits of ancient travelers to witness the phenomenon from the ninth year of Nero, A. D. 63, to the reign of the Emperor Severus, when it became silent.

Colossus of Rhodes.—The gigantic Colossus of Rhodes was a statue of Apollo, so placed as to bestride the entrance to the harbor. It is said to have been commenced by Chares of Lindus, a famous pupil of Lysippus, and was completed by Laches. It was formed of metal which was cast in separate pieces, a process which lasted for twelve years, and was finished in 280 B. C. The Colossus was over 100 feet high, and its thumb was so large that a man could not clasp it with his arms. It cost 300 talents, and sixty years after its erection it was thrown down by an earthquake. When, after lying on the ground for centuries, it was removed, the metal that composed it loaded 900 camels. The Colossus of Rhodes ranks as one of the Seven Wonders of the World.

Comets.—The word "comet" is derived from the Greek *kome*, a title which had its origin in the hairy appearance often exhibited by the haze or luminous vapor, the presence of which is at first sight the most striking characteristic of the celestial bodies called by this name. The general features of a comet are a definite point or nucleus, a nebulous light surrounding the nucleus, and a luminous train preceding or following the nucleus. Anciently, when the train preceded the nucleus—as is the case when a comet has passed its perihelion and recedes from the sun—it was called the "beard," being only termed the "tail" when seen following the nucleus as it approached the sun. This distinction has disappeared from all modern astronomical works, and the latter name is given to the appendage, whatever its apparent position. The nucleus, or body, is generally distinguished by its forming a bright point in the center of the head—conveying the idea of a solid, or at least a very dense, portion of matter. The envelope, or coma, is nebulous light around the nucleus, which frequently renders the edge of the nucleus so indistinct that it is extremely difficult to ascertain its diameter with any degree of precision. Now, neither the tail nor the nucleus is considered absolutely necessary to a comet, but all bodies are classed as comets which have the peculiar motions of comets and an extremely eccentric orbit. Planets move in the same direction from west to east, which is called "direct" motion; but the movements of comets are sometimes from east to west. The orbits of all the planets are limited to a comparatively narrow zone on either side of the ecliptic; but the paths of comets cut the ecliptic in nearly every direction, some being even perpendicular to it. Some comets seem to consist in part of vaporized carbon or hydrocarbon gases, although observations with the spectroscope have failed to give satisfactory evidence of their chemical constitution. They shine by the reflected light of the sun. The tail usually increases very much as it approaches the sun, and in receding from the sun it again contracts, and nearly or quite disappears before the body of the comet is quite out of sight. The tails of comets extend in a direct line from the sun, more or less curved like a long quill or feather, being convex on the side next to the direction in which they are moving.

Comets, Composition of.—According to Professor Newcomb, a theory relating to the physical constitution of comets, to be both complete and satisfactory, must be founded on the properties of matter as made known to us here at the earth's surface; that is, we must show what forms and what continuations of known substances would, if projected into celestial space, permit the appearance of a comet. This, it is held by the professor, has never yet been completely done. The simplest form of these bodies, Professor Newcomb says, is seen in the telescopic comets, which consist of minute particles of a cloudy or vaporous appearance. Now, we know that masses that present this appearance at the surface of the earth, where we can examine them, are composed of detached particles of solid or liquid matter. Clouds of vapor, for instance, are composed of minute drops of water and smoke of minute particles of carbon. Analogy would lead us to suppose that the telescopic comets are of the same constitution. The only alternative to this theory is that the comet is a mass of true gas, continuous throughout its entire length. This gaseous theory derives its main support from the spectroscope, which shows the spectrum of the telescopic comets to consist of bright bands, the mark of an incandescent gas.

Commune, Paris, was an organized band of Socialists who attempted to establish a revolutionary government in Paris in 1871. Before they were suppressed by the army of the republic they became absolute masters of Paris, and committed atrocious acts of cruelty and vandalism. They arrested the Bishop of Paris and other prominent citizens and imprisoned them. They set fire to the public buildings, and endeavored to destroy the ancient monuments and treasures of art. Among the buildings which were destroyed were the Tuileries, the Palais de Justice, the Palais Royal and the Hotel de Ville, and the Louvre Gallery was partly burned. The Column Vendome, erected in honor of Napoleon, was one of the first monuments to fall. Darboy, the Archbishop of Paris, Bonjean, President of the Court of Cassation, and others whom they held as hostages, were shot. In short they seemed to be possessed with a very frenzy of hatred against all government and all order, and wantonly destroyed property and human life. The revolution was finally suppressed on May 27th, and 25,000 of the Communists were taken prisoners, some of whom were put to death, while a large number were banished. In justice it must be said that the more intelligent and honest leaders of the Commune were discarded before the most atrocious acts were committed.

Communism and Socialism.—Communism is the doctrine that society should be reorganized on the basis of abolishing individual ownership of property and control of wages, and most of the now generally admitted rights of individuals in their private and domestic relations, and substituting therefor community ownership and control of every person and everything. Attempts to realize Communism have been made in both England and France, but in all cases resulted in disaster to the communities. The Communistic leader in England was Robert Owen, who made two attempts to carry out his views in that country. Fourier and St. Simon, French Communists, made similar efforts in France, but the results were not more fortunate. A community of St. Simonians established a college or corporation at Menilmontant, with a "supreme father" at their head. The leaders were brought to trial by Louis Philippe on a charge of undermining morality and religion. They were subjected to imprisonment, and not having public feeling with them, they were unable to bear up against contumely thus thrown on them. Socialism is a sort of limited Communism. It would not entirely abolish individual rights of property and personal self-control), but seeks to force a more equitable distribution of property and level the present extreme distinction between men of various classes. Historically considered, Socialism, like many of the significant phenomena of our age, is a product of the French Revolution. It is objected to Socialism, under its various forms, that it makes human happiness too dependent on material gratifications; that it robs man of that energy that springs from ambition; that it unphilosophically ignores an individualism and inequality to which Nature herself has given her inviolable sanction; and that by the abolition of social rewards and punishments it neither holds out any hope to the industrious nor excites any apprehension among the indolent. Yet, on the other hand, it must be admitted that the vigorous assertion of Socialistic principles has led men to a more liberal and generous view of humanity as a whole. Moreover, it has more forcibly called public attention to numerous evils that have sprung up along with the modern development of industry for which no remedy—not even a name—has been provided. Socialism has been fostered to a much greater extent in Germany than in any other country, although there are large numbers of Socialists in the United States.

Compass, The.—The directive power of the magnet seems to have been unknown in Europe until late in the twelfth century. It appears, however, on very good authority, that it was known in China and throughout the east generally at a very remote date. The Chinese annals assign its discovery to the year 2634 B. C., when, they say, an instrument for indicating the south was constructed by the Emperor Hon-ang-ti. At first, they would appear to have used it exclusively for guidance in traveling by land. The earliest date at which we hear of their using it at sea is somewhere about A. D. 300. According to one account, a knowledge of the compass was brought to Europe by Marco Polo on his return from Cathay. It was long contended that the compass as a nautical instrument was first invented by Flavio Gioja, a native of Amalfi, about the year 1362, and that part of the Kingdom of Naples where he was born has a compass for its arms. For this there is no authority whatever, as the compass was well known as a nautical instrument before his time. The phenomena of the magnetic needle which perplex scientists most are that in every place it is subject to variations. By observation at Paris it was found that in 1681 the needle varied 2 degrees 30 minutes to the west; in 1865, 18 degrees 44 minutes to the west. At London, between 1580 and 1692, the needle varied from 10 degrees 15 minutes east to 6 degrees west. In Dakota the average variation is 12 degrees 30 minutes east, in Minnesota 11 degrees east, while in Montana it is 20 degrees east. In a work on Government Surveys it is stated that "The needle does not point due north except in a few localities, and at no place does it continue to point with a given angular distance from the north for any stated length of time. It changes secularly, annually, diurnally and hourly, and is, further, subject to fluctuations reducible to no method of tabulation." In the vicinity of iron in any shape, or magnetic sands, the needle is deflected toward the material attracting it.

Compressed-Air Engines.—The arrangements of atmospheric engines is largely identical with that of non-condensing steam-engines, and they are used very generally both in the United States and Europe in the construction of tunnels, their great advantage being that in place of escaping heat and steam, which would seriously vitiate the close air in the shaft, the working of the engine gives out pure cold air, serving also the purpose of ventilation. An engine worked by compressed air, however, can never be a prime motor in itself, since the air which propels it must be compressed by another power—either steam, electricity, falling water or animal force. There are several ways of applying this compressed air. One is to fill with it a large, strong cylinder or reservoir, and use it to work a piston in the same way that steam is used. Another is to conduct the air from the prime motor in tubes to several smaller engines. In the construction of the Mont Cenis Tunnel the hydraulic power of a cataract near the entrance of the tunnel was used as a prime motor to compress air in reservoirs, whence it was conducted by flexible tubes to work the rock-boring machines. When this boring is done by percussion of steel drills, the atmospheric pressure moves a piston connected with them. When the boring is performed by rotation, as is the case with the diamond drill, the atmospheric engine is either a rotary or reciprocating one. Compressed air is also used with steam as a motor. Air when compressed greatly becomes very hot, and if it is then forced through hot water it becomes saturated with steam, and this steam and air are found to have enormous expansive power. This motive-power has been very successfully applied to the propulsion of street cars. In the working of electric-light machinery compressed air is used to a considerable extent.

Concordat, French.—The first French Concordat—the latter word being one used to signify an agreement between the Pope and some government or sovereign for the settling of ecclesiastical relations—was concluded between Francis I and Pope Leo X in 1516, which continued in force until the French Revolution. From that time until 1801 religious and civil interests were wholly separated, and in 1795 the French Government, by proclamation, refused to recognize any form of religion. But in 1801 the connection between religion and state was renewed, and a new Concordat was concluded between Napoleon Bonaparte as First Consul and Pius VII which gave more power to the state than the previous one. A still more liberal Concordat was obtained, however, in 1813, when Napoleon imprisoned the Pope at Fontainebleau until his signature to it was secured. Under this Concordat the state holds a very important degree of control of Church affairs. Germany, many of the German States individually, several of the Italian States, and Portugal and Spain, have similar compacts with the Pope.

Confederate Treasure.—Upon the evacuation of Richmond, April 2, 1865, President Davis and his Cabinet had in their possession a sum in gold coin belonging partly to the Richmond banks and partly to the Louisiana banks, the latter having previously sent their money to Richmond for safe keeping. It was the purpose of Mr. Davis to distribute this money among the soldiers who formed his escort during his flight. The particulars of the final disposition of the money is given by Lieutenant C. E. L. Stewart, of Davis' staff, in his book, "History of the Last Days and Final Fall of the Rebellion." He says: "At Washington [Ga.] there was a scramble for the specie. It was determined to give the cavalry a few dollars each. They were impatient, and helped themselves as soon as they discovered where to get it. The result was a great irregularity of distribution. Many got too much, many nothing, and 'dust-hunters' picked up a good deal the following day—a good deal that was trampled under foot in the contemptible scramble."

Confucianism is termed a religion, but it ought rather to be regarded as a system of social and political life built upon a slight foundation of philosophy. It contains no trace of a personal God. There are, indeed, a number of allusions to a certain heavenly agency or power—Shang-te—whose outward emblem is Tien, or the visible firmament; but this Shang-te, in the opinion of the most enlightened Chinese scholars, is nothing more than a verbal personification of "the ever-present Law and Order and Intelligence which seem to breathe amid the wonderful activities of physical creation, in the measured circuit of the seasons, in the alternation of light and darkness, in the ebb and flow of tides, and in the harmonious and majestic revolutions of the heavenly bodies." Confucius lived about 550 B. C. He strove to direct the attention of men to the duties of social and political life, and Confucianism is epitomized in the following words of the great teacher: "I teach you nothing but what you might learn yourselves, viz., the observance of the three fundamental laws of relation between sovereign and subject, father and child, husband and wife, and the five capital virtues—universal charity, impartial justice, conformity to ceremonies and established usages, rectitude of heart and mind, and pure sincerity." Confucianism appeals to "practical" men. It lauds the present world; rather doubts, than otherwise, the existence of a future one; and calls upon all to cultivate such virtues as are seemly in citizens—industry, modesty, sobriety, gravity, decorum and thoughtfulness.

Congress.—In order to find the number of a Congress sitting in any given year, subtract 1789, the year in which the first Congress was held, from the year. Should the result be an even number, half that number will give the Congress of which the year in question will be the closing year. If the result is an odd number, add one to it, and half the result will give the Congress of which the year in question will be the first year.

Constitutional Amendments, Dates of.—The first ten amendments to the Constitution of the United States were added before the adoption of the Constitution, in 1791; the eleventh in 1798, the twelfth in 1804, the thirteenth in 1865, the fourteenth in 1868, and the fifteenth in 1870.

Constitution, Ratification of the.—The Constitution of the United States was framed in 1787, and all the States were represented by delegates with the exception of North Carolina and Rhode Island. At the first session of Congress, in order to relieve the hapless condition of these States outside of the Union, their vessels were relieved for a limited time from the burden of a foreign tonnage-duty; and this forbearance, with the persuasion of her neighbors, secured North Carolina. Rhode Island, however, still remained stubborn, owing to the fact that her Assembly was mainly composed of men of limited education, wholly intent upon wiping out private and public debts by the agency of paper money. This condition of affairs continued until 1790, when the United States Senate passed a bill prohibiting all commercial intercourse with the State, and requiring her to pay her quota of the Continental debt. Threatened with Federal coercion on one hand and the open secession of Providence and Newport, who were in favor of the ratification, on the other, the anti-Federalists were forced to succumb, and the Constitution was ratified at Newport, May 24th, 1790, by a majority of two.

Consuls-General, Salaries of.—The salaries of the Consuls-General of the United States are as follows: Berlin, $4,000 per annum; Calcutta, $5,000; Cairo, $5,000; Constantinople, $3,000; Frankfort, $3,000; Halifax, $3,000; Havana, $6,000; Honolulu, $4,000; Kanagawa, $4,000; London, $6,000; Matamoras, $2,000; Melbourne, $4,500; Mexico City, $2,500; Montreal, $4,000; Panama, $4,000; Paris, $6,000; Quito, $3,000; Rio de Janeiro, $6,000; Rome, $3,000; St. Petersburg, $3,000; Vienna, $3,000.

Consuls, Salaries of.—The salaries of the United States Consuls at the principal foreign cities are as follows: Amsterdam, $1,500 per annum; Antwerp, $3,000; Birmingham, $2,500; Bordeaux, $2,500; Bremen, $2,500; Brussels, $2,500; Canton, $3,500; Cork, $2,000; Dublin, $2,000; Florence, $1,500; Glasgow, $3,000; Hamburg, $2,000; Havre, $3,000; Hong-Kong, $5,000; Liverpool, $6,000; Lyons, $2,500; Manchester, $3,000; Marseilles, $2,500; Montevideo, $2,000; Munich, $1,500; Naples, $1,500; Nice, $1,500; Prague, $3,000; Quebec, $1,500; Rotterdam, $2,000; Southampton, $1,500; St. John's, N. B., $2,000; Stockholm, fees; Toronto, $2,000; Trieste, $2,000; Valparaiso, $3,000; Vera Cruz, $3,000.

Continental Currency.—The bill authorizing the issue of Continental currency passed the Continental Congress June 22, 1775, the day on which Congress received the news of the battle of Bunker Hill. The amount to be issued was not to exceed

$2,000,000, for whose redemption the twelve Confederate colonies —Georgia not being then represented—were pledged. The plates of the bills were engraved by Paul Revere, of Boston. The size of the bills averaged 3 1-2 by 2 3-4 inches, and they were printed on thick paper. New issues of this currency were made from time to time until the close of 1779, when the aggregate amount was $242,000,000, and the bills had so much depreciated in value that $100 in specie would purchase $2,600 in paper money. In 1781 the same amount in specie would buy $7,500 in paper. Strenuous efforts were made by Congress to keep up the credit of this currency, but as a pledge from the States to redeem it in specie could not be obtained, and as that was the one essential to save it, the money was bound to go down. Early in 1777 a convention of representatives of the New England States agreed upon a scale of prices for all goods. This was strongly opposed by merchants, but the new States soon after enacted it into a law, and a similar law was adopted soon after by the Middle States, including Maryland and Virginia. This scheme was approved of by Congress, who passed a resolution declaring that the bills of credit ought to pass current in all payments, trade and dealings, and be deemed equal in value to the same nominal sum in Spanish dollars; and it further resolved, that all persons refusing to take them "should be considered enemies of the United States," on whom "forfeitures and other penalties" ought to be inflicted by the local authorities. The depreciation of the money, however, was not checked, but as it was gradual, it operated as a tax, and undue suffering was thus prevented.

Copperhead.—The term "copperhead," as applied to a person, originated during the civil war, and was used to denote one who, while belonging or residing in the Northern States, was yet an open sympathizer with the cause of the rebels. .

Corday, Charlotte, the assassin of Marat, the French revolutionist, was born at St. Saturnin, in Normandy, in 1768, and was of noble parentage. In 1793, when the Girondists were driven from Paris, many of them fled to Caen, in Normandy, where Charlotte at that time lived. She was greatly interested in current events; had studied affairs through the medium of the papers issued by the Girondists; attended their meetings; and was confirmed in the belief that Marat was the chief agent of their overthrow, and conceived the idea of going to Paris and assassinating him. On July 15th, while Marat was bathing, she obtained admission to his room and assassinated him with a dinner-knife. She was tried on the morning of July 17th, and sentenced and guillotined the evening of the same day.

Corner-Stones.—The custom of laying the corner-stone of a public building with ceremonies was practiced by the ancients. We are told that at the laying of the corner-stone when the capitol of Rome was rebuilt a procession of vestal virgins, robed in white, surrounded the stone and consecrated it with libations of living water. A prayer to the gods followed, and then the magistrates, priests, senators and knights laid hold of the ropes and moved the mighty stone to its proper position. In a hollow cut in the stone were placed ingots of gold, silver and other metals which had not been melted in any furnace. With the Jews the corner-stone was considered an emblem of power, and they also performed ceremonies at its laying. In mediæval times the rite was taken up by the Order of Free Masons, and has by them been brought down to modern days. The Masonic ceremony of laying a corner-stone is symbolical. The form of the stone, a square on the surface and a perfect cube; its place, at the northeast corner of the structure; the testing it with a square, level and plumb, and the pouring of libations of corn, wine and oil over it—all have their hidden meaning. The custom of laying the corner-stone with ceremonies is usually observed at the commencement of any public building, when coins of the current year, newspapers and important documents are placed within the stone to serve as valuable historical relics when the building shall be destroyed.

Coronation-Stone.—The Scottish Coronation-Stone—the *Lia Fail*, or Stone of Destiny—which now forms a part of the Coronation-Chair of England, was said by tradition to have been the stone which Jacob used for a pillow, and to have been brought to Ireland, and from Tara to Scotland, where it found a resting-place at Scone. From there it was taken to Westminster by Edward I.

Corsets.—An article of dress somewhat resembling the corsets now worn by women was used in Germany and France as early as the thirteenth century, and it found its way into England in the latter half of the fourteenth century. It contained rods and plates of whalebone and steel, and was designed, we are told, to conceal the defects and exaggerate the beauties of the figure. This stiff arrangement was discarded at the time of the French Revolution owing to the Greek costume having been brought into vogue, and its place was taken by a smoothly-fitting under-waist.

Coulees.—This name should properly be restricted to a small ravine at the bottom of which is the bed of a dry creek, but has come to be applied in certain sections of the Western States, by settlers, to all low places. The word is evidently taken from the geological term coules, from the French verb couler, to flow, and pronounced as though written koo-lay—which means a stream of lava either flowing or consolidated.

Council of Ten was established about the middle of the fourteenth century, at a time when Venice was greatly disturbed. Their rigid despotism, says one writer, had the effect of giving a stern unity of purpose to the proceedings of government, and doubtless contributed in some degree to consolidate the various accessions of territory, which had been made, into one whole. The council is said to have been, at first, at least, more terrible to the nobility than to the commoners, doubtless from the fact that the conspiracies which were then frequent were creations of that class, and the best authorities generally hold the opinion that the Ten preserved the external dignity and independence of the republic better than their predecessors. Eventually there were selected from the ten three inquisitors, in whom all the powers of the state were vested, and who formed a court whose proceedings have so often been called in question by historians. A notable fact is that the height of the prosperity of Venice was reached when the council were in power; and when their despotism passed away, with it departed the greatness of the city.

Councils of Nice.—The first Council of Nice was held in the Emperor Constantine's palace, June 19, A. D. 325, and was attended by 318 bishops of the Catholic Church, and resulted in the adoption of the Nicene Creed, expounding the faith of the Church. August 17, A. D 786 the second Council of Nice was convened by order of the Empress Irene and her son Constantine, at which there were 376 bishops present. This Council was held for the purpose of establishing the use of images in the churches, which had been interdicted by the Emperor Leo and his son Constantine, but was dissolved owing to the tumults raised by the party in opposition. It was reconvened September 24, A. D. 787, when the use of images was restored.

Coventry, Sent to.—The expression "Sent to Coventry," meaning to ignore a person's existence totally, originated as follows: The citizens of Coventry, England, had at one time so great a dislike to soldiers that a woman seen speaking to one was regarded as outside the pale of respectable society ever after. No intercourse was ever allowed between the garrison and the town; hence when a man was sent to Coventry he was cut off from all social enjoyments.

Cow-Tree is found in the mountains of South and Central America, and is an evergreen. Its sap almost exactly resembles milk, and flows copiously from wounds made in the bark. It was first brought to the notice of Europeans by Alexander von Humboldt. The natives of the country where the tree is found are in the habit of drinking freely of the milk, and find it both palatable and nourishing.

Creasote, or, as it is also called, kreasote, is an artificial organic substance generally obtained as a product in the destructive distillation of wood. It is used to a considerable extent for the preservation of vegetable and animal matter. Thus, ordinary meat treated with only one-hundredth of its weight of creasote, and exposed to the air, does not putrefy, but becomes hard and dry, and assumes the taste and odor of smoked meat; and timber treated with creasote does not suffer from dry-rot or other disease. It has a great power of coagulating albumen, and hence is used with advantage in toothache. It is very poisonous to plants and animals. The principal supplies are obtained from Stockholm, Archangel, and the United States.

Credit Mobilier.—The Credit Mobilier of America was a joint stock company organized in 1863 for the purpose of facilitating the construction of public works. In 1867 another company, which had undertaken to build the Union Pacific Railroad, purchased the charter of the Credit Mobilier, and the capital was increased to $3,750,000. In 1872 a lawsuit in Pennsylvania developed the startling fact that much of the Credit Mobilier was owned by members of Congress. A suspicion that those members had voted corruptly in the legislation affecting the Pacific Railway at once seized the public mind, and led to a Congressional investigation, in the course of which many scandalous transactions were brought to light, and the reputation of many public servants suffered greatly. The investigation showed that some of the members of Congress who had this stock in their possession had never paid for it; in other words, that their votes had probably been obtained by giving them stock. In other cases it was shown that persons whose integrity could not be questioned had been reported as stockholders, for the purpose of influencing others to subscribe or to regard the project favorably. The report of the committee exonerated many whose names had been used without authority in connection with the scheme. Owing to the profitableness of the work in which the company was engaged, the stock rose rapidly in value previous to the investigation, and enormous dividends were paid to the shareholders

Cremation.—The reduction of the human body to ashes by fire was a very early and widespread usage of antiquity. The early Aryans, as opposed to the non-Aryan aborigines of India, Greeks, Romans, Sclavs, Celts and Germans, burned their dead; therefore cremation may be regarded as the universal custom of the Indo-European races. The graves of North Europe throughout the "bronze age" contain only jars of ashes. The advocates of disposing of the dead by cremation are at the present time numerous, their principal arguments in favor of it being of a sanitary nature. According to the method which is most favored by modern cremationists, the body is placed in an oblong brick or iron-cased chamber, underneath which is a furnace. The air of the chamber is raised to a very high temperature before the body is put in, and a stream of heated hydro-carbon from a gasometer is then admitted, which on contact with intensely-heated air within immediately bursts into flame. The chamber is, of course, so constructed as neither to admit draughts of air from without nor to permit the escape of gas from within. The noxious gases which are evolved in the beginning of the combustion-process are passed through a flue into a second furnace, where they are entirely consumed. By this process a body weighing 144 pounds can be reduced in about fifty minutes to not more than four pounds of lime-dust. In the cremation of each body about 200 pounds of fuel is used.

Crescent, The, was originally used by the early Christians of Constantinople and the eastern provinces of the Roman Empire as a symbol of the growing influence of Christianity and the extension of imperial sway. In the fourteenth and fifteenth centuries, when the Turks overran Asia Minor and southeastern Europe, and especially after they had captured Constantinople in 1453, partly in derision, and partly as an omen of future victories and the extension of the Mohammedan faith, they adopted the crescent as a national emblem, notwithstanding the fact that the use of images, symbols, religious, martial or civic decorations were prohibited by the Koran.

Crockery.—The materials used in the manufacture of crockery are kaolin, pipe-clay, quartz or flint, and feldspar—the kaolin and quartz to give hardness, and the pipe-clay and feldspar to yield a flux sufficient to bind the masses firmly together. The materials are ground into a fine powder and then mixed with water in a machine called a "blunger," which is a box containing paddles worked very rapidly. When the matter has been thoroughly mixed it is drawn off and forced by a hydraulic pump through a series of sieves and then worked up in what is called a pug-mill, after which it is cut by a fine wire into rectangular blocks. These blocks are then molded into the shape of the article desired, some by the use of a lathe, and some by simply shaping them with the hands. The pieces are thus partially dried, turned on a lathe with a sharp tool to give them a uniform surface, dried slowly in a drying-room, then baked in an oven. In baking, the ware is kept at a white heat for thirty-six hours. The pieces are then glazed by being dipped in a mixture of ground feldspar, ground flint, sal soda, plastic clay and boracic acid, the whole pulverized and mixed with a small proportion of white lead and a little cobalt blue. This glaze is mixed with water, the articles are dipped in it one by one, receiving a deposit like a thin paste on the surface, which, when placed in the oven again, fuses and flows over it, making a coating of glassy smoothness. Fine white china or porcelain is of course made of finer material than crockery, but the process of manufacture is similar.

Cryolite is a snow-white mineral, partially transparent, of a vitreous luster and of brittle texture. It is so named from its fusibility in the flame of a candle. It is a compound of sodium, fluorine and aluminum, and is used for the preparation of the metal aluminum. It occurs in veins in gneiss with pyrites and galena, and has been found in western Greenland and at Miyask in the Ural Mountains. It is extensively employed in the United States in the manufacture of white porcelain glass, and also in the preparation of caustic soda.

Crystal Palace.—The present Crystal Palace is situated at Sydenham, seven and a half miles from London Bridge. The building was erected in 1854, chiefly from the materials of the building of the same name wherein was held the first great World's Fair in 1851—[see *World's Fairs*]—and is 1,600 feet long, 380 feet wide, and at the center transept 200 feet high. It is surrounded by beautiful and extensive parks and grounds, and has two towers, from the top of which 10,000 square miles of England may be seen. There are also an opera-house and theatre, art galleries, two great concert-rooms, within the larger of which performances have taken place at which there were 5,000 vocalists and instrumentalists, a zoological collection, an exhibition department, and a large number of other attractions. The parks and gardens occupy nearly 200 acres; and are adorned with sculptures, stone balustrades, etc., and fountains which are perhaps the finest in the world. The Palace cost about $7,250,000.

Curacoa is a *liqueur* made either from the small Curacoa oranges and limes, or from their peel, by digesting in sweetened spirits, along with a little cinnamon, and often a little mace and cloves. The spirits used are generally reduced to about 56 under proof, and contain about 3 1-2 pounds of sugar per gallon. Curacoa is often colored by digesting in it for a week or ten days a little powdered Brazil-wood, and mellowing the color by means of burned sugar.

Curfew Bell.—The ringing of the curfew bell is commonly believed to have been introduced in England by William the Conqueror, who ordained, under severe penalties, that when the bell rang all lights and fires should be extinguished. In those days it was the custom to place the fire in a hole in the middle of the floor, and when the family retired for the night the fire was extinguished by covering it up; hence the term couvrefeu, or curfew. At first the common hour was seven o'clock; then it was advanced to eight o'clock, and in some places to nine o'clock; while in Scotland ten o'clock was not an unusual hour. This law was abolished by Henry I in 1100; but the practice of tolling a bell at a certain hour in the evening was continued, and in fact is still extant in some places.

Cyclones, Cause of.—The theories regarding the cause of cyclones greatly conflict. Professor Tice of St. Louis, Mo., in describing the tornado which proved so destructive at Mansfield, Mo., a few years ago, stated that he considered it an electrical, and not, as commonly considered, a wind-storm. Among the evidence of the electrical nature of that storm he noted the fact that it destroyed every building which had a tin roof, or which had metal of any kind in its roof, and passed directly over several buildings with shingle roofs which were equally exposed. A mill, situated over a quarter of a mile away from the center of the cyclone had its iron chimney torn out and carried a long distance, while the mill itself suffered very little damage. The cupola of a school-building which had a tin roof was wrecked, but the building, which was roofed with shingles, was not injured. Even more remarkable, he considered, were the phenomena manifested in connection with trees and bushes. The bark was stripped from them on all sides, and the ends were not only denuded of their branches and leaves, but were rifted into fine fibers, so that they presented the appearance of little brooms. The active agency in such cases, he insisted, was not wind, but electricity. General evidence of the electrical character of all tornadoes is found by Professor Tice in the fact that, as a rule, they follow railroads and water-courses, and either begin or expend their greatest energy upon them.

Cyclopean Architecture, the name which has come to be generally used for massive walls of large, irregular stones, unhewn and uncemented. The term originated in Greece, where structures of this kind were found, and were fabled to have been the work of the Cyclopes, or one-eyed giants.

Damascus Steel.—The skill of the Damascenes in the manufacture of steel became famous in Europe at the time of the crusades, but the secrets of their process have never been revealed. A Russian mining engineer, General Anosoff, by analysis and examination, however, succeeded in making steel that could scarcely be distinguished from it in appearance. The essential point of his process was melting the iron in crucibles with graphite and a small quantity of dolomite; but the details of working these materials with success were of course known only by himself, and the quality of the steel produced by the works since his death has very much deteriorated. An imitation of Damascus steel is also made in America and is often known by that name, though its proper appellation is damask steel, so called from the peculiar damask figures on its surface.

Danegelt, or Danegold, a tax which was originally levied upon the Saxons in England for purchasing peace from the Danes in the year 991; but it soon became a permanent tax upon landed property, and remained in force until 1173, when the last instance of its payment is recorded.

Dardanelles, The, are four castles or forts situated on opposite shores of the passage which joins the Sea of Marmora with the waters of the Ægean Sea, but the name, by association, is also given to the channel of water between them. For many years the Turkish Government maintained that no foreign vessel of war should at any time be allowed to pass the Dardanelles forts. This restriction was recognized by Great Britain and France in 1809, and in consequence of which, in 1832–'33 the British and French fleets were not permitted to enter the straits, though a Russian fleet from the Black Sea was anchored in the Bosphorus. This claim on the part of Turkey was fully recognized by all the great powers of Europe in 1841, and was reaffirmed in the Treaty of Paris in 1856. Two years later, however—November, 1858—the United States frigate Wabash passed the Dardanelles and anchored at Constantinople, the commanding officer claiming that the United States, not being a party to the Treaty of Paris, were not bound by its stipulations. Although no positive acknowledgment was made as to the correctness of this position, the vessel was received in a friendly manner by the Turkish Government. This clause of the Treaty of Paris was abrogated in 1876, and in times of peace there is now no restriction on the navigation of this strait. The two castles at the entrance of the strait from the side of the Ægean Archipelago were built by Mohammed IV in 1659, and are still in excellent repair; but the other two castles are of much older construction, and though once very solidly built, now show signs of decay.

"**Dark as Egypt's Night.**"—The origin of this phrase is found in the tenth chapter of Exodus, the 21st, 22d and 23d verses: "And the Lord said unto Moses, stretch out thine hand toward heaven, that there may be darkness over the land of Egypt, even darkness that may be felt. And Moses stretched forth his hand toward heaven; and there was a thick darkness in all the land of Egypt for three days. They saw not one another, neither rose any from his place for three days; but all the children of Israel had light in their dwellings."

Dark Day, The.—So called on account of a remarkable darkness on that day, May 19, 1780, extending all over New England. In some places persons could not see to read common print in the open air for several hours together. Birds sang their evening song, disappeared and became silent; fowls went to roost; cattle sought the barn-yard, and candles were lighted in the houses. The obscuration began about ten o'clock in the morning and continued through the entire day, and was followed by an unusually intense degree of blackness during the ensuing night. The most intense and prolonged darkness, however, was confined to Massachusetts, especially to the eastern half of the State, when the people, believing that the end of all things had come, betook themselves to religious devotions. As to the explanation of this phenomenon, scientists have been much puzzled. It was plain from the falling of the barometer that the air was surcharged with heavy vapor. The darkness, then, it might be said, was only the result of a dense fog; but the question of the cause of so remarkable a fog was still unanswered. Large fires may have prevailed that spring in the forests of western New York and Pennsylvania —a region then an absolute wilderness—the smoke of which was borne through the upper regions of the atmosphere, to fall, when it came to a locality of less buoyant air, down to the lower strata. We say these fires may have recently preceded this day, and served as its sufficient cause, but we have only presumptive evidence that they did occur.

Dark Horse, The.—The custom of referring to the unexpected winner of a coveted honor as a "dark horse" probably originated from the practice of certain horse-jockeys who not infrequently, by coloring or painting some celebrated horse, were enabled to bring him into a race under another name, bet large sums of money upon him, and win the race. They were generally dark, and thus the term probably originated. The "dark horse" in politics is applied to the successful nominee of a party who is little known or thought of as a nominee. President Hayes was a "dark horse."

Dauphin, at one time the title of the eldest son of the King of France. It was originally the title of the sovereign lords of the Province of Dauphiny. Humbert II, the last of these, dying childless, bequeathed his possessions to Charles of Valois, grandson of Philip VI, of France, on condition that the heir-apparent to the throne of France should bear the title of Dauphin of Vienne, and govern the province. Almost sovereign rights were conferred on the Dauphin by Louis IX, but these were gradually abridged by later kings, until Dauphiny was placed under the same laws as the rest of the kingdom, and the title became merely honorary. It was abolished altogether after the Revolution of 1830, Louis, son of Charles X, being the last who ever held the title.

Dead Sea, The, is situated in the southeast of Palestine, and is called by the Arabs Bahr Loot, or *Sea of Lot.* It is about 40 miles long, with an average breadth of 9 miles. Its depth varies considerably. It is fed by the Jordan from the north, and by many other streams, but has no apparent outlet, its superfluous water being supposed to be entirely carried off by evaporation. The north shores of the sea are marked by the blackened trunks and branches of trees which are encrusted with salt, as is everything that is exposed to the spray of this sea. On the southern shore is the remarkable mass of rock called Udsum (Sodom). It is a narrow, rugged ridge of hill extending five miles northwest, and consisting of rock-salt. To the north of Udsum, and at no great distance, is the supposed site of the ancient Sodom. On the borders of the Dead Sea a curious plant grows which yields fruit called the "Apple of Sodom," beautiful on the outside but bitter to the taste, and, when mature, filled with fiber and dust.

Deaf Mutes, Instruction of.—It is recorded in history that a deaf mute was taught to pronounce words and sentences by an English bishop in the year 685, and from that time isolated cases of the same kind are mentioned till the latter part of the eighteenth century, when a school for the teaching of articulate speech to mutes was started in Germany. The method used is exceedingly simple, and consists merely in training the pupil, by imitating the position and action of the vocal organs of the teacher, to utter articulate sounds. Of late years another system has been introduced into English and American schools which has been found more generally successful than the lip-teaching of Germany. It is called visible speech, and was invented by A. Melville Bell, a professor of vocal physiology in England, about 1848. Mr. Bell's method consists of a species of phonetic writings, based not upon sound, but upon the action of the vocal organs in producing them. The characters of this alphabet reveal to the eye the position of these organs in the formation of any sound which can be produced by the human mouth. This alphabet was first applied in England to the instruction of deaf mutes in 1869, and it was introduced in America in 1872 by Professor Abraham Bell, a son of the inventor, and was at once put into practical and successful use in the Clark Institution at Northampton, Mass.

Debatable Land.—A tract of land situated on the western border of England and Scotland, and for many years the residence of thieves and banditti. It was at one time claimed by both kingdoms. It was divided by royal commissioners appointed by the two crowns in 1542, but its unsavory reputation clung to it for a long time afterward. It is frequently referred to in the works of Sir Walter Scott.

Debt, Imprisonment for.—During late years the laws of most countries bearing upon imprisonment for debt have been greatly modified. In England the old harsh laws concerning debtors, which made the issuance of 101,000 writs for debt in one year, 1825, possible, were abolished in 1838; and in 1869, by the passage of the "Debtor's Act," still more lenient regulations were adopted. Imprisonment is still possible there, in certain cases, as when it is believed a debtor intends leaving the country, or when a debtor refuses, when he is able, to settle a claim decided against him by the courts, or when there is palpable evidence of premeditated fraud. The imprisonment cannot continue, however, longer than a specified time—usually one year. Imprisonment for debt was abolished in France by a decree of March 9, 1793, was re-enacted several years later, was again abolished in 1848, and was again re-established the same year. Since that time, however, the law has been greatly modified, and now imprisonment is permitted for a limited period only, and certain classes are exempted from the law; as, for instance, those under twenty years or over seventy years of age, ecclesiastics, and women not engaged in commerce. In France, as in most all continental countries, the entire cession of the property of the debtor to his creditors will procure immunity from personal process, even though it may not cover the amount owed. New York was the first State in the United States to abolish imprisonment for debt. This was done in 1831, and the example was shortly followed by the other States; and though there is great difference in the insolvent laws of the several States, they all permit debtors their freedom except in cases wherein dishonesty or peculation render the debtor also amenable to the Penal Code. Both in Greece and in Rome, in ancient times, the creditor had a claim to the person of the debtor. In Rome, thirty days after judgment was pronounced against the debtor he was given into the hands of his creditor, who kept him sixty days in chains, exposing him on three market-days, and proclaiming his debt. If no one stepped in to release him, the debtor, at the end of that time, might be sold for a slave or put to death. If there were several creditors, the letter of the law permitted them to cut their debtor in pieces, sharing him in proportion to their claims. The common practice, however, was to treat him as a slave and make him work out the debt. The children in his power, in accordance with the constitution of society at Rome, followed his condition.

December.—In the old Roman calendar, before the time of Julius Cæsar, the year began with March, and that which is now twelfth was then the tenth month; hence the name *decem*, ten. It was called midwinter month and yule-month by the Anglo-Saxons.

Decemviri.—The most famous body known under this title were the ten patricians who were appointed as a sort of legislative committee to draw up a code of laws at Rome, and who were intrusted with the whole government of the State during the year for which they were to hold office. The experiment proved eminently successful, the work of legislation was carried on with zeal and success, and the State was governed with prudence and moderation. At the expiration of the year, their labors not being quite finished, a new body of Decemviri was appointed—only *one*, the notorious Appius Claudius, belonging to the previous commission. The new Decemviri acted in a most tyrannical manner. Every species of outrage was committed on the persons and families of the plebeians, and when their term of office expired they not only refused to retire, but to allow successors to be appointed. They were finally driven from office, and the tribunes and other ordinary magistrates of the republic were reappointed. One of the last outrages, which aroused the indignant populace to overthrow them, was the tragic fate of Virginia, related by Macauley in his "Lays of Ancient Rome."

Decisive Battles of the World.—The most decisive battles that have been fought from the fifth century B. C. to the beginning of the nineteenth century are, according to Prof. Creasy, the battle of Marathon, B. C. 490; the defeat of the Athenians at Syracuse, B. C. 413; the battle of Arbela, in which the Greeks under Alexander the Great defeated the Persians, B. C. 331; the battle of the Metaurus, in which the Romans overthrew the Carthaginians, B. C. 207; victory of the German tribes under Arminius over the Roman legions under Varus, A. D. 9; battle of Chalons, when the Romans under Ætius repulsed Attila, the King of the Huns, A. D. 451; battle of Tours, in which the Franks under Charles Martel overthrew the Saracen Turks, who had invaded western Europe, A. D. 732; battle of Hastings, by which William the Conqueror became ruler of England, October 14, 1066; victory of the French under Joan of Arc over the English at Orleans, April 29, 1429; defeat of the Spanish Armada by the English naval force, July 29 and 30, 1588; battle of Blenheim, in which the allied armies of Great Britain and Holland defeated the French and Bavarians, August 2, 1704; battle of Pultowa, in which the Russians under Peter the Great defeated the Swedes under Charles XII, July 8, 1709; battle of Saratoga, in which the American army under General Gates defeated the British under General Burgoyne, October 17, 1777; battle of Valmy, when the armies of Prussia and Austria were defeated by the French, September 20, 1792; battle of Waterloo, when the allied forces of the British and Prussians defeated the French under Napoleon, June 18, 1815. From the battle of Waterloo to the present date only four important battles have been fought—that of Gettysburg, Pa., by which the invasion of the North by the Confederate army was checked, July 1, 2 and 3, 1863; battle at Chattanooga, in which the Confederates in the Southwest were defeated by the Northern troops, November 23 and 25, 1863; battle of Sedan, in the Franco-Prussian war, September 1, 1870, and the battle of Plevna, in the Russo-Turkish war, when Osman Pasha surrendered, December 10, 1877.

Della Cruscan School.—The Della Cruscan school of so-called poetry came into existence at Florence about the year 1785. At that time a number of English people resident at Florence published, under the title of "The Florence Miscellany," a collection of verses written by themselves. These productions were insipid, affectatious and silly in the extreme; yet they found a crowd of admirers and imitators. The Della Cruscans (so-called from an academy at Florence) printed their effusions in England in two daily newspapers, called *The World* and *The Oracle*, and one of the brotherhood—a Mr Robert Merry—came over from Florence and "immediately announced himself by a sonnet to Love." According to Gifford, "the fever now turned to a frenzy; Laura, Maria, Carlos, Orlando, Adelaide and a thousand other nameless names caught the infection, and from one end of the kingdom all was nonsense and Della Crusca." Gifford produced in 1794 his "Baviad," and in 1796 his "Mæviad;" and those poems, by their keen satire, completely killed the Della Cruscan school.

Delphi, Temple at.—The edifice known to have existed at Delphi, Greece, at the beginning of the historic period, is said to have been the work of two architects named Trophonius and Agamedes. In 548 B. C., this temple having been destroyed, the Amphictyons undertook to build another for the sum of 300 talents, of which the Delphians were to pay one fourth, and the remainder was to be contributed by other cities of Greece. The temple is said to have been of the Doric order without, and the Ionic within. The front was built of Parian marble, and the sculptured decorations were rich and beautiful. The arches above the entrances were adorned with representations of legends of mythology, and similar adornments were carved on the panels of the walls. Images and statues in brass and marble enriched the interior, and the golden shields taken at Marathon, and also in battles with the Gauls, adorned the architraves. The attempts of the Persians in 480 B. C., and of the Gauls in 279 B. C., to rob the temple, were both, it was said, prevented by the miraculous interference of Apollo, and the sacred character of the place long protected it from other would-be plunderers. It was, however, eventually plundered by Sulla, and again by Nero, who silenced the oracle. It was restored by Hadrian, and then despoiled of many of its most beautiful works of art by Constantine the Great, and finally destroyed in the latter part of the fourth century.

Department of Justice, Salaries in.—The salaries of the officials of the Department of Justice of the United States are as follows: Attorney-General, $8,000 per annum; Solicitor-General, $7,000; three Assistant Attorney-Generals, $5,000 each, and one at $4,000; Chief Clerk, $2,450; Solicitor of the Treasury, $4,500; Solicitor of Internal Revenue, $4,500.

Dervishes are members of religious orders in Mohammedan countries, somewhat resembling the Christian monks. They are divided into many different brotherhoods and orders, and it is difficult to say when they originated. Tradition refers the origin of these orders to the earliest times of Islam, making the califs Abubekr and Ali founders of such brotherhoods; but it is more probable that they arose later. The dervishes live mostly in well-endowed convents, called Tekkije or Changah, and are under a chief with the title of Sheik, i. e., "elder." Some of the monks are married and allowed to live out of the monastery, but must sleep there some nights weekly. Their devotional services consist in meeting for worship, prayers, religious dances, and "mortifications of the flesh." As the convent does not provide them with clothing, they are obliged to work more or less. Many Mohammedan princes and Turkish sultans have held dervishes in high respect and bestowed rich endowments on their establishments, and they are still held in high veneration by the people. The orders are generally named after their founders. The Kadris, founded in 1165, are commonly known as "the howling dervishes," from the excited chant of their religious services; and the Mevelevis, founded in 1273, are called the "dancing dervishes."

Deus ex Machina.—The tragic poets of Greece, in conformity with the popular mythological beliefs of their age, instead of bringing about the denouement of their plots by natural means, had often recourse to a more expeditious mode, viz.: the intervention of a god, who descended upon the stage by a mechanical contrivance and abruptly solved whatever difficulty barred the proper termination of a piece. Hence, whenever a person or incident is introduced arbitrarily in modern tragedy or comedy merely to remedy some inartistic negligence in its construction, such a contrivance is metaphorically called a *Deus ex machina*.

Dew.—For any assigned temperature of the atmosphere there is a certain quantity of aqueous vapor which it is capable of holding in suspension at a given pressure. Conversely, for any assigned quantity of aqueous vapor held in suspension in the atmosphere there is a minimum temperature at which it can remain so suspended. This minimum temperature is called the dew-point. During the daytime, especially if there has been sunshine, a good deal of aqueous vapor is taken into suspension in the atmosphere. If the temperature in the evening now falls below the dew-point, which after a hot and calm day generally takes place about sunset, the vapor which can be no longer held in suspension is deposited on the surface of the earth, sometimes to be seen visibly falling in a fine mist. Another form of the phenomenon of dew is as follows: The surface of the earth, and all things on it, and especially the smooth surfaces of vegetable productions, are constantly parting with their heat by radiation. If the sky is covered with clouds, the radiation sent back from the clouds nearly supplies an equivalent for the heat thus parted with; but if the sky be clear, no equivalent is supplied, and the surface of the earth and things growing on it become colder than the atmosphere. If the night also be calm, the small portion of air contiguous to any of the surfaces will become cooled below the dew-point, and its moisture deposited on the surface in the form of dew. If the chilled temperature be below 32 degrees Fahr., the dew becomes frozen, and is called *hoar-frost*. The above two phenomena, though both expressed in our language by the word "dew"—which perhaps helps to lead to a confusion of ideas on the subject—are not necessarily expressed by the same word. For instance, in French, the first phenomenon—the falling evening dew—is expressed by the word *serein;* while the latter—the dew seen in the morning gathered in drops on the leaves of plants or other cool surfaces—is expressed by the word *rosee*. Similar to *rosee* is the moisture which condenses on the outside surface of pitchers or glasses of ice-water. The air in immediate contact is cooled below the dew-point and deposits the suspended moisture.

Diamonds, Celebrated.—The discoverer of diamonds is unknown. From references in "Exodus" it is apparent that the diamond was a precious stone in Egypt in those early times; and even before that it was known in India, where probably it was first obtained. The name is a corruption from the Greek word *adamant*, meaning untamable, unconquerable. The art of cutting and polishing diamonds, although long practiced in India and China, was not known in Europe till after the middle of the fifteenth century, when it was introduced by Louis von Berguen, of Bruges. Some particular diamonds, from their unusual magnitude, or from circumstances of their history, are of more than usual interest. The largest diamond certainly known is that belonging to the Rajah of Mattan, weighing 367 carats. It is egg-shaped, with an indented hollow near the smaller end. Many years ago the Governor of Borneo offered for it $500,000, two war brigs fully equipped, a number of cannon, and a quantity of powder and shot; but the rajah refused to part with it, the fortunes of his family being supposed to be connected with it, and the Malays ascribing to water in which it had been dipped the power of healing all diseases. Perhaps the most famous diamond is the Koh-i-noor, once a boasted possession of the Great Mogul, and now belonging to the Crown of Great Britain. It is said to have weighed 900 carats in the rough; but now, after various cuttings, weighs 106 carats, and is estimated to be worth $2,000,000. The Orloff diamond, belonging to the Russian Emperor, and which was once the eye of an Indian idol, is said to have weighed, when rough, 779 carats, but is now cut egg-shape and weighs 192 1–4 carats. It is valued at $500,000. The Regent or Pitt diamond, which weighs in its cut state 136 3–4 carats, is unrivaled in its limpidness and its form, its diameter and depth being nearly equal. It was found in Golconda, was brought from India by an English gentleman named Pitt, the grandfather of the first Earl of Chatham, and by him sold to the Duke of Orleans for £130,000. It decorated the hilt of the sword of state of the Emperor Napoleon, was taken by the Prussians at Waterloo, and now belongs to the Crown of Prussia. It is valued at $600,000. The Sanci diamond, weighing 106 carats, has a still more interesting history. It belonged to Charles the Bold, Duke of Burgundy, who wore it in his hat at the Battle of Nancy, where he fell. It was found by a Swiss soldier and sold to a clergyman for a gulden. It afterward passed into the possession of Anton, King of Portugal, who was eventually obliged to sell it for 100,000 francs. It was then owned by a French gentleman named Sanci, and was sent as a pledge to Henry III. The servant carrying it was attacked by robbers and slain, but swallowed the diamond; and his master, causing his body to be opened, found it in his stomach. It came into the possession of the Crown of England, and was carried to France in 1688 by James II, and it was worn by Louis XIV at his coronation. In 1835 it was sold to a Russian nobleman for £80,000.

Diet of Worms was an assembly convoked by Emperor Charles V, for the purpose of considering state affairs, and principally the course to be pursued toward the Reformation and Martin Luther. It was composed of the princes and other leading representatives of the several states of the German Empire. Luther appeared before this august body, and his defense of himself and his followers against the charge of heresy was dignified and eloquent, and compelled the admiration of the assembly and many of his former foes. He was allowed to leave the city under escort, and at the instigation of his friend, the Elector of Saxony, who feared that he might be assassinated if he continued in active life, he was taken to the Castle of Wartburg, where he remained, virtually a prisoner, for about one year. When his adherents had become numerous enough and strong enough for him to advocate his principles without fear of molestation, he was restored to liberty.

Discovery of Coal in America.—It is generally believed that coal was first discovered in America in Illinois by the early French explorers some time between the years of 1673 and 1680. On a map published by Father Hennepin in 1698, a coal-mine is located in the bluff of the Illinois River near Ottawa.

Diving-Bells.—The principle of the diving-bell is extremely simple, and can be seen by pressing any hollow vessel mouth downward into water. Although some species of diving-bell was probably used in the time of Aristotle—for it is recorded that divers took with them a vessel which enabled them to remain under water—and in mediæval times, it was not until about 1715 that any practical method of supplying the bell with air while under water was discovered. About that year this want was met by a Doctor Halley. He used two water-tight barrels, each supplied with a hose, also attached to the diving-bell, and these, attached to heavy weights, were dropped on each side of the bell, and the diver could, therefore, remain under water as long as the air supplied by the barrels was fit to breathe. The diver's cap, which was made of metal and fitted with a tube for conveying air to it from the bell, so that the wearer could leave the bell and walk around the bottom of the sea, was soon after devised by the same inventor. In 1779 the air-pump, which forced down air from above, was applied to diving-bells by an engineer named Smeaton. The most practical bell in use at present is a sort of submarine boat called the Nautilus, with double sides, between which water is forced to cause the boat to descend and air to cause it to rise. Air is supplied by means of an air-pump worked above water.

Dog-Days are so called from Sirius, the most brilliant of the fixed stars in the head of the constellation Caius Major, or the Greater Dog, and include the period from July 3d to August 11th. During this period this star and the sun rise within the same hour, and the ancients who worshiped the dog attributed the extreme of summer to the influence of this constellation—a superstition which has been perpetuated to the present day in the use of this term.

Doge was the name of the chief magistrate, possessing princely rank, in the republics of Venice and Genoa. On Ascension-Day the Adriatic Sea was married to the Doge of Venice as a symbol of the dominion that republic had gained over the seas. A special ship called the Bucentaur [see *Bucentaur*] was kept for this ceremony, and from its deck the Doge dropped a ring into the water to show that as a wife is subject to her husband, so is the Adriatic Sea to the republic of Venice. As a symbol of princely dignity the Doge wore a horned cap and had the title of " Serenity." With the fall of the Venetian Republic, 1797, the dignity of Doge also disappeared, and it was finally done away with in Genoa in 1804.

Dollar-Mark, Origin of.—There are numerous theories regarding the origin of the $ sign. One is that it is a modification of the figure 8, the dollar being formerly a "piece of eight," and designated by the character 8—8. Another is that it is a combination of U. S., the initials of the United States. The third theory is that it is a combination of H. S., the mark of the Roman unit; while a fourth is that it is a combination of P. and S., from the Spanish, *peso duro*, which signifies "hard dollar." In Spanish accounts, *peso* is contracted by writing the S over the P and placing it after the sum. The best theory regarding the origin of the sign is that offered by the editor of the London *Whitehall Review*.

"It is taken," he says, "from the Spanish dollar, and the sign is to be found, of course, in the associations of the Spanish dollar. On the reverse of the Spanish dollar is a representation of the Pillars of Hercules, and round each pillar is a scroll with the inscription 'Plus Ultra.' This device in course of time has degenerated into the sign which stands at present for American as well as Spanish dollars—'$.' The scroll around the pillars, I take it, represents the two serpents sent by Juno to destroy Hercules in his cradle."

Domesday-Book.—William the Conqueror, desiring to know how many hundred hydes of land England contained, and what lands the King had in it, what cattle was in the several counties, and how much revenue he ought to get yearly from each, ordered that a survey of the country be made. This was done by commissioners called the King's Justiciaries, who seem to have had the help of the chief men of every shire. By a sworn assize or jury of the sheriffs, lords of manors, presbyters of churches, reeves of hundreds, bailiffs, and six villeins of every village, they made inquest as to the name of the place; who held it in the time of King Edward; who was its present possessor; how many hydes there were in the manor; how many plow-gates in the demesne; how many homagers or vassals; how many villeins; how many cottars; how many serfs; what freemen; how many tenants in socage (by hereditary right); how much wood; how much meadow and pasture; what mills and fish-ponds; how much had been added or taken away; what was the gross value in King Edward's time; what was the present value; and how much each freeman or soc man has or had. The returns thus gathered in the several shires, and their hundreds and other subdivisions, were arranged and digested in the record which is now known as the Domesday or Doomsday-Book, and the mere statement which has been made of its contents is enough to show the immense value of the book for all purposes of inquiry into the ancient condition of England. The survey was completed in 1086. The name bears reference to the supreme authority of the book in "doom" or judgment on matters contained in it.

Don Juan.—Like Dr. Faustus, Don Juan is a legendary and mythical personage. He gives himself up so entirely to the gratification of sense, especially to the most powerful of all the impulses, that of love, that he acknowledges no higher consideration. Ultimately he is compelled to acknowledge the worthlessness of a merely sensuous, godless and immoral existence. The legend of Don Juan has furnished a theme for numbers of poets, playwrights, and writers of romance—among others Byron, Dumas, Mozart, and Prosper Merimee.

Doom-Book, or Dom-Boc.—The code of laws compiled by King Alfred, chiefly from the West-Saxon collection of his own ancestor, Ina, but comprising also many portions of the Kentish collection of Ethelbert, with the supplements of his successors, and of the Mercian laws of Offa. Alfred's peculiar Christian character is strongly impressed on his code, which begins with extracts from the Bible: "The Lord spake all these words, saying, I am the Lord thy God." Then follow the Ten Commandments, the part of the Mosaic law relating to criminal offenses, and passages from the New Testament, including the Golden Rule. Alfred made few, if any, original laws, but contented himself with restoring, renovating, and improving those which he found already in existence.

Draco's Laws.—Draco, an Athenian lawgiver and archon, was the author of the first written code of laws at Athens, which he is supposed to have published in the fourth year of the 39th Olympiad, 621 B. C. He was of distinguished birth, honored for his severe manners and his large experience in public affairs, and the people of Athens, a prey to anarchy, besought him to give them ε code of laws. These, however, effected little change in the form of the state, but by being committed to writing put an end to the arbitrary administration of justice on the part of the archons, and resulted in the establishment of a court of appeals—that of the Ephetæ. The system which he proposed linked together civil and moral duties. He took the citizen at the moment of his birth, prescribed the manner in which he should be nourished and educated, and followed him with directions through the different epochs of life. His legislation had a beneficial and permanent effect upon the political development of Athens. The extraordinary severity of these laws, however, which punished the slightest theft, or even laziness, with death, no less than sacrilege, murder and treason, caused them to be often neglected, and made them so hated that Solon was appointed to draw up a new code. Solon, though he softened their severity in some instances, retained that law which punished a murderer with death. Draco, at a later period, went to Ægina, where, after having introduced his laws, he is said to have been stifled in the theater by the garments thrown upon him as a mark of respect by the people. Extremely severe and sanguinary laws are still called *Draconic*, and in ancient Greece it was commonly said that Draco's laws "were written in blood."

Draft Riots.—The draft riots in New York City began on the morning of July 13, 1863. The original cause of the trouble was unquestionably the uncertainty which was felt by the poorer classes regarding the fate of their wives and children should they be drafted, and the unwillingness of the large numbers of foreigners in the city to submit to the harsh conditions of conscription; and these two classes were no doubt incited to resistance by those who opposed the draft for political reasons. When the draft was begun, on the date mentioned above, the building was surrounded by a mob who smashed in the windows and doors, and finally set it on fire, causing the officers to fly for their lives. The success of the rioters here added large numbers to their ranks, and in a few hours a great army, reinforced by all the rough element in the city, was tramping the streets, burning, destroying, plundering and murdering wherever resistance was offered them. Through race-hatred or political animosity, negroes were singled out as special victims, and the Colored Half-Orphan Asylum on Fifth Avenue was plundered and fired and the children beaten by an army of ruffian boys. The riot lasted three days, during which business was entirely suspended, and it was estimated that the number killed was nearly 1,000. This, however, was probably an exaggeration, but $1,500,000 was paid by the county authorities as damages for the property destroyed. The draft was for the time abandoned, and was not again undertaken until after the City Council had passed a relief bill to pay $300 commutation or substitute-money for every drafted man of the poorer classes who had a family dependent upon him.

Dred Scott Case.—Prior to 1834 Dred Scott, a negro, was held as a slave in Missouri by Dr. Emerson, a surgeon in the United States army. In that year the master was transferred to the military post at Rock Island, Ill., and Scott went with him. In 1836 Dr. Emerson was transferred to Fort Snelling, Minn., then an organized Territory of the United States. At that military post Dr. Emerson bought a female slave named Harriet from Major Taliaferro, and held her and Dred as his slaves, they having been married with his consent soon after Emerson's arrival at Snelling. They subsequently moved back to Missouri. After two children had been born to them Dr. Emerson sold them to John F. A. Sanford, of New York City. On first returning to Missouri, and while still owned by Dr. Emerson, Scott unsuccessfully sued for his freedom on the ground that he had been taken into a free State. After his purchase by Mr. Sanford he again sued in the Circuit Court of St. Louis County, and obtained a favorable decision; but the case was finally appealed to the Supreme Court, the decision of which was that if Scott was free he was not a "citizen" because he was a negro, and a negro could not be a "citizen," and that he was still a slave. The court held, in reaching this conclusion, that the law was unconstitutional and void which prohibited a person from holding slaves in the Territories of the United States north of 36 degrees 30 minutes. The Chief Justice (Taney), when delivering the opinion of the court, made an historical survey of the public opinion of the civilized world at the time of the formation of the American Constitution, concerning the African race. Among other statements, he said: "They (the Africans) had for more than a century before been regarded as beings of an inferior order and altogether unfit to associate with the white race, either in social or political relations, and so far inferior that they had no rights which the white man was bound to respect." After this decision Personal Liberty bills were passed in several of the free States for the purpose of defeating the action of the Fugitive Slave law;

Drinking-Usages.—Drink-offerings were made a solemn religious service by the Hebrews. To mark the spot where he communed with God, Jacob set up a pillar of stones and "poured a drink-offering thereon." Among the Greeks and Romans the pouring out of a libation to the gods was a common religious observance. [See *Libations.*] The ceremonial observance of drinking healths, or the uttering of a pious, heroic or friendly sentiment before quaffing liquor on festive occasions, sprung from these and similar usages. The application of the word "toast" is modern, having had its origin in the practice of putting a piece of toasted bread in a jug of ale, hence called a "toast and tankard." The custom of so using the word is said to have had its rise at Bath, in the reign of Charles II. It happened that on a public day a celebrated beauty of those times was in the cross, or large public bath, and one of the crowd of her admirers took a glass of the water in which the fair one had stood, and drank her health to the company. There was in the place a gay fellow, half-tipsy, who offered to jump in, and declared, though he liked not the liquor, he would have the toast; and from this circumstance came the application of the word. There were at one time drinkings on the occasion of births, baptisms, marriages, and even deaths; these last, which included the gloomy festivities of the *Lykwake,* or wake over the corpse of the deceased, being a relic of a very ancient custom, as was that, at least in Scotland, of drinking the *dredgy* (dirge) after the funeral solemnities were completed. There were also numerous drinking-usages connected with departures. We need only notice the *bonailie,* or, as it is sometimes called, a *foy,* a festive drinking at the going-away of servants, or of persons in a still higher degree, once common in the Lowlands of Scotland; also the *stirrup-cup,* or, as it is called in the Highlands, *deoch an dorris,* or drink on getting on horseback and being ready to set off.

Druidism.—The Druids, beyond all things, according to Cæsar, were desirous to inspire a belief that men's souls do not perish, but transmigrate after death from one individual to another, and they held that people are thereby most strongly urged to bravery, as the fear of death is thus destroyed. Druidism is commonly spoken of as the religious system of the Gauls and Britains. Beside being priests and teachers of religion, the Druids appear also to have been adepts in the magic arts, and were versed in the mysterious powers of animals and plants. The oak-tree was especially sacred among them, and their rites were frequently performed in oak-groves. They also had a special reverence for the mistletoe when growing on an oak. According to Pliny, a Druid, clothed in white, mounted the tree, and with a knife cut the mistletoe, which was received by another standing on the ground in his white robe. The same author gives a curious account of the "serpent's egg" worn as a distinguishing badge by the Druids. It was formed, he says, by the poisonous spittle of a great many serpents twined together. Gathered at moonlight, and afterward worn in the bosom, it was a mighty talisman. In all the countries anciently inhabited by the Celts there are found rude structures of stone, and the older archæologists assumed that these were Druidical altars; but there is no proof that such was their object or origin. Similar structures are found in Scandinavia and many parts of Germany, and to assume in all these countries the presence of Celts seems too hazardous. The same doubts prevail as to the larger monuments of this kind—the supposed Druidical temples of Amesbury, of Carnac in Brittany, and of Stonehenge. [See *Stonehenge.*]

Dry Tortugas.—These islets form part of a county of Florida, are ten in number, and are situated at the extreme end of the Florida Keys. They are of coral formation and low and barren, except when partly covered with mangrove bushes. They are defended by fortifications, and on Bush or Garden Key is Fort Jefferson, which was used during the Civil War as a penal station for rebel prisoners. A lighthouse has also been erected upon the same islet.

Dynamite.—As generally manufactured, dynamite consists of infusorial earth, porcelain earth, coal-dust, siliceous ashes or the like, saturated with about three times its weight of nitro-glycerine, a compound which is produced by the action of a mixture of strong nitric and sulphuric acids on glycerine at low temperatures, though the proportions vary with different makers. According to its elements, it is to the eye a grayish-brown, reddish or blackish powder, damp and greasy to the touch, and without smell. Its explosive power is about eight times greater than that of powder. The manufacture of dynamite is attended with great danger, owing to the proneness of nitro-glycerine to explosion even at the slightest shock. The explosive force of the latter substance, which has the appearance of common oil, is about ten times greater than that of gunpowder.

Dynamite Gun.—The nitro-gelatine or dynamite gun, known as the "Zalinski gun," was the invention of Lieutenant Zalinski and Captain Bartlett of the United States army. It is a long tube made of wrought iron, lined with seamless brass tubing one-eighth of an inch thick. The projectile used is shaped like a huge rocket, five or six feet in length. The stick of the rocket has a wooden or metal base large enough to fill the bore of the gun, and against this base the pressure of the air (the propelling force being compressed air)—1,000 pounds to the square inch—is exerted. The head of the rocket contains from fifty to sixty pounds—or more—of nitro-gelatine, a new explosive made of nitro-glycerine and gun-cotton. The projectile, being shot from the gun, is exploded, after reaching its mark, by electricity. A small battery is fixed in the head of each shot, and the discharge is effected by concussion if the shot strikes, or by action of water on a sensitized surface if the shot lights in the sea. It is thought that a submarine explosion within 100 feet of a ship will be disastrous in eight cases out of ten. The gun is from 40 to 75 feet in length, and of caliber from 6 to 10 inches. The mechanical arrangement for compressing the air in the gun and discharging the piece is said to be taken from an invention of B. T. Babbitt, patented in 1878.

Eagle as an Emblem.—In ancient mythology the eagle was believed to carry the souls of the dying to their abode on Mount Olympus, and was called the Bird of Jove. The eagle was first taken as a symbol of royal power by the ancient Etruscans, who bore its image upon their standards. In the year 87 B. C. a silver eagle, with expanded wings, poised on the top of a spear, with a thunderbolt held in its claws, was adopted as the military standard to be borne at the head of their legions by the Romans. At the time of Hadrian a golden eagle was substituted for the silver one. A two-headed eagle was adopted by the Byzantine Emperors as a symbol of their control of both the East and the West. The double-headed eagle of Russia was adopted on the marriage of Ivan I with a Grecian princess of the Eastern Empire; that of Austria was first used when the Emperor of Germany took the title of the Roman Emperor. The national standard of Prussia bears a black eagle, that of Poland a white one. Napoleon I took a golden eagle for his standard, modeled of pure gold, and bearing a thunderbolt, after the pattern of the eagle of the Romans. This standard was disused under the Bourbons, but was restored by a decree of Louis Napoleon in 1852. The eagle was first used on American coins in 1788, on cents and half-cents issued from the Massachusetts mint. It was adopted in the plan of a national coinage as a design upon all gold coins, and on the silver dollar, half-dollar, and quarter-dollar. The design of an eagle was at one time suggested for the national flag, but was abandoned.

Earthquakes.—The phenomena connected with earthquakes have been variously described. Many writers refer to appearances in the heavens, or changes in the atmosphere, which to them seem to have some connection with the catastrophes they narrate. They tell of irregularities in the seasons preceding or following the shock; of sudden gusts of wind, interrupted by sudden calms; of violent rains at unusual seasons or in countries where such phenomena are almost unknown; of a reddening of the sun's disk; of a haziness in the air, often continued for months; and similar phenomena. But these are so irregular in their appearance, and have been so seldom observed associated with more than a single earthquake, that in the absence of any decided reason to the contrary there seems good ground for believing they have no real connection with the earthquake. The general opinion of investigators is that these agitations proceed from within outward, and are not of atmospheric or other external origin. True, Professor Alexis Perry, of Dijon, France, thought he discovered relations between the ages of the moon and these occurrences which seemed to sustain the theory of Zantedeschi that the liquid nucleus of the earth responds to the moon's attraction in tides, somewhat as the coast does; but the theory that the earth has a liquid nucleus covered with only a thin, solid crust is losing adherents continually. All theorists are agreed, as to the connection between volcanoes and earthquakes, that they are produced by the same subterraneous agency. Mr. Mallet, in an elaborate report on the subject presented to the British Association, proposed an ingenious theory. He assumes that volcanoes and the centers of earthquake disturbances are near the sea or other large supplies of water; and he says that when an eruption of igneous matter takes place beneath the sea-bottom the first action must be to open up large fissures in its rocky material, or to lift and remove its incoherent portions, such as sand, mud, gravel, etc. The water, on meeting the heated surface, assumes the spheroidal state. While in this condition the intestine motion may be great, but little steam is generated; but no sooner have the surfaces cooled than the water comes into close contact with them, and a vast volume of steam is evolved explosively and blown off into the deep and cold water of the sea, where it is condensed, and thus a blow of the most tremendous sort is given at the volcanic focus, and, being transferred outwardly in all directions, is transmitted as the earthquake shock. Whatever their origin, whether of one cause or various causes, the prevailing opinion still is that the vibrations of every earthquake can be traced to a focus within the earth, and that this lies directly beneath the point of greatest disturbance on the earth's surface. There are creditable records of between 6,000 and 7,000 earthquakes, between 1606 B. C. and A. D. 1842. In the great Lisbon earthquake no less than 60,000 perished, while in that of Calabria, in the end of the last century, 40,000 were destroyed. It is estimated that at least 13,000,000 of the human race have perished in this way.

Easter.—The festival of the Resurrection of Christ probably derives its Teutonic name from the festival of the Goddess Ostara —in Anglo-Saxon, Eastre—which the Saxons of old were wont to celebrate about the same season at which the Christian festival of Easter occurs. In the second century a dispute arose as to the proper time for celebrating Easter between the Eastern and Western Churches. The great mass of Eastern Christians celebrated Easter on the 14th day of the first month or moon, considering it to be equivalent to the Jewish Passover, when Christ was crucified. The Western Christians celebrated it on the Sunday after the 14th, holding that it was the commemoration of the Resurrection of Jesus. The Council of Nice, A.D. 325, decided in favor of the Western usage. At the time of the introduction of the Gregorian Calendar it was debated whether Easter should continue a movable feast or whether a fixed Sunday after the 21st of March should not be adopted. In deference to the ancient custom, the ecclesiastical authorities decided to adhere to the method of determining the day by the moon. It must be understood, however, that it is not the actual moon in the heavens, nor even the mean moon of the astronomers, that regulates the time of Easter, but an altogether imaginary moon, whose periods are so contrived that the new (Calendar) moon always follows the real new moon—sometimes by two, or even three, days. The effect of this is that the 14th of the Calendar moon—which had from the time of Moses been considered full moon for ecclesiastical purposes—falls generally on the 15th or 16th of the real moon, and thus after the real full moon, which is generally on the 14th or 15th day. With this explanation, then, of what is meant by "full moon," viz., that it is the 14th day of the Calendar moon, the rule is that Easter-Day is always the first Sunday after the Paschal full moon, i. e., the full moon which happens upon or next after the 21st of March ; and if the full moon happens on a Sunday, Easter-Day is the Sunday after.

Easter-Eggs.—The most characteristic Easter-rite, and the one most widely diffused, is the use of Pasch, or Easter-eggs. They are usually stained of various colors with dye-woods or herbs. They are sometimes given as presents, sometimes kept as amulets, and sometimes eaten. In some moorland parts of Scotland it used to be the custom for young people to go out early on Pasch-Sunday and search for wild-fowls' eggs for breakfast, and it was considered lucky to find them. There can be but little doubt that the use of eggs at this season was originally symbolical of the revivification of nature, the springing forth of life in spring. From the Christian point of view this feast of eggs has been usually considered as emblematic of the resurrection and of a future life. The custom is not confined to Christians, as the Jews used eggs in the Feast of the Passover; and we are told that the Persians, when they keep the festival of the solar new year, in March mutually present each other with colored eggs.

East India Company.—In the year 1600 a company of London merchants, influenced by the reports of the great opportunity for commercial adventure in the Indian Peninsula, obtained a charter from Queen Elizabeth and began trading, and shortly afterward established numerous stations for the transaction of their business. In 1620 the capital of the Company had increased to £400,000 and its prospects for continued commercial prosperity were good. Other European traders, however, had begun to perceive the great possibilities of Indian commerce, and the Englishmen were soon involved in irritating competition with Dutch, Portuguese and French rivals. Although the only object of the English Company was peaceful trade it soon became evident that a resort to force would be necessary to retain this, and in 1645 the Company built a fort at Madras and garrisoned it with native warriors. From this time until about the middle of the eighteenth century the country continued fairly peaceful and the Company steadily grew in wealth and power. About this time, however, the troubles between the French and English in India culminated in a war, in which the English under General Clive were successful. Soon after the Company began to have trouble with the natives, and after conquering one of the native princes they adopted the plan of taking possession of his territory At the close of the century the East India Company had become one of the governing powers of the world, keeping great armies on foot, fighting great battles, and controlling vast revenues. The British Government now appointed a board of control to supervise the civil and military government exercised by the Company. In 1833, by the terms of a new charter granted by the Government, the East India Company ceased to be a trading association and was intrusted with the government of all the affairs of the Indian Empire, subject to the Board of Control. Indian trade was made free to all British subjects, and all the property owned by the Company was vested in the Crown, to be held and managed by the Company in trust for the Crown, the Government guaranteeing to them an annual dividend of ten and a half per cent. on their stock. In 1858 all the functions and powers of the East India Company were transferred to the Crown, the Indian mutiny having convinced Parliament that a reform was needed in the administration of Indian affairs.

Ecole Polytechnique, a celebrated military academy of France established in 1794 through the instrumentality of M. Lamblardie, director of the *Pons et Chaussees.* The academy was first called the *Ecole Centrale des Travcaux Publics;* but in the following year, 1795, the name was changed to *Ecole Polytechnique,* and numerous alterations were made in its organization. It was dissolved in 1816, again in 1830, and again in 1832, on account of the impetuous way in which the scholars mixed themselves up with the political disturbances of those years; but it was re-established on each occasion, after the restoration of tranquility. Candidates are admitted by competitive examination, which takes place yearly. To be eligible as a candidate the youth must be French, and must be more than sixteen and less than twenty years of age before the 1st of January following; but soldiers are admissible up to twenty-five, provided they can give proof of service in the regular army. The course of instruction lasts for two years, when graduates have the privilege of choosing, from the various public services supplied from this school, the particular branch they wish to enter. The school was last reorganized by a decree of the 15th of April, 1873.

Edda.—There are two works which bear this title—the *Edda Saemundar hins Froda,* or " Edda of Saemund the Wise," and the *Edda Snorra Sturlusonar.* The former and older of these is a collection of the most ancient mythological and heroic Scandinavian songs, the dates of whose composition may probably be referred to the different periods between the sixth and eighth centuries. These songs, which are supposed to have been collected and arranged by Saemund Sigfusson, surnamed Frodi, an Icelandic priest, were discovered and first brought before the notice of European scholars in 1643 by Brynjulf Sveinsson, Bishop of Skalaholt, who applied to them the name of Edda, or "grandmother." The "Snorra Edda" is a prose composition, and treats of Scandinavian mythology, and of the language and modes of composition of the ancient Skalds. As the name implies, it refers to. Snorri Sturluson, the learned author of the *Heims Kringla*. [See *Heims Kringla*.] This Edda was first published by P. J. Resen in 1665.

Edelweiss is a native of the Alpine ranges of southern Europe, and is found on the loftiest peaks of the Jura hills. Its botanical name is *Cona topedium Alpinum* (the lion's foot). It is a perennial, and grows six to eight feet high. It has oblong, yellow, woolly leaves, and bears pale-yellow or white flowers in a crowned head, surrounded by a whorl of woolly leaves. The *edelweiss* was taken to England in 1776, and is cultivated there to some extent in gardens.

Eden, Garden of.—The question of the locality of the Garden of Eden, or of the exact sense in which the Mosaic narrative is to be understood, is involved in inexplicable mystery. Josephus and several of the Fathers conceived that Eden was a term denoting the entire region between the Ganges and the Nile. Calvin, Huet, Bochart and Wells have, with slight differences of detail, concluded in favor of Kornah, in Babylonia, not far from the Persian Gulf; while Armenia, near the sources of the Tigris and Euphrates, and the region near Damascus, have been selected by other celebrated scholars. The modern German school of Biblical critics, convinced that the Hebrew account is traditional, and, in its present form, of very late composition, and impressed, beside, with the vast antiquity of the far East, have, almost without exception, sought the cradle of the human race in Bactria or Cashmere, or the region lying to the north of it, a part of which is to this day called Audyana, the Garden. The Mohammedans, it may also be mentioned, believe Eden to have been in one of the seven heavens—some say the moon—and that the expulsion from Paradise consisted in Adam being cast down upon earth after the fall. The endeavor to positively identify the river-system of Eden with anything known at present is useless. There is no river on the face of the globe of which the Euphrates and Tigris (Hiddekel) are separate "heads," as they are said to be in the second chapter of Genesis; for, although the Euphrates and Tigris *now* unite for a short space on their way to the Persian Gulf, yet until the time of Alexander the Great they kept entirely distinct courses, and therefore it has been assumed that the Deluge completely altered the physical character of the region denoted by the term Eden. This was Luther's notion, to which, however, it has been objected that the narrative in Genesis is so worded as to convey the idea that the countries and rivers spoken of were existing in the time of the historian. Beside, the science of geology has thrown so much doubt on the universality of a deluge so late as the period assigned to Noah that it is hazardous to argue on the hypothesis of any extensive physical changes having taken place since the first appearance of man on the planet—at least if that be dated only some six thousand years back. In all the theories which have been advanced regarding the location of Eden two things have not been explained by anyone; these are the statement that the four rivers flow from one river, and the river Pison " compasseth the whole land of Havilah." Until these are solved the location of the Garden of Eden will continue to remain a mystery.

Edible Birds' Nests of China are an important article of commerce between the Eastern Islands and China, and of luxury in China. The nest is made by a species of swallow, being shaped like that of the common swallow, and adheres to a rock, vast numbers being found together, often in absolute contiguity, in caves of the Eastern Archipelago. The nests themselves are formed of grass, sea-weed fibers, small leaves, etc., and are attached to the rock by a sort of bracket made of a gelatinous substance, which is the part really eaten. This was formerly thought to be made of sea-weeds, but is now known to consist of saliva, which the swallow exudes from the salivary glands under the tongue. The nests are collected by means of ladders, and often by means of ropes, which enable the gatherers to descend from the summit of a precipice, like the rock-fowlers of the north. The gathering of the nests takes place after the young are fledged, twice a year. They are rated as a great delicacy, sometimes selling as high as thirty dollars a pound, and are only seen on the tables of the wealthiest classes.

Egyptian Labyrinth was situated at Crocodilopolis, near Lake Mœris, in the vicinity of the present pyramid of Biahhmu. It was built of polished stone, with many chambers and passages, said to be vaulted, having a peristyle court with 3,000 chambers, half of which were under the earth and the others above ground, which formed another story. The upper chambers were decorated with reliefs; the lower were plain, and contained, according to tradition, the bodies of the twelve founders of the building and the mummies of the sacred crocodiles, conferring on the building the character of a mausoleum, probably conjoined with a temple—that of Sebak, the crocodile-god. The Labyrinth stood in the midst of a great square. Part was constructed of Parian marble and of Syenitic granite; it had a staircase of ninety steps, and columns of porphyry, and the opening of the doors echoed like the reverberation of thunder. There is great difference of opinion among authors as to the name of the king under whom this remarkable work was constructed and the purpose for which it was intended, and it is probable that it was not built in a single reign. According to some ancient authorities it was supposed to have been inhabited by the Dodicarchy, or twelve kings, who conjointly ruled

Egypt before Psammetichus I; while others claim it to have been the place of assembly of the governors of nomes, or districts—twelve in number, according to Herodotus; sixteen, according to Pliny; and twenty-seven, according to Strabo. The Labyrinth was extant in the time of Pliny, A. D. 78, and was then, according to that author, 3,600 years old. The ruins of the foundations or lower chambers have been found at the modern village of Howara, in Fayoom. The next labyrinth in renown to the Egyptian was the Labyrinth of Crete, supposed to have been built by Dædalus for the Cretan monarch, Minos, in which the Minotaur was confined by his orders. The third of the labyrinths of antiquity was the Samian, constructed by Theodorus and artists of his school, in the age of Polycrates, 540 B. C., supposed to be a work of nature embellished by art, having 150 columns erected by a clever mechanical contrivance. Other inferior labyrinths existed at Nauplia, at Sipontum in Italy, at Val d'Ispica in Sicily, and elsewhere.

Eiffel Tower.—The monster Tower designed by Engineer Eiffel for the Paris Exposition of 1889 has three stories or divisions. The first story is sixty meters high (a meter equals thirty-nine inches), and rests on the arches which join the four foundation-columns that carry upon them the entire weight of the huge structure. The Tower has four distinct sections. Each wing is provided with a refreshment-saloon that may be reached by means of winding staircases under the foundation-piers. Notwithstanding the center of the space has been set apart for the elevator, there still remain 4,200 square meters of floor-room for the accommodation of visitors who desire to promenade; and an iron railing about four feet high, with an arched roof to exclude the intense rays of the sun, surrounds the extreme edge of the promenade. The second story, which is sixty meters above the first one, is also reached by four staircases built inside of the supporting columns, which make a sharp inward bend, leaving but 1,400 square meters for the platform and promenade. Here, too, is a commodious and handsomely-decorated cafe. This story is ninety-one meters above the tip of the Notre Dame steeple, and higher than the tower of the palace of the Trocadero, on the other side of the river, and the view to be had of the surrounding country is almost indescribable. From here on the columns of the Tower fall in toward each other until they ascend a distance of 275 meters above the ground, where the third and last story is situated. Only one staircase leads to this story, which is for the exclusive use of the persons employed in the Tower, visitors being expected to use the elevators. The platform here is eighteen meters square. The story is equipped with reflecting mirrors and a large supply of field-glasses for those who wish to use them. The Tower terminates in what is known as the lantern, twenty-five meters above the third section; but this place has been set aside for the use of scientists for making observations. Some additional idea of the vast proportions of the Tower may be obtained when it is said that the ground-distance from the axis of one of its four pedestals across the drive-way to the axis of the other upon the same front is 100 meters, or about 3,000 feet. Bunker Hill Monument could be easily carried, lying on its side, through the archway. The Tower is built entirely of iron girders and pillars, in the simple construction of four great shafts, consisting of four columns each, starting from the four corners of the base and merging into the single shaft which forms the main part of the Tower. It is 1,000 feet high, or nearly twice as high as the Washington Monument, and its estimated cost is about $1,300,000. Its weight is about 15,000,000 pounds, or 7,500 tons.

Eisteddfod, The.—At Caerwys, Aberfraw, and Mathraval, in Wales, there were held from time to time great competitions in minstrelsy, which were called Eisteddfods. The beginning of these meetings is by some thought to date back to the fourth century, while others hold that they began about A. D. 940, when the privileges of the bards were defined and fixed by King Howel Dha. At these meetings only minstrels of skill performed, and degrees were conferred according to the branch in which the victors had perfected themselves. After the conquest of Wales by Edward 1, of England, in 1283, royal commissioners were appointed who presided as censors over the eisteddfods and allowed no bardic poem to be circulated which appealed to the patriotic sentiments of the conquered race. The last eisteddfod under royal commission was held in Caerwys in 1569, during the reign of Queen Elizabeth. The victor of this occasion received a silver harp, and there were five degrees given for skill in music and four for skill in poetry. Since then, exertions for the revival of national Welsh poetry and the bardic profession have been made by several societies—the Gwyneddigion, founded in 1770; the Cambrian, in 1818; and some years later the Cymmoridian, or Metropolitan Cambrian institution. Annual meetings are held by these societies for the recitation of prize poems and for performances upon the harp.

El Dorado, or the gilded land, was a name given by the Spaniards in the sixteenth century to an imaginary country supposed to be situated in the interior of South America, between the rivers Orinoco and Amazon, and to abound in gold and all manner of precious stones. Expeditions were fitted out for the purpose of discovering this fabulous region; and, though all such attempts proved abortive, the rumors of its existence continued to be believed down to the beginning of the eighteenth century. The Spainards found an imitator in Sir Walter Raleigh, who twice visited Guiana, where he believed El Dorado was situated.

Electricity, Discovery of.—Thales as far back as 600 B. C., and Theophrastus in 321 B. C., mention the power of amber, when rubbed, to attract light substances. Pliny, in A. D. 70, writes concerning the same phenomena; and it is from the Greek name of amber—"elecktron"—that we call this force electricity.

Dr. Gilbert, of Colchester, may be considered the founder of the *science* of electricity, for it was he that carefully repeated the observations of the ancients and experimented in various ways, and published these experiments in a book during the period between 1540 and 1603. Sir William Watson (1715 to 1807) distinctly announced the theory of *positive* and *negative* electricity, which was afterward elaborated by Dr. Benjamin Franklin. Dr. Franklin also established the fact that the lightning was an electric spark similar to that made by an electric machine or Leyden jar. In 1790 Galvani discovered that the contact of metals produced muscular contraction in the legs of a dead frog, and in 1800 Volta discovered the art of generating electricity by contact of metals with damp cloths. From these he obtained the galvanic battery and the voltaic pile. It remained for H. C. Oersted, of Copenhagen, however, to bring forth the most important fact, viz.: the magnetic action of the electrical current. This was in 1820. As soon as this discovery reached France, the eminent French philosopher Ampere set to work to develop the important consequences it involved. Faraday discovered electric magnetic rotation in 1820. From this time up, experimentists and theorists were busy searching for ways and means by which the electrical energy could be utilized as mechanical power; and to-day the galvanic battery and electric dynamo are rapidly superseding steam, and in a thousand ways doing its work with less noise, expense, and better results.

Electricity, Storage of.—The storage of electricity is the conversion of electricity into chemical energy under such circumstances that it may be readily converted back into electricity. The secondary batteries, which are used for storing-purposes, are termed "accumulators." The first battery of this kind was made by Ritter about 1840, and it consisted of a series of disks of a single metal, alternated with cloth or card moistened in a liquid by which the metal would not be affected chemically. In 1859 Mr. Gaston Plante made a secondary battery, for which he used plates of lead instead of plates of platinum. Passing a current through these, lead-oxide was deposited, and after the charging-current was removed the lead and lead-oxide were found to yield a very slight current. To increase this, Plante devised the plan of first charging the plates, then discharging, then charging again with the battery-current reversed, and so on, until, by repeated oxidations and subsequent reductions of the oxidized material, very porous plates were made. These, by their porosity, exposed a large surface to the oxidizing action of the current, so that a small porous plate took up as much electricity as one of large superficial area. Plante found that by connecting a number of cells together, and, after charging them, arranging them in series— that is, the positive plate of one connecting with the negative plate of another, and so on—he could store for use quite powerful currents of electricity. In 1880 another electrician, M. Camille Faure, devised the plan of coating Plante's lead-plates with red-lead, and then incasing them in flannel. The advantage of the red-lead is that it is very quickly made porous, and therefore the process of repeated charging of the plates, known as the 'forming" process, was reduced from weeks to days, and even to hours. This discovery, by reducing the time and expense of making the secondary battery, gave it a commercial value that it never had before, and it was hailed as a great advantage. Since that time a number of patents have been obtained for storage-batteries, and they now exist in different forms, but generally modeled on the inventions of Plante and Faure. The efforts of inventors have been mainly directed toward reducing the weight of the cells and to devising new ways of holding red-lead on the plates. This last-named substance, becoming porous, drops off readily, and for this reason the incasements of flannel, etc., were first devised. In some of the storage-batteries a plate or frame of cast lead is used, with receptacles, cells, etc., which are filled with the red-lead.

Electric Light, The, was first invented by Sir Humphry Davy in the early part of this century, who produced the arc-light with a battery of 2,000 cells. It was not in practical use, however, until 1844, when improvements in its manner of construction were made by a Frenchman named Foucault, and it was used to illuminate the Place de la Concorde, in Paris. In 1855 Jules Duboscq's electric lamp—thus far the most perfect of the kind—was shown at the Paris Exposition; but, though improvements were made in the invention during the twenty years following, little was accomplished toward practical electric lighting until the invention of Jablochkoff's candle. Paul Jablochkoff was a Russian who resigned his position under the Government in 1875 to devote his time wholly to scientific study. It was his intention to visit the Centennial Exposition in America, but was induced to remain in Paris, where, in 1876, he produced the electric candle, whose discovery made a great sensation. The light given by this candle was soft and steady, and a great many of them speedily came into use in Europe. In the last fifteen years great progress has been made, and there are now many different styles and forms, but in their essential features they nearly all come under two general classes—the arc-light and the incandescent light. The arc-light is, in principle, the same as that invented by Davy, the improvements consisting in different devices for regulating and maintaining at a constant distance the tips, and in different preparations for the substance of these tips, which are generally of carbon. The light is produced as follows: Two tips connected with the opposite poles of a strong battery are brought near to each other. The electricity, overcoming the resistance of the air, jumps from one tip to the other, and in so doing generates such an intense heat that the particles on the end of the one tip are volatilized and carried to the other in a condition of white heat, forming an arc of light of intense brilliancy.

Thus one tip is slowly consumed and the other somewhat increased, and hence the necessity of regulators for the tips, whence these lights are sometimes called regulated lamps. The Brush patent is the arc-light, best known and most used in America. In lights of the incandescent class a lighter current is used, and the luminous substance is not consumed, being inclosed in a sealed glass bulb from which the air has been exhausted. It consists of a loop of a thin fiber of some infusible substance (carbon has been found the best), inclosed in a vacuum, as just stated. The ends of this fiber are carried through the neck of the bulb and connected with the opposite poles of the battery; then the current, in passing through such a small conductor, has to overcome a high resistance, and in so doing generates a heat sufficient to maintain the entire loop at a steady temperature of white heat. The principal forms of the incandescent light are those of Edison, Swan, Maxim and Siemens. It is perhaps worthy of note that the great impetus given to electric lighting by the work of Thomas Edison has been not so much in improving the lamp as in cheapening the process of generating the electricity and inventing a ready mode of dividing the light. Hitherto the two principal barriers in the way of applying the electric light to public use had been the expense attendant upon the production of the electric force and the difficulty of using it simultaneously at a large number of illuminating points.

Electric Railways.—There are now in many parts of the country street-railways in operation in which the motive power is electricity, supplied to the electro-motors in the cars by continual contact with a wire extended over the entire length of the line, this wire carrying a strong current, which is generated by dynamos at the termini of the route. This system is not altogether satisfactory, and the great problem now presented to electrical engineers is the invention of a cheap and practical system of storing the electricity, in order that the car or locomotive may carry with it the necessary force to drive the motor. There are several systems now in experimental use, and some of them appear to work satisfactorily, so that there is every prospect that in the near future electricity will supplant all other forces for locomotive power.

Electroplating.—The first to gild the baser metals by means of the galvanic current was Brugnatelli, in 1803; but the first to make the process a success was the chemist De la Rive, and it has since been greatly improved by later inventions. The process depends upon the peculiar power which the electric current possesses of separating certain compound bodies into their constituent parts. For instance, if a current from a galvanic battery is passed by means of platinum electrodes through water to which sulphuric acid has been added, this chemical separation, which is called electrolysis, will take place, the water being resolved into its constituent gases, oxygen and hydrogen. Now, if some sulphate of copper be thrown into the liquid electrolysis will still go on, with a double result: the water will be separated into its elements, and the hydrogen, by its stronger affinity, will form a new compound with the sulphur in the sulphate, setting the copper free; and the liberated copper, being electro-positive in character, will be deposited on the platinum electrode, which is negative. On this general principle the process of electroplating or electrotyping depends, and its art consists in applying the metals thus released from their solutions to artistic and useful purposes. To carry on electroplating on a large scale oblong vats are used, which hold 200 gallons of solution. Silver plates connected with a powerful galvanic battery are placed at intervals in the vats; they form the positive electrodes and correspond in extent of surface with the articles to be coated, and face them on both sides. These articles act as the negative electrodes, and are suspended by copper wire from brass rods laid lengthwise over the vats and connected with the battery. The articles are prepared for plating by being first boiled in a solution of potash to free them from all grease; they are then quickly dipped in red nitrous-acid to remove any oxide that may have formed on the surface, and after this are well washed in water to remove every trace of the acid; they are then dipped into a solution of mercury and then washed in water again. The effect of this latter operation is to make the film of silver adhere more readily. The articles are then weighed and suspended in the solution, and are left there until a sufficient amount of silver has been deposited upon them. This amount is tested by weight. If the additional weight is not gained within the expected time the article is put in the solution again. When finally taken out, the articles are rubbed with brushes of fine wire and cleaned with fine sand; they are then polished on revolving brushes with rotten-stone, then with chamois-leather and rouge. The process of electro-gilding is essentially the same, with the exception that gold is substituted for silver.

Elemental Spirits.—According to the peculiar belief of the middle ages, the elemental spirits presided over the four "elements" living in and ruling them. The elemental spirits of fire were called Salamanders, those of water, Undines; those of air, Sylphs, and those of the earth, Gnomes. Descriptions of each will be found under their respective heads.

Eleusinian Mysteries.—Ceres, the goddess of grain and harvests, in her wanderings in search of her daughter Proserpine, who had been stolen by Pluto, arrived at Eleusis, and in return for some acts of kindness, and to commemorate her visit, she taught Triptolemus the use of corn on the Rharian plain, near the city, and instituted the mystic rites with which her festival was annually celebrated, and which are known as the Eleusinian Mysteries. The festival of Ceres consisted of two parts, the greater and lesser mysteries. The less important feast, serving as a sort of preparation for the greater, was held at Agra, on the Ilissus. The celebration of the great mysteries began at Eleusis on the 15th day of Bœdromion, the third month of the Attic year, and lasted over nine days. On the first day the neophytes, already initiated at the preparatory festival, met and were instructed in their sacred duties. On the second day they purified themselves by washing in the sea. On the third day sacrifices, comprising, among other things, the mullet-fish and cakes made of barley from the Rharian plain, were offered with special rites. The fourth day was devoted to the procession of 'the sacred basket of Ceres. The fifth day was known as the "day of the torches," and was thought to symbolize the wanderings of Ceres in quest of her daughter. The sixth day, called Iacchus, in honor of the son of Ceres, was the great day of the feast. On that day the statue of Iacchus was borne in pomp along the sacred way from the Ceramicus, at Athens, to Eleusis, where the votaries spent the night and were initiated in the last mysteries. Till this time they had been only *mystæ*, but on the night of the sixth day they were admitted into the innermost sanctuary of the temple, and from being allowed to behold the sacred things became entitled to be called *epoptæ*, or, "ephori," i. e., spectators or contemplators. They were once more purified, and repeated their original oath of secrecy with an imposing and awful ceremonial, somewhat resembling, it is believed, the forms of modern freemasonry. The festival was celebrated on the three succeeding days with lesser ceremonies. The eighth day, called Epiduuria, was named in honor of Æsculapius. The mysteries were celebrated with the most scrupulous secrecy. No initiated person might reveal what he had seen under pain of death, and no uninitiated person could take part in the ceremonies, under the same penalty. Initiation into the Eleusinian Mysteries was compulsory on every free-born Athenian. During the period of the festival none of those taking part in it could be seized or arrested for any offense.

Elgin Marbles are the most precious collection of specimens of Greek art in its purest state. They were brought from Greece by Thomas, seventh Earl of Elgin, and purchased from him for the British Museum by the English Government in 1816, for £35,000. They originally adorned certain buildings in the Acropolis of Athens. They consist of portions of the statues of Theseus or Hercules, Ilissus or river-god, upper portions of the torsos of Neptune and Minerva, Iris, torso of Cecrops, Ceres and Proserpine, the Fates, heads of the horses of Hyperion, one of the horses of Night, fifteen metopes, executed in high relief, representing the battle of the Centaurs and Lapithæ, and a large portion of the frieze of the outer wall of the cella. This work represents the solemn procession to the Temple of Minerva during the Panathenaic festival. This exquisite frieze occupied, slab after slab, a space of 524 feet in length. The remains of it in the British Museum on slabs and fragments of marble are to the extent of upward of 249 feet. Of the statues, the Theseus and the head of the horse of Night are the most perfect, the former wanting only the hands and feet and part of the nose, while even the surface of the latter is very little injured.

Emancipation in Great Britain.—The system of slavery was abolished thoughout all the British Colonies by act of Parliament in 1833, when a bill was passed which gave freedom to all classes and indemnified their owners with an award of £20,000,000. According to this act, slavery was to cease on August 1, 1834, but the slaves were to continue with their former owners as apprentices for a certain period. This apprenticeship, however, did not work satisfactorily to either side, and complete emancipation took place in 1838. In 1787 the subject of the suppression of the slave-trade was agitated in London and received the support of Mr. Pitt, the Prime Minister, and William Wilberforce, a member of Parliament, and in 1791 a bill forbidding the further importation of slaves was offered by Wilberforce in Parliament, but was not passed. The conquest of the Dutch colonies in America by the British led to such an increase in the British slave-trade that in 1805 the traffic was forbidden in the conquered colonies; and in 1806 the friends of emancipation gained still another step by the passage of an act forbidding British subjects to engage in the trade, and the following year a general abolition bill making all slave-trade illegal after January 1, 1808, was adopted by Parliament. This, however, did not have the desired effect, as British subjects still continued the trade under the flags of other nations. So, in 1811, it was made a felony, punishable with imprisonment at hard labor or transportation; and subsequent laws made it piracy, to be punished with transportation for life. From this time until the passage of the Emancipation bill the subject was continually pressed upon the attention of Parliament. Slavery existed in Great Britain in Saxon and Norman times, when the peasantry were sold in the market like cattle for exportation, and were looked upon as mere chattels, to be bought and sold with the land upon which they toiled. In Scotland, even as late as 1780, a law existed which compelled colliers, on entering a mine, to perpetual service there, the right to their labor passing with the mine to an inheritor or purchaser, and their children being in like manner attached to the mine, and forbidden under severe penalty to seek other employment.

Emancipation Proclamation, Localities not Affected by.— The Emancipation Proclamation, being a war measure, did not affect the condition of slavery in any portions of the United States not in rebellion against the Government; hence the slaves held in certain parishes in Louisiana, certain counties in Virginia, and in the forty-eight counties which form West Virginia, were not freed until the passage of the thirteenth amendment. The parishes excepted in Louisiana were St. Bernard, Plaquemines, Jefferson, St. John, St. Charles, St. James, Ascension, Assumption, Terre Bonne, Lafourche, St. Mary, St. Martin, and Orleans, including the city of New Orleans. The counties in Virginia were Berkeley,

Accomack, Northampton, Elizabeth City, York, Princess Anne and Norfolk, including the cities of Norfolk and Portsmouth.

Ember-Days are days set apart in the calendar of the Romish and Episcopal Churches for the purposes of fasting and prayer, imploring a divine blessing upon the fruits of the earth, and upon the ordinations performed at that time. Wednesday, Friday and Saturday in the week following the first Sunday in Lent, Whitsunday, the 14th of September, and the 13th of December, are called ember-days, and the weeks in which they occur are called ember-weeks.

Emery is found, upon analysis, to be composed of alumina, oxide of iron, and silica with a little lime. It is a dull, opaque substance, sometimes of a grayish-black, sometimes of a bluish color, and it is prepared for use by crushing the lumps in a stamp-mill, and then passing the powder through sieves of different degrees of fineness. For the most delicate uses of opticians the powder is graded by the process known to chemists as elutriation. Emery was for a long time brought from the Island of Naxos, in the Grecian Archipelago. The Greek Government granted a monopoly of its trade to an English merchant. In 1847 Dr. J. Lawrence Smith, an American explorer in the employ of the Turkish Government, found deposits of the mineral at various points in Asia Minor, and the monopoly was destroyed and the price lowered. Deposits of emery have since been found in Bohemia, in the Ural Mountains, in Australia, and in North Carolina, Georgia and Montana. The supply from these deposits is too small, however, to compete with that which is brought from Turkey and Naxos.

English Crown Jewels.—The present collection of crown jewels of England consists of the crown made for Charles II, the crown made for the Queen of James II and his ivory scepter, the crown made for George IV, Prince of Wales, and that of the late Prince Consort; also the crown made for the coronation of Queen Victoria, which contains gems valued at $600,000, numerous articles of gold and silver studded with gems, the royal spurs, swords, bracelets, the basin in which all royal infants are christened, and the spoons and cups with which they are fed. The most celebrated and remarkable diamond in the collection is known as the Koh-i-noor, or Mountain of Light, which weighed, after cutting, 106 carats. This stone once belonged to Runjee Singh, the ruler of Lahore, India, but on the annexation of the Punjab in 1849 was surrendered to the British Government. The collection also contains a ruby diamond that was worn by the Black Prince, and numbers of other precious stones. With very few exceptions all the articles in the present collection are of comparatively modern date, as during the time of the Commonwealth the royal regalia was sold. The crown jewels are kept in an immense glass case in the Tower of London, and are on exhibition to visitors.

Ensilage is fodder preserved in a silo. A silo is a cistern or vat, air and water-tight on the bottom and sides, with an open top, constructed of masonry or concrete. It may be square, rectangular, round or oval in shape, with perpendicular sides. Corn, sorgho, rye, oats, millet, clover, and all the grasses are taken directly from the fields, run through a cutter which cuts them into pieces less than half an inch in length, and trampled down solidly in the silo and subjected to heavy and continuous pressure. The fodder thus treated retains all its natural juices, and is used for feeding stock during the winter.

Escurial is a famous monastery of New Castile, situated thirty miles northwest of Madrid, Spain. It was built, so it is said, in fulfillment of a vow made by Philip II during the battle of St. Quentin. On that occasion he implored the aid of St. Lorenzo, on whose day (August 10, 1557) the battle was fought, and vowed that should victory be granted him he would dedicate a monastery to the saint. The Escurial is built in the form of a gridiron, in allusion to the instrument of St. Lorenzo's martyrdom, and forms a huge rectangular parallelogram, 744 feet from north to south and 580 feet from east to west, and divided into long courts, which indicate the interstices of the bars. Towers at each angle of this parallelogram represent the feet of the gridiron, which is supposed to be lying upside down; and from the center of one of the sides a range of buildings abut, forming the royal residence and representing the handle. The Escurial was begun in 1563 and finished in 1584, and was intended to serve as a palace, mausoleum and monastery. It has a splendid chapel, built in general imitation of St. Peter's at Rome, with three naves, 320 feet long and 320 feet in height to the top of the cupola. The *pantheon* or royal tomb, from a design after the Roman pantheon, is a magnificently-decorated octagonal chamber, 36 feet in diameter by 38 feet high, in the eight sides of which are numerous black marble sarcophagi. Kings only and the mothers of kings are buried here. It is stated that the Escurial has 14,000 doors and 11,000 windows, and that its cost was 6,000,000 ducats. Its library, previous to 1808, when the Escurial was sacked by the French, contained 30,000 printed and 4,300 manuscript volumes, chiefly treasures of Arabic literature. These were sent to Madrid at the time referred to, and upon their return it was found that nearly one-third of them had been lost. The buildings were seriously damaged by fire in 1872. The correct name of the Escurial is *El real sitio de San Lorenzo el real del Escorial.*

Etching, Art of.—About the middle of the fifteenth century Tomaso Finiguerra, a Florentine, introduced the art of etching. In Germany, Italy and France its value met with prompt recognition, but it was not carried to a state of perfection till later times. It was at first regarded as an industrial art, but it soon grew to have a higher value, reproducing in graceful freedom and precision of touch the very feeling of the artist. The first step in etching is to cover the plate with a composition of wax, asphaltum, gum-mastic, resin, etc., dissolved by heat. An outline of the design, made on paper in pencil or red chalk, is then "transferred" to the surface of this composition by being passed through a press. The subject is then drawn on the ground with the etching-point, which cuts through it and exposes the copper. Etching-points or needles resemble large sewing-needles shortened and fixed into handles four or five inches long. Some are made oval, to produce broader lines. A rim of wax being put around the plate, acid is poured on, and corrodes the copper not protected by the ground. If the acid is found not to have acted sufficiently, it may be applied again to the whole design, or only to portions of it, by stopping up, with a mixture of lampblack and Venice turpentine, applied with a camel's-hair pencil, what has been sufficiently *bitten-in*. When a series of parallel lines are wanted, as in backgrounds, etc., an ingenious machine called a ruler is employed, the accuracy of whose operation is exceeding perfect. This is made to act on the etching-ground by a point or diamond connected with the apparatus, and the tracings are bit in with *aqua fortis* in the ordinary way. The art of etching was popularized by Sandro Botticello, who embellished an edition of "Dante" with etching illustrations about the end of the fifteenth century. The great German etchers of that time were Shoengauer, Bechellin and Wohlgemuth, and the Italian representatives were Bacio Baldini, Pollajuoli and Montegna. In the succeeding century Goltzius and others reproduced the works of the old masters, through etching, with wonderful mobility. Toward the latter end of the seventeenth century the art was carried to a high degree of perfection by Le Bas and by the Spanish school. Then, for a time, the art declined, its place being taken by steel-engraving, which in turn gave way to the chromo, and that to the lithograph. The revival of the art in England is largely due to Philip Gilbert Hamerton. At that time Seymour Haden was the leading etcher in England, as was Count de Gravesande in France. Whistler, the eccentric American, is now one of the leading lights in the art in England, and Hamilton Hamilton is probably the most popular etcher in America. Among the greatest of modern etchers are Salonne, Couteau, Waltner, Rajon, De Baines and Koepping.

Ethiopia, Ancient.—Very little is known concerning the people of ancient Ethiopia, their customs and laws; but the inscriptions on temples and tombs in their country strongly resemble those of the Egyptians, and it is probable that the manners, religion, etc., of the two nations had many points of agreement. The country is supposed to have contained great wealth, as within its limits have been discovered the ruins of large cities and architectural monuments which are not surpassed by those of Upper Egypt. Ancient Ethiopia included modern Nubia, Sennaar and Abyssinia, together with as much of the country west of the White

Nile as was then habitable and inhabited. The Abyssinians are believed to be descendants of the ancient race of Ethiopians.

European Cathedrals.—Among the most noted and magnificent cathedrals in Europe are St. Peters, in Rome; the Cathedral of Cologne, and that of Milan; St. Mark's, in Venice; Westminster and Saulsbury, in England; Rouen and Notre Dame, in France; Seville and Strasburg, in Spain and Germany respectively. St. Paul's, in London, though architecturally much inferior to the others, is yet so noted as to deserve a brief description. It is built in the form of a cross, 514 feet long and 287 feet wide. The cost of the whole building, which is of Portland stone, was nearly $4,-000,000, being the proceeds of a tax on the coal brought into the port of London during its erection. The edifice was built under the direction of Sir Christopher Wren, was thirty-five years in course of erection, and was commenced and finished under the same bishop, the same architect and the same mason. The great bell of this cathedral is only tolled on the occasion of a death in the royal family. St. Peter's, at Rome, was commenced about the year 1503 by Julius II under the direction of Bramanti, but the present form of the basilica is due almost entirely to Michael Angelo. The interior is 613 feet in length, the height of the nave 152 1-2 feet; the length of the transepts is 446 1-2 feet; the interior diameter of the dome is 139 feet, the exterior 195 1-2. The colonnades around the piazza inclose a space 787 feet in diameter, and are connected with the facade by two galleries 296 feet in length. The facade is 379 feet long and 148 1-2 high, and contains five doors, which admit to the grand entrance, which occupies the whole width of the church, 468 feet long, 66 high and 50 wide. The heighth from the pavement to the top of the cross is 476 feet. The Cologne cathedral is one of the noblest specimens of Gothic architecture in Europe. It is said to have had its origin in an erection by Archbishop Hildebold, during the reign of Charlemagne, in 814. Frederic the Red-bearded bestowed upon it, in 1162, the bones of the three holy kings, which he took from Milan, and this gift contributed greatly to the increase of its importance. The bones are retained as precious relics to this day, but the old structure was burned in 1248. According to some accounts the present cathedral was begun in the same year, but others fix the date of its commencement in 1270–'75. To whom the design of this noble building is to be ascribed is uncertain. The work was carried on, sometimes more actively, sometimes more slowly, till the era of the Reformation, when it was suspended; and during the subsequent centuries not only was nothing done to advance it, but what had been already executed was not kept in repair. In the beginning of the present century, however, attention was directed to its unrivaled beauties, and the necessary funds to repair and complete it according to the original designs were raised. The body of the church measures 500 feet in length and 230 feet in breadth; the towers are above 500 feet high. Since 1823 $4,500,000 have been expended on the building; the total cost of the whole is estimated at $10,000,000. The cathedral at Milan is also of Gothic architecture, but the facade is marred by classic doors and windows, and the altars within are in the same style. The edifice is nearly 500 feet long and 250 feet wide through the transepts, and the height of the nave is about 150 feet. The central spire is more than 350 feet high. The throng of statues (some 4,500 in all) and the many pinnacles are marked features of the exterior. [See *St. Sopia* for a description of the famous church of that name in Constantinople.]

European Railways.—The railways in most European countries are partially under the control of the Government. In Great Britain they are managed by private corporations, subject, however, to inspection at stated intervals by an officer appointed by the Government. In Switzerland they are entirely in the hands of private companies, except one which is owned by the canton of Berne. Those in Spain and Portugal have all, or nearly all, been built by private companies, aided by the Government. In France the railroad system is largely under the control of six great companies. In Austria-Hungary, Belgium, Denmark, Germany, Italy, Holland, Russia, Sweden, Norway and other countries of lesser importance, the whole or a portion of their railway system is under the control of the Government.

Evolution Theory, The.—Ancient writers occasionally seemed to have a glimmering knowledge of the fact of progress in nature, but as a theory " evolution " belongs to the enlightenment of the nineteenth century. In the latter part of the seventeenth century Leibnitz expressed the opinion that the earth was once in a fluid condition, and about the middle of the eighteenth century Kant definitely propounded the nebular hypothesis, which was enlarged as a theory by the Herschels. About 1750 the transmutation of species among animals was suggested by Buffon, and other writers followed out the idea. The eccentric Lord Monboddo was the first to suggest the possible descent of man from the ape, about 1774. The evolution theory declares the universe as it now exists to be the result of a long series of changes, which were so far related to each other as to form a series of growths analogous to the evolving parts of a growing organism. Herbert Spencer defines evolution as a progress from the homogeneous to the heterogeneous; from general to special; from the simple to the complex elements of life; and it is believed that this process can be traced in the formation of worlds in space, in the multiplication of types and species among animals and plants, in the origin and changes of language and literature and the arts, and also in all the changes of human institutions and society. Asserting the general fact of progress in nature, the evolution theory shows that the method of this progress has been (1) by the multiplications of organs and functions; (2) according to a definite unity of plan, although with (3) the intervention of transitional forms, and (4) with modifications dependent upon surrounding conditions. The two great apostles of the evolution theory were Charles Darwin and Herbert Spencer. The latter began his first great work, the "First Principles of Philosophy," showing the application of evolution in the facts of life, in 1852. In 1859 appeared Darwin's "Origin of Species." The hypothesis of the latter was that different species originated in spontaneous variation, and the survival of the fittest through natural selection and the struggle for existence. This theory was further elaborated and applied by Spencer, Darwin, Huxley, and other writers in Europe and America; and though, to-day, by no means all the ideas upheld by these early advocates of the theory are still accepted, still evolution as a principle is now acknowledged by nearly all scientists. It is taken to be an established fact in nature—a valid induction from man's knowledge of natural order.

Exchequer, Court of, is an ancient Court of Record in England, instituted by William the Conqueror as a branch of the *Aula Regia*, or great council of the nation. A separate and independent jurisdiction was given to it by Edward I, the special functions thus assigned being to order the revenues of the Crown, and to recover the King's debts and duties. The court was then denominated the *Scaccarium*, Exchequer—a word derived from *scaccus*, or *scaccum*, a chess-board; and it was so called from the checked cloth laid upon the table in the Exchequer chamber, and upon which, when certain of the King's accounts were made up, the sums were marked and scored with counters. The judges of the Exchequer consisted originally of the Lord Treasurer, the Chancellor of the Exchequer, and the puisne judges. These last were called Barons of the Exchequer. This court is now merged in the High Court of Justice. The office of Chancellor of the Exchequer in modern times is, strictly speaking, that of under-treasurer, the office of Lord High Treasurer being now vested in the Lords Commissioners of the Treasury.

Expeditions, Arctic, American.—The first American expedition to the Arctic regions was made in 1850, when the ships Advance and Rescue started in search of the lost explorer Sir John Franklin and his party. In October of the following year, after an absence of nineteen months, they returned, having discovered only supposed traces of the objects of their search, and leaving in entire uncertainty their actual fate. The second American expedition, having for its object the same humane purpose, was due in a great measure to Dr. Kane, and was made under the auspices of the Navy Department, the Smithsonian Institute, the Geographical Society of New York, the American Philosophical Society and other scientific associations. The ship Advance left New York May 30, 1853, on her second expedition, and two winters were spent in the Arctic regions by this party, who reached latitude 80 degrees 56 minutes north; but their efforts were entirely fruitless so far as ascertaining any information regarding the fate of Franklin. In 1855 the Vincennes, Commander John Rodgers, reached latitude 72 degrees 5 minutes north. In 1860 the George Henry, Commander Charles F. Hall, reached Frobisher Bay, latitude 62 degrees north; and in the same year a party from the ship United States, Commander I. I. Hayes, reached by sledge latitude 81 degrees 35 minutes north. During 1864-'69 the Monticello, Commander Charles F. Hall, reached King William's Land; and in 1871 the Polaris, under the same commander, reached latitude 82 degrees 16 minutes north. The next expedition of particular importance was that of the Jeannette, Commander Lieutenant De Long, 1879-'81. This unfortunate vessel was crushed June 13, 1881, in latitude 77 degrees 14 minutes 57 seconds north. In 1880 the Corwin, Commander Captain C. L. Hooper, who had sailed for the relief of the Jeannette, reached Wrangell Land; and in the same year the Rodgers, Commander Lieutenant R. M. Berry, reached latitude 73 degrees 28 minutes north. The Greely expedition of 1881 reached the highest latitude yet attained—83 degrees 24 1-2 minutes north; and the island there found was named Lockwood Island, in honor of Lieutenant Lockwood, who was in charge of the exploring party.

Fabian Policy.—The policy of wearing out the enemy in war by delays, misleading movements, feints of attack, etc., while avoiding open battle, is called the " Fabian policy " from the following circumstance: Fabius Maximus was a Roman General in the second Punic War. Having been appointed just after the Roman army had suffered severe defeat at Lake Thrasymene, he perceived that his disheartened troops and bands of raw recruits could not oppose successfully a trained army flushed with victory and led by their great commander, Hannibal. He therefore avoided pitched battles, moved his camp from highland to highland, and tired out the enemy with marches and counter-marches. This he continued until thwarted in his calculations by the impatience of the Roman Senate.

Fakir is a member of an order of mendicants and penitents in India and the neighboring countries. The word is also used for Moslem priests and dervishes in Persia and Turkey. Originally the fakirs were not only pious men, but occasionally saints, workers of miracles, and healers of all ills; but the ready worship accorded them by the people attracted to their ranks, at a very early date, many whose motives were anything but pure, and who, under a garb of humility and mendicity, collected fabulous treasures. The present number of fakirs is said to exceed 3,000,000. They live either separately, as hermits or solitary mendicants, or unite in large gangs, carrying arms and a banner, beating drums and sounding horns as they approach a town or village. Their appearance is disgusting in the extreme. They are said to go naked, besmeared with the dung of the holy animal, the cow. Some bedeck themselves with the skins of serpents, some with human bones; others array themselves in the garb of women.

Their fearful shrieks and the hideous rollings of their eyes add to the disgust of their appearance. The height to which self-torture is frequently carried by these wretched fanatics, and of which we meet with signs even so far back as the Ramayana, where a penitent is described as perpetually sitting with upraised arms between four fires, the sun forming the fifth, is so appalling that human nature shrinks from the mere description. The origin of fakirism is lost in mythical darkness. The word fakir is derived from the Arabic *fakhar*, poor.

Falconry is of very ancient origin, and has been traced back, as an Eastern sport, to a period anterior to the Christian era. In Britain it seems to have been followed before the time of the heptarchy; and in the celebrated Bayeux Tapestry, Harold is figured with a hawk upon his hand. It seems, however, to have been practiced in eastern countries and central Europe long before it became established in Great Britain. But after the Norman Conquest it took rapid strides in that country, being much indulged in by kings, nobles and ladies; and in those days the rank of an individual was indicated by the particular species of hawk carried upon his wrist. Thus, an earl carried a peregrine falcon. The sport declined somewhat in the seventeenth century but revived in the eighteenth century; but with the introduction of fowling-pieces and the art of shooting on the wing it went entirely out of fashion in England. The hawks were trained to mount and pursue game and bring it to their masters or mistresses, coming and going at the call of the latter with marvelous docility. They were tricked out with gay hoods, and held, until ordered to pursue the "quarry" or game, by leathern straps fastened with rings of leather around each leg, just above the talons, and silken cords called "jesses." To each of these leather straps, or "bewets," was attached a small bell, shaped in most cases like the nearly-closed sleigh-bells of the present day. In India, Persia and other eastern countries falconry is still practiced, the methods there followed being, for the most part, nearly similar to those of Great Britain.

Fastest Locomotive.—The largest and fastest passenger-locomotive ever built is the one lately constructed by the Rhode Island Locomotive Works for the New York, Providence and Boston Railroad Company. The main driving-wheels are six feet in diameter and set but seven feet six inches apart. This arrangement makes the engine run easily on curves. The cylinders are eighteen inches in diameter, with twenty-four-inch stroke. The boiler is fifty-four inches in diameter at the smoke-stack, with a wagon top. It extends to the very end of the cab, and necessitates the elevation of the engineer's seat to a height far above the fire-door. The fire requires three tons of coal before the engine pulls out of the round-house to make her trips, and four tons are carried on the tender. The tank of the latter will hold 4,000 gallons of water, and the total weight of the engine proper is

93,000 to 95,000 pounds. The weight on the driving-wheels is 66,000 pounds. The engine looks to be enormously high, as it sets well up in the air, and the short smoke-stack adds to the apparent height. Everything about her is steel. There is not a particle of brass or bright work. She makes the run from Providence to Groton, Conn., a distance of 62.5 miles, including a dead stop at Mystic draw-bridge, as required by the statute of Connecticut, in just 62.5 minutes, pulling at the same time eight cars, four of which are Pullmans.

Fates, The.—In Grecian mythology the Parcæ or Fates were three women, the daughters of Night, who had control over the universe and particularly over human destinies, presided over all great events in the lives of men, and executed the decrees of Nature. Or, to speak more properly, they personified the decrees of Nature; for, according to the poets, even the "immortal gods," and the "cloud-compelling, mighty Jove" himself, were unable to disobey or set aside a decree of the Fates—Clotho, the spinner of the thread of life; Lachesis, who determines the lot of life; and Atropos, who presides over death. They were usually represented as young women of serious aspect—Clotho with a spindle, Lachesis pointing with a staff to the horoscope of man on a globe, Atropos with a pair of scales, or sun-dial, or an instrument to cut the thread of life. In the oldest representations of them, however, they appear as matrons, with staffs or scepters. Places were consecrated to them throughout all Greece, at Corinth, Sparta, Thebes, Olympia, etc.

Feast of Asses was a ceremonial of the Roman Catholic Church during the middle ages which was peculiar to Rouen and a few other French cities. The event which it commemorated was the flight of the Virgin and her child into Egypt. A young woman bearing an infant was seated upon an ass. Behind her marched the bishops and clergy in solemn procession to the cathedral, where services were held in honor of the beast that had aided in that perilous flight "in the reign of King Herod." This performance occurred at about Christmas-time at Rouen; in other cities it was in June. Finally it came to be so offensive to the better classes in the Church that it was entirely suppressed by the Council of Basle in the fifteenth century.

Feast of Fools.—This grotesque masquerade survived the pagan creed which gave it birth, and not only kept its place among the Christians, but, in the face of solemn anathemas of fathers and councils, found its way into the ceremonials of the Christian Church. It was called at different times and places by many different names, but has latterly come to be best known as the Feast of Fools. The circumstances of the observance were almost infinitely varied, but it was everywhere marked by the same spirit of broad, boisterous drollery, and coarse but not ill-natured caricature. The donkey played a frequent part in the pageant. [See *Feast of Asses*.] In every instance there was more or less attempt at dramatic representation, the theater being generally the chief church of the place, and the words and actions of the drama being ordered by the Book of Ceremonies. The chief point of the farce, when an ass was not brought on the stage, lay in the selection of a mock pope, patriarch, cardinal, archbishop, bishop or abbot. These mimic dignitaries took such titles as "Pope of Fools," "Archbishop of Dolts," "Cardinal of Numskulls," "Boy Bishop," "Patriarch of Sots," "Abbot of Unreason," and the like. On the day of their election they often took possession of the churches, and even occasionally travestied the performance of the church's highest office, the mass, in the church's holiest place, the altar. In some convents the nuns disguised themselves in men's clothes, chanted mock services, and elected a "little abbess," who for that day took the place of the real abbess. The Feast of Fools maintained itself in many places till the Reformation, in the sixteenth century. At Antibes, in the south of France, it survived till the year 1644, when it was described by an eyewitness in a letter to the philosopher Gassendi. The scene was, as usual, a church; and the actors, dressing themselves in priests' robes turned inside out, read prayers from books turned upside down, through spectacles of orange-peel, using coal or flour for incense, amid a babbling of confused cries, and the mimic bellowings of cattle and grunting of pigs.

February was so called from the circumstance that during this month occurred the Roman festival called the Lupercalia, and Februalia, from *februare*, to purify. It had originally twenty-nine days in an ordinary year; but when the Roman Senate decreed that the eighth month should bear the name of Augustus, a day was taken from February and given to August, which had then only thirty, so that it might not be inferior to July.

Felucca is a small vessel, propelled by from ten to sixteen oars and a lateen sail, which is used in the Mediterranean. From their speed in smooth water they have at different times been armed with one or two heavy guns and operated as gunboats against the becalmed vessels of an enemy.

Female Pope.—It is related that a female named Joan (others say Gilberta or Agnes), of English descent, but born in Ingelheim or Mainz, Germany, fell in love with a young Benedictine monk named Felda, and in order to be admitted into the monastery of Fulda, where he was cloistered, assumed male attire. She afterward went with him to Athens, where he died while they were pursuing their studies. Soon after this she went to Rome, where her great learning brought her into distinction, and from a successful career as a professor she was elected by general consent of the College of Cardinals to be the successor of Pope Leo IV, who died A. D. 885. Others say she was the immediate successor of Pope Adrian II, who died A. D. 872. Her title was Pope John VIII—a title which, in the Roman *Notizie*, or official calendar of the Roman Pontiffs, is ascribed to a different person. It is further related of this "female Pope," that she administered the pontifical office with great ability until her sex was discovered by her giving birth to a child during the excitement and fatigue of a procession to the Lateran Palace, which was quickly followed by her death—some say from puerperal fever, while other narratives declare that she was stoned to death. It is generally believed that the pontificate of Joan was a mediæval fiction.

Fiasco is a term borrowed from the Italian theater. Originally it signified a failure to please on the part of an actor or singer, and is thus the opposite of *furore*—although why the word, which simply means a bottle, should come to be thus applied is more than anybody knows. The usual meaning of the word as used now is *fizzle*, or the failure of any pretentious undertaking.

Field of the Cloth of Gold was so called from the extravagance and display attendant upon a meeting of Henry VIII of England and Francis I of France in June, 1530. The Kings met in the field near the small town of Ardres, in France, which was owned by England, and the meeting was held by the request of Francis I, who desired to gain the friendship of Henry to aid him in his projects for curbing the power of his great rival Charles V, of Germany. The ceremonial was under the direction of Cardinal Wolsey, and the nobility of France and England vied with each other in the gorgeous decoration of themselves, their banners and tents, and their retinues of followers.

Fifth-Monarchy Men is an English political-religious society which sprung into existence in 1654. In politics they were republicans of the extremest section, and in 1657 were detected in a conspiracy to murder Cromwell and revolutionize the government. They believed in the four great monarchies of anti-Christ marked out by the prophet Daniel, and they added to them a *fifth*, viz., the kingdom of Christ on earth. They believed in the immediate, or at least in the proximate, advent of Christ, and they held that the fulfillment of God's promise to this effect must be realized by the forcible destruction of the kingdom of anti-Christ. Every obstacle which opposed itself to the setting up of the Messiah's throne was to be thrown down, and what those obstacles were was a question for the solution of which the only criterion which presented itself was their own fanatical prejudices and hatreds. They became extinct as a society shortly after the Restoration.

Filibuster.—This name was originally given to a small vessel used by the buccaneers of the West Indies in their depredations on Spanish commerce. The term was first used in the United States to designate certain expeditions made by adventurers, after the close of the Mexican war, against the Spanish-American colonies to the south of the United States, the most notorious of which was that under William Walker against Nicaragua. The term is now used in legislative assemblies to designate various trivial measures that are resorted to by one party to weary the other in order to defeat a measure or gain time.

Fingal's Cave is a wonderful grotto on the southwest coast of the Island of Staffa, about seven miles off the west coast of Mull, Scotland. It is 212 feet deep, 33 feet wide at the entrance, and 22 feet wide at its inner end. At the opening it is 60 feet high, and the walls meet in a beautiful arch above basaltic pillars which flank it on both sides. The floor of the cave is the sea, and at low tide the water is 20 feet deep. There are many stalactites of various beautiful tints between the pillars of dark-gray basalt. The cave can be readily entered by small boats excepting at extreme high tide. It probably takes its name from Fingal, the legendary hero of Gaelic poetry.

Fire-Losses.—The losses by fire in the United States during the past five years have averaged $110,000,000 annually (an amount equal to double the annual interest charged on the national debt). The principal reported causes of fires, and the numbers of fires from each cause, in 1887, were as follows: Incendiarism, 1,927; defective flues, 1,309; sparks (not locomotive), 715; matches, 636; explosions of lamps and lanterns, 430; stoves, 429; lightning, 369; spontaneous combustion, 326; forest and prairie fires, 280; lamp and lantern accidents, 238; locomotive sparks, 211; cigar-stubs and tobacco-pipes, 203; friction, 179; gas-jets, 176; engines and boilers, 150; furnaces, 135; fire-crackers, 105. There were 4,356 fires classified as "not reported," and 2,672 as "unknown."

First College in the United States.—About six years after the first settlement, by the English, of Boston and the surrounding country an entry was made on the Colony's records, under date of October 28, 1636, that "The Court agreed to give 400*l.* towards a schoale or colledge, whearof 200*l.* to bee paid the next yeare, and 200*l.* when the work is finished, and the next Court to appoint wheare, and what building." The following year the Court ordered that the college should be at "Newetowne," and the Governor and Deputy-Governor, with ten others, including the principal laymen and ministers of the Colony, among whom were John Cotton and John Winthrop, were designated to have charge of the undertaking. This was the origin of Harvard College, the oldest college in the United States. In 1638 the Rev. John Harvard bequeathed his library to the college and £700 in money; and the school—for previous to that time it had been nothing more than a school—was called Harvard College, and the name of the town was changed from Newtown to Cambridge, in honor of the university town in England of that name, and in the same year a class began a course of college studies there under the instruction of Nathaniel Eaton. The first graduating class, in 1642, consisted of nine members. Considering that, owing to the feeble condition of the Colony's resources, it is more than doubtful whether more than a small part of the grant of £400 was ever paid, the real founder of the college must unquestionably be looked upon as the Rev. John Harvard.

First Oil Well.—In 1853 the use of petroleum for lighting and lubricating purposes was suggested by a Doctor Brewer of Titusville, Pa., and in the following year, 1854, the first oil company was formed, and the first well was sunk by Messrs. Drake and Bowditch of that company, which produced from 400 to 1,000 gallons of oil per day. The "boom" thus given caused thousands to flock to the oil regions of Pennsylvania, and the industry rapidly grew to its present vast proportions.

First Railroads.—The first railroad ever built for general traffic was the Stockton and Darlington in England, which was thirty-five miles long, constructed in 1825 by Edward Pease and George Stephenson. In the same year a railroad was projected in America by Gridley Bryant, but it was not constructed until the following year, when Bryant secured the assistance of Col. T. H. Perkins in the enterprise. This road was four miles long, and was used for carrying granite from the quarries in Quincy, Mass., to the site of the Bunker Hill Monument. In 1827 the Mauch Chunk Railway, a coal road, thirteen miles long, was built, and February 27th of the same year the Maryland Legislature granted a charter to the Baltimore and Ohio road. The first locomotive which proved of practical value was invented by George Stephenson, the celebrated English engineer, and was used on the Stockton and Darlington Railway. In 1829 a railway line was built between Liverpool and Manchester, of which Stephenson was the principal engineer, and for this road he constructed the engine known as the Rocket, which accomplished the till then undreampt-of speed of thirty-five miles an hour. The first locomotive built in America was used on the Baltimore and Ohio Railroad.

First Slaves in America.—Slaves were introduced into the United States in 1619, when a Dutch man-of-war entered James River and landed twenty negroes, who were offered for sale.

Fleet Prison derived its name from the Fleet rivulet, so named from its rapidity, and was situated on the east side of Farrington Street, London. As far back as the twelfth century it was the King's Prison and a receptacle for debtors. It acquired a high historical interest in the sixteenth and seventeenth centuries from its having been the prison of the religious martyrs of the reigns of Mary and Elizabeth, and of the political victims of the Courts of the Star Chamber and High Commission in that of Charles I. It was the scene of every kind of atrocity and brutality during the eighteenth century from the extortion of the keepers and the custom of the warden underletting it. The Fleet was abolished by the Act 5 and 6 Victoria.

Flies Walking on the Ceiling.—For a long time it was supposed that the ability of the fly to walk on the ceiling was owing to each of his feet being a miniature air-pump. This, however, was proved to be fallacious, and then a theory was propounded that it was by means of a viscous substance exuded from the hairs on their feet. Some eight years or so ago this theory was thoroughly investigated by Dr. Rombouts, who demonstrated that it was only partly sound; for, though the hairs with which the foot-cushion is covered do certainly exude an oily liquid, the liquid is not sticky, and does not harden when dry. Dr. Rombouts proved by his experiments that the true theory of the walking of flies on smooth substances is that they hang on by the help of capillary adhesion—the molecular attraction between solid and liquid bodies. By a series of nice calculations, such as weighing hairs and measuring their diameters, and sticking the cut end of hair in oil or water to make it adhere when touched to glass, this scientist proved that capillary attraction would uphold a fly were it four-ninths as heavy again as it is at present. It is true that the foot-hairs are very minute, but as each fly is said to be furnished with 10,000 to 12,000 of these, we need not be surprised at what they can do. Reasoning from this theory, we would conclude that flies find it difficult to mount a glass slightly dampened, because of the repulsion between the watery surface and the oily liquid exuding from the feet; and they are likewise impeded by a slight coating of dust, because the interspaces between the hairs are filled with dust, and observation seems to show this to be the case. When we see a fly making his toilet, he is not, as we might suppose, cleaning his body, but his feet, so that they may the more readily adhere.

Florida, Discovery of.—In 1512 the celebrated Spanish explorer Juan Ponce de Leon, with a company of adventurers, sailed from Porto Rico, of which he was then Governor, in search of a fountain whose waters would restore youth and beauty, which a tradition of the natives asserted was to be found on a distant island. After visiting the Bahamas and seeking for the fabled fountain in vain, he descried, on Easter Sunday, land, which he supposed to be another island. This, from the day of its discovery (Easter-Day being called, in Spanish, *Pascua Florida*), and also because of the luxuriant vegetation and flowers that covered its banks, he called Florida. On April 8, 1512, he landed some miles north of the present site of St. Augustine, and took possession of the country in the name of the Spanish King. Some months were spent by de Leon and his followers in searching for the fountain of youth both in this country and on the Tortugas; but he finally returned, disappointed, to Porto Rico, leaving the search to be continued by one of his followers. In 1513 he was appointed Governor of Florida and in 1521 he took a colony thither; but shortly afterward he was severely wounded in a conflict with the natives and returned to Cuba, where he died.

Florida Shell-Mounds.—The mounds of shells which are found in different portions of Florida are unquestionably of human construction, and were probably built by some race of people who inhabited the country about the beginning of the Christian era. These mounds were found overgrown with herbage and forest as long ago as when the first red man set foot in Florida, and the fact that the deposit of earth above them was sufficient to give place to the roots of trees proved their great age. The shells which these mounds contain have, through the process of time, become wholly deprived of organic matter, and to a certain degree calcined, so that they form a kind of conglomerate, which is used extensively for building. It is called "coquina." The inland mounds contain only the shells of fresh-water mollusks; the coast mounds are composed of oyster-shells. There have been found in all these mounds pieces of pottery imbedded in the shell conglomerate; also articles made of shell and bone, rude stone implements, and many bones of animals, such as deer, terrapin, rabbits, alligators and others, and bones of birds and fishes. They vary in size from circular heaps 15 to 20 feet in diameter, and a few inches high, to ridges several hundred feet in length, and varying in height from a few inches to 15 feet and over. There are in the entire State about 40 mounds, the most important of which are those of King Philip's Town, near the outlet of Lake Harney, which are 450 feet long, from 100 to 150 feet broad, and with an average height of 8 feet; the Black Hammock Mounds, on the St. John River, which form a line, though several times broken, 1,200 feet in length, and 150 to 200 feet broad, and vary in height from 10 feet to 3 or 4 inches; Old Enterprise Mounds, on Lake Monroe, 160 feet long on the water-line, in places 15 feet high; and Horse Landing Mounds, on the St. John River, 300 feet long by 100 feet in their widest part, and about 8 feet high.

Flotsam and Jetsam are terms frequently used to designate miscellaneous articles which have been cast away or are found littered around without an owner. In legal usage, the words "flotsam" and "jetsam" designate the position of wreckage found in the water—the first signifying that the goods were found floating on the water, the second that they were found at the bottom.

Flying Dutchman, The, is the name given by sailors to a phantom ship, supposed to cruise in storms off the Cape of Good Hope. According to tradition, a Dutch captain, bound home from the Indies, met with long-continued head-winds, and heavy weather off this cape, and refused to put back, as he was advised to do, swearing a very profane oath that he would beat round the cape if he had to beat there till the Day of Judgment. He was taken at his word, and doomed to beat against winds all his days. His sails are believed to have become threadbare, and his ship's sides white with age, and himself and crew reduced almost to shadows. He cannot heave to nor lower a boat, but sometimes hails vessels through his trumpet, and requests them to take letters home for him. The superstition has its origin, probably, in the looming or apparent suspension in air of some ships out of sight—a phenomenon sometimes witnessed at sea, and caused by unequal refraction in the lower strata of the atmosphere. [See *Mirage.*]

Fogs, Newfoundland, are caused by the mingling of the Arctic current, with its burden of icefields and icebergs, with the warm waters of the Gulf Stream, thereby generating enormous masses of vapor. When westerly winds prevail, this vapor is carried out to sea; but when the wind is from the south or southeast the fog is rolled in on the shores of the island, covering the bays and headlands. In winter there is but little fog.

Foolscap Paper was so called because, when it was first made, in the thirteenth century, it had a water-mark representing a fool's head ornamented with a cap and bells such as jesters used to wear. The use of this water-mark was discontinued about the beginning of the eighteenth century.

Fools' Gold, the popular name applied to a group of minerals known to mineralogists as pyrites, which resemble gold ore in appearance, and which have often been mistaken for that ore. The name "pyrites" originally belonged to the sulphuret of iron, known as iron pyrites, and was given to it in consequence of its striking fire with steel, so that it was used for kindling powder in the pans of muskets before gun-flints were introduced. It is now much used for the manufacture of sulphuric acid, and sulphur is obtained from it by sublimation. Of the other varieties of pyrites we may mention copper pyrites, from which is obtained a large proportion of the copper used in the world, and nickel pyrites, used as an ore of nickel. The early settlers of Virginia, mistaking pyrites for gold-ore, sent a ship-load of it to England, to the subsequent disgust of the London Company.

Foreign Population, Our.—Previous to the year 1820 the foreign emigration to America was comparatively light, but between that year and the end 1879 there was an influx of 10,138,758 emigrants. During the succeeding five years—1880-'85—this number was still further increased by an influx of 3,432,940 persons. The census of 1880 showed 14,922,744 persons of foreign birth, or having one parent foreign-born. Of these, 6,679,943 were born abroad. Adding to these the emigration of the last eight years, without taking any account of the children born after the arrival of the emigrants, we have in the foreign-born and their children a total of about 19,490,000 individuals; of purely foreign birth, about 11,247,199.

Fortune Bay Outrage, The.—On a Sunday in January, 1878, the crews of some American fishing smacks were attacked in Fortune Bay, Newfoundland, by some fishermen of the island. They compelled the Americans to desist from seining herring, in which they were engaged, and in the struggle the nets and fishing tackle were cut and destroyed. The fishing fleet then sailed for home, and laid the case before the authorities at Washington. They presented a bill for damages, which included not only the cost of their tackle and equipments, but the probable loss sustained by not being able to fish through the entire season, making a total claim of $103,000. This claim was formally presented to the British Government; but Lord Salisbury, then Minister for Foreign Affairs, refused to consider it. He gave his reasons in a communication in November, and these were based on the ground that the Americans were at the time engaged in drawing their seines from the shore, which was an infringement of the treaty-agreement, which forbids American fishermen to trespass on private property. He also pleaded that the Americans were violating a provincial law against fishing on Sunday, and other laws prohibiting seining for herring on the coast between October 20th and April 26th, and requiring that seines shall be drawn immediately after being set. Secretary Evarts, in reply, contended that the rights given to the American fishermen by the treaty could not be limited by statutes of the local Legislature. The final reply from the British Government was not made until April, 1880, shortly before the retirement of the Beaconsfield Ministry. In this the claim was refused on the same plea as above, that the Americans in pulling their seines from inshore were violating treaty stipulations. It was also claimed that the local laws violated were in force when the treaty was concluded, and were part of the conditions under which treaty privileges were accorded. In answer to a further communication from the United States State Department, Lord Granville also insisted on the construction that local laws must be binding on both American and Canadian fishermen.

France, Territory Purchased From.—In 1800 Louisiana was retroceded to France by Spain, and in 1803 it was sold to the United States for $15,000,000 by the former Government. The region comprehended in this purchase included all the country west of the Mississippi River, not occupied by Spain, as far north as the British Territory, and comprised the whole or part of the present States of Arkansas, Iowa, Kansas, Louisiana, Minnesota, Missouri, Nebraska, Oregon, the Indian Territory, Colorado, Montana, Washington, and the Territories of Dakota, Idaho and Wyoming.

Franchise in Great Britain.—Through the efforts of Disraeli, a bill was passed by Parliament in 1867 somewhat extending the franchise law which had been in force since 1832, but yet did not give general satisfaction because of the distinction made between agricultural laborers and workingmen in towns. The clause which brought about this dissatisfaction provided that in towns in England all male householders paying a poor-rate, and all lodgers resident for one year paying not less than £10 a year rent, should be entitled to a vote. This extension of the franchise was unquestionably of great importance, as it gave the voting privilege to a large number of workingmen; but as it *did*, with apparent injustice, discriminate to the detriment of agricultural laborers, a reform was eventually brought about through the efforts of Mr. Gladstone, who in 1884 succeeded in having passed by Parliament a bill which he called the "Household Suffrage Bill," through the provision of which the franchise was extended to agents, stewards, gamekeepers or servants living with those who owned or paid the necessary amount of rental (as provided for in the bill of 1867) for their houses who could claim the name of householders; and this increased franchise was granted in the counties as well as the boroughs, and in Ireland and Scotland, thus making the basis of representation uniform throughout the kingdom. With the exception of the reform noted above, the general franchise law of Great Britain is that of 1867, which states that every man is entitled to vote who is of full age and not subject to any legal incapacity, provided he is on the last day of July in any year, and has during the whole of the preceding twelve months been, an " inhabitant occupier," as owner or tenant, of any dwelling-house within the borough; has during the time of such occupation been rated (or taxed) " as an ordinary occupier in respect of the premises so occupied by him within the borough to all rates made for the relief of the poor in respect of such premises," and has paid the said rate; or has occupied as a lodger in the same borough separately, and as sole tenant for the time above designated, "a part of one and the same dwelling-house, of a clear yearly value, if let unfurnished, of £10 or upward." For representatives of counties any man may be registered as a voter who is of full age, and not subject to any legal incapacity, who shall be in possession at law or in equity of any lands or tenements, of copyhold, or any other tenure whatever, except freehold, for his own lifetime or for the life of another, or for any larger estate of the clear yearly value of not less than £5 over and above all rents and charges, who is on the last day of July of any year (and has been during the preceding twelve months) the occupier as owner or tenant of lands or tenements within the county of the ratable value of £12 and upward, and has paid all pool rates rated to him. The qualifications of city electors do not differ materially from those given above. In Scotland the burgher franchise is given to every man of full age who has been for twelve months an occupier, as owner or tenant, of any dwelling, and has paid his poor-rates, and has not been in receipt of parochial relief during that time. The lodger franchise consists in the permission of any lodger to vote who has occupied in the same burgh separately, and as sole tenant for twelve months, a lodging worth £10. In the counties the ownership franchise requires the property to be worth an annual net rental of £5, and a residential qualification of six months. In Ireland the borough franchise requires a lodging of the value of £4. The other qualifications are similar to those required in England.

Freedman's Bank was established in March, 1865, as a charitable enterprise, to encourage frugality and thrift among the newly-liberated slaves. The institution was started at first in Washington, but afterward branch banks to the number of thirty-four were located in different parts of the Union. The bank was not intended to be a money-making concern, either for bankers or for depositors, but as a place of deposit for the savings of negroes, which savings were to be invested in the stocks, bonds, Treasury-notes and other securities of the United States. During the existence of the bank, nine years, it handled no less than $56,000,-000 of deposits, the negroes being led to believe that the safety of the institution was guaranteed by the Government, which was untrue. The institution was managed by a number of trustees of unsavory financial reputation, and as a consequence, at the expiration of nine years it suspended payment. At the investigation which was made by a committee appointed by Congress a most scandalous condition of affairs was discovered. The regulations of the charter had been completely ignored, and the funds had been dissipated by loans made upon inadequate securities. By law the investments of the bank were confined to Government securities alone. Unimproved real estate, unsalable stocks and personal notes were among the assets of the bank. Deficits and embezzlements at the branch banks also produced many losses. The unsecured debts owed to the depositors amounted to $2,900,-000, and the assets yielded about $1,700,000. For some years three bank commissioners were employed, at a salary of $3,000 each, to wind up the affairs of the institution. After $475,000 had been expended in this "winding-up" process the affairs of the bank were all turned over to the Comptroller of the Currency. Dividends have been paid at various times; but many small depositors, through ignorance and despair, forfeited their dividends by not calling for them. In all, 77,000 dividends, amounting to $112,000, were thus forfeited.

Freedmen's Bureau.—March 3, 1865, Congress passed an act organizing in the War Department the "Bureau of Refugees, Freedmen and Abandoned Lands," which was popularly known as the "Freedmen's Bureau." This remained in operation, with somewhat enlarged powers, until July 1, 1869, when its functions ceased, excepting the educational department, which continued until July 1, 1870, and that for the collection of claims. The bureau exercised a general supervision over the freedmen, as also over loyal refugees, protecting their rights, deciding their disputes, aiding them in obtaining work, extending facilities of education, and furnishing them with medical treatment. It was discontinued about five years after its organization, as the chief object for which it was organized had by that time been accomplished.

French Academy, The, had its origin in a literary coterie which held meetings in Paris during the time of Louis XIV, and its purpose and unity were given to it by Cardinal Richelieu. His object was to have a fixed standard of grammar and rhetoric given to the language, believing that this would tend to the unification and peace of France. The duties which were imposed upon the members of the Academy were "to purify and fix the national tongue, to throw light upon its obscurities, to maintain its character and principles, and at their private meetings to keep this object in view. Their discussions were to turn on grammar, rhetoric and poetry; their critical observations on the beauties and defects of classical French authors, in order to prepare editions of their works, and to compose a new dictionary of the French language." The original Academy was swept away in 1793, and the present Academy preserves but little of its original character of a mere coterie of grammarians. This present Academy came into existence with the restoration of the Bourbons. It meets at the Palace Mazarin, Paris. Its chief officer is its secretary, who has a life-tenure of his position. He receives a salary of 12,000 francs a year, the society being allowed by the Government 85,000 francs a year for the payment of its officers and the care of its library. The Academy is always to consist of forty members, all vacancies being filled by the votes of those already composing the body. To belong to it is regarded as a high honor, the members being spoken of as "the forty immortals."

French Renaissance.—"Renaissance" is the name given to the style of art, especially architecture, in Europe which succeeded the Gothic and preceded the rigid copyism of the classic revival in the first half of the present century. It is also used to denote the time during which this style of art prevailed, and also to include the development of the European races in other lines as well as art. The name signifies the "new birth." The date of the beginning of this period coincides with that of the fall of the Byzantine Empire, and the latter was no doubt the cause of the former; for when the Turks took possession of Constantinople all the memorials, paintings, books, etc., that could be removed from the destroying hand of the invaders were hastily conveyed to Italy. These inspired just admiration among the Italian people, and aroused not only a desire to emulate the construction of such worthy works, but also an interest in ancient works and models. In 1494 Charles VIII, King of France, made a warlike expedition into Italy, and on his return brought some Italian workmen to supervise the construction of the royal buildings. This was the first introduction of the renaissance into France. Communication between France and Italy was also stimulated by this expedition, and the growth of Italian ideas among the French was steady, though slow. In the reign of Louis XII, 1498–1515, the work was further stimulated by the founding of a school of architecture under an artist from Verona. But it was under Francis I, 1515–'47, that the new growth was most stimulated and aided. This prince was possessed both of learning and intellectual power. He had a sincere love for literature, science and art, and a keen appreciation of the beautiful in these departments. He invited a number of Italian artists to his court. Among the most famous of these were Leonardo da Vinci and Benvenuto Cellini. These and others introduced Italian details in their designs, which native architects applied to old forms, with which they were familiar; so that the French renaissance was similar to that of Italy, but different from it in many important respects. All lines of art felt the renaissance spirit; and not merely architecture, painting and sculpture, but also music, poetry and literature were stimulated. The minor plastic and decorative arts, engraving, working in wood and metals, pottery, tapestry, etc., were cultivated with eagerness and skill. The study of the classics also received a new impulse, and this era had, in France, some of the greatest scholars of the times. Historical writers usually consider the renaissance period as one of the most important influences in hastening the growth of individuality and the work of the Reformation, and in ushering in the progress that has marked the modern history of the world. In Germany, Russia, and every country in Europe, the renaissance prevailed in a manner similar to that above described.

Friday, the name of the sixth day of the week, has come down to us from the Saxon, the early form being *Frigi dæg*, or day of Frigga, or Freyja, who are probably the same, although often alluded to in Norse mythology as two distinct goddesses. She was the supreme goddess and wife of Odin. The Romans called the day *dies Veneris*, or day of Venus.

Funded and Floating Debt.—"Funded debt" is government or corporation indebtedness in the form of bonds or other evidences of money stipulated to be paid at stated intervals, and usually bearing interest payable annually or oftener. "Floating debt" is indebtedness, such as unsettled accounts, scrip in the nature of due-bills, etc., not funded. A sinking fund is money set apart out of taxes, earnings or other income, for the redemption of government or corporation bonds or other specific tokens of indebtedness.

Funeral Rites among the most primitive peoples always involved extravagant expressions of grief, as tearing the hair, beating and sometimes cutting the body. Funeral feasts have prevailed from the most barbarous ages down to the present time. These had their origin, no doubt, not simply in a desire to do honor to the dead, but in a belief that the departed spirit also took part in the good cheer. The rude music which usually formed a part of the funeral ceremony among uncivilized races was undoubtedly intended to ward off the evil spirits which were supposed to be in the vicinity of a corpse. Funeral dirges were adopted as an expression of poignant grief. These were an important part of funeral rites among the Greeks. The Egyptians held a tribunal over the dead. Any one was allowed to bring to this tribunal accusations against the corpse, and if it was shown that he had lived an evil life, burial was refused. If no accusation was brought, the relatives ceased lamenting and pronounced encomiums on the dead, enlarging upon his many virtues. The laudations of the dead, to which we may trace the funeral sermons of the present day, probably originated with the Jews. The

Greeks had funeral orations in which they gave a full history, not only of the deceased, but of all his ancestors. The funeral customs of the early Christians were partly adopted from the Romans, and modified so as to express the belief in a resurrection. They adopted the custom of vigils also, in which the survivors were expected to ponder upon the shortness and uncertainty of life and "the narrow house appointed for all living." A service also took place at the grave, the object of which was originally to declare the belief of the survivors in the future rising of the body.

Fur Trade, American.—The Northwest Fur Company, a British organization, practically controlled the fur industry along the great lakes and westward at the beginning of this century. A rival company, composed of American and French, and called the Mackinaw Fur Company, was formed about that time; but the importance of the American fur trade is undoubtedly due to the commercial genius of John Jacob Astor. In 1783 Mr. Astor landed in America with a few hundred dollars' worth of musical instruments, which he immediately exchanged for furs. This action was brought about through a conversation with a furrier during the voyage, who impressed upon the young emigrant the great profit to be gained in the fur traffic. From that time until 1809 he made repeated visits to the scattered settlements of western New York and Canada for the purchase of furs, and did much business with the Northwest Fur Company. All direct trade between the United States and Canada was then forbidden by laws of the British Government; hence furs purchased in the latter had first to be taken to London before they could be brought to New York. These restrictions on trade with Canada were removed by treaty in 1794. In 1809 the American Fur Company, an organization with $1,000,000 capital, was granted a charter by the New York Legislature, and it was generally understood that the capital for this enterprise was furnished by Mr. Astor—in fact that he was the company. In 1811 Mr. Astor, in connection with certain parties formerly connected with the Northwest Fur Company, purchased the Mackinaw Fur Company and merged it, with the American Fur Company, in another organization known as the Southwest Fur Company. Four years later, 1815, Mr. Astor bought all the shares of this company and pushed the American Fur Company to the front again, and in the same year succeeded in having a bill passed through Congress excluding all foreigners from taking any part in the fur trade of the United States—thus securing at one stroke a monopoly of the business. From that time he accumulated enormous wealth.

Fustian, a cotton fabric having a pile like velvet, but shorter, and which is manufactured in nearly the same manner as velvet, viz., by leaving loops standing upon the face of the fabric, and then cutting them through so as to form upright threads, which are afterward smoothed by shearing, singeing and brushing.

Moleskin and corduroy, velveteen, velveret, and other stout cotton cloths for men's apparel, are varieties of fustian—a class of goods largely manufactured in Lancashire, England.

Galleon.—The Galleon was originally a war ship of three or four gun-decks. The name was subsequently applied to the Spanish treasure-ships which brought from the Spanish possessions in Mexico and South America gold, silver and other wealth to Spain. They were large, unwieldy vessels, and were eagerly sought after as prizes during times of war on account of the immense wealth which they carried.

Galley-Slaves.—During the sixteenth and seventeenth centuries the galleys of France, Spain and the Italian republics were used as the means of punishment for all criminals, even those who had committed capital crimes. Heretics were particularly sought out for this purpose. Galley-slaves were subjected to the greatest indignities and cruelties. Their heads and faces were shaved, they were always chained to their benches, and they rowed entirely naked, being only allowed to wear clothing when in port. They were seldom released, even when their time of service was accomplished. Henry IV ordered the captains of all galleys to retain prisoners for six years, even although condemned for a shorter time, and under Louis XIV galley-slaves sentenced for only two or three years were often retained for fifteen years and more. In the most ancient times, to row in the galleys was considered honorable; but as the work was very laborious, and it was difficult to procure voluntary recruits for it, prisoners of war were put to this service. Then it became customary to condemn criminals to the work. The galley was a long, low, narrow vessel of war, having sails, but chiefly propelled by rows of oars on each side. It drew but little water, and was especially convenient for coast service. They were abolished in France in 1748, having been gradually going out of use in that and other countries for a number of years.

Galvanized Iron is merely ordinary iron which has been dipped in molten zinc and retains a surface-coating of the zinc when removed. It has come to be of great importance and usefulness, as by this simple process any article may be made to combine the strength and cheapness of iron, and yet be entirely free from rust, as the zinc is unaffected by air or water, oxidizing only at a high temperature.

Gambrinus.—According to one fable, Gambrinus was a poor fiddler, who sold his soul to the Devil on the promise of unlimited wealth. Satan taught him to make chiming-bells and lager-beer. The Emperor of Rome, on the first trial of the beverage, made its inventor Duke of Brabant and Count of Flanders. According to contract, Gambrinus was to enjoy his great wealth for thirty years. At the end of that time Satan sent a messenger for him, but he made the messenger drunk and so escaped, and lived on comfortably for a couple of centuries more. The Gambrinus of

German folk-lore flourished at some remote period, and was the first to brew beer. A tradition of mediæval times made him one of the very ancient German kings—the seventh in descent from Noah—who flourished about 1730 B. C. Gambrinus, as the inventor of beer, also figures in the legends of Denmark. Jean Primus (John the First), Duke of Brabant, who was born in 1251 and died in 1294, was a generous patron of the arts, and was made an honorary member of the guild of brewers in Brussels. In their place of meeting they had his portrait suspended, showing him in his official robes bearing a tankard of beer in his hand. In course of time the memory of the liberal duke perished, and later generations regarded his portrait to represent a mythical inventor of beer, and the name Gambrinus is probably a corruption of the name of the duke, Jean Primus.

Garter, Order of the, was founded in 1344, some writers say 1350, by Edward III. The original number of knights was twenty-five, his majesty himself making the twenty-sixth. It was founded in honor of the Holy Trinity, the Virgin Mary, St. Edward the Confessor, and St. George. The last, who had become the tutelary saint of England, was considered its special patron, and for this reason it has always borne the title of "The Order of St. George," as well as that of "The Garter." The emblem of the order is a dark-blue ribbon edged with gold, bearing the motto *Honi soit qui mal y pense* in golden letters, with a buckle and pendant of gold richly chased. It is worn on the left leg below the knee. Regarding the adoption of this emblem and motto, the story is that the Countess of Salisbury let fall her garter when dancing with the King, and that he picked it up and tied it round his own leg, but that, observing the jealous glances of the Queen, he restored it to its fair owner with the exclamation *Honi soit qui mal y pense.* The Order of the Garter, though not the most ancient, is one of the most famous military orders of Europe. It is said to have been devised for the purpose of attracting to the King's party such soldiers of fortune as might be likely to aid in asserting the claim which he was then making to the crown of France, and intended as an imitation of King Arthur's Round Table. The officers of the order are the Prelate, the Chancellor, the Register, the Garter King of Arms, and the Usher of the Black Rod.

Gasoline is simply air which has been impregnated with very volatile hydro-carbons. Previous to 1836 it was made by passing air over benzol made from coal-tar, but between that year and 1858 numerous machines were patented for its manufacture. The cost of benzol was at first a great obstacle in the manufacture of gasoline, but the discovery of petroleum rendered it possible to make air-gas at 25 cents per gallon, the former price, when benzol was used, having been $1.50. The machines used for making this gas include a "generator," a large vessel more or less complicated in construction, in which a quantity of liquid petroleum or naphtha is exposed in shallow trays for evaporation. **A current of air** is introduced which mingles with the distilled vapor and forms air-gas. This is a dangerous substance, as it bursts into flame with a sharp explosion upon contact with fire. If the generator, however, is placed at some distance from the point where the gasoline is to be used, conveying it thither in air-tight pipes, the danger is removed. Gasoline is extensively used for the lighting of hotels, factories and private residences in small towns or rural districts.

Gate of Tears.—The straits of Babelmandeb, the passage from the Persian Gulf into the Red Sea, are called by the Arabs the "Gate of Tears." These straits are very dangerous in rough weather. The channel is very rocky, and is only about twenty miles wide. It received its melancholy name from the number of shipwrecks that occurred there.

Geodes are rounded, hollow stones, either empty or having the cavity filled with crystallized matter, or sometimes with water and silex or sand. They are most commonly found filled with quartz crystals, perfect in form, and all pointing toward the center. Geodes with crystals of amethyst, agate, chalcedony, garnet and other valuable stones are also occasionally found. The word "geode" means earth-form; and they are supposed to have been formed by the consolidation of the fused rock about a few drops of water holding silex in solution. In the lapse of time, through the influence of extreme heat or cold, or both, the silex has become crystallized in beautiful forms within its prison. Geodes are found in the river-beds, and also imbedded in quartz and other crystalline rocks. In the latter case the nodules are of various shapes, but when found on the banks or in the beds of rivers they are usually smooth, round stones, having been worn to this shape and condition by erosion. They are sometimes known by the name of "potato-stones."

Geological Divisions of Time.—The divisions of time established by geologists are based upon the formations of rock strata and the advents of different forms of life. The grand divisions are five in number, and are named Archæan or Eozoic era; Paleozoic era; Mesozoic era; Cenozoic era, and Psychozoic era. There are seven "Ages" belonging to the eras respectively, as follows: Archæan age, subdivided into Huronian and Laurentian periods; Silurian age, or age of invertebrates or mollusks; Devonian age, or age of fishes; and Carboniferous age, or age of acrozens and amphibians; Age of Reptiles, subdivided into the Triassic, Jurassic and Cretaceous periods; Age of Mammals, subdivided into Tertiary period, embracing the Eocene, Miocene and Pliocene epochs; and Quarternary period, embracing the Terrace, Champlain and Glacial epochs; Age of Man, Human period and Recent epoch. The names of the eras are all derived from the Greek, and signify —Eozoic, life of the dawn; Paleozoic, ancient life; Mesozoic, middle life; Cenozoic, recent life; and Psychozoic, life of the soul and mind.

German Chancellor.—The office of Chancellor, in Germany, is one of great responsibility and power. The incumbent is, by virtue of his office, President of the Bundesrath or Federal Council. He is also the head of the administration for the Empire; and the chancery office, the foreign office, the post and telegraph office are under his absolute authority, unless interfered with by the Emperor. Being the leader of the dominant party, he has much influence in the legislative assembly. All measures which have passed both houses, the Bundesrath and the Reichstag, must be countersigned and promulgated by him to become laws, after they have been signed by the Emperor. The functions of a cabinet are performed by the Federal Council, and it acts, under the direction of the Chancellor, as a supreme administrative and advisory board. The Chancellor is appointed by the Emperor, and holds office during his pleasure.

German Philosophers.—Leibnitz, the founder of modern German philosophy, was a marvelous specimen of precocious genius, his first philosophical treatise being written at the age of seventeen. His system of philosophy supposed the mind and body to be two distinct machines, acting independently of but in harmony with each other. He also held to the theory of "monads"—that is, the indestructible entities of matter and of mind—claiming the Deity to be the prime monad, and asserted that all ideas were innate. He lived from 1646 to 1716. The great opponent of Leibnitz was Christian Wolf, who founded all his philosophy on logical propositions, and set aside those very doctrines on which Leibnitz grounded all his reasoning. After these two philosophers had passed away there was a term of quiescence in German philosophy, broken by the teachings of Emanuel Kant, the philosopher of "Pure Reason," and the father of modern philosophical criticism. The central point of his system lies in the proposition that before we can know anything concerning objects we must understand how we perceive objects, and what degree of knowledge perception can give us. Fichte was a disciple of Kant, but went beyond his master in transforming all knowledge into pure idealism. Schelling was the next writer to gain a general influence. He was at first simply an expounder of Fichte, but gradually developed a philosophy of his own, founded on the theory that the true sources of knowledge are not experience or reflection, but intellectual intuition. Hegel, who succeeded Schelling as the leader in German philosophy, was a more vigorous and logical thinker. The foundation of his system is that the union of assertion and negation, the harmonizing of every proposition with its contradictory, is the source of all knowledge. The Hegelian system has been modified largely by the speculations of Schleiermacher, Schubert and others, but it still remains the most powerful school of German philosophy. The principal opposing system is that of Schopenhauer, whose fundamental doctrine is that the only essential reality in the universe is *will*, all phenomena being but manifestations of the single original will.

Gesta Romanorum, as the oldest legendary work of the middle ages is called, is a collection of short stories, written in Latin, with which the monks were wont to beguile their leisure hours, and which were appointed to be read in the refectory. Their attractiveness lies in the charm of their naivete and childlike simplicity, although their artless piety often passes into a deep mysticism. The *Gesta Romanorum* was one of the most widely-read books among the learned down to the sixteenth century, and it was translated into French, English, German and Dutch. For a long period the authorship of the book was credited to Petrus Berchorius, or Bercheur of Poitou, who died Prior of the Benedictine Abbey of St. Eloi, in Paris, in 1362; but it is now believed that the principal author of the work was a monk named Elinandus.

Giant's Causeway.—The name Giant's Causeway is often applied to the entire range of cliffs in the County Antrim, on the northeast coast of Ireland, but it properly belongs to only a small portion of them, which is a platform of basalt in closely-arranged columns, from fifteen to thirty-six feet high, which extend from a steep cliff down into the sea till it is lost below low-water mark. This platform is divided across its breadth into three portions, the Little, Middle and Grand Causeway, these being separated from each other by dikes of basalt. The columns are generally hexagonal prisms, but they are also found of five, seven, eight and nine sides, in almost every instance being fitted together with the utmost precision, even so that water cannot penetrate between adjoining columns. The name "causeway" was given to the platform because it appeared to primitive imagination to be a road to the water, prepared for the convenience of giants.

Gibraltar of America.—Quebec is often so called, because by its position and natural and artificial means of defense it is the most impregnable city in America.

Girondists, the name given to the moderate republican party during the French Revolution. Their leaders at first acquired great influence by their rhetorical talents and political principles, which were derived from a rather hazy notion of Grecian republicanism. The encroachments of the populace and the rise of the Jacobin leaders compelled the Girondists to assume a conservative attitude; but though their eloquence still prevailed in the Assembly, their popularity and power out-of-doors were wholly gone. The principal things which they attempted to do were to procure the *arrestement* of the leaders of the September massacres, Danton, etc.; to overawe the mob of Paris by a guard selected from all the departments of France; to save the King's life by first voting his death and then by intending to appeal to the nation; and, finally, to impeach Marat, who, in turn, induced the various sections of Paris to demand their expulsion from the Assembly and their *arrestement*. Thirty Girondists were arrested, but the majority escaped to the provinces. The people rose in their defense in the departments of Eure,

Calvados, and all through Brittany, and under the command of General Wimpfen formed the so-called "federalist" army, which was to rescue the republic from the hands of the Parisian populace. Movements for the cause of the Girondists took place likewise at Lyons, Marseilles and Bordeaux. The progress of the insurrection was, however, stopped by the activity of the Convention, and a number of the leaders were brought to the guillotine.

Glacial Period is a term used in geology to designate the period when the greater part of the northern hemisphere was enveloped in one great ice-sheet. This period belongs to the post-tertiary or later formations in the geological succession, and is important in its relations to the general question of the earth's history, and especially to the appearance of man upon the earth. Geologists are generally agreed that long before the advent of man, parts of the northern hemisphere were elevated several thousand feet higher than they are at present, causing the cold of the Arctic zone to extend far southward into present temperate regions, and that a vast glacier rising in the vicinity of Hudson Bay covered the American continent north of the fortieth parallel. The loose soil which covers so large a part of the surface of the northern continent to a depth varying from 30 to 100 feet, over which lie the vegetable deposits of later ages, is considered by geologists the effects of glaciers that in the quaternary or latest geological age slowly moved southward across the country. Upon examination it is found that the erratic bowlders scattered over the Western prairies and other Northern regions are unlike the native rocks of the same regions, being entirely foreign to the localities where they now appear. Sometimes the nativity of the rock is traced hundreds of miles north of where it now rests, showing that some powerful agency has carried it southward. Again, if the native rock be uncovered and closely examined, it will be observed to be polished and grooved with parallel marks, running north and south, as if chiseled out by some coarse and heavy instrument. These marks are attributed to sharp, hard rocks projecting through the lower surfaces of the glaciers. That glaciers do produce such markings is proven by examination of the rocks which the moving ice-fields of Switzerland and other glacial regions have worn and are marking to-day; also, the general appearance of the loose, unstratified, heterogeneous deposit is similar to that of the moraines that the modern glaciers leave as they slowly melt away. In New York and other Eastern States the rocks are scratched from a northwesterly direction, in Ohio from a northerly direction, showing in each State the direction of the origin of the glacier. Scotland, Ireland and the major portion of England were enveloped in this great ice-sheet, and Scandinavia was invested with a sheet of ice which filled up the Baltic and extended into Northern Germany. The Glacial Period, or Ice Age, as it is also called, is estimated to have begun upward of 200,000 years ago, and lasted for 160,000 years.

Glass, Discovery of.—There is comparatively little known in regard to the invention of glass. Some of the oldest specimens are Egyptian, and are traced to about 1500 years before Christ (by some, 2300 B. C.). Transparent glass is believed to have been first used about 750 years before the Christian era. The credit of the invention was given to the Phœnicians by the ancient writers. The story of the Phœnician merchants who rested their cooking-pots on blocks of natron (subcarbonate of soda), and found glass produced by the union, under heat, of the alkali and the sand on the shore, is a familiar one. The world no doubt owes the art of glass-making to the Egyptians. It was introduced into Rome in the time of Cicero, and among the Romans attained a high degree of perfection. Some of the most beautiful specimens of glass ever manufactured were made in Rome before the Christian era; as, for instance, the exquisite Portland vase in the British Museum. [See *Portland Vase.*] During the middle ages the Venetians were the most famous makers of fine glassware, and after them the Bohemians. Though the art of making glass and blowing it into all kinds of shapes was known so early, this material does not seem to have been used for windows until about A. D. 300.

Glucose, termed also grape-sugar, starch-sugar and diabetic sugar, is a natural organic compound consisting of carbon, hydrogen and oxygen. It is found to some extent in the animal kingdom and very largely in the vegetable kingdom, being a constituent of the juice of almost all sweet fruits and vegetables. The name "diabetic" is due to its large occurrence in the urinary secretion and other fluids of the body in the disease called diabetes. It is manufactured in large quantities from starch, and is used in the manufacture of beer and a coarse kind of alcohol. It is in taste much the same as ordinary sugar, but less sweet. It has a peculiar effect upon a ray of polarized light, passing through it; and there are two varieties comprising fruit-sugar, one of which turns the plane of polarization to the right, and is called dextro-glucose, and the other turning the plane of polarization to the left, and called laevo-glucose, or dextrose and laevulose respectively.

Gnadenbrutten Massacre.—In 1760 the Moravian missionaries, who had met with great success in converting the Indians to their faith, established three villages of converts on the Tuscarawas River, Ohio. One of these, on the east side of the river, was called Gnadenbrutten, and was about midway between the white settlements on the Ohio River and the villages of the warlike Wyandots and Delawares on the Sandusky. The Christian Indians were Delawares, but they were friends of peace, and endeavored to maintain, as far as they could, a neutral position between the Americans on the one side and the savage Indians, who were generally under British influence, on the other. In March, 1782, there were murders committed near Pittsburg by wandering bands of Shawnees, and the Christian Indians were suspected, though apparently without any real reason, of having incited them, and a band of volunteer militia, under Colonel Williamson, of the British army, set out to take vengeance. The Indians were found pursuing peaceful occupations, but they were, notwithstanding, all taken prisoners (the village contained about one hundred souls), bound and confined—the men in one house, the women in another. A council of war was then held to decide whether the prisoners should be taken to Fort Pitt or immediately put to death. The latter fate was decided on, and the helpless Indians were murdered and scalped and their village laid in ruins. Only sixteen out of ninety white men voted for mercy, the others all voting for immediate death.

Gnomes.—According to mediæval mythology, a class of beings which are supposed to be the presiding spirits in the mysterious operations of nature in the mineral and vegetable world. They have their dwelling within the earth, where they preside specially over its treasures, and are of both sexes, male and female. The former are often represented in the form of misshapen dwarfs. Pope, in the " Rape of the Lock," and Darwin, in the " Loves of the Plants," have drawn upon the more pleasing associations of this curious branch of mythology. [See *Undine* and *Sylph*.]

Gnostic, a word sometimes confounded with *agnostic*, and employed in a loose and general way to designate a freethinker. Correctly speaking, gnosticism is the term applied to various forms of philosophical speculation which sprung up in the early history of the Church. They were generally regarded as heretical, but the term itself means simply *knowledge*, and does not contain any idea of antagonism to Judaism or Christianity. There were three main schools or centers of gnostic speculation: the Syrian of Antioch; the Alexandrian of Egypt, and that of Asia Minor, represented by Marcion of Pontus. Gnosticism represents the first efforts to construct a philosophical system of faith, and the main questions with which it concerned itself were the same which in all ages have agitated inquiry and baffled speculation—the origin of life and origin of evil, how life sprung from an infinite source, how a world so imperfect as this could proceed from a supremely perfect God. All of the schools agreed in the existence of an infinitely Supreme Being, their differences arising in their various speculations to account for the passage from the higher spiritual world to this lower material one. In the Alexandrian thought, evil is but degenerated good. The Syrian school assumed the existence of two living, active, independent principles, good and evil. The former system embraced Judaism as a divine institution, although inferior and defective in its manifestation of the divine character; the latter rejected it as being wholly the work of the Spirit of Darkness. The anti-Judaical spirit was developed to the extreme in Marcion and his followers. The gnostics accepted Christ, but in different and modified lights. According to the Alexandrian school, He is a higher Divine Being, proceeding from the Spiritual Kingdom for the redemption of this lower material kingdom; but however superior, He is yet allied to the lower angels and the Demiurgos, who is an inferior manifestation of Deity partaking of the Divine nature, the intermediary between the Infinite Spirit and the material world, and the immediate Creator and governor of this world. The Syrian school, on the other hand, regarded Christ as a being totally distinct from the Demiurgos, who was in their system not the representative and organ of the Supreme Spirit, but a rival Spirit of Darkness; and hence, in coming into this lower world, He was invading the realms of the powers of darkness, in order to seek out and rescue any higher spiritual natures who were living here under the power of the Evil One. Gnosticism has been well termed an extraordinary conglomeration of Monotheism, Pantheism, Spiritualism and Materialism. It was vague, confused and irrational for the most part, and yet its influence in the world was not altogether bad. It compelled Christian teachers to face the great problems of which it attempted the solution in so many fantastic forms. It expanded the horizon of controversy within as without the Church, and made the early fathers feel that it was by the weapons of reason and not of authority that they must win the triumph of Catholic Christianity. It may be said to have laid the foundations of Christian science; and Antioch and Alexandria, the centers of half-pagan and half-Christian speculation, became the first centers of rational Christian theology. The several schools began to decline after the middle of the third century. Their doctrines were revived several times by certain sects in the middle ages, but have had no considerable body of adherents since the thirteenth century.

Godiva, Lady, the wife of Leofric, Earl of Mercia and Lord of Coventry. About 1040 the earl imposed certain onerous services and heavy exactions upon the inhabitants of Coventry, who, in consequence, loudly complained. Lady Godiva, having the welfare of the town at heart, eagerly besought her husband to give them relief; and he, in order to escape from her importunities, said he would grant the favor, but only on condition that she would ride naked through the town. Greatly to her husband's surprise she agreed to the conditions; and on a certain day, after having ordered all the inhabitants to remain within doors and behind closed blinds, she rode through the town clothed only by her long hair. This circumstance was commemorated by a stained-glass window, mentioned in 1690, in St. Michael's Church, Coventry; and the legend that an unfortunate tailor, the only man who looked out of a window, was struck blind, has also found commemoration in an ancient effigy of "Peeping Tom of Coventry," still to be seen in a niche of one of the buildings. For many years occasional representations were given of the ride of Lady Godiva, the character being taken by some beautiful woman, clothed, however, in considerable more than her hair, and attended by other historical and emblematic personages. The ceremony has now fallen into disrepute.

Gods, Garden of the, comprises a tract of land about 500 acres in extent, lying four miles northeast of Colorado Springs. It is hemmed in by mountains on the north and west, bordered by ravines on the south, and on the east by a line of old red sandstone cliffs, which shut it entirely from the plains. The road enters the valley through the "Beautiful Gate," a narrow passage-way between two lofty but narrow ledges of cliffs which is still further narrowed by a rock pillar thirty feet high, standing nearly in the center. The remarkable features of the Garden are a number of isolated perpendicular rocks, some of them 350 feet high, mainly of a very soft, brilliantly red sandstone, though several ridges are of white sandstone. The foot-hills in the vicinity are many of them capped by similar upheavals.

God's Truce.—During the middle ages a custom prevailed in France and the German Empire, and for a time in other countries of Europe, whereby for a stated time, and at stated seasons and festivals, the right of private feud for the redress of wrongs, which under certain conditions was recognized by mediæval law, was suspended. This period was known as "God's Truce," and was brought about through the influence of the Church, which endeavored in this way to check the disorganization of the social frame-work which was brought about by these private feuds. A council assembled at Limoges, in the end of the tenth century, at which the princes and nobles bound themselves, by solemn vows, not only to abstain from all unlawful feuds, but also to keep the peace mutually toward each other, and to protect from violence all defenseless persons, clerics, monks, nuns, women, merchants, pilgrims and tillers of the soil. In 1016 a similar engagement was entered into in a council at Orleans. A plague which visited a great part of Europe soon afterward gave a fresh impulse to the movement; and in the year 1033 the "Holy Peace" was almost universally received, and for a time continued to be religiously observed. In 1041, in order to give the observance more weight, the bishops of Aquitaine limited the God's Truce to the week-days specially consecrated by the memory of the Passion and Resurrection of Christ—that is, from the sunset of Wednesday to sunrise of Monday. In 1054 the same decree was renewed at Narbonne, and in 1093 at Troyes. At Clermont, in 1095, it was extended to the whole interval from the beginning of Advent to the Epiphany, and from the beginning of Lent to Pentecost, to which times were afterward added several other festivals. At later councils these enactments were adopted or renewed, and although they were often disregarded, it is impossible to doubt that they exercised a wide and beneficial influence. When the right of private redress was restricted and finally abolished by law, the institution of God's Truce disappeared.

Gold-Beater's Skin.—In preparing the skin used by gold-beaters, the large intestine of an ox is first subjected to a partial putrefaction, by which the adhesion of the membranes is sufficiently diminished to allow them to be separated. The outer membrane is then removed, cleaned from the adhering muscular fibers, dried, beaten and pressed between paper, beside being treated with alum, isinglass and white of egg, the object of which is to obtain the continuous membrane in a clean condition without being weakened by the putrefactive process. The skin, after having passed through this process, becomes a delicate membrane of such firm yet elastic texture that it can be beaten for months with a twelve-pound hammer without material injury. The skin is usually sold in packages containing 900 leaves, for which the intestines of 500 oxen are required, and, in addition to being used by gold-beaters, is used as the fabric for court-plaster.

Golden Fleece, The.—According to Greek tradition, Pelias, King of Iolcos, in Thessaly, dethroned the rightful King Æson and endeavored to kill his son Jason, who was, however, saved by his parents, who conveyed him by night to the cave of the centaur Chiron, to whose care they committed him, and then gave out that he was dead. He remained with Chiron until he was twenty years of age and then went to claim his father's crown. Pelias agreed to surrender the kingdom to Jason provided he brought him the golden fleece from Colchis, expecting that he would never attempt it, or, if he did, would surely perish in the rash adventure. One of the myths of the fleece is that Ino, second wife of Athamas, King of Orchomenus, in Bœotia, wished to destroy Phrixus, son of Athamas; but he and Helle were saved by their mother, Nephele, who gave them a golden-fleeced ram she had obtained from Mercury, which carried them through the air over sea and land. Helle fell into the sea, and it was named Hellespontus. Phrixus went on to Colchis, where he was kindly received, and sacrificed the ram to Jupiter Phyxius, and gave the golden fleece to Æetes, who nailed it to an oak in the grove of Mars, where it was watched over by a sleepless dragon. Jason, by heralds, announced the great undertaking throughout the land, and all the heroes of Greece flocked to his assistance, and the famous company were called the "Argonauts," from the name of their ship, Argo, which was built for them by Argus, with the aid of Minerva. After a voyage of varied adventure the heroes reached Colchis, and Jason explained the cause of his voyage to Æetes; but the conditions on which he was to recover the golden fleece were so hard that the Argonauts must have perished had not Medea, the King's daughter, fallen in love with their leader. She had a conference with Jason, and after mutual oaths of fidelity Medea pledged herself to deliver the Argonauts from her father's hard conditions if Jason would marry her and carry her with him to Greece. He was to tame two bulls which had brazen feet and breathed flame from their throats. When he had yoked these, he was to plow with them a piece of ground, and sow the serpent's teeth which Æetes possessed. All this was to be performed in one day. Medea, who was an enchantress, gave him a salve to rub on his body, shield and spear. The virtue of this salve would last an entire day, and protect alike against fire and steel. She further told him that when he had sown the teeth a crop of armed men would spring up and prepare to attack him. Among these she desired him to fling stones, and while they were fighting with one another about them, each imagining that the other had thrown the stones, to fall on and slay them. All of these things were done by Jason, but Æetes refused to give the fleece, and meditated burning the Argo, Jason's vessel, and slaying her crew. Medea, anticipating him, led Jason by night to the golden fleece; with her drugs she put to sleep the serpent which guarded it; and then, taking her little brother Absyrtus out of his bed, she embarked with him in the Argo, and the vessel set sail while it was yet night. They were pursued by Æetes, when Medea killed her brother and threw his body into the sea piece by piece, thus delaying the King, who stopped to gather up the remains, leaving the Argonauts to escape. After many months of toil and numerous trials they at last reached Iolcos, and the Argo was consecrated by Jason, on the Isthmus of Corinth, to Neptune.

Gold, Price of.—Between the years 1861 and 1879 the highest and lowest price of gold for each year was as follows: 1862, 139—101 1-8; 1863, 172 1-2—122 1-2; 1864, 285—151 1-2; 1865, 234 1-2—128 1-2; 1866, 167 3-4—125 1-8, 1867, 146 3-8—132 1-8; 1868, 150—132; 1869, 162 1-2—119 1-2; 1870, 123 1-4—110; 1871, 115 3-8—108 1-2; 1872, 115 5-8—108 1-2; 1873, 119 1-8—106 1-8; 1874, 114 3-8—109; 1875, 117 5-8—111 3-4; 1876, 115—107; 1877, 107 7-8—102 1-2; 1878, 102 7-8—100. Specie payment was resumed January 1, 1879.

Gordian Knot.—The expression "Gordian knot," or "to cut the Gordian knot," signifies to overcome any great difficulty, or by some prompt and decisive act to dispose of it, and is derived from the following legend: Gordius was a legendary king of Phrygia, Asia Minor. He was, the story relates, a peasant, and one day while plowing, an eagle alighted on his yoke of oxen and remained there until evening. A prophetess, whom he consulted to learn the meaning of this sign, explained it as presaging that his family would rise to greatness and power, and he married her in return for her good wishes. Some years later, the country of Phrygia was greatly torn by civil dissensions, and an oracle declared that a new king, who would end all disturbances, would be brought in a peasant's cart. While the wise men were deliberating on these utterances, Gordius and his wife and son suddenly appeared in a cart, and he was hailed by the councilors as the people's king. The new ruler consecrated the yoke of his team to Jupiter, and fastened the yoke to a beam with a rope of bark so ingeniously tied that no one could loosen it, and an oracle declared that whoever should untie this knot would become master of Asia. When Alexander the Great visited the Acropolis at Gordium, in Phrygia, this knot was shown and the words of the oracle were repeated to him. "Then," said the conqueror, "I will perform the task," and thereupon cut the knot in two with his sword.

Gotham.—The origin of the name "Gotham," as applied to the city of New York, is contained in a humorous book called "Salmagundi," written by Washington Irving, his brother William, and James K. Paulding, and is used to signify that the inhabitants were given to undue pretensions to wisdom. This definition of the word is taken from a story regarding the inhabitants of Gotham, a parish in Nottinghamshire, England, who were as remarkable for their stupidity as their conceit. The story relates that when King John was about to pass through Gotham toward Nottingham he was prevented by the inhabitants, who thought that the ground over which a king passed became forever a public road. When the King sent to punish them they resorted to an expedient to avert their sovereign's wrath. According to this, when the messengers arrived they found the people each engaged in some foolish occupation or other, so they returned to court and reported that Gotham was a village of fools. In time a book appeared, entitled "Certain Merry Tales of the Mad Men of Gotham," compiled in the reign of Henry VIII by Andrew Borde, a sort of traveling quack, from whom the occupation of the "Merry-Andrew" is said to be derived. Among these tales is the story of "The Three Wise Men of Gotham" who went to sea in a bowl.

Goths and Vandals.—The Goths and Vandals were among the leading Germanic or Teutonic tribes. They possessed the roving spirit natural to barbarism, and from the second to the fifth century overran southern Europe. They invaded Italy, Spain and Africa, and the temples of the Romans were repeatedly stripped to buy their favor. In the fifth century the Goths under Alaric took Rome three times, and once placed their leader upon the throne as a rival emperor to Honorius. The recognized chief of the Vandals was Genseric, who also took Rome, and gave the city up to be pillaged by his soldiers for fourteen days. The Roman army at one time was largely composed of Goths and Vandals, and the downfall of the city in A. D. 476 was accomplished by the combined hosts of the Goths, Vandals, Huns, Franks and Alarii. The Goths were the first of the Teutons to come under the influence of Christianity. A considerable time before the fall of the western empire they had been converted from paganism to the form of Christianity called Arianism. The Huns were probably of Mongolian or Tartar stock, the theory being that they were directly descended from the Hiong-now, whose ancient seat was an extensive and barren territory north of the great wall of China. It was to keep these people out of the Chinese country that the great wall was built. In the third century the Huns crossed the river Volga and invaded the territory of the Alarii, a pastoral people living between the Volga and the Don Rivers, conquered this race and united it with themselves. In the fifth century the Huns under Attila attained to a high degree of power, and included or governed all the tribes from the Volga to the Rhine; but at Attila's death the empire fell to pieces, and the people were swallowed up by other tribes. The Huns are described by Roman historians as hideous in appearance, with broad shoulders, flat noses, and small black eyes deeply buried in the head; and so great was the terror inspired by the repulsive appearance and savage manners of this barbarous race that a legend ascribing their ancestry to the union of the witches of Scythia with infernal spirits was readily believed.

Go to Halifax.—The expression "Go to Halifax" originated in the terror with which rogues were once wont to view the law of Halifax, Yorkshire County, England. This law, as may be gathered from a letter of Lord Leicester's, quoted by Motley in his "History of the United Netherlands," was that criminals should be "condemned first and inquired upon after." Halifax lay within the forest of Hardwick, the customary law of which was, that if a felon were taken with 13 1-2 pence worth of goods stolen within that liberty, he should be tried by four frith burghers from four of the precinct towns, and, if condemned by them, be hanged next market-day; after which the case might be sent to a jury. From these facts it can readily be seen that when it was desired to express the wish that a person might be in a place where he would be summarily dealt with, it was quite appropriate to tell him to "Go to Halifax."

Government Receipts and Expenditures.—The total receipts of the United States from the beginning of the Government, 1789, to 1888 have been: From customs, $6,078,062,850; internal revenue, $3,692,586,329; direct tax, $28,131,994; public lands, $262,079,181; miscellaneous, $618,753,294; total, excluding loans, $10,679,613,625. The total expenditures from 1789 to 1888 have been: For civil and miscellaneous, $2,103,985,880; war, $4,636,513,386; navy, $1,138,021,573; Indians, $242,290,230; pensions, $1,055,002,615; interest, $2,577,424,978; total, $11,846,960,227.

Governors, Salaries of.—The salaries of the Governors of the several States and Territories of the United States are as follows: Alabama, $3,000 per annum; Alaska, $3,000; Arizona, $2,600; Arkansas, $3,500; California, $6,000; Colorado, $5,000; Connecticut, $2,000; Dakota, $2,600; Delaware, $2,000; Florida, $3,500; Georgia, $3,000; Idaho, $2,600; Illinois, $6,000; Indiana, $5,000; Iowa, $3,000; Kansas, $3,000; Kentucky, $5,000; Louisiana, $4,000; Maine, $2,000; Maryland, $4,500; Massachusetts, $5,000; Michigan, $1,000; Minnesota, $3,800; Mississippi, $4,000; Missouri, $5,000; Montana, $2,600; Nebraska, $2,500; Nevada, $5,000; New Hampshire, $1,000; New Jersey, $5,000; New Mexico, $2,600; New York, $10,000; North Carolina, $3,000; Ohio, $4,000; Oregon, $1,500; Pennsylvania, $10,000; Rhode Island, $1,000; South Carolina, $3,500; Tennessee, $4,000; Texas, $4,000; Utah, $2,600; Vermont, $1,000; Virginia, $5,000; Washington Territory, $2,600; West Virginia, $2,700; Wisconsin, $5,000; Wyoming, $2,600.

Grangers, or Patrons of Husbandry, as they are properly called, were organized December 4, 1867, by Mr. O. H. Kelley and Mr. Wm. M. Saunders, both of the Department of Agriculture at Washington. Mr. Kelley was commissioned by President Johnson, in 1866, to travel through the Southern States and report upon their agricultural and mineral resources. He discovered agriculture in a state of great depression, consequent upon the changes made by the Civil War. There was also at the time serious dissatisfaction among the farmers of the West and Northwest in regard to the alleged heavy rate and unjust discriminations made by railroad companies in their transportation of farmers' products. It was also claimed that middle-men exacted exorbitant prices for agricultural implements, etc. Mr. Kelley concluded that an association made up of those who were dissatisfied might be organized on some such plan as the Order of Odd-Fellows or Masons. He and Mr. Saunders devised a plan for an organization to be known as the "Patrons of Husbandry," and its branches to be called "Granges," and on December 4, 1867, the National Grange was organized at Washington. In the spring of 1868 granges were founded at Harrisburg, Pa.; at Fredonia, N. Y.; at Columbus, Ohio; at Chicago, Ill., and six in Minnesota. The movement became very popular, and they were, in a few years, organized in nearly every State and Territory in the Union. The order has its greatest strength, however, in the Northwestern and Western States.

Graphite.—The name is derived from the Greek *graphein,* to write. It is also commonly but incorrectly called black-lead and plumbago. It contains no lead, but is an allotropic form of carbon, and therefore identical in composition with charcoal and diamonds. It occurs as a mineral both massive and disseminated through the rock, generally in granite, gneiss, mica, schist and crystallized limestone It is also a product in the destructive distillation of coal, and can be artificially obtained by other methods in the laboratory. It is lighter than water, and this property is made use of in separating it from the rock in which it is found. The ore is pulverized and then thrown into large, shallow tanks; the particles of rock sink, while the particles of graphite float and are taken from the surface free from the rock, and are formed into solid blocks by great pressure. The mine at Burrowdale, in Cumberland, England, has been known since the time of Queen Elizabeth, and probably furnished the first lead-pencils ever made, but became exhausted many years ago. Large deposits of graphite have been found in the northeastern part of Siberia, and in Germany, France, Austria, and in several portions of the United States. Its most important use is in the manufacture of lead-pencils. [See *Lead-Pencils.*] But, as it is infusible and a good conductor of electricity, it has found other important applications, as for crucibles and the linings of small furnaces, and in the process of electrotyping. It is unctuous to the touch, and has a high metallic luster, and is used also in polishing and lubricating-compounds, but for this latter purpose has been found too hard to be satisfactory.

Graphophone.—This instrument is, in its essential features, identical with Edison's phonograph. [See *Phonograph.*] The graphophone now in experimental use is the invention of Mr. Sumner Tainter, aided by Professor Bell. In a correct nomenclature the phonograph would represent a machine for making a record of speech, the record made would be termed a phonogram, and the graphophone would be a machine for reproducing speech from the phonogram. The words are all derived from the same two Greek roots, which mean "write" and "speak."

Grass-Widow.—This expression was originally taken from a similar phrase in the French, and meant a woman who was a mother though not a wife—otherwise, a widow by grace or courtesy. In the United States, however, the term is applied to a woman who, though lawfully married, is living apart from her husband. When the California gold excitement prevailed and a man broke up his home, put his wife to board, and hurried to the gold-regions, he was said to have "turned his wife to grass."

Great Bells.—In the manufacture of great bells Russia has always taken the lead. The "Giant," which was cast in Moscow in the sixteenth century, weighed 288,000 pounds, and it required 24 men to ring it. It was broken by falling from its support, but was recast in 1654. On June 19, 1706, it again fell, and in 1732 the fragments were used, with new materials, in casting the "King of Bells," still to be seen in Moscow. This bell is 19 feet 3 inches high, measures around the margin 60 feet 9 inches, weighs about 443,732 pounds, and its estimated value in metal alone is at least $300,000. St. Ivan's bell, also in Moscow, is 40 feet 9 inches in circumference, 16 1-2 inches thick, and weighs 127,830 pounds. The bells of China rank next to those of Russia in size. In Pekin there are seven bells, each of which is said to weigh 120,000 pounds. The weight of the leading great bells of the world are as follows: "Great Bell of Moscow," 443,732 pounds; St. Ivan's, Moscow, 127,830 pounds; Pekin, 120,000 pounds; Vienna, 40,200 pounds; Olmutz, Bohemia, 40,000 pounds; Rouen, France, 40,000 pounds; St. Paul's, London, 38,470 pounds; "Big Ben," Westminster, 30,350 pounds; Montreal, 28,560 pounds; St. Peter's, Rome, 18,600 pounds.

Great Britain, Elections in.—There is no general election-day in Great Britain. Upon the dissolution of Parliament, because of a ministerial crisis or by the expiration of its term, a new election is ordered by the Queen. This is done by means of writs, and the law provides that an election shall have been held at all polls within not less than nine nor more than twenty-one days after their issuance. The number of members of Parliament is not regulated strictly according to population, but upon a compromise between ancient rights and the modern demand for representation for all classes. According to the system in force at the present time, boroughs or towns of at least 15,000 inhabitants are entitled to one representative ; towns having 50,000 inhabitants are allowed two; and over that, one member to each 50,000 of population. According to this plan, many small country towns which have been represented from time immemorial have now no member; but the representation of the large cities has been greatly increased. There are 670 members of Parliament in all. Ireland elects 104, Scotland 70, and England and Wales 496. A plurality of votes cast is sufficient to elect a member, and all members of the House of Commons are chosen at each election.

Great Eastern, The.—The largest ship in the world, the Great Eastern, was constructed by the Eastern Navigation Company of London. The work of construction commenced May 1, 1854, and the work of launching her, which lasted from November 3, 1857, to January 31, 1858, cost £60,000, hydraulic pressure being employed. Her extreme length is 680 feet ; breadth 82 1-2 feet, and including paddle-boxes 118 feet; height 58 feet, or 70 feet to top of bulwarks. She has 8 engines, capable in actual work of 11,000 horse-power, and has, besides, 20 auxiliary engines. The ship's history presents a singular series of vicissitudes. She left the Thames September 8, 1859, on her trial-trip across the Atlantic ; an explosion of steam-pipes took place off Hastings; seven persons were killed and several wounded; and the voyage abruptly came to an end at Weymouth. After a winter spent in costly repairs the ship started again on June 17, 1860. Leaving Southampton on that day, she crossed the Atlantic in eleven days, and reached New York on the 28th. During the remainder of 1860 and the greater part of 1861 she made many voyages to and fro, losing money by the insufficiency of the receipts to meet the current expenses, and constantly required repairs. In December of the latter year she was used as a troop-ship to convey troops to Canada. The years 1862 to 1864 were a blank as concerns the history of the steamer. In 1864 she was employed by the Atlantic Telegraph Company as a cable-laying ship, and continued in such service during 1865 and 1866. In 1867, when the preparations for the Paris International Exhibition were approaching completion, a body of speculators chartered the Great Eastern for a certain number of months, to convey visitors from New York to Havre and back; but the speculation proved an utter failure, there being neither wages for the seamen and engineers nor profits for the speculators. In 1868 the ship was again chartered by the Telegraph Construction and Maintenance Company. On October 28, 1885, the Great Eastern was sold at public auction for $126,000.

Great Fires.—In 1729 a fire in Constantinople destroyed 12,000 houses, and 7,000 people perished. The same city suffered a conflagration in 1745, lasting five days; and in 1750 a series of three appalling fires occurred—one in January consuming 10,000 houses;

another in April destroying property to the value of $15,000,000; and in the latter part of the year another, sweeping fully 10,000 houses more out of existence. In 1771 2,500 houses were burned; another fire in 1778 consumed 2,000 houses. In 1782 there were 600 houses burned in February; 7,000 in June; and on August 12th, during a conflagration that had lasted three days, 10,000 houses, 50 mosques and 100 corn-mills, with a loss of 100 lives. Two years later, a fire on March 13th destroyed two-thirds of Pera, the loveliest suburb of Constantinople; and on August 5th a fire in the main city, lasting 26 hours, burned 10,000 houses. In this same fire-scourged city, in 1791, between March and July there were 32,000 houses burned, and about as many more in 1795; and in 1799 Pera was again swept by fire, with a loss of 13,000 houses, including many buildings of great magnificence. In 1848 2,500 buildings were consumed, with a loss of $15,000,000; and in 1870 Pera was again partially consumed, with a loss of $26,000,000. At the great fire in New York, which occurred in 1835, property to the value of $15,000,000 was burned. In 1851, 2,500 buildings, of the value of $11,000,000, were consumed by fire in St. Louis. In 1866 half the city of Portland, Me., was laid waste by fire, and the loss was estimated to be at least $11,000,000. The five greatest fires on record, reckoned by destruction of property, are: Chicago fire of October 8 and 9, 1871, when there were 17,430 buildings burned, 250 lives lost, and the loss was $192,000,000; Paris fires of May, 1871; loss $160,000,000; Moscow fire of September 14–19, 1812; 30,800 houses burned; loss $150,000,000; Boston fire of November 9–10, 1872; loss $75,000,000; London fire of September 2–6, 1666, in which were consumed 13,200 houses, with St. Paul's Church, 86 parish churches, 6 chapels, the Guild Hall, the Royal Exchange, 52 companies' halls, many hospitals, libraries, and other public edifices, and the loss was estimated at $53,652,500; and the Homburg fire of May 5–7, 1842, when 4,219 buildings were burned, 100 lives were lost, and the loss was $35,000,000.

Great Hammers.—The weights of the great steam-hammers used in the iron-works of Europe and their dates of manufacture are as follows: At the Terni Works, Italy, the heaviest hammer weighs 50 tons, and was made in 1873; one at Alexandrovski, Russia, is of like weight, and was made in the following year. In 1877, one was finished at Creusot Works, France, weighing 80 tons; in 1885, one at Cockerill Works, Belgium, of 100 tons; and in 1886, at the Krupp Works, Essen, Germany, one of 150 tons, which is the heaviest hammer in the world.

Great Salt Lake is situated in the northern portion of Utah Territory. It lies in one of the great valleys or basins of the Rocky Mountains, and is about 75 miles long and 45 miles broad. Its mean depth is about 12 feet, and its maximum depth is variously given at 60 feet and 78 feet. It is 4,200 feet above the level of the sea. It contains numerous rocky islands, the longest of

which (Antelope) is 15 miles.   The Bear, the Weber and the Jordan
Rivers empty into this lake; but it has no outlet, being for the most
part absorbed by the sandy plain or evaporated by the dry air of the
Great Fremont Basin.   The waters of the lake contain about 20 per
cent. of common salt, and abound with animal life, insects,
shrimps, but not fish, although the experiment of stocking it
with salt-water fish has been made by the United States Fish
Commissioners with some success.   This lake is like the Dead Sea
and the Aral Sea in Asia in having no outlet, and in some respects
is considered the most remarkable body of water in the world.

   Greek Fire was a composition which the Greeks of the Byzantine Empire used as a means of defense.   It is supposed to have
been composed of niter, sulphur and naphtha as principal ingredients.   It was highly inflammable, and was said to have the power
of burning under water.   It was projected either on blazing tow,
tied to arrows, or through a tube, and wherever it fell it made
great havoc, from the inextinguishable nature of the fire.   At
Constantinople the process of making Greek fire was kept a profound secret for several centuries; but at the time of the discovery
of gunpowder it formed a recognized defensive element in most
wars from western Europe to Asia Minor.   The invention of this
material has usually been ascribed to Callinicus of Heliopolis, in
A. D. 668; but there seems to be reason to believe that it was
rather imported from India.

   Greely Expedition.—In the summer of 1881 a party composed
of three officers of the United States army, one acting surgeon and
nineteen enlisted men, under the command of Lieutenant A. W.
Greely, sailed from St. Johns, N. F., on the steamship Proteus,
taking materials for a house, and stores for twenty-seven months,
for the head of Lady Franklin Bay, in the Arctic regions, where a
station was to be established for scientific observations.   The expedition was undertaken in pursuance of a plan of the International Geographical Congress for the establishment of a number of
circumpolar stations for scientific purposes, and was authorized by
Congress in March, 1881.   The Proteus left Greely and his party
at their station, which was called Fort Conger, on August 18th.
In April of the following year Lieutenant Lockwood and three
others made an expedition to the north coast of Greenland, and
succeeded in reaching the most northernmost point ever reached
by man, which they called Lockwood Island, latitude 83 degrees
24 1-2 minutes north; longitude 44 degrees 5 minutes west, on the
13th of May.   August 9, 1883, no relief vessel having arrived, the
party left Fort Conger in their boats, leaving most of their provisions behind them in case they should be obliged to return, and
relying for future supplies on what they should find deposited by
previous relief expeditions.   Eventually they were compelled to
abandon their boats, and were adrift on an ice-floe for nearly
thirty days.   They landed on the north side of Baird's Inlet, where
supplies were found, and shortly afterward reached a point near

Cape Sabin, where they established a camp. At this time their fuel was so scarce that they did not dare use it for anything but to warm their food, and their only light was a wick dipped in seal-oil. On May 14, 1884, their provisions gave out entirely, and from that time till rescued the party lived upon boiled strips from their seal-skin clothing, lichens, and what shrimps they were able to catch. While Greely and his command were undergoing such extreme suffering the United States authorities were doing all in their power for their relief. In the summer of 1883 the steam-whaler Proteus and the United States gunboat Yantic sailed for Lady Franklin Bay to fetch the expedition back; but the Proteus was nipped by the ice and sunk, and the Yantic was left in the rear at Upernavik. A new expedition was then fitted out, consisting of the steam-whalers Thetis and Bear, and the Arctic exploring vessel Alert, which was contributed by the British Government. On June 22, 1884, the crew of the Bear discovered papers at Brevoort Island locating Greely's camp, and the launch of the Bear succeeded in finding the party before evening. Only seven men, including Greely, were found alive, and two of them died soon afterward. The others had all perished of cold, exposure and lack of food, most of them having expired within a few days of the arrival of succor.

Gretna Green Marriages.—The English Marriage Act, which required the consent of parents and guardians, publication of bans, and the presence of a priest, was evaded by the contracting couple passing over to Scotland, where the marriage-law required nothing but a mutual declaration of marriage to be exchanged in presence of witnesses—a ceremony which could be performed instantly—and it was immaterial whether the parties were minors or not. Gretna Green, being the first convenient halting-place, after crossing the Scottish border, for runaway couples from England, gave the name to this kind of marriage. The declaration generally took place in the presence of a blacksmith, who in reality was no more necessary than any other witness, but who gradually assumed an authority which imposed on the credulity of the English strangers and materially increased his income. Of late years the English marriage-laws have been modified to a considerable extent in order to discourage Scottish marriages, and the Scotch law has been altered, so that now it is necessary for at least one of the contracting parties to live in Scotland for twenty-one days next preceding the day of marriage, to make the ceremony valid.

Griffins.—According to Herodotus, griffins were animals which guarded the gold found in the vicinity of the Arimaspians, a Scythian race, from the attempts of the people to possess themselves of it. The griffin is variously described and represented, but the shape in which it most frequently appears is that of an animal generated between a lion and an eagle, having the body and legs of the former, with the beak and wings of the latter. In this form it appears on antique coins, and as an ornament in classical architecture. Like all other monsters, griffins abound in the legendary tales of the Teutonic nations, and the name in various forms, slightly differing from each other, is to be found in most Teutonic dialects. In the science of heraldry the griffin occupies an important position; and that they were not always regarded by the patriarchs of that science as creatures of the imagination is evidenced by the fact that Gerald Leigh, a herald of great reputation in the time of Queen Elizabeth, stated, with entire sincerity, " I think they are of great hugeness, for *I have a claw of one of their paws* which show them to be as big as two lions."

Guelphs and Ghibellines.—At the great battle of Weinsberg in Suabia, A. D. 1140, the Emperor Conrad of Hohenstaufen, and Welf, uncle of Henry the Lion, Duke of Saxony, rallied their followers by the respective war-cries "Hie Waiblingen!" "Hie Welf!" As the chief theater of the conflict of these parties was Italy, the original names took the Italian form of Ghibellini and Guelfi, and under these names they became two great parties, whose conflicts may almost be said to make up the history of Italy and Germany from the eleventh till the fourteenth century. The Ghibellini may, in general, be described as the supporters of the imperial authority in Italy, the Guelphs as the opponents of the emperors and adherents of the popes. Five great crises in the strife of the Guelph and Ghibelline parties are commonly noted by historians : Under Henry IV, in 1055; under Henry the Proud, in 1127; under Henry the Lion, in 1104; under Frederick Barbarossa, in 1159; and in the pontificate of the great champion of Church temporal power, Innocent III. The cities of northern Italy were divided between the two parties—Florence, Bologna, Milan, and other cities, as a general rule, taking the side of the Guelphs; while Pisa, Verona and Arezzo were Ghibelline. In general it may be said that the nobles of the more northern provinces of Italy inclined to the Ghibelline side, while those of the central and southern provinces were Guelph. After the downfall of the preponderance of the German emperors in Italy the contest ceased to be a strife of principles and degenerated into a mere struggle of rival factions. From the fourteenth century the Guelphs or Ghibellines are seldom heard of as actually existing parties; but in the sense already explained, the conflict of principles which they represented is found in every period of political history.

Guerrillas.—The name "guerrilla" is from the Spanish, and signifies "a little war." The term was first used during the Peninsular War, 1808–'14, and was applied to bands of armed Spanish peasants who at times were successful in harassing Napoleon's armies. The name was subsequently used in Central America and the United States. During the Mexican War guerrilla bands were a source of great annoyance in Mexico and Texas. They appeared again during the Civil War, but were officially known as "partisan rangers." They were commanded by officers duly commissioned by the Confederate President for such service. April 12, 1862, the Confederate Congress passed an act which provided that these "partisan rangers" should be paid the full pay of regular soldiers, and be paid the full value of all arms and munitions of war captured by them. February 15, 1864, this act was repealed, and the guerrillas were joined to the regular army.

Gun-Barrels.—The finest musket-barrels are made of iron which contains a portion of steel or undergoes some steeling process. Laminated, twisted or Damascus steel is used in the manufacture of the best barrels. Scraps of saws, steel-pens, files, springs and steel tools are collected from various workshops, for the material of laminated steel. These are cut in small and nearly equal pieces, cleansed and polished by revolving in a cylinder, fused into a semi-fluid state, and gathered into a "bloom" or mass. This bloom is forged with a three-ton hammer, and hardened and solidified with a tilt-hammer. It is then rolled into rods, each rod is cut into pieces six inches long, and these pieces are welded together. The rolling, cutting and welding process is then repeated several times, and thus finally the metal is brought into a very hard, tough, fibrous and uniform state. Twisted steel for barrels is made by taking thin plates of iron and steel, laying them alternately one on another in a pile, welding them by heat and hammering, and twisting them by very powerful mechanical agency until there are twelve or fourteen complete turns to an inch. The length becomes reduced one-half and the thickness doubled by this twisting. Barrels made of Damascus steel are manufactured of steel which has undergone a still further series of welding and twisting operations. Some barrels are made of a mixture of old files with old horseshoe nails; these are called stub Damascus barrels. The files are heated, cooled in water, broken with hammers, and pounded in a mortar into small fragments. Three parts of these fragments are mixed with five of stub and the mixture is fused, forged, rolled and twisted. An inferior kind of Damascus-twist is made by interlaying scraps of sheet-iron with charcoal and producing an appearance of twist, but without the proper qualities. Inferior kinds of barrel-iron are known as "threepenny-skelp" and "twopenny-skelp;" but the worst of all is "sham-dam skelp." The finest barrels are all twisted in form. The skelps, or lengths of prepared steel, are twisted into a close spiral a few inches long; several of these spirals are welded end to end, and the fissures are closed up by heating and hammering. The rough barrel, with a core or mandrel temporarily thrust in it, is placed in a groove and hammered cold until the metal becomes very dense, close, strong and elastic. The interior is then bored truly cylindrical by a nicely-adjusted rotating cutting-tool. If, on close inspection, the interior is found to be straight and regular, the exterior is then ground on a rapidly-revolving stone and finally turned in a lathe. The skelps for the commoner barrels are heated, laid in a semi-cylindrical groove, hammered until they assume the form of that groove, placed two and two together, and heated and hammered until one barrel is made from the two halves. These are browned externally with some kind of chemical stain. The finest barrels are rubbed externally with fine files and polished with steel burnishers.

Gunpowder, Discovery of.—It is generally conceded that gunpowder was used by the Chinese as an explosive in prehistoric times. When they first discovered or applied its power as a propellant is less easily determined. There is an account of a bamboo tube being used, from which the "impetuous dart" was hurled a distance of 100 feet; this was at a very early period, but it is difficult to say precisely when. It is alleged, however, that in the century before the Christian era a cannon was employed bearing the inscription "I hurl death to the traitor and extermination to the rebel." It has also been asserted that India has equal claims with China to the first acquaintance with gunpowder. The ancient Sanscrit writings appear to point very plainly to the operation of some primitive sort of cannon, when, in recording the wars of the Egyptian Hercules in India, it is stated that the sages remained unconcerned spectators of the attack on their stronghold till an assault was attempted, when they repulsed it with whirlwinds and thunders, hurling destruction on the invaders; and a Greek historian of Alexander's campaign testified that the Hindus had the means of discharging flames and missiles on their enemies from a distance. According to Meyer, the preparation of gunpowder was described by Julius Africanus, A. D. 215. In 1073 King Solomon of Hungary bombarded Belgrade with cannon, and in 1085 the ships of Tunis, in the naval battle near Toledo, were said to shoot "fiery thunder." All of which would go to prove that the custom of ascribing the discovery of gunpowder to Bertholdus Schwartz in 1330, or even to Roger Bacon in 1267, is open to considerable objection, although these men probably introduced it in European warfare.

Gutta-Percha.—The name "gutta-percha" is Malayan, *gutta* signifying the concrete juice of a plant, and *percha* the name of the particular tree from which it is obtained. It is the dried milky juice of the tree which is found in the peninsula of Malacca and the Malayan Archipelago. Its use was first discovered by Europeans about 1843. It is imported in blocks and lumps of five to ten pounds weight in various forms, chiefly like large cakes, or rounded into gourd-like lumps. It has a cork-like appearance when cut, and a peculiar cheese-like odor. Before it can be used it has to undergo some preparation. This consists in slicing the lumps into thin shavings, which are placed in a *derilling* or tearing machine revolving in a trough of hot water. This reduces the shavings to exceedingly small pieces, which, by the agitation of the tearing teeth, are washed free from many impurities, especially fragments of the bark of the tree, which, if not separated, would interfere with the compactness of its texture. The small fragments, when sufficiently cleansed, are kneaded into masses which are rolled several times between heated cylinders, which press out any air or water and render the mass uniform in texture. It is then rolled between heated steel rollers into sheets of various thicknesses for use, or is formed into rods, pipes for water or speaking-tubes, and an endless number of other articles. The great value of gutta-percha arises from the ease with which it can be worked, and its being so complete a non-conductor of electricity. It softens in warm water, and can be molded into any form in that state, as, when soft, it is not sticky, and turns well out of molds.

Gypsies.—The weight of evidence in the language, physiognomy and habits of this vagrant people is in favor of their Indian origin. There is to-day a wandering tribe in upper India known as the Zingarro, and the name of the gypsies in the first European country which they visited was the Zingari, and it is clearly impossible that this similarity of names should be a chance coincidence. The first appearance of the gypsies in Europe occurred when the Mongol conqueror Timour was laying waste the fruitful countries of southern Asia and marking the trail over which his army passed with rivers of human blood. The Zingarro, the tramps of Oriental society—the poorer classes, who had no possessions to excite the cupidity of the invaders—fled in bands to the westward, while the conquering party marched to the east. The first bands of these people came to Italy in the first decade of the fifteenth century, and in 1442 there were about 14,000 of them in that country. In 1417 they made their first appearance in the provinces of the Danube, and in 1427 a band of them came to Paris. They appeared in England about 1506 and in Sweden about 1514. Spain banished them in 1492, and a century later renewed the decree strenuously. They were exiled from England for their thieving proclivities by Henry VIII, and also by Elizabeth; and the same measures were eventually taken against them in Italy, Denmark, Sweden and Holland. All efforts to civilize them have been, in the main, unsuccessful, and they have intermarried but little with other races. The majority of the severe laws enacted against them have been repealed. Their language differs greatly in different countries, although everywhere preserving forms of unmistakable Indian origin. The number of these people in Europe is estimated to be about 700,000.

Hades.—The word "hades" is from the Greek. Its etymology is somewhat doubtful, but it is generally believed to have come from the verb *eidein*, meaning to see, and the negative particle *a*. Hence it may mean what is out of sight, the invisible, or, where nothing can be seen, the place of darkness. In Homer the name is applied to Pluto, the lord of the lower regions, perhaps because he was the deity who had the power of making mortals invisible. The Greeks, however, gave up the latter application of the word, and when the Greek Scriptures were written the word was always used to designate the place of departed spirits.   It was the common receptacle of departed spirits, the good as well as the bad, and was divided into two parts—the one an Elysium of bliss for the good, the other a Tartarus of punishment and grief for the wicked, and its locality was supposed to be underground, in the mud regions of the earth. In the very early stages of Grecian history no complete theory of punishments or rewards in Hades had found its way into the popular creed.   The prevalent belief was merely that the souls of the departed—with the exception of a few who had personally offended against the gods—were occupied in the lower world in the unreal or shadowy performance of the same actions that had employed them when in the region of day.   The poets and dramatists introduced the accessories of tribunals, trials of the dead, a paradise for the good and place of torture for the bad. The modes of punishment imagined were ingenious, such as that of Ixion, who was bound to an ever-revolving wheel; that of Sisyphus, who was set to roll a huge stone up a steep hill, a toil never ending and still beginning, for as soon as it reached the summit it rolled back again to the plain; or that of Tantalus, who was placed up to his chin in the water, but was unable to quench his thirst, as the water constantly slipped away from him as he raised it to his lips.   Over his head also hung a branch loaded with fruit, but as he stretched forth his hand to grasp it, it sprang from him toward the clouds.   It is plain that these punishments had their origin in the imagination of poets rather than of priests or religious teachers.

Hail.—Hailstorms occur in the greatest perfection in the warmest season, and at the warmest period of the day, and are generally most severe in the tropical climates.   A fall of hail generally precedes, sometimes accompanies, and rarely, if ever, follows a thunder-storm.   Hailstones are reported to have fallen in tropical countries sometimes as large as a sheep, sometimes as large as an ox, or even an elephant!   But it is probable that the aggregation in these cases was produced by regelation at the surface of the earth, when a series of large masses had impinged on each other, having fallen successively on the same spot.   A curious instance of the fall of large hail, or rather ice-masses, occurred on an English man-of-war off the Cape in January, 1860.   Here the stones were the size of half-bricks, and beat several of the crew off the rigging, doing serious injury.   One of the most disastrous hailstorms that has ever occurred in Europe passed over Holland and France in 1788.   It traveled simultaneously along two lines nearly parallel—the eastern one had a breadth of from half a league to five leagues, the western of from three to five leagues.   The space between was visited only by heavy rain; its breadth varied from three to five and a half leagues.   At the outer border of each there was also heavy rain, but we are not told how far it extended.

The general direction of the storm was from south-west to north-east. The length was at least one hundred leagues. It seems to have originated near the Pyrenees, and to have traveled at a mean rate of about sixteen and a half leagues per hour toward the Baltic, where it was lost sight of. The hail only fell for about seven and a half minutes at any one place. The hailstones were generally of irregular form, the heaviest weighing about eight French ounces, and an official inquiry fixed the damage at about 24,690,-000 francs—nearly $5,000,000.

Halacha is the term for the Jewish oral law, and is supposed to be, like the written law contained in the Bible, of divine origin. It embraces the whole field of juridico-political, religious and practical life down to its most minute and insignificant details. It began to be written down when the sufferings to which the Jews were almost uninterruptedly subjected from the first exile downward had made many portions of it already very uncertain and fluctuating, and threatened finally to obliterate it altogether from memory. The first collection of laws was instituted by Hillel, Akiba and Gamaliel. But the final reduction of the general code, Mishna, is due to Iehudah Hanassi, A. D. 220. The Halacha was further developed in subsequent centuries by the Saboraim, Geonim, and the authorities of each generation.

Halberd.—A halberd was a weapon in use up to the close of the eighteenth century. It was a strong wooden shaft about six feet in length, surmounted by an instrument resembling in form a bill-hook, constructed alike for cutting and thrusting, with a cross-piece of steel, less sharp, for the purpose of pushing. One end of this cross-piece was turned down as a hook, for use in tearing down works against which an attack was made. The invention of the halberd is claimed by both the Swiss and the Danes, and probably each produced something resembling it. Its name appears to be derived from the Teutonic *hild*, battle, and *bard*, ax. It appeared first in England about the time of Henry VIII, and was borne by all sergeants of foot, and by companies of halberdiers in the various regiments. It maintained its position for upward of two centuries.

Halcyon Days, a phrase which has come to signify "times of peace and tranquility." Originally the name Halcyon Days was given by the ancients to the seven days which precede and the seven days which follow the shortest day of the year. Alcyone, or Halcyone, daughter of Æolus, married Ceyx, who was drowned as he was going to consult the oracle. The gods apprised Alcyone in a dream of her husband's fate, and when she found, on the morrow, his body washed on the sea-shore, she threw herself into the sea. To reward their mutual affection the gods changed them into halcyons or kingfishers, and, according to the poets, decreed that the sea should remain calm while these birds built their nests upon it. According to Pliny the halcyons only showed themselves at the setting of the Pleiades and toward the winter solstice, and even then they were but rarely seen. They made their nests, according to the same authority, during the seven days immediately preceding the winter solstice, and laid their eggs during the seven days that followed.

Hallows' Eve, or Halloween, is the night of October 31st, the eve of All-Saints' or All-Hallows'-Day, which is November 1st, and is probably a relic of pagan times or of mediæval superstitions, as it has nothing whatever to do with the Church festival. In England and Scotland it is especially selected as the time for trying spells and divinations in love affairs. The tradition of superstition regarding it is that it is the night of all others when supernatural influences prevail; when spirits of the invisible and visible world walked abroad, for on this mystic evening it was believed that the human spirit was enabled by the aid of supernatural power to detach itself from the body and wander through the realms of space. There is a similar superstition in Germany concerning " Walpurgis-night "—the night preceding the first of May. On this night, the German peasants believe that there is a witch-festival, or gathering of evil spirits, on the summit of the Brocken, in the Hartz Mountains, and the malign influence of this convocation was believed to be felt all over the surrounding country. It was an old custom, and still observed in some places, to light great bonfires of straw or brush on that night to drive away the spirits of darkness supposed to be hovering in the air. Considering that All-Saints'-Day was originally kept on May 1st, there would appear to be but little doubt that All-Hallow-eve and Walpurgis-night have a common origin which, doubtless, dates back to the earliest belief in a personal and all-powerful Evil One —the Chaldean's Power of Darkness.

Hampshire Shakers.—This community of Shakers settled in the New Forest, near Lymington, Hampshire, England, in 1872 or 1873, and consisted of eighty-three persons. Their leader, a Mrs. Girling, wife of an Ipswich builder, declared herself to be the woman of the twelfth chapter of Revelations, who was "clothed with the sun, and the moon under her feet." These Girlingites, or Bible Christians, as they called themselves, believed that the earth and the fullness thereof belonged to the elect, and that they were the elect. They professed to take the literal Scriptures for their guide in all things, yet were so little inclined to earn their bread by the sweat of their brow that they got into debt, mortgaged the cottages which had been secured for them by a Miss Wood, a convert, and finally lost their property in 1878, when, as a community, they passed out of existence.

Hanging Gardens of Babylon.—The Hanging Gardens of Babylon, so celebrated among the Greeks, contained a square of four plethra—that is, 400 feet on every side—and were carried up aloft into the air in the manner of several large terraces, one above another, till the height equaled that of the walls of the city. The ascent was from terrace to terrace by stairs ten feet wide. The whole pile was sustained by vast arches, raised upon other arches, one upon another, and strengthened by a wall, surrounding it on every side, of twenty-two feet thickness. On the top of the arches were first laid large flat stones, sixteen feet long and four broad; over these was a layer of reeds, mixed with a quantity of bitumen, upon which were two rows of bricks, closely cemented together with plaster. The whole was covered with thick sheets of lead, upon which lay the mold of the garden; and all this flooring was contrived to keep the moisture of the mold from running away through the arches. The mold, or earth, laid thereon was so deep that the greatest trees might take root in it; and with such the terraces were covered, as well as with all other plants and flowers that were proper for a garden of pleasure. In the upper terrace there was an engine or kind of pump by which water was drawn up out of the river, and from thence the whole garden was watered. In the spaces between the several arches, upon which the whole structure rested, were large and magnificent apartments that were very light, and had the advantage of an exceedingly beautiful prospect.

Hari-Kari, sometimes called "Happy Dispatch," was a curious Japanese system of official suicide, obsolete since 1868. All military men and persons holding civil offices under the Government were bound, when they had committed any offense, to rip themselves up. This they performed by two gashes, in the form of a cross; but they might not set about it until they had received an order from the court to that effect, otherwise their heirs would run the risk of being deprived of their places and property. Not infrequently, upon the death of superiors or masters, the same operation was self-inflicted by those who desired to exhibit devotion and attachment; sometimes, also, in consequence of a disgrace or affront, it was resorted to when no other resource was left.

Harpsichord was introduced into England early in the seventeenth century, but the date of its invention is uncertain. It was exactly like a grand piano in shape, and its internal arrangements were somewhat similar. The sound from the strings was produced by a small piece of crow-quill, or a piece of hard leather, which projected out of a slip of wood, called the jack, that stood upright between the strings, and was pushed upward by the key till the quill or leather twitched the string, causing a brilliant but somewhat harsh sound. It was entirely lacking in any means of modification, in respect to loudness or softness. The harpsichord and spinnet were of a similar character, although the latter was a much weaker and smaller instrument, and both went out of use at the invention of the piano-forte.

Hashish is the Oriental name of the plant, or rather of the tops and tender parts of the plant, which is scientifically known as *Cannabis Indica*, and which we term Indian hemp. It is cultivated in India, and has long been employed as a medicine in Asia. Arabs, Persians, Indians, Chinese and South Africans esteem it for its intoxicating powers. Various preparations of the plant are employed for the purpose of producing this effect. A favorite mode of extracting its active principle is by boiling the tops and flowers with water, to which butter of oil has been added, evaporating, and thus forming an oleaginous solution or fatty substance. The effect produced by hashish is that of happiness, and by that is meant an enjoyment entirely moral and by no means sensual. The hashish-eater is happy, not like the gourmand or the famished man when satisfying his appetite, or the voluptuary in the gratification of his desires, but like him who hears tidings which fill him with joy. One of the first appreciable effects of the drug is the gradual weakening of the power of controlling and directing the thoughts. Then comes the stage already described; and accompanying, and in part following it, there are observed errors of sense, false convictions, and the predominance of one or more extravagant ideas. These ideas and convictions are generally not altogether of an imaginary character, but are suggested by external impressions which are erroneously interpreted by the perceptive faculties. Finally, if the dose is sufficiently powerful, there is a complete withdrawal of the mind from external things.

Hats and Caps.—A covering for the head was early adopted by the inhabitants of the northern climes, and was usually a hood made of fur; but it was not until the Phrygians had conquered Asia Minor that the people of warmer latitudes wore any headcovering. The Phrygians were the first to adopt the fashion, and they did it in order to distinguish themselves from the conquered race with whom they lived. Their head-dress was a small, close-fitting cap, which was also soon adopted by the Roman free citizens. In 1404 a Swiss manufacturer of Paris invented the first hat.

Hearse.—The word "hearse," or *herse,* is of French origin, and means a harrow or frame for setting candles in, and was originally applied to a bar or frame-work with upright spikes for the reception of candles; and it was used at the ceremonies of the Church and at funeral services. In the fifteenth and sixteenth centuries hearses of great splendor came into use, and were erected in the churches over the bodies of distinguished personages. The framework was of iron or brass, sometimes of beautiful workmanship, square, octagonal, etc., in plan, with pillars at the angles, and arched frame-work above forming a canopy. The whole was hung over with rich cloths and embroidery, and lighted up with hundreds of wax-candles and decorated with wax images. From this the transition to the modern hearse can easily be traced. In Roman Catholic churches of the present day the hearse still exists as a triangle with spikes on which candles are placed.

Heather is found on arid places, and also in bogs. The flowers are of a lilac-rose or purple color, rarely white. They afford abundance of honey, and beehives are therefore transported to the moors when the heather is in bloom. In the Highlands of

Scotland the plant is applied to various uses. Cottages are often thatched with it, and some of the poorest are mostly built of it, in layers, with the roots inward, and mixed with earth and straw. Beds are also made of it placed in a sloping direction, with the tops upward, and are said to be very soft and elastic, and it is used in the making of besoms and scrubbing-brushes. In the Island of Islay, ale is made by brewing one part of malt and two of the young tops of heather, and this is supposed to be the same beverage which was anciently used by the Picts.

Heat, Summer.—The first cause of summer heat is the verticality of the sun's rays, which, being distributed on a smaller space than when more oblique, cause a more intense heat; the second cause is the longer day of summer. When the sun is above and below the horizon for an equal time the same amount of heat is received and radiated, and the temperature is little changed. When the sun is more than twelve hours above the horizon more heat is received than is radiated, and the general temperature rises. The maximum of heat, however, is not the greatest at the summer solstice. To be sure, the sun's rays are then the most direct, the daily increase of heat is the largest, the nightly loss least, and the net increase for one day is the greatest; but on succeeding days the net increase of heat, though not as great, is still greater than the expenditure, and therefore the aggregate increases. This increase in accumulated heat will continue until the maximum is reached, when the loss at night equals the gain by day and begins to exceed it. The maximum of heat is gained when the sun's declination is 12 degrees north, about August 20th; the maximum of cold when it is 12 degrees south, February 10th. For similar reasons the warmest part of the day is about 2 o'clock P. M., and the coldest part of the night shortly before sunrise. This reasoning is of course reversed when applied to the southern hemisphere, and does not in any case take account of the modifying influences of bodies of water, mountain ranges, etc.

Hecatomb.—In the Greek and other ancient religions a hecatomb meant a sacrifice of a large number of victims, properly, by the meaning of the word, although by no means necessarily one hundred. The practice originally was to burn the entire victim; but as early as the time of Homer this had been changed so far that only the legs wrapped up in fat and certain parts of the intestines were burned, while the rest of the victim was eaten at a feast which succeeded the sacrifice. In the hecatomb, strictly so called, the sacrifice was supposed to consist of one hundred bulls; but other animals were frequently substituted.

Hedjrah (*Hegirah*), the date of the flight of Mohammed. On the 13th of September, A. D. 622, Mohammed secretly left Mecca, owing to the fact that the tribe of Koreish had resolved to slay him, and repaired to Medina, where he was well received and vigorously supported in the wars which he began to wage against his adversaries. The rise and progress of Mohammedanism was said to date from this time. The Hedjrah, therefore, was made the starting-point of a new era—the Mohammedan—by Calif Omar, who, in 639 or 640, with the aid of a Persian, Harmozan, instituted the new Moslem calendar. It does not, however, as is generally supposed, begin from the day of the flight itself, but from the first of the Moharram (the first month of the year) preceding it—a date corresponding to our 15th or 16th of July, A. D. 622. The Mohammedan year, as a lunar year, is shorter than ours by 10 days, 21 hours, and 14 2-5 seconds—a circumstance which renders the transfer of Mohammedan dates into dates of our own calendar a decidedly difficult task.

Height of Waves.—The measurements of waves by Scoresby, which are regarded as very accurate, proved that during storms waves in the Atlantic rarely exceed 40 feet from hollow to crest, the space between the crests being 560 feet, and their speed 32 1-2 miles an hour. More recent observations taken in the Atlantic give from 44 to 48 feet as the highest measured waves; but such heights are rarely reached, and, indeed, waves exceeding 30 feet are very seldom encountered. The monsoon waves at Kurrachee breakwater-works were found to dash over the wall to the depth of thirteen feet, or about forty feet above the mean sea-level. The greatest height of waves on the British coast were those observed in Wick Bay—so famous for the exceptionally heavy seas which roll into it—being thirty-seven and one-half to forty feet. Green seas to the depth of twenty-five feet poured over the parapet of the breakwater at intervals of from seven to ten minutes, each wave, it is estimated, being a mass of 40,000 tons of water, and this continued for three days and three nights. During severe storms the waves used to ride above the top of Smeaton Eddystone tower; while at the Bell Rock the seas, with easterly storms, envelop the tower from base to balcony, a height of 400 feet.

Heimskringla, or "Mythic Ring of the World," is a poem recording the history of the kings of Norway from the earliest times to the death of Magnus Erlingsson, in 1177. It was the work of Snorri Sturlesson, a learned historian and a distinguished Icelandic politician, and was compiled from ancient genealogical tables and other documents. It was translated into Danish about 1559 by Peder Clauson, and published first by Olaf Worm in 1633.

Heliography.—The idea of first conveying signals by means of mirrors, which is the meaning of heliography, is said to have been employed by Alexander the Great, 333 B. C. The heliostat, an instrument invented by a Hollander early in the eighteenth century, and the heliograph, invented by Mr. Mance in 1875, have both been used by the British army in their Eastern campaigns. The instruments differ somewhat in construction, but the result arrived at is the same in both. Signals are produced by causing a reflected ray of the sun to appear and disappear alternately at a distant point, the intervals of appearance and obscuration being carried in length so as to produce the combination of long and short signals, known as the Morse alphabet. The reflecting body is a glass mirror which varies in size according to the distance to which it is desired to signal. A five-inch mirror has given, when atmospheric conditions were favorable, distinct signals at a distance of sixty miles. The heliograph has also been found of great service in defining distant points for large surveys, and was used for verifying the arc of the meridian by the astronomers at the Cape of Good Hope.

Hellenists was the name given to Jews who, either by birth, or by residence and the adoption of the Greek language, manners, etc., were considered Greeks in opposition to the Hebrews properly so called, whether of Palestine or the dispersion. The Hellenists formed a distinct body, and stood in a relation of rivalry, if not antagonism, to the Hebrews. Among the Jews settled in Alexandria the Hellenizing tendency found its freest development, and it was there that the peculiar dialect of the Greek language which is known as the Hellenistic was formed, and also the singularly acute and speculative philosophy which exercised so large an influence on those early Christian schools of which Origen is the most famous exponent.

Hercules, Twelve Labors of.—As Hercules, by the will of Jupiter, was subjected to the power of Eurystheus, and obliged to obey him in every respect, the latter, acquainted with his success and rising power, commanded him to achieve a number of enterprises the most difficult and arduous ever known, generally called the Twelve Labors of Hercules. The first labor was to destroy the lion which haunted the forests of Nemea and Cleonæ, and could not be wounded by the arrows of a mortal. Hercules boldly attacked him with his club, but in vain; and he was finally obliged to strangle him with his hands. From this time he wore the lion's skin as armor. The second was to destroy the Lernæan hydra, which he accomplished with the assistance of his friend Iolaus [see *Hydra*]; but because he received assistance in this labor, Eurystheus refused to count it. His third was to catch the hind of Diana, famous for its swiftness, its golden horns and brazen feet. The fourth was to bring alive to Eurystheus a wild boar which ravaged the neighborhood of Erymanthus. The fifth was to cleanse the stables of Augeas, King of Elis, where 3,000 oxen had been confined for many years, which he accomplished in one day by turning the rivers Alpheus and Peneus through the stable. His sixth was to destroy the carnivorous birds with brazen wings, beaks, and claws, which ravaged the country near the lake Styphalis, in Arcadia. The seventh was to bring alive to Peloponnesus a bull remarkable for his beauty and strength, which Poseidon, at the prayer of Minos, had given to Minos, King of Crete, in order that he might sacrifice it; but Minos afterward refusing to do so, Poseidon made the bull mad and it laid waste the island. Hercules brought the bull on his shoulders to Eurystheus, who set it at liberty. The eighth labor was to obtain the mares of Diomedes, King of the Bistones in Thace, which fed upon human flesh. The ninth was to bring the girdle of Hippolyta, queen of the Amazons. The tenth was to kill the monster Geryon and bring his herds to Argos. These were all the labors which were originally imposed on Hercules; but as Eurystheus declared the second and fifth unlawfully performed, he was ordered to perform two more. The eleventh was to obtain the golden apples from the garden of the Hesperides. Atlas, who knew where to find the apples, brought them to Hercules, who meanwhile supported the vault of heaven. The last and most dangerous labor was to bring from the infernal regions the three-headed dog Cerberus. Pluto promised him Cerberus on condition that he should not employ arms, but only force. When Hercules had brought the monster to Eurystheus, the latter, pale with fright, commanded him to be removed. Hercules set him at liberty, whereupon Cerberus immediately sunk into the earth. The hero, having performed the twelve labors, was now free from his state of servitude.

Hero and Leander.—Hero was a priestess of Venus. Leander was a youth of Abydos, a famous city on the Asiatic side of the strait of the Hellespont, nearly opposite the city Sestos, on the European coast. At a festival of Venus and Adonis, held at Sestos, Hero and Leander first saw each other, and were immediately inspired with a mutual passion; but Hero's office as a priestess and the opposition of her parents stood in the way of their union. Undaunted by these obstacles, Leander every night swam across the Hellespont to visit his beloved, who directed his course by holding a burning torch from the top of a tower on the sea-shore. After many meetings Leander was drowned in a tempestuous night, and his body was cast up at the foot of the tower where Hero stood expecting him. Heart-broken at the sight, she flung herself from the tower into the sea, and passed with her lover into the immortality of art and song.

High Seas, The.—By the "high seas," referred to in Article I of the Constitution of the United States, is meant the open sea; that is, the waters outside of the civil jurisdiction of any country, which the law of nations limits to one marine league, or three geographical miles, from shore. The great lakes beyond the limits above designated are regarded as high seas. In the event of crimes committed on the high seas, parties charged therewith are subject to the jurisdiction of the Federal or United States courts in the district which the vessel first enters after the commission of the crime, or in the district where the offender is found.

Hobson's Choice.—Tobias Hobson, it is said, was the first man in England that let out hackney-horses. When a man came for a horse he was led into the stable where there was a great choice, but Hobson obliged him to take the horse which stood nearest to the stable-door, so that every customer was alike well served, according to his chance; from whence it became a proverb, when what ought to be one's choice was forced upon them, to say it was "Hobson's choice."

Holiday Customs, Old.—St. George's Day was celebrated with considerable pomp in Great Britain as late as 1614, and it was the custom of fashionable gentlemen to wear blue coats on that day. In localities in England the famous dragon annually went in procession with the Mayor and corporation on the Tuesday preceding the eve of St. John the Baptist. The animal was a magnificent reptile, all glittering in green and gold. He was witty, also, cracking jokes with his admirers. He went with the procession to the cathedral door, but never entered, but sat upon a stone—the dragon's stone—till the service was concluded and the procession again formed. This custom was broken up in 1835. Michaelmas Day, or the Day of St. Michael and All Angels, has for centuries been observed as a great festival by the Church of Rome and as a feast by the Church of England. Michaelmas is one of the four quarterly terms or quarter-days on which rents are paid in England, and it was usually celebrated with a good dinner, of which the goose formed an important part. This custom, it is said, "originated in a practice among the rural peasantry of bringing a good stubble goose at Michaelmas to the landlord, when paying their rent, with a view of making him lenient."

Holy Alliance, The, was a league formed by the Emperors Alexander I of Russia, Francis of Austria, and King Frederick William III of Prussia, after the second abdication of Napoleon. The main principles of the alliance were: 1. That the different Governments of Europe belonged to one family of nations. 2. That all the different creeds of Christiandom were to be accorded full and equal rights in the alliance. 3. That the Christian religion was to be regarded as the moral principle governing in the international conduct and comity of the states. 4. That the Christian religion was to regulate the whole system of public law. 5. That the allied sovereigns were to give one another united aid in all cases when required. A special article of the treaty also provided that no member of the Bonaparte family should ever sit upon a European throne. Alexander of Russia drew up the agreement and gave it a name. It was signed by the three monarchs September 26, 1815, but it was not wholly made public until February 2, 1816. All the Governments of Europe except Rome, which had not been invited, probably through fear that the Pope would claim the first place in its councils, and thus revive the old difficulty of the supremacy of the Church over Christian Governments, and England, which had declined, became members of the alliance. The alliance accomplished but little, and after Alexander's death, in 1825, the compact lost authority, and the French Revolution of 1830 caused a wide breach between the parties to it. The formation of the Prussian Diet, in 1847, the European uprising in 1848, the re-establishment of the Napoleon dynasty in 1850, and finally the war of Russia against England, France and Turkey in 1854 brought about the complete dissolution of the alliance.

Holy Coat, a garment which is alleged to be the seamless coat of our Saviour, and to have been discovered in the fourth century by the Empress Helena on her visit to Palestine. It was deposited by her at Treves, where it is preserved in the cathedral of that city with the greatest reverence. The Treves relics were concealed from the Normans in the ninth century in crypts; but the Holy Coat was rediscovered in 1196, and then solemnly exhibited to the public gaze, which did not take place again till 1512, when Leo X appointed it to be exhibited every seven years. In 1810 the exhibition was attended by 227,000 people, and in 1844 by still greater multitudes. The exhibition of the Holy Coat in this latter year led to the secession of the German Catholics from the Church of Rome.

Holy Grail.—The Holy Grail was one of the leading themes of mediæval romance, fabled to have been the cup or chalice used by Christ in the Last Supper, and in which he changed the wine into blood. This chalice, preserved by Joseph of Arimathea, had also received the blood which flowed from the side of Christ on the cross. This is what the apocryphal gospel of Nicodemus says, but no early mention is made of it by either profane or ecclesiastical writers. In the twelfth century it reappears as the central subject of the prophecies of Merlin and the object of the adventurous quest of the Knights of the Round Table. It was also mixed up, by romance, with the struggles in Spain between Moors and Christians, and with the foundation of the Order of Templars in Palestine.

"Home, Sweet Home."—John Howard Payne, the author of "Home, Sweet Home," was born in New York City June 9, 1792. At the age of seventeen he adopted the theatrical profession, and in 1818 he went to England, and for twenty years thereafter was engaged as an actor, manager and playwright. He was appointed United States Consul at Tunis, Africa, in 1841, held office for three years, was reappointed in 1851, and died there April 10, 1852. It is said that the words of the song by which he is most widely known—"Home, Sweet Home"—were composed as he wandered through the streets of London without food or shelter.

Host.—In conformity with the doctrines of the Roman Catholic Church the consecrated bread of Eucharist is called the Host. In the Latin Church it is a thin circular disk of unleavened bread, made of the finest flour, and generally bearing some emblematic device. In the Greek and other Oriental churches, as well as in the various Protestant communities, the Eucharist is celebrated in leavened bread, only differing from ordinary bread in being of finer quality.

Hotch-Potch.—A Scottish dish composed of meat—usually mutton or lamb—and a variety of vegetables. The term also has, to a certain extent, the same literary significance as the French *pot-pourri* [see *Pot-Pourri*] and the Spanish *olla-podrida* [see *Olla-Podrida*].

Howe's Cave is situated thirty-nine miles from Albany, New York, and after the Luray Cave, Virginia, and the Mammoth Cave, Kentucky, is probably the most remarkable cavern known. The entrance is about fifty feet above the valley, and the rock chambers known as the Reception-room, Washington Hall, the Bridal Chamber, and the Chapel, are successively reached. Then the Harlequin Tunnel is traversed, and the visitor passes through Cataract Hall, Ghost Room, and Music Hall. The Stygian Lake is 10 feet deep, and is 30x20 feet in extent. Fine stalagmites appear both above and below the lake. The lake is crossed in a small boat, and a path which begins at Plymouth Rock, the landing-place, and follows a small brook, traverses the chambers and passages known as the Devil's Gateway, Museum, Geological Room, Uncle Tom's Cabin, Giants' Study, Pirates' Cave, Rock Mountains, and Valley of Jehoshaphat. Then the Winding Way is succeeded by the Rotunda. The stalactites and stalagmites are abundant and beautiful. The cave was discovered by Lester Howe, for whom it was named, in 1842. He penetrated it to a distance of eleven or twelve miles, it is said, but visitors do not generally go farther than about four miles. It is also called the Otsgaragee Cave, and is considered one of the wonders of the continent.

Hudson's Bay Company was started in 1670 by means of a charter granted to Prince Rupert and seventeen other noblemen and gentlemen by Charles II. The original corporation was known as the "Governor and Company of Adventurers of England Trading into Hudson's Bay." This charter secured to them the absolute proprietorship, subordinate sovereignty, and exclusive traffic of an undefined territory which, under the name of Rupert's Land, comprised all the regions discovered, or to be discovered, within the entrance of Hudson's Strait. In 1821 Hudson's Bay Company and the Northwest Fur Company of Montreal [see *American Fur Trade*] amalgamated, obtaining a license to hold for twenty-one years the monopoly of trade in the vast regions lying to the west and northwest of the first-named company's grant. In 1838 Hudson's Bay Company acquired the sole right for itself, and obtained a new license for twenty-one years. This expired in 1859 and was not renewed, and the district covered by that license has since been open to all. The license to trade did not affect the original possessions of the company, which it retained until 1869, when they were transferred to the British Government for £300,-000, and in 1870 they were incorporated with the Dominion of Canada. The loss of territorial control has not, however, in the least affected the Hudson's Bay Company as a trading community.

Its organization is still complete. It has various posts which have from time to time been erected around the central one, at distances varying from about 200 to 500 miles. These settlements are supplied with goods which are given to the Indians in the fall in payment for such furs as they obtain during the winter. These are transmitted in the spring to the central post, and from thence either to England or to Canada. If to the former, they are sold at auction.

Humanities are those branches of education or study which are included in what are called polite or elegant learning, as languages, grammar, philosophy and poetry, with that pertaining to what is called polite literature, including the ancient classics. The name implies that the study of these branches, in opposition to the physical sciences, which especially develop the intellectual faculties, has a tendency to humanize man, to cultivate particularly those faculties which distinguish him as man in all his relations, social and moral; that is, which make him a truly cultured man.

Hunker and Barnburner.—In 1845 the Democratic party in New York State, owing to internal squabbling, became divided into two pronounced factions. These were the administration Democrats, calling themselves Conservatives, and the sore-heads of those days, stigmatized as Radicals, because, among other things, they were affected with anti slavery or "free-soil" sentiments, whereas the administration party was strongly pro-slavery. In the Democratic State Convention held at Syracuse early in 1847, the latter faction, by political manipulation, secured the organization of that body, and decided nearly all the contested seats in their own favor, and made the State ticket and the State committee to suit themselves; in other words, "carried off the hunk," and fairly won the name of "Hunkers." The other faction refused to support the ticket, and as a consequence the Whigs carried the State by over 30,000 majority in the gubernatorial election. One of the Hunker orators likened the other faction to the Dutch farmer who burned his barn to rid himself of rats, and thenceforward the name Barnburners was fastened on them, and the two nicknames, Hunker and Barnburner, were bandied back and forth until after the latter joined with the Liberty party, in 1852, to support Mr. Van Buren as the Free-Soil candidate for the Presidency. Hunk is evidently a corruption of the Dutch *honk*, or *home*, and was used to signify that the administration faction had reached their goal or home.

Hurdwur Pilgrimage.—Hurdwur stands on the west bank of the river Ganges at the point where it emerges from the sub-Himalayas into the plains of Hindustan, and from its position on the sacred stream it attracts immense numbers of pilgrims for the purpose of ablution. The orthodox time for the pilgrimage is the end of March and the beginning of April, at which time a great fair is held, thus grafting commerce on religion. The attendance amounts, in ordinary years, to 200,000 or 300,000, but every twelfth year the festival attracts about 2,000,000 people.

Hydra was a fabulous monster, who, according to different historians, had from seven to one hundred heads, which immediately grew up again as fast as they were cut off. It inhabited the marshes of Lernæa, in Argolis, and its destruction was one of the twelve labors of Hercules. Hercules mounted his chariot, which was driven by Iolaus, son of Iphiclus, and on coming to Lernæa stopped the horses and went in quest of the hydra, which he found on a rising ground near the springs of Amymone, where its hole was. He shot at the animal with fiery darts till he made it come out, and he then grasped and held it while it twisted itself about his legs. The hero crushed its heads with his club, but to no purpose, for when one was crushed two sprung up in its place. A huge crab also aided the hydra, and bit the feet of Hercules. He killed the crab and then called upon Iolaus to come to his assistance. Iolaus immediately set fire to the neighboring wood, and with the flaming brands seared the necks of the hydra as the heads were cut off, effectually checking their growth. Hercules then cut off the last head, which was immortal, and buried it under a heavy stone. He cut the body of the hydra into pieces and dipped his arrows in its gall, which made their wounds incurable.

Hydraulic Cement.—Hydraulic cements are those which set or become hard under water. The stone from which these cements are made in the United States is found in stratified rocky beds of aqueous deposits. It is a species of limestone containing 8 to 25 per cent. of alumina, magnesia and silica, which yields a lime when burned that does not slack when moistened with water, but forms a mortar with it. This does not become solid in the air, but hardens with great rapidity under water, becoming more and more insoluble the longer it is immersed. The cement is prepared by burning the stone, breaking it in a crush-mill, and then pulverizing it between millstones. When it is to be used it is made into a paste with water. Deposits of this limestone are found in Western Vermont, New York, New Jersey, Pennsylvania, Maryland, East Tennessee, Ohio and Illinois. The greater part of the hydraulic cement of commerce, however, comes from Central New York.

Hydraulic Ram is a simple and conveniently-applied mechanism by which the momentum or weight of falling water can be made available for raising a portion of itself to a considerable height. It was invented by Montgolfier, but its details have been greatly improved since. Its action depends upon the property of inertia which water, in common with all bodies, possesses. A body moving with a given velocity performs, while being brought to rest, an amount of mechanical work sufficient to raise the body to the height producing the velocity. A car, for instance, moving upon a track with a velocity of 48 feet per second, or nearly 38 miles per hour, and reaching a steep incline, would mount it to a height of 35.82 feet, friction and resistance of air not counted, that being the height which a heavy body must fall to acquire a velocity of 48 feet per second. The mechanical work performed by a moving body in coming to rest is represented by the resistance opposed to its motion multiplied by the distance which the body moves against this resistance; so that the resistance necessary to stop a running body, or the pressure which it can exert while stopping, is great or small according as its motion is arrested suddenly or slowly. In the hydraulic ram the moving body is the mass of water contained in a long pipe, the exit of which is alternately opened and closed. The resistance opposed to the water's motion when its exit is closed is the elastic force of air confined in a closed vessel, and the work performed by it consists in compressing this air, which, by its tendency to expand, forces the water to a higher level. For raising comparatively small quantities of water—such as are necessary for the supply of single houses, farm-yards, etc., when water at the lower level is plentiful and cheap—the hydraulic ram is a most useful piece of mechanism.

Hymen.—According to Grecian mythology, Hymen was the god of marriage, and was said to be the offspring of the muse Urania; but the name of his father was unknown. By the Latin poets he is presented to us arrayed in a yellow robe, his temples wreathed with the fragrant plant *Amaracus*, his locks dropping perfume, and the nuptial torch in his hand. Originally, the word "hymen" seems to have denoted only the bridal-song which was sung by the companions of the bride as she went from her father's house to that of the bridegroom. The god Hymen is first mentioned in the poems of Sappho.

Ice, Artificial.—Until recently, the modes of producing artificial ice have been too costly to be practically useful; but applied science, in its great progress in every line, in the last few years, has supplied the desideratum. There are now in use several systems and machines, both economical and practical [see *Refrigerating Machines*], and ice is made in Peru under the equator, one machine producing as much as ten tons a day, where ice was never before known. They are used also in India and other warm countries, and to some extent on ocean steamers. Efforts are now being made to construct a small refrigerator for family use, containing a simple ice-making apparatus, so that ice may be made at any time and in any amount desired right in the kitchen or cellar of every house. A contrivance of this nature has been lately patented, and appears to work satisfactorily. The next few years will probably see various improvements incorporated and the improved machine in general use.

Icebergs are huge fragments of glaciers which have become detached by the action of the water from the lower end of the glacier. Greenland has been called the fatherland of icebergs, having very many glaciers. It is generally accepted that but one-eighth of the iceberg is above the surface of the water; so that when one is seen that rises over fifty feet its size can be easily computed, and the dangers attending an encounter with a berg can be appreciated. These bergs carry with them in their journeys from the north masses of rocks, earth, and sometimes plants; and upon them the denizens of the polar regions, such as the bear and seal, are occasionally transported from one place to another. Icebergs occur in the North Atlantic in the summer, usually the latter part of the season, and are quite dangerous at times to transatlantic navigation. The ocean currents bear them from the Atlantic to the temperate zone, and they are far more numerous in the northern than in the southern polar regions.

Ice, Formation of.—The formation of ice usually begins at the surface of the water—first, because ice is lighter than water just about to freeze, and thus floats in it; and, secondly, because of the peculiar law of its expansion. The general law is that cold induces contraction. This law holds good with water only to a certain point. When it has cooled down to within 7.4 degrees (Fahr.) of freezing it ceases to contract, as before, with increase of cold, and begins to expand till it freezes. This expanding would naturally cause the coldest parts of the water to rise to the surface. The formation of ground-ice, or anchor-ice, as it is called, is only an apparent exception to this rule. The whole body of water is at the same time cooled below the freezing-point, and the substances at the bottom, the rock and stones of the river-bed, serve as points of congelation or crystallization for the water; but as soon as these layers of ice are detached from the bodies which hold them they immediately rise to the surface.

Ides, Nones and Kalends.—The Romans reckoned the days of the month from three periods known as kalends, nones and ides. The kalends always fell upon the 1st of the month; the nones in March, May, July and October, on the 7th; and the ides on the 15th; and in the remaining months the nones on the 5th and the ides on the 13th. The kalends were so named because it was an old custom of the College of Priests on the first of the month to *call* (or assemble) the people together to inform them of the festivals and sacred days to be observed during the month; the nones received their name from being the ninth day before the ides, reckoning inclusively; and the ides from an obsolete verb, signifying to divide, because they nearly halved the month. This threefold division also determined the reckoning of the days, which were not distinguished by the ordinal numbers first, second, third, etc., but as follows: Those between the kalends and the nones were termed the days before the nones; those between the nones and ides the days before the ides; and the remainder the days before the kalends. Under the Empire the Senate sat regularly on the ides and on the kalends, with the exception of the ides of March, the anniversary of Cæsar's death, which was regarded as a *dies ater*—a day of mourning.

Igneous Rocks are those which have been produced from materials fused by heat. They differ from the sedimentary rocks in their origin, structure and position. They invariably come from below upward, breaking through the older rocks, and are generally ejected in a melted state from volcanic vents or from fissures opened to some seat of fires within or below the earth's crust. The materials of sedimentary strata are fragments of pre-existing rocks worn by the action of water either into a fine mud or into rounded particles of greater or less size; whereas igneous rocks exhibit either a vitreous structure, as when they have been quickly cooled, or a granular structure composed of more or less minute crystals, according to the rate of cooling, or a vesicular structure when they have been expanded by the contained gases, or by being brought into contact with water. In position, also, they may be distinguished from the sedimentary rocks, very seldom occurring regularly stratified with parallel upper and under surfaces, but generally local, thinning out into wedge-shaped beds or having that irregular stratification which may be seen in modern lava. They are also found as upright walls and columns, of which the famous Giant's Causeway and Fingal's Cave are notable examples. Igneous rocks when filling a narrow fissure in an older stratum, and also when spreading beyond the fissure and forming an extensive superstratum, is called a *dike*. The rocks above mentioned are *dikes*, as are also the Palisades on the Hudson, Salisbury Crags near Edinburgh, many rocks around Lake Superior, over the western slope of the Rocky Mountains, and numerous other localities. The outflow in some cases has been very large, the lava floods of Oregon, Nevada and Northern California being estimated to comprise a total area of not less than 200,000 square miles, with a maximum thickness of 3,500 feet, the average being probably 2,000 feet. The most common rocks of *dikes* are *doleryte* (often called trap) and peri-dotyte: both sometimes called *basalt* when not granular in texture.

Ignis-Fatuus.—A number of theories have been advanced in explanation of the luminous appearance which is frequently seen in marshy places, church-yards and stagnant pools, and which is known as ignis-fatuus. Of these it is only necessary to mention two. The first is that the ignis-fatuus is due to *phosphoretted hydrogen gas*, which possesses the power of spontaneous ignition on coming in contact with dry atmospheric air; the gas would be generated by the decomposition of animal matter present in a marshy soil. The motion of the ignis-fatuus (it floats in the air at about two feet from the ground, is sometimes fixed, and sometimes travels with great rapidity) is accounted for by the flame being communicated along the line of a stream of gas. The second is that it is due to the combustion of *light-carburetted hydrogen gas* arising from the decomposition of vegetable matter; but, though this supposition satisfactorily accounts for many appearances connected with the ignis-fatuus, the gas itself is not spontaneously combustible, and an additional supposition requires to be made to account for its ignition. The ignis-fatuus generally appears a little after sunset as a pale, bluish-colored flame, varying in size and shape; sometimes it shines steadily till morning, at other times disappears and reappears within about half-hourly intervals. In general it recedes on being approached, and *vice versa*, though several successful attempts have been made to light a piece of paper by it. In former times, under the names of *Will-o'-the-Wisp, Jack-a-Lantern, Spunkie*, etc., it was an object of superstition among the inhabitants of the districts where it appears, and was believed to be due to the agency of evil spirits attempting to lure the traveler to his destruction; and unfortunately there are many instances on record of travelers mistaking the ignis-fatuus for a lamp, and being thus decoyed into marshy places, where they perished. The ignis-fatuus is not a common phenomenon, but it is not unfrequently seen in the north of Germany, the swampy and moorland districts in the south and northwest of England, and in the lowlands of Scotland.

Illiteracy.—According to the census of 1880 there were 4,923,-451 persons of ten years of age and upward in the United States who were unable to read, or 13.4 per cent. of the entire population; those who could not write numbered 6,239,958, or 17 per cent. The ratio of adults unable to write in foreign countries is as follows: England, 16 per cent.; Scotland, 12 per cent.; Ireland, 33 per cent.; France, 22 per cent.; Germany, 6 per cent.; Russia, 89 per cent.; Austria, 51 per cent.; Italy, 59 per cent.; Spain and Portugal, 66 per cent.; Switzerland, 12 per cent.; Belgium and Holland, 14 per cent.; Scandinavia, 13 per cent.

Incubation, Artificial.—From time immemorial the Egyptians have hatched eggs by artificial warmth in peculiar stoves called mammals. In 1777 a Frenchman named Bonnemain devised an apparatus by which, for several years before the French Revolution, he supplied the Parisian markets with excellent poultry at a period of the year when the farmers had ceased to supply it. In 1825 M. d'Arcet obtained chickens and pigeons at Vichy by artificial incubation effected by the thermal waters there. Of late years artificial incubation has been carried on in the United States with average success. In a climate incident to such sudden and extreme changes the experiment demands, as an essential to success, skill and constant attention. None but absolutely fresh eggs must be selected; a temperature hardly varying from 103 degrees, and a proper degree of moisture must be maintained with sleepless vigilance. Let the eggs be chilled, even for a few moments, and the consequences are disastrous. After the eggs have been in the incubator two, or at most three days, every egg that is not fertile can be told by placing the small end to the eye, looking toward the sun, and moving the head up and down. If the egg is fertile a dark spot will be seen floating on the top. Any egg that remains perfectly clear after being in the incubator until the fourth day may as well be taken out, since it will never hatch. After the third day the eggs should be taken out of the egg-drawer once a day and allowed to cool down to about 70 or 80 degrees, but not below 65 degrees. They should also be turned every four or five hours during the day, and once during the night. This is done by moving the frames on which the eggs rest backward or forward a couple of inches. After the third day two or more soup-plates, or tin pie-pans, of water should be set on the sawdust in the ventilator, under the eggs, to moisten them; and from the ninth to the twelfth day a little tepid water should be sprinkled on the eggs by hand. From the twelfth to the fifteenth day they should be hand-sprinkled twice a day, and thereafter three times a day until they hatch. The water acts on the lime of the shells and makes it brittle. When the eggs are hatched the chickens should be kept in the incubator till they are dried, anywhere from twelve to eighteen hours, but not longer. They should then be placed in the brooder, or "artificial mother," but not fed until they are eighteen or twenty hours old. As before remarked, the temperature should not be allowed to rise above 105 degrees, as there is even more danger of killing the eggs by overheating than by letting the temperature run a little low.

Indians, Status of.—The legal status of the Indians, under the fourteenth and fifteenth amendments, was defined by a decision in the United States Supreme Court, November 4, 1884, which was to the effect that an Indian who was born a member of one of the tribes within the United States (said tribe still existing and recognized as a tribe by the Government), and who has voluntarily separated himself from his tribe and taken up his residence among the white citizens of a State, but who has not been naturalized or taxed, or recognized as a citizen either by the United States or the State, is not a citizen within the meaning of the fourteenth amendment, and cannot sustain a claim to the elective franchise under the amendment. In Michigan, Minnesota and Wisconsin the franchise has been granted to civilized Indians who have severed their connection with tribal organizations. The United States has also, by treaty or legislative enactment, admitted the following tribes or portions of tribes to full rights of citizenship: The Pottawatomies, Wyandots, and a remnant of the Kickapoos and Delawares in Kansas, the Winnebagoes of Minnesota, the Stockbridges of Wisconsin, the Ottawas and Chippewas of Michigan, the Ottawas of Blanchard's Fork, Indian Territory, and a band of friendly Sioux in Dakota. Of these, however, a large number have disposed of the lands granted them, and are known to have again connected themselves with their original tribe. The law in different States varies as to the necessary qualifications for citizenship. In some, naturalization papers must be taken out by the Indian as by any other alien. In others, a declaration before the courts of an intent to become a citizen is required; while in still others the ownership of taxable property is sufficient.

Indian Summer.—Scientists differ regarding the cause of this phenomenon which is peculiar to North America and certain parts of Central Europe. A change in the condition of the upper strata of the atmosphere, confining the radiating heat-rays in the lower strata, is generally held to be the true explanation. A theory to account for the smoky appearance, which appears plausible, is that it is due to the decay or slow chemical combustion of leaves, grass and other vegetable matter under the action of frost and sun. It was to forest and prairie fires kindled by the Indians that the early settlers attributed the smoky appearance of the season. Hence the name "Indian Summer."

Indulgences.—Originally indulgences meant a release from the temporal penalties which remained due after the sin itself had been remitted by confession and absolution, and were granted during the first centuries of the Christian Churches, not only by the Pope, but by all bishops, to infirm persons or to those penitents who showed extraordinary contrition. By degrees the practice of remitting punishment for money was introduced, the bishops allowing the offenders to buy off canonical penalties by bestowing gifts for some religious purpose, and from this time the popes began to reserve for themselves the right of granting, or rather selling, indulgences. In the fourteenth and fifteenth centuries this right was extended to an enormous degree. After the establishment of the doctrine of *opera supererogatore* the Pope abrogated not only the privilege of releasing from temporal penalties, but the power of forgiving sin; and this enormous extension was accompanied in the fifteenth and sixteenth centuries with the most scandalous practices.

Infusoria are minute animalcules, some large enough to be barely visible to the naked eye (1.100 inch), but most of them altogether microscopic and almost exceeding the power of the glass to detect. They belong to the lowest order of animal life, have neither vessels nor nerves, and are made up of a uniform tissue called by Huxley *protoplasm*. The body has some well-defined form, of which the varieties are very great in different species. Many in the higher orders are furnished with hairs, the motion of which carries them with great rapidity through the fluid in which they live, and by means of which, also, currents are created in the fluid to bring food to the mouth. Some infusoria have a few slender filaments instead of hairs, which they agitate with an undulatory movement. Others move by contractions and extensions of their bodies. Some have stiff, bristle-like organs, which they use as feet for crawling on the surfaces of other bodies, and some have hooks, by which they attach themselves to foreign bodies. The food of the infusoria consists of organic particles of various kinds, and the different species have been remarked to show a preference, like those of higher animals, for particular kinds of food. The numbers of the infusoria are prodigious. They are found in all parts of the world, and both in fresh and salt water, in stagnant ponds and ditches, in mineral and hot springs, and in moist situations. Any infusion or other liquid containing vegetable or animal matter, if left exposed to the atmosphere, is sure to be full of them. In multitude they are so great that leagues of the ocean are sometimes tinged by them. Some, which, instead of swimming freely like most of their class, become surrounded with a gelatinous substance, are found adhering together in masses, sometimes four or five inches in diameter, although the individual animals are so small that a cubic inch of the mass may contain 8,000,000. The infusoria contained in a single cup of putrid water may exceed in number the whole human population of the globe.

Infusorial Earth.—The term is a misnomer, as true infusoria have no hard structure which is capable of preservation. The large deposits known by this name are the fossil siliceous shells of diatoms, organisms formerly included in infusoria, but now generally conceded to belong to the vegetable kingdom, and classed as a sub-order of *Algæ.* They are exceedingly minute, a single cubic inch of the fine, earthy slate being estimated to contain the fossil remains of forty-one thousand million organisms. They are found in the strata of every age, but especially in those of the tertiary, in which extensive deposits occur. The substance is as fine and white as chalk, which it somewhat resembles, and contains a fine siliceous grit, which has led to its extensive use as a polishing-powder. The first used for this purpose came from Bilin, in Bohemia, where there is a hill whose top is entirely composed of fine white diatomaceous earth; it became well known under the name of Tripoli-stone. Electro-silicon, the common polishing-powder in general use, is simply this same diatomaceous earth as it may be dug from the side of a hill. The City of Richmond, Va., is built upon a stratum of this earth, which is thirty feet thick and many miles in extent. There are other large beds in different parts of the United States, and in Great Britain and Europe.

Inns of Court.—The societies known as the Inner Temple, the Middle Temple, Lincoln's Inn and Gray's Inn possess under the name of the Inns of Court the exclusive right of calling persons to the English bar. These inns are each governed by a committee or board, called benchers, who are generally Queen's counsel or senior counsel, self-chosen; i. e., each new bencher is chosen by the existing benchers. Each inn has a local habitation, consisting of large tracts of houses or chambers occupied by barristers, sometimes by attorneys. The inns are distinct from each other and self-governing. It is entirely in the discretion of an inn of court to admit any particular person as a member, for no member of the public has an absolute right to be called to the bar, there being no mode of compelling the inn to state its reasons for refusal. But, practically, no objection is ever made to the admission of any person of good character.

Interior Department, Salaries in.—The salaries of the officials of the Interior Department of the United States are as follows:

Secretary of the Interior, $8,000 per annum; two Assistant Secretaries, $4,000 each; Chief Clerk, $2,750; Commissioner of Patents, $5,000; Commissioner of Pensions, $5,000; Commissioner of Land Office, $4,000; Commissioner of Indian Affairs, $4,000; Commissioner of Railroads, $4,500; Commissioner of Education, $3,000; Commissioner of Labor, $3,000; Director of Geological Survey, $6,000; Chief of Census Division, $2,000.

Inquisition, The, was a tribunal in the Roman Catholic Church for the discovery, repression and punishment of heresy, unbelief, and other offenses against religion. From the very first establishment of Christianity as the religion of the Roman empire, laws more or less severe existed, as in most of the ancient religions, for the repression and punishment of dissent from the national creed, and the Emperors Theodosius and Justinian appointed officials called "inquisitors," whose special duty it was to discover and to prosecute before the civil tribunals offenders of this class. For several centuries cases of heresy were tried before the ordinary courts, but in course of time the examination of those accused of this crime was handed over to the bishops. Special machinery for the trial and punishment of heretics was first devised in the eleventh and twelfth centuries against the various sects who had separated from the Church, and who became known under the general term of Albigenses. Heresy was then regarded as a crime against the state as well as the Church, and the civil, no less than the ecclesiastical, authorities were arrayed against those sects. The murder of a papal legate in 1205 gave a pretext for declaring against the Albigenses a war in which thousands perished, and in 1299 the Council of Toulouse decreed the "Inquisition" for their extermination. The searching out of heretics was first given to the bishops of the Church, but the Pope (Gregory IX), fearing that these would not be active enough, transferred their work to the Dominican friars. A guild was also formed called the "Militia of Jesus Christ," whose object was to aid inquisitors in their work. The Church found the heretics, examined and sentenced them, and then called in the civil authority to put its sentence into execution. The inquisitorial courts at first only held occasional sessions, but after 1248 they sat permanently. A person, if suspected of heresy or denounced as guilty, was liable to be arrested and detained in prison, only to be brought to trial when it might seem fit to his judges. The proceedings were conducted secretly. He was not confronted with his accusers, nor were their names, even, made known to him. The evidence of an accomplice was admissible, and the accused himself was liable to be put to torture, in order to extort a confession of guilt. The punishments to which, if found guilty, he was liable, were death by fire, as exemplified in the terrible auto-da-fe, or on the scaffold, imprisonment in the galleys for life or for a limited period, forfeiture of property, civil infamy, and in minor cases retraction and public penance.

Inquisition, Spanish.—The Inquisition was introduced in Spain in 1232 by Pope Gregory's appointment of the Dominicans of Arragon as inquisitors, and it ultimately came to be viewed by the people with most abject terror. At first it passed no sentence more severe than the confiscation of property, but toward the close of the fifteenth century the zeal of Mendoza, the Archbishop of Seville, gave a new impulse to the institution. At that time there was a real or pretended alarm lest the Jews and Moors in Spain should unite against the Christians. Bishop Mendoza proposed to King Ferdinand, in 1477, that an inquisition should be established in Castile, with the primary object of searching out the Jews who had relapsed into Judaism after having professed Christianity, or who simply feigned conversion. Of course, under this was the true purpose of the scheme—to keep in check the power of the Jews and extort their wealth by persecution. The King readily assented to the scheme, and Queen Isabella also approved of it. The Inquisitorial Court of Seville was established in September, 1480, in the person of two Dominican friars; their first edict was issued January 2, 1481, for the arrest of six " new Christians," as Jewish converts were called, and January 6th all these were burned at the stake. Other executions followed, though many appeals were sent to the Pope (Sixtus IV), who endeavored to check the bloody work, and counseled milder measures. But in 1483 King Ferdinand made the infamous Torquemada the Grand Inquisitor General of all Spain, and at the same time appointed a Royal Council of the Supreme Inquisition, of which the Grand Inquisitor was President, of right and for life, with a bishop and two lawyers as counselors. The Spanish Inquisition, by its compact organization, became very powerful. Though the Inquisitor General was appointed by the King and approved by the Pope, he was, in reality, independent of both. He named the subaltern officers, and had an absolute control over all the lower courts. The Jews were expelled from Spain in 1492, and the Moors in 1500; and the fact that many of these persons of alien race endeavored to avoid expatriation by accepting Christianity brought many victims to the tortures of the Inquisition. According to the estimate of Llorente, the celebrated historian of the Spanish Inquisition, the number of persons burned alive under Torquemada (1483-'98) amounted to 8,800; those under Deza (1499-1506), to 1,664; and those under Cardinal Ximenes (1507-'17), to 2,536. The following is the record given by him for the time from 1483 to 1808: Burned alive, 31,912; burned in effigy, 17,659; subjected to rigorous pains and penances, 291,456. By the beginning of the seventeenth century, the Inquisition, having completely exterminated Protestantism in Spain, became more lenient. Its efforts were then principally directed against heretical books, and only occasionally decreed an execution. The jurisdiction of the Inquisition had been greatly restricted when Joseph Bonaparte abolished it in December, 1808. It was restored by

Ferdinand VII in 1814, but was again abolished by the Constitution of the Cortes in 1820. After the second restoration an inquisitorial junta was appointed in 1825, and in 1826 a tribunal, much on the old plan, was re established at Valencia. It was finally abolished, however, in 1834, and in 1835 all its property was confiscated for the public debt.

Iron, Discovery of.—The actual discovery of iron was probably made so early in the history of the human race that it cannot now be accurately placed. The Bible ascribes the discovery of working iron to Tubal Cain. The Egyptians ascribe it to one of their early mythological kings, Hephæstus, who has been identified by students with the Hephæstus of Greek and the Vulcan of Roman mythology. The Egyptians and the Assyrians made iron at a very early period of their history. In ancient tombs and ruins but recently unearthed many implements of iron are found, cooking-utensils, and weapons of various kinds. The Chalybes, a Scythian tribe living south and east of the Black Sea, who attained great skill in iron-working, are accredited by ancient writers with being the first to use coal in their furnaces, the inventors of steel or hardened iron, and the discoverers of magnetic iron. The books of Moses mention the use of iron some eleven centuries before the Christian era, and the Arundelian marbles fix a date for it before 1370 B. C.

Iron Crown, The, was a crown of gold, having inside of it a ring of iron which was said to have been forged from the nails of Christ's Cross. It was made by order of the Princess Theudelinde for her husband Agilulf, King of the Lombards, in the year 591. It was afterward given by the queen to the church at Monza. The iron crown was used by Charlemagne at the ceremony of his coronation, and after him by all the emperors who were also kings of Lombardy. The Order of the Iron Crown, which is now regarded as a high honor in Austria, was founded by Napoleon. It fell into disuse after his fall, but was revived by Francis 1 of Austria, in 1816. In 1859 the Iron Crown was taken by the Austrians to Vienna, but was presented to the King of Italy in 1866, and is now among the royal treasures in Naples.

Iron Mask, The Man with the.—The story of the prisoner, so called, confined in the Bastile and other prisons in the reign of Louis XIV has long kept up a romantic interest. About the year 1679 he was carried with the utmost secrecy to the Castle of Pignerol, and wore, during the journey, a black mask, which was not of iron, but of black velvet, strengthened with whalebone, and secured behind with steel springs, or by means of a lock, as some say. The orders were that if he revealed himself he was to be killed. In 1686 he was conveyed to the Isle of Sainte Marguerite, and during the passage watch was kept that he might not allow himself to be discovered. In 1698 the unknown prisoner was transferred to the Bastile, and was, as before, hidden behind the mask. In that prison he remained until his death in 1703.

On November 20th, the day after his death, he was buried in the cemetery of St. Paul under the name of Machioti. Many conjectures have been hazarded as to who "The Man with the Iron Mask" could have been. Voltaire advanced the belief that he was an elder brother of Louis XIV, and other writers have ascribed his parentage to Anne of Austria and the Duke of Buckingham, and still others to the Queen and Cardinal Mazarin. The first conjecture of what at one time seemed to be the truth is contained in a letter dated 1770, written by a Baron d'Heiss to the *Journal Encyclopedique* and repeated by Louis Dutens in his "Intercepted Correspondence" (1789), which declares that there is no point of history better established than the fact that the prisoner with the iron mask was a Minister of the Duke of Mantua. This minister, Count Matthioli, had pledged himself to Louis XIV to urge his master, the Duke, to deliver up to the French the fortress of Casale, which gave access to the whole of Lombardy. Though largely bribed to maintain the French interests, he began to betray them; and Louis XIV, having got conclusive proof of the treachery, contrived to have Matthioli lured to the French frontier, secretly arrested April 23, 1679, and conveyed to the fortress of Pignerol. A still more recent work by a French officer, M. Th Jung, has, however, conclusively shown that Matthioli could not have been the mysterious prisoner, and endeavors to prove that the man in the iron mask was the unknown head of a wide-spread and formidable conspiracy, working in secret for the assassination of Louis XIV and some of his ablest ministers.

Irvingites.—The Rev. Edward Irving, a minister of the Scotch Church, London, delivered in the winter of 1829-'30 a series of lectures on spiritual gifts, in which he maintained that those which we are in the habit of calling "extraordinary" or "miraculous" were not meant to be confined to the primitive Church, but to be continued through the whole period of the present dispensation. About the same time, as if to confirm the views of the preacher, there occurred certain strange phenomena in the west of Scotland and in his own church which brought many converts to his manner of belief. The Church of Scotland eventually deposed Irving from his office for heresy; but meanwhile the sect with which his name is associated had been assuming a more definite and ecclesiastical shape, and the final result was the Catholic Apostolic Church. In this Church there are, as in the apostolic times, *four* ministries—first, that of "Apostle;" second, that of "Prophet;" third, that of "Evangelist," and fourth, that of "Pastor." The apostles are invested with spiritual prerogatives; they alone can minister the Holy Ghost by the laying on of hands; to them the mysteries of God are revealed and by them unfolded to the Church, and they decide on matters of order and discipline. Nothing that transpires in any church in the way of "prophetic utterance" can be authoritatively explained save by them, and the various "angels of the churches" are bound to bring all such utterances under their cognizance, in order that they may be rightly interpreted. The work of an "evangelist" mainly consists in endeavoring to "bring in" those who are without. The "angel" of the Catholic Apostolic Church corresponds with the bishop of other Christian denominations. The ministers of each full congregation comprise an angel, with a fourfold ministry (consisting of elders, prophets, evangelists and pastors), and a ministry of deacons to take charge of temporal affairs. This ministry is supported by tithes, the people giving a tenth of their income for the support of the priesthood. In regard to the common doctrines of the Christian religion the Catholic Apostolic Church does not differ from other Christian bodies; it only accepts the *phenomena* of Christian life in what it considers to be a fuller and more real sense. It believes that the wonder, mystery and miracle of the apostolic times were not accidental, but are essential to the divinely instituted Church of God, and its main function is to prepare a people for the second advent of Christ. In regard to the sacrament of the Lord's Supper the doctrine of the objective presence is held, but both transubstantiation and consubstantiation are repudiated. A special feature of the Catholic Apostolic Church is its extensive and elaborate symbolism. The Church has established itself in England, Scotland, the United States, Canada, Prussia, France, Switzerland, Ireland, Belgium, Russia, Denmark, Sweden, Austria and India.

Isidorian Decretals, a spurious compilation of the ninth century which probably originated at Mentz, at some time between the years 840 and 847. It was introduced under the name of Isidore of Seville as a part of the genuine collection known as his, and was believed to have been brought from Spain by Riculf, the Archbishop of Mentz. Up to the ninth century the only authentic collection of decretals, that of Dionysius Exiguus, commenced with the decrees of Pope Siricius in the end of the fourth century. The so-called Isidorian Decretals stretch back through the predecessors of Siricius up to Clement himself, and comprise no fewer than fifty-nine decrees or epistles anterior to the time of Siricius. In a later part of the Isidorian collection, however, are interpolated nearly forty similar documents, unknown until the time of that compilation. All these documents are presented not merely as authentic, but as the genuine productions of the particular popes to which they are attributed. From the first circulation of the false decretals down to the fifteenth century no doubts were raised regarding them. Nicholas of Cusa and Cardinal Turrecremata were the first to question their genuineness, but after the Reformation the question was fully opened. The centuriators of Magdeburg demonstrated their utter apocryphal character. Their utterly fraudulent character may be said to have been finally settled by Blondel.

Isinglass.—The raw material of isinglass is the air-bladders or sounds of fish. In Russia, where the finest isinglass is made, the sounds of the sturgeon are cut open and steeped in water until the outer membrane separates from the inner, and then the latter is washed and dried in the sun. The sounds of the common cod, the hake, and other *Godidæ* are also used for isinglass.

Isis, the name of an Egyptian deity, and the sister and wife of Osiris. She was said to have first taught men the art of cultivating corn, and was regarded as the goddess of fecundity; hence the cow was sacred to her. The annual festival of Isis in Egypt lasted eight days, during which a general purification took place. The priests of the goddess were bound to observe perpetual chastity. Their heads were shaved and they went barefoot. This deity was often represented as a woman with the horns of a cow. She also appears with the lotus on her head and the sistrum in her hand; and in some instances her head is seen covered with a hood. Heads of Isis are frequently ornaments of Egyptian capitals on the pillars of the temples. As the worship of Isis passed into foreign lands it assumed a foreign character and many foreign attributes, as we see from the Greek and Roman writers. Sometimes she is represented like Diana of Ephesus, the universal mother, with a number of breasts. The worship of Isis was introduced into Rome by Sulla, 86 B. C., from Tithorea, and shared the fate of that of other Egyptian deities, being associated with that of Serapis, Anubis and others, and the temples from time to time destroyed. It flourished under the Flavians and Hadrians. At this time Isis was represented with a sistrum or rattle, a bucket, and a dress with a fringed border, knotted at the chest. The festivals, seclusion and rules of chastity attracted many followers, but the worship was not altogether considered reputable by the Romans. It was more extended and respected in Asia Minor and the provinces, but fell before Christianity, A. D. 391. Isis was worshiped as the giver of dreams, and in the twofold character of restorer of health and inflicter of diseases.

Islam, or, as it is also called, Eslam, is the proper name of the Mohammedan religion. The word is Arabic, and means "Submission to God," or, according to some authorities, "Salvation." Islam, it is held, was once the religion of all men; and every child, it is believed, is born in Islam, or the true faith, and would continue in it till the end were it not for the wickedness of its parents, "who misguide it early and lead it astray to Magism, Judaism or Christianity." Whether wickedness and idolatry came into the world after the murder of Abel, or at the time of Noah, or only after Amru Ibn Lohai, one of the first and greatest idolators of Arabia, are moot-points among Moslem theologians.

Isothermal Lines are lines laid down on the map to connect places of the same mean temperature, and were first brought into use in 1817, by Baron von Humboldt. They are named according to the mean temperature which they indicate, according to the Fahrenheit thermometer, as the line of 50 degrees, or 60 degrees, etc. These lines would agree exactly with the parallels of latitude if the surface of the earth were uniform, that is, if there were no great inequalites of land and water upon it to modify the climatic conditions; but since there are so many causes that affect temperature they do not correspond at all. In the isothermal lines, as given on the map, the local influences of elevation of land are eliminated and the temperatures reduced to what they would be were all places at the level of the sea. These lines are not parallel with each other, but show great deviations of curve that seem to indicate two northern and two southern poles, or centers, of greatest cold. The curvatures are greatest in the extra-tropical parts of the northern hemisphere. In the northern hemisphere the isothermal lines descend to a lower latitude in the eastern part of the two great continents, while rising to a comparatively high latitude on the western coasts of both. The distances of the isothermal lines are also remarkably various in different parts of the world. Thus, in the east of North America, from Charleston to Labrador, the mean annual temperature varies more than a degree and a half for every degree of latitude; while in central Europe the variation is only about nine-tenths of a degree, and on the western coast of Europe still less.

Jacobins were members of a political club which exercised a very great influence during the French Revolution. It was originally called the Club Breton, and was formed at Versailles, when the States-General assembled there in 1789. The club originally consisted exclusively of members of the States-General, all more or less liberal or revolutionary, but of very different shades of opinion. On the removal of the Court and National Assembly to Paris the club began to acquire importance. It now met in the hall of the former Jacobin convent in Paris, when it received the name of the Jacobin Club, which was first given to it by its enemies, the name which it adopted being the *Société des amis de la Constitution.* There were many distinguished men among the members, and, as their opinions were spread abroad in the columns of a journal of their own, the influence of the club was very great. Every political question and every motion was debated there before being presented to the National Assembly. As the club grew more powerful its principles became more radical, until in the spring of 1790 Talleyrand, Lafayette, and many other moderate members withdrew, and founded the "Club of 1789." In nearly every town and village in France revolutionary societies on the Jacobin model were formed, and affiliated to the original club, whose orders they implicitly obeyed. The club reached the zenith of its power when the National Convention met in 1792. The agitation for the death of the King, the storm which destroyed the Girondists, the excitement of the lowest classes against the *bourgeois,* or middle classes, and the reign of terror all over France were the work of the Jacobins. But the overthrow of Robespierre gave also the death-blow to the club. The magic of its name was destroyed, and the Jacobins sought in vain to contend against a reaction, which increased daily, both in the convention and among the people. A law of October 16, 1794, forbade the affiliation of clubs, and on November 9, 1794, the Jacobin Club was finally closed, and soon after its place of meeting was demolished.

Jacquard Loom.—The Jacquard apparatus, for the purpose of pattern-weaving, was invented by M. Joseph Marie Jacquard, a native of Lyons, France, in 1801. Being necessitated to carry on the weaving business of his father, for which he had a distaste, he endeavored to improve the existing machinery, and the Jacquard loom was the result. He enabled, by his invention, an ordinary workman ·to produce, with comparative ease, the most beautiful patterns in a style which had only previously been accomplished by skilled labor. The reception of his great invention by the public, however, was most discouraging, for although rewarded with a small pension by Napoleon, the silk-weavers offered such violent opposition to its introduction that on one occasion he narrowly escaped with his life. The machine was destroyed by the weavers on the public square of Lyons. The merit of the invention, however, was too great to admit of its being long suppressed, and when its value was once fairly recognized it effected a complete revolution in the art of weaving, especially in the finer kinds of figured silk fabrics. The Jacquard apparatus can be adjusted to almost every kind of loom, its office being merely to direct those movements of the warp-threads which are required to produce the pattern, and which previously were effected by the weaver's fingers. Its arrangements generally are very complicated, but its principles are remarkable for their extreme simplicity and certainty. On the same spot where the first machine was publicly destroyed a statue now stands, to show the gratitude of a more enlightened people.

January was among the Romans held sacred to Janus [see *Janus and Jana*], from whom it derived its name, and was added to the calendar, along with February, by Numa. It was not till the eighteenth century that January was universally adopted by European nations as the *first* month of the year, although the Romans considered it as such as far back as 251 B. C.

Janus and Jana, Latin divinities, male and female, whose names are merely different forms of *Dianus* (probably the sun) and *Diana* or *Luna* (certainly the moon). The former was worshiped by the Romans, and in every undertaking his name was first invoked. He presided not only over the beginning of the year, but over the beginning of each month, each day, and the commencement of all enterprises. The pious Romans prayed to him every morning. He is represented with a scepter in his right hand and a key in his left, sitting on a beaming throne. He has always two faces (whence the expression applied to a deceitful person, "Janus-faced"), one youthful and the other aged, the one looking forward and the other backward. Numa dedicated to him the passage close by the Forum, on the road connecting the Quirinal with the Palatine. This passage (erroneously called a temple, but which was merely a sacred gateway, containing a statue of Janus) was opened in times of war and closed in times of peace. It was shut only thrice in 700 years—first by Numa himself, again at the close of the first Punic war, and for the third time under Augustus. January, the first month of the year, derived its name from Janus.

Jelly-Fishes consist of a jelly-like mass, containing a cavity which generally has a mouth from which extend tentacles, varying in length from 30 to 100 feet. From the center, tubes pass to connect with other tubes around the circumference. Their food is smaller marine animals, which they catch with thread-like lassos attached to their tentacles. Agassiz divided jelly-fishes, or *medusæ*, into three orders: *Beroid medusæ, medusæ* proper, and *hydroidæ*. Of the beroids the most curious are the pleurobrachia, found off the north-east-coast of America. It is melon-shaped, and, like a melon, its surface is striped, being divided by eight rows of fringes. Its two tentacles are plume-like in appearance, and exceedingly graceful, sweeping about in curves near the surface of the sea. The medusæ proper, known as the "sunfish," when large is one of the most beautiful of the jelly-fishes. This is disk-shaped, from 8 to 12 inches in diameter, with tentacles 100 feet in length. The young are hatched in the spring, reach full growth by midsummer, and die in the fall. Soon after hatching the little jelly-fish attaches itself to a shell or piece of sea-weed. Later the body divides horizontally, the segments become more and more separate, and finally each one floats away by itself as an ephyra, which eventually develops into a perfect "sunfish." The Gulf of Mexico furnishes the finest of the hydroids. Tenney thus describes the "Portuguese man-of-war:" It consists of an elegantly-creased air-sac, floating upon the water and giving off numerous long and varied appendages. These are the different members of the community, and fulfill different offices, some eating for the whole, others producing medusæ buds, and others being locomotive or swimming members, and having tentacles that stretch out behind the community to the length of twenty or thirty feet. All of these and many other species of the jelly-fish are beautifully colored, and their phosphorescence by night, as they rapidly glide about, has given them the name "Lamps of the Sea."

Jerked-Beef is beef preserved by drying in the sun. The cattle are slaughtered when in good condition, and the fleshy parts are dexterously pared off in such a manner as to resemble a succession of skins taken from the same animal. These sheets of flesh, which are rarely more than an inch in thickness, being exposed to the sun, dry before decomposition commences, and in that state can be kept almost any length of time. The beef is sometimes dipped into brine or rubbed with salt before being dried. Jerked-

beef is properly called *charqui*, and, like its name, is of Chilian
origin, although now made in large quantities in Montevideo,
Buenos Ayres, and other places in South America. It is very
largely used in Cuba, where it is called *tasajo*.

Jesuits, Society of, was founded by Ignatius of Loyola, assisted
by Peter Le Feyre, a Savoyard; James Lainez, Francis Xavier,
Nicholas Bobadilla, Spaniards, and a Portuguese named Rodriguez,
in the year 1534. The society, when first conceived, had for its
object a pilgrimage to the Holy Land and the conversion of the
infidels. This purpose, however, was abandoned owing to the
warfare existing at that time between the Turks and the Western
powers, and Loyola and his associates turned their attention to an
organization designed to labor zealously in resisting the spread of
the Reformation. In 1539 the rule of the proposed order—"To
the greater glory of God"—and the vow by which they bound
themselves to go as missionaries to any country which the Pope
might indicate was submitted to Paul III, and Loyola was made
the first General of the order. The Society of Jesuits is one of the
most celebrated religious orders of the Roman Catholic Church,
and its history has been closely identified at times with that of
several of the leading countries of Europe. Many good Roman
Catholics, however, denounce this order, claiming that Jesuitism
is the synonym of craft and duplicity—a reputation resulting from
their avowed principle that "the end justifies the means." However that may be, it remains a fact that the Jesuits have been
driven out of France, Italy, Spain, and many other countries.

Jewish Year.—It is supposed that the Jewish year was instituted about the time of the Exodus. Though the characteristics
of any single year cannot be fixed from the Sacred Record, the
essential points of division for years in general are known. The
year was undoubtedly solar—that is, it included the time of the
sun's apparent revolution in the ecliptic. Had this been otherwise the feast of the first fruits, when the offerings of harvest-
time were made, which was fixed by law at a certain time of the
year, would in the lapse of a few years be thrown quite out of its
proximity to the harvest season. But the months, it is quite as
certain, were lunar, each beginning with a new moon; therefore
there must have been some method of adjustment. After the captivity the custom of inserting an intercalary or thirteenth month
was followed, and this extra month was inserted seven times in a
cycle of nineteen years. The method by which the Jews fixed the
commencement of each year is not exactly known, but probably
the rising or setting of some star which was known to mark the
right time of the solar year was used to determine it. The time
from one Passover to another, therefore, varied. It usually included twelve lunar months of thirty days each, but occasionally
had thirteen months. After the captivity the Jews had two reckonings for each year—the sacred and the civil reckonings. By the
sacred reckoning, which had been instituted at the Exodus, the

first month of the year was the month Abib, occurring about the time of the vernal equinox. By the civil reckoning the first month was Tazri, the seventh of the sacred year, beginning at near the time of the autumnal equinox.

Jingo and Jingoism.—The word "Jingoes" came into use in England during the closing days of the late war between Turkey and Russia, and was applied to those whose attitude toward Russia was hostile. It originated, according to Justin McCarthy, in the following manner: "Some Tyrtæus of the tap-tub, some korner of the music-halls, had composed a ballad which was sung at one of those caves of harmony every night amidst the tumultuous applause of excited patriots. The refrain of this war-song contained the spirit-stirring words 'We don't want to fight, but, by jingo, if we do, we've got the ships, we've got the men, we've got the money, too;' and some one whose pulses this lyrical outburst of national pride failed to stir called the party of enthusiasts the Jingoes—a name which was caught up at once."

Journalism, Beginning and Growth of.—The first printed newspaper was the *Gazette*, published in Nuremberg, Germany, in 1457; and the oldest paper extant is the *Neue Zeitung aus Hispanien und Italien*, printed in the same city in 1534. Other countries followed Germany in issuing printed newspapers in the following order: England, in 1622; France, in 1631; Sweden, in 1644; Holland, in 1656; Russia, in 1703; Turkey, in 1827. The first American paper consisted of three pages of two columns each and a blank page, and was published in Boston, September 25, 1690, under the name of *Publick Occurrences, both Foreign and Domestic*, but it was immediately suppressed. In 1704 the Boston *News Letter* appeared, printed on one sheet of foolscap paper. It flourished for seventy-two years. The oldest newspaper in the United States is the *Weekly Massachusetts Spy*, published at Worcester, Mass. This paper was established at Boston, March 3, 1771, by Isaiah Thomas, the historian of American printing. It was removed to Worcester in 1775, where it has been issued continuously ever since. The total number of newspapers published in the world at present is estimated at about 43,000, distributed as follows: United States, 17,000; Germany, 5,500; Great Britain, 6,000; France, 4,092; Japan, 2,000; Italy, 1,400; Austria-Hungary, 1,200; Asia, exclusive of Japan, 1,000; Spain, 850; Russia, 800; Australia, 700; Greece, 600; Switzerland, 450; Holland, 300; Belgium, 300; all others, 1,000. Of these, about half are printed in English. The whole number of periodicals published in the United States in 1887 was 16,310. The whole number of copies printed during the year was 2,497,354,000. The first printing-office in the United States was established in 1639, the first political newspaper was published in 1733, the first daily paper in 1784, the first penny paper in 1833, and the first illustrated paper in 1853.

Juggernaut.—The temple in the town of Juggernaut, one of the chief places of pilgrimage in India, contains an idol of the Hindu god, called *Jaggernaut* or *Juggernaut*, a corruption of the Sanscrit word *Jagannatha*, i. e., lord of the world. The legend regarding the building of the town, the erection of the temple and the formation of the idol is as follows: A king desirous of founding a city sent a learned Brahmin to pitch upon a proper spot. The Brahmin, after a long search, arrived upon the banks of the sea, and there saw a crow diving into the water, and, having washed its body, making obeisance to the sea. Understanding the language of birds, he learned from the crow that if he remained there a short time he would comprehend the wonders of this land. The king, apprised of this occurrence, built on the spot where the crow had appeared a large city and a place of worship. The Rajah one night heard in a dream a voice saying, "On a certain day cast thine eyes on the sea-shore, when there will arise out of the water a piece of wood 52 inches long and 1 1-2 cubits broad; this is the true form of the Deity; take it up and keep it hidden in thine house seven days; and in whatever shape it shall then appear, place it in the temple and worship it." It happened just as the Rajah had dreamed, and the image, called by him Jagannatha, became the object of worship of all ranks of people, and performed many miracles. The car-festival, when Jagannatha is dragged in his car on a yearly visit to his country quarters, is currently believed to be the occasion of numerous cases of self-immolation, the frantic devotees committing suicide by throwing themselves before the wheels of the heavy car. This has been proved, however, upon good authority, to be untrue.

July was the fifth month in the Roman calendar, and was called Quintilis, the fifth. Originally it contained 36 days, but was reduced by Romulus to 31, by Numa to 30, but was restored to 31 by Julius Cæsar, in honor of whom it was named July, on account of his birth having happened on the twelfth of this month. It was called *Mæd-monath*, or mead-month, and *litha-æftera*, or after-mild-month, by the Anglo-Saxons.

June, the fourth month among the Romans. It consisted originally of 26 days, to which four were added by Romulus, one was taken away by Numa, and the month again lengthened to 30 days by Julius Cæsar. It was so called from the goddess Juno. Among the Anglo-Saxons it was called *sear-monath*, or dry-month, and *midsumer-monath*.

Jungfrau.—The word jungfrau, which signifies "the maiden," is the name of one of the highest mountains of the Bernese Alps. It rises on the boundary-line between the cantons of Bern and Valais, and attains a height of 13,720 feet. It received its name either from the unsullied purity and dazzling brightness of the snow, by which its summit is covered, or from the fact that no traveler had ever reached its highest point. Its summit was first reached by two Swiss gentlemen in 1811, and since by Agassiz, Professor Forbes and many others.

Junk, a Chinese vessel, often of large dimensions. It has a high forecastle and poop, and ordinarily three masts. Junks, although clumsy vessels, incapable of much seamanship or speed, have proved themselves sea-worthy on voyages extending even to the United States and Europe. The junk of Japan is considerably superior to that in use in China.

Kelp is the crude alkaline matter produced by the combustion of sea-weeds. These become thoroughly saturated with the salty ingredients in the sea-water, which are the principal constituents of the ashes remaining after combustion. A ton of good kelp will yield about eight pounds of iodine (which is solely obtained from this source), large quantities of chloride of potassium, and, additionally, by destructive distillation, a large quantity (from four to ten gallons) of volatile oil, from four to fifteen gallons of paraffine oil, three or four gallons of naphtha, and from one and a half to four hundred weight of sulphate of ammonia. At one time many thousand tons were obtained annually on the shores of Great Britain, and employment was given to great numbers of people. This, however, was when kelp was the great source of soda (the crude carbonate); but as this salt can now be obtained at a lower price and of far better quality from the decomposition of common salt, the kelp industry is far less important than formerly.

Kensington Gardens.—The gardens at first were only twenty-six acres in extent, but have been frequently enlarged, and are now two and a half miles in circuit. It is traversed by walks and ornamented with rows and clumps of noble trees. Near the western border of the park stands Kensington Palace, an edifice of brick, originally the seat of Heneage Finch, Earl of Nottingham and Lord Chancellor of England, and afterward bought by King William III. William III, Queen Mary, Queen Anne and George II all died in this palace, and Queen Victoria was born here. The gardens extend on the west side of Hyde Park, London, from which it is partly separated by the Serpentine.

Keystone State.—The keystone is the middle stone of an arch which, when slipped into place, completes the arch and gives stability and strength to it. Pennsylvania is called the Keystone State from its having been the central State of the Union at the time of the formation of the Constitution. If the names of the thirteen original States are arranged in the form of an arch, Pennsylvania will occupy the place of the keystone.

King Arthur and His Knights.—The story of King Arthur and his knights, as embodied in romance or ballad, is, no doubt, wholly fabulous—"a curious instance of a mythical period interposed between two ages of certain history." But there is good reason to believe that there was a King of Cornwall by this name, and that he did ably defend Britain against the invasions of the Saxon Chief Cerdic. The legend says that he overthrew the Saxons in twelve pitched battles, and the localities and circumstances of these battles are given, some of them, no doubt, founded on fact. The Arthurian romances occupy an important part in English literature. They owe their origin to the legendary chronicles of Wales and England, made during the ninth and tenth centuries, these largely founded on floating traditions and ballads current among the people. Twelve knights, according to the legend, the bravest of the brave, formed the center of the king's retinue, and sat with him at a round table; these were the famous Knights of the Round Table, whose knightly mission it was to protect woman, chastise oppressors, liberate the enchanted, and enchain giants and malicious dwarfs. The round table was an enchanted table which was made for Prince Arthur's father, Uther Pendragon, by the magician Merlin. Uther gave it to King Leodegraunce, and this king gave it to Arthur when the latter married Guineve, his daughter.

King's Evil.—The belief that the disease of scrofula, which was called the king's evil, could be cured by the touch of the reigning sovereign began in England during the reign of Edward the Confessor, 1042-'66. The custom, however, was taken from the French kings, who had claimed the divine power ever since the time of Anne of Clovis, who reigned in the year 481. It is recorded that on Easter Sunday, 1686, Louis XIV touched 1,600 people in the royal chapel in Paris. In England Henry VII introduced the practice of presenting the person touched with a small gold or silver coin called a touch-piece, and this was kept up until the custom was dropped by George I, 1714. In the reign of Charles II 92,107 persons were touched; and according to Wiseman, the king's physician, they were nearly all cured.

Kissing the Book.—The custom of swearing on the Bible comes from the ancient Jews, who at first touched their phylacteries—small cases containing strips of parchment inscribed with texts from the Old Testament—in taking oaths, and later laid their hands upon the Book of the Law; and the various customs of taking oaths in different countries have all a similar origin. The early Anglo-Saxons regarded stones as sacred to their gods, therefore laid their hands on a pillar of stone. In mediæval times it was customary to touch a relic, and this was regarded as giving the oath more sacredness than when sworn upon the missal, or prayer-book. Another custom of the same times was swearing by churches. A certain number were mentioned, and the attestor was obliged to go to each one, take the ring of the church-door in his hand and repeat his oath. The custom of kissing the cross to attest an oath has been observed in Russia from very early times and has extended into other countries. According to the laws of the Order of the Garter in the time of Henry VIII, Knights Templar were required in taking oath to touch the book and kiss the cross. Since the Reformation the taking of oaths by kissing the Bible has not been permitted in Scotland. In other portions of Great Britain it is the common method.

Knighthood, originally a military distinction, came, in the sixteenth century, to be occasionally conferred on civilians, as a reward for valuable services rendered to the crown or community. The first civil knight in England was Sir William Walworth, Lord Mayor of London, who won that distinction by slaying the rebel, Wat Tyler, in the presence of the king. The ceremonies practiced in conferring knighthood have varied at different periods. In general, fasting and bathing were in early times necessary preparatives. In the eleventh century, the creation of a knight was preceded by solemn confession and a midnight vigil in the church, and followed by the reception of the eucharist. The new knight offered his sword on the altar, to signify his devotion to the Church and determination to lead a holy life. The sword was redeemed in a sum of money, had a benediction pronounced over it, and was girded on by the highest ecclesiastic present. The title was conferred by binding the sword and spurs on the candidate, after which a blow was dealt him on the cheek or shoulder, as the last affront which he was to receive unrequited. He then took an oath to protect the distressed, maintain right against might, and never by word or deed to stain his character as a knight or a Christian. Upon the infringement of any part of his oath a knight could be degraded, in which case his spurs were chopped off with a hatchet, his sword broken, his escutcheon reversed, and some religious observances were added, during which each piece of armor was taken off in succession and cast from the recreant knight. Knighthood is now generally bestowed by a verbal declaration of the sovereign, accompanied with a simple ceremony of imposition of the sword.

Knights Bachelors.—Persons who are simply knights without belonging to any order are called in England Knights Bachelors. Originally the distinction was conferred for military services, but eventually came to be bestowed upon civilians for no mightier service than carrying a congratulatory address to court. It is generally conferred by the sovereign by a verbal declaration accompanied with the imposition of the sword, and without any patent or instrument. The person who is to receive the honor kneels down before the sovereign, who touches him on the shoulder with a naked sword, saying, in French, "*Sois chevalier au nom de dieu*"—be a knight in God's name—and then adds, "Rise, Sir A. B."

Knights Banneret, a degree of knighthood formerly existing in England and France, which was given on the field of battle in reward for the performance of some heroic act. It was so called because the pennon of the knight was exchanged for the banner, a proceeding which was effected by rending the points from the pennon. The ceremony of the creation of a Knight Banneret was very impressive. The king, or his general, at the head of his army, drawn up in order of battle after a victory, under the royal standard displayed, attended by all the officers and nobility of the court, received the Banneret elect, who was not necessarily a knight previously, led between two knights of note, or other men famous in arms, carrying his pennon in his hand, the heralds walking before him and proclaiming his valiant achievements for which he deserved to be made a Knight Banneret and to display his banner in the field. The king, or general, then said to him "Advance, Banneret!" and caused the point of his pennon to be torn off. The new knight, with the trumpeters sounding before him, and the nobility and officers bearing him company, was sent back to his tent, where a noble entertainment was provided by the king. The first Banneret in England is said to have been made by Edward I, and the last by Charles I, after the battle of Edgehill, when the honor was bestowed on one John Smith for rescuing the royal standard from the hands of the rebels. George III twice conferred the title on occasion of a review, but the proceedings were considered irregular, and the rank of the knights was not generally recognized.

Knights of Bath is the second order in rank in England, and previous to 1847 was a purely military order. The present organization consists of three classes—first class, Knights of the Grand Cross (K. G. C.); the number not to exceed, for military service, 50, exclusive of the royal family and foreigners; and for the civil service, 25. Second class, Knights Commander (K. C. B.); military, 202, and civil, 50, exclusive of foreigners. These, like the first, have the title *Sir*, and take precedence of Knights Bachelor. Third class, Companions (C. B.); military, 525, and civil, 200. They take precedence of Esquires, but are not entitled to the distinctive appellation of knighthood. No officer can be nominated to the military division of this class unless his name has been mentioned in the London *Gazette* for distinguished service in action. The ancient ceremony of bathing, which used to be practiced at the inauguration of a knight, as an emblem of the purity henceforth required of him by the laws of chivalry, gave to the order its name. The last Knights of the Bath created in the ancient form were at the coronation of Charles II in 1661. The order fell into oblivion from that period until the accession of the House of Hanover. In 1725 it was revived by George I. By the statutes then framed for the government of the order, it was declared that besides the sovereign, a prince of the blood, and a great master, there should be thirty-five knights. On January 2, 1815, the limits of the order were extended for the purpose of rewarding the merits of many distinguished officers, both military and naval. In 1847 it was further extended by the admission of civil knights, as stated above.

Knights of Our Lady of Mercy, a Spanish order of knighthood founded by James I, of Aragon, in 1218. The order was instituted for the redemption of Christian captives from the Moors, each knight at his inauguration vowing that, if necessary for their ransom, he would remain himself a captive in their stead. During the first six years of the order about 400 captives are said to have been ransomed by its means. The labors of the knights were transferred to Africa on the expulsion of the Moors from Spain. In 1261 the order was extended to ladies.

Knights of Our Lady of Montesa an order of knighthood founded for the protection of Christians by James II, of Aragon, in 1316. Some time after the abrogation of the Order of Templars, Pope John XXII granted to James all the estates of the Templars and the Knights of St. John situated in Valencia, Spain. Out of these was founded the new order, which King James named after the town and castle of Montesa, which he assigned as its head-quarters. The order is now conferred merely as a mark of royal favor, though the provisions of its statutes are still nominally observed on new creations.

Knights Templar.—The Order of Knights Templar was founded in the twelfth century at Jerusalem, for the protection of pilgrims to the holy sepulcher, by seven French knights, together with Hugues de Paganes and Geoffrey de St. Omer. Governors, known as Masters of the Temple, were appointed in every country. At first the order was composed of wealthy laymen; but by degrees the ranks were thrown open to "spiritual persons not bound by previous vows," and finally laymen of humble birth were admitted as "serving brothers." With added wealth and power the vices and arrogance of the knights increased so rapidly that within two centuries Pope Clement V, at the instigation of Philip IV, of France, confiscated their lands and scattered the members of the order. Finally, the order was suppressed throughout Europe in 1312, and its property was given to the Knights of St. John. The Knights Templar of Freemasonry are representatives of these ancient knights.

Koran, the sacred book of the Mohammedan religion. According to that belief a copy of it, in a book bound in white silk, jewels and gold, was brought down to the lowest heaven by the angel Gabriel, in the blissful and mysterious night of Al-Khadr, in the month of Ramadan. Portions of it were, during a space of twenty-three years, communicated to Mohammed, both at Mecca and Medina, either by Gabriel in human shape, "with the sound of bells," or through inspirations from the Holy Ghost "in the Prophet's breast," or by God himself, "veiled and unveiled, in waking or in the dreams of night." Mohammed dictated his inspirations to a scribe, not, indeed, in broken verses, but in finished chapters, and from this copy the followers of the Prophet procured other copies. The chief doctrine laid down in the Koran is the unity of God and the existence of one true religion with change-able ceremonies. When mankind turned from it at different times, God sent prophets to lead them back to truth; Moses, Christ and Mohammed being the most distinguished. Both punishments for the sinner and rewards for the pious are depicted with great diffuseness, and exemplified chiefly by stories taken from the Bible, the Apocryphal writings, and the Midrash. Special laws and directions, admonitions to moral and divine virtues, more particularly to a complete and unconditional resignation to God's will, legends principally relating to the patriarchs, and almost without exception borrowed from the Jewish writings, form the bulk of the book, which throughout bears the most palpable traces of Jewish influence. The outward reverence in which the Koran is held throughout Mohammedanism is exceedingly great. It is never held below the girdle, never touched without previous purification; and an injunction to that effect is generally found on the cover. It is consulted on weighty matters; sentences from it are inscribed on banners, doors, etc. Great lavishness is also displayed upon the material and the binding of the sacred volume. The copies for the wealthy are sometimes written in gold, and the covers blaze with gold and precious stones. Nothing, also, is more hateful in the eyes of a Moslem than to see the book in the hands of an unbeliever.

Ku-Klux Act.—The object of the "Ku-Klux Act" or "Force Bill," was to enforce more rigidly the provisions of the fourteenth amendment in the Southern States. It was passed by the Forty-second Congress, April, 1871. By this act any person depriving another of the right of a citizen could be sued in the Federal Courts, and it was a penal offense to interfere to prevent another from exercising the right to vote or to conspire in any way to deprive another of his civil rights. The act also provided that inability, neglect or refusal on the part of State Governments to suppress these conspiracies, or their refusal to call upon the President for aid in overthrowing them, should be regarded as a denial by such States to its citizens of the equal protection of the laws; that the existence of such conspiracies should be regarded as a rebellion against the Government of the United States, and authorized the President, whenever in his judgment the public safety required it, to suspend the privileges of the writ of *habeas corpus*, and to call out the army and navy for the forcible suppression of such conspiracies. The section of the act referring to the writ of *habeas corpus* was to remain in force only to the next regular session of Congress, and in May, 1872, a bill to further extend this section failed to pass both Houses. The second section of the act, making it a penal offense to conspire to deprive another of his civil rights, was declared unconstitutional by the United States Supreme Court, January 22, 1883. The bill originally was passed by a strict party vote in the House, no Democrat voting for it and no Republican against it. In the Senate two Republicans voted against the bill. The entire act is now virtually a dead letter.

Ku-Klux Klan was organized for the alleged purpose of "redeeming the South," and was first started, it is believed, in the State of Tennessee about the beginning of the year 1868. From the month of January to May the organization spread so rapidly over the Southern States that, according to some of the best authorities, by the middle of the year it numbered at least 500,-000 men. In order to bring about this so-called redemption, the Klan were to oppose the enforcement of the Reconstruction act, the elevation and education of the colored race in the South, to prevent colored men from exercising the right of suffrage, to maintain the rule of the Bourbon whites in the South, and to prevent the emigration of whites into the South from the North, and the introduction of Northern industries. Each member was bound under the most solemn oath to assist in the accomplishment of these purposes, and the deeds perpetrated by them at length became so devilish that an investigation was ordered by Congress, and ultimately stringent measures were resorted to to suppress the order and punish the innumerable murders and outrages which had been committed by them. [See *Ku-Klux Act.*] The organization was divided into districts, and at the head of each division or district was a grand officer, who, with numerous assistants, was given power to appoint the work and duty of each man in his division.

Kummel, or, as it is also called, *Doppel Kummel,* is chiefly made at Riga, and is the principal *liqueur,* or cordial, of Russia and Germany. It is made with sweetened spirit, flavored with cumin and caraway seeds, the latter usually so strong as to conceal any other flavor. There is a finer variety of kummel, but it is only manufactured in small quantities at Weissenstein, in Esthonia. That made at Riga is the quality in common use.

Lace-Making.—The application of machinery to lace-making has cheapened lace that would otherwise always have remained expensive, and has consequently deprived a large number of the inhabitants of towns in France and elsewhere of a lucrative source of income. The great centers of the manufacture of real lace, as hand-made lace is called to distinguish it from machine-made or imitation lace, are Belgium, France and England. In the former country there are at least 900 lace schools, and over 150,000 women find employment in this trade. Brussels lace, which is of very fine thread and intricate design, has a world-wide reputation. Mechlin lace, a fine and transparent web, is made at Mechlin, Antwerp, Lierre and Turnbrout. Valenciennes is largely made in Flanders, but is extinct in its native city, from which it derived its name. The towns of Ypres, Bruges, Courtrai, Menin, Ghent and Alost produced this lace in large quantities and fine quality. Before the introduction of machinery the number of lace-makers in France was estimated to be at least 250,000, but this number has been greatly reduced within the last few years. The celebrated Point d'Alençon lace, which is made entirely by hand with a small needle, in small pieces, which are afterward united by invisible seams, is made chiefly at Bayeux. Another favorite lace, the Chantilly, which was formerly made almost altogether at Chantilly, is now made at Bayeux and Caen. Lille lace, which though simple in design is fine and beautiful, is the production of the town of Lille. The lace of Bailleul is strong and cheap, and extensively used for trimming. In the district of Auvergne, of which the town of Le Puy is the center, over 100,-000 women are employed in lace-making, and nearly every kind of lace is made. The industry is considered more extensive and more ancient in this district than in any other portion of France. In England the counties of Buckingham, Devon and Bedford are the centers of lace-making. The most widely known of the English lace is Honiton, so called from the town of this name in Devonshire. The manufacture of hand-made laces was an important industry in Nottingham some years ago, but it has been almost entirely destroyed by the introduction of machinery. Lace is made to a limited extent in Limerick, Ireland; also in Scotland, and in fact in nearly every country in Europe. The imitation or machine-made lace is manufactured in Caen, France; in Nottingham, England; and also in the United States.

Lake School.—Toward the close of the last century the poets Wadsworth, Coleridge and Southey took up their residence in the Lake district of Cumberland and Westmoreland, in England, for the purpose, as they said, of seeking the sources of poetical inspiration in the simplicity of Nature, rather than in the works of their predecessors and the fashions of the time. On this account they were given the name of the Lake School by the "Edinburgh Review."

Lapis Lazuli, or, as it is sometimes called, azure stone, is a mineral of beautiful ultramarine or azure color, consisting chiefly of silica and alumina, with a little sulphuric acid, soda and lime. It is found in primitive limestone and granite in Siberia, China, Thibet, Chili, etc. It is generally found massive, and is translucent at the edges, with uneven, finely granular fracture, but sometimes appears crystallized in rhombic dodecahedrons, its primitive form. It was called by the Greeks and Romans *sapphire*, and was highly esteemed by them as an ornamental stone. It is employed now in ornamental and mosaic work, and the valuable pigment called ultramarine is made from it. The finest specimens of lapis lazuli are brought from Bokhara.

Lares, Manes and Penates.—The derivation of the names Lares, Manes and Penates, who were tutelary spirits or deities of the ancient Romans, is not quite certain; but the first is generally considered the plural of *lar*, an Etruscan word signifying "lord" or "hero;" the second is supposed to mean "the good or benevolent ones," and the third is connected with *penus*, "the innermost part of a house or sanctuary." The Lares were divided into two classes—*Lares domestici* and *Lares publici*. The former were the souls of virtuous ancestors set free from the realms of shades by the Acherontic rites and exalted to the rank of protectors of their descendants. They were, in short, household gods, and their worship was really a worship of ancestors. The first of the Lares in point of honor was the *Lar familiaris*, the founder of the house, the family Lar, who accompanied it in all its changes of residence. The *Lares publici* had a wider sphere of influence, and received particular names from the places over which they ruled. The images of these guardian spirits were placed (at least in large houses) in a small shrine or compartment called *ædiculæ*, or *lararia*. They were worshiped every day. Whenever a Roman family sat down to meals a portion of the food was presented to them; and at festive gatherings the *lararia* were thrown open, and the images of the household gods were adorned with garlands. The Manes and Penates do not appear to have been regarded as essentially different beings from the Lares, for the names are frequently used either interchangeably or in such a conjunction as almost implies identity. Yet some have thought that a distinction is discernible, and have looked upon the Lares as earthly, the Manes as infernal, and the Penates as heavenly protectors—a notion which has probably originated in the fact that Manes is a general name for the souls of the departed; while among the Penates are included such great deities as Jupiter, Juno, Vesta, etc. Hence we may infer that the Manes were just the Lares viewed as departed spirits, and that the Penates embraced not only the Lares, but all spirits, whether daimons or deities, who exercised a "special providence" over families, cities, etc.

Largest Rivers.—The Amazon River, although it is 300 miles shorter than the Missouri River, and 100 miles shorter than the Nile, is considered the largest river in the world from the fact that it discharges a far greater amount of water than either of the others. Its length is estimated to be 4,000 miles. Its breadth at 2,000 miles above its mouth is 1 1-2 miles; at Santarem, 500 miles from its mouth, it is 10 miles, and 30 miles from the ocean it broadens into an estuary 150 miles in width. It is estimated that the Amazon drains 2,000,000 square miles of territory.

Latin Union was formed in 1865 and originally embraced France, Italy, Belgium and Switzerland, but was joined by Greece in 1868, Spain in 1871, and subsequently Servia and Roumania. The object of this combination was to regulate the amount of silver to be coined yearly in each country, and to secure a uniform coinage which would be received without discount throughout the Union. The unit of coinage in the Latin Union is the franc, and although it is known in other countries under different names the value is always the same. The perfect decimal system of France is also used. The convenience of this coinage system has led to its adoption by about 148,000,000 people. In 1874 the States, by mutual consent, practically suspended the coinage of silver.

Latter-Day Saints, or Mormons, were founded by Joseph Smith, the son of a Vermont farmer, who claimed to have received from the hands of an angel of the Lord certain plates on which were engraved God's revelation to the New World. This was the famous Book of Mormon, believed by the followers of Smith to be of equal authority with the Jewish and Christian Scriptures and to form an indispensable supplement to them. It was published in 1830, with the names of Oliver Cowdery, Martin Harris and David Whitmer appended to a statement that an angel of God had come down from Heaven and shown them the original plates. Eight other witnesses testified that they had been shown the plates by Smith. These, however, are the only persons who have been so privileged. The first Mormon settlement was at Manchester, N. Y., in 1830, but the following year Smith and his followers moved to Kirtland, Ohio. Their missionaries were full of zeal, converts were made in great numbers, and churches were established in Ohio, Pennsylvania, Indiana, Illinois and Missouri. Toward the close of 1838 the whole body of Saints, about 15,000, took refuge in Illinois at a place which they called Nauvoo, or the City of Beauty. Here, for a space of years, the Mormons lived in quietness, gathering to themselves many new converts; but ultimately the doctrine of "sealing wives" aroused the wrath of the neighborhood, and Smith and his brother Hiram were thrown into prison at Carthage, where, on June 27, 1854, they were shot by a mob who broke into the jail. Previous to this event, however, the main body of the Mormons had removed to Salt Lake City, Utah, and upon Smith's death Brigham Young was chosen to succeed him. The points of the belief of the Mormon Church have been somewhat altered since first received from Joseph Smith, that teacher having taught, for instance, the dogma of a Trinity, while modern Mormonism holds that there is a duality of persons in the Godhead, the Holy Ghost being merely a spiritual soul. They also teach that God has parts resembling the body of man, and not materially differing from him in size. They deny the doctrine that "all men sinned in Adam," but accept the atonement through Christ for sins committed by men. They hold that the ordinances of the gospel are: (1) Faith in Christ; (2) Repentance; (3) Baptism by immersion for remission of sins; (4) Laying on of hands for the gift of the Holy Ghost. They believe that a man is called to preach by "prophecy and the laying on of hands," and claim to have the same organization in respect to teachers that the primitive church held. They further hold a twofold priesthood, which they call the Melchisedek and the Aaronic, and they believe in a "baptism for the dead;" that is, that a living person may save a dead friend by being immersed for him, unless he has committed the unpardonable sin. They believe that the gift of tongues, revelations, visions, etc., is still granted to men, and that many things are still to be revealed concerning the kingdom of God. They further believe in the literal gathering of the tribes of Israel and in the restoration of the Ten Tribes; that Zion will be built upon this continent; that Christ will reign personally upon this earth, and that the earth will be renewed and receive its paradisal glory. The doctrine of polygamy was not a part of the original revelation of Mormonism, but was introduced later, and came to be not simply tolerated, but enjoined as a positive duty, a man's rank in Heaven being alleged to be largely dependent on the number of his children. Children are taken into the Church at the age of eight years; never before.

Lazulite, or Azulite, a mineral consisting chiefly of phosphoric acid and alumina, with magnesia and protoxide of iron. It is found imbedded in quartz, or in fissures in clay-slate, in Styria, North Carolina, Brazil, etc. Lazulite was long confounded with lapis lazuli, but although somewhat similar in color it is very different in composition. [See *Lapis Lazuli.*]

Lead-Pencils.—The manufacture of lead-pencils from graphite has become an important industry, about 250,000 pencils being used up per day by the people of the United States alone. The method of making pencils is as follows: The graphite is taken in lumps to the stamp-mills, and there pulverized under water. It is then taken to the factory in the form of dust, and there separated according to fineness by repeated washings. The coarsest and heaviest particles settle to the bottom of the first tub, and so on to the last, which has only the very finest powder. This is so fine and soft that it can be taken up in the hand like water, but can scarcely be retained in the hand any more than water can. This powder is now mixed with clay—a peculiar pipe-clay brought from Germany being used by the best manufacturers—in proportions varying according to the degree of hardness required. The more clay used, the harder the pencil. The graphite and clay are mixed together with water to the consistency of thick cream, and the mixture is fed to the grinding-mills, which consist of two flat stones about two feet in diameter placed horizontally, only the upper one revolving. Between these the mass is ground like paint, for the finest pencils as many as twenty-four times, thus securing the most perfect strength, uniformity and freeness from grit in the leads. After grinding, the mass is inclosed in stout canvas bags, and the clear water forced out by hydraulic pressure until it becomes a thick dough. It then goes to the forming-press. This is simply a small, vertical, iron cylinder, having a solid plunger or piston, driven by a screw. A plate is inserted in the bottom, having an opening of the size and shape of the lead desired, and the graphite is slowly forced through the hole, exactly as water is forced from a syringe, coiling itself round and round, like a coil of wire, on a board set beneath the press. The coil is taken up at intervals, "rove" off straight by the hands in lengths sufficient for three leads, which are straightened out, laid in order on a board, and pressed flat by putting a cover over them. They are finally hardened by placing them in a crucible and baking in a kiln. The handling must be done expeditiously, as the leads begin drying immediately, and become brittle as they dry; but on first issuing from the press they are so plastic that knots may be tied loosely in them. The leads are now ready for their wooden cases. At the saw-mills the wood is cut into blocks about seven inches long, and these are sawed into strips about three and one-half inches wide and three-sixteenths of an inch thick. These boards are shaped by machinery and grooved. The lead is then placed between them, and the parts are glued together.

Leaning Tower of Pisa.—This celebrated and beautiful bell-tower is situated in the city of Pisa, Italy, and was built during the twelfth century by the German architect William of Inuspruck. It is cylindrical in shape, 50 feet in diameter, 180 feet high, and leans about 14 feet out of the perpendicular. It is entirely of white marble, and consists of seven stories, divided by rows of columns. The top, which is surmounted by a flat roof and an open gallery, commanding a splendid view of the surrounding country, is reached by 300 steps. The tower was not originally intended to lean, but the foundation settled more on one side than on the other until it reached the present inclination, which it has maintained with scarcely any perceptible increase for hundreds of years. The upper part of the structure was built in a manner to counteract in part the inclination; and the grand chime of bells, seven in number, of which the largest alone weighs 12,-000 pounds, is mounted with reference to counteract this fault still further.

Legal Terms, Dictionary of.—[See Appendix.]

Lemon-Grass, a beautiful perennial grass, three or four feet high. It is a native of India, Arabia, etc., and is extremely abundant in many places. It has a strong lemon-like fragrance, oppressive where the grass abounds. It is too coarse to be eaten by cattle except when young. An agreeable stomachic and tonic-tea is made of the fresh leaves by Europeans in India. By distillation an essential oil is obtained which is employed externally as a stimulant in rheumatic affections, and is yellow, with a strong lemon-like smell. This oil is used in perfumery, and is often called oil of verbena by perfumers.

Leprosy.—The terrible disease of leprosy is more loathsome and more dreaded than any other malady with which mankind is afflicted. A little blotch appears, often on the face of the victim, which, gradually extending, covers the greater part of the body. Scales drop from the sufferer; his limbs become frightfully swollen; his voice grows hoarse and his eyes almost burst from their sockets. His body is numb, but his appetite is as good as ever, and he sleeps with as much relish as he did when in health. Although leprosy does not fill the air with contagion, yet the possible inoculation by personal contact, or by handling objects which have been touched by lepers, has led to their banishment not only from communities but from their homes. The disease prevailed in the middle ages and down to modern times in Europe, and is now prevalent in various warm climates. The western portion of the Island of Molokai, one of the Hawaiian group of islands, contains over 2,000 lepers who are shut out from all hope of ever seeing their friends, unless the latter become similarly afflicted. There have been a few isolated cases of leprosy discovered in the United States, principally among Chinese. Although nothing certain is known regarding the causes of this disease, the investigations of physicians have led to the conclusion that it is due to the use of semi-putrid meat and fish and of rancid oils, to insufficient vegetable food, and to want of cleanliness and exposure to cold and damp. It has also been determined that it is hereditary, and that women are less liable to it than men.

Lettres de Cachet, the name given to the famous warrants of imprisonment issued by the kings of France before the Revolution. The use of *lettres de cachet* became much more frequent after the accession of Louis XIV than ever before, and it was very common for persons to be arrested upon such warrants and confined in the Bastile or some other state prison, where some of them remained for a very long time, and some for life, either because it was so intended, or, in other cases, because they were forgotten. The *lettres de cachet*, or *lettres closes*, as they were also called, were sealed with the king's little seal (*cachet*).

Libations.—The practice of spilling the first few drops of wine from a bottle on the floor is a survival of the very ancient custom of pouring out wine before the gods as an act of homage or worship, a custom nearly identical with the drink-offering of the ancient Hebrews. Among the Greeks and Romans, nearly all sacrifices to the gods were accompanied with libations, wine being poured over them. But libations were also made independent of sacrifices, as before solemn prayers, and on many occasions of public and private life, as before drinking at meals and the like. With the Romans the libation was a sort of grace before meat; as before each meal they made an offering of this kind to the *lares* or household gods   Libations usually consisted of unmixed wine, but milk or honey diluted with water was also used for the purpose. The household libation is distinctly heathen in its origin, as the Hebrews never offered the drink-offering separate from the sacrifice.

Liberty Bell was cast in London in 1752 by order of the Pennsylvania Assembly, for use in their State House. The bell reached Philadelphia the following year, but it cracked without any apparent reason when it was rung to test the sound, and it was necessary to have it recast. This was done by Philadelphia workmen, and in June, 1753, it was again hung in the belfry of the State House. On July 4, 1776, when the Continental Congress declared the colonies independent of Great Britain, the bell was rung for two hours, so the story goes, by the old bellman, who was so filled with enthusiasm and excitement that he could not stop. It was taken down when the British threatened Philadelphia in 1777, and removed to Bethlehem, Pa., but was returned to the State House in 1778, and a new steeple was built for it. A few years afterward it cracked under a stroke of the hammer, and although an attempt has been made to restore its tone by sawing the crack wider, it has been unsuccessful. During the World's Fair in New Orleans in 1885, the bell was sent there for exhibition. It left Philadelphia January 24th, in the charge of three custodians appointed by the Mayor of the city, who did not leave it day or night until it was returned in June of the same year. The train carrying the bell was preceded over the entire route by a pilot engine. The following words are inscribed around it: "By order of the Assembly of the Province of Pennsylvania, for the State House, in the City of Philadelphia, 1752," and underneath, "Proclaim liberty through all the land unto all the inhabitants thereof—Levit. xxv. 10." Its weight is about 2,000 pounds.

Liberty Cap was first used in the United States as one of the devices on a flag of the Philadelphia Light Horse Guards, a company of militia organized some time prior to the Revolution. August 31, 1775, a resolution providing a seal for the use of the board was passed by the Committee of Safety at Philadelphia. On this seal was engraved a liberty cap and the motto, "This is my right, and I will defend it." The cap is of very ancient origin, and was first worn by the Phrygian conquerors of the eastern part of Asia Minor. They adopted it to distinguish themselves from the people they had conquered. The Romans took the fashion from them, and it became customary in Rome to place a red cap called the *pileus* upon the head of a slave when he was given his freedom. In the year 263, when Saturninus took the capital, a red cap was set up on the top of a spear as a promise of liberty to all slaves who would join him. A cap on a spear was also carried by the conspirators as a token of liberty to Rome when Cæsar was murdered; and a medal, which is still extant, with the same device, was also struck. As an emblem of liberty the cap has been adopted by England, and also by France. The liberty cap was blue, with a white border; the French cap was red; and the American is blue, with a border of gilt stars on white.

Libraries, Foreign.—First among the libraries of Great Britain, and second to few, if any, on the continent, is that of the British Museum. It contains about 1,300,000 printed volumes, besides rare and extensive collections of manuscripts, maps, prints and drawings. Next in rank is the Bodleyan or Bodleian Library at Oxford, which contains 300,000 volumes in addition to 20,000 to 30,000 in manuscript. The third and fourth places are occupied by the Public or University Library of Cambridge, and the Library of the Faculty of Advocates at Edinburgh, which are nearly on a par as regards extent and value, containing not less than 265,000 volumes each. The Library of Trinity College, Dublin, with about 192,000 volumes, is the largest and most valuable in Ireland. These five libraries have long been, and still are, entitled by statute to a free copy of every book published in the empire. The great National Library of France—*La Bibliotheque* *du Roi,* as it used to be called, *La Bibliotheque Nationale,* as it is called at present—is one of the largest and most valuable collections of books and manuscripts in the world. The number of printed volumes contained in it is estimated at nearly 2,500,000, and of manuscripts at about 150,000. Among libraries of the second class in Paris, the Arsenal Library with 300,000 volumes, the Library of Ste. Genevieve with 200,000, and the Mazarine Library with 160,000, are the chief. In Italy the Library of the Vatican at Rome stands pre-eminent. The number of printed volumes is only about 200,000, but the manuscript collection is the finest in the world. The Casanata Library, also at Rome, is said to contain 120,000 volumes; the Ambrosian Library at Milan, 140,000 volumes; the Magliabechi Library at Florence, 200,000 volumes; the Royal Library at Naples, 200,000 volumes; the Library of St. Mark's at Venice, 120,000 volumes and 10,000 manuscripts. The Laurentian Library at Florence consists almost entirely of manuscripts. The principal libraries of Spain are the Biblioteca National at Madrid, numbering nearly 430,000 volumes, and the Library of the Escorial, which contains numerous manuscript volumes, treasures of Arabic literature. The Imperial Library at Vienna is a noble collection of not fewer than 400,000 volumes, of which 15,000 are of the class called *incunabula,* or books printed before the year 1500. The Royal Library at Munich contains 900,000 volumes, including 13,000 *incunabula,* and 22,000 manuscripts. The Royal Library at Dresden is a collection of 500,000 volumes, among which are included some of the scarcest specimens of early printing, among others the Mainz Psalter of 1457, the first book printed with a date. The Royal Library of Berlin contains about 700,000 volumes of printed books, and 15,000 volumes of manuscripts. Of the other libraries in Germany, that of the University of Gottingen contains upward of 500,000 volumes, the Ducal Library of Wolfenbuttel about 270,000 volumes, and the University Library at Strasburg over 513,000 books and manuscripts. In Holland, the principal library is the Royal Library at the Hague, containing about 200,000 printed volumes. The Royal Library at Copenhagen contains nearly 550,000 volumes. The largest library in Sweden is that of the University of Upsala, consisting of nearly 200,000 volumes. One of its chief treasures is the famous manuscript of the Gothic Gospels of Ufilas, commonly known as the *Codex Argenteus.* The number of volumes in the Imperial Library of St. Petersburg, Russia, is estimated to be at least 900,000, in addition to 35,000 manuscripts.

Libraries in the United States.—Previous to the Revolutionary War there were only five public libraries in all the colonies, outside of the libraries of colleges. Of these, two were in Philadelphia—the Library Company of Philadelphia, founded in 1731, and the American Philosophical Society, in 1742; one in Charleston, S. C.—the Library Society, established in 1748;

one in Providence, R. I.—the Athenæum, established in 1753; and one in New York—the Society Library, founded in 1754. There are now, according to recently compiled statistics, 5,338 public libraries in the United States, each containing 300 volumes and upward. These include all the libraries of colleges and academies. Three hundred and eighty-six libraries on this list have 10,000 volumes each and upward, 268 being libraries that are free to the public under certain restrictions, and 118 charge a subscription-fee for their privileges. Of the 10,000-volume libraries 120 are libraries of schools and colleges, and 266 are libraries belonging to States, cities or societies. There are eleven libraries in the United States having over 100,000 volumes each, among which are the Library of Harvard College, 260,000 volumes and over; the Astor Library, New York, 200,000 volumes; the Library of Congress, 400,000 volumes and 130,000 pamphlets; the Library of the Boston Athenæum, 123,000 volumes; the Boston Public Library, 260,000 volumes, and the New York Mercantile Library, 200,000 volumes.

Lick Observatory was founded in January, 1877, in pursuance of a deed of trust made by Mr. James Lick of San Francisco, Cal., September 21, 1875. This deed authorized the expenditure of $700,000 in the building of an observatory and equipping it with a telescope "superior to and more powerful than any yet made." The observatory was to become the property of the University of California, and any surplus that might remain after its completion was to go toward its endowment. The land upon which the observatory is built—Mount Hamilton—was granted by the United States, and an excellent road from the valley to the top of the mountain was built by Santa Clara County, in which it is situated, at a cost of $78,000. The observatory was first used, though still incomplete, in noting the transit of Mercury, November 7, 1881. The telescopes were made by Alvin Clark & Sons, Cambridgeport, Mass. The smaller of these, of twelve-inch aperture, was placed in position in 1881. The larger one, of thirty-six inches, was completed in 1886. The lenses of this telescope are the largest and most perfect ever made.

Life Insurance, Origin of.—The rise of life insurance may be traced to several sources. The doctrine of probabilities developed by Pascal and Huyghens as to games of chance was applied to life contingencies by the great Dutch statesman Jan De Witt in 1671, but it was not till some time after that it was applied to life insurance. In 1696 there was a hint at modern life insurance in a London organization, and this was followed by another association two years after. The operators of these two seem to have passed away without giving to their successors any clear account of their plan of operations. In 1706 the Amicable Society for a Perpetual Assurance Office was founded in London, and this is considered the first actual life insurance company established. Its plan was mutual—that is, each member, without reference to age, paid a fixed admission fee and a fixed annual payment per share on from one to three shares; at the end of the year a portion of the fund was divided among the heirs of deceased members in proportion to the shares held by each. In after years the limitations as to age, occupation and health were added.

Lilies, Throne of the.—The throne of France is so called because of the old national emblem—the fleur-de-lis, a species of lily. The story of the adoption of the fleur-de-lis is partially historical and partially legendary. According to history, Clovis, King of the Franks, married the Princess Clotilde of Burgundy in A. D. 493. The young Queen, who was a Christian, earnestly desired the conversion of her husband, who, like the most of the Frankish nation, was a heathen. Her arguments, however, had but little effect upon him. In 496 the Franks and the Allemanni (Germans) were at war, and at the battle at Tolbiac, near Cologne, Clovis was so hard pressed by his enemies that in desperation he called upon the God of the Christians for help, vowing that should he obtain victory he would himself become a Christian. The Allemanni were routed, and on Christmas-day of the same year Clovis and several thousand of his soldiers were baptized. The continuation of the story, which is legendary, is that on the eve of his baptism an angel from heaven presented King Clovis with a blue banner embroidered with golden fleur-de-lis, which he was to adopt as the banner of France. However this may have been, the fact remains that from the time of Clovis to the French Revolution the kings of France bore as their arms, first an indefinite number, and latterly three golden lilies on an azure field.

Lilith.—According to the Talmud, Adam had a wife before Eve by whom he became the father of demons. She refused to submit to the authority of her husband, and left Paradise for a region of the air, which she still haunts as a specter, and lies in wait for and kills children. It is said that our word lullaby is a corruption of the words "Lilla, abi," or "Begone Lilith." Lilis, or Lilith, also became a legendary witch of the middle ages. The superstition that a child must wear an amulet to be safe from Lilith's evil intentions still exists among the ignorant Jews.

Liquor, Consumption of.—The annual consumption of alcoholic drink by all nations is as follows: Austria, wine, 300,000,-000 gallons; beer, 245,000,000 gallons; spirits, 30,000,000 gallons. Belgium, wine, 4,000,000 gallons; beer, 170,000,000 gallons; spirits, 10,000,000 gallons. British Colonies, wine, 108,000,000 gallons; beer, 81,000,000 gallons; spirits, 20,000,000 gallons. Denmark, wine, 1,000,000 gallons; beer, 25,000,000 gallons; spirits, 8,000,-000 gallons. France, wine, 760,000,000 gallons; beer, 190,000,000 gallons; spirits, 34,000,000 gallons. Germany, wine, 120,000,000 gallons; beer, 880,000,000 gallons; spirits, 60,000,000 gallons. Holland, wine, 3,000,000 gallons; beer, 35,000,000 gallons; spirits, 12,-000,000 gallons. Italy, wine, 480,000,000 gallons; beer, 20,000,000 gallons; spirits, 10,000,000 gallons. Portugal, wine, 60,000,000 gallons; beer, 1,000,000 gallons; spirits, 1,000,000 gallons. Russia, wine, 30,000,000 gallons; beer, 63,000,000 gallons; spirits, 145,000,000 gallons. Spain, wine, 220,000,000 gallons; beer, 2,000,000 gallons; spirits, 3,000,000 gallons. Sweden and Norway, wine, 2,000,000 gallons; beer, 35,000,000 gallons; spirits. 27,000,000 gallons. United Kingdom, wine, 15,000,000 gallons; beer, 1,007,000,000 gallons. England, spirits, 21,600,000 gallons. Ireland, spirits, 6,610,000 gallons. Scotland, spirits, 8,800,000 gallons. United States, wine, 30,000,000 gallons; beer, 440,000,-000 gallons; spirits, 76,000,000 gallons.

"**Little Bird Told Me So, A.**"—This common popular expression is not a literal quotation, but is borrowed from the 20th verse of the 10th chapter of Ecclesiastes: "Curse not the king, no not in thy thought; and curse not the rich in thy bedchamber: for a bird of the air shall carry thy voice, and that which hath wings shall tell the matter."

Liverpool Docks.—The docks, at Liverpool, England, extend on the city side of the river Mersey 6 1-4 miles, and have a water area of 333 1-2 acres, and a lineal quayage of 22 miles. The great landing-stage at Liverpool is the finest structure of the kind in the world. It was originally built in 1857, and was greatly enlarged in 1874, but shortly after its completion, July 28, 1874, it accidentally caught fire and was entirely consumed. It was again built in the most substantial manner. Its length in 2,063 feet, and its breadth is 80 feet. It is supported on floating pontoons, which rise and fall with the tide, and is connected with the quay by seven bridges, beside a floating bridge 550 feet in length for heavy traffic. The great system of docks at Liverpool was commenced by the corporation in 1709, and were for a century under the control of the City Council, but since 1856 their management has been in the hands of a board. The amount of capital invested in these docks is £10,000,000, of which £7,000,000 is in Liverpool proper, and the revenue derived from them is over £1,250,000 annually. They are constructed as water-tight inclosures, with flood-gates, which are opened during the flowing and closed during the ebbing of the tide, so that vessels within can be kept afloat and at the same level while being loaded and unloaded.

Llano Estacado, or the Staked Plain of Texas, forms part of the western plateau of that State, and is so called from the great number of bare yucca-stems, resembling stakes, seen there. The plain extends from the headwaters of the Colorado, Brazos and Red Rivers on the east to the Red Pecos in New Mexico on the west, and from the valley of the Canadian on the north to the Pecos on the south. Its surface is gently undulating, but owing to the lack of water there is almost a total absence of vegetation, the yucca being the only plant that grows there.

Locker, Davy Jones'.—This expression alludes to death, according to sailors' vernacular. Jones is probably a corruption of Jonah, and Davy is said to come from the West Indian negro's word duffy, meaning devil or evil spirit. A locker is any receptacle where a sailor keeps his private stores. Sailors attribute any evil which overtakes the ship or crew to an evil spirit, and Duffy Jonah is considered the evil spirit of the sea.

Locomotives, Weight and Cost.—The average weight of the locomotive engines now on the standard-gauge roads is from twenty-five to thirty-five tons. As locomotives are now built, anything above thirty-five tons would be considered heavy, although there have been locomotives built weighing seventy tons. The cost of a locomotive for the standard-gauge roads is about $10,500. It is usually computed by railroad men that in weight and cost the locomotives on the narrow-gauge roads are from one-third to one-half less than those of the standard-gauge lines.

Locusts as Food.—In certain portions of the globe some species of this insect are eaten, and are considered a delicacy. The Arabs in the kingdom of Morocco boil them. The Bedouins roast them a little, then dry them in the sun, and then pack them into large sacks with salt. Other inhabitants of the Eastern countries, when bread is scarce, pulverize them and make bread of them. This is the food referred to in the Scriptures as having been eaten by John the Baptist.

Lollards, or Lollhards, acquired their name from their practice of singing dirges at funerals—the low-German word *lullen,* or lollen, signifying to sing softly or slowly. The Lollards were a semi-monastic society formed in Antwerp about the year 1300, the members of which devoted themselves to the care of the sick and the dead. They were also called, from their frugal life and the poverty of their appearance, *Matemens*; also, from their patron saint, *Brethren of St. Alexius*; and on account of their dwelling in cells, *Fratres Cellitæ.* In the frequent pestilences of that period the Lollards were useful and everywhere welcome, and the order spread through the Netherlands and Germany. Owing to the fact that they were persecuted and reproached with heresy by the clergy and begging-friars, their name was afterward very commonly given to different classes of religionists; and in England it became a designation of the followers of Wycliffe.

London Monument was built in 1671-'77 by Sir Christopher Wren to commemorate the great London fire of 1666. It is placed about 200 feet from the spot where the fire first began in Pudding Lane. The pedestal of the monument is 40 feet high, and the whole structure 202 feet. Until the building of the Washington Monument, the London Monument was noted as being the loftiest isolated column in the world. It was erected at an estimated cost of £14,500. The staircase leading to the top of the column has 345 steps. There were originally four inscriptions on the monument—three in Latin, and the following in English: "This pillar was set up in perpetual remembrance of that most dreadful burning of this Protestant city begun and carried on by ye treachery and malice of ye Popish faction, in ye beginning of September, in ye year of our Lord, 1666, in order to ye carrying on their horrid plot for extirpating ye Protestant religion and old English liberty, and ye introducing popery and slavery." This charge was wholly unfounded, and in 1831 these lines were finally obliterated by order of the Common Council of London.

Longevity of Tradesmen.—The average ages to which men of different occupations live are shown by statistics to be as follows: Agate polishers, 45-48 years; blacksmiths, 55.1 years; brass founders, 60.4 years; brass workers, 52.2 years; brewers, 50.6 years; britannia workers, 42.2 years; butchers, 56.5 years; cabinet makers, 49.8 years; carpenters, 55.7 years; cloth weavers, 57.5-59 years; workers in coal, 55.1 years; confectioners, 57.1 years; coppersmiths, 48.6 years; cotton operatives, 47-50 years; dyers, 63.7 years; engravers, 54.6 years; fertilizer makers, 51 years; gasmen, 62-65 years; gilders, 53.8 years; glass-cutters, 42.8 years; glass-makers, 57.3 years; goldsmiths, 44 years; hatters, 51.6 years; laborers in bleaching-works, 52-53 years; copper forgers, 60.5 years; day laborers, 52.4 years; lead-miners, 41 years; laborers in distilleries, 63.5 years; locksmiths, 49.1 years; machinists and stokers on railroads, 35 years; machinists and stokers on steamships, 57 years; masons, 55.6 years; millers, 45.1 years; workers in oil, 64 years; painters, 57 years; paper-makers, 37.6 years; potters, 53.1 years; printers, 54.3 years; railroad employees, 39.7 years; saddlers, 53.5 years; salt boilers, 67 years; scavengers, 58-60 years; stone-cutters, 36.3 years; tanners, 61.2 years; workers in tobacco, 58.3 years; varnishers, 45 years; watchmakers, 55.9 years.

Lord Dundreary is the name of the character which was assumed by Sothern, the celebrated English actor, in the play called "Our American Cousin."

Lotus-Eaters.—According to Homer, the Lotus-Eaters were a people who lived on the northern coast of Africa, visited by Ulysses in his wanderings, and who endeavored to detain his companions by giving them the lotus to eat. Whoever ate of this fruit wished never to depart. The Arabs call the fruit of the lotus the "fruit of destiny," which they believe is to be eaten in Paradise. The lotus is a shrub of two or three feet high, and its fruit, which is produced in great abundance, is a drupe of the size of a wild plum, which has a pleasant sweet taste. The name lotus has also been given to several beautiful species of water-lily, especially to the blue water-lily and the Egyptian water-lily. In the mythology of the Hindoos and the Chinese the lotus, as a flower, plays a distinguished part. The Hindoo deities of the different sects are often represented seated on a throne of its shape, or on the expanded flower. The color in Southern India is white or red, the last color fabled to be derived from the blood of Siva when Kamadeva, or Cupid, wounded him with the love-arrow. It symbolized the world; the *meru*, or residence of the gods; and female beauty. Among the Chinese the lotus had a similar reputation and poetic meaning, being especially connected with Buddha, and symbolizing female beauty, the small feet of their women being called *kinleen*, or "golden lilies."

Louisiana Returning Board.—It has been claimed with apparent truth that the State Constitution of Louisiana in no way warranted the extensive powers granted to the Returning Board which made itself notorious in 1876; but the historian Johnson calls attention to the fact that the United States Constitution directs the appointment of the electors of a State "in such manner as the Legislature thereof may direct." As far as the choice of Presidential electors went, therefore, the limitations of the State Constitution had no restraining force whatever over powers granted by the Legislature. The Returning Board was, by act of the State Legislature passed in 1872, to be made up of "five persons, elected by the Senate from all political parties," with power "to make the returns of all elections." A majority of the Board was to be a quorum, and any vacancy was to be filled by the residue of the Board. In cases of violence or bribery in any district the local election officers were to certify the facts to the Returning Board, these certificates to be sent within twenty-four hours after the election. Within ten days after the election the Returning Board was to meet in New Orleans and canvass and compile the returns having no certificates attached; then it was to investigate the certificates and take evidence thereon, being empowered to send for persons and papers; and finally, if convinced that the charges of bribery from any place were sustained, was to throw out the returns from that place. There being some apprehension that the Board would not conduct its operations altogether "on the square," or that perhaps it might be interfered with, two deputations were sent down to New Orleans—one by the National Democratic Committee and one by President Grant. The Returning Board invited five gentlemen from each deputation to be present at its meetings, but reserved the right to exclude by its rules other spectators, and to go into secret session for the consideration of "motions, arguments and propositions." A number of protests were entered against the "secret session" plan, against the continued refusal of the Board to fill up their number by the appointment of a Democrat (it was composed entirely of Republicans), as provided by the law under which it was organized, and also against other irregular methods, especially against counting ballots for all the electors when such ballots only bore the names of part of them. No attention, however, was paid to these protests; they were simply filed by the Board, and the work of compiling the returns went on. On December 6th it declared the election of the Republican candidates for State offices and Presidential electors, four Republican and two Democratic Congressmen, nineteen Republicans and seventeen Democrats in the State Senate, and seventy-one Republicans, forty-three Democrats and three Independents in the lower House. Its principal changes had been made by counting for all the eight Hayes electors some 1,200 ballots which bore the names of only three, and by throwing out about 3,000 Democratic and 2,000 Republican votes in parishes where intimidation of the negro vote had been asserted. Soon after the meeting of Congress in December a special committee was appointed by each House, its members drawn from both parties, to make an investigation of the Louisiana election, and sent to New Orleans for that purpose. The officers of the Returning Board protested against this invasion of the rights of a State by committees of the Federal Congress and declined to give up their records, but agreed to allow them to be copied for the committee. More than a month was spent in the examination of witnesses and papers, and upon the return of the committees majority and minority reports were made by both, the division being made on strict party lines. All the Republicans were convinced that the actions of the Returning Board were legal and right, and all the Democrats were equally firm in their conviction of the contrary. The members of the Returning Board were J. Madison Wells, T. C. Anderson, L. M. Kenner and G. Cassanave, all Republicans. The fifth member of the Board—Oscar Arroyo, a Democrat—had, for some unexplained reason, resigned immediately after the election, and the others refused to fill his place.

Lucky Horseshoe.—Most of the houses in the West End of London were protected against witches and evil spirits in the seventeenth century, says John Aubrey, the English antiquary, by having horseshoes fastened to them in various ways. It was the belief that then no witch or evil genius could cross the threshold which was protected by the shoe. The custom of nailing horseshoes, for luck, to all kinds of sailing craft is still, to a certain extent, in vogue, and we all know how fortunate it is considered for any one to find a horseshoe, the good-luck being increased by the number of nails that are attached to the shoe when it is picked up. This superstition can be traced back to about the middle of the seventeenth century, and then we find it lost in the obscurity of the ages.

Luray Caves are three in number, and are situated in Page County, in the Shenandoah Valley, Virginia. Upon their discovery in 1879, the cavern explored was found to contain bones of men and animals, and the walls were blackened, as though from smoke, thus showing conclusively that it had at some time been occupied, but at what period it was of course impossible to determine. The floors were found smooth and even, showing that the stalagmites had been removed by some human agency for this purpose. Stalagmites and stalactites of great size and variety abound in the cave. One, the Empress Column, is a pure white mass of alabaster seventy feet high, reaching from the floor nearly to the roof. Another pendant formation, nearly equal to the former in length, vibrates for a minute when struck; and in one of the rooms, called the cathedral, are twenty slender columns, which sound part of a scale when struck successively. At the Smithsonian Institute at Washington many remarkable specimens from this cave are on exhibition.

Lynch Law.—This term, which signifies the infliction of punishment on persons charged with crimes by persons without legal authority, is supposed to have derived its name from John Lynch, a farmer of North Carolina, who, with his neighbors, tortured and even put to death fugitive slaves and criminals who at that time, the beginning of the last century, infested the Dismal Swamp. What is known as the Lidford Law in England has the same significance.

Macaroni, Manufacture of.—Italian macaroni is made from a peculiar kind of wheat named grano duro, or hard grain. At first it was imported at considerable expense from the Russian territories on the Black Sea, but is now extensively grown by the farmers of Southern Italy. After the wheat has been washed it is hulled and ground, and passed through several sieves to separate the finer from the coarser flour. Five qualities are obtained by as many siftings, the last the finest that can be made. The flour is mixed with hot water to the consistency of a stiff dough, and is then kneaded by means of a wooden pole fastened to a post and worked up and down upon the paste; or the cheaper grades are often made by treading the dough with the feet. When the paste has been kneaded for a long time it is put into a trough or iron vessel containing a large number of small holes of two sizes, the part passing through the smallest becoming vermicelli. Over the larger holes are little copper bridges, from which copper wire passes through each hole, and this makes the hollow tubes of the macaroni. When this vessel is filled with the dough a press is driven in upon it, and as fast as it is forced through the holes a workman takes up the macaroni, or vermicelli, as the case may be, and lays it across a line to dry in lengths of two or three yards, after which it is ready for the market.

Machpelah, Cave of, is one of the Bible sites that are positively known, and was situated on the western slope of a hill in Hebron. A large structure called "El Harum," or "The Sacred Inclosure," surrounds the ancient cave. It stands high up the slope on the eastern side of the valley. The outer wall is 194 feet long, 109 feet wide, and from 48 to 58 feet high. The stones, which are dressed and fitted with great care, are of enormous size, some of them 30 to 38 feet in length and 4 feet thick. This wall, it is generally believed by scholars, was erected probably about the time of David or Solomon. Within the inclosure is a building, which is supposed to have been built for a Christian church in the time of the Emperor Justinian; but it is now used as a Mohammedan mosque. In separate apartments of the mosque are tombs or cenotaphs purporting to be those of Abraham, Isaac, Jacob, Sarah, Rebekah and Leah. These tombs are of stone, and overhung with cloths embroidered with gold and silver. Between the tombs of Isaac and Rebekah is a circular opening into a cavern below, which is supposed to be the real Cave of Machpelah. It is thought probable that the embalmed body of Jacob will really be found in the cave, and explorers have desired to enter it; but the superstitions of the Mohammedans prevent this, as they will allow no one to go into this cavern, believing that any one who should attempt it would be instantly killed.

Madrigal.—The musical madrigal, which originally was a simple song sung in a rich, artistic style, but afterward was an instrumental accompaniment, is believed to have originated with the Flemings, and dates from the middle of the sixteenth century. It went out of fashion about the beginning of the eighteenth century, but the later *glee* may be regarded as a similar composition. The madrigal, as a poem, denotes a short lyric, adapted to the quaint and terse expression of some pleasant thought, generally on the subject of love. The proper madrigal consists of three verses or strophes, generally bound together by rhymes; but this form is not always adhered to, and the name is often applied to little love poems of any form. The best writers of madrigals among the Italians are Petrarch and Tasso; among the French, Montreuil, Lainez and Moncrif; among the Germans, Ziegler (the earliest), Voss, Mansa, Goethe and A. W. Schlegel; and among the English the poets of the Elizabethan and Caroline ages, several of whom, such as Lodge, Withers, Carew and Suckling, have written verses, sometimes called madrigals, sometimes songs, the grace and elegance of which have never been matched. The etymology of the word madrigal is uncertain.

Madstone is a light, porous stone of a greenish color, which is said to possess the property of drawing the venom from the bite of a dog or other animal afflicted with hydrophobia. They are quite rare, being only occasionally found in the South.

Maelstrom, The, which means, literally, " grinding stream," is situated on the Norwegian coast, south-west of the Loffoden Isles, and is the most remarkable whirlpool in the world. It runs between the island of Moskenes and a large solitary rock in the middle of the straits. The strong currents rushing between the Great West Fjord and the outer ocean through the channels of the Loffoden Isles produce a number of whirlpools, of which the maelstrom is by far the most dangerous. During severe storms from the west, for instance, the current runs continually to the east at the rate of six knots an hour, without changing its direction for rising or falling tide, and the stream will boil and eddy in such mighty whirls that the largest steamer could hardly contend successfully with the waters. The depth of the whirlpool is only 20 fathoms, but just outside the straits soundings reach from 100 to 200 fathoms. The great danger to vessels is of course not of suction into the heart of the whirlpool, as legends have supposed, but of being dsahed to pieces against the rocks.

Magnet.—The iron ore which possesses the property of attraction was given the name of *magnet* by the Greeks, because it was first found in Magnesia in Asia Minor, or according to another account because it was first discovered by a shepherd named Magnes, who had iron tips on his shoes, and while walking over some rocks found that his feet stuck to them in a mysterious way. The ore is now called magnetite, and is an oxide of iron containing about seventy-three per cent. of iron when pure. It is a very valuable ore, and supplies a large amount of the finest iron and steel of commerce. Large deposits occur in Norway and Sweden, Finland and the Ural; in the Adirondack region in northern New York; in northern New Jersey; in eastern Pennsylvania, the most noted locality being Cornwall, Lebanon County, where the mines have been worked for over a hundred years; in North Carolina, California and Oregon, and several places in Canada. It is also found in the form of sand in some places in North America, India and New Zealand. One of the largest occurrences of magnetic sand is on the south shore of Long Island, near Quogue, where a furnace was built and an attempt made to work it; but the enterprise proved unsuccessful and was abandoned.

Mahdi.—This word means "The Guided" (by God), and denotes a kind of Mohammedan Messiah who is to come at the end of the world and utterly destroy sin and disbelief and the anti-Christ (Ed-Dejjal). This doctrine is not set forth in the Koran, but it was undoubtedly taught by Mahomet, and the character, easily lending itself to imposture, has played a prominent part in the sectarian revolutions of the East. There have been many pretenders, and some of them have led successful rebellions and established powerful dynasties. The name is best known to the world at large through the late prophet of the Soudan, Mahomet Ahmed, or Achmet, born in the province of Dongola in 1843. This man has had a remarkable career. As a boy he showed a great aptitude for learning, and when twelve years old knew the Koran by heart. At an early age he went away to Khartoum and joined the free school, or "Medressu" of a faki, which was attached to the tomb of Sheikh Hoghali, the patron saint of that city. He studied religion, the tenets of his Sheikh, etc., and after a time left and went to Berber, where he entered another free school; and here, under the Sheikh Ghubush, completed his religious education. Subsequently he became a disciple of Sheikh Dur-el-Daim (continuous light), and was by him ordained a sheikh or faki. He was now twenty-five years old, and like his prototype, the great Arabian Prophet, he retired from the world for a period of solitary meditation, taking up his abode on the Island of Abba, near Kana, in the White Nile. Here he made a small subterranean excavation into which he made a practice of retiring, to repeat by hours one of the names of the Deity, and to fast and pray and burn incense. His fame for wisdom and sanctity by degrees spread far and wide, and he became wealthy, collected disciples and married several wives, all of whom he was careful to select from among the daughters of influential sheikhs. In May, 1881, he began to write to his brother fakis (religious chiefs), and to teach that he was the Mahdi foretold by Mahomet, and that he had a divine mission to reform Islam, to establish a universal equality, a universal law, a universal religion, and a community of goods; also that all who did not believe in him should be destroyed, be they Christian, Mohammedan or pagan. He at once left his place of retirement and publicly announced his appearance, being then about forty years old, and thus again following the career of Mahomet. There were many circumstances calculated to strengthen and support his pretensions; he had made his life closely correspond to that of the founder of Islam; he bore the same name, and his parents also, Abdallah and Amina, bore the names of the parents of Mahomet. Moreover, the year of his appearance, 1300 of the Hegira, was one fraught with anxious apprehension to all true and pious Moslems, who believed that the world would come to an end before its close. Consequently the Mahdi soon had a large and fanatically devoted body of adherents. After some delay, Raouf Pasha, Governor General of the Soudan, sent a small force of 200 men to suppress him; they shot one dervish, and were slaughtered to a man. In August, 1881, Geighe Pasha sent against him the garrisons of Senaar, Feshuda and Kordofan, in all 7,000 men, of whom only 150 escaped. In January, 1883, Senaar joined the Mahdi, and El-Obeyd was captured and became his headquarters. In November, 1883, another Egyptian army under an English officer, Hicks Pasha, was destroyed; and this same fall the Egyptian gendarmerie, advancing under Baker Pasha from Suakim to relieve the loyal garrisons of Sinkat and Tokar, was completely overthrown by Osman Digna (Othman Dakana, or Othman of the black beard), the Mahdi's lieutenant in Eastern Soudan. Two British expeditions from Suakim gained signal victories shortly afterward, but they made no impression on the Mahdi in El-Obeyd, and in January, 1884, the English Government dispatched General Charles George Gordon (the famous Chinese Gordon) to the seat of war. The unique and peculiar prestige of this General among the Soudanis was cunningly counterbalanced by the Mahdi by declaring that he was the Dejjal, and he was after a short while shut up in Khartoum. After much delay another English army under Lord Wolseley was sent to his relief, September, 1884, but it arrived two days too late. General Gordon, after withstanding the determined siege of the Mahdi for 326 days, had surrendered January 26, 1885. The English expedition was at once recalled and the Soudan definitely separated from Egypt and abandoned to the Mahdi, who had, however, but a short while to enjoy his triumph, dying of fever in the following June. Apart from his divine pretensions he was probably a man of considerable ability, shrewd, determined and energetic; he was of medium height and coffee-colored complexion, wore a black beard, and had three scars on each cheek. Abdallah Et-Taashi succeeded him as Khalif of the Soudan.

Mahomet and the Mountain.—The origin of the expression, "If the mountain will not come to Mahomet, Mahomet must go to the mountain," probably is contained in the story that the Arabs demanded from Mahomet some supernatural proofs of his divine commission, when he reluctantly commanded Mount Safa to come to him, and when it did not stir at his bidding, exclaimed: "God is merciful. Had it obeyed my words, it would have fallen upon us to our destruction. I will, therefore, go to the mountain, and I thank God that he has had mercy on a stiff-necked people."

Maiden, The.—From about the middle of the sixteenth century to nearly the end of the seventeenth century the machine in use in Scotland for beheading criminals was called "The Maiden." In construction it was like the French guillotine, except that it had no turning-plank on which to bind the victim. It would seem at first to have been called indifferently "The Maiden" and "The Widow," both names, it may be conjectured, having their origin in some such pleasantry as that of the Earl of Argyle, one of The Maiden's last victims, when he protested that it was "the sweetest maiden he had ever kissed."

Majolica Ware was first manufactured in the island of Majolica, and from thence the art was taken to Italy, where, during the fourteenth and fifteenth centuries, it was carried on to a considerable extent. A factory for manufacturing this ware was established in Fayenza, France, in the latter century, and the name *faience* was substituted for that of *majolica*. About 1530, plates and other ware were manufactured in Italy, decorated with subjects derived from the compositions of Raphael and Marc Antonio, painted in gay and brilliant colors. The establishment was abandoned in 1574, but pieces of majolica continued to be fabricated in various cities of Italy till the eighteenth century. During the decadence of the art of making enameled pottery in Italy, it flourished greatly in France at the famous Palissy pottery works at Paris and the factories at Nevers and Rouen, where it was manufactured till the end of the seventeenth century. The term "majolica" is now applied to vessels made of colored clay and coated with white opaque varnish.

Malachite, a mineral, essentially a carbonate of copper, of a green color. It is valuable as an ore of copper, although seldom smelted alone, not only because it is found along with other ores, but because the metal is apt to be carried off with the carbonic acid. It is sometimes passed off in jewelry as turquois, although easily distinguished by its color and much inferior hardness. It is used for many ornamental purposes. Slabs of it, chiefly from the mines of Siberia, are made into tables, mantels, etc., of exquisite beauty.

Mamalukes, an Arabic word, signifying slaves. When Ghengis Khan desolated great parts of Asia, in the thirteenth

century, and carried away a multitude of the inhabitants for
slaves, the Sultan of Egypt bought 12,000 of them and formed
them into a body of troops. These slaves, or Mamalukes, soon
found their own power so great that in 1254 they made one of
their own number Sultan of Egypt. In 1517 the Mamaluke
kingdom was overthrown by Selim I, but he was compelled to
permit the continuance of the twenty-four Mamaluke Beys as
governors of the provinces. This arrangement continued until
the middle of the eighteenth century, when the number and
wealth of the Mamalukes gave them such a preponderance of
power in Egypt that the Pasha named by the Porte was reduced
to a merely nominal ruler. Their last brilliant achievements were
on the occasion of the French invasion of Egypt, and during the
time immediately following the retirement of the French. They
were foully massacred in 1811 by Mohammed Ali, afterward Vice-
roy of Egypt. The Mamalukes, in general, were able and energetic rulers, and Egypt under their sway arrived at a degree of
prosperity and power to which she had been a stranger from the
days of Sesostris.

Mammoth Cave, The, is situated in Edmonson County, near
Green River, Kentucky, and extends some nine miles. It contains
a succession of wonderful avenues, chambers, domes, abysses, grot-
toes, lakes, rivers and cataracts. One chamber, the Star, is about
500 feet long, 70 feet wide and 70 feet high; the ceiling is composed of black gypsum, and is studded with innumerable white
points, that by a dim light resemble stars; hence the name.
There are avenues one and a half and even two miles in length,
some of which are incrusted with beautiful formations, and present a most dazzling appearance. There is a natural tunnel about
three-quarters of a mile long, 100 feet wide, covered with a ceiling of smooth rock, 45 feet high. Echo River is some three-
fourths of a mile in length, 200 feet in width at some points, and
from 10 to 30 feet in depth, and runs beneath an arched ceiling of
smooth rock about 15 feet high; while the Styx, another river, is
450 feet long, from 15 to 40 feet wide, and from 30 to 40 feet deep,
and is spanned by a natural bridge. Lake Lethe has about the
same length and width as the river Styx, varies in depth from 3
to 40 feet, lies beneath a ceiling some 90 feet above its surface,
and sometimes rises to a height of 60 feet. There is also a Dead
Sea. The entrance to the cave is reached by passing down a wild,
rocky ravine through a dense forest. To visit the portions of this
wonderful cave already traversed requires, it is said, 150 to 200
miles of travel.

Mammoth Trees.—The most famous of the big trees of California are in the Calaveras and Mariposa groves. In the former
there are ninety-three of these mammoth trees, and the highest
now standing is called the "Keystone State." It is 325 feet high
and 45 feet in circumference. In the same grove there are 4
others over 300 feet in height and from 40 to 61 feet in circum-

ference. An idea of the immensity of these monarchs of the forest can be formed from the fact that a house thirty feet in diameter has been built upon the stump of a tree cut down in the Calaveras grove, and that the hollow trunk of a tree, prostrate in the Maraposa grove, will admit of the passage through it of three horsemen riding abreast. The average height of the Mariposa trees is less than that of the Calaveras, the highest being 272 feet; but the average size is greater. The "Grizzly Giant," the most noted of the trees in this grove, is 94 feet in circumference, and its first branch is nearly 200 feet from the ground and is 6 feet in diameter. In addition to these two main groves there are the Tuolumne grove with about 30 big trees, and the Fresno and Stanislaus groves with about 800 each. In this connection should be mentioned the petrified forest which is considered one of the great natural wonders of California. This forest is situated near Calitoga, and contains portions of nearly 100 distinct trees of great size. They are scattered over an area of 3 or 4 miles in extent, and the largest is 60 feet long and 11 feet in diameter at the base. These forests, however, are by no means confined to California, as they have been discovered in the eastern portions of Nebraska, and in Kansas, Colorado, New Mexico, Wyoming, and other States and Territories. It is supposed that these trees were silicified during what is known as the drift period. Silica, which in its crystallized forms is called quartz, agate, flint, etc., becomes gelatinized under certain conditions, and even liquid. In this state it permeates the pores of the wood, and as the woody fiber decays replaces it. Lime and other minerals replace woody structures in the same manner.

Mandarin is derived from the Portuguese *mandar*, to command; the Chinese equivalent is *kuan*. The term is applied by foreigners to every grade of Chinese officers. The mandarins are divided into nine ranks, each distinguished by a different colored ball or button placed on the apex of the cap, by a peculiar emblazonry on the breast, and a different clasp of the girdle. They are not allowed to hold office in their native provinces, nor to marry in the jurisdiction under their control, nor own land in it, nor to have a near relative holding office under them; and when they are remiss or guilty of crime they are required to accuse themselves and to request punishment. A mandarin is seldom continued in office in a station or province for more than three years. It is incumbent on every provincial officer to report the character and qualifications of all under him to the Board of Civil Office. The points of character are arranged under six different heads, viz.: those who are not diligent, the inefficient, the superficial, the untalented, superannuated and diseased. According to the opinions given in this report, officers are elevated or degraded so many steps in the scale of merit, like boys in a class.

Man-in-the-Moon is a name popularly given to the dark lines and spots upon the surface of the moon which are visible to the naked eye, and which, when examined with a telescope, are discovered to be due to depressions and mountains on the surface. It is one of the most popular and perhaps one of the most ancient superstitions in the world that these lines and spots are the figure of a man leaning on a fork, on which he carries a bundle of thorns or brushwood, for stealing which, on a Sunday, he was confined in the moon. Some of those versed in such lore explain that this story undoubtedly had its origin in the account given in the fifteenth chapter of the Book of Numbers, thirty-second verse, of a man who was stoned to death for gathering sticks upon the Sabbath-day. With the Italians Cain appears to have been the offender. The Jews have some Talmudical story that Jacob is in the moon, and they believe his face is visible. Bishop Wilkins writes that "as for the forme of those spots, some of the vulgar thinke they represent a man, and poets guess 'tis the boy Endymion, whose company she loves so well that she carries him with her."

Maraschino, a *liqueur* or cordial distilled from a fine, delicate variety of cherry, called *marazques*, grown only in Dalmatia. This cherry is largely cultivated around Zara, the capital, where the *liqueur* is chiefly made. Great care is taken in the distillation to avoid injury to the delicate flavor, and the finest sugar is used to sweeten it.

March, the first month of the Roman year, was named from Mars, the god of war. It was considered as the first month of the year in England until the change of style in 1752. The Anglo-Saxons called it *Hlyd monath*, stormy month, and *Hræd monath*, rugged month.

Mardi-Gras.—The Mardi-Gras is the festival preceding the first day of Lent, or Ash-Wednesday. Most of the distinctive ceremonies now annually performed in New Orleans were originally introduced by the French population as early as 1827. The day is a legal holiday, and the entire city is for the time ostensibly placed under the control of a king of the carnival, the great "Rex." There are two principal pageants. The first, in the day-time, is the escort of the "beloved Rex" through his favorite city; the other, or night pageant, is known as the "Mystick Krewe of Comus." This has a character altogether unique. The first display was in 1857. On Twelfth-night (January 6th) the "Knights of Momus" have a display analogous to the Mardi-Gras, but more exclusively burlesque, and in which they satirize the follies of the age. The arrangements for these celebrations come within the control of quite an elaborate organization. The Mardi-Gras is held on Shrove-Tuesday, a day of pleasure in most Roman Catholic countries. It is the Carnival of the Italians, the Mardi-Gras of the French, and the Pancake-Tuesday of former times in England.

Mason and Dixon's Line, a name given to the southern boundary-line of the State of Pennsylvania, which separates it from the

States of Maryland and Virginia. It was run, except about twenty-two miles, by Charles Mason and Jeremiah Dixon, two English mathematicians and surveyors, between November 15, 1763, and December 26, 1767. During the exciting debate in Congress, in 1820, on the question of excluding slavery from Missouri, the eccentric John Randolph, of Roanoke, made great use of this phrase, which was caught up and re-echoed by every newspaper in the land, and thus gained the celebrity which it still maintains.

Massachusetts Blue-Laws.—In regard to the so-called "blue-laws" of Massachusetts it is difficult to determine just where the line between fact and fancy is to be drawn. It is claimed that the founders of Connecticut borrowed most of their laws and judicial proceedings from Massachusetts. Many of these laws were enacted previous to 1640, and a number were the orders and sentences of the Massachusetts Court of Assistants and General Court. For instance, one order we find is as follows: "It is ordered, that all Rich. Clough's strong water shall presently be seazed upon, for his selling greate quantytie thereof to several men servants, which was the occasion of much disorder, drunkenes, and misdemeanor." Another record, in March, 1631, is to the effect that "Nich. Knopp is fyned 5£ for takeing upon him to cure the scurvey, by a water of noe worth nor value, which he solde att a very deare rate, to be imprisoned till hee pay his fine or give securitye for it, or else to be whipped; and shal be lyable to any man's action of whome he hath receaved money for the said water." In September, 1634, a number of restrictions regarding the fashions of dress were enacted. One of them was as follows: "The court, takeing into consideration the greate, superflous, and unnecessary expences occasioned by reason of some newe and immodest fashions, as also the ordinary weareing of silver, golde, and silke laces, girdles, hatbands, etc., hath therefore ordered that noe person, either man or woman, shall hereafter make or buy apparell, either woollen, silke or lynnen, with any lace on it, silver, golde, silke, or threed, under the penalty of forfecture of such cloathes." That there was restraint put upon the tongue is shown by the following, under date of September, 1636: "Robert Shorthose, for swearing by the blond of God, was sentenced to have his tongue put into a cleft stick, and to stand so by the space of haulfe an houre." And here is one against cakes and buns: "It is ordered, also, that no person shall sell any cakes or buns, either in the markets or victualing houses, or elsewhere, upon paine of 10s. fine; provided that this order shall not extend to such cakes as shal be made for any buriall, or marriage, or such like spetiall occasion."

Masque, the favorite form of private theatricals in England in portions of the sixteenth and seventeenth centuries. It originated in the practice of introducing in any solemn or festive procession men wearing masks, who represented either imaginary or allegorical per sonages. At first it was simply an "acted pageant," but it gradually expanded into a regular dramatic entertainment, which in the hands of men like Fetcher and Ben Jonson attained a high degree of literary beauty. Although the masque as a source of amusement was not in fashion during the reign of Charles I, yet to the time of that monarch belongs the finest masque and one of the most splendid poems ever written—the "Comus" of Milton.

Matador, a Spanish word signifying "slayer." The Matador is the principal performer in a bull-fight. He is handsomely dressed, and holds in the right hand a naked sword, in the left the *muleta*, a small stick with a piece of scarlet-colored silk attached. After a bull has been driven into a state of frenzy by the inferior performers, the matador enters the arena alone to complete the tragic business. As soon as the bull's eye catches the *muleta* he generally rushes blindly at it; and then the matador, if he is well-skilled, dexterously plunges the sword "between the left shoulder and the blade," and the animal drops dead at his feet. The victorious matador is greeted with acclamations, and not less the bull, should he wound, or even kill his antagonist; in which case a new matador steps into the arena and the sport is continued.

Matches, Invention of.—Previous to 1829 the matches in use consisted of a slender stick with a pointed end, which had been dipped in sulphur; and they were lighted by touching them to a spark struck into tinder by flint and steel. In that year, however, what was known as the "Instantaneous Light-Box" was invented. It consisted of a small tin box containing a bottle, in which was placed some sulphuric acid, with sufficient fibrous asbestos to soak it up and prevent its spilling out of the bottle, and a supply of properly prepared matches. These consisted of small splints of wood about two inches long, one end of which was coated with a chemical mixture prepared by mixing chlorate of potash, powdered loaf-sugar and powdered gum-arabic, the whole colored with a little vermilion, and made into a thin paste with water. The splints were readily inflamed by dipping the prepared ends into the sulphuric acid. These were succeeded by the lucifer, or loco-foco match, which was ignited by friction; and that, in turn, by the Congreve, which was similar to the sulphur matches now in use; and this, shortly afterward, by the present parlor match.

Mauna Loa, Volcano of, is on the Sandwich Islands. It has two craters, one of which, Kilauea, is the largest active volcanic crater in the world. The mountain is 14,100 feet high, and Kilauea is situated on the eastern side, about 4,000 feet above the sealevel. This crater is a vast lake of boiling lava, which rises and falls continually by the action of subterranean forces, and it produces large quantities of glassy lava in the form of filaments. This seems to be caused by the passage of steam through the molten lava, which throws small particles or shots of glass into the air, and these leave behind them fine, gleaming filaments, like a tail. The natives call this substance "Pele's hair," Pele being the name of the goddess of the mountain.

Maundy-Thursday, the Thursday of Holy-week. The name is derived from *mandatum*, the first word of the service chanted at the washing of the feet of the pilgrims on that day, which is taken from John xiii, 34. The washing of the pilgrims' feet is of very ancient usage, being referred to by St. Augustine; and both in ancient and modern times it was accompanied by a distribution of "doles," which were handed to the pilgrims in small baskets, thence called "maunds." In the royal usage of maunds in England, the number of doles distributed was reckoned by the years of the monarch. The custom was retained in that country till the year 1838, since which period the "Maundy" men and women receive a money-payment from the clerk of the Almonry office, instead of the dole.

Maxim Self-Acting Gun was invented by Hiram S. Maxim of England. The peculiar features of this gun are: Every round after the first is fired by the recoil of the previous explosion; the cartridges are picked out of the cartridge-belt, one end of which is placed in the gun-mechanism on one side by the automatic action of the gun, and the belt and cartridge-shells are ejected after firing; every recoil of the gun brings the next cartridge into position, forces it into the barrel, cocks the hammer, pulls the trigger, extracts the empty shell and ejects it from the gun—all these processes going on with such marvelous rapidity that 600 rounds are fired in a minute. The gun can be turned in any direction by means of a crank, and the rate of discharge is regulated by a controlling chamber, ingeniously contrived so that the gun may be fired rapidly or slowly, as desired. At the moment of firing, the recoil drives the barrel back about three-quarters of an inch, and it is this recoil which directs the mechanism of the gun and makes its discharges continuous.

May, Latin *Maius,* is from a root *mag,* or *mah,* to grow. The notion that it was named Maius by the Romans in honor of Maia, the mother of Mercury, is quite erroneous, for the name was in use among them long before they knew anything either of Mercury or his mother, who were Greek deities. The outbreak into new life and beauty which marks nature at this time instinctively excites feelings of gladness and delight; hence it is not wonderful that the event should have at all times been celebrated. Among the Romans the feeling of the time found vent in their *Floralia,* or Floral Games, which began on the 28th of April and lasted a few days. In England, as we learn from Chaucer and other writers, it was customary, during the middle ages, for all, both high and low—even the court itself—to go out on the first May morning at an early hour "to fetch the flowers fresh." Hawthorn-branches were also gathered. These were brought home about sunrise, with accompaniments of horn and tabor, and all possible signs of joy and merriment. By a natural transition of ideas they gave the hawthorn-bloom the name of the "May;" they called the ceremony "the bringing home the May;" they spoke of the expedition to the woods as "going a-Maying;" the fairest maid of the village as the "Queen of the May." The most conspicuous feature of these festive proceedings was the erection in every town and village of a fixed pole, called the Maypole, on which they suspended wreaths of flowers, and round which the people danced in rings pretty nearly the whole day. A severe blow was given to these merry customs by the Puritans, who caused the Maypoles to be uprooted. They were, however, revived after the Restoration, and held their ground for a long time; but they have now almost disappeared.

Mean and Solar Time.—Owing to the inclination of the earth's axis and its unequal movement in its orbit, solar days vary in their length. The average solar day corresponds to the twenty-four hours of our clocks, which keep what is called mean time. If a clock were so constructed as to give the real solar time for all periods of the year, it would be observed that sometimes when the solar clock pointed at noon, the ordinary clock, keeping mean time, would be pointing at figures between 11:45 and 12, or at other times between 12 and 12:15. Four times each year, however, the two clocks would coincide, and correct noon-marks can be made December 24, April 15, June 14 and September 1, and the shadow of a dial or noon-mark would point due south at noon by the clock.

Medes and Persians, Laws of.—Several references are to be found in the Scriptures relating to the laws of the Medes and Persians. The phrases which have become so familiar to Bible and other readers regarding the unchangeableness of these laws are taken from the Books of Esther and Daniel. When the enemies of Daniel were afraid of his popularity they formed a conspiracy against him, obtaining an idolatrous decree, which Daniel was accused of breaking. They pressed the king to sign the decree, saying, "Know, O king, that the law of the Medes and Persians is that no decree or statute which the king establisheth may be changed." It is not to be understood from this, however, that a royal decree was in every sense irrevocable, or beyond the possibility of modification or repeal, but rather that edicts could not be capriciously altered, and that the despot was bound and regulated by past decisions and precedents. How a decree could be neutralized, even though it could not be reversed, is shown in the Book of Esther.

Medical Terms, Dictionary of. [See Appendix.]

Meerschaum is a mineral existing in many parts of the world. In Europe, it is found chiefly at Hrubschitz in Moravia, and at Sebastopol and Kaffa in the Crimea; and in Asia it is found abundantly just below the soil in the alluvial beds at Kittisch and Bursa in Natolia; and in the rocks of Eske-Hissar, in the same district, it is mined so extensively as to give employment to nearly a thousand men. Meerschaum, from its having been found on the sea-shore in some places, in peculiarly-rounded snow-white lumps, was ignorantly imagined to be petrified froth of the sea, which is the meaning of its German name. It is composed of silica, magnesia and water. When first dug from the earth it is quite soft and soap-like to the touch, and as it lathers with water and removes grease, it is employed by the Turks as a substitute for soap in washing. After being molded into pipes, these are boiled in oil or wax and baked until hard.

Melrose Abbey is a celebrated ruin in Roxburghshire, Scotland, near the Tweed, about thirty-one miles southeast of Edinburgh. It was founded in 1136 by David I, completed in 1146, and dedicated to the Virgin Mary. In 1322 it was destroyed by the English army of Edward II, but it was soon rebuilt by Robert Bruce in a style of magnificence which ranks it among the most perfect ecclesiastical constructions in the best age of Gothic architecture. In 1385, and again in 1545, it suffered severely at the hands of the English armies, and during the Reformation its choicest sculptures were mutilated. In later times many of the stones have been taken away to use in other buildings, but the church still remains, and a part of the cloister square. After five centuries, these show plainly the original beauty of the building. As an abbey, the history of Melrose is but meager. Its first occupants were Cistercian monks. In its line of abbots there was but one saint, St. Waltheof, who was a stepson of King David. King Alexander II was buried within its walls at his own request. Bruce left it the legacy of his heart, and it gave tombs to that flower of Scottish chivalry, the Knight of Liddesdale, and to his cousin the heroic Douglass, who fell at Otterburn.

Menthol.—The peculiar virtues possessed by menthol, and in fact the drug itself, is comparatively a new discovery in America; but the Chinese and Japanese have made use of it for a long time. It is a white crystalline substance deposited from oil of peppermint, and is obtained by freezing and thawing the oil a number of times, the crystals being deposited during the congealing process. These crystals melt at 97 degrees Fahrenheit, are slightly soluble in water, and entirely soluble in ether and the volatile oils. In the manufacture of menthol the Japanese oil is generally used, as it yields the crystals more richly than the others. The drug is used for external application, and often gives much relief in cases of headache. The effect produced is mainly a sensation of intense cold, caused by the rapid evaporation of the thin coating of the substance which is left on the skin when the menthol pencil has been rubbed over it.

Merchants' Marks.—In the middle ages it was the practice for merchants, traders and others, to whom the proper use of heraldry was not conceded, to be allowed by the heralds to bear devices indicative of their trades or occupations. A cutler might bear his knife, a tailor his shears, a mason his trowel and compasses. These insignia were in strictness ordered to be borne only in "targets hollow at the chief flankes," yet we often find them on shields, and sometimes even impaled and quartered with arms. Merchants, along with a monogram of their initials, often bore a mark composed of a cross and a figure resembling the figure 4 turned backward—perhaps a symbol of the Holy Trinity, though it has also been explained to represent the mast and yard of a ship. The insignia of their companies were frequently borne by merchants in a *chief* above their marks, and occasionally quartered with them. These merchants' marks were probably the origin of the trade-marks of the present time.

Mesmerism was first brought into notice by Frederick Anton Mesmer, a German physician, in 1766, when he published a thesis on "The Influence of the Planets on the Human Body," claiming that the heavenly bodies diffused through the universe a subtle fluid which acts on the nervous system of animated beings; and he further stated that he regarded the new force, which, he said, could be exerted by one living organism upon another, as a means of alleviating or curing disease. In 1778 he left Vienna for Paris, where he gained numerous proselytes and much money. His discovery was fostered by Dr. D'Elson, physician to the King's brother, and in 1784 the French Government ordered the medical faculty of Paris to investigate Mesmer's theory. A committee was appointed, who subsequently reported that "The violent effects which are observed in the public practice of magnetism are due to the manipulations, to the excitement of the imagination which leads us to repeat anything which produces an impression upon the senses." One year later, 1785, Mesmer's popularity had so far declined that he left Paris and retired to Switzerland, where he spent the balance of his life. Mesmerism excited some attention again in 1848, when Miss Harriet Martineau and others announced their belief in it.

Meteoric Stones.—A meteoric stone, which is described by Pliny as being as large as a wagon, fell near Ægospotami, in Asia Minor, in 467 B. C. About A. D. 1500 a stone weighing 1,400 pounds fell in Mexico, and is now in the Smithsonian Institute at Washington. The largest meteoric masses on record were heard of first by Captain Ross, the Arctic explorer, through some Esquimaux. These lay on the west coast of Greenland, and were subsequently found by the Swedish Exploring Expedition of 1870. One of them, now in the Royal Museum of Stockholm, weighs over 50,000 pounds, and is the largest specimen known. Two remarkable meteorites have fallen in Iowa within the past thirteen years. On February 12, 1875, an exceedingly brilliant meteor, in the form of an elongated horseshoe, was seen throughout a region of at least 400 miles in length and 250 in breadth, lying in Missouri and Iowa. It is described as "without a tail, but having a sort of flowing jacket of flame. Detonations were heard, so violent as to shake the earth and to jar the windows like the shock of an earthquake," as it fell, at about 10:30 o'clock P. M., a few miles east of Marengo, Iowa. The ground for the space of some seven miles in length by two to four miles in breadth was strewn with fragments of this meteor, varying in weight from a few ounces to seventy-four pounds. On May 10, 1879, a large and extraordinarily luminous meteor exploded with terrific noise, followed at slight intervals with less violent detonations, and struck the earth in the edge of a ravine near Estherville, Emmet County, Iowa, penetrating to a depth of fourteen feet. Within two miles other fragments were found, one of which weighed 170 pounds and another thirty-two pounds. The principal mass weighed 431 pounds. All the discovered parts aggregated about 640 pounds. The one of 170 pounds is now in the cabinet of the State University of Minnesota. The composition of this aerolite is peculiar in many respects; but, as in nearly all aerolites, there is a considerable proportion of iron and nickel.

Mica consists of a silicate of aluminum combined, according to species, with small proportions of potash, soda, lithia, oxide of iron, oxide of manganese, etc. The most common and serviceable variety is known as potash mica. It is a constituent of granite, gneiss, mica slate, and several other kindred rocks. It is found both disseminated and in veins. It is very widely distributed, especially in composition with other minerals, but there are comparatively few localities where it is known to exist in such quantities and form as to be mined with profit. Its most valuable form is that of muscovite, in which it appears in translucent laminæ or plates. The larger and clearer these plates, the greater the value of the mine or quarry. In Siberia they have been found more than three feet across, and they have been obtained of great size in Sweden and Norway. This is also the case at Acworth, Grafton and Alstead, N. H. Mica is used largely for the doors of stoves and the sides of lanterns. It is employed in some countries as a substitute for window-glass, and its toughness recommends it for this purpose on board vessels of war. Lithia mica contains a small proportion of lithia, which gives it in many cases a fine rose or peachblow color, so that it is used for ornamental purposes. Potash mica, when ground in a fine powder, is used to give a brilliant appearance to walls, and as a sand for drying ink or paper.

Microphone, The, is the black carbon button used in telephones, and is an instrument for magnifying sound. The most sensitive substance, so far as yet discovered, to have the peculiar power, when placed in the electric current, of magnifying sound, is willow charcoal plunged, when at white heat, into mercury. A piece of such charcoal an inch long, placed vertically between two blocks of carbon, hollowed to receive its ends, wires connecting the blocks with an electric battery, and the ordinary receiving-instrument of a telephone, constitute one of the simplest forms of a microphone. The invention of the microphone is claimed by

Professor Hughes of England, and Thomas Edison, the American inventor.

Microscope, Invention of the.—It is generally believed that the first compound microscope was made in 1590 by a Hollander named Zacharias Jansen. Pocket microscopes were first made in London in 1740 by Benjamin Martin. The discovery of the magnifying power of the simple lens was undoubtedly made long before the Christian era, as it is known that the Greeks used magnifiers of glass which they called "reading-glasses," and rude lenses of crystal have been found in Egyptian ruins.

Midnight Sun, Land of the.—In his book on the travels and explorations which led up to the discovery of the remains of the famous and ill-fated Franklin expedition to the Polar regions by the expedition under Lieutenant Schwatka in 1878, Mr. Gilder, the second in command, writes as follows regarding the midnight sun: "We were beginning to get used to the phenomena of the Arctic region, not the least among which is the 'midnight sun.' It is difficult for one who has not witnessed it himself to understand the meaning of this portent. The idea of the long Arctic night seems to be much more generally comprehended. Nearly all writers upon the subject, whether those who have themselves experienced its effects or those whose knowledge is derived from study, dwell with great force on the terribly depressing effect upon the physical organization of natives of the median zones caused by the long Arctic night whenever brought within its influence. Though much less has been written or said concerning the interminable day, its effects are almost as deleterious upon the stranger as the prolonged night. Indeed, to the sojourner in high latitudes the day is much more appreciable, for at no point yet visited by man is the darkness the total darkness of night throughout the entire day, while the 'midnight sun' makes the night like noon-day. Even when the sun passes below the horizon at its upper culmination the daylight is as intense as at noon in lower latitudes, when the sun's disk is obscured by their clouds. The long twilight in the north, where the sun's apparent path around the earth varies so little in latitude at its upper and lower culminations, takes some of the edge off of the prolonged night at the highest latitude ever attained by the Arctic explorer; but there is nothing to relieve the long weary day of its full power upon the system. There (in the north), in the spring, the sun never sets. There is no morning and no night. It is one continuous day for months. At first it seems very difficult to understand this strange thing in nature. The world seems to be entirely wrong, and man grows nervous and restless. Sleep is driven from his weary eyelids, his appetite fails, and all the disagreeable results of protracted vigils are apparent. But gradually he becomes used to this state of affairs, devises means to darken his tent, and once more enjoys his hour of rest. In fact, he learns how to take advantage of the new arrangement, and when traveling pursues his journey at night, or when the sun is lowest, because then he finds the frost that hardens the snow a great assistance in sledging."

Military Divisions and Departments.—The United States are divided into three military divisions and six military departments. The Division of the Atlantic, also the Department of the East, includes the New England States and all States east of the Mississippi River except Illinois, Arkansas and Louisiana. The Division of the Missouri comprises the Department of the Platte, States of Iowa and Nebraska, and Territories of Utah, eastern Idaho and southern Wyoming; the Department of Dakota, States of Minnesota, North and South Dakota and Montana, and the northern part of Wyoming Territory; the Department of Texas, comprising the State of Texas. The Division of the Pacific comprises the Department of California, States of California and Nevada; the Department of Arizona, Territories of Arizona and New Mexico; and the Department of the Columbia, States of Oregon and Washington, and Territories of Idaho and Alaska.

Millennium.—The idea of the Millennium, literally a thousand years' time, originated proximately in the Messianic expectation of the Jews; but more remotely, it has been conjectured, in the Zoroastrian doctrine of the final triumph of Ormuzd over Ahriman, and was connected by the Christians with the second coming of Christ. The notion of a golden age, preserved by the converts from heathenism to Christianity, as well as the oppression and persecution to which they were long subjected by the state authorities, were naturally calculated to develop and strengthen such hopes. The chief basis of the millennium idea in Judaism as well as in Christianity, however, is the ardent hope for a visible Divine rule upon earth, and the identification of the Church with that of which it is merely a symbol. In the Mosaic account of creation we find the primitive ground for making the victorious era of the Church last a thousand years. By a strictly literal interpretation of the 4th verse of the 90th Psalm it was supposed that a day of God was arithmetically equal to a thousand years; hence the six days of creation were understood to indicate that the earth would pass through 6,000 years of labor and suffering, to be followed by a seventh day—that is, 1,000 years of rest and happiness. In the Book of Revelation this view is presented. Still, the rabbinical traditions differ widely among themselves as to the duration of the happy period. During the civil and religious wars in France and England the belief in millenniumism was prominent. The Fifth-monarchy men of Cromwell's time were millennarians of the most exaggerated and dangerous sort. [See *Fifth-Monarchy Men.*] Their peculiar tenet was that the millennium *had* come, and *they* were the saints who were to inherit the earth. Great eagerness and not a little ingenuity have been exhibited by many persons in fixing a date for the commencement of the millennium. The celebrated theologian Johann Albrecht

Bengel asserted, from a study of the prophecies, that the millennium would begin in 1836. This date was long popular. Swedenborg held that the last judgment took place in 1757, and that the new Church, or "Church of the New Jerusalem," as his followers designate themselves — in other words, the millennium era—then began. In America considerable agitation was excited by the preaching of one William Miller, who fixed the second advent of Christ about 1843. Of late years the most noted millennarian was Dr. John Cummings of England, who originally placed the end of the *present* dispensation in 1866 or 1867; but as the time drew near without any millennial symptoms he was understood to have modified his views considerably, and came to the belief that the beginning of the millennium will not differ so much after all from the years immediately preceding it, as people commonly suppose.

Mineral Veins were Filled, How.—The latest theory, and the one generally accepted by the best-informed students of science as to the manner in which the minerals of the earth have been deposited in veins, is that the deposition of mineral matter is due to chemical precipitation. According to this theory, the fissures are first filled with water, usually flowing from sources deep in the earth, where, highly heated and under great pressure, it becomes charged with mineral substances. As it approaches the surface, and the temperature and pressure are reduced, the minerals which it had in solution are precipitated on the sides of the channel. The extensive deposits of various minerals on the walls of thermal springs seem to show that this theory is sufficient for mineral veins. Water or steam, holding in solution sulphur, fluorine and chlorine, and highly heated, might dissolve any minerals with which it came in contact. The formation of geodes and of stalactites in caves seem to prove that solutions of mineral matter are constantly flowing through the rocks beneath the surface of the earth. Out of the numerous theories that have been advanced in explanation of this matter there are four others which are worthy of note—the theory of injection, of aqueous deposition, of lateral secretion, and of sublimation. The theory of injection was held at the time when philosophers were accustomed to ascribe all the great changes in the earth's surface to the action of heat. It should be noted, however, that there are very few mineral veins whose materials can be regarded as even the possible product of fusion, and most of them contain minerals that never could have been formed in the presence of great heat. When the veins on the south shore of Lake Superior, which contain great masses of copper, were first described, they were considered as remarkable examples in proof of the igneous theory; but as masses of native silver are formed in these copper veins, both metals being distinct and nearly pure chemically, it was plain that the veins could not have been filled by the action of heat, as these metals in that case would have united in the form of an alloy.

After the theory of heat-action came the theory which ascribed all or nearly all geological phenomena to the action of water. It was suggested that fissures opened up into seas and other water basins, and that the vein material was deposited from water as limestone and other sedimentary rocks are laid down. According to the third theory, that of lateral secretion, the materials of mineral veins have been derived from the adjacent rocks by percolation through the walls of the vein. The fourth theory accounted for the filling of fissure veins on the supposition that the metals therein were deposited in the form of vapor. In regard to all of these four theories, it has been found that from one circumstance or another their principles are untenable.

Mineral Waters have been used from a very early period as remedial agents. The oldest Greek physicians had great faith in their curative power, and the temples erected to Æsculapius were usually in close proximity to mineral springs; they had recourse to the sulphurous thermal springs of Tiberias (now Tabareah), which are still used by patients from all parts of Syria in cases of painful tumor, rheumatism, gout, palsy, etc., and to the warm baths of Calirrhœ, near the Dead Sea, which are mentioned by Josephus as having been tried by Herod during his sickness. We are indebted to the Romans for the discovery not only of the mineral thermic springs in Italy, but of some of the most important in other parts of Europe, among which may be mentioned Aix-la-Chapelle, Baden-Baden, Bath, Spa in Belgium, and many others; and Pliny, in his "Natural History," mentions a very large number of mineral springs in almost all parts of Europe.

Ministers Plenipotentiary, Salaries of.—The salaries of the Ministers Plenipotentiary of the United States are as follows: Austria-Hungary, $12,000 per annum; Brazil, $12,000; Central America, $10,000; Chili, $10,000; China, $12,000; Colombia, $7,500; France, $17,500; Germany, $17,500; Great Britain, $17,500; Italy, $12,000; Japan, $12,000; Mexico, $12,000; Peru, $10,000; Russia, $17,500; Spain, $12,500; Turkey, $7,500.

Ministers Resident and Consuls-General, Salaries of.—The salaries of the Ministers Resident and Consuls-General of the United States are as follows: Argentine Republic, $7,500 per annum; Belgium, $7,500; Bolivia, $5,000; Corea, $7,500; Denmark, $5,000; Hawaii, $7,500; Hayti, $5,000; Liberia, $5,000; Netherlands, $7,500; Persia, $5,000; Portugal, $5,000; Roumania, $6,500; Siam, $5,000; Sweden and Norway, $7,500; Switzerland, $5,000; Venezuela, $7,500.

Minnesingers, derived from the word *minne,* or love, and is a designation applied to the earliest lyric poets of Germany in the twelfth and thirteenth centuries, their productions being almost exclusively devoted to love romances. Henry of Veldig, who flourished at the court of Frederick Barbarossa, Emperor of Germany, in the beginning of the twelfth century, is regarded as the father of the minnesingers; the last of them was Walther von der

Weide. Besides songs in praise of women, the minnesingers composed odes on public or private occasions of lament or joy, distiches or axioms, and *wachtlieder*, or watch-songs, in which the lover was represented as expostulating with the watchmen who kept guard at the gate of the castle within which his lady-love was imprisoned. These songs and odes were recited by the composer, to his own accompaniment on the viol; and as few of them could write, their compositions were preserved mostly by verbal tradition only, and carried by wandering minstrels from castle to castle throughout Germany, and even beyond its borders. The works of the minnesingers are for the most part superior to those of their more generally known contemporaries, the troubadours (see *Trouvere* and *Troubadour*), both in regard to delicacy of sentiment, elegance and variety of rhythmical structure and grace of action. The glory of the minnesingers may be said to have perished with the downfall of the Swabian dynasty, under which greater liberty of thought and word was allowed among Germans than they again enjoyed for many ages.

Minotaur, one of the most repulsive conceptions of Grecian mythology, is represented as the son of Pasiphaë and a bull, for which she had conceived a passion. It was half-man, half-bull—a man with a bull's head. Minos, the husband of Pasiphaë, shut him up in the labyrinth of Crete, and there fed him with youths and maidens, whom Athens was obliged to supply as an annual tribute, till Theseus, with the help of Ariadne, slew the monster. The minotaur is, with some probability, regarded as a symbol of the Phœnician sun-god.

Mirage.—This phenomenon is extremely common in some localities and is simple in its origin, being merely the difference in density of contiguous strata of the atmosphere. It usually occurs when from any cause, as the radiation of heat from the earth, the stratum of air lying near the surface of the earth in any locality is rendered less dense than the stratum above it. In this case rays of light from a distant object situated in the denser medium, that is a little above the earth's level, coming in a direction nearly parallel to the earth's surface, will strike the rarer medium at a very obtuse angle, and instead of passing into it be reflected back to the dense medium. Thus if a spectator be situated on an eminence and looking at an object situated, like himself, in the denser stratum of air, he will see the object by means of directly transmitted rays; and besides this, rays from the object will be reflected from the upper surface of the rarer stratum of air beneath his eye. The image produced by the reflected rays will appear inverted and below the real object. In particular states of the atmosphere, reflection of a portion only of the rays takes place at the surface of the dense medium, and thus double images are formed—one by reflection and the other by refraction—the first inverted and the second erect. Sometimes objects that are distant and beyond the range of vision because of the curved surface of the earth are made visible; this is caused simply by the refraction of the atmosphere. The mirage of the desert, which takes the appearance of a lake or sheet of water, is the reflection of the sky or a cloud. As the reflecting surface is irregular and constantly varies its position, owing to the continual communication of heat to the upper stratum, the reflected image will be constantly varying, and present the appearance of water ruffled by the wind. This form of mirage, which even experienced travelers have found to be completely deceptive, is of common occurrence in the arid deserts of Lower Egypt, Persia, Tartary, etc. In the Arctic regions it is of no uncommon occurrence for whale-fishers to discover the proximity of other ships by means of their images seen elevated in the air. A mirage frequently seen in the Straits of Messina is known as the "Fata Morgana." The "Specter of the Brocken" in Hanover is another celebrated instance of mirage.

Mirrors, Manufacture of.—In the making of mirrors a large stone table, which can be inclined by means of a screw underneath it, is used. Around the edge of this table is a groove, which allows the superfluous mercury to run off into a receptacle at one end. While the surface of the table is perfectly level tin-foil is carefully laid all over it. A strip of glass is then placed on each of three sides of the foil, and the molten quicksilver is poured from ladles upon the foil until nearly a quarter of an inch deep, the affinity of the mercury for the tin-foil and the obstruction of the glass keeping it from flowing off. The plate of glass for the mirror, which has been cleaned with especial care, is now dexterously slid upon the molten metal in the open side—that is, the side on which no glass strip has been placed. When exactly in its place it is held till one edge of the table has been raised by the screw and the superfluous mercury has run off. The table is then tilted back to a level, heavy weights are placed on the glass, and it is left thus for several hours. It is then turned over and put in a frame, the side covered with amalgam—that is, tin-foil and mercury—placed uppermost. In this position the amalgam becomes hard enough to allow the glass to be set on edge, but it must stand for several weeks to be thoroughly hardened. There are other methods of manufacturing mirrors, but the finest are still made by the method described, which was invented by the Venetians in the sixteenth century.

Mississippi Scheme.—The gigantic commercial scheme commonly known by this name was projected in France by the celebrated financier John Law of Edinburgh in 1717, and collapsed in 1720. Its primary object was to develop the resources of the Province of Louisiana and the country bordering on the Mississippi, a tract at that time believed to abound in the precious metals. The company was incorporated in August, 1717, under the title of the "Company of the West," and started with a capital of 200,000 shares of 500 livres each. They obtained the exclusive privilege of trading to the Mississippi, farming the taxes and coining money. The prospectus was so inviting that shares were eagerly bought; and when, in 1719, the company obtained the monopoly of trading to the East Indies, China and the South Seas, and all the possessions of the French East India Company, the brilliant vision opened up to the public gaze was irresistible. The "Company of the Indies," as it was now called, created 50,000 additional shares; but a rage for speculation had seized all classes, and there were at least 300,000 applicants for the new shares, which consequently rose to an enormous premium. Law, as director-general, promised an annual dividend of 200 livres per share, which, as the shares were paid for in the depreciated *billets d'etat*, amounted to an annual return of 120 per cent. The public enthusiasm now rose to absolute frenzy, and Law's house and the street in front of it were daily crowded by applicants of both sexes and of all ranks, who were content to wait for hours—nay, for days together—in order to obtain an interview with the modern Plutus. While confidence lasted a factitious impulse was given to trade in Paris, the value of manufactures was increased fourfold, and the demand far exceeded the supply. The population is said to have been increased by hundreds of thousands, many of whom were glad to take shelter in garrets, kitchens and stables. But the Regent had meanwhile caused the paper circulation of the National Bank to be increased as the Mississippi scheme stock rose in value, and many wary speculators, foreseeing a crisis, had secretly converted their paper and shares into gold, which they transmitted to England or Belgium for safety. The increasing scarcity of gold and silver becoming felt, a general run was made on the bank. The Mississippi stock now fell considerably, and despite all efforts it continued to fall steadily and rapidly. In 1720 the National Bank and the Company of the Indies were amalgamated; but, though this gave an upward turn to the share-market, it failed to put the public credit on a sound basis. The crisis came at last. In July, 1720, the bank stopped payment, and Law was compelled to flee the country. The French Government was nearly overthrown, and great and widespread financial distress and bankruptcy was occasioned.

Mississippi, Steam on the.—The introduction of steam in the navigation of the Mississippi River was first made in October, 1811, by Nicholas J. Rosevelt, who, under an arrangement with Fulton and Livingston, had a stern-wheel steamboat built in Pittsburg, Pa. It was of 200 tons burden, and was called the New Orleans. The hull was 138 feet long, 30 feet beam, and the cost of the whole was $40,000, including engines. The boat carried sails on two masts.

Mistletoe.—Many of the cherished superstitions and observances of the pagans were, in the early days of Christianity, grafted upon the new religion by the priests, who believed that thereby their cause would be rendered more acceptable to the masses; and as the mistletoe was intimately connected with many of the superstitions of the Druids in Britain and of the ancient Germans, the special custom connected with this plant on Christ-mas-eve is an indubitable relic of the days of Druidism. This custom allows any of the daughters of Eve who passes under a suspended branch of the mystic plant to be then and there kissed by any gallant present.

Mitrailleuse.—The modern mitrailleuse was invented by a Belgian about 1864, was adopted by the French Government in 1868, and was extensively used by the French during the Franco-German war. It has twenty-five rifled barrels, and is loaded at the breech. The American invention of the Gatling gun is on the same principle, only much lighter and more effective. Guns of a somewhat similar character were made as early as the fourteenth century, and well-preserved specimens of these ancient imple-ments—then called killing organs—are still to be seen in the arsenals and museums of Vienna, Rome, Berlin, Moscow and Con-stantinople. In the modern guns of this type the peculiar feature and advantage over other kinds is, that the whole number of barrels may be fired without reloading, and in rapid succession.

Mnemonics.—The oldest method of rendering artificial aid to the memory is said to have been invented by the Greek poet Simonides, who lived 500 B. C. It is called the topical or local-ity plan, and was in substance as follows: Choose a spacious house, containing numerous differently furnished apartments. Impress on the mind whatever is conspicuous in it, so that the thought can readily go over all its parts. Then if one has to re-member a series of ideas, place the first in the hall, the second in the parlor, and so on, going over the windows, the chambers, to the statues and several objects. Then, when one wishes to recall these ideas in their proper succession, commence going through the house, and in connection with each apartment will be found the idea attached to it. Much labor has been spent on mnemonic devices for the assisting in the recollection of numbers, and ulti-mately a system was invented by Gregor von Feinaigle, a German monk, and was taught by him in various parts of Europe, and finally published in 1812. His plan was to connect letters with figures having some association with each other. Thus, for the figure 1 he used the letter t, a single stroke; for 2, n, two strokes; 3, m, or three strokes; 4, r, because this letter is found in the word denoting "four" in all European languages; 5, l, because the Roman numeral L signifies fifty, or five tens; 6, d, from the fancied similarity; 7, k, because two 7s joined at the top would somewhat resemble this letter; 8, b or w, from supposed similar-ity; 9, p, from similarity, and also f, both of which are united in the word puff, which proceeds from a pipe like a 9 figure; 0, s, x or z, because it resembles in its roundness a grindstone which gives out a hissing noise like these letters. Vowels are used in connection with these letters, but always with the express stipulation that they have ńo significance. Suppose, then, that a number is given, say 547; 5 is l, 4 is r, 7 is k, which makes l, r, k; among these we insert an unmeaning vowel, as a, to make up an intelligible word, lark, which remains in the memory far more readily than the numerical form. The word mnemonic is derived from the Greek, signifying "artificial memory."

Mock Suns and Moons.—The former are sometimes called sun-dogs; the scientific names are respectively parhelia and paraselenæ. They occur usually with the phenomena of halos, and are explainable under the same laws, the crystallization of water and the refraction and dispersion of light passing through the minute ice-crystals. In high northern latitudes halos and parhelia are very frequent; but whether in higher or lower latitudes, they are only seen when there intervene between the luminary and the observer those highest thread-like forms of cloud, the cirrus or cirro-stratus. The cold prevailing in the higher spaces occupied by these clouds render it quite certain that their particles must be in the frozen condition—a fine ice-mist. These crystals incline chiefly to the form of regular hexagonal prisms, and are suspended in innumerable different positions between the eye of the spectator and the sun, but, owing to the resistance of the air, taking up especially vertical and horizontal directions. The refraction of the light, passing through these, results in an appearance of a colored ring with the sun as a center, the red within and quite distinct, the other colors overlapping one another and indistinctly seen, or resulting in white. Light is also reflected from the surface of these prisms, which remains white and is diffused with uniformity about the sun. The parhelia may be considered as the intensified effects at certain points of a greater condensation of the dispersed rays, taking the form of colored images of the sun. If the sun is near the horizon they appear generally in the halo, and if it is higher, they are thrown beyond the halo. There is another form of the mock sun, which is a single white image, occasionally seen after the sun has set or before it has risen. This is caused by the reflection of the light from the horizontal edges of ice-prisms. Mock moons are similar phenomena, but are rarely seen. In a general way the above explanation is satisfactory, referring these halos and images to the reflection and single and double refraction of which light is capable, and to the probable effects of extraordinary forms and combinations of the ice-crystals; but the exact and scientific explanation of the complicated and peculiar details of the phenomena is extremely difficult. If the general views be correct, then these appearances prove what is the temperature of the highest cloud-region and the condition of cloud occupying it. They are certainly connected closely with some meteorological changes, and when occurring in summer indicate rain or wind, while in winter they precede snow, or sometimes frosts.

Modern Athens, a name often given to the city of Boston,

Mass., owing to the superior intellectuality which is supposed to be possessed by its citizens, and also for its many excellent literary, scientific and educational institutions and publications.

Molly Maguires.—The first organization of this name was formed in Ireland, with the object, it is believed, of generally misusing process-servers and others engaged in the prosecution and eviction of tenants, and was composed of young men who, in some localities, assumed women's clothing, blackened their faces, and otherwise disguised themselves. It remained, however, for the American "Mollies" to terrorize whole counties and leave a blood-red trail behind them in the coal regions of Pennsylvania. To give even a record of the murders and outrages they committed would require an entire volume; but they were numbered by hundreds, and the unfortunate victims were, in most cases, well known and respected men. The American organization was composed of the restless and reckless element drawn to the coal regions through the opening of the coal-fields. There is no recorded instance where the disguise of women's clothes was assumed in the United States. Through the efforts of James Mc-Parlan, a detective, the secrets of the order were finally revealed and many of its members were brought to justice.

Monday, the second day of the week, derives its designation from the Romans, who called it *Lunæ Dies,* or day of the moon. In most European countries it has been held as sacred to the moon, and bears a corresponding name—in German, *Montag;* in French, *Lundi;* Danish, *Mandag.* The English word comes from the old Anglo-Saxon *Monandæg.*

Monitor, The.—This vessel, which played so important a part in the Civil War, was constructed under the direction of Captain John Ericsson, with its turret invented by Theodore Timbey. Its length was 174 feet, breadth of beam 41 feet, and its cost was $275,000. In the engagement with the Merrimac the Monitor was commanded by Lieutenant, afterward Admiral, John L. Worden. She was lost off the coast of North Carolina, December 31, 1862. Four of her officers and nine men went down with her.

Monroe Doctrine.—The United States had recognized the independence of South American States, and desired to foster republican governments in the western hemisphere. It was the conviction that the less the European powers had to do in the control of the governments of America the safer would be republican institutions. In the year 1823 President Monroe enunciated the doctrine which came afterward to be known by his name. The doctrine was as follows: "That we consider any attempt on the part of European powers to extend their system to any portion of this hemisphere as dangerous to our peace and safety; that we could not view any interposition for the purpose of oppressing or controlling American governments or provinces in any other light than as a manifestation by European powers of an unfriendly disposition toward the United States." This doctrine had an important effect upon the course of foreign powers, and since its enunciation has been generally accepted by the leading statesmen of the country.

Monsoon, the name of the winds prevailing in the Indian Ocean, which blow from the south-west from April to October, and from the north-east from October to April. Similar, though less- strongly-marked, winds prevail off the coasts of Upper Guinea, in Africa and Mexico. During the summer, half of the year the north of Africa and the south of Asia are heated to a higher degree than the Indian Ocean. As the heated air expands and rises and the colder air flows in to supply its place, a general movement of the atmosphere of the Indian Ocean sets in toward the north, thus giving a northerly direction to the wind; but as the air comes from those parts of the globe which revolve quicker to those which revolve more slowly, an easterly direction will be communicated to the wind, and the combination of these two directions results in the south-west monsoon. As the conditions are reversed in the winter, the general motion of the atmosphere sets in toward the south and west, the result being the north-east monsoon.

Monuments and Towers, Heights of.—The heights of the principal monuments and towers in the world are as follows: Eiffel Tower, Paris, 1,000 feet; Washington Monument, Washington, D. C., 555 feet; Cathedral at Cologne, 542 feet; Pyramid of Cheops, 486 feet; Antwerp Cathedral, 476 feet; Strasburg Cathedral, 474 feet; Pyramid of Cephrenes, 456 feet; St. Peter's, Rome, 448 feet; St. Martin's Church at Landshut, 411 feet; St. Paul's, London, 365 feet; Salisbury Cathedral, 400 feet; Cathedral at Cremona, 397 feet; Cathedral at Florence, 386 feet: Church at Fribourg, 386 feet; Cathedral of Seville, 360 feet; Cathedral of Milan, 355 feet; Cathedral of Utrecht, 356 feet; Pyramid of Sakkarah, 356 feet; Cathedral of Notre Dame, Munich, 348 feet; St. Mark's, Venice, 328 feet; Assinelli Tower, Bologna, 272 feet; Trinity Church, New York, 284 feet; Column at Delhi, 262 feet; Church of Notre Dame, Paris, 224 feet; Bunker Hill Monument, 221 feet; London Monument, 202 feet; Leaning Tower of Pisa, 179 feet; Washington Monument, Baltimore, 175 feet; Monument, Place Vendome, Paris, 153 feet; Trajan's Pillar, Rome, 151 feet; Obelisk of Luxor, Paris, 110 feet.

Mosaics.—The origin of the art of producing artistic designs by setting small square pieces of stone or glass of different colors, so as to give the effect of painting, is obscure, but it was much practiced by the Romans, especially for ornamental pavements, specimens of which are almost always found wherever the remains of an old Roman villa are discovered. Under the Byzantine empire it was also much used for the ornamentation of churches, in which it formed a large portion of the wall-decoration. Christian mosaics admit, says one writer, of two general divisions, the later Roman and the Byzantine styles, the material in use being in general cubes of colored glass, inlaid, in the Roman school, on a ground of blue and white, although in the latter the tesseræ are frequently irregular in size and the workmanship coarse. The former style flourished in Italy chiefly in the fifth and sixth centuries, the most splendid specimens being found in the churches of Rome and Ravenna. The Florentine mosaic dates from the time of the Medici, and is made entirely of precious or semi-precious stones, such as amethyst, agate, jasper, onyx, and others, cut and inlaid in forms or thin veneers best suited to produce the effects desired. The objects represented are most frequently birds, flowers, fruits, vases, sometimes buildings, and more rarely portraits and landscapes. In reference to the present Roman mosaics, it may be said that the smalti or small cubes of colored glass which compose the pictures are stuck into the cementing paste, or mastic, in the same manner as were the colored glass, stone, and marble sectilia and tesseræ of the ancients. Within quite recent years mosaics of surpassing beauty, both in design and material, have been produced by Russian artists in the Imperial Glass Manufactory of Russia.

Moscow, Great Bell of, was cast in 1733, and is the largest bell in the world. Its circumference at the bottom is nearly 68 feet, its height about 21 feet, and its weight has been computed to be 443,772 pounds. It was never hung, owing to the fact that it was cracked before finished, and remained in the pit where it was cast until the Czar Nicholas caused it to be raised and set upon a platform in 1836, where it now stands, serving as a chapel.

Mosquito Reservation.—The territory known by the name of the Mosquito Reservation is a strip of land on the eastern coast of Nicaragua, extending from the Wawa River on the north to the Rama River on the south, and from the sea inland to the meridian of 84 degrees 15 minutes west. It contains an area of nearly 9,000 square miles. The western part of the reservation is hilly, but the part near the coast is low, and it is all generally covered with forest. It has a population of from 8,000 to 10,000 aboriginal Indians, whose chief calls himself the King of the Musquito Nation. The first King of the Mosquitos was crowned at Balize in 1825. At his death, several years later, he appointed as Regent the British agent at Balize. From this time Great Britain, who had maintained a foothold in the Honduras country since 1740, claimed a protectorate over the Mosquito Kingdom. In 1848 she seized the port of San Juan, and made an attempt to extend her protectorate over all the adjacent coast. This led to a diplomatic quarrel with the United States, which joined the Central American Republics in refusing to acknowledge the claims of Great Britain. This was settled by the Clayton-Bulwer treaty in 1850. The points at issue between Nicaragua and Great Britain were settled by the convention of Managua in 1860, when San Juan was constituted a free port, and Nicaragua assumed the protectorate over the Mosquitos.

Mother Goose, Author of.—The universally popular stories which are now known under the title of "Mother Goose's Melodies" were most of them composed by the celebrated French writer Charles Perrault in the year 1697, and were issued as the work of his son, who was then a mere child. In 1715 a Boston printer named Thomas Fleet was married by Cotton Mather to Elizabeth Goose, and in due time a son was born to him. This little stranger was the particular delight of his maternal grand-mother, who was known as Mother Goose; and she, to amuse the infant, was accustomed to relate to him in song and otherwise the wonderful ditties which had been familiar to her in her younger days. These eventually were collected and published by Fleet, who, in derision of his mother-in-law, called them "Songs for the Nursery, or Mother Goose's Melodies for Children," under which title they have become famous.

Motor, Keely, The, was the subject of much popular talk and some scientific discussion a few years ago. Keely claimed to have discovered a hitherto unknown *etheric* force which would accomplish more than any other known power, and with it to have solved the problem of perpetual motion. The opinions of skilled engineers in regard to this so-called discovery were not encouraging. Mr. Edison said that nothing had been done yet by the Keely motor that could not just as well be done by compressed air, and a practical engineer who had seen it at work said "that it is clearly nothing more nor less than a generation of an elastic condition of air, gas or vapor produced by causing the molecules of the gas acted upon to vibrate violently in a containing vessel, from whence it is allowed to escape in this strained condition, in order to produce a development of power in any way desirable." Keely showed great perseverance and persistency in keeping the subject before the public and in his endeavor to establish his marvelous discovery; but it is now almost forgotten, and has proved its worthlessness by being so quickly consigned to oblivion.

Mottoes of the States.—The mottoes of the various States are: Arkansas, *Regnant Populi;* California, *Eureka;* Colorado, *Nil Sine Numine;* Connecticut, *Qui Transtulit Sustinet;* Delaware, Liberty and Independence; Georgia, Constitution; Illinois, State Sovereignty—National Union; Indiana, Constitution; Iowa, Our Liberties We Prize—Our Rights We Will Maintain; Kansas, *Ad Astra Per Aspera;* Kentucky, United We Stand, Divided We Fall; Louisiana, Justice; Maine, Dirigo; Maryland, *Crescite et Multiplicamini;* Massachusetts, *Ense Petit Placidam Sub Libertate Quietem;* Michigan, *E Pluribus Unum—Tuebor—Si Quæris Peninsulam Amænum Circumspice;* Minnesota, *L'Etoile du Nord:* Missouri, United We Stand, Divided We Fall—*Salus Populi Suprema Lex Esto;* Nebraska, Equality Before the Law; Nevada, All For Our Country; New York, Excelsior; Ohio, *Imperium in Imperio;* Oregon, The Union; Pennsylvania, Virtue—Liberty—Independence; Rhode Island, Hope; Tennessee, Agriculture—

Commerce; Vermont, Freedom and Unity; Virginia, *Sic Semper Tyrannis;* West Virginia, *Montani Semper Liberi;* Wisconsin, Forward.

Mound-Builders.—It is generally believed that the Mississippi Valley and the Atlantic coast were once populated by an agricultural and partially civilized race quite different from the nomadic Indians, though possibly the progenitors of some of the Indian tribes, and that, after centuries of occupation, they disappeared—at least a thousand, and perhaps many thousand years before the advent of Europeans. The theory has been advanced that these people migrated from Asia; that they passed over Asia to Siberia, across Behring Straits, down the Pacific coast of America from Alaska and to the Mississippi Valley, and down to Mexico, Central America and Peru. The remains of the Mound-Builders, as this vanished people are called, are scattered over most of the States of the Central and lower Mississippi Valley, along the banks of the Missouri, and on the sources of the Allegheny. They are most numerous in Ohio, Indiana, Illinois, Wisconsin, Missouri, Arkansas, Kentucky, Tennessee, Mississippi, Alabama, Georgia, Florida, Texas, and are found in the western part of New York, and in Michigan and Iowa. These mounds vary greatly in size, in some instances are very extensive and exceedingly intricate, notably those of the Licking Valley, near Newark, Ohio, which cover an area of two square miles; in other localities there are some which reach a height of ninety feet. It is not believed that these people had any written language, as no inscriptions or tablets yet discovered indicate this. Many of these mounds have been found to contain skeletons, numerous implements and ornaments, usually composed of stone, sometimes of copper—in its native state—and occasionally shell and bone; also coarse and rude pottery of curious design. In substantiation of the belief that these people came from Asia is the fact that in Siberia mounds have been found similar to those in the Mississippi Valley.

Mount Ararat.—The mountains of Ararat, referred to in the Scriptures, overlook the plain of Arexas in Armenia, and are divided into two peaks, Great Ararat and Little Ararat. The summit of the former is 17,323 feet above the level of the sea, and of the latter 13,000 feet. It is believed that the resting-place of the Ark was upon some lower portion of this range rather than upon the peaks, and in support of this view is the fact that at an elevation of 6,000 or 7,000 feet the climate is temperate, the harvests are quick to mature and abundant; while the peaks, for more than 3,000 feet below their summits, are continuously covered with ice and snow.

Mountain Meadow Massacre.—In September, 1857, a party of emigrants known as "The Arkansas Company" arrived in Utah from the East, on their way to California, and while on their way through the Territory a conspiracy was gotten up by the Mormon leaders, among whom were "Bishop" Dame, George A.

Smith (Brigham Young's right-hand man), and two church dignitaries named Haight and Lee, to massacre the entire company.
The "Saints" claimed that emigrants who had passed through
Utah en route to California had on several occasions treated them
and their people with indignities, had stolen or destroyed their
property, and had given them just cause of complaint. The
followers of Young and his "bishops" and head men had won
over to their interests the Indians residing near and among them,
and had sent out Mormon runners, who gathered in the Indians to
the number of several hundred to aid them in the butchery. Under
the lead of the Mormons the Indians attacked the emigrants, killing some and wounding many more. Then there was a lull in the
fight. The emigrants had defended themselves behind their
wagons and in pits thrown up hastily in their camp. At first, the
Mormons determined to starve them out, but finally it was decided
to send a flag of truce to them with the advice that they put their
arms away in their wagons and depart by another road which was
marked out for them. The emigrants, strange to say, accepted
this advice, and marched into an ambush which had been prepared
for them. Men, women and children were slaughtered, and the
bodies of the slain were stripped and left nude for the time, and
later were thrown into shallow graves, where they were soon
scented and unearthed by the wolves. The bones of the victims
were given a decent burial by the military authorities, and some
one carved on a rude stone raised over the graves the words
"Vengeance is mine; I will repay, saith the Lord." Several of
the instigators of the massacre were brought to trial and subsequently punished.

Mountains, Highest.—So far as known, Mount Everest, in the
Himalayas, is the highest mountain in the world, rising 29,002
feet above the sea. Dapsang in Siberia is probably the next highest, 28,300 feet. Then follows Kanchinjinga, Himalayas, 28,156
feet; Illampu, 24,744 feet; Aconcagua, 22,422 feet; Chimborazo,
21,424 feet—all in the Andes range. Hindoo Koh, Hindoo Koosh
Mountains, 20,000 feet; Ararat, in Armenia, 17,260 feet; St. Elias,
in Alaska, 19,500 feet; Kilimanjaro, 18,715 feet, and Kenia, 18,000
feet, both in the Mountains of the Moon in Africa; Popocatapetl,
17,853 feet, and Orizaba, 17,176 feet, in Mexico; Elburg, in the
Caucasus range, 18,570 feet, and Blanc, in the Alps, 15,784 feet;
Whitney, 14,887 feet, and Shasta, 14,442 feet, in California; and
Howard, 14,383 feet, and Pike's Peak, 14,174 feet, both in the
Rocky Mountains.

Mourning Customs.—From the earliest times the manner of expressing grief at death has differed in different countries. The
Hebrew period of mourning was usually seven days; but in some
instances, as at the death of Moses and Aaron, it was extended to
thirty days. The mourners tore their clothing, cut off the hair
and beard, strewed ashes on their heads and cast themselves on
the ground, weeping and smiting their breasts. The **Greeks**

mourned thirty days, except in Sparta, where the mourning period was limited to ten days, and wore coarse black garments, cut off their hair, and secluded themselves from the public gaze. In the event of the death of a great general the whole army cut off their hair, and also the manes of their horses. The Roman mourning period lasted only a few days; but if the death was that of some great ruler or general all business was stopped, and the forum and the schools were closed. Among the Fiji Islanders the women are required to burn their bodies on the death of a chief, and in the Sandwich Islands the people go into mourning by knocking out the front teeth and by painting the lower part of the face black. The mourning color among the Romans under the republic was black or dark blue for both sexes, but during the empire the women wore white. In Europe and America the color is black; in Turkey it is violet; in China, white; in Egypt, yellow; in Ethiopia, brown. It is customary for the courts in all European countries to go into mourning on the occasion of the death of a member of a royal family. The custom of draping buildings on the death of a great man or a hero of national reputation has always prevailed in the United States.

Mufti is an Arabic word, signifying an expounder of the law, and is the name of a religious and civil functionary who is to be found in every large town of the Ottoman empire. He manages the property of the Church, and watches over the due observance and preservation of its rites and discipline. In his civil capacity he pronounces decisions in such matters of dispute as may be submitted to him. Matters of police, disputes between families, and generally questions involving private interests of no great importance, are decided by the Mufti without the intervention of advocates or any legal expense. The Mufti of Constantinople, or Grand Mufti—called also Sheikh al Islam (Lord of the Faith)—is the highest religious authority of the empire and the supreme head of the Ulemas (servants of religion and laws). He ranks next to the Grand Vizier; he is the chief interpreter of the law, and his authority and influence, though only advisory, were formerly very great. He is appointed, and may be deposed by the Sultan, and his position has in late years lost much of its dignity and importance; but he is exempt from death or any degrading punishment, and his property cannot be confiscated.

Mumming.—The practice of mumming, or masquerading, as it means, is very ancient. It was practiced by the Romans during the Saturnalia, or days of festival and revel, when Saturn was believed to rule the earth. When paganism was replaced by Christianity, Christmas festivities took the place of the ancient Saturnalia; but in spite of the efforts of the priests to suppress it, the practice of masquerading was continued. The players dressed in the most outlandish costumes obtainable, sported in halls or paraded the streets, not unfrequently entering private houses. In England and Scotland mumming is not confined to the Christmas season. Candlemas, Twelfth-night and other festivals are observed by similar revels. In France, Italy and other countries mumming is practiced at their carnivals; and it is a conspicuous feature of the Mardi-Gras at New Orleans, Memphis and other places in America.

Munchhausen, Baron.—There is a simple and natural foundation for the fact that Munchhausen has become a by-word for all wild and improbable tales. There lived in the eighteenth century a certain Karl Friedrich Hieronymus, Baron von Munchhausen, a member of an ancient and noble German family, who attained a remarkable celebrity as a relater of ridiculous and untrue exploits and adventures. A collection of his marvelous stories was first compiled by Rudolf Erich Raspe, and it is probable that a number of the tales credited to the Baron were taken from older books or manufactured outright by the compiler.

Murderous Nations.—Italy takes the lead, with an average annual crop of murders of 2,470, a ratio per 10,000 deaths of 29.4; Spain follows, with a ratio of 23.8 and 1,200 murders; the United States, ratio of 21.5 and 2,100 murders; Austria, ratio of 8.8 and 600 murders; France, ratio of 8.0 and 662 murders; England, ratio of 7.1 and 377 murders. The number of murders and homicides in the United States during the year 1888 was 2,184, classified by causes as follows: Quarrels, 1,033; jealousy, 214; liquor, 192; by highwaymen, 143; highwaymen killed, 82; insanity, 51; infanticide, 66; resisting arrest, 64; strikes, 12; riots, 34; self-defense, 38; outrage, 6; duels, 2; unknown, 247.

Muses, The.—The nine muses were Clio, the muse of history; Euterpe, of lyric poetry; Thalia, of comedy; Melpomene, of tragedy; Terpsichore, choral dance and song; Erato, of erotic poetry; Polyhymnia, of the sublime hymn; Urania, of astronomy; and Calliope, of epic poetry.

Musical Terms, Dictionary of.—[See Appendix.]

Mythological Terms, Dictionary of.—[See Appendix.]

Nabob, the title belonging to the administrators under the Mogul empire of the separate provinces into which the district of a *subahdar* was divided. In Europe, and particularly in England, it came to be applied derisively to those who, having made great fortunes in the Indies, returned to their native country, where they lived in Oriental splendor.

Nails.—It is only since 1810 that machinery has been employed to any extent in the manufacture of nails. Previous to that date they were made by hand by forging on an anvil, and great numbers of men were employed in the industry, there having been as many as 60,000 nailers in the neighborhood of Birmingham alone. It appears that as early as 1606 a patent was obtained for cutting nail-rods by water-power, by Sir Davis Bulmer. An improvement on this was patented in 1618 and a new invention in 1790, which last was the first nail-machine in actual use; it was patented by Thomas Clifford, and used in French's factory at

Wimburn, Staffordshire, in 1792. Toward the close of the last century many patents were obtained in the United States for new machines and improvements on old ones. Many of the first inventors spent large sums of money on their machines, and it has been estimated that it cost fully $1,000,000 to bring them to the perfection attained in 1810, when a machine made 100 nails a minute. The machine invented by Jesse Reed of Massachusetts about 1800 is the one which first came into general use, and this, with some improvements, is the one most largely used to-day. In 1810, Joseph C. Dyer of Boston, then a merchant in London, took out patents in England for the nail-machinery invented in Massachusetts; it was at once widely introduced, and large manufacturing establishments were soon established. Some factories at Birmingham are now capable of making over 40,000,000 nails a week. The term *penny*, used to indicate the size of nails, is supposed to be a corruption of pound; thus a fourpenny nail was one such that 1,000 of them weighed four pounds; a tenpenny, such that 1,000 weighed ten pounds. Originally the "hundred," when applied to nails, meant six score or 120; consequently the thousand was 1200. In France the greater part of the nails used in carpentry-work are made of soft iron-wire, pointed with the hammer, and the head is formed by pinching them in a toothed vise.

Namby-Pamby.—The term "namby-pamby," which has come to be applied to a person of vacillating character, as well as to weak literary productions, was originated by the poet Pope. He applied it to some puerile verses that had been written by an obscure poet—one Ambrose Phillips—addressed to the children of a peer. The first half of the term is meant as a baby way of pronouncing Amby, a pet nickname for Ambrose, and the second half is simply a jingling word to fit it.

Natural Bridge of Virginia is situated in Rockbridge County, and spans the mountain chasm in which flows the little stream called Cedar Creek, the bed of which is more than two hundred feet below the surface of the plain. The middle of the arch is 45 feet in perpendicular thickness, which increases to 60 at its juncture with the vast abutments. It is 60 feet wide, and its span is almost 90 feet. Across the top is a public road. For many years the name of Washington, cut in the rock forming one of the abutments when the Father of his Country was a lad, stood high above those of all others; but in 1818 a student of Washington College, Virginia, Piper by name, climbed from the foot to the top of the rock and placed his name above that of Washington.

Natural Gas.—The earliest use of natural gas of which there is any record is in China, where for centuries it has been conveyed from fissures in salt-mines to the surface through hollow bamboos and used for burning purposes. There are also places in Asia, near the Caspian Sea, where it is seen to issue from the earth, and a similar phenomenon is to be seen in the Szalatna salt-mine in

Hungary.   The first discovery of natural gas made in America was in the neighborhood of Fredonia, Chautauqua County, New York, early in this century.   In 1821 a small well was bored in the village and the gas was conducted through pipes to the houses and used for illuminating purposes, and on the occasion of Lafayette's visit in 1824 it is said that the village was illuminated with this gas.   Although this discovery was widely known it did not lead to any further experiments, either in the neighborhood or in other places, till fully twenty years after.   In the early part of the present century it was found that the wells which were bored for salt in the Kanawha Valley yielded large quantities of gas, but it was not utilized as fuel until 1841.   In 1865 a well which was sunk for petroleum at West Bloomfield, New York, struck a flow of natural gas.   An effort was made to utilize this, and it was carried in a wooden main to the city of Rochester, a distance of twenty-four miles, in 1870, for the purpose of illuminating the city, but the experiment was a failure.   In 1873 a well in Armstrong County, Pennsylvania, was so arranged that the gas could be separated from the water with which it was discharged, and conveyed through pipes to several mills in that vicinity, where it was extensively used for manufacturing purposes for the first time.   From that date to the present day the use of natural gas, both for fuel and illuminating, has increased very rapidly, it having been discovered in other parts of Pennsylvania, Ohio and Indiana.

Natural Storm-Signals.—A continuous south wind in most localities will in a few days cause rain, because, being warm, dense and charged with moisture, it is rarified and cooled by the atmosphere of more northern or elevated sections, and thus its capability of sustaining moisture is lessened.   On the other hand, a continuous north wind dispels all rain signs for the time being.   Flaky clouds, or low-running ones, from any direction but the north, denote rain or snow.   Salmon, leaden or silvery-colored clouds denote falling weather; bright red, clear.   When the sunset is followed by bright lances or streaks of light of various hues radiating from the point where the sun disappeared, continuing across the heavens and converging to a common point in the opposite horizon, there exists a storm-cloud in line with the sun, though it may be so distant as to be for a while entirely hidden from view by the rotundity of the earth.   If the rays of light are evenly divided north and south of the line between the observer and the radiating point, and continue so until they have faded out, the cloud is approaching.   When "heat-lightning" is visible there is a storm-cloud in the same direction, though it may not be seen nor thunder be heard.   When the lightning is continuous and very brilliant the storm is a violent one, though the track of the destructive elements may be from 100 to 200 miles away.

Nautical Terms, Dictionary of.—[See Appendix.]

Naval Academy.—There are allowed at the United States

Naval Academy at Annapolis one cadet for each member or delegate of the United States House of Representatives, one for the District of Columbia and ten at large. The appointment of cadets at large and for the District of Columbia are made by the President. Candidates must be actual residents of the districts from which they are nominated. The course of naval cadets is six years, the last two of which are spent at sea. All cadets at the time of their examination for admission must be between the ages of 14 and 18 years, and physically sound, well formed and of robust condition. They enter the academy immediately after passing the prescribed examinations, and are required to sign articles binding themselves to serve in the United States Navy eight years, including the time of probation at the Naval Academy, unless sooner discharged. The pay of the naval cadet is $500 a year, beginning at the date of admission.

Navies of Europe.—The number of vessels comprising the navies of the several European countries are as follows: Germany, armored ships, 14; unarmored ships, 81; torpedo-boats, 130; armored gun-boats, 18; unarmored gun-boats, 11. France, armored ships, 60; unarmored ships, 59; torpedo-boats, 128; unarmored gun-boats, 51; armored gun-boats, 8. Italy, armored ships, 23; unarmored ships, 14; torpedo-boats, 76; unarmored gun-boats, 34. Russia, armored ships, 23; unarmored ships, 36; torpedo-boats, 160; unarmored gun-boats, 79. Austria, armored ships, 12; unarmored ships, 14; torpedo-boats, 40; unarmored gun-boats, 18. Great Britain, armored ships, 82; unarmored ships, 109; torpedo-boats, 300; armored gun-boats, 3; unarmored gun-boats, 133. Netherlands, armored ships, 17; unarmored ships, 46; torpedo-boats, 50; armored gun-boats, 7. Spain, armored ships, 20; unarmored ships, 39; torpedo-boats, 21; armored gun-boats, 4; unarmored gun-boats, 74. Sweden and Norway, armored ships, 4; unarmored ships, 6; torpedo-boats, 24; armored gun-boats, 11; unarmored gun-boats, 18. Turkey, armored ships, 17; unarmored ships, 48; armored gun-boats, 5; unarmored gun-boats, 11. Denmark, armored ships, 7; unarmored ships, 6; armored gun-boats, 5; unarmored gun-boats, 3.

Navigation Acts, The.—In 1650 an act was passed by the British Parliament with a view to stop the gainful trade of the Dutch, prohibiting all ships of foreign nations from trading with any English plantation without a license from the Council of State. In 1651 the prohibition was extended to the mother-country, and no goods were suffered to be imported into England or any of its dependencies in any other than English bottoms, or in the ships of that European nation of which the merchandise was the genuine growth or manufacture. In the year 1660 foreign vessels were prohibited from entering the colonial ports. In 1663 a duty was laid upon goods shipped from one colony to another, and two years later the colonists were forbidden to manufacture any goods which would be likely to compete with English ones in their own as well as foreign markets. These laws, like all others, were enacted by a power which supposed it could enforce them; but they were, in part or as a whole, denounced and disregarded by the people of the colonies as unjust and tyrannical, and were one of the causes of the Revolutionary War.

Navy Department, Salaries in.—The salaries of the officials of the Navy Department of the United States are as follows: Secretary of the Navy, $8,000 per annum; Chief Clerk, $2,500; Chief, Bureau of Yards and Docks, $5,000; Chief, Bureau of Equipment, $5,000; Chief, Bureau of Navigation, $5,000; Chief, Bureau of Ordnance, $5,000; Chief, Bureau of Construction, $5,000; Chief, Bureau of Steam-Engineering, $5,000; Chief, Bureau of Provisions and Clothing, $5,000; Chief, Bureau of Medicine, $5,000; Superintendent, Nautical Almanac, $3,500; Colonel Commanding Marines, $4,500; Hydrographer, $3,000; Superintendent, Naval Observatory, $5,000.

Navy Officers, Salaries of.—The salaries of the officers of the United States Navy are as follows: Admiral, $13,000 per annum; Vice-Admiral, $9,000; Rear-Admiral, $6,000; Commodores, $5,000; Captains, $4,500; Commanders, $3,500; Lieutenant-Commanders, $2,800; Lieutenants, $2,400; Masters, $1,800; Ensigns, $1,200; Midshipmen, $1,000; Cadet-Midshipmen, $500; Mates, $900; Medical and Pay Directors and Medical and Pay Inspectors and Chief Engineers, $4,400; Fleet-Surgeons, Fleet-Paymasters and Fleet-Engineers, $4,400; Surgeons and Paymasters, $2,800; Chaplains, $2,500.

Navy Yards.—The several navy yards of the United States are named and located as follows: Brooklyn Navy Yard, Brooklyn, N. Y.; Charlestown Navy Yard, Boston, Mass.; Gosport Navy Yard, near Norfolk, Va.; Kittery Navy Yard, opposite Portsmouth, N. H.; League Island Navy Yard, seven miles below Philadelphia, Pa.; Mare Island Navy Yard, near San Francisco, Cal.; New London Naval Station, New London, Conn.; Pensacola Navy Yard, Pensacola, Fla.; Washington City Navy Yard, Washington, D. C.; Norfolk Navy Yard, Norfolk, Va. In addition to the above there are naval stations at Port Royal, S. C., and Key West, Fla., and a torpedo station and naval war college at Newport, R. I.

Nebular Hypothesis.—The Nebular Hypothesis assumes that the solar system was once an enormous mass of gaseous substance. Rapid rotation arising in this gaseous mass, it took the form of a disk, and at last inertia (popularly but erroneously called centrifugal force), overcoming cohesion, whole rings and fragments flew off from this disk, and by gravitation contracted into spheroid masses. As, in the original mass, the velocity of the outer circle of each body thrown off is greater than the inner circle, this causes each spheroid to revolve on its own axis. This process goes on, and the central mass continues to cool and shrink until we have at last a central body with a number of smaller spheroidal bodies revolving around it in orbits; the smaller, the nearer they are to the central orb. Certain points are assumed in this hypothesis to explain the distribution of matter in our solar system. It is assumed that in throwing off great masses from the central disk, immense quantities of minute particles were also thrown, which continue to revolve, in the same plane with the large mass, around the central body. By slow degrees these minute atoms, by the law of gravitation, were aggregated into the mass nearest to them. These subordinate aggregations would form with most difficulty nearest the large central mass, because of the superior attractive force of the latter, wherefore the interior planets— Mercury, Venus, the earth, and Mars—are smaller than the two great orbs in the zone beyond them. These two enormous planets, Jupiter and Saturn, occupy the space where conditions are most favorable to subordinate aggregations; but beyond them the gravity of aggregating material becomes reduced, and so the planets found in the outer zone, Uranus and Neptune, are smaller than the planets of the middle zone. This hypothesis was first suggested by Sir William Herschel, and was adopted and developed by Laplace.

Needfire is fire obtained by the friction of wood upon wood, or the friction of a rope on a stake of wood, to which a widespread superstition assigned peculiar virtues. With varieties of detail, the practice of raising needfire in cases of calamity, particularly of disease among cattle, has been found to exist among most nations of the Indo-European race. It has been supposed effectual to defeat the sorcery to which the disease is assigned. When the incantation is taking place all the fires in the neighborhood must be extinguished, and they have all to be relighted from the sacred spark. In various places in the Scottish Highlands, the raising of needfire was practiced up to a few years ago. The sacrifice of a heifer was thought necessary to insure its efficiency. The ways of obtaining fire from wood have been various; one is by an apparatus which has been called the "fire-churn," a cylinder turning on a pivot, and furnished with spokes by means of which it is made to revolve very rapidly, and fire is generated by the friction. In its origin, the fire-churn was considered a model of the apparatus by which the fires of heaven were daily rekindled.

Nemesis.—According to Greek mythology, Nemesis was a female divinity who was regarded as the personification of the righteous anger of the gods. According to Hesiod she was the daughter of Night, and was originally supposed to personify the moral feeling of right and a just sense of criminal actions—in other words, the conscience. She was in an especial manner looked upon as the avenger of family crimes and the humbler of the overbearing. There was a celebrated temple sacred to her at Rhamnus, one of the boroughs of Attica, about sixty studia distant from Marathon; the inhabitants of that place considered her the daughter of Oceanus. According to a myth preserved by Pausanias, Nemesis was the mother of Helen by Jupiter, and Leda, the reputed mother of Helen, was only in fact her nurse; but this myth seems to have been invented in later times to represent the divine vengeance which was inflicted on the Greeks and Trojans through the instrumentality of Helen. Nemesis was represented in the olden times as a young virgin resembling Venus; in later times as clothed with the tunic and peplus, sometimes with swords in her hands and a wheel at her foot, a griffin also having his right paw upon the wheel; sometimes in a chariot drawn by griffins.

Newgate Prison.—The celebrated London prison known as Newgate stands at the western extremity of Newgate Street. The exterior presents high, dark stone walls, without windows. The earliest prison here was in the portal of the *new gate* of the city as early as 1218, and hence the name. About two centuries afterward it was rebuilt by the executors of Sir Richard Whittington, whose statue, with a cat, stood in the niche till its destruction by the great fire of London in 1666. Shortly after, it was reconstructed, from which time till 1780, the date of the erection of the present edifice, its condition was, in a sanitary point of view, horrible. It is stated that in the spring of 1750 the jail distemper, spreading to the adjoining Sessions House, caused the death of two of the judges, the lord mayor, and several of the jury and others, to the number of sixty persons and upward. The *Newgate Calendar* contains biographical notices of the most notorious murderers, burglars, thieves and forgers who have been confined within its walls.

New Testament Money.—The American equivalent of the Roman money mentioned in the New Testament is as follows: A mite, 00.343 cents; a farthing, about 00.687 cents; a penny or denarius, 13.75 cents; a pound or mina, $13.75.

New York Elevated Railways.—In 1848 an elevated railroad extending a half-mile was constructed on Greenwich Street, New York, as an experiment. Three years later the West Side Elevated Railroad Company obtained a charter, but shortly afterward sold its right to the New York Elevated Railroad Company. The new organization proceeded rapidly to erect its roads, and in December, 1879, its rolling stock consisted of 131 locomotives, 292 passenger cars, and 8 service cars. In May, 1879, the road was leased to the Manhattan Railway Company. The Metropolitan Elevated Railroad was first called the Gilbert Elevated Railroad, in honor of its projector, Dr. Rufus H. Gilbert. Although the company obtained its charter in 1872, work was not commenced until March, 1876. In two years it expended $10,300,000 in constructing its lines. In 1879 the road with its rolling stock, consisting of 56 locomotives, 180 passenger cars, and 2 freight cars, was leased to the Manhattan Elevated Railroad Company, which now controls and manages the entire elevated railroad system of New York.

Nibelungenlied, one of the most finished specimens of the genuine epic of Germany belonging to the middle ages. Nothing certain is known of the author or authors of the work beyond the fact that it was put in its present form by a wandering minstrel in Austria about or prior to the year 1210, which is the date of the oldest accredited manuscript. In the more authentic manuscripts the poem consists of only twenty parts. The epic cycle embraced in the Nibelungenlied may be specially regarded as the fusion of the history of the mythical people, called in the poem the Nibelungen, with five leading groups of myths, in which are incorporated the adventures of some of the most universally popular personages belonging to the semi-historical myths of mediæval German folk-lore; as, for instance, the hero Siegfried, with his mantle of invisibility, and the lovely Icelandic Brunhild; King Gunther of Burgundy, and his fair sister, Kriemhild, the wife of Siegfried; Hagen of Norway, Dietrich of Berne, and Etzel (Attila), King of the Huns. The loves and feuds, and the stormy lives and violent deaths of these national heroes and heroines, are skillfully intertwined in the Nibelungenlied, and artistically made to center round the mythical treasure of the Nibelungen, which after the murder of Siegfried, who had brought it from the far north, is secretly buried by his murderer, Hagen, beneath the Rhine, where it still remains. The poem, in its rude but strict versification, tells the tale of Kriemhild's vengeance for her husband's death with a passionate earnestness that carries the sympathies of the reader with it, until the interest culminates in the catastrophe of the fierce battle between the Bulgarians and Huns at the court of Etzel, whose hand Kriemhild has accepted, the better to accomplish her purpose of revenge. The tale of horrors fitly closes with the murder of Kriemhild herself, after she has satisfied her vengeance by slaying with Siegfried's sword his murderer, Hagen.

Nicaragua Canal.—The great incentive to the voyages of the early American explorers was the discovery of a direct route to the far East. The existence of a natural strait, connecting the two oceans, was a settled conviction in the minds of those brave navigators, and it was reluctantly abandoned only after a most minute and thorough examination of the whole coast. When the fact was at last forced upon men's minds that there was *not* a passage provided by nature, the more intelligent and far-seeing at once suggested the idea of an artificial channel. Even Balboa and Cortez touched upon it, and the project was definitely urged upon Philip II by Gomara, the Spaniard, in 1551; but there was not then in Spain the energy and ability to grasp so vast an undertaking. For a long time afterward there was no thought of an interoceanic canal until Humboldt awakened new interest in the subject, and indicated the Valley of the Aratro and the Isthmus of Darien as points where, in his opinion, examinations should first be made. In 1825 Nicaragua invited the co-operation of the United States in the construction of a canal by way of Lake Nicaragua and the river San Juan, but with no satisfactory results. In the course of the following years many other attempts were made, and all possible routes, methods and plans were examined and discussed: but nothing came of them until the construction of the Panama Railway, which was the first actual achievement in the line of direct interoceanic communication. This success, however, though of great service to commerce, has, by providing an imperfect system, retarded the realization of the greater project of a water-way between the oceans. Precise instrumental surveys have reduced the possible lines of transit to three, Panama, Nicaragua and Tehuantepec (see articles on *Panama* and *Tehuantepec*), and the prospect indicates the survival of Nicaragua only as the fittest of all. Louis Napoleon thoroughly believed in this route, and at one time, before he became Emperor, was prepared to assume the presidency of the "Canal Napoleon de Nicaragua." In a magazine article published at that time he said: "The State of Nicaragua can become the necessary route of the great commerce of the world, and is destined to attain an extraordinary degree of prosperity and grandeur." This, to-day, bears a prospect of immediate fulfillment, and it is more than probable that the 400th anniversary of Columbus' discovery, 1892, will see his dream accomplished of a direct water-way to the Indies. The enterprise is now well under way, all the preliminary work has been completed and active construction work begun. In 1888 the Maritime Canal Company of Nicaragua and Costa Rica was incorporated by Act of Congress, with a capital of $100,000,000. Important rights and concessions have been obtained from the Governments and ratified by the Congresses of Nicaragua and Costa Rica, which have a common boundary for some distance in the San Juan River. These include all privileges for the canal and a railroad and telegraph line along its route; also land grants amounting to a million and a quarter acres, mostly on the line of the canal. These are now vested rights and the property of United States citizens, which our Government is bound to protect; hence there is no apparent obstacle to the steady progress and early completion of the work. The route, operations and constructions, as at present projected, are as follows: The course is to be from Greytown on the Atlantic to Brito on the Pacific, a total distance of 169.67 miles, of which 140.78 miles are free navigation and 28.89 actual excavation and construction. At the highest point of the route is the great inland sea, Lake Nicaragua, providing a vast water supply at the summit level, and obviating by its size as a reservoir those destructive freshets, such as characterize the Chagres River, which have been one of the greatest difficulties at Panama. This lake is very deep and affords free navigation to the largest ships for 56.50 miles of the course; it is only 15 miles from the Pacific; but, singularly, has only one outlet, the San Juan River, which empties into the Atlantic. To the west of the lake a cut of 8¼ miles carries the canal to the Tolo basin, where, by damming the Rio Grande River, five miles of free navigation are secured at the altitude of the lake 110 feet above the sea-level. At this dam two locks lower the level 85 feet, and the canal continues in excavation down the valley of the Rio Grande for two miles to the last lock, a tidal one of 30 feet lift, below which it enters the upper part of the harbor of Brito, one and a-half miles from the Pacific. The eastern course follows the San Juan for 84 miles, then continues for 12.73 miles through the San Francisco and Machado basins, a rock-cut of three miles, and the Descado basin four miles—the required depth of water and the level of the lake being maintained for this entire distance by means of dams and embankments. Then by a series of three locks the canal is brought down to the sea-level, and after 12.37 miles of soft excavation reaches the Atlantic at Greytown. Among the leading engineering feats is the formation of good harbors at Greytown and Brito. It is proposed to protect Brito and the western mouth of the canal from the long swell of the Pacific by two long breakwaters. Greytown harbor is now obstructed by a sandbar, which is to be removed by dredging the entrance, protected by a stone jetty. The estimated cost for building and equipping the canal is $60,000,000. The commercial value and far-reaching results of this great enterprise almost exceed the limits of thought. The traffic ready to use the canal as soon as opened will give a net revenue of about $15,000,000 annually; and once opened, the traffic will without doubt be vastly increased. It will reduce the water distance from New York to the Pacific ports, now 13,000 to 14,000 miles, to 4,500 to 5,500 miles; the distance from Europe to Japan by 3,000 miles; and besides this saving of mileage it lies directly in the path of the great belt of steady trade-winds, which will carry a ship almost all the way from Europe to Japan without tempest or calm.

Nickel was first obtained as a metal in Germany about 1751; but the ore had been previously known to miners, who called it *kupfernickel*, or Old Nick's copper, for the reason that, though it looked like copper ore, no copper could be obtained from it. Nickel, when pure, is silvery white, and does not oxidize or tarnish in the air. It is found in many parts of the world, but the principal mines are in Russia, Sweden, Germany, Austria, England and Scotland, and in the States of Pennsylvania and Connecticut in America. Its chief use is for plating other metals, but it is also used in alloys.

Nihilism.—The term "Nihilist" was probably first used by the Russian novelist Turgeneff, and was given to the party now known as Nihilists in derision, because its members sought the destruction of all existing order and government without proposing and apparently without intending to substitute any defined scheme or organization in its place. The earliest advocate of this doctrine was Michael Bakunin, who as early as 1847 advocated a Russian republic, and in 1868 founded the "International Alliance of Revolution," a secret society having for its object a popular uprising against all monarchical governments. This society was undoubtedly the parent of the many secret organizations that have since sprung into existence throughout Europe. Though Alexander II introduced a much more liberal policy than any of his predecessors, it came so far short of the desires of the party of progress that the spirit of discontent seemed stimulated, and the existence of a revolutionary conspiracy was proved in 1877, when, after a great trial lasting eighteen months, 135 persons out of 183 arrested were found to belong to such an organization. In 1878, when Vera Sassulitch shot General Trepoff, chief of the secret police, the Nihilists began to attract attention as a really formidable society. Her acquittal was followed by a series of outbreaks and assassinations which were only checked after the Czar himself had fallen at the hands of a Nihilist assassin. The doctrines and objects of the Nihilists must be taken from the declarations of their leaders. Bakunin, in a speech at Geneva in 1868, announced that he was the bearer of a new gospel, whose mission was to destroy the *lie* at the beginning of which was God. Having got rid of this belief, the next *lie* to be destroyed was *right*, a fiction invented by *might* to strengthen her power. "Our first work," he said, "must be destruction of everything as it now exists, the good and the bad; for if but an atom of this old world remains, the new will never be created."

Nirvana is, in Buddhistic doctrine, the term denoting the final deliverance of the soul from transmigration. The word is from the Sanscrit *nir*, out; and *vana*, blown; hence, literally, that which is blown out or extinguished. [See *Buddhism*.]

No Man's Land was ceded by Texas to the United States, and has been classed geographically with the Indian Territory for convenience. It extends from the 100th to the 103d meridian, and is about seventy-five miles in width. It lies between Colorado and Kansas on the north and Texas on the south. The following account has been given of its condition and settlement: "For forty years or more the country has been without a name and without law. Even the land-laws of the United States do not cover its nearly 4,000,000 fertile acres. Its well-watered valleys have been a vast herding-ground. Those who are now living there enjoy to the fullest extent the squatter sovereignty extolled by Stephen A. Douglas, and the great Illinois Senator is responsible for it. In fixing up the boundaries during the territorial legislation in which he took a leading part, this strip of land, containing 5,761 square miles, was left out entirely, and from that day has been absolutely without government. It is one of the most fertile spots in the United States, but for the reason that the land and other laws of the nation do not apply to it, settlers have been chary about going on to it. Two years ago some adventurous persons went in and took up lands. They are simply 'squatters.' They have no title whatever to the land, and can get none. The population has grown to 10,000, which lives without law or lawyers. Several small villages have grown up." A provisional government was established in March, 1887, and the name of Cimarron, after its principal river, was given the territory. The provisional council was re-elected November 8, at which time Owen G. Chase was elected a delegate to Congress. A bill for the organization of this land into a Territory had been brought up at the second session of the Forty-ninth Congress, but failed. Soon after the opening of the Fiftieth Congress, a bill for its organization under the name of Cimarron was brought, and was referred to the Committee on Territories.

North and West Riding.—The word "riding" is a corruption of the Anglo-Saxon trithing or thriding, meaning a third. This term is applied to three divisions of Yorkshire County, England, which are known as the North, East and West Ridings, and each retains its own government and officers, as in the early times.

Notable Literary Hoax.—A certain bookseller of London found himself with a large edition of a book called "Drelincourt on Death" on his hands, and consulted Daniel De Foe, the author of "Robinson Crusoe," as to some means of disposing of it. A few days after, this fertile author furnished the manuscript of a pamphlet entitled "The True History of an Apparition of One Mrs. Veal, the Next Day After Her Death, to One Mrs. Bargrave, at Canterbury, the 8th of September, 1705." The business-like, homely, commonplace air of truth that pervaded the whole story was irresistible to the average reader. He felt compelled to believe it. Especially was it convincing to the ladies. The apparition wore a washed silk gown. Her friends did not know that she had had that particular gown washed, but afterward learned that she had. What a convincing air was in this small detail! "Don't tell me," said a lady to her husband, who doubted the story, "that you know anything about washed silk!" And the point of this ghost-story was that this good woman had returned to her neighbor's tea-table to declare that Dr. Drelincourt's book on death was the wisest and truest volume ever written on the subject. This pamphlet was circulated and brought an immediate demand for the book. The copies, to borrow an illustration used by Sir Walter Scott, who was very fond of telling this little story, "which had hung on the bookseller's hands like a pile of leaden bullets, now traversed the town in every direction like the same bullets discharged from a field-piece." A new edition of the book was soon printed, with which was bound the remarkable pamphlet. Of this volume fifty editions have since been sold; it has made fortunes for both publisher and bookseller, and thousands of people in England still buy it, and still quote Mrs. Veal's case as one of the authentic supernatural appearances on record.

November, Latin *novem*, nine, the ninth month of the year among the Romans at the time when the year consisted of 10 months, and then contained 30 days. It subsequently was made to contain only 29 days, but Julius Cæsar gave it 31; and in the reign of Augustus the number was restored to 30. November was one of the most important months in connection with the religious ritual of the Romans, and continues in the same position, though for other reasons, in the Roman Catholic ritual. It was known among the Saxons at *Blot-monath*, "blood-month," on account of the general slaughter of cattle at this time for winter provisions and for sacrifice.

Obelisks.—The word is from the Greek, and signifies a prismatic monument of stone or other material terminating in a pyramidal or pointed top. They are found principally in Egypt, and date back to the most remote periods of antiquity. They were placed before the gateways of the principal temples, and correspond in Egyptian art to the columns of the Romans and stelæ of the Greeks, and appear to have been erected to record the honors or triumphs of the monarchs. They are also called "monoliths," being cut out of a single piece of stone, and have four faces, broader at the base than at the top, the width at the base being one-tenth the height of the shaft to the beginning of the pyramidion, or cap, which is also one-tenth of the same height. The sides are generally sculptured with one vertical line of deeply-cut hieroglyphs and representations. Some of them were originally capped with bronze or gold. Their height varied from a few inches to upward of one hundred feet, the tallest known being that of Karnak, which rises to 105 feet 7 inches. A number of them were removed to Rome by Augustus and later emperors, and they were afterward transported to various cities of Italy and France, and used to adorn squares and public parks. Among the most notable of these relics of ancient art are the two known as Cleopatra's Needles, which, from the inscriptions on them, appear to have been set up at the entrance of the Temple of the Sun, in Heliopolis, Egypt, by Thothmes III, about 1831 B. C. Two centuries after their erection the stones were nearly covered with carvings, setting out the greatness and achievements of Rameses II. Twenty-three years before the Christian era they were moved from Heliopolis to Alexandria by Augustus Cæsar and set up in the Cæsarium, a palace which now stands, a mere mass of ruins, near the station of the railroad to Cairo. In 1819 the Egyptian Government presented one of them to England, but it was not taken to London until 1878. The other was transported to New York in 1880, it having been presented to the United States, and was raised on its pedestal in Central Park, New York, January 22, 1881. The material of these, and indeed of most of the obelisks, is granite brought from Syene, near the first cataract of the Nile. They were cut at the quarry, and floated into and down the Nile during one of the annual overflows.

Occupations of the Inhabitants of the United States.—According to the census of 1880 the occupations of the inhabitants of the United States were as follows: Agriculture, 7,670,493; professional and personal services, 4,074,238; trade and transportation, 1,810,256; manufacturing, mechanical trades and mining, 3,837,112; miscellaneous occupations, 17,392,099.

Oceans, Areas of.—The area of the several oceans is as follows: Pacific, 71,000,000 square miles; Atlantic, 35,000,000 square miles; Indian, 28,000,000 square miles; Antarctic, 8,500,000 square miles; Arctic, 4,500,000 square miles.

Oceans, Depth of.—The average depth of all the oceans is from 2,000 to 3,000 fathoms. Soundings have been made in the Atlantic Ocean, ninety miles off the Island of St. Thomas, in the West Indies, which showed a depth of 23,250 feet, or about four and one-half miles. In 1872–'74 the ship Challenger made a voyage around the world for the purpose of taking deep-sea soundings, and the results showed that the greatest depth in the Pacific Ocean was between four and one-half and five miles, while that of the Atlantic was probably as given above.

Ocean Steam Navigation.—The first ocean steam navigation in the world was by the steamboat Phœnix, built by Colonel John Stevens and navigated from Hoboken, N. J., to Philadelphia in 1808 by Robert L. Stevens. In 1819 the Savannah, an American vessel of 380 tons burden, built at Corlear's Hook, N. Y., made the first steam voyage across the Atlantic. The steamer went from New York to Savannah, Ga., and thence to England. From England she proceeded to St. Petersburg, Russia, where an effort was made to dispose of her to the Czar. The sale not being consummated, she returned to New York, and was afterward converted into a sailing-vessel.

October was the eighth month of the so-called "Year of Romulus," but became the tenth when (according to tradition) Numa changed the commencement of the year to the first of January. October preserved its ancient name, notwithstanding the attempts made by the Roman Senate and the Emperors Commodus and Domitian, who substituted for a time the terms Faustinus, Invictus, Domitianus. Many Roman and Greek festivals fell to be celebrated in this month, the most remarkable of which was the sacrifice at Rome of a horse (which was called October) to the god Mars. The name is from the Latin *octo*, eight. Among the Saxons it was styled *Wyn-monath*, or the wine month.

Odin was the chief god of the ancient Danish, Swedish, Norwegian, and in fact all the North Germanic races, having his seat in Valaskjalf, where he receives, through his two ravens, tidings of all that takes place in the world. As a war-god he holds court in Valhalla, where all brave warriors arrive after death. Under the name of Wuotan or Wodin he was also worshiped by the Saxons. Wednesday derives its name from this god. There is another Odin, who, according to tradition, was a chief of what is known as the Scandinavian branch of the Teutonic family of nations which migrated from Asia into Europe. In the time of Pompey and Julius Cæsar, 70 B. C., he ruled, it is said, over a portion of

Scythia, near the Black Sea. Later, having been driven from that region, he fought his way across Europe, conquered Denmark, and made that country the seat of his kingdom. He was the author of the older "Edda," one of the sacred mythological books of the Scandinavians, which was reduced to writing from oral tradition by one of the Icelandic writers more than a thousand years later. Whether Odin, "the supreme god," and Odin, "the conqueror," were the same individual or not it is difficult to determine. Possibly the warrior-king may have claimed to be an incarnation of the god and assumed his name, or his followers may have deified him after his death.

"**O-Grab-Me Act.**"—This term was applied to the Embargo Act of December 27, 1807. This embargo, laid by the United States on all its own ports and vessels in retaliation for certain decrees of England, sorely restricting the rights of neutral vessels, bore particularly hard on New England, which had been increasing its shipping very rapidly. Inverting the word "embargo," the malcontents called it the "O-grab-me Act," referring to the fact that it operated to the advantage of one part of the country at the expense of the shipping interests in another. The act was repealed in February, 1809.

Ohm's Law is so named from its discoverer, Georg Simon Ohm, a German physicist, born 1787, died 1854. He devoted himself particularly to the investigation of the laws governing galvanic currents, and by a combination of mathematical and experimental investigation, carried on for many years, he at length discovered and established the law which forms the basis of the mathematical theory of electricity. His discoveries were first announced in scientific journals in 1825-'26. This fundamental theorem, known as Ohm's Law, may be briefly stated as follows: The strength of a galvanic current is equal to the electro motive force divided by the resistance. The term *ohm* is now used to designate the standard measure or unit of galvanic resistance, and is equal to the resistance of a cylindrical wire of pure copper one-twentieth of an inch in diameter and 250 feet long.

Old Abe, the War Eagle.—The eagle that has a national reputation as "Old Abe" was captured on Flambeau River, near the line between Ashland and Price Counties, in Wisconsin, in 1861, by a Chippewa Indian named Chief Sky, and was sold by him for a bushel of corn, and subsequently disposed of for $5 to a Mr. Mills, who presented him to Company C of the Eighth Wisconsin Regiment. The bird was named in honor of President Lincoln, and the men of Company C were known as the Eau Claire Eagles, and the Eighth Regiment as the Eagle Regiment. Old Abe accompanied the regiment to the South and occupied a conspicuous position on a perch which was carried alongside of the colors. His first pitched battle was at Farmington, Miss. He was wounded in front of Corinth and before Vicksburg, and was injured *en route* from Memphis to Helena. From the time he joined the regiment until it was finally mustered out of service Old Abe was engaged in thirty-six battles. He always announced the approach of an enemy by a note of alarm; and at the siege of Corinth the rebel general, Price, is said to have ordered his men to capture or kill the bird, at the same time remarking that he would rather capture Old Abe than a whole brigade. When Company C was mustered out it was resolved that Old Abe should be presented to the State of Wisconsin, and in the autumn of 1864 he was carried back to his native State, and on September 26 he was formally accepted by Governor Lewis on behalf of the State. During the winter of 1864–'65 he was exhibited at the Sanitary Fair in Chicago, and the sale of his picture and a little pamphlet history of his exploits netted to the fund for sick and disabled soldiers the sum of $16,000. From that time until his death, which occurred in 1881, he was exhibited at fairs, political conventions and soldiers' reunions without number. A model of him was taken by the sculptor, Leonard W. Volk, and several magnificent monuments have been graced with his counterfeit presentment. He died March 26, 1881, presumably from the effects of smoke inhaled at a fire in the Capitol at Madison in the earlier part of the year. He was stuffed and now stands in the war museum of the State Capitol.

Oldest Library.—The oldest approximations to libraries of which any records exist were brought to light by the Assyrian discoveries of a few years ago, and consist of the Babylonian books inscribed on clay tablets, supposed to have been prepared for public instruction about 650 B. C. It is said that Pisistratus founded a library at Athens about 537 B. C., though there is no clear evidence of the fact. Strabo says Aristotle was the first known collector of a library, which he bequeathed to Theophratus, 322 B. C., and this library at length found its way to Rome.

Oleomargarine.—The belief which is prevalent among the masses that the ingredients which constitute oleomargarine are unclean is fallacious, as will be seen by the following description: Clean beef fat and a proportionate quantity of salt are by process of machinery and heat transformed into what is called white stearine and butter oil, otherwise the oil which has been pressed from the fat. This oil is then churned in the proportion of about 442 pounds of butter oil, 120 pounds of milk, 87½ pounds of cream-made butter and 1¼ ounces of bicarbonate of soda. To this some coloring matter is added, and the mixture churned for some fifty minutes, giving as a result a smooth mass resembling an emulsion of cream. This is put into ice-cream freezers and kept constantly agitated until it solidifies. It is then worked over with revolving butter-workers to get the necessary amount of salt well into it, and is then packed in firkins or made into molds. Science shows that, chemically, pure oleomargarine butter differs but slightly from pure cream butter. By analysis the constituents of cream butter are: Water 11.968, butter solids 88.032. Those of oleomargarine are: Water 11.203, butter solids 88.797. The process of making oleomargarine was invented by M. Hippolyte Niege, a French chemist, about 1872; but later experiments, made by Doctor Mott of New York, added to the commercial value of the original process. The name is derived from two words—oleine and margarine. Oleine is the thin, oily part of fats, and margarine is a peculiar, pearl-like substance extracted from some vegetable oils, and also from some animal fats, the name being of Latin origin, from margarita, a pearl.

Olla-Podrida, a term which has come to be figuratively applied to literary productions of very miscellaneous contents. Originally the term, which is Spanish, and whose literal meaning is a *putrid pot,* signified an accumulation of remains of flesh, fish, vegetables, etc., thrown together in a pot; but it was also used to designate a favorite national dish of the Spaniards, consisting of a mixture of different kinds of meat and vegetables stewed together. The French equivalent is *pot-pourri* [see *Pot-Pourri*], and the Scotch *hotch-potch.* [See *Hotch-Potch.*]

Olympic Games.—The Olympian games were events of paramount interest among the Greeks, and were celebrated in honor of Zeus, the father of gods. They were held every fifth year, sometimes in the month Apollonius (July), and sometimes in the month Parthenius (August). During the continuance of the games, which were athletic in character, heralds proclaimed the cessation of all intestine hostilities throughout Greece, and the territory of Elis, in which the plain of Olympia was situated, was declared inviolable. The great Olympic festival lasted five days, and originally none were allowed to participate in it except those of pure Hellenic blood; but after the conquest of Greece by the Romans the latter sought and obtained the honor of admission to the games. Women were at first forbidden to be present, on pain of being thrown headlong from the Tarpeian rock, but eventually they took part in the chariot races. A victory at Olympia was considered the highest honor which a Greek could obtain, and conferred so much glory upon the state to which he belonged that successful candidates were often solicited to allow themselves to be proclaimed citizens of states to which they did not belong. When a victor returned home he was received with extraordinary distinction; songs were sung in his praise; a place of honor was given him at all public spectacles; frequently statues were erected to him, not only in his native city but also in the sacred grove at Olympia; and he was in general exempted from public taxes, and at Athens was boarded at the expense of the state in the Prytaneion. The fifth or last day of the festival was set apart for processions, sacrifices, and banquets to the victors, who were crowned with a garland of wild olive twigs cut from a sacred tree which grew in the Altis, or sacred grove, and presented to the assembled people, each with a palm-branch in his hand, while the heralds proclaimed his name and that of his father and country.

The space of time which intervened between the holding of these festivals was called an Olympiad, and they began to be reckoned from the year 776 B. C., which was the beginning of the histor ical period in Greek history. The last Olympiad, the 292d, fell in the 392d year of the Christian era. The origin of the Olympic games is hidden in the mists and obscurity of the mythic period of Grecian history. The first glimpse of anything approaching to historic fact in connection with them is their so-called revival by Iphitus, King of Elis, with the assistance of the Spartan lawgiver, Lycurgus, about 884 B. C., or according to others, 828 B. C.—an event commemorated by an inscription on a disk kept in the Heræum at Olympia, which was seen by Pausanias in the second century.

Oneida Community is a society of Perfectionists, or Bible Communists, founded by John Humphrey Noyes, who was born at Brattleborough, Vt., in 1811. He was originally a lawyer, then studied theology at Andover and Yale, and became a Congregationalist minister, but soon lost his license to preach on account of the views which he adopted. The Community is situated on Oneida Creek, in Lenox township, Madison County, N. Y., where it owns a fine estate, several mills and manufactories, and is said to be in a prosperous condition. The cardinal principles of the Community are four in number: reconciliation to God, salvation from sin, recognition of the brotherhood and equality of man and woman, and the community of labor and its fruits. The last-named principle embraces a scheme by which all the male and all the female members of the Community are held in a sense to be married to each other. This has led to the charge being made against them of being "free-lovers;" but says one writer, "The system, as regulated by the 'principle of sympathy' and controlled by that free public opinion which constitutes the supreme government of the society, is far from being amenable to the reproach of immorality in any sense of the word." The Community reject all rules of conduct except those which each believer formulates for himself, subject to the free criticism of his associates. They hold that the Mosaic law and ordinances were abrogated by the second coming of Christ, which they place at A. D. 70, and at which time the reign of sin was concluded; and true believers have since been free to follow the indications of the Holy Spirit in all things, nothing being good or bad in itself. While all the males and females are united by a "complex marriage,". their intercourse—which, in theory, is unfettered by any law—is, in practice, subject to a good deal of regulation. Like everything else, it is subject to the opinion of the society, and certain principles have been so steadily applied to it that they have gained the force of laws. First there is the principle of the ascending fellowship. There should be contrast, the Perfectionists say, between those who become united in love. That there should be differences of temperament and of complexion has, they say, been well ascertained by physiologists. They hold that there should be a difference in age also, so that the young and passionate may be united to those who have, by experience, gained self-control. In virtue of this principle, the younger women fall to the older men, and the younger men to the older women. A second principle is that there should be no exclusive attachment between individuals; a third, that persons should not be obliged to receive the attentions of those whom they do not like; and lastly, it is held indispensable that connections should be formed through the agency of a third party; because, without this, the question of their propriety might be open to criticism, and also because this affords the lady an easy opportunity of declining.

Opium War.—In 1757, the monopoly of opium cultivation, which had been in the hands of the Great Mogul of Bengal, by the victory of Lord Clive at Plassey, passed into the control of the East India Company, and the annual importation of the drug into China was increased from 200 chests in 1773 to 4,054 chests in 1790. This, however, was in direct opposition to the wishes of the Chinese Government, and in 1796 the Emperor forbade its importation, and strenuous laws were passed against opium-smoking. The trade, notwithstanding, increased, and by 1830 had reached an importation of 16,877 chests yearly. In 1834 severer laws against the trade were passed, and Government officials waged open war upon the opium ships. Five years later, March 18, 1839, the Chinese authorities, who were in earnest regarding the absolute stoppage of the traffic, ordered the seizure of all the opium in the hands of English merchants in Canton. Resistance to this order caused riots; but on April 20th 20,283 chests of opium of 143½ pounds each were destroyed by the mandarins, the English owners having previously received a promise from their Government of the full value of all destroyed. The intelligence of these seizures was received with great indignation in England, and when the Chinese emperor passed an edict, January 4, 1840, forbidding all trade and intercourse with England forever, the British Government declared war. A British fleet shortly after captured Chusan, and in the following year the Bogue Forts fell, and Hong Kong was ceded to the British, and an indemnity of $6,000,000 was paid by the Chinese. Canton was taken in May, and ransomed with a similar indemnity. Other cities also fell, and a treaty was finally signed in August, 1842, by which China agreed to pay $21,000,000 indemnity; to throw open to the British the ports of Canton, Amoy, Foochoofoo, Ningpo and Shanghai, and to allow consuls to reside at these cities; to cede Hong Kong to the British in perpetuity; to unconditionally release all British prisoners, and to pardon all Chinese who had been in the British service. In spite of the frequent protests of the Chinese Government, the increase of the opium trade since has been very great. Opium was used in China as a medicine for many years before the opium-trade proper began, and was probably introduced by the

Arabs in the latter part of the thirteenth century, though it is thought by some that it might have been supplied by the Dutch traders, as they are known to have purchased the drug from India long before the East India Company was established.

Oracles dated from the highest antiquity, and flourished in the most remote ages. The word signifies the response delivered by a deity or supernatural being to a worshiper or inquirer, and also the place where the response was delivered. These responses were supposed to be given by a certain divine afflatus, either through means of mankind, as in the organism of the Pythia, and the dreams of the worshiper in the temples, or by its effect on certain objects, as the tinkling of the chaldrons at Dodona, the rustling of the sacred oak, the murmuring of the streams, or by the action of sacred animals, as exemplified in the Apis or sacred bull of Memphis, and the feeding of holy chickens of the Romans. These responses, however, had always to be interpreted to the inquirer by the priesthood. It is probable that all the Egyptian temples were oracular, although only a few are mentioned by Herodotus, as the oracles of Latona in the City of Buto; those of Hercules, Mars, Thebes, and Meroe. Oracles were also used by the Hebrews. The Grecian oracles enjoyed the highest reputation for truthfulness, and the most renowned of all was the Delphic Oracle. Sacrifices were offered by the inquirers, who walked with laurel crowns on their heads, and delivered sealed questions; the response was deemed infallible, and was usually dictated by justice, sound sense and reason, till the growing political importance of the shrine rendered the guardians of it fearful to offend, when they framed answers in ambiguous terms, or allowed the influence of gold and presents to corrupt the inspirations. There were numerous other oracles in Greece and in Asia Minor, and written ones existed of the prophecies of celebrated seers. Those of the Sibyls or prophetic women enjoyed great popularity. [See *Sibyls.*]

Ores are minerals containing a sufficient quantity of metal to make their working a profitable transaction. A rock containing only one per cent. of iron is never called an ore; on the other hand, one containing the same proportion of gold is a very rich ore.

Oriflamme, of France, was a banner which originally belonged to the Abbey of St. Denis, and was borne by the Counts of Vexin, patrons of that church. In 1082 Philip I attached the County of Vexin to the crown, and the oriflamme became the property of the king. It was first used as a national banner in 1119. It was a crimson-silk flag on a gilt staff. The loose end was cut in three wavy Vandykes, to represent triangles of flame, and a silk tassel was hung in each cleft. The name was from the Latin *auriflamma,* the flame of gold. When the oriflamme was displayed on the battle-field it indicated that no quarter was to be given, and therefrom it was called "the oriflamme of death." The battle of

Agincourt, in 1415, is believed to have been the last engagement in which it was carried.

Origin of Mugwump.—This term arose in the Presidential campaign of 1884 as an appellation of the Independent Republicans who seceded from their party and supported the Democratic candidate, Grover Cleveland, chiefly owing to a strong feeling against their own candidate, James G. Blaine. The word is said to be derived from the language of the Algonquin Indians, among whom it meant a Chief or person of importance. It came to be applied derisively to persons who exaggerated their wisdom and importance, and was used in this sense to designate the Independents; but they adopted the name themselves, ignoring the reproach it had been intended to convey. Another explanation of the word derives it from the vernacular of the old Virginia families, where the word is applied to a bull-frog in its intermediate stage from a tadpole, when it is really neither one thing nor the other—a kind of nondescript; whence the name was thought to characterize very aptly the Independents.

Orpheus and Eurydice.—Orpheus was said to have been the son of Apollo and the muse Calliope, or, according to another account, of Œagrus and a muse. He was one of the Argonauts, to whom he rendered the greatest service by his skill in music; the enchanting tones of his lyre made the Argo move into the water, delivered the heroes from many difficulties and dangers while on the voyage, and mainly contributed to their success in obtaining the golden fleece. The skill with which Orpheus struck the lyre was fabled to have been such as to move the very trees and rocks, and the beasts of the forest assembled round him as he touched its cords. He had for his wife a nymph, Eurydice, who died from the bite of a serpent as she was flying from Aristæus. Orpheus, disconsolate at her loss, determined to descend to the lower world to endeavor to mollify its rulers, and to obtain permission for his beloved Eurydice to return to the regions of light. Armed only with his lyre, he entered the realms of Hades, and gained an easy admittance to the palace of Pluto. At the music of his "golden shell" the wheel of Ixion stopped, Tantalus forgot the thirst that tormented him, the vulture ceased to prey upon the vitals of Tityos, and Pluto and Proserpina lent a favoring ear to his prayer. Eurydice was allowed to return with him to the upper world, but only on condition that Orpheus did not look back upon her before they reached the confines of the Kingdom of Darkness. He broke the condition and she vanished from his sight. The common account of his death is that he was torn to pieces by the Thracian women at a Bacchic festival in revenge for the contempt which he had shown toward them through his sorrow for the loss of Eurydice.

Ostracism, the banishment for a time of a person whose presence is considered dangerous to the liberty of his fellow-citizens. This right was first exercised by the people of Athens, and was introduced by Clisthenes about the beginning of the sixth century B. C., after the expulsion of the Pisistratidæ. The people were annually asked by the Prytanes if they wished to exercise this right, and if they did, a public assembly was held and each citizen had opportunity of depositing, in a place appointed for the purpose, a potsherd or small earthen tablet (whence the name), on which was written the name of the person for whose banishment he voted. Six thousand votes were necessary for the banishment of any person; but the greatest men of Athens—Miltiades, Aristides, Themistocles, Cimon, Alcibiades, etc., were subjected to this treatment. There is a famous story connected with the ostracism of Aristides. By his rigid integrity he had gained, among the people, the name of "The Just." When political excitement rose high at Athens in the contest between Themistocles and Aristides, and the banishment of Aristides rested with the vote of the people, a man not knowing the famous statesman approached him, while walking on the sea-shore, and asked him to write on a *shell* the name of Aristides. "And why," said the orator, "do you wish to banish Aristides?" "Oh," replied the man, "I am tired of always hearing him called 'The Just'!" Aristides was banished; but the uncertainty of political life at Athens shortly afterward reversed the situation, and Aristides was recalled to be honored by his state, while his rival, Themistocles, was ostracized, and finally ended his days in exile. The banishment was at first for ten years, but the period was afterward restricted to five. Property and civil rights or honors remained unaffected by it. Ostracism was finally abolished through the exertions of Alcibiades.

Ostrich Feathers.—The feathers of the male bird are more valuable than those of the female. In the male the long feathers of the wings and hinder parts are white, and the short feathers of the body are jet black. In the female the rump and wing-feathers are white, tinged with a dusky gray, the general body color being the latter color.

Oxford University is one of the two greatest seats of learning in Great Britain. It is situated at Oxford, fifty-two miles from London, and comprises twenty colleges and six halls—the latter for the residence of students. The colleges, their founders, and the dates thereof, are as follows: University College, founded by William of Durham, 1249; Balliol, by John Balliol and Devorgilla, his wife, between 1263 and 1268; Merton, by Walter de Merton, Bishop of Rochester, at Malden, in 1264, and removed to Oxford before 1274; Exeter, by Walter de Stapleton, Bishop of Exeter, 1314; Oriel, by Edward II, 1326; Queen's, by Robert Eglesfield, chaplain to Phillippa, queen of Edward III, 1340; New, by William of Wykeham, Bishop of Winchester, 1386; Lincoln, by Richard Fleming, Bishop of Lincoln, 1427; All Souls', by Henry Chichele, Archbishop of Canterbury, 1437; Magdalen, by William of Waynflete, Lord Chancellor, 1456; Brasenose, by William

Smith, Bishop of Lincoln, 1509; Corpus Christi, by Richard Fox Bishop of Winchester, 1516; Christ Church, by Henry VIII, 1546–'47; Trinity, by Sir Thomas Pope, 1554; St. John's, by Sir Thomas White, 1555; Jesus, by Queen Elizabeth, 1571; Wadham, by Nicholas Wadham, 1613; Pembroke, by James I, at the expense of Thomas Tisdale and Richard Wrightwick, 1620; Worcester, by Sir Thomas Cookes, 1714; Keble, as a memorial to the Rev. John Keble, by public subscription in 1870.

Pagodas are in most instances pyramidal-shaped temples consisting of various layers of stones piled one upon another in successive recession, and covered all over with the richest ornamentation. They are among the most remarkable monuments of Hindoo architecture. The pilasters and columns, which take a prominent rank in the ornamental portion of these temples, show the greatest variety of forms; some pagodas are also overlaid with strips of copper, having the appearance of gold. Though the word pagoda is used to designate but the temple, it is in reality an aggregate of various monuments, which in their totality constitute the holy place sacred to the god. Sanctuaries, porches, colonnades, gate-ways, walls, tanks, etc., are generally combined for this purpose according to a plan which is more or less uniform. Several series of walls form an inclosure; between them are alleys, habitations for the priests, etc.; and the interior is occupied by the temple itself, with buildings for the pilgrims, tanks, porticoes, and open colonnades. The walls have, at their openings, large pyramidal gate-ways higher than themselves, and so constructed that the gate-way of the outer wall is always higher than that of the succeeding inner wall. These gate-ways are pyramidal buildings of the most elaborate workmanship, and consist of several, sometimes as many as fifteen, stories. The pagoda of Chalambron, in Tanjore, is one of the most celebrated and most sacred of these monuments in India. The buildings of which this pagoda is composed cover an oblong square 360 feet long and 210 wide. The pagodas of Juggernaut on the north end of the coast of Coromandel are three in number, and are surrounded by a wall of black stone, whence they are called by Europeans the Black Pagodas. The height of the principal one is said to be 344 feet; according to some, however, it does not exceed 120–123 feet. The term pagoda is also applied, but not correctly, to those Chinese buildings of a tower form, as the Porcelain Tower of Nankin. [See *Porcelain Tower of China*.] These buildings differ materially from the Hindoo pagodas, not only as regards their style and exterior appearance, but inasmuch as they are buildings intended for other than religious purposes. The word pagoda is, according to some, a corruption of the Sanscrit word *bhagavata*, from *bhagavat*, sacred; but according to others, a corruption of *put-gada*, from the Persian *put*, idol, and *gada*, house.

Palace of the Cæsars.—The palace of Augustus, built upon the site of the houses of Cicero and Catiline, was the beginning of the magnificent pile of buildings known as the Palace of the Cæsars, and each succeeding Emperor altered and improved it. Tiberius enlarged it, and Caligula brought it down to the verge of the Forum, connecting it with the Temple of Castor and Pollux, which he converted into a vestibule for the imperial abode. Nero added to it his "Golden House," which extended from the Palatine to the Cœlian Hill, and even reached as far the Esquiline. This latter portion was afterward used by Titus for his famous baths. The ruins of the palace extend over three hills of Rome, and cover an area of 1,500 feet in length and 1,300 feet in width. The Golden House, as can be imagined from its name, was a building of extraordinary magnificence. It was surrounded by a triple portico a mile in length, and supported by a thousand columns; and within this lay an immense lake, whose banks were bordered by great buildings, each representing a little city, about which lay green pastures and groves, where sported "all animals, both tame and wild." The ceilings of the banqueting-rooms were fretted into ivory coffers made to turn, that flowers might be showered down upon the guests, and also furnished with pipes for discharging perfumes. The principal banqueting-room was round, and by a perpetual motion, day and night, was made to revolve after the manner of the universe. The interior walls of the palace were covered with gold and precious stones, and adorned with the finest paintings that the world afforded. In the vestibule stood a statue of Nero, 120 feet in height.

Palanquin, a vehicle used in Hindustan by travelers. It consists of a wooden box, about 8 feet long, 4 feet wide and 4 feet high, with wooden shutters, which are constructed like Venetian blinds, and can be opened or shut at pleasure. At each end of the palanquin, on the outside, two iron rings are fixed, and the *hammals*, or bearers, of whom there are four, two at each end, support the palanquin by a pole passing through these rings. The interior is furnished with a cocoa-mattress and two small bolsters. Similar modes of traveling have been at various times in use in western Europe, as the French "chaise a porteurs," the Roman "litter," and the "sedan-chair," but only for short distances.

Palissy, Bernard, was born in France in 1510. He was apprenticed to a potter, and after laboring at great expense and hardship for sixteen years he succeeded in discovering the method of enameling pottery. Owing to his religious beliefs, being a Protestant, he was arrested and imprisoned during the reign of Henry II, and again toward the end of the reign of Henry III. He died in the Bastile in 1590. There are several collections in Paris of his pottery-ewers, vases, jugs, salvers, etc., generally small in size, but highly finished, which are greatly valued for their fineness of material, elegance of form, and beauty of decoration. Probably the most remarkable of his glass paintings is a representation of the myth of Psyche, after Raphael.

Pall-Mall, the famous locality in London, is so called from the fact that in earlier times it was an alley for tennis-playing, and took its name from the name by which the mallet was known—pell-mell, or pall-mall.

Pan, the chief Grecian god of pastures, forests and flocks. He was, according to the most common belief, a son of Hermes by a daughter of Dryops, or by Penelope, the wife of Ulysses; while other accounts make Penelope the mother, but Ulysses himself the father—though the paternity of the god is also ascribed to the numerous wooers of Penelope in common. The original seat of his worship was the wild, hilly and wooded solitudes of Arcadia, whence it gradually spread over the rest of Greece, but was not introduced into Athens until after the battle of Marathon. He is represented as having horns, a goat's beard, a crooked nose, pointed ears, a tail and goat's feet. He had a terrible voice, which, bursting abruptly on the ear of the traveler in solitary places, inspired him with a sudden fear (whence the word panic). He is also represented as fond of music, and of dancing with the forest nymphs, and as the inventor of the syrinx or shepherd's flute, also called Pan's pipe. The fir-tree was sacred to him, and he had sanctuaries and temples in various parts of Arcadia, at Trœzene, at Sicyon, at Athens, etc. When, after the establishment of Christianity, the heathen deities were degraded by the church into fallen angels, the characteristics of Pan—the horns, the goat's beard, the pointed ears, the crooked nose, the tail, and the goat's feet—were transferred to the devil himself. And thus the "Auld Hornie" of popular superstition is simply Pan in disguise.

Panama Canal.—Since 1528, when first the idea of an artificial channel between the oceans was suggested, the Isthmus of Panama, being in its narrowest part only thirty miles across, has been regarded as one of the most practicable localities for this purpose. A route using the Chagres and Grande Rivers, emptying into the Atlantic and Pacific respectively, and connecting them by an excavated canal, was first examined by two Flemish engineers under the orders of Philip II of Spain; but this monarch discarded the project, and ordered that no one should revive the subject under penalty of death. [See *Nicaragua Canal.*] Many surveys of many different routes have been made during the present century by Frenchmen, Colombians and Americans. Finally, in 1874, two expeditions were sent out by the United States Government—one to survey a line between the Aratro and the Pacific across the Colombian State of Cauca, the route first suggested by Humboldt, and the other a line parallel to the Panama Railway, between Panama and Aspinwall, a distance of 47½ miles. [See *Panama Railway.*] After a careful examination it was decided that on this latter line a lock-canal was possible though difficult, and would cost over $100,000,000. A canal at the level of the sea was deemed impracticable, the violence of the freshets in the Chagres River placing it beyond successful engineering control. No move was made by the United States; but in 1876 French enterprise took hold of the project, and in that year the "International Society of Interoceanic Canal" was formed in Paris. Certain French speculators had obtained the necessary concessions and privileges from the United States of Colombia, of which Panama is a State; they interested M. De Lesseps in the scheme, and he assumed the leadership of the Panama sea-level canal. Then they sold to his company the concessions which they had obtained from Colombia, and retired from the enterprise with their own pockets well filled. In 1879 De Lesseps caused the French Geographical Society to assemble, by invitation, an Inter-oceanic Canal Congress. This was thoroughly under his control as to committees, and largely so as to the body of the congress, and decided, against the earnest protest of the ablest engineers in the world, to approve the sea-level canal at Panama. The plan contemplated a direct cut from sea to sea, with a nominal depth of 29.52 feet below the sea-level, and a width at the bottom of 72.16 feet; also the excavation of a side-basin 3.1 miles long, at about the central point, to facilitate the passage of ships in either direction. Work was begun in 1881, and it was at first estimated that the canal would be in operation in 1888; but quite another result was reached in that year, the work being then finally abandoned, after $250,000,000 had been expended in actual work on the Isthmus, including vast sums for machinery and materials, which were afterward found useless and cast away, to become monuments to the reckless extravagance of the management. At the time of its suspension, the total liabilities of the company were $422,000,000, with an annual interest and fixed charge of $22,000,000. The Chagres River has repeatedly, by its great overflows, completely destroyed parts of the work already done, and at its final abandonment De Lesseps himself only claimed thirty per cent. of the work done, while fifteen per cent. would probably be a more exact estimate. Early in 1888 a change had been made in the plan, and it was proposed to construct a temporary or provisional lock-canal; but the necessary funds for continuing the work could not be obtained even by De Lesseps, whose name had been for almost ten years an *open sesame* to the pockets of Frenchmen. We can hardly question the honesty of the motives of De Lesseps, and can only attribute his persistent obstinacy and willful blindness to a strange fatuity such as sometimes dominates a great man. He was unquestionably a man of determined and energetic character and vigorous intellect; but he was trained as a diplomat, and not an engineer, and was totally ignorant of the true nature of the topographical and climatic difficulties at Panama. Flushed with the success of Suez, he would listen to no arguments or objections; *that* had been called impossible, and *this* would be an equally brilliant triumph and vindication for De Lesseps, and bring great money returns to all who believed in and supported him. Thus a noble French project, executed by Frenchmen in the face of the opposition of the whole world, appealed to the national pride of his countrymen. They loyally supported their famous De Lesseps, and the $422,000,000 squandered in this colossal fiasco have been mainly drawn from France and from the small savings of the middle classes.

Panama Railway is owned and controlled by an American company. It extends from Panama to Aspinwall, a distance of 47½ miles, was begun in 1850, completed in 1855, and cost $7,500,-000. The finest work on the road is the iron bridge over the Chagres River, which frequently submerges large parts of the road. This bridge is 625 feet long, 40 feet above the normal level of the water, and cost $500,000. In connection with the railway are lines of steamships between Aspinwall and New York and Panama and San Francisco. Other lines, also—British, French and Chilian—touch at one or the other of these ports.

Pandects, called also by the name *Digestum* or *Digest*, and one of the celebrated legislative works of the Emperor Justinian. In its relations to the history and literature of ancient Rome it is invaluable, and taken along with its necessary complement the *Codex Justinianus*, after which it was compiled, it may justly be regarded as of the utmost value to the study of the principles not alone of Roman but of all European laws. The work of compilation was performed by a commission, of which Tribonianus was the head, consisting of 17 members, who were occupied from the year 530 till 533 in examining, selecting and compressing, and systematizing the authorities, consisting of upward of 2000 treatises; and some idea of its extent may be formed from the fact that it contains upward of 9000 separate extracts, selected according to subject from the 2000 treatises referred to above.

Pandora's Box.—Pandora was the first created female, celebrated in one of the early legends of the Greeks as having been the cause of the introduction of evil into the world. Jupiter was incensed at Prometheus for having stolen the fire from the skies, and resolved to punish men for this deed. He therefore directed Vulcan to knead earth and water, to give it human voice and strength, and to make it assume the fair form of a virgin, like the immortal goddess. Minerva was to endow her with artist-knowledge, Venus to give her beauty, and Mercury to inspire her with an impudent and artful disposition. Then she was attired by the Seasons and Graces, and each of the deities having bestowed upon her the commanded gifts, she was named Pandora, or the All-Gifted, and conveyed by Mercury to the dwelling of Epimetheus. This man had been warned by his brother Prometheus to be on his guard and to receive no presents from Jupiter; but when he saw Pandora he was dazzled by her charms, and took her into his house and made her his wife. In this dwelling was a closed jar which Epimetheus had been forbidden to open. Pandora's woman's curiosity got the better of all other considerations and the lid was raised, and out flew all the evils, till then unknown to man, and spread themselves over the earth. When she saw the monsters she was terrified, and shut down the lid just in time to prevent the escape of Hope, which thus remained to man.

Panics, American.—The three great financial crises of the United States occurred in 1837, 1857 and 1873. The panic of 1837 was immediately traceable to a fever of speculation superinduced by the ease with which money had been obtained from the wildcat banks, and there had been large importations of foreign goods under the compromise tariff act, and much American capital had been driven out of business. In the month of May of that year the crash which had been anticipated for some time was precipitated by the suspension of the New York banks. The condition of firms and houses of high credit was alarming; hundreds of business firms were ruined; many corporations closed up their works; even States became bankrupt, and the President of the United States was at times unable to obtain his salary when it fell due. The panic of 1857 began with the failure of the Ohio Life Insurance and Trust Company. The number of bank failures was exceedingly large and public confidence was greatly shaken. Land speculation had again assumed reckless proportions, paper cities were numerous, and many unproductive railroads had been undertaken, all of which combined to produce disastrous results. The panic of 1873 began on September 19, when the failure of Jay Cooke & Co. was announced in the New York Stock Exchange, and for a time pandemonium reigned. Failure succeeded failure; firms that had been supposed to be of great financial strength were swept away like so much chaff, and it required nearly four years to restore public confidence.

Pantheon of Rome, a famous temple of circular form, built by M. Agrippa, son-in-law of Augustus, in his third consulship, about 27 B. C. The edifice was called the Pantheon, not, as is commonly supposed, from its having been sacred to all the gods, but from its majestic dome, which represented, as it were, the *"all-divine"* firmament. It was dedicated to Jupiter Ultor. Beside the statue of this god, however, there were in six other niches as many colossal statues of other deities, among which were those of Mars and Venus, the founders of the Julian line, and that of Julius Cæsar. The Pantheon is by far the largest structure of ancient times, the external diameter being 188 feet, and the height to the summit of the upper cornice 102 feet, exclusive of the flat dome or calotte, which makes the entire height about 148 feet. It has a portico, in the style of the Corinthian architecture, 110 feet in length and 44 feet in depth, made up of 16 granite columns, with marble capitals and bases, placed in three rows, each column being 5 feet in diameter and 46½ feet high. These columns supported a pediment with a roof of bronze. The Pantheon stands near the ancient Campus Martius, and, after the lapse of 1900 years, is still the best preserved of the old Roman buildings. It was given to Boniface IV by the Emperor Phocas in 609, and was dedicated as a Christian church to the Virgin and the Holy Martyrs, a quantity of whose relics was placed under the great altar. In 830 Gregory IV dedicated it to all the saints. It is now known as the Church of Santa Maria Rotunda. This consecration of the edifice, however, seems to have afforded it no defense against the subsequent spoliations, both of emperors and popes. The plates of gilded bronze that covered the roof, the bronze bassi-relievi of the pediment and the silver that adorned the interior of the dome were carried off by Constans II, A. D. 655, who destined them for his imperial palace at Constantinople; but, being murdered at Syracuse when on his return with them, they were taken by their next proprietors to Alexandria. Urban VIII carried off all that was left to purloin—the bronze beams of the portico, which amounted in weight to more than 45,000,000 pounds. During eight centuries it has suffered from the dilapidations of time and the cupidity of barbarians. The seven steps which elevated it above the level of ancient Rome are buried beneath the modern pavement. Its rotunda of brick is blackened and decayed; the marble statues, the bassi-relievi, the brazen columns have disappeared; its ornaments have vanished, its granite columns have lost their luster, and its marble capitals their purity. Yet, under every disadvantage, it is still pre-eminently beautiful. No eye can rest on the noble simplicity of the matchless portico without admiration. Its beauty is of that sort which, while the fabric stands, time has no power to destroy.

Pantomime.—Originally the word pantomime denoted a person, not a spectacle, who acted not by speaking, but wholly by mimicry. They were in high favor among the Romans. The dress of the actors was made to reveal, and not to conceal, the beauties of their persons; and as, after the second century, women began to appear in public as pantomimes, the effect of the esthetical costumes, as may easily be supposed, was injurious to morality. The subjects represented were always mythological, and consequently pretty well known to the spectators. The pantomimes were shown great favor by the Emperors Augustus, Caligula and Nero. The modern pantomime was first introduced by a dancing-master of Shrewsbury, England, named Weaver, in 1702, and met with great success.

Paper Car-Wheels were invented and first used in 1869 by Richard N. Allen, a locomotive engineer, who tested them on a wood-car belonging to the Central Vermont Railroad. In 1871 the Pullman Palace Car Company gave the first order for 100 wheels; twelve years later the Allen Paper Car-Wheel Company were manufacturing 20,000 wheels annually. The body of the wheel only is made of paper. The advantages of these wheels over those of solid iron are their greater cheapness, their much increased elasticity, and a much lessened susceptibility to the effects of extreme cold, which so affects the crystalline structure of iron, sometimes, as to make it exceedingly brittle. The wheels are made as follows: The paper is sent to the works in circular sheets of 22 to 40 inches diameter. Two men, standing by a pile of these, rapidly brush over each sheet an even coating of flour paste, until a dozen are pasted into a layer. A third man transfers these layers to a hydraulic press, where a pressure of 400 tons or more is applied to a large pile of them, the layers being kept distinct by the absence of paste between the sheets. After solidifying under this pressure for two hours the twelve-sheet layers are kept for a week in a drying-room heated to 120 degrees Fahrenheit; several of these layers are in turn pasted together, pressed and dried for a second week; and still again these disks are pasted, pressed, and given a third drying of a whole month. The result is a circular block, containing from 120 to 160 sheets of the original paper, compressed from $5\frac{1}{2}$ to $4\frac{1}{2}$ inches in thickness, and of a solidity, density and weight suggesting metal rather than fiber. The rough paper blocks are turned accurately in a lathe—when shavings like leather and a cloud of yellow dust fly off—to a diameter slightly greater than the inner circle of the tire. The hole in the center is also made on the lathe, and after the paper has received two coats of paint, to prevent moisture working its way within, the cast-iron hub is pressed through by the aid of a hydraulic press, and the wrought-iron back-plate is clamped on. The suasion of enormous hydraulic power now drives the paper center into the tire by the help of the bevel, and the wheel is completed.

Paper, Hand-Made.—Previous to the invention of paper-making machinery, hand-making of paper was practiced in all countries. The substance to be used—rags, bark, or the like—was first reduced by water and heating to a fine, smooth pulp. The workman then took his mold, which was a sheet of net-work attached to a frame, placed on it a deckle, a thin frame corresponding in size to the mold, and dipped both into the pulp, the deckle forming a ridge which retained just enough of the liquid pulp for the sheet of paper. When the water of the pulp had completely drained through the wire gauze, the face of the sheet was applied to a piece of felt stretched on a board called the couch, and pressed. The pressure caused the sheet to leave the mold and adhere to the couch. Each successive sheet was treated in the same way, and all were piled together with a sheet of felt upon each, and the piles, when they contained several quires each, were put one by one in a powerful press. The pieces of felt were removed when taken from the press and the sheets of paper were hung up in the drying-room. When thoroughly dried they were put into hot *size*, then pressed again, and glazed by being passed through hot rollers of polished iron or steel. The molds, of course, varied in design, according to the style of paper which it was desired to produce.

Paper, History of.—It is generally conceded that the Egyptians were the first manufacturers of paper, which they made from papyrus, a species of reed. In former times this plant grew in abundance on the banks of the Nile, but it is now said to have disappeared from Egypt. It was called by the Egyptians " papu," from which the Greeks gave it the " papyrus," and our word paper comes   Herodotus named it " byblus," whence came the Greek " biblion " (book), and our word Bible. The ancient Mexicans used a kind of paper prepared from the maguey plant that grows on table-lands and closely resembles the Egyptian papyrus. This paper took ink and color well, as is attested by specimens which have been preserved. The credit of being first to form from fiber the web which constitutes modern paper belongs to the Chinese, and the art was known to them as early as the commencement of the Christian era.   In the seventh century the Arabians learned the art of making it from cotton from the Chinese, and the first manufactory was established at Samarcand, about A. D. 706. From thence it was taken into Spain, where under the Moors paper was made, it is thought, of hemp and flax as well as cotton. Just when linen rags were first used in the composition of paper is uncertain; but the best evidence is offered by the Arabian physician Abdollatiph, who writes, in an account of his visit to Egypt in the year 1200, "that the cloth found in the catacombs and used to envelop mummies was made into garments or sold to the scribes *to make paper for shop-keepers;*" and as there is no doubt that these mummy-cloths were linen, it proves the use of this material to be of considerable antiquity.   Of the use of linen rags in Europe, the earliest proof is the celebrated document found by Ichwandner in the monastery of Goss, in Upper Styria, which purports to be a mandate of Frederick II, Emperor of the Romans, and is dated 1242. It is written on paper which has been proved to have been made of linen. The practice of making a distinctive water-mark on paper was also of very early date, as manuscripts as old as the thirteenth century bear it. There is, however, no really satisfactory information respecting the exact time or place of the introduction of paper-making into Europe. By some it is supposed that Spain was the first to receive the art, and that thence it spread to France and Holland, and subsequently to England; but it is quite certain that England was a long time behind the other countries. As proof of this we find that the first patent for paper-making was taken out in 1665 by one Charles Hildeyerd, but it was for "the way and art of making blew paper used by sugar-bakers and others." Ten years later, 1675, a patent was taken out by Eustace Barneby for "the art and skill of making all sorts of white paper for the use of writing and printing, being a new manufacture, and never practiced in any way in any of our kingdomes or dominions." Paper is now made out of cotton and linen rags, waste paper, straw, esparto grass, wood, cane, jute and manilla.

Papier-Mache has been in use for more than a century in Europe, and it is thought probable that it was first suggested by some of the beautiful productions of Sinde and other parts of India, where it is employed in making boxes, trays, etc., as well as in China. Its first application, as far as is known, was to the manufacture of snuff-boxes by a German named Martin in 1740, who learned it of a Frenchman named Lefevre. The cheaper articles of papier-mache are made of paper reduced to a pulp with water and glue, and pressed in oiled molds. Better articles are produced by pasting together sheets of paper, and when a proper degree of thickness is attained it is pressed into the shape desired. When moist this substance may be made to take any form, and when dry may be planed into any shape. A brilliant surface can be had by polishing with rotten-stone and oil. Papier-mache is much used to make architectural ornaments, both for exterior and interior decorations. The sheets of paper, placed in layers with glue, are pressed into metal molds for some hours; then they are removed, and a composition of paper-pulp, mixed quite thin with resin and glue, is poured in, and the paper impressions are again put in and subjected to powerful pressure. This causes the composition to adhere to the molded articles, and gives them the rough surface that is desired. Papier-mache can be made water-proof by adding to the pulp sulphate of iron or some of the silicates, and fire-proof by mixing with clay and borax, phosphate of soda, or any alkali.

Parchment.—The ordinary writing-parchment is made from the skins of the sheep and she-goat; the finer kind, known as *vellum*, is made from those of very young calves, kids and lambs. The thick, common kinds of parchment, which are used for drums, tambourines, battledoors, etc., are made from the skins of old he-goats and she-goats, and in northern Europe from wolves; and a peculiar kind, which is used for tablets, is made from asses' skins. Parchment, as a writing material, was known at least as early as 500 B. C. Herodotus speaks of books written upon skins in his time. Pliny, without good grounds, places the invention as late as 196 B. C., stating that it was made at Pergamos (hence the name *Pergamena*, corrupted into English parchment). Possibly the Pergamian invention was an improvement in the preparation of skins, which had certainly been used centuries before. The manufacture rose to great importance in Rome about a century before Christ, and soon became the chief material for writing on; and its use spread all over Europe, and retained its pre-eminence until the invention of paper from rags.

Parsees, the followers of the ancient Persian religion as reformed by Zerdusht, or Zoroaster, as he is commonly called. According to Zerdusht there are two intellects, as there are two lives—one *mental* and one *bodily;* and, again, there must be distinguished an *earthly* and a *future* life. There are two abodes for the departed—Heaven and Hell. Between the two there is the

Bridge of the Gatherer, or Judge, which the souls of the pious alone can pass. There will be a general resurrection, which is to precede the last judgment, to foretell which Sosiosh, the son of Zerdusht, spiritually begotten, will be sent by Ahuramazdao. The world, which by that time will be utterly steeped in wretchedness, darkness and sin, will then be renewed. Death, the arch-fiend of Creation, will be slain, and life will be everlasting and holy. The Parsees do not eat anything cooked by a person of another religion. Marriages can only be contracted with persons of their own caste and creed. Their dead are not buried, but exposed on an iron grating in the Dokhma, or Tower of Silence, to the fowls of the air, to the dew and to the sun, until the flesh has disappeared, and the bleaching bones fall through into a pit beneath, from which they are afterward removed to a subterranean cavern. The temples and altars must forever be fed with the holy fire, brought down, according to tradition, from heaven, and the sullying of whose flame is punishable with death. The priests themselves approach it only with a half-mask over their faces, lest their breath should defile it, and never touch it with their hands, but with holy instruments. The fires are of five kinds; but, however great the awe felt by Parsees with respect to fire and light, they never consider these as anything but emblems of Divinity. There are also five kinds of "sacrifice," which term, however, is rather to be understood in the sense of a sacred action.

Parthenon, a celebrated temple at Athens, on the summit of the Acropolis, and sacred to Minerva. The Parthenon in beauty and grandeur surpassed all other buildings of the kind, and was constructed entirely of Pentelic marble. It was built during the splendid era of Pericles, and the expense of its erection was estimated at 6,000 talents. It contained innumerable statues raised upon marble pedestals and other works of art. The colossal statue of Minerva, which was in the eastern end of the temple, was 39 feet high, and was composed of ivory and gold, the value of the latter being 44 talents, or about $465,000. The temple was reduced to ruins in 1687. A part of the matchless friezes, statues, etc., of the Parthenon now form the most valuable and interesting portion of the British Museum, they having been taken from the temple by Lord Elgin in 1800, and by him sold to the British Government. [See *Elgin Marbles.*]

Partition of Poland was accomplished by the then Allied Powers of Russia, Prussia and Austria under the monarchs Catherine II, Frederick William and Maria Theresa respectively, each annexing the provinces adjoining its own territory. By three successive divisions, the final one being effected in 1795, the very existence and name of Poland as an independent state were annihilated. The Poles were a brave and independent people, and made a fierce and heroic struggle for their national existence, their greatest leader being Kosciusko, whose name has now a world-wide fame as a national hero and great General; but they were crushed by the superior strength of their combined enemies inclosing them on all sides. Since their complete overthrow in 1795, their country has been the scene of many desperate and bloody insurrections and rebellions. Early in the present century they invoked the aid of Napoleon against Russia, and had strong hopes of the restoration of the whole or Poland; but this prospect soon vanished, and the territorial limits of the divided country were rearranged by the Congress of Vienna, which created a shadow of Polish independence in the miniature republic of Cracow but gave the lion's share to Alexander of Russia. Further uprisings afterward occurred, and Cracow was finally annexed to the Austrian province of Galicia in 1846. The Russian provinces were the scenes of almost continued warfare until 1864, when thousands of the insurgents were transported to Siberia, their government reorganized on a rigid and systematic provincial basis, the franchise extended to the inhabitants who were left, the Russian language and calendar, Russian schools and universities, established, and the entire country thoroughly and forcibly Russianized.

Pasha.—The name Pasha or Pacha is said to be derived from two Persian words—*pa*, foot or support, and *shah*, ruler—and signifies "the support of the ruler." In the Ottoman empire it is applied to governors of provinces, or military and naval commanders of high rank. In the early period of that empire the title was limited to princes of the blood, but was subsequently extended. The distinctive badge of a pasha is a horse's tail waving from the end of a staff crowned with a gilt ball. The three grades of pashas are distinguished by the number of the horse-tails on their standards; those of the highest rank are pashas of three tails, and include in general the highest functionaries, civil and military. All pashas of this class have the title of Vizier. The pashas of two tails are the governors of provinces, who are generally called by the simple title "Pasha." The lowest rank of pasha is the pasha of one tail; the sanjaks, or lowest class of provincial governors, are of this class.

Passion-Flower.—It was so called by the first Spanish settlers of America because they imagined that they saw in its flower a representation of Our Lord's passion, the filamentous processes being taken to represent the crown of thorns; the nail-shaped styles, the nails of the cross; the anthers, the marks of the five wounds; the leaf, the spear that pierced the Saviour's side; the tendrils, the cords or whips by which He was scourged; the column of the ovary, the upright of the cross; the stamens, the hammers; the calyx, the glory or halo; the white tint, purity; the blue tint, heaven. The passion-flower is a native of the warm parts of America, and its flowers are large and beautiful.

Passion-Plays.—The first composition of moralities, or miracle-plays, from which passion-plays originated, is ascribed to Ezekiel, a Jew, who in the third century adapted the story of Israel's exodus from Egypt to the Grecian stage. St. Gregory Nazianzen,

Bishop of Constantinople, having noticed that the Grecian drama had had a good effect upon Ezekiel's desponding countrymen, concluded that the readiest method of extending the Church of Christ was the dramatic presentation of the sufferings of its author, and in the fourth century he presented a drama entitled "The Passion of Christ." Next followed six Latin plays on subjects connected with the lives of the saints, by Roswitha, a nun of Gandersheim, in Saxony. On the establishment of the Corpus Christi festival by Pope Urban IV, in 1264, miracle-plays became one of its adjuncts, and every considerable town had a fraternity for their performance. Throughout the fifteenth and following centuries they continued in full force in England. Designed at first as a means of religious instruction for the people, they had, long before the Reformation, so far departed from their original character as to be mixed up in many instances with buffoonery and irreverence, and to be the means of inducing contempt rather than respect for the church and religion. These plays were as popular in France, Germany, Spain and Italy, as in England. Soon after the Reformation the miracle-plays began to decline, and now they are performed in only a few places, mostly in Southern Bavaria and the Tyrol. The passion-play of Oberammergau is famed throughout the world, and attracts an immense concourse of visitors whenever it is presented In 1633 the flax in that neighborhood became diseased and unfit for the spindle. To prevent the recurrence of any such calamity the Oberammergau peasants made a vow to God that every ten years they would present the sufferings of Christ upon the stage in this way. This vow was kept until the beginning of the present century, when the further performance of the play was prohibited, owing to the representation in it of the devil and comic personages. The pleading of a deputation of Ammergau peasants with Max Joseph of Bavaria saved their "mysterie" on condition that everything that could offend good taste should be expunged. The play commences with Christ's triumphal entry into Jerusalem, and closes with a scene previous to the Ascension. The personator of Christ considers his part an act of religious worship; he and the other principal performers are said to be selected for their holy life, and consecrated to their work with prayer. The players, about 500 in number, are exclusively the villagers, who, though they have no artistic instruction except from the parish priest, act their parts with no little dramatic power and a delicate appreciation of character. The New Testament narrative is strictly adhered to, the only legendary addition to it being the St. Veronica handkerchief. The acts alternate with tableaux from the Old Testament and choral odes. The last performance took place in 1880. There is an all but unanimous feeling of opposition both in the United States and England to having the passion of the Saviour, the solemn tragedy of Calvary, mimicked on the stage by ordinary stage-performers, and no successful efforts have been made to give a representation of a passion-play in either country in late years.

Passports are not used within the countries of England and the United States, nor are they required by these countries from visitors to their shores, except in the case of Chinese visiting the United States. The governments of these countries, however, give passports to those of their citizens who wish to travel abroad. These documents give the name, age, residence and occupation of the holder, with a description of his person and appearance, which is meant to give the means of identifying him if necessary. They also assure to the holder the support of his own government in any difficulty, and claim for him the protection of all governments at peace with his own. They are issued in America by the United States Secretary of State, who also regulates their issue by the government's agent abroad. Passports are required by all vessels of the United States sailing for foreign ports. The system is of considerable advantage in Europe in the detecting and tracking of suspicious and troublesome characters.

Paul Pry was written by John Poole, an English dramatist. For some time it was supposed that the original of the character was Thomas Hill, the eccentric editor of the *Dramatic Mirror*, but in a biographical sketch of himself Poole relates that "The character of Paul Pry was suggested by the following anecdote, related to me several years ago by a beloved friend: An idle old lady, living in a narrow street, had passed so much of her time watching the affairs of her neighbors that she at length knew the sound of each particular knocker within hearing, and could tell to which house it belonged. It happened that she fell ill and was for several days confined to her bed. Unable to observe in person what was going on outside, she stationed her maid at the window as her substitute for the performance of that task. But Betty soon grew weary of the occupation; she became careless in her reports, impatient and *tetchy* when reprimanded for her negligence. 'Betty, what are you thinking about? Don't you hear a double knock at No. 9? Who is it?' 'The first-floor lodger, ma'am.' 'Betty! Betty! I declare I must give you warning. Why don't you tell me what that knock is at No. 24?' 'Why, Lord, ma'am, it's only the baker with the pies.' '*Pies!* Betty, what *can* they want with pies at No. 24? They had pies yesterday.' Let me add that Paul Pry was never intended as the representative of any one individual, but of a class."

Pawnbroker's Sign, Origin of.—It is generally held that the three golden balls used by pawnbrokers as a sign were adopted from the armorial bearings of the Medici family of Italy by the Lombard merchants, among whom were several representatives of that family. This sign was used in London in very early times by some of those merchants who had emigrated from Italy and established the first money-lending establishments in England.

Pearl Fisheries.—The cause of the pearl is the introduction of a grain of sand or other foreign substance into the shell of the pearl oyster. This causes an irritation of the delicate tissues of the oyster, which immediately deposits the pearly matter around it for protection. Advantage of this fact has been taken to put substances within the shells of young oysters to induce the formation of pearls, and the Chinese by this method force a species of fresh-water mussels to produce the jewel. The most important pearl fisheries of the world are those of Ceylon and Coromandel, in the Indian Sea, whence pearls have been obtained since the earliest times of history. The divers are natives, trained to the pursuit, who are accustomed to descend to the depth of six or eight fathoms some forty times a day, and remain under water from a minute to a minute and a half. The fishing season begins in March or April and lasts but one month. A single shell may contain from eight to twenty pearls, varying in size from that of a small pea to about three times that size. The coasts of Java, Sumatra, Japan, and also Colombia and other points on the shores of South America, have yielded large quantities of pearls; but they are usually smaller than the Oriental pearls, and inferior to them in lustre.

Peat is decomposed vegetable matter which accumulates in swamps, morasses, and low places in localities where the climate is moist and the subsoil is impervious to water. These accumulations are composed mainly of mosses, ferns, reeds, sedges and rushes; but there are great differences in peat-beds, some peats being without traces of vegetation, therefore burning readily, while others retain much vegetable matter that is but slightly advanced in the peaty decomposition. In Holland, Holstein, Friesland and Denmark a substance called mud-peat is taken from the bottoms of ponds, which on drying becomes hard and dense, partaking of the nature of " pitch-peat," which is found in Germany. This latter peat, when moist, resembles clay, and may be cut and molded to any shape. On drying it becomes hard and can be burnished.

Pegasus was, according to Greek mythology, a winged horse, the offspring of Neptune and Medusa, and which sprung forth from the neck of the latter after her head had been severed by Perseus. He is said to have received his name because he first made his appearance beside the springs of Oceanus. As soon as he was born he flew upward, and fixed his abode on Mount Helicon, where with a blow of his hoof he produced the fountain Hippocrene. He used, however, to come and drink occasionally at the fountain of Pirene, and it was here that Bellerophon caught him. The myth concerning Pegasus is interwoven with that of the victory of Bellerophon over the Chimæra. [See *Bellerophon.*] Pegasus is also spoken of in modern times as the Horse of the Muses, which, however, he was not. The ancient legend on this subject is that the nine Muses and the nine daughters of Pieros engaged in a competition in singing by Helicon, and everything was motionless to hear their song save Helicon, which rose ever higher and higher in its delight, when Pegasus put a stop to this with a kick of his hoof, and from the print arose Hippocrene, the inspiring spring of the Muses.

Pen-and-Ink Fish.—*Sepia*, a pigment used as a water-color, is prepared from the secretion of a peculiar organ, called the ink-bag, found in the cuttle-fish. This secretion is black at first, and insoluble in water, but extremely diffusible through it; it is therefore agitated in water to wash it, and then allowed slowly to subside, after which the water is poured off and the sediment, when dry enough, is formed into cakes or sticks. In this state it is called India ink. If, however, it be dissolved in a solution of caustic potash it becomes brown, and is then boiled and filtered, after which the alkali is neutralized with an acid, and the brown pigment is precipitated and dried. This constitutes the proper *sepia*. It is usually prepared in Italy, great numbers of the species which yield it most abundantly being found in the Mediterranean. The black kind, called India ink, is prepared in China, Japan and India, and forms the common writing-ink of those countries. From the form of the cuttle-bone of the fish it is often popularly referred to as the pen-and-ink fish.

Penny Weddings was the name given to festive marriage ceremonials in Scotland, at which the invited guests made contributions in money to pay the general expenses and leave over a small sum, which would assist the newly-married pair in furnishing their dwelling. This practice, now disused, was prevalent in the seventeenth century; and, as leading to "profane minstrelsing and promiscuous dancing," was denounced by an act of the General Assembly of the Kirk, 1645, as well as by numerous acts of presbyteries and kirk-sessions about the same period.

Perambulation of Parishes.—The ancient custom in England of perambulating parishes in Rogation week appears to have been derived from a still older custom among the ancient Romans, called Terminalia and Ambarvalia, which were festivals in honor of the god Terminus and the goddess Ceres. On its becoming a Christian custom, the heathen rites and ceremonies were discarded and those of Christianity substituted. The object of the custom as practiced in England was to supplicate the Divine blessing on the fruits of the earth, and to preserve in all classes of the community a correct knowledge of, and due respect for, the bounds of parochial and individual property. It was appointed to be observed on one of the Rogation days, which were the three days next before Ascension-Day. Before the Reformation parochial perambulations were conducted with great ceremony. The lord of the manor with a large banner, priests in surplices and with crosses, and other persons with hand-bells, banners and staves, followed by most of the parishioners, walked in procession round the parish, stopping at crosses, forming crosses on the ground, "saying or singing gospels to the corn," and allowing "drinking and good cheer." At the Reformation, the ceremonies and practices deemed objectionable were abolished, and only the useful and harmless part of the custom retained. The necessity or determination to perambulate along the old track often occasioned curious incidents. If a canal had been cut through the boundary of a parish, it was deemed necessary that some of the parishioners should pass through the water. Where a river formed part of the boundary line, the procession either passed along it in boats or some of the party stripped and swam along it, or boys were thrown into it at customary places. If a house had been erected on the boundary line, the procession claimed the right to pass through it. A house in Buckinghamshire, still existing, has an oven passing over the boundary line. It was customary in the perambulations to put a boy into this recess, to preserve the integrity of the line. The custom of perambulating parishes continued in England to a late period, but the religious portion of it was generally, if not universally, omitted. Perambulation was the formal legal term, the more common and later expression being Beating the Bounds. [See *Beating the Bounds*.]

Percussion Caps, Composition of.—The explosive which is used in the making of percussion caps is a fulminate of mercury, made by first dissolving 100 parts mercury in 1,000 parts of nitric acid—or 740 parts by measure. When the solution is heated to 130 degrees Fahrenheit it should be slowly poured through a glass funnel-tube into 830 parts alcohol, sp. gr. .830—or 1,000 parts by measure. After effervescence, filtering, washing and drying, the explosive is dropped into the copper cap.

Perfectionists, or Bible Communists, as they call themselves, are a small religious sect which was founded by John Humphrey Noyes of Brattleborough, Vt. The peculiarities of their belief will be found under the head *Oneida Community.*

Peri.—According to the mythical lore of the East, a Peri is a being begotten by fallen spirits which spends its life in all imaginary delights; is immortal, but is forever excluded from the joys of Paradise. They take an intermediate place between angels and demons, and are either male or female; when the latter, they are of surpassing beauty. One of the finest compliments to be paid to a Persian lady is to speak of her as Perizadeh (born of a Peri; Greek, *Parisatis*). They belong to the great family of genii, or jin, a belief in whom is enjoined in the Koran, and for whose conversion, as well as for that of man, Mohammed was sent.

Peter-Pence, the name given to a tribute offered to the Roman pontiff in reverence to the memory of St. Peter, whose successor the Pope is believed by Roman Catholics to be. The first idea of an annual tribute appears to have come from England. It is ascribed by some to Ina (A. D. 721), King of the West Saxons, who went as a pilgrim to Rome, and there founded a *hospice* for Anglo-Saxon pilgrims, to be maintained by an annual contribution from England; by others, to Offa and Ethelwulf, at least in the sense of their having extended it to the entire Saxon territory. The tribute consisted in the payment of a silver penny by every family possessing land or cattle of the yearly value of thirty pence, and it was collected during the five weeks between St. Peter's and St. Paul's-Day and August 1st. Since the total annexation of the Papal States to the Kingdom of Italy the tribute has been largely increased in France, Belgium, England and Ireland.

Peter the Hermit was the apostle of the first crusade, and was born in the diocese of Amiens, France, about the middle of the eleventh century. After engaging in several pursuits he became a hermit, and in 1093 undertook a pilgrimage to Jerusalem, where the oppression he witnessed and experienced determined him to arouse the people of Christendom to undertake a war for the liberation of the holy sepulcher. The first host of crusaders was led by Peter in person, and was unsuccessful. He was associated with the expedition under Godfrey of Bouillon. While the crusaders were besieged in Antioch he deserted, but was captured and brought back. On the conquest of Jerusalem he preached a sermon to the crusaders on the Mount of Olives. After this he returned to Europe and founded the Abbey of Neufmoutier, near Huy, where he died in 1115.

Petrified Bodies.—Petrifaction is simply the substitution of the organic substance by the inorganic, atom by atom. As a molecule of wood or bone decays, a molecule of stone takes its place. This can only occur when the air or earth or water surrounding the organic substance holds in solution some readily precipitated mineral. In the case of a woody substance, or of bone, while decomposition goes on there yet remains a frame-work whose interstices are gradually filled by the mineral substance; but in the case of flesh no such frame-work exists. The very rapid decay of flesh also makes it impossible for the very slow process of petrifaction to have any effect upon it. The stories of petrified bodies found in graveyards, that float periodically through the press, are usually made up of "whole cloth," as the saying is, though it is true that bodies of both men and animals have been found incrusted with silicious substance so as to resemble petrifactions. These, however, when veritable finds, are fleshless skeletons, the soft parts of the body having decayed while the slow process of incrustation was going on. It may be noted here that but one true human bone petrifaction has ever been found, and that is the "Fossil Man of Mentone," discovered in 1873–'74. The majority of fossils, be it remembered, are of great age, antedating the existence of man on the earth. In places where the silicious deposits have been rapid, as in limestone caverns, human bones, fossilized, have been discovered. Two human skeletons were found in an apparent state of comple petrifaction on the Island of Guadaloupe early in the present century. One of these was placed in the British Museum, and the other in the museum at Paris. But examination showed that in these the bony structure still remained, though it was completely incased in the calcareous deposits. In excavating in the caverns of Mentone, in France, on the coast of the Mediterranean, some fifteen years ago, M. Riviere, a noted French scientist, found a number of human bones and a complete skeleton in a true fossil condition, which were complete evidence of the existence of men upon the earth at a period of very great antiquity.

Philippics, originally the three orations of Demosthenes against Philip of Macedon. The name was afterward applied to Cicero's orations against the ambitious and dangerous designs of Marc Antony. It is now commonly employed to designate any severe and violent invective, whether oral or written.

Phlogiston is a term which was invented in 1697 by Stahl, professor of chemistry at Halle, to designate a hypothetical element, whose existence in any substance rendered it combustible, combustion being the disengagement of this element, the residue being always an acid or an earth. This phlogistic theory was universally and unquestioningly accepted by scientists until the time of Lavoisier, who substituted for it the true theory of oxygenation (1775–1781), proving that combustion was not a disengagement of phlogiston, but a combining with oxygen. The great chemists, Priestley and Scheele, late in the last century, adhered to the phlogiston theory, and when they discovered the gases oxygen (1774) and chlorine (1776), respectively, they called them *dephlogisticated air* and *dephlogisticated marine acid gas,* on account of their non-combustible properties. Lavoisier's views have been thoroughly confirmed in modern times by the use of the balance, to which chemistry owes much of its marvelous progress in the last half century.

Phœnix, a mythical bird of gorgeous plumage that was believed to live in Arabia, and which, as the legend goes, was seen in Egypt once in every 500 years, when it built a funeral-pile of wood and aromatic gums, and, lighting it by the fanning of its wings, was consumed to ashes, out of which arose a new Phœnix.

Phonograph was invented in 1877 by Thomas A. Edison, and brought into public notice early in the following year. Its principle is extremely simple, and is based upon the fact that as all sound is produced by vibrations of the air, any sound can be reproduced by reproducing its vibrations. The apparatus is a small brass cylinder, made to turn on a metal shaft, which has a spiral groove cut on its surface corresponding to threads cut on the shaft. Over the cylinder is spread a sheet of tin-foil, secured on its edges by some highly adhesive substance. In the later and improved machines wax or some other plastic substance is used on the cylinder, as it is found to retain the impressions better. This cylinder is called the phonogram. A crank attached to the shaft turns the cylinder, giving it at the same time a rotary and horizontal motion. In front of the cylinder is a mouth-piece, having on its bottom (next the cylinder) a very thin plate or diaphragm of metal, to which is attached a round, steel point. When the lips are applied to the mouth-piece, and any sentence is spoken, the crank at the same time being turned, the vibrations imparted to the metal plate by the voice will cause the steel point to come into contact with that part of the foil overlying the groove, and to make on it a series of indentations as it revolves and is carried forward laterally before the mouth-piece. The cylinder is then brought back to its starting-point, and a resonator is substituted for the mouth-piece. The steel point is now held by a screw close to the foil, and as the cylinder moves the point retraces the indentations from beginning to end, and communicates to the metal diaphragm the same vibrations which it had received from it; and these vibrations, communicated to the resonating apparatus, are reproduced as spoken words. If the crank is turned with exact regularity, the exact pitch and tone of the speaker's voice will be given back.

Phosphorescence is the property which some bodies possess of being luminous in the dark without the emission of sensible heat. There are five kinds distinguished by physicists, and designated as follows: Spontaneous phosphorescence; phosphorescence from the effects of heat; from mechanical action; from the action of electricity; by insolation or exposure to the light of the sun. The first is by far the most common and familiar phenomenon, being exhibited by certain living organisms both in the vegetable and animal kingdoms. There are flowers of a bright red or yellow color which have been observed to emit light flashes in the dark, and other plants which give out a faint, continuous light, caused probably by the oxidation of some hydro-carbon which they secrete. The best known examples, however, are those seen in animals, as the glow-worm or fire-fly, and the myriads of minute animalcule which cause the magnificent displays of phosphorescence that are often seen at sea by night, especially in the tropics, and in temperate zones during the summer. Various causes have been assigned for this animal phosphorescence, and they doubtless vary with different animals. In the glow-worm and fire-fly it is thought to be produced by an act of the will. M. Jousset discovered the liquid which exudes from the crushed eggs of the glow-worm to be phosphorescent, and to remain so until dried up. In the marine animalcula, it is believed that a subtle luminous matter is thrown off as a secretion supplied by glands having this special function; and some naturalists assert that it contains epithelial cells in a state of fatty degeneration, the decomposing fat being the cause of the phosphorescence. That phosphorescence seen in decaying fish and other animal matter, and in wood (called "fox-fire"), is due to a species of slow combustion by which vibrations are excited capable of emitting luminous rays. The other kinds of phosphorescence are, for the most part, seen only in scientific experiments, except the last, which is now receiving some application in articles of every-day use, as matchboxes, clock-faces, etc.; they are covered with a preparation possessing this property, and remain luminous, and therefore easily visible in the dark. Certain compounds have been discovered which exhibit the property in a high degree, as Canton's phosphorus, Bolognese phosphorus, etc. It is probably due to the absorption of the energy of the vibrations falling upon them, which is afterward radiated from them again. It is probable that all bodies possess the quality in a greater or less degree; but with the great majority the duration of the phenomenon is very short—rarely more than a small fraction of a second. The phenomenon has no connection with ordinary phosphorus, but the name is thence derived from the similar light emitted by phosphorus in the dark, which is due to the slow combustion of this element, which oxidizes at a very low temperature.

Photo-Engraving. [See *Photogravure.*]

Photogravure.—The earliest attempt at photographic engraving dates back to 1827, which was six years previous to the introduction of the daguerreotype process, and was the invention of M. Nicephore Niepce of Paris, who first discovered that thin plates of bitumen were curiously affected by light. He therefore coated metal plates with a thin layer of bitumen of the kind called Jew's pitch and placed them in a *camera obscura*, so arranged that he could insure their exposure to the same image for several hours. The plate was then submitted to the action of oil of spike, which readily dissolved those portions not acted upon by the light, but exerted little action upon the remainder. The metal exposed by the solution of the bitumen was then acted upon by acid, which produced a complete etching-plate, the picture-part being protected by its bituminous varnish from the action of the acid. The art, which can now be performed by several different methods, is also known by the names of photo-zincography and process-engraving. In ordinary zincography the picture is laid, by the help of transfer paper, on a zinc plate; the parts to be protected are then covered with a varnish that will resist acid, and the whole is then dipped in a bath of dilute nitrous acid. This is repeated until the *biting-in* is sufficient, when the plate is dried and the ink taken off with benzine. In another process brass plates are used, which are covered with white wax, the design being drawn with an etching-point upon the wax. The plate is then submitted to a powerful acid, which acts upon the parts of the metal exposed by the lines, but does not affect the wax. In photo-zincography the drawing is photographed to the right size, and an ordinary negative on glass is taken. This is then laid on a sensitized zinc plate, on which the picture is printed by the action of light. The zinc is coated with bitumen, and after the picture is printed, so much of the bitumen as has not become insoluble by the action of light is removed by a wash of turpentine. In another process—the photographic etching process—the negative is printed on a sensitized carbon-paper, which is then laid on a polished zinc plate, and, being wet, all the carbon-paper that does not hold the lines of the drawing is readily removed. The plate is then *bitten-in* in an acid bath. In what is called the Ives process a negative is applied to a gelatine plate, sensitized with bichromate of potash. This plate is then put into water, and all the parts not touched by the negative will swell. A cast is then taken of this in plaster of paris, which serves to form a base for electrotypes. The lines of engraving can also be reproduced by photography, and a late process produces successfully intaglio plates. Photo-engraving has enormously cheapened the reproduction of pictures, but it does not give plates that print with the clearness and distinctness of those taken from wood-engravings.

Pictured Rocks are a series of sandstone bluffs, rising in many places abruptly out of the water to a height varying from 50 to 200 feet, and are situated about 70 miles west of Whitefish Point, on the southern shore of Lake Superior. Two features impart to the scenery its remarkable appearance—the one, the strange style of the cliff excavations, worn away by the action of the lake; and the other, quite as strange, the way in which large portions of the surface of the bluffs have been colored by bands of brilliant color. It is to this latter circumstance that their name is due. The "Grand Portal" is the most imposing feature of the series It is 100 feet high by 168 feet broad at the water-level, and the cliff it is cut in rises above the arch, making the whole height 185 feet. The great cave, entered through the Portal, extends back in the shape of a vaulted room, the arches of the roof built of yellow limestone, and the sides fretted into fantastic shapes by storm-driven waves. About a mile west is "Sail Rock," a group of detached rocks which bear a resemblance to the mainsail and jib of a sloop. The height of this is about 40 feet. The "Chapel" is a vaulted apartment in the rock, 30 or 40 feet above the lake-level. An arched roof of sandstone rests on four columns of rock, so as to leave an apartment about 40 feet in diameter and the same in length; within are a pulpit and altar. West a short distance from the Chapel is Chapel River, which falls over a rocky ledge 15 feet high into the lake. Miner's Castle, 5 miles west of the Chapel, and just west of Miner's River, is the western end of the Pictured Rocks, and resembles an old turreted castle with an arched portal. The height of the advanced mass in which the Gothic gateway may be recognized is about 70 feet, and the height of the main wall forming the background is 140 feet.

Piers Plowman, or more properly, "The Vision of William Concerning Piers the Plowman," is a remarkable poem of very early date, by William Langland, or Langley, an Englishman. It is in vigorous alliterative verse, and describes a series of nine dreams, in certain of which a person called Piers the Plowman appears. Under allegorical covering the *Vision* exposes the manifold corruptions of the State, of the Church, and of existing social arrangements. From the forty-three manuscripts which remain,

it is evident that the poem, originally written about 1362, was repeatedly revised, altered and extended, and that it continued to
occupy the author all his lifetime.

Pilgrim Fathers and Mothers.—The names of the passengers
who came over to America in the Mayflower on her first trip in
the year 1620, and were the founders of New Plymouth, which
led to the planting of the other New England colonies, were Mr.
John Carver, who was chosen the first Governor, and Katherine,
his wife; Desire Minter; Mr. William Brewster, their Ruling Elder, Mary, his wife, and Love and Wrestling Brewster, his sons;
Mr. Edward Winslow, some time Governor, and Elizabeth, his
wife; Mr. William Bradford, the second Governor, and Dorothy,
his wife; Mr. Isaac Allerton, Mary, his wife, Bartholomew, a son,
and Remember and Mary, daughters; Mr. Samuel Fuller, physician; Richard More, his brother and two boys; Captain Myles
Standish and Rose, his wife; Mr. Christopher Martin and his
wife; Mr. William Mullens, his wife, a son Joseph, and a daughter Priscilla; Mr. William White, his wife, Susanna, and a son
Resolved; Mr. Stephen Hopkins, his wife, Elizabeth, two sons,
Giles and Damaris, and two daughters, Constantia and Oceanus;
Mr. Richard Warren; John Billington, his wife, Ellen, and two
sons, John and Francis; Edward Tillie, his wife, Ann, and daugh-
ter, Elizabeth; Francis Cooke; Thomas Rogers and son Joseph;
Thomas Tinker, wife and son; John Rigdale and his wife Alice;
James Chilton, his wife and daughter, Mary; Edward Fuller, his
wife and son, Samuel; John Turner and his two sons; Francis
Eaton and his wife Sarah; John Howland; Roger Williams; Wil-
liam Latham; Jasper Moore; George Soule; Elias Story; Ellen
More; John Hook; John Crackston and his son John; Solomon
Prower; John Langemore; Robert Carter; William Holbeck; Ed-
ward Thompson; Edward Doty; Edward Lister; Moses Fletcher;
John Goodman; Thomas Williams; Digeric Priest; Edmond Mar-
geson; Richard Britterige; Richard Clark; Peter Brown; Richard
Gardiner; Gilbert Winslow and John Alden.

Pillar Saints were a remarkable class of ascetics who, to
separate themselves more completely from earth and their fellow-
men, took up their abode on the tops of pillars, on which they remained without ever descending to earth, exposing themselves to
all the variations of the weather. The earliest of them and the
most celebrated was a Syrian monk, called Simeon the Stylite,
who, previous to taking up his abode on a pillar, had lived in his
monastery for nine years without ever moving from his cell.
About the beginning of the fifth century, increasing in enthusiasm,
he withdrew to a place about forty miles from Antioch, where he
built a pillar, on the top of which, only a yard in diameter, he
took up his position. From this pillar he removed to several
others in succession, each higher than the last, till he eventually
attained to one 40 cubits or 60 feet in height. In this manner of
life he spent 37 years, his neck loaded with an iron chain and

engaged in constant prayers, during the recitation of which he bent his body so that his forehead touched his feet. His powers of fasting also were marvelous; he is said to have limited himself to a single meal a week, and during the forty days of Lent to have entirely abstained from food. In consequence of an ulcer, which formed on one of his legs, he was obliged to remain, it is said, for the last year of his life on one foot. In this position he died in 460, aged 72 years. Daniel, a disciple of Simeon, built a pillar about four miles from Constantinople, upon which he lived for 33 years. Here at times for days together he was covered with snow and ice, and the emperor eventually insisted upon a covering being placed over the top of the pillar. There were many pillar saints in Syria as far down as the twelfth century.

Pillars of Hercules.—"The Pillars of Hercules" was the name given in ancient times to the mountains of Calpe and Abyla, standing opposite to each other, the one on the European, the other on the African shore of the straits which connect the Mediterranean Sea with the Atlantic Ocean. These mountains are now called the Rock of Gibraltar and Jebel Zatout. The word Gibraltar, also applied to the straits in modern times, is derived from "Jeb-el-Taric," meaning "Mount of Taric," Taric being the name of the leader of the first Mohammedan band which crossed at this point over to Spain in A. D. 710.

Pitching, Curved.—A ball thrown through the air is retarded in its forward motion by the resistance of the air, which not only exerts a pressure on the face of the ball, but also a resisting force on its sides by friction. If the ball is simply thrown forward without any special bias being given it, the friction of the air is equal on each side of it; but if one side be made to move forward faster than the other—that is, if the ball be made to rotate on its own axis from right to left, or left to right—so as to increase the lateral friction, the result is naturally a curve in the line of its delivery in the direction of the side on which its progress has been retarded. Hence what is known as a "curved ball."

Pitch, Tar and Turpentine.—Pitch is the residuum obtained by boiling tar in an open pot, or in a still, until the volatile and liquid portion is driven off. It is soft and sticky when warm, but becomes solid and brittle when cold. Tar is obtained from pine wood by the process of charring. The wood is packed in kilns or pits, or may be laid in mounds and covered closely with ashes. Fire is then applied and the wood slowly carbonizes. The tar as formed trickles down into a gutter beneath the wood, and is conveyed thence by pipes into proper tanks. Turpentine is an oily, resinous substance flowing from the pine and other coniferous trees. An excavation, which has a capacity of about three pints, is made in the trunk of the tree, and in this the exuded juice accumulates. It becomes stiff very soon on exposure to the air, and is taken from the tree, washed with warm water, then heated and purified by straining through straw filters. When this crude product is distilled with water the oil of turpentine is removed, and the residue left is the resin of commerce. The different cone-bearing trees furnish different grades and kinds of turpentine.

Place of Fire, The, is a spot on the peninsula of Apsheron, on the west coast of the Caspian Sea. It is considered sacred by the Guebres and Persian Fire-Worshipers, who visit it in large numbers, and bow before the holy flames which issue from its bituminous soil. It is about a mile in diameter, and from its center, in clear, dry weather, creeps forth a blue flame, caused by the ignition of naphtha, which shines with great brightness by night.

Plants, Sap Circulation.—During the winter months there is an almost entire suspension of the sap-secreting power. In the spring, summer and autumn the sap which rises in the stems of plants is of a watery nature, containing the various inorganic matters absorbed by the roots; also some sugar, dextrine, and other organic substances. This undergoes considerable alteration during its passage to the leaves, but when it reaches them is still unfitted for the requirements of the plant, and hence is called "crude sap." This sap again undergoes important changes in the leaves through the action of light and air, and becomes adapted for the nourishment of the plant. It is then called "elaborated sap."

Playing-Cards.—The invention of playing-cards has been variously attributed to India, China, Arabia and Egypt. There seems to be but little doubt that they originated in Asia, and were introduced into Europe by the Saracens about the close of the thirteenth century. There is historical mention of the game of cards in Germany in 1275, in Italy in 1299, but not in France until 1393. An active trade in cards sprung up in Germany as early as the fifteenth century, where they were manufactured for other portions of Europe. One hundred years later we find the manufacture of cards a flourishing business in England, and under Edward IV their importation was forbidden, thus protecting the home industry. Owing to their supposed immoral influences they were at times prohibited by various European governments. The marks upon the suits of cards are believed to have been chosen to represent symbolically the different classes of society. Thus, the hearts stood for the clergy, clubs for the soldiery, spades for the serfs, and diamonds for the merchants. In the early French cards the kings were pictures of David, Alexander, Cæsar and Charlemagne, representing the monarchies of the Jews, Greeks, Romans and French; the queens were Argine, Esther, Judith and Pallas. The number of the cards, the ace and the knave, were probably based on similar ideas. The suits of the earliest German cards were designated by hearts, bells, leaves and acorns. Italian cards had swords, batons, cups and money. The court cards at first were the king, chevalier and knave. The queen was first substituted for the chevalier by the Italians. The English cards in the seventeenth century were embellished with heraldic designs, the king of clubs bearing the coat-of-arms of the Pope of Rome, and those of hearts, diamonds and spades being adorned respectively with the armorial device of the kings of England, Spain and France. The club of modern cards derived its form from the trefoil, a French design. A pack of Hindustani cards in the possession of the Royal Asiatic Society of England is supposed to be fully 1,000 years old. It consists of eight suits of divers colors. The kings are mounted on elephants; the viziers, or second honors, upon horses, tigers and bulls; and some of the common cards have such curious marks as a pineapple in a shallow cup, and a something like a parasol without a handle, and with two broken ribs sticking through the top.

Plumed Knight.—The title of "The Plumed Knight" was conferred upon James G. Blaine by Colonel Robert G. Ingersoll in a speech made at the National Republican Convention at Cincinnati, in 1876. Colonel Ingersoll said: "This is a grand year—a year filled with the recollection of the Revolution; filled with proud and tender memories of the sacred past; filled with the legends of liberty; a year in which the sons of freedom will drink from the fountain of enthusiasm; a year in which the people call for a man who has preserved in Congress what our soldiers won upon the field; a year in which we call for the man who has torn from the throat of Treason the tongue of slander; a man who has snatched the mask of Democracy from the hideous face of Rebellion; a man who, like an intellectual athlete, stood in the arena of debate and challenged all comers, and who, up to the present moment, is a total stranger to defeat. Like an armed warrior, like a *plumed knight,* James G. Blaine marched down the halls of the American Congress and threw his shining lance full and fair against the brazen forehead of every defamer of this country and maligner of its honor."

Polyandry, or Polyandria.—In Thibet, in the Himalayan and sub-Himalayan regions adjoining and under the influence of Thibet, and among numerous other semi-civilized people, a form of polygamy known as polyandry, which permits a woman to have several husbands, is practiced. A wife is commonly the wife of a whole family of brothers, the elder brother being chief husband. The origin of this peculiar institution is believed to be connected with the want of balance between the numbers of the sexes, due to the practice of female infanticide, which is its almost invariable accompaniment. From ancient history we learn that the area over which polyandry at one time existed was very extended; and in certain cantons of Media, according to Strabo, a woman was allowed to have many husbands, and they looked with contempt upon those who had less than five. Cæsar informs us that in his time polyandry also prevailed among the Britons.

Polyglot, a term almost exclusively applied to manifold versions of the Bible, although the word means in general an assemblage of versions in different languages of the same work. The polyglot versions are, as a rule, united in parallel columns, often having also interlinear Latin translations. They are divided into two classes, the greater and the lesser polyglots. To the former belong four works: the Complutensian Polyglot, containing, besides the Hebrew text, the Septuagint Greek and the Chaldee (each with a literal Latin version) and the Latin Vulgate; the Antwerp Polyglot, containing in the Old Testament, the Hebrew, the Greek, the Targum of Onkelos and the other Chaldee paraphrases and the Latin Vulgate, and in the New Testament the Greek and Latin text and a Syriac version, printed both in Syriac and in Hebrew characters; the Parisian Polyglot, containing, in addition to the contents of the Antwerp Polyglot, another Syriac version and an Arabic version, together with the Samaritan version and the Samaritan text of the Pentateuch, each of these being accompanied by a literal Latin translation; and the London Polyglot, containing the Bible, or portions of it, in nine languages —Hebrew, Samaritan, Chaldee, Syriac, Arabic, Ethiopic, Persic, Greek and Latin. Of the minor polyglots, the chief are the Heidelberg Polyglot, Hebrew, Greek and Latin; Wolder's Polyglot, Hebrew, Greek, Latin and German; Hutter's Polyglot, Hebrew, Chaldee, Greek, Latin, German and French; Reineccius' Polyglot, Syriac, Greek, Latin and German; and Bagster's Polyglot, a very valuable collection of modern versions, Hebrew, Greek, English, Latin, French, Italian, Spanish and German in the Old Testament, and in the New, Syriac, in addition to those mentioned.

Popular Names of Cities.—The nicknames given to the various prominent cities in the United States are as follows: Brooklyn, N. Y., City of Churches; Boston, Hub of the Universe; Baltimore, Monumental City; Buffalo, Queen City of the Lakes; Chicago, Garden City; Cincinnati, Queen City; Cleveland, Forest City; Detroit, City of the Straits; Hannibal, Bluff City; Indianapolis, Railroad City; Keokuk, Gate City; Louisville, Falls City; Lowell, City of Spindles; New York, Gotham, Empire City; New Orleans, Crescent City; Nashville, City of Rocks; New Haven, City of Elms; Philadelphia, Quaker City, City of Brotherly Love; Pittsburg, Iron City; Portland, Me., Forest City; Rochester, Flour City; St. Louis, Mound City; Springfield, Ill., Flower City; Washington, D. C., City of Magnificent Distances.

Population of the United States.—The population of the United States and Territories of the Union, according to estimates made by the officials of the States and Territories, was on January 1, 1889, as follows: Alabama, 1,500,000; Alaska, 40,000; Arizona, 50,000; Arkansas, 1,140,000; California, 1,350,000; Colorado, 350,000; Connecticut, 670,000; Dakota, 700,000; Delaware, 150,000; District of Columbia, 220,000; Florida, 450,000; Georgia, 1,752,711; Idaho, 100,000; Illinois, 3,750,000; Indiana, 2,500,000; Iowa, 1,800,000; Kansas, 1,518,552; Kentucky, 2,200,-000; Louisiana, 1,100,000; Maine, 660,139; Maryland, 1,100,000; Massachusetts, 2,078,625; Michigan, 2,195,692; Minnesota, 1,250,-

000; Mississippi, 1,300,000; Missouri, 2,750,000; Montana, 130,000; Nebraska, 1,400,000; Nevada, 61,000; New Hampshire, 346,000; New Jersey, 1,463,404; New Mexico, 160,000; New York, 6,500,-000; North Carolina, 1,650,000; Ohio, 4,500,000; Oregon, 250,-000; Pennsylvania, 5,400,000; Rhode Island, 304,284; South Carolina, 1,350,700; Tennessee, 1,700,000; Texas, 2,060,000; Utah, 210,000; Vermont, 333,000; Virginia, 1,700,000; Washington Territory, 309,000; West Virginia, 800,000; Wisconsin, 1,700,000; Wyoming, 85,000. Total 65,088,107.

Population of the World.—The number of individuals in the entire world is about 1,438,680,000. Europe, with an area of 3,756,970 square miles, supports a population of 331,972,000; Asia has an area of 17,212,680 square miles and 795,591,000 inhabitants; Africa has an area of 11,514,700 square miles and a population of 205,825,000 souls; North America, in an area of 7,900,350 square miles, supports 72,500,000 inhabitants; South America, in an area of 6,854,000 square miles, supports a population of 28,400,000; Oceanica, having an area of 3,456,700 square miles, supports a population of 4,310,000; and the Polar regions, in an area of 1,730,000 square miles, supports 82,000 inhabitants. The white people of the human race are estimated at about 550,000,000, the black at some 250,000,000, the rest of intermediate color. Of the entire race some 500,000,000 are comfortably clothed, 700,000,000 are partly clothed, and the rest are practically naked. About 500,000,000 may be said to live in houses partly or wholly furnished with the appointments of civilization, 800,000,000 live in huts or caves, with no attempt at furnishing them with any luxuries or scarcely conveniences, and the balance have nothing that can be called a home. The Christians in the world number 395,000,000, divided as follows: Protestants, 110,000,000; Roman Catholics, 175,000,000; Communion of the Greek Church, 90,000,-000; all other Christian sects, 20,000,000; Buddhists, 400,000,000; Brahmins, 220,000,000; Mohammedans, 160,000,000; Fetish worshipers number 150,000,000; Jews, 7,000,000; and there are among the Aboriginal tribes and others of various beliefs 100,000,000.

Porte.—The name Sublime Porte, or Ottoman Porte, given to the Turkish Government, is derived from the ancient Oriental custom of making the gates of cities, and of kings' palaces, places of assembly in connection with the affairs of government and of the administration of justice. The Turks found the term in common use among the Byzantines some time previous to their establishment at Constantine, and adopted it on the organization of their empire. The use among European nations of the French term *Sublime Porte* (Lofty Gate) is accounted for by the fact that French is the language of European diplomacy.

Porter-House Steak.—The origin of the name porter-house steak is stated by Colonel Thomas F. De Voe, author of the "Market Book," etc., to have been as follows: "Martin Morrison kept a favorite porter-house at No. 327 Pearl Street, New York, near the old Walton House. It was a popular resort with many of the New York pilots, because here they were always sure of a pot of ale or porter and 'a hot bite,' including one or two substantial dishes. On one occasion, in 1814, Morrison had enjoyed an unusual number of calls for steaks, and when an old pilot, who dropped in at a late hour, called for something substantial to eat, he was forced to cut from a sirloin roasting-piece which he had got for the next day's family dinner. The old pilot relished his steak amazingly and called for another. This disposed of, he squared himself in front of his host and vociferated : ' Look ye here, messmate; arter this I want my stakes off the roasting-piece ! Do you hear that ? So mind your weather-eye, old boy !' The old pilot's companions soon learned to appreciate these cuts, and it was not long before they were all insisting on having them. Accordingly, Morrison's butcher, Thomas Gibbons of the Fly Market, asked him why he had ceased to order the large sirloin steaks. Morrison explained that he had found that cuts from the small end of the sirloin of the beef suited his customers best, both in size and quality, and directed that thereafter, instead of sending him the sirloin roasts uncut, he have them cut into chops or steaks, as he should direct. Gibbons' daily order, 'Cut steaks for the porterhouse,' soon gave these the name of porter-house steaks, by which they became known all through the Fly Market, particularly as this excellent cut rapidly became popular in all the public houses in the city." The name is now familiar wherever the English language is spoken.

Portland Vase.—The celebrated Portland Vase, which is one of the most valued relics of antiquity in the British Museum, was made, it is believed, to hold the ashes of the Roman Emperor Alexander Servius, and was discovered during the sixteenth century in a rich sarcophagus on Monte del Grano, where it had been for about thirteen hundred years It is an urn, ten inches high. The groundwork is of blue glass, enameled with white glass cut in cameo, to represent the wedding of Thetis and Peleus. It was placed in the museum by the Duke of Portland in 1810, and in 1845 was maliciously broken by a man named Lloyd. The pieces, however, were collected and cemented together, but the vase has not been on exhibition since that date. It was at one time known as the Barberina Vase, and was owned by Sir William Hamilton, who found it in the Barberina Palace, and purchased it in 1770. In time it passed into the possession of the Duchess of Portland, and was disposed of as related.

Postage-Stamps, Designs On.—The portrait on the two-cent stamp now used, in terra-cotta color and green, is the same as that formerly used on the three-cent letter-stamp, both in green and red—that of Washington, after Houdon's celebrated bust. On the old two-cent stamp, in vermilion, was the head of Andrew Jackson, from a bust by Hiram Powers. The old one-cent stamp, in ultramarine blue, is that of Benjamin Franklin, after a profile bust by Rubricht; the new one also has Franklin, from the bust by Ceracchi, the noted Italian sculptor. The old five-cent stamp, in blue, bore the portrait of Zachary Taylor; and the later one, in drab, has the head of Garfield. The Lincoln profile, in red, on the six-cent stamp, is after a bust by Volk. The old seven-cent stamp, in vermilion, had the head of Stanton, after a photograph. The head of Jefferson, on the ten-cent stamp, in chocolate, is drawn from a life-size statue by Hiram Powers. The portrait of Henry Clay, in neutral purple, on the twelve-cent stamp, was after a bust by Hart. The head of Webster on the fifteen-cent stamp, in orange, is after the Clevinger bust. The portrait of General Scott on the twenty-four-cent stamp, in purple, was after a bust by Coffee. The head of Hamilton on the thirty-cent stamp, in black, is after the Ceracchi bust. The portrait of Commodore Oliver Hazard Perry, in carmine, on the ninety-cent stamp, is after Wolcott's statue. The seven, twelve and twenty-four-cent stamps were retired a few years ago, though one may still be occasionally seen. In 1869 there were a series of stamps issued, of which the three-cent letter-stamp was designed in commemoration of the completion of the Pacific Railroad. It was shorter and wider than the usual stamp size, and had on its face the picture of a locomotive. For some reason it was shortly retired from use. In England and the British Colonies there are nearly 200 different stamps which have the portrait of Queen Victoria. Of the countries which do not use the conventional portrait we may mention France and several South American States, which have the Goddess of Liberty; British Guiana, which has a ship; Colombia, a shield; and the Central American States a series of landscapes, generally including a volcano. Egypt, also, has the Pyramids and Sphinx; Turkey, the Sultan's sign-manual; and Rome, the papal tiara and keys.

Postage-Stamps, First.—Postage-stamps in the form of stamped envelopes were first used by M. de Velayer, who owned a private post in the city of Paris in the reign of Louis XIV. Over a century later, in 1758, M. de Chamouset, also the proprietor of a post, issued printed postage-slips to be attached to letters. In Spain, in 1716, and in Italy also, stamped covers for mail-matter were tried; but it was not until 1840 that stamps, as we know them now, were put in use. This was in England, the Government adopting the system devised by Rowland Hill. Brazil was the first country to take up the new invention. Russia adopted the postage-stamp next, in 1845; then Switzerland in 1846; and March 3, 1847, the Congress of the United States authorized the issue of postage-stamps. These were at first a five-cent stamp and a ten-cent stamp. The reduction of rates in 1851 gave a new set of stamps, valued at 1, 3 and 12 cents respectively. Other stamps of different values were added from time to time to meet the exigencies of postal arrangements, reduction of postage to foreign countries, etc. Before 1845 the postal rate on letters in the United States varied from 6 cents for carrying a distance of 30 miles to 25 cents for over 400 miles. By the reduction of that year the postage was made 5 cents for 300 miles or less, and 10 cents for any distance above that. In 1851 the rate was fixed at 3 cents for every half-ounce for 3,000 miles, and 6 cents for any greater distance within the United States. In 1883 the postage was reduced to 2 cents for half an ounce for letters sent less than 3,000 miles, and in 1885 to 2 cents an ounce.

Postage-Stamps, Language of.—Of late years the postage-stamp has been invested with a language of its own. When a stamp is inverted on the right-hand upper corner, it means the person written to is to write no more. If the stamp be placed on the left-hand upper corner inverted, then the writer declares his affection for the receiver of the letter. When the stamp is in the center at the top it signifies an affirmative answer to a question or the questions, as the case may be; and when it is at the bottom it is a negative. Should the stamp be on the right-hand corner, at a right-angle, it asks the question if the receiver of the letter loves the sender; while in the left-hand corner means that the writer hates the other. There is a shade of difference between desiring one's acquaintance and friendship. For example: the stamp at the upper corner at the right expresses the former, and on the lower left-hand corner means the latter. The stamp on a line with the surname is an offer of love; in the same place, only reversed, signifies that the writer is engaged. To say farewell, the stamp is placed straight up and down in the left-hand corner.

Postal Business.—Since the last reduction in the rate of postage the postal business has shown a large deficiency, and at the present time is by no means self-supporting. The operations of the years 1885 and 1886, after the reduction took effect, resulted in a cash deficiency of nearly $7,000,000 each year. For the fiscal year 1887 this deficiency was reduced to $4,000,000. The total revenue for 1887 was $48,837,609.39, against $43,948,422.95 for 1886, and $42,560,843.83 for 1885. The expenditures in the same time have increased from $49,534,788.65 in 1885 to $50,854,109.12 in 1886, and $52,814,113.61 in 1887. There were but ten States in which the postal business was run at a profit in 1887. These were Connecticut, Delaware, Illinois, Massachusetts, Michigan, New Hampshire, New Jersey, New York, Pennsylvania and Rhode Island.

Postmasters, Salaries of.—Postmasters are divided into four classes, and the salaries are as follows: First-class, $3,000 to $4,000, excepting New York City, which is $8,000; second-class, $2,000 to $3,000; third-class, $1,000 to $2,000; fourth-class, less than $1,000. The first three classes are appointed by the President and confirmed by the Senate. Those of the fourth-class are appointed by the Postmaster-General.

Post-Office Department, Salaries in.—The salaries of the officials of the Post-Office Department of the United States are as follows: Postmaster-General, $8,000 per annum; First, Second and Third Assistant Postmaster-Generals, $4,000 each; Superintendent of Railway Mail, $3,500; Chief Clerk, $2,200; Superintendent of Foreign Mail, $3,000; Superintendent of Money Order Department, $3,500.

Post-Offices, Origin of.—The name post-office originated in the posts placed at intervals along the roads of the Roman Empire, where carriers were kept in readiness to bear dispatches and intelligence; but the posts of ancient times were never used for the conveyance of private correspondence. The first letter-post seems to have been established in the Hanse towns in the early part of the thirteenth century. A line of letter-posts followed, connecting Austria with Lombardy, in the reign of the Emperor Maximilian, which are said to have been organized by the princes of Thurn and Taxis; and the representatives of the same house established another line of posts from Vienna to Brussels, connecting the most distant parts of the dominions of Charles V. In England, in early times, both public and private letters were sent by messengers, who, in the reign of Henry III, wore the royal livery. They had to supply themselves with horses until the reign of Edward I, when posts were established where horses were to be had for hire. Camden mentions the office of "Master of the Postes" as existing in 1581, but the duties of that officer were probably connected exclusively with the supply of post-horses. A foreign post for the conveyance of letters between London and the Continent seems to have been established by foreign merchants in the fifteenth century; and certain disputes which arose between the Flemings and Italians regarding the right of appointing a postmaster, which were referred to the privy-council, led to the institution of a "Chief Postmaster of England," who should have charge both of the English and the foreign post. Thomas Randolph was the first Chief Postmaster of England, appointed in 1581. In 1635 a mail was established to run weekly between London and Edinburgh, and soon eight other lines were instituted. Far back in the twelfth century the University of Paris, whose students, gathered from all the civilized nations, employed footrunners to carry letters for its members to all parts of Europe. But not until 1524 was permission granted to the Royal French posts to carry other letters than those for the Government and the nobility. In the United States, Massachusetts was the first colony to provide by legislation for a postal-system. This was done in 1639, and Virginia followed in 1657. In 1762 a monthly post was instituted between Boston and New York. In the beginning, letters arriving in this country from beyond the seas were delivered on board the ship. Letters not called for were left by the captain at a coffee-house near the wharf, where they were spread on a table or shelf, awaiting call. These coffee-houses gradually grew into common use for letters between cities and the interior, until **regular posts were instituted.** The establishment of a general post-office department was one of the first acts of the Continental Congress, and Benjamin Franklin was appointed as the first Post-master-General.

Potatoes.—The potato was used as a food in America long before the advent of Europeans, and was probably indigenous from Chili to Mexico. It was taken from Peru to Spain, and thence into the Netherlands, Burgundy and other parts of Europe early in the sixteenth century. In 1563 or 1565 it was carried from Virginia to Ireland by Sir John Hawkins, and Sir Francis Drake introduced it into England in 1585. Its importance as a vegetable was not recognized, however, until the time of Sir Walter Raleigh, who cultivated it on a considerable scale on his estates in the County of Cork, Ireland. Through the exertions of Raleigh it was developed in quality and popularized as food to such an extent in Ireland that its cultivation spread into England, where it became known as the "Irish potato." The potato mentioned by early English writers before the seventeenth century was the same as the Spanish batatas, or sweet-potato.

Pot-Pourri, a French term which, when applied to music, signifies a selection of favorite pieces strung together without much arrangement so as to form a sort of medley. It is also the name of a mixture of sweet-scented materials, chiefly flowers, dried and usually placed in a vase with a perforated lid, in order that their perfume may be diffused through rooms in which it is placed. It also signifies a dish of different sorts of viands, and corresponds in this sense to the *hotch-potch* of Scotland [see *Hotch-Potch*], and the *olla-podrida* of Spain [see *Olla-Podrida*].

Precious Stones, Language of.—The superstition that each month of the year has a gem associated with it, and that the influence of qualities attributed to different gems controls the destinies of persons born in the various months, is taken from the folk-lore of Poland. According to this superstition January has a jacinth or garnet, which denotes constancy and fidelity. February—amethyst, preventive against violent passions. March—a blood-stone, courage and wisdom. April—sapphire or diamond, signifying repentance and innocence. May—emerald, typical of successful love. June—an agate, meaning long life and health. July—ruby, corrects evils resulting from mistaken friendship. August—sardonyx, a happy married life. September—chrysolite, preserves from folly. October—opal, denotes both misfortune and hope. November—topaz, prevents bad dreams, denotes hope, and sharpens the sight and faith of the possessor. December—torquois, signifies prosperity in love.

Preserving Wood.—The processes for preserving wood which have been patented are numerous. One of them, very generally used, consists in immersing the timber in a bath of corrosive sublimate. Another process consists in first filling the pores with a solution of chloride of calcium under pressure, and next forcing in a solution of sulphate of iron, by which an insoluble sulphate of lime is formed in the body of the wood, which is thus rendered nearly as hard as stone. Wood prepared in this way is now very largely used for railroad ties. Another way is to thoroughly impregnate the timber with oil of tar containing creasote and a crude solution of acetate of iron. The process consists of putting the wood in a cylindrical vessel, connected with a powerful air-pump. The air is withdrawn and the liquid subjected to pressure, so that as much of it as possible is forced into the pores of the wood. Yet another process consists in impregnating the wood with a solution of chloride of zinc.

Preserving or Canning.—The process for preserving provisions by boiling and inclosing them in a vessel from which the air is excluded was first patented by M. Epert, a Frenchman, in 1808.

Presidents' Ages at Inauguration.—George Washington, inaugurated April 30, 1789, aged 57 years. John Adams, inaugurated March 4, 1797, aged 62 years. Thomas Jefferson, inaugurated 1801, aged 58 years. James Madison, inaugurated 1809, aged 58 years. James Monroe, inaugurated 1817, aged 59 years. John Quincy Adams, inaugurated 1825, aged 68 years. Andrew Jackson, inaugurated 1829, aged 62 years. Martin Van Buren, inaugurated 1837, aged 55 years. William II. Harrison, inaugurated 1841, aged 68 years. John Tyler, inaugurated April 4, 1841, aged 51 years. James K. Polk, inaugurated March 4, 1845, aged 50 years. Zachary Taylor, inaugurated 1849, aged 65 years. Millard Fillmore, inaugurated July 10, 1850, aged 50 years. Franklin Pierce, inaugurated March 4, 1853, aged 49 years. James Buchanan, inaugurated 1857, aged 66 years. Abraham Lincoln, inaugurated 1861, aged 52 years. Andrew Johnson, inaugurated April 15, 1865, aged 57 years. Ulysses S. Grant, inaugurated March 4, 1869, aged 47 years. Rutherford B. Hayes, inaugurated 1877, aged 55 years. James A. Garfield, inaugurated 1881, aged 50 years. Chester A. Arthur, inaugurated September 20, 1881, aged 51 years. Grover Cleveland, inaugurated March 4, 1885, aged 48 years. Benjamin II. Harrison, inaugurated 1889, aged 55 years.

Presidents, Burial-Places of.—George Washington died December 14, 1799, at Mount Vernon, Va., and was buried at Mount Vernon. John Adams died July 4, 1826, at Quincy, Mass., and was buried at Quincy in a room beneath the Unitarian Church. Thomas Jefferson died July 4, 1826, at Monticello, Va., and was buried in a thick grove of woods near a road leading from that place to Charlotteville. James Madison died June 28, 1836, at Montpelier, Va., and was buried in the center of a large field at that place. James Monroe died July 4, 1831, at New York, and was finally buried in Hollywood Cemetery in Richmond, Va. John Quincy Adams died February 21, 1848, at Washington, D. C., and was buried in the room under the Unitarian Church at Quincy, Mass. Andrew Jackson died June 8, 1845, at the Hermitage, near

Nashville, Tenn., and was buried there. Martin Van Buren died July 24, 1862, near Kinderhook, N. Y., and was buried in the cemetery there. William II. Harrison died April 4, 1841, at Washington, D. C., and was buried at North Bend, Ohio. John Tyler died January 8, 1862, at Richmond, Va., and was buried in the Hollywood Cemetery, where Monroe lies. James K. Polk died June 15, 1849, at Nashville, Tenn., and was buried in the garden of the old family homestead in that city. Zachary Taylor died July 9, 1850, at Washington, D. C., and his remains are now in the cemetery at Frankfort, Ky. Millard Fillmore died March 8, 1874, at Buffalo, N. Y., and was buried at Forest Lawn Cemetery, near that city. Franklin Pierce died October 8, 1869, at Concord, N. H., and was buried in the old cemetery in that city. James Buchanan died June 1, 1868, at Wheatland, Pa., and was buried at Woodward Hill Cemetery, near Lancaster, Pa. Abraham Lincoln died April 15, 1865, at Washington, D. C., and his resting-place is Oak Ridge Cemetery, Springfield, Ill. Andrew Johnson died July 31, 1875, at Greenville, Tenn., and was buried there on a spot selected by himself. James A. Garfield died September 19, 1881, at Elberon, N. J., and was buried in Lakeview Cemetery, Cleveland, Ohio. Ulysses S. Grant died July 23, 1885, at Mount McGregor, N. Y., and was buried at Riverside Park, New York City. Chester A. Arthur died November 18, 1885, and was buried in the Albany Rural Cemetery, Albany, N. Y.

Presidential Flag has a blue ground, with the arms of the United States in the center. It was designed and first used by President Chester A. Arthur in 1883, and is now hoisted at the main whenever the President of the United States is on board any Government vessel.

Presidential Succession, The, is fixed by chapter 4 of the acts of the Forty-ninth Congress. In case of the removal, death, resignation or inability of both the President and Vice-President, then the Secretary of State shall act as President until the disability of the President or Vice-President is removed, or a President is elected. If there be no Secretary of State, then the Secretary of the Treasury will act; and the remainder of the order of succession is: the Secretary of War, Attorney-General, Post master-General, Secretary of the Navy and Secretary of the Interior. This act applies only to such Cabinet officers as shall have been appointed with the advice and consent of the Senate and are eligible under the Constitution to the Presidency.

Printer's Devil.—The origin of this term is ascribed to the fact that in the early days of printing the apprentice's duties included the inking of the forms with bags containing ink or besmeared with it. In the performance of this work his face and hands became so daubed with the ink that in appearance he suggested the devil. Hence the name.

Printing Crockery.—Common crockery, when it is in the state called biscuit-ware—that is, when it has been whitened by baking but has not been glazed—is figured upon or decorated by applying to its surface a design freshly printed upon paper. The ware absorbs the enamel ink, and the paper is removed by water. It is then fired in seggars, or a muffle, to fix the color, dipped in glaze, and then again fired, which converts the glaze into a perfectly transparent glassy covering all over the surface of the pottery. Porcelain decoration has long held a high rank as a fine art; and the exquisite skill shown in some of the finest works of the continental manufacturers, and also in those of Great Britain, has fairly entitled it to that rank. The colors employed are all colored glasses ground to impalpable powder, and mixed with borax or some other fluxing material; for use they are generally made liquid with oil of spike, and they are laid on with hair-pencils in the same way as oil colors. The whole process is exactly the same as in painting or staining glass, the glaze on the biscuit-porcelain being true glass, and the enamel colors being exactly the same as those used by the glass decorator. Peculiar and beautiful metallic lusters are produced upon pottery by precipitated platinum and other metals. The manufacture of pottery is carried on with great activity in Trenton, Philadelphia, Liverpool (in Ohio), and other places in the United States.

Prohibitory Laws.—The first actual prohibitory law was enacted in Maine in 1851. This was the famous Maine Liquor Law, and it is still in force in that State, and in 1884 its specifications were put in the form of a Constitutional amendment, and adopted by a large popular majority. Vermont enacted a prohibitory law in 1852, its provisions, however, being much less stringent than those of the Maine law. It was strengthened by the passage in 1869 of a civil-damage act, which provided that damages might be collected from the liquor-seller for injuries inflicted by his customers, while in a state of intoxication, upon themselves or others. A mild prohibitory law was also passed by New Hampshire in 1855, which has been strengthened by enactments since adopted. Damages are assessed on the liquor-seller for the acts of drunkards in that State also, by an act passed in 1870. In Massachusetts the temperance excitement of 1852 resulted in the passage of a prohibitory law by the Legislature, but the courts decided the law was unconstitutional, and in 1853 it was repealed. In 1855, the Know Nothing party being in power in the Assembly, another prohibitory law was passed. This was on trial for several years before the courts, but at length its constitutionality was affirmed. In 1868 this law was repealed because of great popular dissatisfaction with its manner of working. A milder law was passed in 1869, but, being even more unsatisfactory, was abolished in 1875, and replaced by a license law which still exists. In Rhode Island, as in Massachusetts, a law passed during the excited state of public feeling in 1852 was declared unconstitutional the following year. The law was then amended so as not to conflict with the Constitution, and the question of its adoption being submitted to the people, it was approved by a small majority. In 1863, however, the law was repealed. In 1874 a similar law was passed, only to be abolished in the next year, when a license law prohibiting the sale of liquors to minors and drunkards, and also on Sundays, and providing for the collection of damages from the liquor-dealer, was passed. An amendment was offered to the people in 1886 which was not adopted, but in the next year a stringent prohibitory law was passed. Connecticut passed a prohibitory law in 1854, but owing to some defect in the law, or to the indifference of the people, it could not be enforced, and became virtually a dead letter. About 1870, therefore, it was superseded by the present license law, which has the local-option feature. This has given opportunity to a large number of towns and districts to positively forbid the sale of liquor in their localities, so that nearly half of the State is under practical prohibition. Michigan in 1853 adopted a prohibitory law which was repealed almost immediately. A similar law, however, was adopted in 1855, which continued on the statute-books for about twenty years. As it had become inoperative through popular indifference, it was replaced by a license law in 1875. This latter was strengthened in 1883 by the adoption of a damage clause. In 1885 New York passed a prohibitory law which shared the fate of many similar enactments, being declared unconstitutional, and was repealed the following year. In 1861 efforts had been made to secure prohibition in the Revised Constitution, but the result was a failure. The extent of New Jersey's prohibition is a law passed in 1797, and still in force, forbidding the distribution or sale of liquors at a public auction. Pennsylvania once had a prohibitory statute on its books for a few months. It was adopted in 1855 and repealed in 1856. This law had been preceded by a "no-license act" which had been enacted by the Legislature in 1846, and had been pronounced unconstitutional by the Supreme Court. In 1872 a law was passed giving local option to the counties, and sixty-seven of them voted against licensing the traffic. In two years that law was repealed and a license law adopted, which is still in force. The prohibition issue was squarely before the people in the spring elections of this year (1889), and was defeated by a large popular majority. Delaware has tried prohibition twice. The first law was passed in 1847, only to be repealed in 1848. The second law was made in 1885; but it was in a few years displaced by a license law which is still in existence. Three other States—Indiana, Illinois and Iowa—adopted prohibitory laws in 1855. That of Indiana was declared void soon after, and has never been re-enacted. The legislative enactment of Illinois was submitted to the people and rejected by them. Since then no effort has been made to make the State prohibitory, but a high-license law was passed by the Legislature of 1882–'83. This law has been declared constitutional by the courts, and has been generally successful in its operation. The Iowa law has stood, with some modifications, and, where public opinion has supported it, has been generally executed. In 1882 a prohibitory clause was put into the Constitution by popular vote. This amendment has been declared void by the Supreme Court on account of certain technical errors in drawing it up. In 1884 a prohibitory law was passed. Ohio put a "no-license" clause in its Constitution in 1851, and the sale of liquors has been virtually free throughout the State. Attempts have been made at several times to regulate the traffic by law, but all have failed. Two of the States adopted prohibitory laws while they were still under territorial organization—Minnesota in 1852 and Nebraska in 1855. In both cases the law was modified to make it fit public sentiment more nearly, and both States now have high-license laws. Kansas adopted a modified prohibitory law in 1866. In 1880 the popular vote added an amendment to the Constitution prohibiting the manufacture and sale of intoxicating liquors in the State "except for medical, scientific and mechanical purposes." In Georgia, ninety-five counties have suppressed the sale of liquor through the privilege of local option. Similar laws are made somewhat effective, also, in Texas, Arkansas and Florida. Other States have laws forbidding the sale of liquor within a certain distance of a school, or to minors, to persons of notoriously intemperate habits, etc.

Prometheus.—According to Greek mythology Prometheus was a son of Iapetus, by Clymene, one of the Oceanides. He was a brother of Epimetheus, Menætius and Atlas, and was fabled to have surpassed all mankind in sagacity. When the gods and men had a controversy at Mecone, Prometheus took an ox, and, dividing it, put the flesh and entrails in the hide, and, wrapping the bones up in the inside fat, desired Jupiter to take which he would. The god, though aware of the deceit, selected the bones and fat, and in revenge he withheld fire from man. But Prometheus stole the fire in a hollow staff, brought it to earth, and gave it to man. Jupiter then sent Pandora on earth to deceive man to his ruin, and he bound Prometheus with chains to a pillar, and sent an eagle to prey without ceasing on his liver, which grew every night as much as it had lost during the day. After a long interval of time, however (according to some, 30,000 years), Hercules slew the eagle and freed the sufferer. On the story of Prometheus has been founded the following very pretty fable: When Prometheus had stolen the fire from heaven for the good of mankind, they were so ungrateful as to betray him to Jupiter. For their treachery they got in reward a remedy against the evils of old age; but, not duly considering the value of the gift, instead of carrying it themselves they put it on the back of an ass and let it trot on before them. It was summer-time, and the ass, quite overcome by thirst, went up to a fountain to drink, but a snake forbade all approach. The ass, ready to faint, most earnestly implored relief. The cunning snake, who knew the value of the burden which the ass bore, demanded it as the price of access to the font. The ass was forced to comply, and the snake obtained possession of the gift of Jupiter, but with it, as a punishment of his art, he got the thirst of the snake. Hence it is that the snake, by casting, annually renews his youth, while man is borne down by weight of the evils of old age.

Protocol.—The word protocol is used in two senses: 1. The rough draft of an instrument or transaction, and more particularly the original copy of a government dispatch, treaty, or other document. 2. A record or register. In Scotland every notary, on admission to office, formerly received from the clerk-register a book called his protocol, in which he was directed to insert copies of all instruments which he might have occasion to execute, to be preserved as in a record. These protocols have often been found serviceable, when regularly kept, to supply the loss of a missing deed. The word is from the Greek *protos*, first, and *kolla*, glue.

Public Lands.—The public lands of the United States still unsold and open to settlement are divided into two classes, one class being sold by the Government for $1.25 per acre as the minimum price, the other at $2.50 per acre, being the alternate sections reserved by the United States in land grants to railroads, etc. Such tracts are sold upon application to the Land Register. Heads of families, or citizens over twenty-one years, who may settle upon any quarter-section (160 acres) have the right under the pre-emption law of prior claim to purchase, on complying with the regulations. Under the homestead laws, any citizen or intending citizen has the right to 160 acres of the $1.25 or $2.50 land after an actual settlement and cultivation of the same for five years. Under the timber-culture law any settler who has cultivated for two years as much as 5 acres in trees of an 80-acre homestead, or 10 acres of a homestead of 160 acres, is entitled to a free patent for the land at the end of eight years.

Public Lands, Division of.—The system by which the public lands of the United States are divided dates back to the earliest days of the nation's existence, and the plan is due in the main to the practical genius of Thomas Jefferson. According to his plan the land was divided into divisions called "hundreds," which were to be ten miles square, each of them to be subdivided into plots one mile square, numbered from one to one hundred. This was embodied in a report to the Tenth Continental Congress in 1785; and an amendment reducing the principal divisions to six miles square, to be called "townships," each township to be subdivided into sections one mile square, containing 640 acres, was offered by James Monroe and was adopted. The general plan of survey remained, however, as it had been originally introduced, and in the same form is still in use.

Public Schools.—The origin of the public school system of America dates back to the time of the settlement of Massachusetts and Connecticut. In the very beginning of their history these colonists made provision for the establishment of schools in every town, and parents were required to send their children to them or educate them otherwise. At first these schools were not entirely free; that is, those who could pay were required to do so; but the evil of separating the children into paupers and rate-payers in time became apparent, and shortly after the colonies became States the school-taxes were increased and the schools were made free. The example of these colonists was quickly followed by other New England colonies; but in other sections of the country schools were either private or parochial for many years, except in cases where a free school was established and supported by private beneficence. When the vast territories west of the Alleghany Mountains came into the possession of the United States, every sixteenth section in each Congressional township was set aside by the Government as a nucleus of a public school fund; later, this was increased to two sections for the benefit of the newer States. The Southern States were the last to embrace the free school system in its entirety, having done so only since the close of the civil war. Maine, Vermont, Massachusetts, Connecticut, New Hampshire, New York, New Jersey, Kansas, Nevada, Wisconsin, Ohio, Michigan, California, Arizona, Wyoming and Washington Territory have compulsory educational laws. The average age up to which school attendance is required is, in the United States, 14½ years, which is older than that in any other country.

Punch, London, or the London *Charivari*, was founded in 1841 under the joint editorship of Mark Lemon and Shirley Brooks, and is at the present time the greatest of English comic magazines. Douglas Jerrold, Tom Hood, Albert Smith and Thackeray were helped to fame through their contributions to *Punch*, as were Doyle, Leech, Tenniel, Du Maurier and Keen by their illustrations in the same publication.

"Puts" and "Calls."—When stocks are thought to be about to decline in market price, and a small operation in them without much risk is desired, a small sum is given for the privilege of delivering an amount of stock at a certain price at a future time; for example, cash price of Erie being 57, a speculator gives $50, we will say, for the privilege to "put," or in other words deliver, a hundred shares at 56½, say in ten days. If the market goes down, as he naturally expects it will when making the transaction, all that it falls below 56 is profit. If it should go up, he can only lose the $50 originally invested. A "call" is a similar transaction on a rising market; for instance, a certain stock is selling at 50, and in the opinion of a speculator is likely to advance, he then purchases the privilege of calling for the stock at a certain price, say 53, on a certain day, expecting the value to rise above 53, all advance on this figure being clear profit.

Pygmies.—The pygmies were a fabulous race of dwarfs, in whose existence the ancients believed. They were said to be about 2½ feet in height, and to be engaged in constant warfare with their inveterate enemies, the cranes. By some writers they are placed at the mouth of the Nile, and by others as inhabiting the region of the Thule, and as living in subterranean dwellings on the eastern side of the Ganges. It was said that they cut down every ear of corn with an ax; that when Hercules came into their country they climbed up his goblet, by the help of ladders, to drink from it; and that when he was asleep, two whole Pygmy armies fell upon his right and another upon his left hand, but were all rolled up by the hero in his lion's skin. Explorations in Africa have, however, thrown light upon the pygmy myth by revealing the existence of a race of very small human beings in southeast Africa. They were found in the mountainous country on the east of the southern great branch of the Ogobai by Du Chaillu. They are called Obongos, are about $4\frac{1}{2}$ feet in height, and live in the midst of negro tribes of ordinary stature. A race of very small men was also discovered in Africa by the explorer Schweinfurth in 1868–'71, none of whom exceeded four feet ten inches is height. Their peculiarities are disproportionately large heads, peculiar-shaped shoulder-blades, and abdomens of enormous size.

Pyramids.—The weight of authority among modern Egyptologists inclines to the view that the Pyramids were a new and bold architectural type, invented in its entirety between the fifth and twelfth dynasties, in Middle Egypt, and not the development from earlier forms of tomb-mounds. " Pyramid," in its strict, geometrical sense, denotes a building having a polygonal base and plain triangular sides which meet in an apex. There are various forms of ancient tomb-mounds of earth and stone and stepped structures, as the *mastaba* in Egypt, and early temples and mausolea in Mexico and Assyria, and there are also some inferior imitations of later date; but the true pyramidal construction is seen only in Egypt, and comprises about seventy structures on the banks of the Nile, none of which are later than the twelfth dynasty (about 2000 B. C.). They are all built upon a square base, with the four sides facing the four cardinal points of the compass, and in the earlier forms are composed of horizontal layers of rough-hewn blocks with a small amount of mortar—degenerating in the buildings of the sixth and succeeding dynasties to a cellular system of retaining-walls filled with loose chips, and finally, in the twelfth dynasty, to a mass of mud bricks. But there was, in all cases, on the outside, a casing of fine stone, beautifully polished and jointed, the inner chambers having a similar finish. These casing-stones were not a mere veneer or film, but were massive blocks, usually greater in thickness than in height. Inside of each pyramid, always low down, and usually beneath the level of the ground, was built a sepulchral chamber, and this was reached by a downward passage from the north side. This passage had a lesser chamber in its course, and was blocked once or oftener with a massive stone portcullis. The interior was probably in every case accessible to the priests for the purpose of making offerings, the passage-way being closed by a stone door turning on a horizontal pivot, the location of which was known to them. The chambers were always roofed by great sloping cantilevers of stone projecting from the north and south sides, on which they rested without pressing on each other along the central ridge, so that there was no thrust, nor indeed any force to disturb the buildings; and now, after a lapse of four thousand years, in spite of the brutal treatment of enemies and the greed of later builders (who have removed almost all of the casing-stones), they still stand as colossal monuments of the work of man. Owing to the loss of the casing-stones, their present appearance presents a series of huge, rough steps, and their height has been considerably diminished by the encroachment of the sand of the desert around their bases. Many archæologists believe these vast piles, especially the great Pyramid of Cheops at Gizeh, to have been constructed under divine inspiration, and to embody in the living rock great astronomical facts and mathematical principles, and memorials of a system of weights and measures for universal use. It is also maintained that Masonic emblems and symbols have been found within them. Whatever the builders embodied in the details of their construction, their immediate object and use was undoubtedly to serve as royal mausolea. As for these theories, future investigations will probably develop or explode them; but that there is great mathematical knowledge and wonderful accuracy of measurement displayed in them is well established. In the great Pyramid at Gizeh, the four sides have a mean error of only 6-10th of an inch, and twelve seconds in angle from a perfect square. This pyramid is the largest of all, and by far the most remarkable in its construction. It is somewhat different from the others in its internal arrangement, having the subterranean chamber, which is but half-finished, and having also an upward passage leading to two large upper chambers, highly finished with great slabs of polished red granite. Probably both of these chambers contained originally a polished sarcophagus of the same Syenitic granite; and the larger one—the "King's"—although in the very heart of this huge pile, is perfectly ventilated by two air-passages about nine inches square, which run to the north and south faces of the Pyramid. It was built by Cheops or Khufu, of the fifth dynasty, and its construction is thought to have employed 100,000 men for thirty years or more—probably half a century. The masonry consisted originally of 89,028,000 cubic feet, and still amounts to 82,111,000. The height is at present 450 feet (originally 479), and the length of the sides 746 feet (originally 764). The King's Chamber is 19 feet 1 inch in height, and in area 34 feet 3 inches by 17 feet 1 inch; the Queen's Chamber is 20 feet 3 inches in height, and in area 17 feet by 18 feet 9 inches. It is now generally agreed that there were no inscriptions on the external surface of any of the pyramids, the casing-stones bearing a smooth polish. The mechanical means employed by the builders have been partly ascertained.

The hard stones, granite, dioryte and basalt were, in all fine work, sawn into shape by bronze saws set with jewels (either corundum or diamond); hollows were made (as in sarcophagi) by tubular drilling with tools like our modern diamond rock-drills, and small articles were turned in lathes fitted with mechanical tool-rests and jewel-pointed tools. The questions of the transport and management of such huge stones, weighing oftentimes more than thirty tons apiece, remain still to be answered.

Pyx, Trial of the, as the annual testing of the standard of the gold and silver coins in the English mint is called, is a custom of very ancient origin, and derives its name from the pyx or chest in which the coins to be examined are kept. In early times the mint-master in England was simply a person under contract with the Government for the manufacture of the coinage, and periodical examinations were consequently necessary to see that the terms of the contract were complied with. The mint-master is now an officer of the Crown, but the manner of conducting the ceremony is substantially unchanged. The finished coins are delivered to the mint-master in weights called journey-weights; that is, 15 pounds, troy weight, of gold, containing 701 sovereigns, or 1,402 half-sovereigns; of silver, 60 pounds, troy. From each journey-weight a coin is taken and placed in the pyx for the annual trial. The examination of the coins is made by the Goldsmiths' Company, under the direction of the Crown and in the presence of the "Queen's Remembrancer," who administers the oath to the jury and presides over the proceedings. The coins are compared with pieces cut from trial-plates of standard fineness, which are in keeping of the Warden of the Standards. If the coins are found to be of standard fineness and weight, within certain limits, a statement to that effect is testified to by the jurors and handed over to the treasurer. The coins to be tested are kept in the ancient chapel at Westminster Abbey, in joint custody of the Lords of the Treasury and the Comptroller-General. A similar ceremony is provided by law in the United States. This trial is made at the Philadelphia mint, yearly, on the second Wednesday in February, before the Judge of the United States District Court, the Comptroller of the Currency, the Assayer of the New York Assay Office, and such other persons as the President of the United States. may designate. A majority of the persons appointed constitute a competent board, and the examination is made in the presence of the Director of the Mint. From each delivery of coins made by the chief coiner a certain number are reserved for trial, deposited in the pyx and kept under the joint care of the Superintendent of the mint and the Assayer, each of these officers securing it by an independent lock. Reserved coins from the coinage of other mints are transmitted quarterly to the Philadelphia mint, or the Director may, if he wishes, take other pieces for the test. The examiners are not sworn, as in England, but they make a certified report of the trial after examination. If this shows the coins to be within the limit of tolerance in fineness and weight, it is simply filed; but if not, the fact is certified to the President of the United States, and if he should deem it proper to do so, he may order all the officers implicated in the error thenceforward disqualified for holding their offices.

Queen's Counsel are barristers who receive from the Queen a patent giving them preaudience over their brethren. The advantage of the appointment is that it enables the most able or successful counsel to take the chief conduct of cases in preference to those of the same or longer standing. The appointment is made on the nomination of the Lord Chancellor. When a Queen's Counsel is engaged in a criminal case against the Crown, as, for example, to defend a prisoner, he requires to get a special license to do so from the Crown, which is given on payment of a small fee. It is sometimes popularly believed that the appointment of Queen's Counsel entitles the counsel to a salary from the Crown, but this is a mistake except as to the Attorney and Solicitor-General. Sir Francis Bacon was the first barrister to receive the appointment.

Queen of the Antilles, an appellation sometimes given to Cuba, which, from its great size, its rich natural productions, its fine harbors, varied and beautiful scenery, and its commanding geographical position, ranks first among all the islands of the West Indian group.

Quintessence.—The word quintessence, which signifies, literally, the fifth essence, is of ancient origin, and dates from the time when it was generally believed that the simple elements or constituents of bodies were *four* in number, viz., fire, air, earth and water, and that earth was the lowest element, being grosser than water, water than air, and air than fire. A fifth element or essence, *ether*, was added by some Pythagorian philosopher, who did not believe that the four elements, or essences, sufficed for the composition of all substances in Nature. This fifth element or essence was supposed to be more subtle and pure than fire (the highest of the four), and was therefore located in the uppermost regions of the sky. The word "quintessence" has thus come down to us in the signification of the subtle and vital ingredient of any body, though in ordinary language it is employed in a figurative sense.

Rabbit's Foot.—The legends of "Br'er Rabbit" among the negroes, his clever devices in outwitting his natural enemies—the dog, fox and wolf—and thwarting every scheme designed for his own punishment, are almost without number. From these legends of the preternatural sagacity of the living rabbit came the idea that the dead rabbit had certain magic powers. The negroes believe that to carry a rabbit's foot in the pocket is not only a talisman for good luck, but is a specific for diseases. The left hind foot of the rabbit is believed to have the most efficacy, and if it be taken from a rabbit that runs in a grave-yard, its supernatural properties are believed to be quite irresistible.

Rack-Rent is a term employed in Great Britain to signify the full yearly value of lands let upon lease, or to an occupier, or held by a tenant for life, as distinguished from the value fixed by the lease or agreement between the parties, and which is often less or greater than the real value.

Railroad Mileage of the World.—The total railroad mileage of the world is 335,099 miles. Of this amount the United States has 147,999 miles; Great Britain and Ireland, 19,332 miles; Germany, 24,197 miles; France, 19,996 miles; Russia, 18,130 miles; Austria-Hungary, 14,335 miles; British India, 13,200 miles; Canada, 11,523 miles; Italy, 7,266 miles; Spain, 5,654 miles; Brazil, 4,955 miles; Sweden, 4,654 miles; Argentine Republic, 4,216 miles, and Mexico, 4,000 miles. The mileage of the other countries is comparatively small, ranging from 2,763 miles in Belgium to 20 miles in San Domingo. The cost of the railroads in the United States has been about $9,000,000,000, and they furnish employment to 1,000,000 persons. The longest mileage operated by a single system is that of the Atchison, Topeka and Santa Fe Railway, being about 8,000 miles, and the highest railroad bridge in the United States is the Kinzan Viaduct, 305 feet high, on the Erie Railroad.

Railroad Time-Tables.—A railroad time-table governing the running of trains on any road is one of the most important things in the management. The preparation of such a table is a very ingenious piece of work. The means employed are of the simplest sort—common pins and spools of colored threads and a large sheet of drawing-paper mounted on an easel. This paper is called the time-chart. The chart is ruled either for two, five or ten minutes' time by perpendicular lines. The "time" is marked above the perpendicular lines, and the distance, or stations and termini, on horizontals, crossing the perpendicular lines. For illustration, 12 midnight is the mark on the first perpendicular line, and each hour is marked until the twenty-fourth or the following midnight hour is reached on the last perpendicular line. Between the hour lines the space is divided into minutes and graduated as fine as desired. On a two-minute chart the space between the hours is divided into ten minutes' time, and the ten minutes' time into two minutes' time. One terminus of the road is marked on the first line beside the first time-mark, 12 midnight. The other stations follow down on the horizontal lines until the other terminus is reached. It is calculated that the running time shall be, say, twenty-five miles an hour, and, for the purpose of illustration, the tracing of one passenger train will suffice to explain the system. A passenger train leaves the first station, say at 8 A. M.; a pin is placed on the first horizontal line at the 8 A. M. time-mark, and the end of the blue thread fastened thereto. If the train runs without stopping for fifty miles the blue thread is stretched over opposite the station at which the stop is made, and directly under the 10 A. M. time-mark another pin is stuck, and the blue thread wrapped about it to keep it taut. If this is a stop of forty minutes the blue thread is stretched to the 10:40 A. M. mark on a direct line with the same station, and another pin stuck and the blue thread wrapped. The train starts, and its entire course is thus timed and distributed along the road; and if the road operates many trains the time chart, when it is completed, looks like a great spider's web, stretched with pins and colored threads. A blue thread is used to represent a passenger train, a red thread a freight train, and if the trains of other roads use part of the track, they are designated by a different colored thread.

Railway Trains, Speed of.—The fastest time made by an American train is claimed to be 92 miles in 93 minutes, on the Philadelphia and Reading Railroad, one mile being made in 46 seconds. The fastest time between Jersey City, N. J., and San Francisco, Cal., was made in June, 1886, when the Jarrett and Palmer special theatrical train made the run in 3 days, 7 hours, 39 minutes and 16 seconds. A West Shore Railroad train ran, in July, 1885, from East Buffalo, N. Y., to Weehawken, N. J., 422.6 miles, in 9 hours and 23 minutes. In May, 1886, the run from New York to Buffalo, 440 miles, was made by a train on the New York Central Railroad in 9 hours and 30 minutes. June, 1884, the Baltimore and Ohio Railroad ran a train from Chicago to Bellaire, 463 miles, in 11 hours and 21 minutes. The weight of engine, tender and cars in these trains was from 250,000 pounds to about 400,000 pounds, and all the trains were very light. In the summer of 1888 the rival trains, running between London and Edinburgh, of the Great Northern Railroad and the London and Northwest Railroad, made the run between those cities, the former in 7 hours and 32 minutes, giving a speed of 52 miles per hour including stops, and the latter in 7 hours and 38 minutes. The distance by the latter route, it must be remarked, is 400 miles, while by the Great Northern it is only 392 miles. So far as the machinery of a railway is concerned—by which we mean the road, the rolling-stock and the signals—there is nothing to prevent an average speed of 60 miles an hour being maintained; yet there is not in the world a train timed to run at that speed, although it is, of course, certain that even a greater velocity is often attained for short distances. The fastest train in the world—that is to say the train whose *regular* running time is faster than that of any other —is undoubtedly the celebrated "Flying Dutchman."

Rainbow.—A rainbow can only be seen when the spectator stands between it and the sun; its center must always be directly opposite the sun, moving with the sun's motion, falling if the sun is rising, and rising if the sun is declining. A rainbow occurs when the sun or moon, not too far above the horizon, throws its beams upon a sheet of falling rain-drops on the opposite side of the heavens. Thus, a ray of light from the sun strikes a rain-drop obliquely; part of it is reflected at the surface of the drop;

the rest, passing into the drop, is refracted; on the other side of the drop part of the ray passes through, and the rest is again reflected; on passing from the drop on the same side that it entered, a second refraction occurs. These successive reflections and refractions separate the ray of white light into its component colored rays, and as the angles of incidence and emergence vary for each color, the eye of a spectator perceives them as distinct bands. Now, every drop in the sheet of falling water which has equal obliquity to the spectator's eye will send to it rays of the same color. But the only drops which can fulfill these conditions of like obliquity of reflected rays are those which define the base of a cone whose apex is the eye, and the center of whose base is in a right line passing through the sun and the eye of the spectator. At or near sunset, when the sun and the observer are in the same horizontal plane, the bow will be seen to form a complete semicircle; when the sun is higher in the sky, a smaller arch is seen; the entire circle could only be visible to a spectator on the top of a very high and narrow mountain peak, which would elevate his plane much above that of the sun's rays without cutting off their light. A complete circle may also be sometimes seen in the rainbow formed by the sunlight on the spray arising from cataracts. The lunar rainbow, which is a comparatively rare but very beautiful phenomenon, differs from the solar simply in the source and intensity of the light by which it is produced; and, as in all cases of feeble light, the distinction of the colors is very difficult. In fact, except under the most favorable circumstances, the lunar rainbows rarely show colors at all, giving a pale, ghostly gleam of apparently white or yellow light.

Rainbows, Artificial.—In the fall of 1883 Professor Tyndale undertook to reproduce in his laboratory the effects of light that he had seen in the Alpine Mountains. His first object was to obtain artificially a mixture of fog and drizzle such as might most nearly resemble the atmosphere of the hills. His account of the experiment and its result is as follows: "A strong cylindrical copper boiler, sixteen inches high and twelve inches in diameter, was nearly filled with water and heated by gas-flames until steam of twenty pounds pressure was produced. A valve at the top of the boiler was then opened, when the steam issued violently into the atmosphere, carrying droplets of water mechanically along with it, and condensing above to droplets of a similar kind. A fair imitation of the Alpine atmosphere was thus produced. After a few tentative experiments the luminous circle was brought into view, and having once got hold of it, the next step was to enhance its intensity. Oil-lamps, the lime-light and the naked electric-light were tried in succession, the source of rays being placed in one room, the boiler in another, while the observer stood, with his back to the light, between them. It is not, however, necessary to dwell upon these first experiments, surpassed as they were by the arrangements subsequently adopted. My mode of proceeding was this: The electric-light being placed in a camera, with a condensing-lens in front, the position of the lens was so fixed as to produce a beam sufficiently broad to clasp the whole of my head and leave an aureola of light around it. It being desirable to lessen as much as possible the foreign light entering the eye, the beam was received upon a blank surface, and it was easy to move the head until its shadow occupied the center of the illuminated area. To secure the best effect it was found necessary to stand close to the boiler, so as to be immersed in the fog and drizzle. The fog, however, was soon discovered to be a mere nuisance. Instead of enhancing, it blurred the effect, and I therefore sought to abolish it. Allowing the steam to issue for a few seconds from the boiler, on closing the valve the cloud rapidly melted away, leaving behind it a host of minute liquid spherules floating in the beam. A beautiful circular rainbow was instantly swept through the air in front of the observer. The primary bow was duly attended by its secondary, with the colors, as usual, reversed. The opening of the valve for a single second caused the bows to flash forth."

Raki, the East Indian name for all sorts of distilled spirituous liquors, but chiefly for that procured from toddy or the fermented juice of the cocoa and other palms, and from rice. The cocoanut-palm is a chief source of toddy or palm-wine, and is obtained from trees ranging from twelve to sixteen years old, or, in fact, at the period when they begin to show the first indications of flowering. After the flowering shoot or spadix enveloped in its spathe is pretty well advanced and the latter is about to open, the toddy-man climbs the tree and cuts off the tip of the flower-shoot; he next ties a ligature around the stalk at the base of the spadix, and with a small cudgel he beats the flower-shoot and bruises it. This he does daily for a fortnight, and if the tree is in good condition a considerable quantity of a saccharine juice flows from the cut apex of the flower-shoot. The juice rapidly ferments, and in four days is usually sour; previous to that it is a favorite drink, known in India by the natives as callu, and to the Europeans as toddy. When turning sour it is distilled and converted into raki, known better to the Hindus as naril, and to the Cingalese as pol, or nawasi. It is probable that the use of raki is more widely diffused among the human race than either wine, brandy, whisky or beer.

Reaper, First in the United States.—In 1803 a reaping machine was patented by Richard French and John J. Hawkins, but it did not prove successful. Prior to 1832 there were granted eight patents for machines for cuttting grain. No inventor, however, succeeded in producing machines that possessed sufficient practical merit to be used otherwise than experimentally until we come to Bell, Hussey and McCormick, whose machines have since become so well known. At the meeting of the British Association at Dundee, September, 1867, the Reverend Patrick Bell stated that he invented his reaping machine in 1826. McCormick's

American machine was patented in 1834, and, with improvements added in 1845 and 1847, received a medal at the World's Fair in London, 1851. In 1833, Obed Hussey, then of Cincinnati, Ohio, patented a machine to which he applied saw-toothed cutters and guards. This machine was at once put into practical operation, and gave general satisfaction. Hussey, in 1847, patented the open-topped slotted finger. The practical use of self-rakers, in this country, dates from the invention of W. H. Seymour of New York, in 1851. He arranged a quadrant-shaped platform directly behind the cutters, a reel to gather the grain and a rake moving over the platform in the arc of a circle depositing the sheaves on the ground. In 1856, Owen Dorsey of Maryland combined the reel and rake, and his improvement has been extensively used here and abroad, with some modifications, one of which was by Johnston in 1865, who arranged it so that the size of the sheaves, or gavels, as they are called, could be regulated at the will of the driver. The names of Haines, Ketchum, Manny and Wood are prominent among inventors of improvements in mowers and harvesters.

Red Snow.—The apparent redness of snow, as seen from a distance, is often an effect of light; but the snow of this color which was seen by some prospectors at the head of Cross Creek in Colorado a few years ago was, it is thought, due to the presence of a minute red animalcule in the snow. It was first seen at the head of Cross Creek, where it was found in patches of intense carmine, varying in area from as large as a man's hat to twenty feet in diameter. Taken in the hand and closely examined, nothing could be detected that gave it color, and it melted into clear red water, leaving no stain. Further on, in some of the steep gulches with which the country abounds, the bottoms were entirely covered with the strange substance. In some places the color was vivid in the extreme, while in others it faded to a faint pink, producing an effect not readily described in words. In the almost inaccessible defiles of Mount Shasta, in California, is the only other known place in the United States where this phenomenon is seen. In the polar regions it is a familiar sight. It may be added that snow is occasionally tinged black, yellow, red or green, as known to Pliny, and has been minutely described by various scientific writers.

Refrigerating Machines.—The great practical and commercial value of refrigerating machines lies in their use for the preservation of food, especially fresh meat. Natural ice, in temperate, and still more, in hot climates, is so rare and expensive as to prevent its use on a large scale and restrict it to the most costly of food-products. The great problem of the successful transportation of fresh meat to distant markets was solved in 1879. In March, of this year, the Anchor Line steamship Circassia delivered in England the first cargo of fresh meat artificially preserved, which was transported in a Bell-Colman dry-air refrigerator, introduced by Mr. J. J. Colman in conjunction with Messrs. H. and J. Bell. These rapidly came into general use, and with some later improvements are now to be found in thousands of steamers and sailing vessels, carrying fresh meat in large quantities to and from all parts of the world. The first shipment from Australia, consisting of thirty-one tons of beef and mutton, was delivered in London in February, 1880; and in June, 1882, the sailing ship Dunedin brought from New Zealand to London 4909 carcasses of sheep and 22 pigs—all in perfect condition, notwithstanding the long voyage of ninety-eight days, and the intense heat experienced during the passage. Dry-air refrigerators are now in general use in passenger-steamers; also for the preservation of fresh provisions. The possibility of producing cold by artificial means has been long known to scientists, and put to various scientific uses, but no successful application in the arts was made until 1850, when the first compressed-air ice-making apparatus was invented by John Gorrie of New Orleans. The Bell-Colman refrigerator was brought out in 1879, and an improvement was invented shortly afterward by A. S. Haslam, in which the temperature of the compressed air is lowered by passing it through pipes cooled externally instead of by a spray of cold water injected into the tubes. One of the latest improved machines of this type is the "Windhausen." The process in these machines is in general as follows: Ordinary atmospheric air is compressed to one-third or one-fourth of its normal bulk by a steam-cylinder; the air, however, in the condensation becomes very hot, and it is therefore necessary to cool it by one of the methods mentioned above. It is then conducted to the expansion-cylinder, where a very rapid expansion produces a great and sudden fall of temperature, and the cold air is thence distributed in pipes throughout the freezing-chamber, in which anything desired may be placed. The rapid expansion of any compressed gas would produce this same result, air being used mainly because the supply is unlimited and the cost is nothing. The fundamental principle underlying the process is the simple physical law that in the passage of any form of matter from a more dense to a less dense condition, heat-energy is necessary, in order to drive the molecules farther apart. Now, in order that a compressed gas may resume its normal volume, an amount of heat-energy is required equal to the mechanical energy which effected the compression. Hence in the above machines the heat of the compressed air itself, and of everything in contact with it, is consumed in the expansion; and as cold is merely the absence of heat, a great fall in temperature is the result. There are two other ways of producing artificial cold, viz.: freezing-mixtures or liquefaction and vaporization. The first is explained by the laws of chemistry, certain substances when mixed in certain proportions always producing cold, and in some cases a great degree. They are not used in ice-machines, chiefly because they are too expensive for consumption on such a large scale. A common example is the mixture of ice and salt in an ordinary ice-cream freezer, which produces a temperature much below that of the ice, and causes at the same time a rapid liquefaction of the ice and solution of the salt. The last process, that by vaporization, depends upon the same physical laws as that by expansion. It has been extensively applied to large machines, the first successful apparatus being one exhibited by M. Carre, a Frenchman, in 1862. Linde's improved machine, invented about 1870, is still in use, and is one of the best. Ammonia is the liquid generally used, but methylic ether and sulphurous acid are also successfully employed. This method is, in general, as follows: A strong galvanized wrought-iron boiler, capable of sustaining a pressure of ten atmospheres, is connected by a tube with a freezing-chamber of similar strength and material, consisting of two compartments, one inclosing the other, the outer one being connected with the boiler by the tube, and the inner one designed for the reception of the substance to be frozen. The freezing-chamber is placed in a cold bath, and to the boiler, into which has been poured a quantity of a saturated solution of ammonium gas, sufficient heat is applied to create a pressure of five or six atmospheres; this pressure expels the ammonium from the water in which it was dissolved and forces it into the outer compartment of the freezing-chamber, when, partly by its own pressure and partly by the cool bath in which the chamber is placed, it is condensed in liquid form along with about one-tenth its weight of water. When enough of the gas has been condensed, the boiler itself is placed in a cool bath, and the cylinder containing the substance to be frozen is placed in the inner compartment of the freezing-chamber. Now, as the temperature in the boiler falls, the pressure in the apparatus is reduced, the liquefied ammonium in the outer compartment vaporizes very rapidly, and thus, in passing into the less dense form of a gas, abstracts heat-energy from everything in its neighborhood, and produces an intense cold in the inner compartment. A machine of this kind can turn out as much as 800 pounds of ice in an hour. [See *Ice, Artificial.*]

Religious Beliefs, Statistics of.—The numbers of followers of the different religious creeds in the world are as follows: Christianity, 338,000,000; Buddhism, 340,000,000; Mohammedanism, 210,000,000; Brahmanism, 175,000,000; Confucianism, 80,000,000; Sintoism, 14,000,000, and Judaism, 7,000,000.

Religious Statistics.—The communicants of the various religious denominations in the United States, according to the latest available reports, are as follows: Adventists, 100,441; Baptists, 3,971,685; Christian Union, 120,000; Congregationalists, 457,584; Episcopalians, Protestant, 437,785; Episcopalians, Reformed, 9,000; Friends, 107,968; German Evangelical, 125,000; Lutherans, 987,-600; Mennonites, 93,000; Methodists, 4,699,529; Moravians, 10,966; Presbyterians, 1,136,685; Reformed, 269,523; Roman Catholics, 7,200,000; Swedenborgians, 5,750; Unitarians, 20,000; Universalists, 37,807.

Representation in Congress, State.—According to the Constitution of the United States, each State, no matter what its population may be, is entitled to have two Senators in the National Congress and at least one member of the House of Representatives. Representation in the lower House of Congress is based upon population; so after each decennial census there is a new apportionment of members of this House among the different States, in order to proportion the membership of each State as nearly as possible to the number of its inhabitants as compared with the aggregate population of all the States. Senators serve for six years, and are chosen by the Legislatures of their respective States. Representatives serve for two years, and are elected by popular vote. According to the last apportionment, each district containing 151,912 of population is a Congressional district, and is entitled to one Representative. The number of Representatives from the several States are at present (1889) as follows: Alabama, 8; Arkansas, 5; California, 6; Colorado, 1; Connecticut, 4; Delaware, 1; Florida, 2; Georgia, 10; Illinois, 20; Indiana, 13; Iowa, 11, Kansas, 7; Kentucky, 11; Louisiana, 6; Maine, 4; Maryland, 6; Massachusetts, 12; Michigan, 11; Minnesota, 5; Mississippi, 7; Missouri, 14; Nebraska, 3; Nevada, 1; New Hampshire, 2; New Jersey 7; New York, 34; North Carolina, 9; Ohio, 21; Oregon, 1; Pennsylvania, 28; Rhode Island, 2; South Carolina, 7; Tennessee, 10; Texas, 11; Vermont, 2; Virginia, 10; West Virginia, 4; Wisconsin, 9. Each Territory is represented by one Delegate in Congress, who is entitled to a seat in the lower House, and the right to take part in debates but not to vote. The salary of Senators and Representatives is $5,000 per annum; mileage, 20 cents per mile of travel to and from Washington, each annual session; allowance for stationery and newspapers, $125 per annum. The President of the Senate and the Speaker of the House receive $8,000 per annum each. When a State fails to re-district before the election following the re-apportionment of Representatives according to the latest census, the additional members of the House from that State are elected by the entire State instead of by districts, and such members are known as Congressmen-at-Large—as, for instance, the four additional Representatives given to Kansas by the last Congressional apportionment. Where the number of Congressmen is reduced, and the State also fails to re-district previous to the election, *all* the Representatives from that State are elected on a general State ticket, and are also known as Congressmen-at-Large.

Revolution, Sons of The.—The society of the "Sons of the Revolution" was organized in New York, December 4, 1883, incorporated May 3, 1884, to "keep alive among ourselves and our descendants the patriotic spirit of the men who, in military, naval or civil service, by their acts or counsel achieved American independence; to collect and secure for preservation the manuscript rolls, records and other documents relating to the war of the Revolution, and to promote intercourse and good feeling among its members now and hereafter." Eligibility to membership is confined to male descendants from an ancestor who, as a soldier, sailor, or civil official, assisted in establishing American Independence during the war of the Revolution. The society numbered 310 members in 1888.

Ribbonism, the name of a system of Irish secret associations which first appeared about 1808 and originated in Armagh, and later spread to Down, Antrim, Tyrone and Fermanagh. The real object of their organization was probably for direct antagonistic action against the Orange confederacy. At first their operations were, for the most part, limited to the counties chiefly in the north and northwest of Ireland, where the Orange associations were sufficiently numerous to be formidable. The Ribbon Association was divided into lodges, and the members of each lodge were bound by a secret oath to "be true to each other," and "to assist each other in all things lawful." Stated meetings of the lodges were held, and small money contributions were exacted both at entrance into the association and on each occasion of meeting. Of late years they have been almost entirely replaced by newer secret organizations. The name by which they are known is supposed to have originated from the badge of ribbon worn by the members.

Rickets is exclusively a disease of childhood, and generally attacks the children of the poor. It is regarded by some writers as a special disease of the bones, and by others as merely one of the various forms of scrofula. The characteristic symptom in rickets is the imperfect development, atrophy, softness and consequent distortion of some or many of the bones. The bones thus affected consist of a sort of gelatinous tissue which will bend without breaking, and they are so soft that they may be cut with a knife. On microscopic-chemical examination the structural arrangement of the bone is found to be unaffected, while there is a great deficiency of the earthy salts to which the normal bones owe their firmness. The weight of the body acting on bones deficient in this earthy salt causes them to bend, and the thighs or shins are abnormally arched, or the spine is curved, or, in slighter cases, only the normal form of the ankle is modified. In aggravated cases the chest is so affected as to give rise to the condition known as *pigeon-breasted.*

Rivers, Velocity of.—The average velocity of a river may be estimated approximately by finding the surface velocity in the center of the current by means of a float which swims just below the surface and taking four-fifths of this quantity as a mean. If the mean velocity in feet per minute be multiplied by the area of the transverse section of the stream in square feet, the product is the amount of water discharged in cubic feet per minute. As most rivers have their sources on very high ground, their velocity is greatest at the beginning of their course. But the velocity does not altogether depend upon the slope of a river's bed; much is owing to its depth and volume. Therefore most rivers flow with varying velocity at different seasons of the year. The bends in a river's course, jutting points of rocks, or other obstacles, whether at the sides or bottom, interfere with its speed; hence its velocity differs at different parts of its bed. The lower Amazon flows at the rate of 3 miles an hour; the Mississippi, in the lower part of its course, has a current of about 3¼ miles an hour; the Congo has for miles above its mouth a current of nearly 7 miles; the Nile has, below the Cataracts at Wady Halfa and beyond, a current of 9 miles. The most rapid river in the world, of any size, is the river Rhone, in France, whose current ranges from as high as 40 to as low as 6 miles an hour. The current of a river is slower at the bottom than at the surface, and at the sides than the middle, and its line of quickest velocity is a line drawn along the center of the current. In cases where this line is free from sudden bends or sharp turns it also represents the deepest part of the channel. The velocity of falls, which is often enormous, cannot properly be included in any estimate of the velocity of rivers, although the impetus given by rapids has an influence on the rate of the currents.

Robes of Office.—The custom of wearing robes by the Justices of the Supreme Court of the United States was adopted from a similar custom in England. The garment is a long, black robe, enveloping the person from the shoulders to the feet. It is made full, with full sleeves and full body, and somewhat resembles clerical vestments.

Robin Goodfellow, a domestic spirit or fairy famous in English folk-lore, and from whom Shakespeare's "Puck" was derived. From the early ballads concerning Robin we learn that he was the offspring of a "proper young wench by a hee fairy," who was no less a person than Oberon, King of Fairyland. In his youth Robin displayed many mischievous tricks. As a specimen of his "mad prankes," Robin went one day to a wedding as a fiddler, and was a welcome guest; but in the evening "then hee beganne to play his merry trickes in this manner: First hee put out the candles, and then, being darke, hee strucke the men good boxes on the ears; they, thinking it had beene those that did sit next them, fell a-fighting one with the other, so that there was not one of them but had either a broken head or a bloody nose. The women did not 'scape him, for the handsomest he kissed, the others he pinched, and made them scratch one the other, as if they had beene cats. Candles being lighted againe, they all were friends, and fell againe to dancing, and after to supper. Supper being ended, a great posset was brought forth. At this, Robin's teeth did water, for it looked so lovely that hee could not keepe from it. To attaine to his wish hee did turne himself into a beare; both men and women seeing a beare amongst them ranne away, and left the whole posset to Robin. Hee quickly made an end of it, and went away without his money, for the sport hee had was better to him than any money whatsoever." Robin, however, was not always mischievous, for it is related that he often performed at midnight household duties for servants who had laid out for him a bowl of milk or curds and cream.

Rob Roy, the popular name of Robert M'Gregor, a celebrated Scottish outlaw, whose singular adventures entitle him to be considered the Robin Hood of Scotland. In Gaelic, the name *Roy* signifies *red*, and was applied to him from his ruddy complexion and color of hair. Rob Roy in his youth was distinguished for his skill in the use of the broadsword, in which the uncommon length of his arms was of great advantage. It was said that he could, without stooping, tie the garters of his Highland hose, which are placed two inches below the knee. Like many of the Highland proprietors of the period, Rob Roy dealt in grazing and rearing black cattle for the English market, and he also protected his neighbors' flocks from the banditti from Inverness, Ross and Sutherland. In return for this he levied a tax, which went under the name of blackmail. [See *Blackmail*.] Numberless stories are still current in the neighborhood of Loch Lomond and Loch Katrine of his hairbreadth escapes from capture by the troops, and many instances have also been recorded of his kindness to the poor, whose wants he often supplied at the expense of the rich. The exploits of Rob Roy have been immortalized by Sir Walter Scott in his celebrated novel of "Rob Roy," written in 1817.

Rocking-Stones, or *Loggans*, as they are called, are numerous in many places in England, Ireland and Scotland, and nearly every other country. One, situated at a place on the island of Magee, in Brown's Bay, Ireland, is popularly believed to acquire a rocking, tremulous motion at the approach of sinners and malefactors. These rocking-stones are large masses of rock so finely poised as to move backward and forward with the slightest impulse. Some of them appear to be natural, others artificial. The former are chiefly granitic rocks, in which feldspar and porphyry are abundantly present; and these ingredients becoming rapidly decomposed, and the dust and sand washed away by rains, what was formerly a solid rock soon assumes the appearance of a group of irregularly-shaped pillars having a rhomboidal horizontal section, and separated into portions by horizontal and vertical fissures. As disintegration proceeds, the edges of the blocks forming the pillars are first attacked and disappear, and finally the pillars become piles of two or more spheroidal rocks resting upon each other. If, now, a mass of rock be so situated as to preserve its equilibrium in spite of the gradual diminution of its base or point of support, a rocking-stone is the result. The artificial ones appear to have been formed by cutting away a mass of rock around the center-point of its base. In Greece, rocking-stones occur as funeral monuments, and are generally found on conspicuous places near the sea. Some rocking stones occur near to the remains of ancient fortifications, which seems to bear out a statement in one of the poems of Ossian that the bards walked round the stone singing, and made it move as an oracle of the fate of battle.

Roman Baths, The, were among the most magnificent and extensive architectural ornaments of the city in the time of the Empire. They were erected by different emperors for the use of the populace, and the vast ruins still existing testify to their great size and the unparalleled luxury of their arrangements. In these great *thermæ*, as they were called, the primitive object of bathing was largely lost sight of, and they became favorite places of general resort for pleasure. The most famous were those erected by the Emperors Titus, Caracalla and Diocletian. Caracalla's baths were 1,500 feet long by 1,250 feet broad, and the swimming-bath or *natatorium* in those of Diocletian was 200 feet long by 100 feet wide; and it is calculated that in this entire establishment 18,000 people could bathe at one time. There were separate structures for the exclusive use of women, and in some cases separate apartments in the same building, but these were generally inferior to those for the men. They were built entirely of stone and polished marble, and all the apartments were beautifully ornamented with mosaic and profusely adorned with painting, stucco-work and statuary. The public baths of Pompeii were uncovered in 1824 and the complete internal arrangement disclosed, which is probably similar to, though on a smaller scale than, those in Rome. The process of bathing was this: After undressing in the *apodyterium*, or "room for undressing," the bather was rubbed and anointed with some of the fragrant oils and ointments used by the ancients, and then proceeded to a spacious apartment devoted to exercises of various kinds, among which games at ball held a prominent place. After exercise he went into the *caldarium*, either merely to sweat or to take the hot bath; and during this part of the process the body was scraped with *strigiles* (small curved instruments usually made of bronze). Being now dried with cloths, and slightly anointed all over with perfumed oils, he resumed his dress, and then passed a short time, successively, in the *tepidarium* and the *frigidarium*, or temperate and cold rooms, which softened the transition from the great heat of the *caldarium* into the open air. The artificial bath has been used from the most ancient times of which we have any record. It is mentioned in Homer, the vessel for bathing being described as of polished marble and the *warm-baths* referred to as effeminate. Public baths were common in Greece during the historic period, and they were in use at Rome from early times; but during the Republic they continued small, dark and inconvenient, and it was not until the time of the Empire that they reached their great size and splendor.

Roman Calendar.—The Romans are said to have had originally a year of 10 months; but in the times of their kings they adopted a lunar year of 355 days, divided into 12 months, with an occasional intercalary month. Through the ignorance of the priests who had charge of this matter the utmost confusion gradually arose, which Julius Cæsar remedied, 46 B. C., by the introduction of the Julian Calendar, according to which the year has ordinarily 365 days, and every fourth year is a leap-year of 366 days—the length of the year being thus assumed as 365¼ days, while it is in reality 365 days, 5 hours, 48 minutes and 50 seconds. Cæsar gave to the months the number of days which they still have. So comparatively perfect was the Julian style of reckoning time that it prevailed generally among Christian nations, and remained undisturbed till the renewed accumulation of the remaining error of eleven minutes or so had amounted, in 1582 years after the birth of Christ, to ten complete days. This shifting of days had caused great disturbances by unfixing the times of the celebration of Easter, and hence of all other movable feasts. Accordingly, Pope Gregory XIII, after deep study and calculation, ordained that ten days should be deducted from the year 1582, by calling what, according to the old calendar, would have been reckoned the 5th of October the 15th of October, 1582; and in order that the displacement might not recur, it was further ordained that every hundredth year (1800, 1900, 2100, etc.) should not be counted a leap-year excepting every fourth hundredth, beginning 2000. In this way the difference between the civil and natural year will not amount to a day in 5,000 years. The Catholic nations in general adopted the style ordained by their sovereign; but the Protestants were then too much inflamed against the Roman See in all its relations to receive even a purely scientific improvement from such hands. The Lutherans of Germany, Switzerland and the Low Countries at length gave way in 1700, when it had become necessary to omit eleven instead of ten days. Scotland adopted the new reckoning in 1600, and England and Ireland in 1751. Russia, Greece, Roumania and the minor countries belonging to the Greek confession still adhere to the old style.

Rome Saved by Geese.—About the year 390 B. C. a number of Gauls, under the command of Brennus, entered Upper Italy and laid siege to several places. Rome interfered, and by this act simply irritated the invaders, who at once marched against her. A battle was fought and the Romans were defeated. Rome was now practically at the mercy of the Gauls. The better account relates that the victors, after slaughtering the helpless inhabitants and plundering the city, besieged the citadel in vain for seven months, and then retired upon the payment of 1000 pounds of gold as a ransom for the defenders of the fortress. Another tradition is that the Senate had not enough men left after the battle to defend the city, and so they congregated all the men capable of bearing arms in the Capitol, and sent away all who were useless; the old men and women and children took refuge in the nearest cities. There remained in Rome only a few pontiffs and ancient Senators, who, not being willing to survive either their country or its glory, gencrously devoted themselves to death, to appease, according to their belief, the anger of the infernal gods. These were found by Brennus, and for a time their splendid habits, their white beards, their air of grandeur and firmness astonished the Gauls and inspired a religious fear in the army. Finally, however, the Gauls massacred the Senators and then attacked the Capitol. While the Gauls plundered the city, the country round was recovering from its defeat. Camillus was chosen leader of the Romans, and while the Gauls were reveling they attacked the invaders and killed many of them. Camillus was proclaimed the saviour of his country, but he refused to do anything as their leader without the order of the Senate and the people shut up in the Capitol. It was almost impossible to gain access to them. A young Roman, however, undertook the perilous enterprise and was successful. Camillus was declared dictator and collected a large army. The Gauls had, however, discovered the traces left by the young Roman, and Brennus attempted during the night to surprise the Capitol by the same path. After many efforts a few succeeded in gaining the summit of the rock, and were on the point of scaling the walls; the sentinels were asleep and nothing seemed to oppose them. Some geese, consecrated to Juno, were awakened by the noise made by the enemy, and began to cry, as they do when they are disturbed. Manlius, a person of consular rank, ran to the spot, encountered the Gauls, and hurled several from the rocks. The Romans were roused and the enemy were driven back, and ultimately were defeated in open battle by Camillus, who has been called Rome's second founder.

Rosa, Saint, was born at Lima, Peru, in 1586. The name of Isabel was given to her in baptism by her parents, who were wealthy Spaniards, but her extreme beauty caused her to be called Rose. On the verge of womanhood her parents lost their wealth, and in order to provide them with support she entered the family of the treasurer Gonsalvo. She received numerous offers of marriage, but in spite of her parents' requests refused them all, and finally adopted the habit of the Dominican Sisters, to strengthen herself in her ascetic resolutions. She spent a life of severe fasting, and wore around her head a circlet of silver studded inside with sharp pins, in remembrance of our Saviour's Passion. She was possessed of a most excitable imagination, and was haunted for years with horrible phantoms and apparitions, all of which she regarded as assaults of the Evil One. She died August 24, 1617, after years of suffering, from a complication of diseases, and was buried in the Dominican Convent at Lima. She was canonized by Clement X, who ordered her festival to be kept on August 30th, and is the only American saint on the canonical record.

Rosetta Stone, the name given to a stone which was discovered in 1799 by M. Boussard, a French officer of engineers, during the French occupation of Egypt under Napoleon, in an excavation made at Fort St. Julien, near the city of Rosetta. It is a piece of black basalt, 3 feet 7 inches in length, and 2 feet 6 inches in width, and contains part of three distinct inscriptions; the first or highest in hieroglyphics, the second in euchorial characters, and the third in Greek. The Greek text, when translated, showed that the inscription was an ordinance of the priests decreeing certain honors to Ptolemy Epiphanes on the occasion of his coronation, 196 B. C. It contained a command that the decree should be inscribed in the sacred letters (hieroglyphics), the letters of the country (demotic), and Greek letters—this for the convenience of the mixed population of Egypt under its Greek rulers. It was natural to conclude that the three texts were the same in substance, and accordingly earnest efforts were made to decipher the hieroglyphics by aid of the Greek. The first clew was obtained by noticing that certain groups of the hieroglyphic characters were inclosed in oval rings, and that these groups corresponded in relative position with certain proper names, such as Ptolemy, etc., in the Greek text. It was by comparison of the group judged, on strong grounds, to be the name Ptolemy, with another group (found on another stone) supposed to stand for the name Cleopatra, that the first great advance was made. By means of other groups the whole alphabet was made out, and finally it was proved that the characters and groups could be resolved into the Coptic language of Egypt, which was already understood by scholars. It has been shown, by more recent excavations, that the Rosetta stone was found on the site of a temple dedicated by Necho II, of the 26th dynasty, to the solar god Atum, or Tum. The great work of deciphering the hieroglyphics was mainly effected by the French savant, Champollion. The stone is now in the British Museum.

Royal Incomes, English.—The annual income of the Queen of England is $1,925,000, out of which must be paid the cost of the royal household, which includes the expenses and salaries of nearly 1,000 officers and servants. The amount set aside for her personal use, or privy purse, as it is called, is $300,000; Prince of Wales receives $200,000; Princess of Wales, $50,000; Crown Princess of Prussia, $40,000; Duke of Edinburgh, $125,000; Princess Christian, $30,000; Princess Louise, $30,000; Duke of Connaught, $125,000; Princess Beatrice, $30,000; Duke of Cambridge, $60,000; Duchess of Teck, $25,000; Duchess of Albany, $30,000; Duchess of Mecklenburg-Strelitz, $15,000; making a total of $2,715,000 per annum, which is supplied by appropriation.

Rubicon, the ancient name of a small stream—thought to be the modern Pisatello—which formed the boundary between Italy and Cisalpine Gaul. It is celebrated from Cæsar's having hesitated about crossing it with his army, and initiating civil war, in the year 49 B. C. When he came to the river he paused upon the brink, but finally, saying "The die is cast!" he spurred-on his horse and dashed into the water. Hence, "To pass the Rubicon" has become a proverbial phrase to denote the taking of the first step in a momentous undertaking from which one cannot or will not recede.

Rubrics, originally the titles or headings of chapters in certain law-books, and so called from the red color of the ink in which these titles were written. In mediæval and modern use the name is restricted to the directions which are found in the service-books of the Catholic churches as to the ordering of the several prayers, and the performance of the sometimes complicated cere-monial by which they are accompanied.

Rump Parliament, the Parliament which, in conjunction with the army, brought about the trial and condemnation of Charles I. On December 6, 1648, Oliver Cromwell sent two regiments under Colonel Pride to coerce the House of Commons. Forty-one mem-bers who were favorable to accommodation were imprisoned in a lower room of the House, 160 were ordered to go home, and only 60 of the most violent of the independents were admitted. This clearance was called *Pride's* Purge, and the privileged members ever afterward passed by the name of the *Rump*, forming, as it were, the fag-end of the Long Parliament. Five years later, the Rump Parliament, forgetting that it was but the creature of the army, attempted to make a stand against certain demands on the part of the soldiers. The result was that Cromwell filled the House with armed men; the Speaker was pulled out of his chair, the mace taken from the table, the room cleared, the door locked, and the Parliament declared to be dissolved. Cromwell then con-voked an assembly, which assumed the name of Parliament, which subsisted five months, and was known as the *Barebones Parlia-ment*, after one of its prominent members, a leather-seller, called Praise-God Barebones. On the death of Cromwell the expulsion of the Rump Parliament was declared illegal, and that assembly was restored to its functions, but was again expelled by the troops on October 13, 1659, a provisional government of officers assuming the direction of affairs. This, however, did not prove satisfactory, and the Rump, which had been twice ignominiously expelled, was once more restored. On March 16, 1660, it solemnly decreed its own dissolution, owing to the fact that the return of a number of the members who had been excluded by Pride's Purge placed the independents in the minority.

Runic Alphabets were the earliest alphabets in use among the Teutonic and Gothic nations of northern Europe. The exact period of their origin is not known. The name is derived from the Teutonic *run*, a mystery; and the original uses of these char-acters seem to have been for purposes of secrecy and divination. The resemblance which some of the runic characters bear to the Phœnician alphabet, and others derived from it, has led to the supposition that they were first introduced to northern peoples by Phœnician merchants who traded on the coasts of the Baltic. Scandinavian and Anglo-Saxon traditions agree in ascribing the invention of runic writing to Odin, or Wodan. The countries in which traces of the use of runes exist are Denmark, Norway, Sweden, Iceland, Germany, Britain, France and Spain; and they are found engraved on rocks, crosses, monumental stones, coins, medals, rings, brooches, and the hilts and blades of swords. Runic letters were also often cut on smooth sticks called *runstafas*, or mysterious staves, and used for purposes of divination. The systems of runes in use among the different branches of the Teutonic stock are not identical, though they have a strong general family likeness, showing their common origin. The Norse alphabet is generally considered the oldest, and the parent of the rest. It has sixteen letters—four vowels and twelve consonants. Each letter is, as in the Hebrew-Phœnician, derived from the name of some well-known familiar object, with whose initial letter it corresponds. Runes being associated in the popular belief with augury and divination, their use was, to a considerable extent, discouraged by the early Christian priests and missionaries; still, we find Christian inscriptions in runic characters in the Anglo-Saxon kingdoms of Northumbria, Mercia and East Anglia of as late date as the middle of the tenth century. Runes are said to have been laid aside in Sweden by the year 1001, and in Spain they were officially condemned by the Council of Toledo in 1115. There is no reason to believe that the runic characters were at any time in the familiar use in which we find the characters of a written language in modern times, nor have we any traces of their being used in books or on parchment.

Russia, Religion of.—The Established Church of Russia, to which the great majority of the inhabitants belong, is identical in doctrine with, and is a branch of, the Greek Church. The liturgy used is the same as that originally used by the Church at Constantinople, but it is read, not in Greek, but in the Sclavonic tongue. Previous to the time of Alexander II, dissent in all its forms was not only discouraged but often rigorously repressed, and it has only been during very late years that general toleration has been permitted. The Roman Catholic Church has been the object of especial severity in the past, particularly during the reign of the Czar Nicholas. Under the laws of Alexander II, all Catholics and Protestants enjoy civil rights with members of the Established Church, and are equally admissible to the highest offices of the empire. Christianity was introduced into Russia in the ninth century.

Saga, an old Norse word, used to denote a tale which, originally depending on, and gradually elaborated by, oral tradition, had at last acquired a definite form in written language. Such sagas, along with the poetical and legislative writings, constitute the chief part of the old Norwegian-Icelandic literature.

Salamander.—In the mythology of the middle ages Salamanders were beings possessing the shape of a man, whose element was the fire, or who at least could live in that element. [See *Elemental Spirits.*]

Salic Law.—The laws of the Salic or Salian Franks were committed to writing in the fifth century, while the people were yet heathens, and that code is known as the "Salic Law." It relates principally to the compensation and punishment of crimes, and there is a chapter containing provisions regarding the succession to what are called "Salic Lands," which seems to have been inserted at a later date. Although the Frankish law did not in general exclude females, the succession to the Salic lands, whatever they were, was confined to males, probably from the importance of securing the military service of the chief proprietors. It was but a doubtful analogy that led the rule of succession to Salic lands to be extended to the succession to the French throne, and it seems to have been only in the fourteenth century that the exclusion of females from the throne became an established principle.

Salt in the Ocean.—Many theories have been advanced to account for the saltness of sea-water, the great problem being to find a satisfactory explanation for the comparatively uniform degree of saltness which has characterized the waters of the ocean during the entire period of man's occupation of the earth. That this saltness is a normal and primeval property of the great bodies of water is a fact thoroughly established by geological researches, the great mineral deposits of rock-salt being clearly the result of the evaporation of great inland shallow salt-seas in past geologic ages. [See *Salt, Sources of.*] In the great chemical changes taking place, in the earliest periods, among the elements which constitute the earth's crust, the great volume of water undoubtedly received a proportion of mineral salts in solution as a part of its original composition. Various causes, especially the many forms of marine life belonging to the animal and vegetable kingdoms, operate to diminish the quantity of salts held in solution; and it is now generally agreed that the average is maintained through the agency of the innumerable rivers, streams and springs which flow into the sea and its arms. These, in their passage through earthy channels, dissolve small quantities of the salts which occur as ingredients of the soil—not enough to be noticeable in the river-water itself, the ocean-water being, consequently, less saline where a large volume of river-water is discharged into it, but furnishing a constant and cumulative supply; for the water is evaporated from the surface of the sea, to be taken up into clouds, and falls again on the land, to find its way to the same great reservoir, carrying more salts, while the salts are not evaporated, but all remain in the sea-water. The main ingredient in sea-salt is chloride of sodium (common salt), comprising about four-fifths of the whole, the remainder consisting of small percentages of magnesium and calcium compounds, and traces of almost all the metallic elements. The average quantity in the open water of the ocean is about $3\frac{1}{2}$ per cent., and it has been estimated that the total amount in all the ocean area is equal to 4,419,360 cubic miles, or $14\frac{1}{2}$ times the entire mass of the Continent of Europe above high-water mark, mountains and all. The constant motion and the circulation of the great ocean currents aid in maintaining a tolerably constant proportion throughout the ocean area; but the polar waters have been found to contain somewhat less, and the equatorial somewhat more, than the average per cent. It is apt to be large where the water is deepest, but does not increase with the depth. It varies in land-locked basins, being less where these bodies of water are fed with fresh water in excess of their evaporation. In the Mediterranean, Gulf of Mexico and Carribean Sea it is greater. The silver in sea-water, though contained in a very minute proportion, yet, in all, has been estimated to be equal to 2,000,000 tons; and in some cases the deposit on old coppered hulls has been large enough to make its separation profitable. The sea-water has always been a large source of the common salt of commerce.

Salt, Sources of.—At one time nearly the whole of the salt used as food and for industrial purposes was obtained from sea-water, and in many countries where the climate is dry and warm and there is a convenient sea-board, large quantities are still so obtained. In Portugal more than 250,000 tons are annually produced, and about the same quantity is obtained on the Atlantic and Mediterranean coasts of France. Spain has salt-works in the Balearic Islands, the Bay of Cadiz, and elsewhere, which turn out annually 300,000 tons; and even the small Adriatic sea-board of Austria produces every year from 70,000 to 100,000 tons. The peninsula and islands of Italy yield about 165,000 tons, and there are still a few establishments in England and Scotland; but in these latter countries the industry has been almost entirely driven out by the rock-salt works. The salt obtained from this source is called "sea" or "bay" salt. The works are generally called salt gardens—*salina* (Spanish)—*salz garten*, in Austria. They consist of a series of large, shallow evaporating reservoirs. The sea-water is admitted, and flows slowly from one to another, all the while evaporating under the heat of the sun, until finally the dry salt remains in crystalline crusts on the salting-tables in the final basins. These reservoirs vary from ten to sixteen inches in depth, the sediment and many of the impurities being deposited in the earlier and deeper basins in the first stages of evaporation. Between the temperatures of 25 and 26 degrees (Baume) pure salt is deposited, equal to about twenty-five per cent. of the whole. This is kept pure by conducting the brine to separate salting-tables at this temperature, and, after it reaches 26 degrees, carrying it on to other basins, where a second quality, equal to about sixty per cent. of the whole, is formed. After the brine reaches 28.5 degrees it is led into still other basins, where the remainder of the salt is deposited. The salt is raked up and sold just as it is formed, with the slight purification resulting from a few months' exposure to the weather, which is customary. The evaporating surface of these shallow basins covers, in many establishments, hundreds of acres. Those at Berre, on the Mediterranean, have an area of 815 acres. Sea-salt has been obtained in this way in many of the sea-board States of the United States, but not to any extent. The other great source of common salt is the vast mineral deposits. Salt also occurs as a mineral in an almost pure state, and associated with the rocks of almost every geologic period. Many of the deposits are of vast extent, and are another great commercial source of this substance. This mineral deposit is called rock-salt, and is evidently the result of the evaporation of great shallow bodies of salt-water in remote ages, as is proved by its generally stratified nature, with beds of clay intervening, and the occurrence of marine shells and fossils in the surrounding rock formation. Large mines are worked in England and all the European countries, and in many places throughout the world. The most famous of all is the mine at Williczka, nine miles from Cracow, in Galicia, which has been worked continuously for upward of six hundred years. It is stopped-out in longitudinal and transverse galleries, with frequent large vaulted chambers supported by massive pillars. These extend on four different levels, and have a total length of 30 miles, the mine being 1 mile 1,279 yards long by 830 yards wide and 284 yards deep. The lower levels contain streets and houses, constituting a complete village; and many of the miners, of whom there are 800 to 1,000, rarely come above ground. The salt is sold just as it is dug out of the mine, and 55,067 tons are annually extracted. The total extent of this deposit is 500 by 200 miles, with an average depth of 1,200 feet. Salt is also obtained in many localities from mineral deposits by means of salt-wells. In some cases the water occurs naturally in the salt-strata, and the saturated brine is reached by deep borings (sometimes 1500 feet); in other cases water is introduced into the borings and then pumped out again, two concentric tubes being employed. After the brine is secured it is evaporated by artificial heat in large iron vats. The salt-wells in Onondaga County, New York, near Syracuse and Salina, are a large and important industry. Michigan has the largest output next to New York, and many other States produce it to some extent; but the home supply is not equal to the demand, and there is a large annual importation into the United States.

Salutation, Forms of.—The custom of shaking hands, which is the most common among civilized nations, comes undoubtedly from remote barbarism, when two men, meeting, gave each other their weapon-hands as a security against treachery or sudden attack. In the East and among the Slavic nations the character of salutations is quite different. Among the Persians, the custom of throwing one's self upon the ground and kissing the feet of the monarch prevails. In China, an inferior upon horseback meeting a superior dismounts and waits until the latter has passed. In Japan the inferior removes his sandals when meeting his superior, crosses his hands by placing the right hand in the left sleeve, and with a slow, rocking motion of his body, cries out " Augh ! Augh !" (Do not hurt me.) In Siam the inferior throws himself upon the ground before his superior; the latter sends forward one of his slaves to see whether the former has been eating anything, or carries with him any smell at all offensive. If he does, he is immediately kicked out without ceremony; but if not, the attendant raises him up. In Ceylon the inferior, on meeting a superior, throws himself upon the ground, repeating the name and dignity of the latter. Among some tribes of the American Indians the custom is to salute by rubbing noses together. This form is also common in the Friendly and Society Islands, where it is returned by each taking the hand of the other and rubbing it upon his own nose and mouth. The Moors of Morocco ride at full speed toward a stranger, as if they intended to run him down, and, on arriving near, suddenly stop and fire a pistol over his head. The Arabians shake hands six or eight times; but if persons of distinction, they embrace and kiss several times, also kissing their own hands. In Turkey it is the custom to place the hand upon the breast and bow to the person saluted. In Burmah, when a gentleman meets a lady or another gentleman he applies his mouth and nose closely to their cheek and draws in a long breath, as if smelling a delightful perfume with both mouth and nose. In the greater portion of Germany it is an act of politeness to kiss the hand of a lady; but this privilege is allowed in Italy only to near relatives, while in Russia it is extended to kissing the forehead. On the European continent it is usual for men who are intimate friends to kiss one another. The Pelew Island inhabitants grasp either the hand or foot of the one they wish to salute and rub their faces against it; while Yemen persons of rank permit their fingers to be kissed, after long refusal.

Salvation Army was founded in London, England, in 1865, by Mr. Booth, now called General Booth, a minister of the Methodist New Connection. Its aim was to bring under the influence of the gospel the classes not reached by the ordinary services of the churches—the inhabitants of the lowest slums of cities, profligates, thieves, drunkards and vagabonds. The organization steadily grew, and in 1878 the name Salvation Army was adopted. The services are highly unconventional; much use is made of processions in the streets, of banners and of music. The doctrines, however, are those of the orthodox evangelical churches, great stress being laid on purity of heart. The army has excited singularly keen antipathy among the roughest parts of the population, and its members have very frequently been assaulted and maltreated, especially on occasions of processions. But notwithstanding this fact the army has grown rapidly, and has numerous branches in the United States, France, and in a number of the British colonies.

Sandhurst.—The Royal Military College at Sandhurst, England, was founded in 1802 at Great Marlow, and in 1812 it was transferred to Sandhurst. Up to 1862 the college was devoted to the education of boys from the age of thirteen upward; but in that year the system was changed, the course limited to one year immediately before entering the army, and the instruction confined to the higher mathematics, modern languages and military sciences. Entrance is on the nomination of the commander-in-chief, and the payment by the cadet's parent or guardian varies from £100 to *nil*. Those for whom no payment is made must be orphans, and are styled "Queen's Cadets." Under the purchase system, which was in vogue in the English army up to 1871, all first commissions in the cavalry and infantry of the line, which were granted without purchase and not to men from the ranks, were given to cadets from the Royal Military College, who competed for these prizes and obtained them in order of merit. The abolition of the purchase system brought about a radical change. The students are no longer boys intending to become officers, but sub-lieutenants, who, having passed by competition for the army, spend a year at Sandhurst in acquiring the theoretical part of the war science. To be confirmed in the army as lieutenant, the officer must pass creditably out of Sandhurst, and then serve a year on probation with a regiment. About two miles distant from Sandhurst is situated another Government institution known as the Staff College. It was founded in 1858 for the purpose of giving higher instruction to a limited number of officers (at first thirty, now forty) aspiring to appointments on the staff. An officer, to be entitled to compete for entrance, must have been five years in active service, must have passed the qualifying examination for a captaincy, and must have the recommendation of his commanding officer. Only one officer is eligible at one time from any battalion. The students receive their regimental pay while at college, and the whole educational charges are borne by the public. The course lasts two years. At the end of each year there is an examination. After passing the Staff College the officer is attached for duty, for a short period, to each of the arms with which he may not have already served. He then becomes eligible for appointment to the staff, as opportunity may occur.

Sanhedrim, as the supreme national tribunal of the Jews was called, was established at the time of the Maccabees, and was the court before which Christ was tried for high treason against the Roman Emperor. It was presided over by the Nasi (Prince), at whose side was the Ab-Beth-Din (Father of the Tribunal). Its members, of which there were seventy-one, belonged to the different classes of society; there were priests, elders—that is, men of age and experience—scribes, or doctors of law, and others exalted by eminent learning, which was the sole condition for admission. The limits of its jurisdiction are not clearly known, but it is believed that the supreme decision over life or death was exclusively in its hands. The regulation of the sacred times and seasons was vested in it. It fixed the beginnings of the new moons; intercalated the years when necessary; watched over the purity of the priestly families by carefully examining the pedigrees of those priests born out of Palestine, so that none born from a suspicious or ill-famed mother should be admitted to the sacred service. The mode of procedure was extremely complicated; and such was the caution of the court, especially in matters of life and death, that capital punishment was pronounced in the rarest instances only. The Nasi had the supreme direction of the court, and convoked it when necessary. He sat at the head, and at his right hand was the seat of the Ab-Beth-Din; the rest of the seventy-one too' their places, according to their dignity, in front of them, in the form of a semicircle, so that they could be seen by both the chief officers. The meeting-place of the court was, on ordinary occasions, in a hall at the south-east corner of the Temple, but on extraordinary occasions it met in the house of the high priest. It met daily, with the exception of Sabbaths and feast days. After the destruction of the Temple and Jerusalem, the Sanhedrim, after many emigrations, was finally established at Babylon.

Sans-Culottes.—At the commencement of the French·Revolution the democratic " proletaires" of Paris were called in derision by the court party sans-culottes, " without breeches;" and the term soon became the distinctive appellation of a " good patriot," particularly as their contempt for the rich was often shown by neglect of apparel and the cultivation of rough manners. This is the English version. The French definition of the word, however, is that the sans-culottes were so called because they gave up knee-breeches with the close of the *ancien regime* and took to wearing trousers, or pantaloons.

Sarcophagus is a Greek word signifying flesh-eater, and is applied to a stone receptacle for the dead. It originated in the property, assigned to a species of stone found at Assos, in Troas, and used in early times, of consuming the whole body, with the exception of the teeth, within the space of forty days. The sarcophagi of Egypt, some of which are contemporary with the Pyramids, are the oldest known. The earliest of these are of a square or oblong form, and either plain or ornamented with lotus-leaves; the latter are of the form of swathed mummies, and bear inscriptions. Persian and Phœnician kings were also buried in sarcophagi. The Roman sarcophagi of the earlier republican period were plain. In the later republic burning was the most general method of disposing of the dead, although sarcophagi were occasionally used.

Sargasso Sea is the name commonly used to designate a region of the Atlantic Ocean which is covered by a peculiar floating sea-weed, either in tangled masses of considerable extent or simply scattered twigs. It was at one time supposed that this enormous mass of sea-weed grew on the Bahama and Florida shores, and was torn thence by the powerful current of the Gulf Stream; but it seems certain that if such was its original source, the Gulf-weed now lives and propagates while freely floating on the ocean surface, having adapted itself by various modifications to its present mode of existence. A Sargasso sea, which bears the same relation to the North Pacific currents that the one in the Atlantic does to the Gulf Stream, is found northward of the Sandwich Islands. Multitudes of small marine animals accompany this floating seaweed, with fishes ready to prey on them. The Gulf-weed is eaten in China, and in other parts of the East it is used in salads and as a pickle.

Saturday.—In the name Saturday we have a reminiscence of Roman mythology which is noticeable, because the names of most of our days come from the old Anglo-Saxon gods of Norse mythology. The full form is Saturn's day; in Latin, *dies Saturin*. It is the seventh day of the week and the Jewish *Sabbath*. In the Roman Catholic Breviary it is called *dies Sabbati*.

"Scalpers."—The selling of railroad tickets at reduced rates by ticket-brokers, or "scalpers," as they are called, has of late years grown to be a business of considerable proportions. Their method of obtaining such tickets is as follows: As the fares between the prominent Eastern and Western railroad centers are usually proportionately lower than to way stations, where there is no competition, travelers often find that they can purchase through tickets at such prices as make it more economical for them to do so, even though they desire to travel only a portion of the distance, and then sell the unused mileage to the "scalpers" at a discount. Again, during excursions many persons use but half of a ticket and sell the "return." In railroad wars "scalpers" can buy quantities of tickets at reduced rates, the railroad companies selling tickets in large quantities at such times to speculators, who, in turn, transfer them to the "scalpers;" and sometimes, while a railroad company is bound by contract not to sell at less than a specified rate, it will offer to "scalpers" a commission large enough to enable them to undersell the regular ticket-agents, who are bound by the agreements entered into by the companies.

Scarabæus, a peculiar beetle held sacred by the Egyptians. Several mystical ideas were attributed to it; the number of its toes, 30, symbolized the days of the month; the time it deposited its ball, which contained its eggs, was supposed to refer to the lunar month; the movement of the clay-ball referred to the action of the sun on the earth, and personified that luminary. It was supposed to be only of the male sex, hence it signified the self-existent, self-begotten generation, or metamorphosis, and the male or paternal principle of nature. In this sense it appears on the head of the Pygmæan deity Ptah - Socharis Osiris, the Demiurgos, and in astronomical scenes and sepulchral formulas. In connection with the Egyptian notions, the Gnostics and some of the Fathers called Christ the scarabæus. The insect during its life was worshiped and after death embalmed.

School, Church and Theater Expenditures.—According to the census of 1880, the total expenditures for salaries of teachers of common schools in the United States were $55,745,029; for buildings and grounds, $6,643,313; for all other school purposes, $16,951,472; making a grand total of $79,339,814. The total expenditures of church societies of America are about $70,000,000 per year, and there are about $40,000,000 per year spent for theatrical entertainments.

Schoolmen and Scholastics are the terms applied to the class of learned theologians and philosophers who flourished in Europe, mainly in France and England, during the middle ages. They were largely given to hair-splitting logic and endless argumentations and speculations on points of the most unimportant and often silly nature. Still, in their number were included men of great learning and ability, as Duns Scotus, Thomas Aquinas, and Albertus Magnus, with whom this system of philosophical theological scholasticism culminated in the fourteenth century. Johannes Erigena Scotus was not strictly a scholastic; he lived in the ninth century, in the preparatory period of scholasticism.

Scot and Lot Voters.—The old legal phrase *Scot* (Anglo-Saxon, *sceat*, pay) and *Lot* embraced all parochial assessments for the poor, the church, lighting, cleansing and watching. Previous to the Reform Act, the right of voting for members of Parliament and for municipal officers was, in various English boroughs, exclusively vested in payers of Scot and Lot.

Scotland Yard.—The world-famed headquarters of the London police, Scotland Yard, is understood to have obtained that name from the fact that a palace formerly occupied the site, which was built for the reception of the Scottish kings when they visited the English capital. According to Pennant, the palace was originally given by King Edgar to Kenneth of Scotland when he went to London to pay homage.

Screw-Propeller, The.—In 1802 Dr. Shorter, an English mechanician, produced motion by the agency of a screw; but his discovery was of no value at the time, as the steam-engine had not then been applied to navigation. In 1832 Mr. B. Woodcroft patented a screw-propeller with an increasing pitch; and four years later Mr. F. P. Smith patented a screw making two whole turns, which he reduced in 1839 to one whole turn. In 1837 he and Captain Ericsson brought the matter practically forward on the Thames, where a small screw-steamer, 45 feet long, 8 feet broad, and of 27 inches draught, towed a vessel of 630 tons against the tide at 4½ knots an hour. This experiment was followed by a number of others, some undertaken under the direction of the British Admiralty, which clearly established the practicability of the screw, and its advantages for ships of war became incontestable. From the entire submergence of the propeller, and the consequent lowness of its engines in the ship, the chances of injury from an enemy's shot were reduced almost to nothing. The screw-propeller is of the same construction as the common screw, but with the narrow thread exaggerated into a broad, thin plate, and the cylinder diminished to a mere spindle. If a screw of this form were turned round in an unyielding substance, as wood, it would for each turn advance as much as the center of the blade (or thread) had moved along the spindle in forming the screw, i. e., the distance. If, on the other hand, the screw itself were prevented from moving longitudinally, and the piece of wood *not* fixed, the latter would be compelled to advance along the screw the same distance. When the screw is fixed beneath a ship and made to revolve in the water, the case lies between the two just supposed—the screw moves forward, and with it the ship, and the water in which it has been working moves backward. The backward motion should only be small proportionately, and the ratio between it and the sum of the backward motion of the water and the forward motion of the ship is called the *slip.* Screws have been formed with two, three, four and six blades, or arms; but the form most commonly used is two blades for ships of war, and three or four blades in the merchant service.

Scriptural Measures of Capacity.—The measures of capacity referred to in the Scriptures, with their English equivalents, are as follows: The Chomer or Homer in King James' translation was 75.625 gals. liquid, and 32.125 pecks dry. The Ephah or Bath was 7 gals. 4 pts., 15 ins. sol. The Seah, 1-3 of Ephah, 2 gals. 4 pts., 3 ins. sol. The Hin=1-6 of Ephah, 1 gal., 2 pts., 1 in. sol. The Omer=1-10 of Ephah, 5 pts., 0.5 in. sol. The Cab=1-18 of Ephah, 3 pts., 10 ins. sol. The Log=7 1-72 of Ephah, $\frac{1}{2}$ pt., 10 ins. sol. The Metretes of Syria (John ii, 6)= Cong. Rom. 7$\frac{1}{2}$ pts. The Cotyla Eastern=1-100 of Ephah, $\frac{1}{2}$ pt., 3 ins. sol. This Cotyla contains just 10 ozs. avoirdupois of rain water; Omer, 100; Ephah, 1,000; Chomer or Homer, 10,000.

Scriptural Measures of Length.—The measures of length used in the Scriptures, with their English equivalents, are as follows: The great Cubit was 21.888 ins.=1.824 ft., and the less 18 ins. A span, the longer=$\frac{1}{2}$ a cubit=10.944 ins.=.912 ft. A span, the less=1-3 of a cubit=7.296 ins.=.608 ft. A hand's breadth=1-6 of a cubit=3.684 ins.=.304 ft. A finger's breadth= 1.24 of a cubit=.912 ins=.076 ft. A fathom=4 cubits=7.296 ft. Ezekiel's Reed=6 cubits=10.944 feet. The mile=4,000 cubits= 7.296 ft. The Stadium, 1-10 of their mile=400 cubits=729.6 ft. The Parasang, 3 of their miles=12,000 cubits, or 4 English miles and 580 ft. 33.164 miles was a day's journey—some say 24 miles; and 3,500 ft. a Sabbath day's journey; some authorities say 3,648 ft.

Scylla and Charybdis.—Scylla, according to Homer, was a fearful monster with a voice like that of a young whelp. "She has twelve feet and six long necks, with a terrific head and three rows of close-set teeth on each. Evermore she stretches out these necks and catches the porpoises, sea dogs and other large animals of the sea which swim by, and out of every ship that passes each month takes a man. She dwells in a cave in a cliff whose height is so great that its summit is forever enveloped in clouds." There are other accounts of Scylla, one of which represents her as having been once a beautiful maiden, beloved by the sea-god Glaucus, but who, by the jealousy of Circe, was changed into a monster, having the upper part of the body that of a woman, while the lower part consisted of the tail of a fish or serpent surrounded by dogs. A rocky cape on the west coast of South Italy, jutting out boldly into the sea so as to form a small peninsula at the north entrance to the Straits of Messina was called by this name. Charybdis is a celebrated whirlpool in the Straits of Messina, nearly opposite to the harbor of Messina, in Sicily, and in ancient writings always mentioned in conjunction with Scylla. The navigation of this whirlpool is, even at the present day, considered to be very dangerous, and must have been exceedingly so to the open ships of the ancients. Homer places it immediately opposite to Scylla, probably taking advantage of the poetic license to exaggerate the danger of the navigation, although it is possible that the whirlpool may have changed its location since his days. The myth connected with it is that under a large fig-tree, which grew out of a rock opposite Scylla, dwelt the monster Charybdis, who thrice every day sucked down the water of the sea, and thrice threw it up again.

Sea-Lions, Uses of.—They are found on the east coast of Kamschatka, around the Kurile Islands, and on the west coast of North America, on rugged shores and desert rocks of the ocean, nearly to latitude 40 degrees north. They are of much value to the natives of the northwest coasts of America, though they are not so accounted in the commercial world. The Indians use their skins for covering boats and for making long boots for protecting the limbs. They make water-proof garments by sewing together their intestines, convert their stomach-walls into oil pouches, dry their flesh for food, and sell their mustache bristles to the Chinese, who use them as pickers for their opium pipes. They are about fifteen feet long, weigh some 1,600 pounds, and the males have stiff, curled hair on the neck, a thick hide, large head, bushy eyebrows, long nose, and are covered with coarse hair of a tawny color.

Sea-Serpents.—It is maintained by some naturalists that there is sufficient creditable evidence to warrant the assertion that there is a species of marine animal characterized by a serpentine neck, a large head, air breather, and propelled by paddles—something not unlike the plesiosaurians found in the fossil state among the rocks of the mesozoic age. In a report of the Linnæan Society of New England a description of an animal supposed to be a sea-serpent, which was seen by eleven creditable witnesses off the coast of Cape Ann, Mass., in 1817, is given. The monster is described as being dark brown in color, with white under the head and neck. Its head was as large as a horse's, but shaped like a serpent's, with a projection in front, in appearance like a single horn. Its length was estimated to be at least fifty feet. One of the latest accounts touching the existence of these animals is given by Captain Seymour of the bark Hope On. He states that while on the watch for whales off the Pearl Islands, between forty and fifty miles from Panama, a strange animal was seen by himself and his crew, which measured at least twenty-five feet in length. It had a horse-like head with two unicorn-shaped horns protruding from it, four legs or double-jointed fins, a bronzed hide profusely speckled with large black spots, and a tail which appeared to be divided into two parts. This description is verified by officers of the Pacific Mail Steamship Company, who state that the animal has been seen by them on several occasions. There are numerous other instances where it is claimed that similar animals have been seen off different coasts, but such claims have been by no means as well substantiated as in the instances above. Norwegian fishermen relate numerous traditions of sea-serpents seen on their coasts, particularly in Moldefjord. Some naturalists assume, however, that these traditions are founded upon stories of the fabulous serpent "Midguardsormen" of the old Scandinavian mythology, who was represented as dwelling in the depths of the ocean and enfolding the foundations of the earth in his coils.

Seasons, Beginning of the.—The civil or tropical year, the one commonly used in the measure of time, is the period which elapses from the sun's appearance on one of the tropical circles to its return to the same. It varies very slightly, and has a mean length of 365 days, 5 hours, 48 minutes and 49.7 seconds. Astronomically considered, the four seasons begin at the equinoctial or the solstitial points. The summer solstice is the meridian passing through the point where the sun touches the tropic of cancer. The winter solstice is the meridian passing through the point where it touches the tropic of capricorn; and the equinoctial points are the points at which the sun's path or equinoctial crosses the celestial equator. All these points shift according to very exact astronomical laws from year to year, and so precise times when the seasons begin are matters of the nicest mathematical calculation.

Secretaries of Legation, Salaries of.—The salaries of the Secretaries of Legation of the United States are as follows: Austria, $1,800 per annum; Chili, $1,500; China, $2,625; France, first secretary, $2,625, second secretary, $2,000; Germany, $2,625; Great Britain, $2,625; Italy, $1,800; Japan, $2,625; Mexico, $1,800; Russia, $2,625; Spain, $1,800; Turkey, $1,800.

Secret Societies in the United States.—There are over three hundred secret societies in the United States, and some of the leading organizations and their memberships are as follows: Free and Accepted Masons, 650,000; Independent Order of Odd Fellows, 594,000; Grand Army of the Republic, 375,245; Knights of Labor, 297,418; Knights of Pythias, 230,000; Ancient Order of United Workmen, 211,750; Independent Order of Good Templars, 210,000; Knights of Honor, 128,000; Royal Arcanum, 85,000; Improved Order of Red Men, 70,000; American Legion of Honor, 62,000;

Knights and Ladies of Honor, 55,000; Sons of Veterans, 50,000; Daughters of Rebekah, 45,000; Ancient Order of Foresters, 40,000; Brotherhood of Locomotive Engineers, 30,000; Independent Order of B'nai B'rith, 27,000; German Order of Harugari, 25,000; Brotherhood of Locomotive Firemen, 18,000; Knights of Maccabees, 17,000; United Ancient Order of Druids, 16,000; Royal Society of Good Fellows, 15,000; Brotherhood of Railroad Brakemen, 15,000; Order of American Firemen, 15,000; Order of Railroad Conductors, 12,000; Independent Order Sons of Benjamin, 11,000; Brotherhood of the Union, 9,000; Benevolent Protective Order of Elks, 8,650.

Semiramis.—The legendary Semiramis is described by the historian Ctesias as the wife of Ninus, the founder of the Assyrian Kingdom, who flourished about 2200 B. C., and as a woman of great beauty and military prowess, who survived her husband, ruled the kingdom for some years with much ability, and finally abdicated in favor of her son Ninyas. This story is now believed to be purely mythical. The true Semiramis, however, according to Rawlinson, was the wife of Iva-Lush, an Assyrian king who ruled from 810 to 781 B. C. She was a Babylonian princess, and the union was sought by the Assyrian ruler to strengthen his claim to the provinces of Babylon. She seems to have enjoyed with her royal husband a sort of co-sovereignty in the government, and from this fact it is thought the legends concerning her great conquests, etc., had their origin. Nothing is certainly known of her life or deeds.

September, from the Latin word *septem,* seven. It was the seventh month of the Roman calendar. The Saxons called it *gerst-*month, or barley-month, because barley, their chief cereal crop, was generally harvested during this month.

Septuagint.—The most ancient Greek translation of the Old Testament that has come down to us, and the one commonly in use at the time of Christ, was the Septuagint. Its origin is shrouded in deep obscurity. There are a number of myths concerning it, but the principal one is that it was made during the reign of Ptolemy Philadelphus, 284–247 B. C. This king, it is stated, anxious to embody in a collection of laws of all nations, on which he was engaged, also those of the Jews, invited 72 men of learning and eminence from Palestine, who performed the task of translation in 72 days. The facts upon which this legend, now rejected as a piece of history, rests, cannot well be ascertained. It seems clear, however, that Ptolemy, aided by his librarian, Demetrius Phalereus, did cause a Greek version of the Pentateuch to be executed, probably during the time of his being co-regent of Ptolemy Lagi; but the translators were not Palestinian, but Egyptian Jews. This is evidenced from the state of the text from which the translation must have been made, and from the intimate acquaintance with Egyptian manners and customs which it evinces. The Septuagint was held in the very highest repute among the Alexandrine Jews, while the Palestinians looked upon it as a dangerous innovation, and even instituted the day of its completion as a day of mourning. Gradually, however, it also found its way into Palestine. It was read and interpreted in the synagogues for some centuries after Christ, until the increasing knowledge of the original, fostered by the many academies and schools, and the frequent disputations with the early Christians, brought other and more faithful and literal translations.

Serfs in Russia.—Serfdom was not known in Russia until the sixteenth century, when the Czar, Boris Godunoff, by an edict forbade the peasants and their descendants from leaving the service of the land-owner for whom they were working when the decree was made. Under Peter the Great, the serfs on private lands were transformed into chattels, to be bought and sold with the land. The peasants on the crown estates were free, but in the event of such lands being given by the czars to private individuals, the peasants upon them became serfs. Serfdom was abolished by Alexander II, March 3, 1861, but it was not until July, 1865, that all the necessary arrangements for this great work were completed.

Serpent-Charming.—In India, and to a certain extent in other Eastern countries, the profession of serpent-charming is hereditary, and has been practiced from remote antiquity. The serpent-charmers of the East possess a power beyond other men of knowing when a serpent is concealed anywhere, long practice having probably enabled them to distinguish the musky smell which serpents very generally emit, even when it is too faint to attract the attention of others. They usually ascribe their power to some constitutional peculiarity, but it has been ascertained beyond a doubt that the poison-fangs, and in some cases even the poison-glands, have been removed by the charmer before he undertakes to perform his tricks. What power the tones of their voices may exert is of course uncertain; but they accompany their words with whistling, and make use also of various musical instruments, the sounds of which certainly have great power over the serpents. In the exhibitions the serpents are made to erect themselves partially from the ground, and in this posture perform strange movements to the sound of a pipe on which the serpent-charmer plays. He exerts also a very remarkable influence over them by his eye, for even before any musical sound has been employed, he governs and commands them by merely fixing his gaze upon them.

Serpentine is a kind of marble, and is composed of silica and magnesia in about equal proportions, combined with about thirteen parts of water and a trace of protoxide of iron. It is a soft mineral of different shades of green, of waxy luster, unctuous to the touch, and susceptible of a high polish. It is better adapted to ornamental work within doors than to be exposed to the action of the weather. Its appearance is frequently spotted, clouded or veined, and the name is accordingly derived from its resemblance to the mottled skin of a snake. It is found abundantly in Canada and Vermont. Verd-antique is a mixture of green serpentine and light-colored limestone. The best varieties come from Tuscany and Egypt, but fine slabs have been obtained from quarries in Connecticut and New York; and it occurs also in Pennsylvania, New Jersey and all of the New England States. Precious serpentine is quite a rare mineral. It is of a rich dark-green color, very hard, translucent, and sometimes contains garnets imbedded in it, which form red spots and add much to its beauty. It is found at Baireuth, Germany; in Corsica; at Potsoy in Banffshire, and at many places in the United States. It was used by the ancient Romans for pillars and many other ornamental purposes; and vases, boxes, etc., are still made of it and much valued. Imaginary medicinal virtues were also ascribed to it by the ancients.

Seven Champions of Christendom.—The Seven Champions of Christendom, who are often alluded to by old writers, were St. George, the Patron Saint of England; St. Denis, of France; St. James, of Spain; St. Anthony, of Italy; St. Andrew, of Scotland; St. Patrick, of Ireland, and St. David, of Wales.

Seven Wise Men of Greece were the authors of the celebrated mottoes inscribed in later days in the Delphian Temple. These mottoes were: "Know thyself."—*Solon*. "Consider the end."—*Chilo*. "Know thy opportunity."—*Pittacus*. "Most men are bad."—*Bias*. "Nothing is impossible to industry."—*Periander*. "Avoid excesses."—*Cleobulus*. "Suretyship is the predecessor of ruin."—*Thales*.

Seven Wonders of America.—The seven wonders of the New World, as they are classed, are: Niagara Falls; Yellowstone Park; the Mammoth Cave; the Canyons and Garden of the Gods, Colorado; the Giant Trees, California; the Natural Bridge, Virginia, and the Yosemite Valley.

Seven Wonders of the World comprise the Egyptian Pyramids, Mausoleum of Artemisia, Temple of Diana at Ephesus, Walls and Hanging Gardens of Babylon, Colossus at Rhodes, the Statue of Jupiter Olympus, and the Pharos or Watch Tower of Alexandria.

Shakers is the popular name given to a religious sect who call themselves the "United Society of Believers in Christ's Second Appearing." They were founded in England about the year 1770 by an Englishwoman named Ann Lee, in whose person they believe that Christ has appeared a second time. Shortly before the outbreak of the Revolutionary War a small band of them, with Ann Lee at their head, emigrated to America, and penetrated far into the wilderness to Niskenna, and there founded the settlement, which still exists at Watervliet, N. Y. In the spring of 1780, when they had been three years and a half at Niskenna, a religious revival took place at Albany, and spread through the surrounding districts; and from Hancock and New Lebanon a deputation was sent to Niskenna, to see what light its inhabitants enjoyed as to the way of salvation. The deputation consisted of Joseph Meacham and Lucy Wright, subsequently the heads of the Shaker Society. These persons became believers in Ann Lee, and through their agency other converts were won, and a Shaker Society established at New Lebanon. Toward the close of 1780, the Revolutionary War being then in progress, notoriety was given to Ann Lee through an incident seemingly unfavorable. On suspicion of being a British spy she was imprisoned for some time at Poughkeepsie, and before she obtained her liberty, in December, 1780, all the colonies had heard of the "female Christ," and in the following year she started on a missionary tour through New England and the adjacent colonies, and made not a few converts. She died in 1784, and was succeeded in the headship of the Society by Joseph Meacham and Lucy Wright. Her death was a surprise to many of her followers, who believed that she was to live with them forever. Their doctrine has been, to some extent, developed as well as systematized since the death of "Mother Ann." They believe that the Kingdom of Heaven has come; that Christ has come upon earth a second time in the form of "Mother Ann," and that the personal rule of God has been restored. Then they hold that the old law has been abolished and a new dispensation begun; that Adam's sin has been atoned; that man has been made free of all errors except his own; that the curse has been taken away from labor; that the earth and all that is on it will be redeemed. Believers, on going "into union," die to the world and enter upon a new life, which is not a mere change of life but a new order of being. For them there is neither death nor marriage; what seems death is only a change of form, a transfiguration, which does not hide them from the purified eyes of the saints; and in union, as in Heaven, there is no marrying nor giving in marriage. They believe that the earth, now freed from the curse of Adam, is Heaven; they look for no resurrection besides that involved in living with them in "resurrection order." The believer, upon entering into union, leaves behind all his earthly relationships and interests, just as if he had been severed from them by death. And since to be in union is heaven, the Shakers hold that no attempts should be made by them to draw men into union. They believe that they live in daily communion with the spirits of the departed believers. The Shaker settlements are composed of from two to eight "families," or households. A large house, divided through the middle by wide walls, and capable of accommodating from 30 to 150 inmates, is erected by each family, the male members occupying one end and the female the other. Their meals are taken in a common room, and in silence. They possess an average of seven acres of land to the member, and are very industrious. The settlements are at New Lebanon and Watervliet, N. Y.; Hancock, Tyringham, Harvard and Shirley, Mass.; Enfield, Conn.; Canterbury and Enfield, N. H.; Alfred and Gloucester, Me.; Union Village, White Water and North

Union, Ohio; and at Pleasant Hill and South Union, Ky., and number, in all, 2,400 members.

Shays' Rebellion was an uprising of people in Massachusetts, in 1786, under the leadership of Daniel Shays. Following the close of the Revolutionary War the financial condition of the country was bad. Taxes were high, and there was an enormous number of suits for debt before the courts. A general feeling of discontent prevailed which, in the fall of the year mentioned, assumed an organized form. Petitions were addressed to the State authorities complaining that the salaries of the Governor and State officers were too high, that the taxes were too burdensome, that lawyers exacted too heavy fees, and they demanded an issue of paper money and the removal of the Legislative Assembly from Boston. Efforts were made to allay this feeling of discontent, but unsuccessfully, and in September an armed force of insurgents interrupted and dispersed the court in session at Worcester. In like manner, courts in session in other sections of the State were broken up by bodies of armed men; and in December the sessions of the Supreme Court at Worcester and Springfield were suspended by 1,000 men under Daniel Shays. In January of the following year a body of 2,000 men, under command of Shays, marched upon Springfield with the object of capturing the arsenal, but were routed by a force of militia under General Shephard; and the following day a large force of militia, under General Lincoln, captured 150 of them at Petersham. This ended the rebellion. A number of the prisoners were tried and sentenced to death, but ultimately a free pardon was extended to all who had participated in the rebellion.

Shekel.—Originally the ancient Hebrews employed the shekel as a standard weight to calculate the value of metal, metal vessels, and other things. From that it gradually became a regular piece of money, both in gold and silver. In the Old Testament, the gifts to the sanctuary, the fines, the taxes and the prices of merchandise are all reckoned by the shekel—not counted, but weighed. There are mentioned three different kinds of the gold, silver and copper shekels: the common shekel, the shekel of the sanctuary (probably of double value), and the shekel of royal weight. There were, beside these, a half-shekel (*beka*) and a fourth-shekel. The sacred shekel was equal to 20 geras (beans), and 3,000 sacred shekels made a talent. The gold shekel is reckoned approximately to contain 161 troy grains, and the silver shekel 275.

Sheol, a Hebrew term of doubtful derivation. It occurs frequently in the Old Testament, and signifies, according to the authorized version, grave, hell, or pit. The use of the word in the original would seem to prove a great fluctuation of the dogma respecting the world to come, during the various periods represented in the special parts of the Bible. Sometimes it does stand unmistakably for a "tomb," although our notions of an artificially prepared grave do not originally belong to it; at other times it is the abode of disembodied spirits, whether good or evil. It is the place where the dead go to be united with their "people," their "ancestors," friends, and all the departed. It was placed in the center of the earth, or below the ocean, and was a dismal, dark place, like the Orcus or Tarturus. It has gates and bars; it has chambers, valleys and rivers; and its inhabitants—the shadows—who ordinarily enjoy deep repose in this "reign of silence," are troubled by being called up to the surface, or tremble at the arrival of some great tyrant. As the receptacle of all things, it contains the shadows even of trees and kingdoms. It is described as all-devouring, remorseless and insatiable.

Shepherd Kings.—According to the historian Manetho, about 2214 B. C., certain invaders from the East conquered Egypt without a battle, destroying the temples and slaying or enslaving the people, and then made one of their number king, who established his rule firmly in Memphis and made all Egypt tributary to him. The Egyptians called these intruders the Hyksos, or "Shepherd Kings." The Hyksos treated the Egyptians with great cruelty. They established their capital at Avaris, on the northeastern frontier, and held the rule for about 511 years, forming the kings of the fifteenth, sixteenth and seventeenth dynasties. One of the later kings of their number was Apophis, supposed to be the monarch under whom Joseph was raised to great power. The Shepherd Kings were finally overthrown by the kings of Thebias, and the greater portion of the shepherds were driven out of Egypt. It is supposed that it was the memory of their hatred of these usurpers that made, in later years, every shepherd "an abomination" to the Egyptians.

Shintuism is the prevailing religion of Japan. Its characteristics are the absence of an ethical and doctrinal code, of idol worship, of priestcraft, and of any teachings concerning a future state. It requires pre-eminently purity of heart and general temperance. The principal divinity is the sun-goddess Amaterasu, whose descendant and vice-regent on earth is the Mikado, who is therefore worshiped as a demi-god. Their temples are singularly devoid of ecclesiastical paraphernalia. A metal mirror generally stands on the altar as a symbol of purity. The spirit of the enshrined deity is supposed to be in a case, which is exposed to view only on the day of the deity's annual festival. The worship consists merely in washing the face in a font, striking a bell, throwing a few cash into the money-box, and praying silently for a few seconds. In addition to the chief deity, there are a legion of canonized heroes and benefactors who are worshiped. Many Japanese temples are magnificent specimens of architecture in wood, and are remarkable for their vast tent-like roofs and their exquisite wood-carving.

Shoddy was at one time simply the waste arising in the manufacture of woolens; but of late years the name has been given a wider significance by being applied to the wool of woven fabrics reduced to the state in which it was before being spun and woven, and thus rendered available for remanufacture. Woolen rags, no matter how old and worn, are now a valuable commodity to the manufacturer; they are sorted into two special kinds, the rags of worsted goods and the rags of woolen goods, the former being made of *combing*, or long-staple wools, and the latter of *carding*, or short-staple wools. The former are those properly known as shoddy-rags, and the latter are called *mungo*. Both are treated in the same way; they are put into a machine called a *willey*, in which a cylinder covered with sharp hooks is revolving, and the rags are so torn by the hooks that in a short time all traces of spinning and weaving are removed, and the material is again reduced to wool capable of being reworked.

Showers of Fishes.—Tropical countries where violent storms, sudden gusts of wind and whirlwinds are most common, often experience showers of fishes. Fish varying in weight from a pound and a half to three pounds have been known to fall in India. Sometimes they are living, but more frequently they are dead and putrefying. They are always of kinds abundant in the sea or fresh waters of the neighborhood; and there can be but little doubt that they are carried up in the air by violent winds, although they sometimes fall at a considerable distance from any water which could supply them. There have been instances where falls of fishes have taken place in countries not tropical. A shower of small three-spined sticklebacks fell near Merthyr-Tydvil, in Wales, sprinkling the ground and house-tops over an area of at least several square miles, some years ago. They were alive when they fell, yet if caught up by a whirlwind from any of the brackish ponds near the sea in which this species of fish abounds, they must have been conveyed through the air a distance of almost thirty miles. At Torrens, in the Isle of Mull, another similar instance occurred, in which herrings were found strewed on a hill five hundred yards from the sea, and one hundred feet above it.

Siberian Exile System.—The system of exile to Siberia is used for two purposes—first, for the punishment of actual criminals, vagrants and other worthless characters; and, secondly, as "a means of preventing crime against the existing imperial order." In the case of criminals there is some preliminary legal process, by which the offender is convicted of crime; but in the case of political or religious exiles, legal forms are generally dispensed with, and the exile is conducted by "Administrative process." "This process," says George Kennan, an American traveler, who two years ago undertook a journey of investigation through Siberia, "means the banishment of an obnoxious person from one part of the empire to another without the observance of any of the legal formalities that, in most civilized countries, precede or attend deprivation of rights and the infliction of punishment. The person so banished may not be guilty of any crime, and may not have rendered himself in any way amenable to any law of the state; but if, in the opinion of the local authorities, his presence in a particular place is 'prejudicial to social order,' he may be arrested without a warrant, and, with the concurrence of the Minister of the Interior, may be removed forcibly to any other place within the limits of the empire, and there be put under police surveillance for a period of five years. He may or may not be informed of the reasons for this summary proceeding, but in either case he is perfectly helpless. He cannot examine the witnesses upon whose testimony his presence is declared to be ' prejudicial to social order.' He cannot summon friends to prove his loyalty and good character without great risk of bringing upon them the same calamity which has befallen him. He has no right to demand a trial, or even a hearing. He cannot sue out a writ of *habeas corpus.* He cannot appeal to the public through the press. His communications with the world are so suddenly severed that sometimes even his own relatives do not know what has happened to him. He is literally and absolutely without any means whatever of self-preservation."

Sibyls were certain females who were supposed to be inspired by Heaven, who flourished in different parts of the world. They are supposed to be ten in number, but the most celebrated one of all was the Cumæan. The Roman legend regarding her is that she came from the east, and appearing before King Tarquin, offered him nine books for sale. The price demanded appeared to the monarch exorbitant, and he refused to purchase them. She then went away, destroyed three, and returning asked as much for the remaining six as for the nine; and when Tarquin again refused to buy them, she burned three more, and still persisted in demanding the same sum of money for the three that were left. This extraordinary behavior astonished the monarch, and, by the advice of the augurs, he bought the books, upon which the sibyl immediately disappeared, and was never seen after. The books were found to contain advice regarding the religion and policy of the Romans, and were preserved in a subterranean chamber of the Temple of Jupiter on the Capitoline. In the year 84 B. C., the Temple of Jupiter having been consumed by fire, the Sibylline books or leaves were destroyed, whereupon a special embassy was dispatched by the Senate to all the cities of Greece, Italy and Asia Minor, to collect such as were current in these regions, and the new collection was deposited in the Temple of Jupiter when it was rebuilt. Toward the close of the Republic, spurious sibylline prophecies, or what were regarded as such, accumulated greatly in private hands, and they were all given up to the city prætor and burned by order of Augustus, who feared they might be used for political purposes. More than 2000 were destroyed on this occasion. The remainder perished during the burning of Rome in the time of Nero. Other collections, however, were made, and as late as the sixth century, when the city was besieged by the Goths, there were not wanting some who pretended to predict the issue from a consultation of these venerable oracles

Sicilian Vespers, the name given to the massacre of the French in Sicily on the day after Easter (March 30), 1282, the signal for the commencement of which was to be the first stroke of the vesper-bell. Charles of Anjou, the brother of Louis IX of France, had deprived the Hohenstaufen dynasty of Naples and Sicily, and parceled out these kingdoms into domains for his French followers; but his cruelty toward the adherents of the dispossessed race, his tyranny, oppressive taxation, and the brutality of his followers, excited among the vindictive Sicilians the deadliest animosity. On the evening of Easter Monday, the inhabitants of Palermo, enraged (according to the common story) at a gross outrage which was perpetrated by a French soldier on a young Sicilian bride, turned on their oppressors, and put to the sword every man, woman, and child of them, not sparing even those Italians and Sicilians who had married Frenchmen. This example was followed, after a brief interval, by Messina and the other towns, and the massacre soon became general over the island; the French were hunted like wild beasts, and dragged even from the churches, where they vainly thought themselves safe. More than 8,000 of them were slain by the Palermitans alone. The 600th anniversary of the Sicilian Vespers was celebrated with much enthusiasm in Palermo in 1882.

Signal - Service Bureau.—February 9, 1870, a joint resolution of Congress imposed upon the Signal-Service Bureau of the United States army the duty of "giving notice by telegraph and signal of the approach and force of storms." The bureau previous to that date had been engaged in military service only. According to the system now in use by the bureau, tri-daily observations are taken at all the stations east and west at 7 A. M., 3 P. M., and 11 P. M., Washington time, and immediately put upon the wires. So nearly are these observations simultaneous, and so carefully are the differences of time calculated, that they are usually all concentrated at the central office within about forty-five minutes. These reports are made the basis of draughting seven graphic charts, the first showing the barometric pressures, temperatures, winds, and states of weather throughout the country; the second showing the dew-points at all stations; the third the cloud-conditions visible from the different reporting-stations; the fourth and sixth charts show the normal barometric pressures and temperatures, and existing variations therefrom, in the same general mode; and the fifth and seventh show the deviations or departures from the normal condition in these particuulars for the previous twenty-four hours. From these charts the signal officer proceeds to calculate the probabilities of the weather at the different points on his chart for the next twenty-four or forty-eight hours. These probabilities or "weather bulletins" are sent by telegraph to all the stations, and are made public through the daily press. Special "farmers' bulletins" are also printed and sent to small towns and villages along most of the railroads radiating from the chief cities of the country, to be posted in some public place.

Signals, Wind and Weather.—A red flag with a black center indicates that a storm of marked violence is expected. A yellow flag with a white center indicates that the winds expected will not be of extreme severity. A red pennant indicates easterly winds—that is, from north-east to south, inclusive, and that, generally, the storm center is approaching. If shown above the red flag, winds from the north-east are more probable; if below, winds from the south-east may be expected. A white pennant indicates westerly winds—that is, from north to south-west, inclusive, and that, generally, the storm center has passed. If shown above the red flag, winds from north-west will probably prevail; if below, winds from south-west. A white flag indicates fair weather. A blue flag indicates rain or snow. A black triangular flag refers to temperature; when placed above the white or blue flag it indicates warmer weather, and when placed below them, colder weather. A white flag with black square in center indicates the approach of a sudden and decided fall in temperature, and is usually ordered at least twenty-four hours in advance of a cold-wave. When displayed on poles, the signals are arranged to read downward; when displayed from horizontal supports, a small streamer is attached to indicate the point from which the signals are to be read.

Silk-Worm.—It is the general belief that the great importance of the silk-worm was first discovered by Se-ling, the wife of the Chinese Emperor Hoangti, who reigned about 2637 B. C., and that she also invented and taught the art of silk-spinning and weaving. The worms are exceedingly tender, and liable to perish from the slightest changes of temperature and dampness. They feed upon the leaves of various trees and bushes, but experiments go to show that the best silk is produced when the worm is fed upon mulberry leaves. The great centers of this industry are China, Japan, India and Southern Europe, and they have been successfully raised in California, Ohio, Kansas, East Tennessee, Northern Georgia, Kentucky, and in some parts of New Jersey.

Sinai.—The exact position of Sinai, the mount on which God gave to Moses the Ten Commandments and the other laws by which the Israelites were bound, is a matter of some dispute, but it is probably to be found in the mountains occupying the greater part of the Arabian peninsula, lying between the Gulf of Suez and Akabah. This mountain mass is divisible into three groups— a northwestern, reaching, in Mount Serbel, an elevation of 6,340 feet; an eastern and central, attaining in Jebel Katherin a height of 8,160 feet, and a southeastern, whose highest peak, Um Shanmer, is the culminating point of the whole Sinaitic range. Serbel, with its five peaks, looks the most magnificent mountain in the peninsula, and is identified with Sinai by the early Church

Fathers, Eusebius, Jerome, Cosmas, etc.; but the requirements of the Hebrew narrative are not met by it, and even as early as the time of Justinian, the opinion that the Serbal was the Sinai of Moses had been abandoned, and to a ridge of the second or eastern range that honor had been transferred, the northern summit of which is termed Horeb; and the southern, Jebul-Musa, or Mount of Moses, continues to be regarded by a majority of scholars as the true Sinai. The famous monastery of Mount Sinai stands at the eastern base of Jebel-Musa, in solitary peace. There were numerous other convents, chapels and hermitages around the mountain in earlier times.

Singing Sand.—The theory concerning singing sand is that the sound is produced by friction between the angular particles. Samples of singing sand have been found in twenty-six places on the American coast. Professor Julian, of Columbia College, New York, who has given the subject of this phenomenon much study, says: "The singing sand may occur in comparatively small patches in the midst of ordinary sand. It always occurs between the limits of high and low tide. The same sand does not produce sound at all seasons, nor does it always give forth like sounds. When it is wet it will emit sounds. When samples were transported in bags they lost their sounding power, but retained it when carried in bottles." One of the most remarkable occurrences of this sand is that of the beach at Manchester, Mass., where the sand for about one-fifth of a mile gives out a distinct sound when it is walked upon, or even when it is stirred by a rod or cane, and a stick driven into it violently will elicit a sound that can be heard 140 feet away, above the roar of the sea.

Sirens, The.—According to Greek mythology the sirens were two—some versions say three—young maidens who sat on the shore of an island near the Island of Caprera, in the Mediterranean Sea, and sang with bewitching sweetness songs that allured the passing sailor to draw near, but only to meet with death; and their tenure of life was dependent on the successful exercise of their charms. It is related by Homer, in the "Odyssey," that when the Greek hero Ulysses, in the course of his wanderings, approached their perilous home, he, by the advice of the sorceress Circe, stuffed the ears of his companions with wax and lashed himself to a mast until he sailed out of hearing of their fatal songs. Others say that it was the Argonauts who got safely past, owing to the superior enchantment of Orpheus' singing, whereupon the sirens threw themselves into the sea and were transformed into rocks. The Latin poets give them wings, and in works of art they are often represented as birds with the faces of virgins, and are provided with musical instruments.

Sizar.—Students at Cambridge and Dublin Universities who are unable to pay the full college charges are admitted on easy terms and are known by the name of sizars. In return for this concession they were originally required to perform some menial service;

but this has long since been abolished. Sizars are not on the foundation, and therefore are not eligible for fellowships so long as they remain such; but they may at any time become pensioners, and generally sit for scholarships immediately before taking their first degrees. If successful, they are on the foundation, and may become candidates for fellowships when they have taken their degrees. The word is from *size*, in university slang, an allowance of victuals from the buttery, or the smallest quantity of anything which can be bought; a word derived from *assize*, formerly the same as *assess*, to apportion. There is a similar order of students at Oxford, who are denominated servitors.

Skald was a name given to Norse poets who exercised their art as a vocation requiring a learned education. The aim of Skaldic poetry was to celebrate the deeds of living warriors or their ancestors, and for this reason princes attached Skalds to their courts, and competed with each other, by magnificent presents, for the possession of the most skillful minstrels. There are very few complete Skaldic poems extant, but a multitude of fragments have been preserved, partly in the younger "Edda," partly in the "Sagas," and partly in the "Heimskringla," which see.

Skating-Rinks.—The first public skating-rink was opened in Newport, R. I., in 1866, under the auspices of a Mr. Plympton of Boston, the inventor of the "Plympton skate." From that city the skating mania spread all over the country, and for a few years raged fiercely. About 1872, and for several years following, the interest in the sport declined in the United States; but in 1879 it was revived in New England, and extended throughout all the towns of the East, South and West. This furor lasted for a few years, during which time large and expensive rinks were erected in almost all the principal cities of the country. Roller-skates were first patented and used in France in 1819, and a few years later they were manufactured in England by an Englishman named Syers. The Syers skate consisted of a sandal mounted on five narrow wheels in a single row, so arranged, however, that only two of them could touch the floor at the same time. Between 1865 and 1872 large rinks were established and successfully maintained at London, Paris, Rome and other foreign cities, and in the East Indies and Australia.

Skeleton in Every Closet, A.—The expression "There is a skeleton in every closet" is supposed to be derived from the following story: A soldier once wrote to his mother, who complained of her unhappiness, asking her to get some sewing done for him by some one who had no care nor trouble. In the course of her search for such an individual the lady came to one who she thought, from all outward appearances, must be content and happy. It appeared, however, that she was mistaken, for when she had told her business, the lady took her to a closet containing a human skeleton. "Madam," said she, "I try to keep my sorrows to myself; but know that every night I am compelled by my husband to kiss this skeleton of him who was once his rival. Think you, then, I can be happy?"

Slave Law, Fugitive.—The first fugitive slave law was approved by President Washington February 12, 1793. It was in four sections, and was entitled " An act respecting fugitives from justice and persons escaping from the service of their masters." By this law, as embodied in sections third and fourth, the owner, his agent or attorney was empowered to seize his fugitive slave, take him before a Federal Court, or before any magistrate of the county, city or town wherein the arrest should be made, and make proof by affidavit or oral testimony of his ownership, and the certificate thereof was to be sufficient warrant for the removal of the fugitive to the State or Territory from which he had fled. In the event of his rescue, concealment, or of the obstruction of his arrest, a fine of $500 could be imposed upon all persons interested therein. The preceding sections of the act referred simply to arrest of fugitive criminals.

Slavery in the North.—The first State to abolish slavery within her borders was Vermont, which adopted a plan for gradual emancipation in 1777, before she had joined the Union, and in 1800 slavery in that State had entirely ceased. The new Massachusetts Constitution, adopted in 1780, contained a clause declaring that " All men are born free and equal, and have certain natural, essential and inalienable rights, among which may be reckoned the right of enjoying and defending their lives and liberties," which had the effect of freeing all the slaves, a very small number, then held within the borders of that State. In 1780 there were 4,000 slaves in Pennsylvania, and in that year their gradual emancipation was provided for by legislative enactment. Sixty-four of these were still living in bondage, however, in 1840. Rhode Island and Connecticut followed the example of Pennsylvania, and the former had but five slaves left in 1840, and the latter seventeen. New York passed a gradual Emancipation Act in 1799, at which time she had upward of 20,000 slaves, and slavery was totally abolished in the State from July 4, 1827. In 1850 there were still 236 persons living in bondage in New Jersey, although the State had adopted the gradual emancipation plan in 1804. The census of 1810 showed that there were no slaves held in Massachusetts, New Hampshire or Vermont, New Hampshire having emancipated the few slaves held in the State between 1800 and 1810. In Pennsylvania, New York and New Jersey, large numbers of slaves who could not be held in those States were nefariously sold to Southern slave-dealers by unprincipled owners, notwithstanding the fact that each State had adopted, at the time of emancipation, the most stringent laws regarding the exportation of slaves. By the census of 1860 it was shown that slavery was entirely abolished north of Mason and Dixon's line.

Slavs are one of the most numerous groups of nations of the Aryan race, and occupy nearly the whole of Eastern Europe and part of Northern Asia. In the earliest times to which the history of the people can be traced, their seats were around and near the Carpathian Mountains, whence they spread north toward the Baltic, west toward the Elbe and the Saale, and finally, after the destruction of the Huns, south across the Danube over the territories of modern Turkey and Greece. The unity of the race was destroyed, and they split into a number of tribes, separated from each other by political organizations and different dialects. The Slavs are now divided into the eastern and western stems. The former of these contains three branches: The Russians, who are subdivided into Russians and Ruthenians; the Illyrico-Servian branch, comprising the Serbs proper, the Hungarian Serbs, the Bosnians, Herzegovinians, Montenegrins, Slavonians, Dalmatians, Croats and Wends, and the Bulgarians. The western stem comprises, the Polish branch, to which belong the Poles, the Slavic Silesians, and an isolated tribe in Pomerania called Kassubs; the Czecho-Slovak branch, which embraces the Bohemians, Moravians and Slovaks in North-west Hungary, and the Lusatian branch, containing the remnants of the Slavs of North Germany. The aggregate number of the Slavs in both divisions is 89,499,683.

Sling-Buoy, or, as it is also called, the *petticoat breeches,* is a life-saving apparatus invented by Lieutenant Kisbee. It consists of a circular cork life-buoy forming the top ring of a pair of canvas breeches. When a rocket has been fired and a line has reached the distressed ship, one of these sling-buoys is hauled over from the shore to the ship, a man gets into it, his legs protruding below the breeches and his armpits resting on the cork buoy, and he is hauled ashore by a block-tackle.

Smallest Railroad.—A young engineer by the name of George E. Mansfield projected and built a short railroad, with but ten-inch-width track, from the elevated village of Hyde Park, Mass., down to the depot, over which he conducted 3,000 people safely in six weeks' time. Shortly afterward a company was formed, and a road was constructed with a ten-inch gauge from North Billerica, Mass., to Bedford, Mass., a distance of 8¼ miles. There are 11 bridges on the road, one of which is over 100 feet long. The cars will seat 30 persons, and weigh but 4½ tons, ordinary cars weighing on an average 18 tons. The trains run at the rate of 20 miles an hour with perfect safety. The engine is placed behind the tender, giving it greater adhesion to the track. They weigh 8 tons, and draw two passenger and two freight cars. The cost of the road was about $4,500 per mile.

Smithsonian Institute is situated in Washington, D. C., and was organized by act of Congress in August, 1846, to carry into effect the provisions of the will of James Smithson. That celebrated English physician bequeathed to his nephew £120,000, the whole of his property, which, in the event of the death of the latter without heirs, was to revert to the United States, to found at Washington an establishment for " the increase and diffusion of knowledge among men," and which was to be named the Smithsonian Institute. The conditions on which the bequest was to take effect in the United States occurred in 1835 by the death of the nephew without issue, and the Hon. Richard Rush was sent to London to prosecute the claim. On September 1, 1838, he deposited in the United States Mint $515,169, being the proceeds of the estate. The Institute is governed by regents appointed by the Federal Government, and contains a museum, library, cabinets of natural history and lecture-rooms. It receives copies of all copyrighted books, and exchanges with other countries, and its museum is enriched with the gatherings of national exploring expeditions. A portion of its funds is devoted to scientific researches and the publication of works too expensive for private enterprise. There are departments of astronomy, ethnology, meteorology and terrestrial magnetism. The courses of public lectures by eminent scientific men are among the attractions of the Capital.

Snap-Dragon.—This game, which is a familiar one at the Christmas holidays in England, is thought by some to be a survival of the "ordeal by fire" of the middle ages, while others find in it a trace of the still older custom of fire-worship among the Druids. However that may be, it is certain that fire plays an important part in the sport, as will be seen. A quantity of raisins are placed in a large shallow dish, and brandy or some other spirit is poured over them and set on fire. The players then endeavor, by turns, to seize a raisin by thrusting their hands through the flames. This requires fearlessness and quickness, particularly the former, as it is customary to extinguish all lights in the room while the game is being played, and the lurid glare from the burning spirits gives a weird aspect to the scene.

Soaps, Natural.—From time immemorial the Egyptian soap-root and the Spanish soap-root have been employed for washing in Southern Europe and Egypt, and are, to some extent, exported for use in cleansing fine articles. In the West Indies and South America a pulpy fruit, which grows on a tree known as the soap-tree, is said to have such cleansing properties that it will clean as much linen as sixty times its weight of manufactured soap. There is also a tree in Peru, *Quillaja Saponaria*, whose bark, in infusion, yields a soapy liquid much valued for washing woolens, and is largely imported to England and other countries for this purpose. The juice of the soap-wort, or, as it is commonly called in the United States and Great Britain, the "Bouncing Bet," strongly possesses the saponaceous qualities. In California the roots of the *Phelangium Pomaridianum*, which grows there abundantly, are much used for washing. This plant has a strong odor of brown soap in its leaves and stems, as well as the roots. The South Sea Islands and the islands of the Caribbean Sea also produce plants which are used as soap substitutes.

Soap-Stone, or steatite, is principally composed of silicon and magnesium, with more or less aluminum and water. It is known under several different names—as pot-stone, reusselaerite, and French chalk. It is found in massive form, and is white or yellow, often reddish or greenish-white, light-green or gray in color. It is put to a great variety of uses, and is found in many countries. The principal quarries in the United States are at Grafton, Athens, Westfield and Marlborough, Vt.; at Francestown, Pelham and Keene, N. H.; at Middlefield and Chester, Mass.; near Baltimore, Md.; near Washington, Va.; and in Loudon County in the same State; in Guilford County, N. C.; also in other places. The earth, which the clay-eaters of Orinoco and New Caledonia devour with much appetite, is a kind of soft soap-stone.

"Soapy Sam."—The name " Soapy Sam " was applied by his enemies to Bishop Samuel Wilberforce at the time of the Tractarian controversy at Oxford. He was a man of great personal magnetism and remarkable eloquence, and took a very active part in the debates of the House of Lords. As he held his opinions very strenuously, and defended them with convincing power, he naturally had many enemies politically, though he was of the most upright character, and there never was the slightest imputation against his integrity. The bishop knew of the cognomen applied to him; and once when a little girl, overcome by curiosity, said, " Please, sir, why do people call you ' Soapy Sam ?' he replied, " Because, my dear, when I get into hot water I always come out clean."

Soda-Locomotive.—The first soda-locomotives ever built in the United States were made in Philadelphia by the Baldwin Locomotive Works, in 1866. The engine is about 16 feet long, entirely boxed in, with no visible smoke-stack nor pipes, as there is no exhaust nor refuse. The boiler is of copper, $84\frac{1}{2}$ inches in diameter and 15 feet long, having tubes running through it as in steam-boilers. Inside the boiler is placed five tons of soda, which, upon being damped by a jet of steam, produces an intense heat. In about six hours the soda is thoroughly saturated, when the action ceases. A stream of superheated steam from a stationary boiler is then forced through the soda, which drives out the moisture, and the soda is ready for use again. These engines were built for service on the streets of Minneapolis, Minn., where steam-engines are forbidden, and they have the same power as the engines in use on the New York elevated roads. Soda-engines are used in Berlin and other European cities very successfully, and they also traverse the St. Gothard Tunnel, under the Alps, where the steam-engines cannot be used, because the tunnel cannot be ventilated so as to carry off the noxious gases generated by the locomotive.

Soluble Glass, also called water glass, is an artificial silicate of sodium or potassium, or a double silicate of both these alkalies, and thus, in its essential ingredients, the same as ordinary glass. But ordinary glass is, to a slight extent, soluble in water, owing to the alkali which it contains, and by varying the proportion of the alkaline constituent the compound becomes readily soluble to any desired degree. Attention was first directed to it by Fuchs, a German chemist, about 1824. It has been used to some extent, and quite successfully, in preventing the decay of stone walls and edifices under the action of the weather; the surface is covered with a coating of a suitable solution, and, the water soon evaporating, leaves a thin, transparent glaze over the stone, effectually protecting it from the disintegrating action of the atmosphere. The Houses of Parliament in London were treated in this way, and several minsters and numerous other buildings in Germany. It is also employed in the fabrication of artificial stone.

Sophia, Saint, Church of.—The celebrated church of St. Sophia, at Constantinople, was originally built by the Emperor Constantine in 325-326, and is so called as being dedicated, not, as commonly supposed, to a saint of that name, but to *Hagia Sophia* (Holy Wisdom); that is, to the Eternal Wisdom of God, or the Logos, the second person of the Trinity. The church was twice destroyed and rebuilt, the present edifice having been built by the Emperor Justinian about 532. It may be described as a square of 241 feet, forming interiorly a Greek cross, and surrounded in the interior by a woman's choir or gallery, supported by magnificent pillars, for the most part borrowed from ancient buildings. In the center rises a dome, which is supported by two great semi-domes, the whole presenting a series of unexampled beauty. The height of the dome is 175 feet. The building is approached by a double porch, which is about 100 feet in depth. The whole of the interior was richly decorated with sculptured marble and mosaics. The building occupied seven years in its erection, and the history of the work and of the details of its material and construction is full of marvels. Ten thousand workmen are said to have been employed upon it. The materials were supplied from every part of the empire, and comprised remains of almost every celebrated temple of the ancient paganism. The sedilia of the priests and those of the patriarchs were of silver-gilt. The dome of the tabernacle was of pure gold, and was surmounted by a gold cross weighing 75 pounds and encrusted with precious stones. All the sacred vessels and other apparatus were of gold. The altar-cloths were embroidered with gold and pearls; and the altar itself was composed of a mass of molten gold, into which were thrown pearls, sapphires, diamonds, onyxes, and every other object which could raise its costliness to the highest imaginable degree. The total cost of the structure is stated by the ancient authorities at 320,000 *pounds.* Some regard this as pounds-weight of silver, others as of gold. If the latter, which is most generally adopted, the cost reaches the enormous sum of $65,000,000. On the capture of Constantinople by the Turks in 1453 St. Sophia was appropriated as a mosque, and has since been put to that use.

South-Sea Bubble was a financial scheme which occupied the attention of prominent politicians, communities, and even nations, in the early part of the eighteenth century. The scheme was originated by Robert Hartley, Earl of Oxford, then Lord Treasurer of England, in 1711, with the view of restoring public credit and providing for the funding of the floating national debt, which at that time amounted to £11,000,000—the interest, about £600,000, to be secured by rendering permanent duties upon wines, tobacco, wrought silk, etc. Purchasers of this fund were also to become shareholders in the "South-Sea Company," a corporation to have the monopoly of the trade with Spanish South America, a part of the capital of which was to be a new fund. The wondrously extravagant ideas then current respecting the riches of the South American continent were carefully fostered and encouraged by the company, who also took care to spread the belief that Spain was prepared, on certain liberal conditions, to admit them to a considerable share in its South American trade; and, as a consequence, a general avidity to partake in the profits of this most lucrative speculation sprung up in the public mind. But Spain, after the Treaty of Utrecht, refused to open her commerce to England, and the privileges of the South-Sea Company became worthless. There were many men of wealth who were stockholders, and the company continued to flourish, while the ill success of its trading operations was concealed. Even the Spanish war of 1718 did not shake the popular confidence. Trusting to the possibility of pushing credit to its utmost extent without danger, the company proposed, in the spring of 1720, to take upon themselves the whole national debt (at that time £30,981,712), on being guaranteed five per cent. per annum for seven and a half years, at the end of which time the debt might be redeemed if the Government chose, and the interest reduced to four per cent. This proposition was accepted by large majorities in both Houses of Parliament, and after that a frenzy of speculation seized the nation, and the stock rose to £300 a share, and by August reached £1,000 a share. Then Sir John Blunt, one of the prominent men in the company, sold his shares; others followed, and the stock began to fall. By the close of September the company stopped payment, and thousands were beggared. An investigation ordered by Parliament disclosed much fraud and corruption, and many prominent persons were implicated, some of the directors were imprisoned, and all of them were fined to an aggregate amount of £2,000,000 for the benefit of the stockholders. This, with the other assets, yielded a dividend of about thirty-three per cent.

Spain, Castles In.—This expression, as used to denote visionary possession, originated in France, and was peculiarly significant from the fact that the style of building designated in that country as a castle, or chateau, was not found in Spain.

Speakers of the House of Representatives.—The Speakers of the House of Representatives from the first Congress to the present have been as follows: F A. Muhlenburg, 1789-'91; Jonathan Trumbull, 1791-'93; F. A. Muhlenburg, 1793-'95; Jonathan Dayton, 1795-'99; Theodore Sedgwick, 1799-1801; Nathaniel Macon, 1801-'07; Joseph B. Varnum, 1807-'11; Henry Clay, 1811-'14; Langdon Cheves, 1814-'15; Henry Clay, 1815-'20; John W. Taylor, 1820-'21; Philip P. Barbour, 1821-'23; Henry Clay, 1823-'25; John W. Taylor, 1825-'27; Andrew Stevenson, 1827-'34; John Bell, 1834-'35; James K. Polk, 1835-'39; R. M. T. Hunter, 1839-'41; John White, 1841-'43; John W. Jones, 1843-'45; John W. Davis, 1845-'47; Robert C. Winthrop, 1847-'49; Howell Cobb, 1849-'51; Linn Boyd, 1851-'55; Nathaniel P. Banks, 1856-'57; James L. Orr, 1857-'59; William Pennington, 1860-61; Galusha A. Grow, 1861-'63; Schuyler Colfax, 1863-'69; James G. Blaine, 1869-'75; Michael C. Kerr, 1875-'76; Samuel J. Randall, 1876-'81; John W. Keifer, 1881-'83; John G. Carlisle, 1883-'89.

Sphinx, according to Egyptian legend, was a fabulous creature with the body of a lion, the head of a man or an animal, and with two wings attached to its sides, and symbolized wisdom and power united. The reigning monarch in Egypt was usually represented in the form of a sphinx. The most remarkable sphinx is the Great Sphinx at Gizeh, a colossal form, hewn out of the natural rock, and lying 300 feet east of the second pyramid. It is sculptured out of a spur of the rock itself, to which masonry has been added, in certain places, to complete the form. It measures 172½ feet long by 56 feet high, but owing to the encroachment of the sand of the desert, only the head can now be seen. The Theban Sphinx is described as having a lion's body, female head, bird's wings and serpent's tail. She was said to be the issue of Orthos, the two-headed dog of Geryon, by Chimæra, or of Typhon and Echidna, and was sent into the vicinity of Thebes by Juno to punish the transgressions of Laius. In Assyria and Babylonia, representations of sphinxes have been found, and they are also not uncommon on Phœnician works of art.

Spilling Salt.—The origin of the superstition regarding the spilling of salt is easily traced to the ancients, who placed salt upon the head of a victim in sacrifice, since it was regarded as an emblem of purity or sanctification. If the salt was spilled in doing this, it was considered a bad omen. The Greeks and Romans took this custom from the Jews, and came eventually to regard the spilling of salt on any occasion as a portent of evil. To avert this, the practice of throwing some of the spilt salt over the right shoulder was adopted by the Romans. Among their augurs, any movement or appearance on the right side was lucky, and any on the left side was unlucky. So the superstition has been handed down to the present age.

Spinning-Wheel.—The invention of the art of spinning was ascribed by the ancients to Minerva, the Goddess of Wisdom. It is said that Arcas, the King of Arcadia, taught his subjects the art about 1500 B. C. The use of the spindle and distaff, however, was known in Egypt even earlier than this, as is shown by pictures upon Egyptian monuments. The distaff was a simple stick, around which the fiber was coiled, and was held in the left hand. The spindle was a species of top, which was set in motion by a twirl of the hand and by combining its rotary motion with a gradual movement away from the spinner. The size of the fiber was equalized by passing it between the finger and thumb of the right hand until the motion of the spindle was exhausted, when the thread was wound around it, and the process was repeated. The improvement upon this method by placing the spindle in a frame, and making it revolve by mechanical action of the hand or foot in connection with a wheel and treadle, constituted the spinning-wheel, which, though probably in use long before, cannot be traced farther back than A. D. 1530. The spinning-jenny, a machine of eight spindles, was first invented in 1767, and subsequent to that time many improvements in spinning by machinery have been made.

Spiritualism.—According to the majority of Spiritualists, spiritualism is the belief that at death the corporeal body is changed for the spiritual, which, through the light and understanding derived from the spirit-world, has been transformed so that all lusts and passions have been transmuted from a material to an immaterial organism, but which is still affected by the same natural laws that affect mortals, modified only by corporeal disinthrallment. Love, in the spirit-world, is the controlling factor; hence the departed, actuated by a benevolent desire to benefit humanity, are believed to communicate with persons susceptible and sensitive to spiritual influences. Spiritualism first came into notice in a small village in western New York on March 31, 1848, when the Fox sisters claimed to hold intercourse with the spirit-world. Since then the doctrines of Spiritualism have found believers in nearly every community.

Sponges and Sponge Fishing.—Sponges belong to the very lowest order of animal life, and are attached like plants to rocks or similar substances. Those fit for use are found generally in the seas of warm climates. They consist of a frame-work, which is sometimes of an elastic fibrous substance, and sometimes is made up of an aggregation of hard, silicious spicules. A sponge, when fixed to a rock, increases in size by a regular process of growth. To free them from the jelly-like animal matter which they contain when first brought, they are buried for some days in the sand, and are then soaked and washed. In the Turkish sponge-fisheries the sponge is obtained by diving, and the diver guides himself beneath the water with a stone, to which a cord from the boat is attached. The best sponges are obtained from eight to ten fathoms below the surface of the water. In the Greek sponge-fisheries of the Morea, and on the Bahama Islands, a pronged fork at the end of a long pole is used to detach the sponges from the rocks below. Two species are found in the Levant, another on the Bahamas, and still another on the coasts of Florida and Mexico. The Turkish sponge-fisheries employ between 4,000 and 5,000 men, and the value of the sponges they gather aggregates nearly $500,000 annually.

Spontaneous Combustion may be defined as the ignition of inflammable bodies without the application of flame, or without obvious cause of increase of temperature, and arises from the well-understood liability of certain bodies to undergo chemical changes which develop sufficient heat to set them on fire. Recently-expressed fixed oils are particularly disposed to oxidize when exposed to light and air. They then absorb oxygen, and give out carbonic acid and hydrogen. If the process goes on rapidly, as it usually does when the oil is diffused through light inflammable substances, as cotton, tow, the waste used in lubricating machinery, oatmeal, etc., the heat may be sufficient to set them on fire. Bituminous coal lying in large heaps is liable to be ignited by the heat evolved in the decomposition of the sulphuret of iron which it commonly contains. The rapid absorption of water by quicklime is also attended with development of heat sufficient to ignite combustible bodies in contact with the lime. Strong nitric acid will act on straw, hay, and such bodies, so as to render them spontaneously combustible.

St. Elmo's Light.—St. Elmo's fire, or light, is the popular name of an appearance sometimes seen, especially in Southern climes, during thunder-storms, of a brush or star of light at the tops of masts of vessels, at the ends of the yards, or on spires or other pointed objects. It is occasionally accompanied by a hissing noise, and is evidently of the same nature as light caused by electricity passing off from points connected with an electric machine. It is said, in Grecian mythology, that Castor and Pollux, who were esteemed mighty helpers of men, calmed tempests, appearing as the light flames on the masts of ships as described, and the ancient mariners took the appearance of these balls of light on their vessels as a sign that they had nothing to fear from the storm.

St. George and the Dragon.—Around the few facts of the history of St. George many traditions and myths have gathered. According to the Roman *Acta Sanctorum* he was born in Cappadocia, and received a careful Christian training. His fondness for war induced him, at an early age, to join the army of the Emperor Diocletian, where he soon rose to high rank, but suffered martyrdom April 23, A. D. 303, because he confessed his faith to the Emperor and remonstrated with him against his cruelty to the Christians. Among the myths and traditions related regarding him is the story of his slaying a dragon which had haunted a certain neighborhood and seized and carried off one of the most beautiful maidens. According to another account he is said to have reappeared nearly seven centuries after his martyrdom and fought with the famous crusader, Godfrey of Bouillon, at the battle of Antioch, and to have revealed himself to Richard Cœur de Lion, at the siege of Acre, predicting victory. St. George is the patron saint of England, and his feast, the 23d of April, was celebrated with jousts and tournaments until after the Reformation. The anniversary of his death is observed by the Catholic Church as a holy-day.

St. Honorat, Monastery of.—The monastery at St. Honorat, on the Island of St. Honorat, near Cannes, France, was founded near the end of the fourth century, and no woman has ever been allowed to enter its gates from that time to the present day.

St. Nicholas and Christmas.—The origin of the idea that presents are presented at Christmas-time by St. Nicholas, or Santa Claus, probably originated from the following circumstance: St. Nicholas is said to have been Bishop of Myra, and to have died in the year 326. He was noted for his fondness for children, and became their patron saint, and the young were universally taught to revere him. He is said to have supplied three destitute widows with marriage portions by secretly leaving money at their windows, and as this occurred just before Christmas, he thus became the purveyor of the gifts of the season to all children in Flanders and Holland, who hung up their shoes and stockings in the confidence that Knecht Clobes, as they called him, would put in a prize for good conduct. Formerly, and still, in some parts of Germany, the practice is made of all the parents in a small village sending the presents to some one person, who, in high buskins, a white robe, a mask and an enormous flax wig, goes from house to house on Christmas eve, and, being received with great pomp and reverence by the parents, calls for the children and bestows the intended gifts upon them after first severely questioning the father and mother as to the character and conduct of the child. As this custom became less frequent, the custom of children hanging up their stockings was substituted; and as the purveyor no longer visited the houses, it was necessary to explain it by telling the children that he came into the house at night, coming down the chimney and leaving their presents and departing. The custom of decking the houses and churches at Christmas with evergreens is derived from ancient Druidical practices. It was an old belief that Sylvan spirits flock to the evergreens and remain unnipped by frost until a milder season, and it was probably on account of the good omen attached to the evergreen that Christmas-trees came into use.

St. Patrick, the patron saint of Ireland, is supposed to have been born at what is now called Dumbarton on the Clyde, and was of noble parentage, his father being the deacon Calpurnius, and his grandfather the priest Potitus. At the age of fifteen years he is said to have been captured by a band of pirates, but after six years' captivity, during which he tended cattle, probably in the County Antrim, made his escape to Britain. He then entered the priesthood and devoted himself to the conversion of the Irish, and at the age of forty-five was made bishop. Patrick's real name, according to tradition, was Succat. The fact that there were three Patricks has greatly puzzled Christian writers. The date of his death is not definitely known, but the place was Saul, near Down-patrick, where his relics were preserved down to the period of the Reformation.

St. Valentine's Day.—The custom of sending valentines can without doubt be traced, in origin, to a practice among the ancient Romans. At the feast of the Lupercalia, which was held on the 15th of February, in honor of the great god Pan, the names of all the virgin daughters of Rome were put in a box and drawn therefrom by the young men, and each youth was bound to offer a gift to the maiden who fell to his lot and to make her his partner during the time of the feast. This custom became allied to the name of St. Valentine, probably, only through a coincidence in dates. St. Valentine was a bishop of Rome during the third century. He was of most amiable nature and possessed remarkable gifts of eloquence, and was so very successful in converting the pagan Romans to Christianity that he incurred the displeasure of the Emperor, and was martyred by his order February 14, A. D. 270. When the saint came to be placed in the calendar his name was given to the day of his death, and this was made a festival, to offset that of the Lupercalia, and an effort was made to substitute the names of saints for those of girls in the lottery, but naturally without success. Many other customs of mediæval and later times which have become allied in name to a holy saint of the Church are unques-tionably of purely secular, even pagan, origin.

Standing-Stones.—In almost every part of the world where man has fixed his habitation are found large, rude, unhewn blocks of stone artificially raised at some remote period to an erect position. In the British Isles they are especially abundant, where they sometimes stand singly, and sometimes in more or less regu-lar groups. It was long the opinion of archæologists that they were connected with the Druidical worship of the Celtic races, but the result of modern investigation has been to throw doubts on that theory. It is believed that many of these monoliths mark the site of a grave or of a battle-field, as human skeletons and bronze and iron weapons have been, in numerous cases, found under-neath them. Another possible purpose is preserved in the Scot-tish name of "hair-stane," or boundary-stone, by which they are occasionally known. A third use of these monoliths is at least as old as the historical books of the Old Testament, for there we read of Abimelech being made king "by a pillar which was in Shechem," and of Joash, when he was anointed king, standing "by a pillar, as the manner was." A like custom prevailed in ancient Britain, when the king or chief was elected at the "Tan-ist-stone" (from *Tanist*, the heir-apparent among the Celts), and there took a solemn oath to protect and lead his people. A very celebrated stone of this kind was the Lia Fail of Ireland, which was brought to Icolmkill for the coronation of Fergus Erc, and after being removed to Scone became the coronation-stone of Scotland, till conveyed away by Edward I to Westminster, where it now forms part of the coronation-chair of the sovereigns of Great Britain. A peculiar degree of sacredness seems to have invested any contracts entered into at some of these stones. At one time a stone with an oval hole large enough to admit a man's head adjoined the monolithic group of Stennis, in Orkney. It was known as the "Stone of Odin," and continued until the middle of the last century to be the scene of the interchange of matrimonial and other vows—he who broke the vow of Odin being accounted infamous. It is said to have been the popular belief that any one who had in childhood been passed through the opening would never die of palsy; and the power of curing rheumatism was ascribed to a perforated stone at Maddorty, in Cornwall. Still more puzzling to archæologists than the single monoliths are the large symmetrical groups of them, of which the most remarkable and imposing is Stonehenge, in Wiltshire, England, [see *Stonehenge*]; and another remarkable description of monument, whose purpose is also utterly unknown to us, is the Rocking-Stone, or Loggan-Stone, for a description of which see *Rocking-Stones*. [See *Coronation Stone*.]

Standard Time.—According to the new standard time, which was adopted by agreement at 12 o'clock on November 18, 1883, by all the principal railroads of the United States, the continent is divided into five longitudinal belts and a meridian of time is fixed for each belt. These meridians are fifteen degrees of longitude, or one hour's time apart. The time divisions are called intercolonial time, eastern time, central time, mountain time and Pacific time. Eastern Maine, New Brunswick and Nova Scotia use the sixtieth meridian; the Canadas, New England, the Middle States, Virginia and the Carolinas use the seventy-fifth meridian, which is that of Philadelphia; Alabama, Georgia, Florida, Texas, Kansas and the larger part of Nebraska and Dakota use the ninetieth meridian, which is that of New Orleans; the Territories to the western border of Arizona and Montana go by the time of the one hundred and fifth meridian, which is that of Denver; and the Pacific States employ the one hundred and twentieth meridian. In passing from one time-belt to another a person's watch will be an hour too fast or too slow, according to the direction in which he is traveling. This new system, which has reduced the time standards from fifty-three to five, was suggested by Professor Abbe, of the Signal Service Bureau at Washington, and was elaborated by Dr. A. P. Barnard of Columbia College, New York.

Staple, Court of, was a tribunal of great antiquity, which had cognizance of all questions which should arise between merchants, native or foreign. It was composed of an officer called the Mayor of the Staple, re-elected yearly by the native and foreign merchants who attended the staple, i. e., the towns in which the chief products of a country were sold; two constables, appointed for

life, also chosen by the merchants; a German and an Italian merchant; and six mediators between buyers and sellers, of whom two
were English, two German, and two Lombard. The law administered was the *lex mercatoria*, and there was a provision that
causes in which one party was a foreigner should be tried by a
jury, one-half of whom were foreigners.

Star-Chamber, an English tribunal which met in the Old
Council-Chamber of the Palace of Westminster. It is said to have
derived its name from the circumstance that the roof of that apartment was decorated with gilt stars. Its notoriety was gained
principally as a criminal court. It could inflict any punishment
short of death, and had cognizance of a variety of offenses. The
form of proceeding was by written information and interrogatories,
except when the accused person confessed, in which case the information and proceedings were oral; and out of this exception
grew one of the most flagrant abuses of this tribunal in the latter
period of its history. Pressure of every kind, including torture,
was used to procure acknowledgments of guilt; admissions of the
most immaterial facts were construed into confessions, and fine,
imprisonment and mutilation were inflicted on a mere oral proceeding, without hearing the accused. During the reign of Charles I
its excesses reached such a height that it was abolished by the
last Parliament of that sovereign

Star Routes.—A "star route" is any route over which the
mail is carried by other power than that of steam—as, for example, on horseback, or by stage or wagon. These are marked in the
route-book of the Post-Office Department with an asterisk (*);
hence the name.

State Department, Salaries in.—The salaries of the officers
of the Department of State of the United States are as follows:
Secretary of State, $8,000 per annum; Assistant Secretary, $4,000;
Second Assistant Secretary, $3,500; Third Assistant Secretary,
$3,500; Chief Clerk, $2,750; Chief, Bureau of Indexes, $2,100; So-
licitor, $3,500; Chief, Bureau of Statistics, $2,100; Chief, Diplomatic Bureau, $2,100; Chief, Consular Bureau, $2,100; Chief, Bureau of Accounts, $2,100.

State Militia of United States.—The strength of the National
Guard of the several States of the Union is as follows: Alabama,
2,365; Arizona, 502; Arkansas, 2,289; California, 3,794; Colorado,
1,211; Connecticut, 2,524; Dakota, 1,014; Delaware, 571; District
of Columbia, 1,418; Florida, 1,008; Georgia, 4,305; Illinois, 3,861;
Indiana, 2,289; Iowa, 2,447; Kansas, 1,800; Kentucky, 1,317;
Louisiana, 1,916; Maine, 1,041; Maryland, 1,948; Massachusetts,
4,751; Michigan, 2,398; Minnesota, 1,747; Mississippi, 1,525; Mis-
souri, 1,447; Montana, 578; Nebraska, 1,217; Nevada, 559; New
Hampshire, 1,279; New Jersey, 3,981; New Mexico, 1,676; New
York, 12,634; North Carolina, 1,196; Ohio, 5,694; Oregon, 949;
Pennsylvania, 8,367; Rhode Island, 1,263; South Carolina, 4,457;
Tennessee, 1,374; Texas, 2,586; Vermont, 790; Virginia, 2,961;

Washington Territory, 913; West Virginia, 233; Wisconsin, 2,188.

States, Names of.—The names of the several States and Territories comprising the United States are in many instances of Indian derivation, and were given to them for descriptive reasons. Alabama is an Indian word meaning "Here we rest," and is believed to have been given by some early French explorers on hearing the word used by one of their Indian guides when a beautiful spot was selected for a camping-place. Arkansas is from Kansas, the name of a tribe of Indians found there, with the French prefix of *arc*, meaning a bended bow. Connecticut is from the Indian phrase Quinnitukut, meaning the long river. Dakota is an Indian word signifying leagued or allied. Illinois is from Illini, the name of an Indian tribe, meaning "men." The *ois* was the French suffix, implying plurality. Iowa is the French form of an Indian word meaning "the sleepy ones." Kansas is from the name of a tribe of Indians inhabiting the country. Kentucky is an Indian word meaning at the head of a river. Massachusetts is an Indian word meaning "about the great hills." California was so named by Cortes in the year 1535, and it is supposed that he took the name from an old Spanish romance in which there is an imaginary island called California, abounding in great treasures of gold. Georgia was named in honor of George II by the English settlers. Florida was so called by Ponce de Leon because he discovered it on Easter Sunday, which is in Spanish Pascua Florida. Colorado is from the Spanish, meaning red or colored, and refers to the hue of much of the soil. Maine is from the name Maenis, given to the country by the French voyagers who touched there in the fifteenth century, and was probably so called after the ancient form of the name of the French province Mayenne. Louisiana was named after Louis XIV by the French colonists. Michigan is an Indian word meaning "a weir for fish," applicable to the number of fresh-water lakes in the State. Minnesota is an Indian word meaning "cloudy water," and was applied by the Indians to the lake-country near the headwaters of the Mississippi. Mississippi is an Indian word meaning "long river." Delaware was named for Lord de la Warr, one of the early Governors of Virginia. Indiana is from the word Indian. Idaho is an Indian word. Arizona means sand-hill, and is descriptive of a large portion of the Territory. Maryland was named in honor of Henrietta Maria, wife of Charles I. Missouri is an Indian word meaning "muddy." Nebraska is an Indian word meaning "shallow river or water-valley." New York was named after the Duke of York, to whom the country was granted by his brother Charles II. North and South Carolina were named in honor of Queen Caroline. Ohio is an Indian word signifying "beautiful." Tennessee is from the Indian name of the stream, meaning "river of the big bend." Vermont is from *verd* (green) and *mont* (mountain). Virginia was named in honor of Queen Elizabeth, the virgin queen, by Sir Walter Raleigh.

Utah was probably named after the Ute tribe of Indians. Texas was the generic title of the many tribes of Indians who inhabited the land. Rhode Island was so called from a fancied resemblance to the Island of Rhodes; also, and probably more accurately, it was derived from the name of the island when in possession of the Dutch, Roodt Eyland. Pennsylvania was named after William Penn, the suffix meaning wooded land. Oregon was the name given by the explorer Carver to the stream, and signifies "river of the west." New Jersey was named in honor of its Governor, Sir George Carteret, who was a native of the Isle of Jersey. New Hampshire was so called from the county of Hampshire, England. Nevada is from the Spanish name of the mountain range Sierra Nevada.

States, Popular Names of.—Arkansas is called the Bear State; California, Golden State; Colorado, Centennial State; Connecticut, Nutmeg or Freestone State; Delaware, Blue Hen or Diamond State; Florida, Peninsular State; Georgia, Empire of the South; Illinois, Sucker or Prairie State; Indiana, Hoosier State; Iowa, Hawkeye State; Kansas, Jayhawker or Garden of the West; Kentucky, Blue Grass or Dark and Bloody Ground; Louisiana, Creole State; Maine, Lumber or Pine-Tree State; Massachusetts, Bay State; Michigan, Wolverine State; Minnesota, Gopher or North-Star State; Mississippi, Bayou State; New Hampshire, Granite State; New York, Empire State; North Carolina, Old North or Turpentine State; Ohio, Buckeye State; Pennsylvania, Keystone State; Rhode Island, Little Rhoda or Rhody; South Carolina, Palmetto State; Tennessee, Big-Bend State; Texas, Lone-Star State; Vermont, Green-Mountain State; Virginia, Old Virginia or Mother State; West Virginia, Panhandle State; Wisconsin, Badger State.

Steam-Engines.—The application of steam as a moving power is claimed by various nations, but the first extensive employment of it, and most of the improvements made upon the steam-engine, the world indisputably owes to the English and the Americans. It would appear that as early as 1543 a Spanish captain named Blasco de Garay showed in the harbor of Barcelona a steamboat of his own invention. It is most likely that Blasco's engine was on the principle of the Æolipile of Hero, invented 130 B. C., in which steam produces rotatory motion by issuing from orifices, as water does in Barker's mill. The preacher Mathesius, in his sermon to miners in Nuremberg in 1562, prays for a man who "raises water from fire and air," showing the early application of steam-power in Germany. An Italian engineer, G. Branca, invented in 1629 a sort of steam windmill, the steam being generated in a boiler, which was directed by a spout against the flat vanes of a wheel, which was thus set in motion. In England, among the first notices we have of the idea of employing steam as a propelling force is one contained in a small volume, published in 1647, entitled "The Art of Gunnery," by Nat. Nye, mathematician, in which he purposes to "charge a piece of ordnance without gunpowder" by putting in water instead of powder, ramming down an air-tight plug of wood and then the shot, and applying a fire to the breech "till it burst out suddenly." But the first successful effort was that of the Marquis of Worcester. In his "Century of Inventions," the manuscript of which dates from 1655, he describes a steam apparatus by which he raised a column of water to the height of forty feet. This, under the name of "Fire-Waterwork," appears actually to have been at work at Vauxhall in 1656. The first patent for the application of steam-power to various kinds of machines was taken out in 1698 by Captain Savery. In 1699 he exhibited before the Royal Society a working model of his invention. His engines were the first used to any extent in industrial operations. In all the attempts at pumping-engines hitherto made, including Savery's, the steam acted directly upon the water to be moved, without any intervening part. To Dr. Papin, a celebrated Frenchman, is due the idea of the piston. It was first used by him in a model constructed in 1690. The next great step in advance was made in 1705, in the "atmospheric engine," conjointly invented by Newcomen, Cawley and Savery. This machine held its own for nearly seventy years, and was very largely applied to mines. The next essential improvements on the steam-engine were those of Watt, which began a new era in the history of steam-power. His first and most important improvement was the separate condenser, patented in 1769. He had observed that the jet of cold water thrown into the cylinder to condense the steam necessarily reduced the temperature of the cylinder so much that a great deal of the steam flowing in at each upward stroke of the piston was condensed before the cylinder got back the heat abstracted from it by the spurt of cold water used for condensing the steam in the cylinder. The loss of steam arising from this was so great that only about one-fourth of what was admitted into the cylinder was actually available as motive power. This difficulty was overcome by Watt's invention. The principal improvements that have been made since Watt's time have been either in matters relating to the boiler, in details of construction consequent upon our increased facilities, improved machinery and greater knowledge of the strength of materials, in the enlarged application of his principle of expansive working, or in the application of the steam-engine to the propulsion of carriages and vessels.

Steam, Shadows From.—Steam is composed of vapor of different degrees of density, intermingled usually with some air, so that the rays of light entering it are not uniformly refracted, and therefore interfere with and neutralize each other to a considerable degree. This accounts for the fact that shadows are cast by steam. Water does not cast a shadow, for the reason that when it is in a state of rest it is of almost uniform density, and the rays of light, although they may be refracted, pass through it, equally impeded, in parallel lines.

Steel, Manufacture of.—Steel, which is a compound of iron and carbon, was used by the Egyptians, Assyrians and Greeks. The oldest method of making it is the pot-steel process, which consists at first in melting wrought-iron with carbon in clay crucibles, and this process is still used to some extent. The direct process of making steel by immersing malleable iron in a bath of cast-iron was first invented in 1722 by Reamur. Improvements in this manufacture were made in the early part of this century by Mushat and Lucas, and the eminent metallurgist, Heath, first successfully melted the ingredients of cast-steel on the open hearth of the reverberatory furnace about 1839. He patented his process in 1845, but it was not regarded as successful until practical conditions were furnished for it by the invention of the Siemens regenerative gas-furnace in 1862. By the Bessemer process, which was first patented in 1855, and which is now the most generally used, twenty tons of crude iron have been converted into cast-steel in twenty-three minutes. Sir Henry Bessemer has received in royalty on this process some $10,000,000. The manufacture of steel has been carried to the highest perfection in the United States, and the output of American steel-works is about 600,000 tons yearly.

Steel-Pens, Invention of.—During the last century many efforts were made to improve the quill-pen, the great defect of which was its speedy injury from use, and the consequent trouble of frequent mending. These efforts were chiefly directed to fitting small metal, or even ruby, points to the nib of the quill-pen; but the delicacy of fitting was so great that but very little success attended the experiments. At the beginning of this century pens began to be made wholly of metal. They consisted of a barrel of very thin steel, and were cut and slit so as to resemble the quill-pen as closely as possible. They were, however, very indifferent, and, being dear, they made but little way. Their chief fault was hardness, which produced a disagreeable scratching on the paper. In 1820 Joseph Gillott perfected the present form of steel-pens and began their manufacture at Birmingham, England. The first gross of steel-pens ever sold at wholesale were sold for $36, in 1820, at Birmingham. In 1830 the price was $2; in 1832, $1.50; in 1860, 12 cents; while an article as good as those manufactured in 1820 was sold at 4 cents. The annual production of steel-pens in Birmingham alone ranges from 8,000,000 to 15,000,000 gross.

Steppes, the name applied to extensive plains in Russia and Siberia. In spring and early summer these plains are clad with a thin covering of green herbage, become parched and barren under the scorching heat and drought of June, and in winter are hid beneath a thick covering of snow, which, raised in huge, white thin clouds, and driven hither and thither by furious storms, brings destruction to every living creature within its sweep. In autumn, when the herbage, withered by the heat of summer, has been rooted up and broken by violent winds, it becomes gathered and rolled together into enormous balls, sometimes of from nine to eleven yards in diameter.

Stereotyping.—The *papier-mache* process, which is the most general, was first used in France in 1848. It is extremely simple. The types being set, corrected, made into pages and fixed in a frame, are laid upon the stone or table used, face upward, and a little fine oil is brushed over them to prevent the *papier-mache* from adhering to the face of the types. This *papier-mache*, which is used for making the matrix or mold, is formed by pasting upon a sheet of tough brown paper several sheets of tissue-paper and a sheet of soft absorbent white paper. It is made in sheets, and usually, to make a matrix of the desired thickness, several sheets are used. It is kept moist for use, and is lightly covered with pulverized French chalk when laid upon the face of the types. Then it is beaten with a stiff brush to force the soft paper into all the interstices of the types. Other sheets of prepared paper are added to secure the desired thickness, and the whole is then covered with a woolen blanket and put into a press, the bed of which is moderately heated, and the press is screwed down. The heat soon dries the matrix, which when taken out of the press is a stiff card showing a perfect reversed impression of the types. A mold of metal is then taken from the matrix, in which the exact face of the types are reproduced for printing. When the plate is to be run on a rotary press, it is cast in a box which is curved inside, so that the form of the plate will fit the cylinder of the press. By this method an entire large plate can be made in a quarter of an hour, or even less time. For fine book-work the matrices are made of plaster of Paris, which is a much slower and more costly way, but produces a finer and cleaner plate when finished. This process was invented about 1731.

Sterling Money.—The origin of the word "sterling," as applied to money, is variously given by different historians. The historian Camden says that men were sent from the Easterling country, as the eastern part of Germany was then called, in the reign of King John, to instruct the British in coining money, and he derives the word "sterling" directly from this circumstance. Others, however, take the word from starling, or little star, and say that it is in allusion to a star impressed on the coin; and still others refer it to Stirling Castle in Scotland, where money was coined in the reign of Edward I. The weight of authority, however, is with the "Easterling" origin, and it is undoubtedly from thence came the term "sterling" as expressive of a standard purity.

Stoics.—This name, applied to the sect of ancient moralists who were opposed to the Epicureans in their views of human life, arose in the following circumstance: Zeno, a Cyprian, 340–260 B. C., the founder of the system, opened his school in a building or porch called the *Stoa Pœcile* ("Painted Porch"), at Athens, whence his disciples soon came to be called the Stoics. Stoicism was the most remarkable and enlightened of pagan philosophical systems. It came, through the Cynics, from Socrates, whose doctrines and life and death were the foundations of Stoic precepts. It prevailed to some extent in Greece and Asia Minor, but most widely in the Roman world—Seneca (6 B. C.–A. D. 65), Epictetus (A. D. 60–140) and the Emperor Marcus Aurelius Antoninus (A. D. 121–180) being the principal Stoic philosophers whose writings have come down to us. The earliest composition which is extant is a fragment of a "Hymn to Jupiter," by Cleanthes (300–220 B. C.), a follower of Zeno. This is a wonderful production, setting forth the unity of God, His omnipotence, and His moral government. Some of the essential doctrines of their philosophy were: a belief in the moral government of the universe by one good and wise God, together with inferior or subordinate deities; the recognition of Reason as a governing intelligence dominating the entire man, and representing in their conception not merely an intellectual faculty, but an active force combining intellect and will; the pursuit of happiness by cultivating this superiority of mind, and a stern endurance which would enable them to bear every vicissitude, every pain and sorrow, with indifference and equanimity; the absolute subordination of self-interest to the good of the many, of the family, country, universe; and the obligation resting upon every man to assume the duties of active citizenship. The Stoics adopted the four cardinal virtues—Wisdom, or the knowledge of good and evil; Justice, Fortitude, Temperance—as part of their plan of a "virtuous life," the "life according to nature." Positive Beneficence had never been preached as a virtue before them; and there is also, in their system, a recognition of duty to God and morality, as based on piety. Not only are we brethren, but "children of one Father." This philosophy has had a large influence on the world through all the ages, and is in harmony with Christian precepts on many points. The limitation of wants, the practice of contentment, the striving after equanimity, the hardening of oneself against the blows of fortune, are all familiar to the moralists of later ages.

Stonehenge, a remarkable structure, composed of large, artificially-raised monoliths, situated near the town of Amesbury, in Wiltshire. The structure when entire, which it was until in the early part of the present century, consisted of two concentric circles of upright stones, inclosing two ellipses, the whole surrounded by a double mound and ditch circular in form. Outside the boundary was a single upright stone, and the approach was by an avenue from the north-east, bounded on each side by a mound or ditch. The outer circle consisted of 30 blocks of sandstone, fixed upright at intervals of 3½ feet, and connected at the top by a continuous series of imposts, 16 feet from the ground. About 9 feet within this peristyle was the inner circle, composed of 30 unhewn granite pillars, from 5 to 6 feet in height. The grandest part of Stonehenge was the ellipse inside the circle, formed of 10 or 12 blocks of sandstone, from 16 to 22 feet in height, arranged in pairs, each pair separate, and furnished with an impost, so as to form 5 or 6 trilithons. Within these trilithons was the inner ellipse, composed of 19 uprights of granite similar in size to those of the inner circle, and in the cell thus formed was the so-called altar, a large slab of blue marble. Regarding the origin and purposes of Stonehenge there has been much speculation, but none of the theories advanced are quite satisfactory. The theory which at one time was most accepted was that, in common with other similar structures elsewhere, it was a temple for Druidical worship; but the discovery of the sepulchral character of many other monuments which had also been presumed to be Druidical has shaken this belief. [See *Standing-Stones.*]

Stone Tower at Newport.—There is considerable difference of opinion among antiquarians both regarding the builders of the round stone tower at Newport and the purpose for which it was erected. It is not referred to in history until 1678, when Governor Benedict Arnold refers to it as "my stone-built windmill." A favorite theory is that it was built by the Norsemen from Iceland and Norway, and that it was intended for a baptistry, and is only part of a large sacred edifice. In substantiation of this theory is the fact that as early as 1002 a party of these daring adventurers reached the American coast and settled for a time at Martha's Vineyard, which they called Vinland; and it has also been shown that the plan of the tower is almost identical with that of certain baptistries built in Europe in mediæval times, some of which are still standing. Those in favor of the windmill theory, however, prove with apparent conclusiveness that it so closely resembles a stone windmill at Chesterton, England, that it was probably modeled from it. Between these two theories the antiquarians fall out; but the old stone tower, overgrown with vines and somewhat decayed, still stands in Newport, a puzzle to the students of antiquities.

Stool of Repentance, the name ordinarily given in Scotland to a low stool, conspicuously placed in front of the pulpit in churches, on which persons who had become subject to ecclesiastical discipline for immoral conduct were required to sit during public worship, in profession of their penitence, or on which they stood at the close of the service to be "rebuked" by the minister. It was also familiarly called the *cutty*-stool, a term applied to small stools of similar form common in houses, but which came to be often employed, in conversation and in humorous verses, with special reference to that which stood in the church. The stool itself has now fallen into complete disuse, but it is quite common to speak of a person who expresses sorrow for some wrong-doing as being on the "stool of repentance."

Storthing, the name of the Legislative Assembly of Norway. Its members are elected by certain deputies, who, in their turn, are chosen by a constituency comprising every native Norwegian of 25 years of age who is a burgess of any town, or possesses property in land to the value of £33; the qualification for being elected, if 30 years of age, being the same. Every member of the storthing is paid a small allowance per day while it is in session. When elected it meets of its own authority, without any writ from the king. and divides itself into two chambers, the *laything* and the *odelsthing*, the former composed of one-fourth and the latter of the remaining three-fourths of the members.

Stoves, American.—Previous to 1745 the stoves in use in America were imported either from Holland or Germany, but in that year a stove was invented by Doctor Franklin which was a great improvement on all that had preceded it. In 1771 he continued his inventions in this line and produced a stove for burning bituminous coal which consumed its own smoke, and another which, after being filled and kindled at the top, could be inverted and made to burn from the base. Between the years 1785 and 1795 several improvements in stoves, ovens, heating and cooking-apparatus were made by Count Rumford, and as early as 1798 his soapstone-lined ranges had been introduced into New York and were gradually coming into use.

Strasburg Clock.—The celebrated astronomical clock of Strasburg is in the minster, or cathedral, and was originally designed by an astronomer named Isaac Habrecht, in the early part of the sixteenth century. Previous to this time, in fact as early as 1354, Strasburg had an astronomical clock. It was in three parts. The lower part had a universal calendar, the central part an astrolabe, and in the upper division were figures of the three Magi and the Virgin. At every hour the Magi came forward and bowed to the Virgin; at the same time a chime was played, and a mechanical cock crew. This Clock of the Magi, as it was called, stopped in the early part of the sixteenth century, and was replaced by the clock made by Habrecht, which ran until 1789, when it stopped, and all attempts to put its works in order failed. In 1838 a clock-maker named Schwilgue undertook to remodel the internal machinery, and finished it in 1842. The case of the clock made by Habrecht was retained. A perpetual calendar, forming a ring around a dial thirty feet in circumference, occupies the central part of the lower division of the clock. At midnight, December 31st, the clock regulates itself (for the new year) for 365 or 366 days, as the case may be—even the omission of the bissextile day every 400 years being provided for. The disk within the calendar shows the eclipses of the sun and moon, calculated for all time to come. On one side Apollo points with an arrow to the date and name of the saint for the day. On the opposite side stands Diana, the goddess of night. Above the calendar is a niche in which, on each day, the mythological deity of the day appears—Apollo on Sunday, Diana on Monday, Mars on Tuesday, Mercury on Wednesday, Jupiter on Thursday, Venus on Friday, and Saturn on Saturday. Above this is a dial marking the mean time in hours and quarters, with two Genii, one on each side, the one striking the first stroke of every quarter, the other turning over the hour-glass at the last stroke of the last quarter. Then follows an orrery, showing the revolution of the seven visible planets around the sun, and above, a globe giving the phases of the moon. Still above this, in a niche, four figures revolve around the skeleton image of Death, in the center. Childhood strikes the first quarter, Youth the second, Manhood the third, and Old Age the last—Death strikes the hour. In a higher niche stands the image of our Saviour. At twelve o'clock the Twelve Apostles pass before Him in line, and He raises His hands to bless them. St. Peter closes the procession, and, as he passes, the mechanical cock on top of the case flaps his wings and crows three times. The left turret of this wonderful clock contains the weights and machinery, and has in its lower part the portrait of Schwilgue, above this the figure of Copernicus, and yet above, the muse Urania. At the foot of the case is a celestial globe, calculated for observation at the latitude of Strasburg. The clock is wound up every eight days. The mythical story of the city fathers of Strasburg put ting out the eyes of the clockmaker to prevent his building a similar clock for any other city refers to Isaac Habrecht.

Strikes, Statistics.—The plan of settling labor difficulties by strikes is a very old one. The first strike in the United States occurred in New York City in 1803, when a number of sailors struck for an advance of wages. According to "Bradstreet's Commercial Reports" there were 697 strikes in 1888, involving 211,841 employees—a decline from 1887 of 23 per cent. in the number of strikes and of 38 per cent. in strikers. Against 1886 the decrease in number of strikers is 52 per cent. Higher wages or fewer hours were the cause of strikes by 68 per cent. of the strikers in 1888, against 62 per cent. in 1887. Trades-union questions were behind the strike of 17 per cent. of the men involved in 1888, against 22 per cent. of the year before. About 45 per cent. of striking was in Pennsylvania in 1888, against 32 per cent. in 1887. Only 38 per cent. of the strikers of 1888, involving 50 per cent. of the whole number who went out, resulted in favor of the employees, against 42 per cent. of the strikes and 38 per cent. of those involved in 1887. In 1888 there were 74,837 employees locked out, against 46,000 in 1887. The number of days' labor lost by striking and locked-out employees in 1888 was 7,562,480, against 10,250,921 in 1887. If the labor be placed at $1.50 per man, the estimated loss of wages to striking and locked-out employees in 1888 would be $11,343,720, against $15,380,881 in 1887 —a decline of 25 per cent.

Styx, a fabulous river of the lower world, the idea of which was probably borrowed from the Styx of Arcadia. It was said to encompass the lower region nine times in its winding course, and is described by the poets as a broad, dull and sluggish stream of but little depth. According to the popular belief, the gods regarded this stream with so much reverence that they were accustomed to swear by it, and deemed such an oath the most binding in its nature. If, however, any deity ever violated an oath thus taken, the punishment was believed to be deprivation of nectar and ambrosia, and the loss of all heavenly privileges for the space of ten whole years. Hesiod, in a curious passage of the "Theogony," gives the particulars of this punishment very minutely, but makes it apply to the case of celestial perjury in general, not merely to the violation of an oath taken in the name of the infernal river. According to the poet, when any one of the gods is guilty of perjury, Iris is sent down to Hades, and brings up thence, in a golden vase, some of the chilling waters of this celebrated stream. The offending deity is compelled to swallow the noxious draught, and thereupon he lies outstretched for one whole year, without sense or motion, nor partakes of the nectar and ambrosia. At the end of this year other troubles are in store for him. For nine whole years he is now separated from the society of the gods, neither attending at the council of Jove nor partaking of the banquet. In the tenth year his punishment ends and he is restored to his former privileges.

Submarine Boats.—The question as to whether submarine navigation is feasible or not has been, in the main, satisfactorily settled by the inventions of M. Nordenfeldt, a Dane, and J. F. Waddington, of Birkenhead, England, as both gentlemen have designed vessels which are capable of being navigated under the sea. The Nordenfeldt invention is a cigar-shaped, steel-plated vessel, 64 feet in length, 12 feet beam, 11 feet deep, and is run by steam. Two propellers working in a vertical direction supply the sinking force, and a system of balanced rudders keep the boat in a horizontal position. The steam is supplied by a marine boiler for traveling on the surface, and is stored up for moving under water. The crew live in the air-space in the hull. This boat has been run 150 miles on the surface, without recoaling, at a maximum speed of eight knots an hour, and under water sixteen miles at a maximum speed of three knots. She has been successfully operated at a depth of sixteen feet, and has remained under water over an hour without inconvenience to the men. The Waddington boat is also cigar-shaped, but somewhat smaller than the other, being 37 feet long and 6 feet in diameter at the center, tapering off to the pointed ends, and is propelled by electricity. A tower is mounted on the boat, and her depth of immersion below the water-surface is regulated by external inclined planes placed one on either side, and controlled from within. The boat is fitted with a rudder placed aft, and a self-acting arrangement serves to keep the vessel in a horizontal position. The electricity, which is stored in fifty cells, drives a screw-propeller, and the charge is sufficient to propel the boat for ten hours at a speed of nearly nine knots an hour either below the water or on its surface. Electricity also furnishes the light and drives a pump for emptying the water-ballast tanks, which are filled for submerging the boat.

Submarine Forests occur at several places around the shores of Great Britain and Ireland. They consist of beds of impure peat, containing the stools of trees which occupy the sites on which they grew, but by change of level the ancient forest surfaces are now covered by the tide, even at low water. No kind of tree has been found in these forests which does not exist at the present day in the country, and the underwood and herbaceous plants, so far as determined, agree specifically with those found now in similar localities. Submarine forests belong to the recent period, and occur above the bowlder clay.

Sub Rosa.—It was customary among the ancient Germans, on occasions of festivity, to suspend a rose from the ceiling above the table as a symbol that whatever was said during the feast by those present would be afterward forgotten, or at least be kept as a secret among themselves. From this custom came the expression "sub rosa;" that is, under the rose, or between ourselves, or in secrecy.

Suez Canal.—About 600 B. C. a ship-canal connecting the delta of the Nile and the Red Sea was projected and partially finished by Pharaoh Necho. The honor of its completion is assigned by some to Darius, King of Persia, and by others to the Ptolemies. It began about a mile and a half from Suez, and was carried, in a north-westerly direction, through a remarkable series of natural depressions, to Bubastis, on the Pelusiac, or eastern branch of the Nile. Early in the second century it became choked with sand, but was cleaned out by the Roman Emperor Trajan. The canal again became useless, and remained so till the conquest of Egypt by Caliph Omar, A. D. 638–'40, who had it cleaned of sand a second time. It then continued in use for over a century, when it was finally blocked up again by the unconquerable sands, and in that condition has remained. The attention of Europe was first called, in modern times, to the idea of building a canal across the Isthmus of Suez by Napoleon during his invasion of Egypt, and in 1854 the exclusive right to build a canal was granted to M. de Lesseps by the Egyptian Government. In 1858 a company with a subscribed capital of 200,000,000 francs, afterward increased by a loan of 100,000,000 francs, was formed, and the work was begun. The canal is 100 miles long—25 miles of this length being through lakes—its width, at the top, from 195 to 325 feet, and its depth 26 feet. It was formally opened on November 16, 1869, with a procession of steamers, in presence of the Khedive, the Empress of France, the Emperor of Austria, the Crown Prince of Prussia, and others. On November 27th the first ship, the Brazilian, passed through the canal. The cost of the construction of the canal was said to have reached, in December, 1869, the total of $55,135,000. The great advantage of the canal is, of course, the shortening of the distance between Europe and India, as by it twenty-four days are saved in the voyage from London or Hamburg to Bombay, thirty from Marseilles or Genoa,

and thirty-seven from Trieste.   The interest of the Khedive was
bought out by the English Government, and it is now under Eng-
l sh control.

Suicide, Statistics of.—The number of suicides in the United
States for the five years, 1882–'87, was 8,226. Of these, 6,363 were
males and 1,813 were females; 2,724 were husbands; 754 wives;
1,796 bachelors; 661 maids; 362 widowers; 155 widows; 107 divorced males; 60 divorced females; 5,386 acts of suicide were committed in the day and 2,419 in the night. The favorite season was
summer; June was the favorite month, and the 11th the favorite
day of the month. Among the curious causes which were assigned
for the act was the possession of a pimple on the nose.   In European cities the annual number of suicides per 100,000 inhabitants
is as follows: Paris, 42; Lyons, 29; St. Petersburg, 7; Moscow,
11; Berlin, 36; Vienna, 28; London, 23; Rome, 8; Milan, 6; Madrid, 3; Genoa, 31; Brussels, 15; Amsterdam, 14; Lisbon, 2;
Christiania, 25; Stockholm, 27; Constantinople, 12; Geneva, 11;
Dresden, 51.   The month in which the largest number of suicides
occurs is July.

Sumptuary Laws.—At an early period in Roman history the
Censors, to whom was intrusted the superintendence of public and
private morality, punished with the *notatio censoria* all persons
guilty of luxurious living; but as the love of luxury grew with
the increase of wealth and foreign conquest, various legislative
enactments were passed with the object of restraining it, and such
enactments were known as "Sumptuary Laws."   The *Lex Orchia*,
161 B. C., limited the number of guests to be present at a feast;
the *Lex Fannia*, 161 B. C., regulated the cost of entertainments,
enacting that the utmost sum which should be spent on certain
festivals was to be 100 asses, 30 asses on certain other festivals,
and 10 asses on an ordinary entertainment, where, also, no other
food than one hen was permitted to be served up, and that not
fattened for the purpose.   From the time of Edward III down to
the Reformation sumptuary laws were in great favor in England.
They prescribed not only the number of courses which it was lawful to have either at dinner or supper, but also the manner of
dress of the various classes, from knights downward.   Scotland
had also a similar class of statutes.   The Scottish Parliament attempted to regulate the dress of the ladies to save the purses of
the "puir gentlement, their husbands and fathers."   There was a
prohibition against their coming to kirk or market with the face
muffled in a veil, and statutes were passed against superfluous
banqueting and the inordinate use of foreign spices "brocht
from the pairts beyond sea, and sauld at dear prices to monie folk
that are very unabil to sustain that coaste."   In France there were
sumptuary laws, as old as Charlemagne, prohibiting or taxing the
use of furs; but the first extensive attempt to resist extravagance
in dress was under Philip IV.   Most of the English sumptuary
laws were repealed during the reign of James I, but a few remained on the statute-book as late as 1856.

Sunday.—The name of the first day of the week is derived from the Saxon *Sunnan daeg*, or day of the Sun; in the Roman calendar, *dies Solis*. We have no definite information as to when the observance of the first day of the week was substituted by the Christians for that of the seventh day, the ancient Jewish Sabbath. It undoubtedly arose among the earliest practices of the Christian Church, and was regarded as the fittest day to be held as sacred, because, in the words of one of the Fathers, "It is the first day in which God changed darkness and matter, and made the world; and on the same day, also, Jesus Christ, our Saviour, rose from the dead." Various additional reasons, taken from the Old Testament, were advanced by others of the early Fathers in support of the observance of this day. The first *law*, either ecclesiastical or civil, by which the sabbatical observance of Sunday is known to have been ordained, is an edict of Constantine, A. D. 321, forbidding all work but necessary husbandry on the "venerable Sunday." In the Theodosian Code it is enjoined that "on the Sunday, rightfully designated by our ancestors as the Lord's Day, all lawsuits and public business shall cease." Since the ninth century, Sunday has been a thoroughly established institution of the Christian Church as a day of rest and religious exercises, and one exempt from any occupations of a purely secular character, except such as were absolutely necessary.

Sunday-Schools.—In the city of Gloucester, England, in 1781, was established by Robert Raikes, an editor, the first regularly organized school for the instruction of children on Sunday. The school was principally intended for the children of the poorer classes, who were instructed in reading and writing and other secular subjects by hired teachers. This great progressive movement spread rapidly, and in 1789 there were schools of a similar character in nearly every town in England, with an attendance of at least 300,000 children. After they had become firmly established, the nature of the instruction was changed from secular to religious; and somewhat later, paid teachers were replaced by volunteers. The first school of this kind started in America was established in Hanover County, Virginia, under the lead of Bishop Asbury, in 1786; but at the close of the century there was a powerful revival in the work of teaching children. Christian workers vied with each other in this missionary work, and as a consequence, schools multiplied in the cities and large towns. In 1791 the first society having for its object the institution and support of Sunday-schools was organized in Philadelphia, Pa. It is, of course, to Raikes that the chief honor of setting this grand movement on foot must be ascribed, notwithstanding the fact that Sunday-schools had previously been taught by both Martin Luther and John Knox, and also the parish priests in England, the latter confining themselves to instruction in the Catechism.

"Sunset" Cox.—The nickname of "Sunset" which has for a number of years been applied to Congressman Samuel S. Cox, was originally given to him owing to a vivid but rather grandilo-quent description of an Ohio sunset which emanated from his pen, and was widely copied by newspapers throughout the country.

Sun-Worship.—The most complete system of sun-worship that we have any account of was that existing in Peru when discovered by the Spaniards in 1526. The Incas, as the Peruvian monarchs were called, claimed to be children of the sun and his representatives on earth. Their Government was a despotic theocracy, of which the Inca was both high-priest and king. In Cuzco, the capital, stood a splendid Temple to the Sun, in which all the implements were of solid gold. On the west end of the interior was a representation of the sun's disk, and rays in the same precious metal. so placed that the rising sun, shining in at the open east end, fell full upon the image, and was reflected with dazzling splendor. In the plaza or square of the Temple a great annual festival was held at the summer solstice. The multitude, assembled from all parts of the empire, and presided over by the Inca, awaited in breathless solemnity the first rays of their deity to strike the golden image in the Temple, when they all prostrated themselves in adoration. Sacrifices, similar to those of the Jews, were offered on the occasion, and bread and wine were partaken of in a manner strikingly resembling the Christian Sacrament. The Moon as the spouse of the Sun, the planet Venus as his page, the Pleiades, and the remarkable constellation of the Southern Cross, were minor deities. The rainbow and lightning were also worshiped as servants of the Sun; and fire, air, earth and water were not without adoration. In fact, there was little in Nature that the Peruvians did not contrive to make a deity.

Surface Condensers.—Previous to the invention of the instrument known as the surface condenser, the incrustation of saline deposits in the boilers of ocean steamers was one of the most difficult incidents of ocean steam-navigation. By this device the labor of scaling and cleaning the salt deposit from the boilers is saved, their durability is increased, the expense of their repairs is greatly reduced, a much greater pressure of steam can be carried, and a far greater expansion of the steam is made possible. As it was, of course, impracticable for a steam vessel to carry large enough reservoirs to supply the boilers with fresh water throughout the voyage, salt water was generally used, which, besides the disadvantages enumerated above, necessitated a considerable loss of fuel and heat in "blowing off" a portion of the brine at intervals and replacing it with the sea-water in order to avoid the accumulation of too dense brine in the boilers. The desired improvement affecting all these points was secured in the surface condenser, invented by S. Hall in 1831, but not brought into general use until much later, by means of which the supply of fresh water with which the vessel leaves port is used over and over again as long as desired. The appliance consists of a large number of small tubes, generally of brass and about three-quarters of an inch in diameter, through which the cold sea-water is made to circulate, while the steam, after being used in driving the pistons, is brought in contact with their outside surfaces and condensed to water, which passes into a tank and then into the boiler again. In some cases the steam is passed through the tubes and the sea-water circulates around them; but in either way it is kept entirely separate from the boiler-water, which remains absolutely pure. The very freedom of the condensed water from dissolved mineral substances was for a time an obstacle to the adoption of surface condensers, for it was found that the boiler, no longer protected by a deposit of scale, became rapidly corroded through the action of acids formed by the decomposition of the lubricating oil. This objection was finally overcome by introducing a sufficient amount of salt water to allow some scale to form, and then the use of marine condensers soon became universal on steamers plying in sea-water.

Sylphs are elemental spirits of the air. They eat, drink, speak, move about, beget children, and are subject to infirmities like men; but, on the other hand, they resemble spirits in being more nimble and swift in their motions, while their bodies are more diaphanous than those of the human race. They also surpass the latter in their knowledge, both of the present and the future, but have no souls, and when they die, nothing is left. In form they are ruder, taller and stronger than men, but stand nearest to them of all the elemental spirits, in consequence of which they occasionally hold intercourse with human creatures, being especially fond of children and of simple, harmless people. They even marry with our race, like the Undines [see *Undine*], and the children of such a union have souls and belong to the human race. This is according to the fantastic system of the Paracelsists. In common usage the term "sylph" has a feminine signification, and is applied to a graceful maiden. How this curious change of meaning occurred is not quite certain, but it is probably owing to the popularity of Pope's "Rape of the Lock," which introduced the term; for although even in Pope the sylph that guards Belinda is a *he*, yet the poet so refined and etherealized his spiritual agents that they soon came to be associated with our ideas of grace and beauty, and this circumstance may have reacted on the popular idea and brought about the change of gender.

Taj Mahal was built by the Shah Jihan of India as a mausoleum for the remains of his wife, Nourmahal, and is situated at Agra. It is of white marble, 100 feet in diameter and 200 feet in height, built in the form of an irregular octagon, and rising from a marble terrace, under which is a second terrace of red sandstone. At the corners of the marble terrace are lofty minarets, and in the center of the main building rises a dome, flanked by cupolas of similar form. Every part, even the basement, the dome and the upper galleries of the minarets, is inlaid with ornamental designs in marble of different colors, principally of pale brown and bluish violet. Here and there, also, the exterior and interior are decorated with mosaics of precious stones. The whole Koran is said to be written in mosaics of precious stones on the interior walls. In the construction of this magnificent building, which, as Bayard Taylor says, alone repays a visit to India, 20,000 men were employed twenty years. Although the labor cost nothing, over $20,000,000 were expended in its construction. The doors are of solid silver, and an enormous diamond was placed upon the tomb itself.

Talisman, a species of charm consisting of a figure engraved on metal or stone when two planets are in conjunction, or when a star is at its culminating point, and supposed to exert some protective influence over the wearer of it. The terms Talisman and Amulet [see *Amulet*] are often considered nearly synonymous, but the proper distinctive peculiarity of the former is its astrological character. Talismanic virtues have often been attributed to a peculiarly marked or formed egg, and instances are recorded, by various authors, of eggs hatched with figures of comets or eclipses on them. A species of talisman at present in use in Asia is a piece of paper on which the names of the Seven Sleepers and their dog are inscribed. Pasted on the walls of houses, it is believed to be a protection against ghosts and demons.

Talking for Buncombe.—The phrase "Talking for Buncombe," often heard among politicians, was first used by a member of Congress from a district in Buncombe County, North Carolina. During a long speech which he made, several members, who had not patience to listen, retired from the hall, and as they were leaving he told the remaining members that they, also, might as well go, to, as he should speak for some time, and was "only talking for Buncombe."

Tammany, Society of, or Columbian Order, was formed in 1789, being the effect of a popular movement in New York, having primarily in view a counterweight to the so-called "aristocratic" Society of the Cincinnati. It was essentially anti-Federalist or Democratic in its character, and its chief founder was William Mooney, an upholsterer and a native-born American of Irish extraction. It took its title from a noted, ancient, wise and friendly chief of the Delaware tribe of Indians named Tammany, who had, for the want of a better subject, been canonized by the soldiers of the Revolution as the American patron saint. The first meeting was held May 12, 1789. The act of incorporation was passed in 1805. The Grand Sachem and thirteen Sachems were designed to typify the President and the Governors of the thirteen original States. The society is nominally a charitable and social organization, and is distinct from the general committee of the Tammany Democracy, which is a political organization.

Tannhauser, Legend of.—Tannhauser was a famous minnesinger who won the affections of a fair maiden, Lisaura; but being filled with a passion for adventure, he set out to visit the Horselberg, in a cavern of which, called the Horselloch, Venus was said to dwell. It was toward dusk that he passed the cliff, and as he rode by he saw a white glimmering figure of matchless beauty standing before him and beckoning him to her. As she spoke to him the sweetest strains of music floated in the air, a soft roseate light glowed around her, and nymphs of exquisite loveliness scattered roses at her feet. Seven years of revelry and debauch were passed by Tannhauser in the heart of the mountain with the goddess. Then the minstrel's heart began to feel a strange void, and he yearned for the pure, fresh breezes of earth, and at the same time his conscience began to reproach him, and he longed to make his peace with God. In vain did he entreat Venus to permit him to depart, and it was only when, in the bitterness of his grief, he called upon the Virgin Mother that a rift in the mountain-side appeared to him and he stood again above ground. The chime of a village church struck sweetly on his ears, and he hurried down the mountain to the church which called him. There he made his confession; but the the priest, horror-struck at his recital, dared not give him absolution, but passed him on to another. And so he went from one to another, till at last he was referred to the Pope himself. Urban IV then occupied the chair of St. Peter. To him Tannhauser related the story of his guilt, and prayed for absolution. Urban was a hard and stern man, and, shocked at the immensity of the sin, he thrust the penitent indignantly from him, exclaiming, "Guilt such as thine can never, never be remitted. Sooner shall this staff in my hand grow green and blossom than that God should pardon thee!" Tannhauser, full of despair, and with his soul darkened, returned to his only refuge—the enchanted mountain. Three days after he had gone, Urban discovered that his pastoral staff had put forth buds and had burst into flower. Then he sent messengers after Tannhauser, but he was never found.

Tantalus, a character noted in Greek mythology for the punishment he suffered in the lower world. He is said to have been the son of Jupiter by a nymph called Pluto, and some accounts describe him as King of Argos, or Corinth. Various reasons are assigned for his undergoing the severe punishment which he did, the most common being that he divulged the divine councils of Zeus, which the latter had communicated to him as secrets. In the lower world he was afflicted with an insatiable thirst, and had to stand up to the chin in a lake, the waters of which receded whenever he tried to drink of them. Clusters of fruit hung over his head, which eluded his grasp whenever he endeavored to reach them, his mind at the same time being kept in a state of constant terror lest a huge rock, suspended above his head, and ever threatening to fall, should crush him. Tantalus, or rather the punishment which he suffered, has supplied the English language with the very significant verb "tantalize."

Tehuantepec Ship-Railway.—In 1881 Captain James B. Eads, a noted American engineer, obtained from the Mexican Government the right to build a ship-railway across the Isthmus of Tehuantepec. He was also promised a large grant of money and land by the Mexican Government, and he immediately made application to Congress for further aid to secure the carrying out of the plan. The matter was referred in the House of Representatives to a committee, and this body, February 12, 1881, made report indorsing the project, and recommending the passage of a bill pledging the protection of the United States to the railway company, and guaranteeing the interest on $50,000,000 of its bonds. This report, however, was laid upon the table by an overwhelming vote, and thus for the time being the considerations of the merits of the project was prevented. There were several strong objections to the scheme at that time. It had been asserted by several competent engineers that the plan was impracticable. Lieutenant-Commander Gorringe said, "However successful Captain Eads may be in moving a laden ship across such a distance, over such varying grades, the ship would not float on reaching the point where the floating would be a matter of some importance. The jarring in motion, no less than the development of strains not provided for in ship-construction, must inevitably open every seam, and cause every rivet to leak." Of course a suspicion of dangers of this kind caused much prejudice against the scheme. Still greater prejudice was aroused by the disposition shown by Mexico to claim a chief right in the railway. By the terms of the agreement under which Captain Eads obtained his right of way, charts and subsidy, from that Government, it was provided that the Mexican Government was to control the railway. The danger urged by the other engineers that vessels would be injured in transportation Captain Eads planned to prevent by a mechanical contrivance which he thus described: "It consists, in brief, of a cradle made up of a number of separate parts, but all of them containing hydraulic jacks, on which the ship is in fact supported. All the jacks communicate by pipes, so that the same hydraulic pressure is evenly distributed along the bottom of the vessel, no matter what may be the vertical irregularity of the track. Carried on this hydraulic cradle, the vessel may, in fact, be said to rest on the water, and there appears to be less injury than there would be in towage through a canal." The cost of the railway over the Tehuantepec route, 112 miles in length, as was estimated by Captain Eads, would be $75,000,000. In the fall of 1881 and in 1882 a corps of engineers were employed in surveying the route, but all that Captain Eads obtained from the Forty-sixth or the two subsequent Congresses were favorable reports. The Forty-ninth Congress, however, partially consented to incorporate his company. A bill was passed by the Senate, February 17, 1887, which constituted James B. Eads and some eighty other persons named as a body politic under the name and title of the Atlantic and Pacific Ship Railway Company The stock was not to exceed $100,000,000, and when 10 per cent. of the stock had been subscribed for and 10 per cent. thereon paid in cash, a meeting of stockholders was to be held in either Washington or New York for the election of directors. If $10,000,000 of stock was not subscribed for and 10 per cent. in cash paid thereon within two years, the charter, so the bill declared, must expire by limitation. This bill did not get through the House, however, being lost in the rush of legislation before adjournment, and as Captain Eads died on March 8th following, nothing has as yet been accomplished with his scheme. The plan, it would seem to be demonstrated, was feasible, and if accomplished would undoubtedly have been one of the greatest engineering triumphs of the century.

Telautograph, an instrument which reproduces at a distance an autograph or personal signature. It is the invention of Professor Gray, and is described as consisting of two current-interrupters at the sending end and a pair of electro-motors at the receiving end. The sender uses either pen or pencil, near the point of which are attached two threads running at right angles to each other. These threads are kept at an even tension automatically, and each one passes to a current-interrupter set into the telegraphic circuit. When the pen moves to the right the current is broken a great number of times for a small movement. When it moves to the left the current is reversed, and is similarly interrupted. The same arrangement prevails on the movement of the pen up and down. The writer can write or sketch as rapidly and as freely as if he had no telegraphic attachment. At the receiving end there are two electro-magnets, fitted with rods set at right angles to each other, so pivoted as to give any motion desired to the pen which they carry at their intersection. When a series of breaks in the current is caused by a motion of a sending pen to the right, the magnet draws a lateral rod also to the right. Similarly, upward motion is given to the vertical rod. Left-handed or downward strokes of the sending pen are reproduced by the receiving pen in the same manner. Consequently, every motion made on the paper at one end of the wire is copied at the other end. When the pen is taken off, or a new line is begun, an automatic device operates with the same result on the receiving pen.

Telegraph is a name derived from two Greek words, and means to "write far away." It has been used to signify any means of conveying intelligence other than by voice or writing—implying also an idea of speed—but now it has come to be applied exclusively to the electric system of communication. Telegraph instruments may be classed under two heads—those which record the signals, and those which only give passing signals to the observer or listener. Among the former are several kinds, namely: those giving a record in arbitrary signs (as the dots and dashes of the Morse alphabet); those which print in ordinary characters, as the type-printing instruments; and those giving a *fac-simile* of the message. [See *Telautograph*.] The two latter classes are not in extensive use, the great bulk of telegraphing in the world being done either by the Morse printer or by the non-recording instruments. The fundamental method upon which these common instruments are constructed is, in bare outline, as follows: A single continuous wire of a material which is a good conductor connects two distant places; a current of electricity, generated by a battery, is made to traverse this wire, which at each end terminates in a plate of metal sunk in the earth, which completes the circuit at the will of the operator; at the receiving end there is inserted in the circuit an electro-magnet, having an armature of soft iron, held at a little distance from the poles by a spring; now when the operator closes the circuit the electricity, instantly passing through the coil of the electro-magnet, generates sufficient magnetic force to attract the armature which, is held down until the operator opens the circuit, when the current instantly ceases, and with it the magnetic attraction, and then the spring causes it to fly up. This motion of the armature indicates by the system of arbitrary signs the message sent by the operator. The current used is not strong enough to move the instruments on a long circuit, but at each station is reinforced by a local battery, technically called a *relay*, which operates the instrument at that station.

Telegraph, Introduction of.—The first telegraph line built in America extended from Washington to Baltimore, and was built by S. F. B. Morse, the inventor of the electric recording telegraph, by means of an appropriation made by Congress. The first message was sent May 27, 1844, was dictated by Miss Anna Ellsworth, and read, " What hath God wrought?" This was followed by the announcement of the nomination of James K. Polk for President by the Democratic Convention. The first telegraph line in operation in England was between Paddington and Drayton, and was built in 1835. The first message that passed over the Atlantic cable, laid in 1866, was the announcement of peace between Prussia and Austria, which had been agreed on at Nicholsburg the day before the completion of the cable.

Telephone.—In 1831 Wheatstone showed that when the sounding-boards of two musical instruments are connected together by a rod of pine wood, a tune played on one will be faithfully reproduced by the other. Somewhat later a toy, called the "lovers' string," was made, and is the simplest form of a mechanical telephone. The toy consisted of two tin cups, the bottoms made of parchment or catgut tightly stretched like a drum-head, and connected, one with the other, by a string or cord. When the string was drawn taut, sounds, such as those of ordinary speech, produced in front of one of the cups were transmitted along the string to the other cup and reproduced there. This was the first telephone. At various times between 1831 and 1876 electricians and scientists

had experimented with electro-magnets as a means of transmitting
sounds a long distance. In 1854 Charles Boursel published an
article on the electrical transmission of speech, and recommended
the use of a flexible plate, at the source of sound, which would
vibrate in response to the atmospheric pulsations, and thus open
and shut an electrical circuit, and would thus operate, by an
electro-magnet, upon a similar plate at a distance connected by
wire with the first, causing it to give out as many pulsations as
there were breaks in the circuit. In 1876 Alexander Graham Bell
first exhibited the speaking-telephone at the Philadelphia Centennial Exposition. It is this telephone, greatly improved however,
which is now in common use. This telephone consists of a compound permanent magnet fitted into the center of a hard rubber
tube, and carrying, at one end, a short electro-magnet. In front
of this electro-magnet is fixed a thin, soft iron disk, about 1¼
inches in diameter. This disk lies at the end of the rubber tube,
where the tube is formed into a mouth-piece. The action of tele-
phoning with this telephone is very simple. The sound, as ordinary speech, is made in the mouth-piece. The atmosphere conveys
the sound-vibrations against the thin, iron disk (commonly
called the diaphragm). The disk vibrates in sympathy, and coming against the electro-magnet, breaks and opens the electric circuit with every vibration. By means of the connecting wire the
electro-magnet in the distant telephone causes the diaphragm to
vibrate corresponding to the breaks in the current. This, of
course, vibrates the atmosphere, and the pulsations are conveyed
to the ear. The telephone thus described is now used as a receiver. The transmitter invented and improved by Edison and
Blake is combined with the Bell telephone, and makes the telephone of general use. Telephonic communications have been
held between Chicago and New York, but not with any great
amount of success.

Temperance Movement.—In 1789 a meeting for the purpose
of discouraging the use of spirituous liquors was held at Litch-
field, Conn., at which 200 farmers determined not to use any distilled liquors in doing their farm-work the ensuing season. This,
however, was not the first meeting of the kind held on the American continent, as it is recorded that a temperance meeting was
held at Sillery, near Quebec, during a movement made by the
priests to prevent the use of liquor among the early settlers and
Indians. This meeting was addressed by a converted Indian, who
exhorted his people to total abstinence, and declared to them the
penalties enacted against drunkenness. The honor of having
organized the first temperance society in America belongs to Dr
" Billy " J. Clarke and the Rev. Lebbeus Armstrong. The society
was started in the town of Moreau, Saratoga County, N. Y., and
was called " The Moreau and Northumberland Temperance Society." The pledge, which was signed by forty-seven men, prohibited the use of rum, gin, whisky, wine, or any distilled liquor

whatever, and a fine of twenty-five cents was imposed for every violation of the pledge. In 1813 "The Massachusetts Society for the Suppression of Intemperance" was formed, but owing to the laxity of its rules it was not very efficient. "The American Society for the Promotion of Temperance" was inaugurated in Boston in February, 1826, and rapidly grew into an extensive organization, having increased in three years to 11 State associations and 1,000 local societies. About this time the name "teetotal" came into use, having originated from the vain attempt of a stuttering reformed Englishman to pronounce the word total. In 1840 the "Washingtonian Society" was formed by six drunkards, in the city of Baltimore, who resolved to avoid their cups and reform their associates. In five years its pledge had been signed by 650,000 persons, most of whom had been tipplers or drunkards. Other societies were soon formed—the "Sons of Temperance" in New York, in 1842; the "Order of Templars of Honor and Temperance," in 1845; and the "Good Templars," in 1851.

Temples of Baalbec.—The Temples of Baalbec, in Syria, stood upon an artificial platform raised above the plain thirty feet, having immense vaults underneath. The style of the foundation is very similar to that of Solomon's Temple at Jerusalem, which has led some to ascribe its erection to the great son of David. Three of the stones in the foundation wall are each 63 feet long by 15 feet wide and 13 feet deep, raised to a height of twenty feet. Outside of this platform, on the southwest corner, there is a wall where many of the stones measure 30 feet long by 15 feet wide by 13 feet deep. On the platform stood three temples, the Temple of the Sun, the Temple of Jupiter, and the Circular Temple. The Temple of the Sun, or Great Temple, was 290 feet long by 160 feet broad, surrounded by Corinthian columns 75 feet high and 7 feet 3 inches in diameter at the base. The stones of the entablature, which reached from column to column, were 15 feet high by 15 feet long, making the total height at the top of the entablature 90 feet. The stones forming the entablature were fastened together by wrought-iron clamps, inserted in the ends, one foot thick. Six only of these immense columns are now standing. The Temple of Jupiter stands on a platform of its own, some ten feet lower than that of the Great Temple, and is the most perfect ruin in Syria. Its dimensions on the outside are 230 feet by 120 feet. As one writer remarks: "Even with arch destroyed, column overthrown, pilaster broken and capital defaced, so vast at once and so exquisitely beautiful in design and sculpture are the ruins which here surround the traveler, that we scarcely wonder at the fond superstition which leads nations to aver and stoutly to maintain that masses so mighty were never transported and upreared by human hands, but that the once magnificent but now ruined Baalbec was built by the Genii, reluctantly yet irresistibly coerced to their Titanic labors by the mighty power of the seal of the wise son of David."

Teocalli.—The word signifies the House of God, and is the name given to the temples of the aborigines of Mexico, many of which still remain in a more or less perfect state. They were built in the form of four-sided pyramids, and consisted for the most part of two, three or more stories or terraces, with the temple, properly so-called, placed on a platform on the summit. The most celebrated and largest is the Pyramid of Cholula, measuring 1,440 feet each way, and 177 feet in height. It is much defaced, and the temple on its summit has been removed. The teocallis in Yucatan are in much better preservation. They are not generally built in terraces, but rise at an angle of 45 degrees to the level of the platform, with an unbroken series of steps from base to summit. The temples on their summits are sometimes ornamented with bas-reliefs in stucco and hieroglyphic tablets, and the roof is formed by courses of stone approaching each other, and furnished with projections like dormer-windows. Not unlike the teocallis are the palaces of the Aztec kings or chiefs, and sometimes a palace and temple are found attached together; and in a few cases, the most remarkable of which is the Casa de las Monjas, at Uxmal, the buildings are arranged around a court-yard.

Terrapin War was a phrase which was applied to the war of 1812 by those who were especially annoyed at the Embargo Acts. They considered that the country, by thus extinguishing commerce, was drawing within its own shell like a terrapin. Caricatures, epigrams and songs were directed against the embargo, and also against the act forbidding intercourse with Canada. In one newspaper-cut the trade of the United States was represented by a bewildered serpent, which had caught itself between two trees, marked, respectively, " Embargo " and " Non-Intercourse." The wondering snake does not understand the trouble, and its head calls out, " What's the matter, Tail?" to which the tail replies, " I can't get out." A cock, supposed to represent France, stands by, crowing joyfully. In the spring and summer of 1812 "The Terrapin War" was a popular campaign song with the Federalists.

Thanksgiving-Day.—In February, 1631, the colony at Charlestown was reduced to the very point of starvation, and when a vessel with supplies arrived a day of public rejoicing and thanksgiving was ordered by the Governor, and this is considered to have been the first Thanksgiving-Day held in America. In June of the following year the colonists of Massachusetts held a day of thanksgiving on account of a favorable measure toward the colonies having been passed by the Privy Council of the King of England. During the following years frequent days of thanks were appointed in the New England colonies. At first these appointments were at different seasons of the year—sometimes twice in one year—and for special reasons: a victory over the Indians, or the arrival of ships with provisions and new colonists; but later the day came to be set apart in the autumn or early winter, to give thanks for the abundant harvests and generally prosperous condition of the colonists. Thanksgiving-Day was a national institution during the Revolution, and was annually recommended by Congress; but after a general thanksgiving for peace, in 1784, there was no national appointment till 1789, when President Washington, by request of Congress, recommended a thanksgiving for the adoption of the Constitution. In 1795 Washington appointed another national thanksgiving on account of the suppression of the insurrection of that year. In 1815 a day of thanksgiving for the restoration of peace was recommended by President Madison; but during the early part of the century thanksgiving remained an institution peculiar to New England, but was not always held either on the same day or in the same month. The Protestant Episcopal Prayer-Book, adopted in 1789, recommended for a day of thanksgiving the first Thursday in November, and this day was observed by the Church generally in States where there was no official thanksgiving appointed. The first official appointment of a Thanksgiving-Day in the State of New York was made in 1817, but the Governors of Western and Southern States did not generally follow the custom until after 1850. Proclamations recommending special thanksgiving for victory were issued by President Lincoln in 1862 and 1863, and in 1863 and 1864 he appointed the annual Thanksgiving-Day by national proclamation. Since that time annual thanksgiving proclamations have been issued by the Presidents, the Governors of the several States and the Mayors of the principal cities. The last Thursday of November is celebrated as Thanksgiving-Day throughout the country.

Thawing in the Ground.—During the approach and continuance of winter the earth throws off by radiation, each night, more heat than it absorbes in the daytime. While this goes on the temperature of the surface of the earth must continue to fall, and the cold of the atmosphere must penetrate deeper and deeper daily into the ground. As spring approaches the condition changes, and each night less heat is radiated than is absorbed during the day. The average temperature of the earth is therefore steadily rising instead of falling, and opportunity is given to the latent heat of the earth to manifest its influence; for, next to the primal source of heat—the sun—a very important source is found in the heat of the globe itself. While the surface is still frozen, therefore, and has not yet absorbed a sufficient surplus of heat to overcome the effect of the nightly loss by radiation, the ground may yet be thawing rapidly and perceptibly from below, through the influence of the earth's latent heat.

Theosophy.—The name "theosophy" is from the Greek word *theosophia*, divine wisdom. The object of theosophical study is professedly to understand the nature of divine things. It differs from both philosophy and theology in that all reasoning processes are excluded as imperfect, and claims to derive its knowledge from direct communication with God. It does not accept the truths of recorded revelation as immutable, but as subject to modification by later direct and personal revelations. It is really but another name for mysticism, although the latter name implies much more; and the direct and immediate knowledge or intuition of God to which the Mystics laid claim was, in fact, the foundation of that intimate union with God, and consequent abstraction from outer things, which they make the basis of their moral and ascetical system. The theosophic system dates from a very high antiquity. Since the Christian era we may class among theosophists such sects as Neoplatonists. the Hesychasts of the Greek Church, and in later times the disciples of Paracelsus, Thalhauser, Bohme and Swedenborg.

Thermal Springs.—Spring water is scarcely ever cooler than the mean temperature of the surface-ground, yet it is often found to possess a much higher temperature, ranging even to that of boiling water. These springs, warmer than the average, are called thermal springs, even though their temperature is but little above that of ordinary springs. The higher temperature, according to some of the most eminent scientists, is imparted to the spring water by the deep-seated layers of rock which are the river beds of the subterranean streams. This view is sustained by the fact that the thermal springs most abound in mountains and in all those regions where the strata of the earth have been disturbed, as in the volcanic districts.

Thermopylæ of Texas.—In the struggle by Texas for independence, the most sanguinary and heroic conflict of the border warfare which merged into the Mexican war occurred at a fort on the San Antonio River, near San Antonio, Texas, called the Alamo This conflict was for years familiarly known as the Thermopylæ of Texas. The fort was about an acre in extent, oblong, and surrounded by a wall eight or ten feet in height by three feet in thickness. Upon the dismantling of San Antonio by Sam Houston, and then Santa Anna, a body of Texans under the command of Colonel William Barrett Travis retired into the fort, where, on February 23, 1836, they were invested by a large force under Santa Anna. The Texans numbered only 140 men, while the Mexican army was 4,000 strong. The Mexicans erected batteries on both sides of the river, and after a siege lasting about twelve days, during which time they were frequently repulsed with severe loss by the handful of Texans, captured the fort. When this was accomplished, however, but six of the devoted band were alive. Among this number was the famous "Davy" Crocket, who, with the others, surrendered under promise of protection. This, however, was not fulfilled, as they were cut to pieces by order of Santa Anna, Crocket being stabbed by at least a dozen swords. It is said that the Mexicans collected the bodies of the slain Texans, and after horribly mutilating them burned them in the center of the Alamo. During the siege it is estimated that the Mexican loss aggregated over 1,600 men. At the battle of San Jacinto, which occurred a few weeks later, Santa Anna was captured and his troops routed with immense loss by the Texans, who raised the war-cry, "Remember the Alamo."

Thunder is caused by the sudden re-entrance of the air into a vacuum which is supposed to be caused by the lightning in its passage through the atmosphere. The electricity exerts a powerful repulsive force upon the particles of air along the path of its discharge. thus making a momentary vacuum. Into this void the surrounding air rushes with a violence proportioned to the intensity of the electricity, and is thus thrown into vibrations, which are the source of the sound.

Thursday is so called from Donar or Thor, who, as god of the air, had much in common with the Roman Jupiter, to whom the same day was dedicated. The Swedish form is *Thorsdag;* the German, *Donnerstag;* the French, *Jeudi*, and the Latin, *Jovis dies.*

Timothy Grass grows extensively in Continental Europe, from the Mediterranean to the North Sea, and it is supposed was brought to the United States from there. It was extensively cultivated and brought into notice by Timothy Hanson of Maryland, from whom it was named. In Europe the grass is wild, and nearly a century ago its seed was taken to England from Maryland as a novelty. In some portions of the United States it is called herd's grass. There is, however, a species of grass which grows in Pennsylvania and some of the Eastern States which is also called herd grass, but is entirely different from timothy. In England timothy is raised to some extent, and is there called cat's-tail grass.

Tobacco.—The name tobacco is thought by some to have been taken from Tobacco, a province of Yucatan; by others from Tobago, an island in the Caribbean Sea; and by still others from Tobasco, in the Gulf of Florida. The plant, although it is asserted that the Chinese have used it from earliest times, was not introduced into Europe until after the discovery of America by Columbus. He first found it in use on the Island of San Domingo in the West Indies. The Indian, among all the tribes from Peru to Upper Canada, smoked it in pipes. The seed of the plant was first introduced in Europe by Gonzalo Hernandez de Oviedo, who took it to Spain and cultivated it for ornamental purposes; but its narcotic qualities were shortly afterward discovered and the practice of smoking it soon became general, and its manufacture into snuff followed in course of time. It was introduced in Italy and France in 1560, and was brought into the latter country by Jean Nicot, the French Embassador to Portugal, in whose honor it received its botanical name *Nicotiana*, whence the name nicotine. The plant was introduced into England by Sir Walter Raleigh. It was along in the seventeenth century before it was known to be used in Asia, but the Oriental nations at the present time are probably the greatest smokers in the world.

Toddy, a name given in the East Indies to the fermented juice of various palms from which raki is distilled. [See *Raki*.] The name has been adopted in England and the United States for a mixture of whisky, sugar and hot-water, which forms a popular drink in winter.

Tower of London is an irregular quadrilateral collection of buildings on rising ground adjoining the Thames, and immediately to the east of the City of London. It is the most celebrated citadel of England, and the only fortress of the British capital. The space occupied is between twelve and thirteen acres. Within its walls some of the most noted political and religious characters have been confined, tortured or beheaded. The oldest part is what is known as the White Tower, which was built by Gundolph, Bishop of Rochester, in the time of William the Conqueror, and which has not been changed inside, but has been remodeled externally. Some of the walls are fourteen feet thick, which made it practically impregnable in its day. The notable places to be seen by the visitor are: The Traitor's Gate, opposite to which is the White Tower, and through which the prisoners like Raleigh were taken to their cells; the Bloody Tower is also nearly opposite, and there the sons of Edward IV were murdered at the instigation of Richard III; Beauchamp Tower is also seen and remembered as the place where Anne Boleyn and the unfortunate Lady Jane Grey were detained; the Bell Tower, where the Governor resides; the galleries known as the Horse Armory and Queen Elizabeth's Armory; and the Jewel Room, where the crown jewels are kept. The old banqueting hall and council chamber have been made the store-house for arms, and St. John's chapel has been transformed into an office for the records and archives. The armories have famous collections of arms of mediæval and modern times. The Tower is surrounded by a moat of fair width but no great depth. This is usually dry, but the garrison have the power of flooding it. Early writers have alleged that Julius Cæsar first built the Tower of London as a Roman fortress; but there is no written evidence to prove the existence of any fortress on this site before the construction of the White Tower in 1078. During the reign of the first two Norman kings the Tower seems to have been used as a fortress merely. In Henry I's time it was already a state prison. That monarch and his successors gradually increased the size and strength of the ramparts and towers, until the whole became a stronghold of the first class for feudal times. The kings frequently resided there, holding their courts, and not unfrequently sustaining sieges from their rebellious subjects. Of the long list of executions for political offenses, real or imputed, those of Lords Kilmarnock, Balmireno and Lovat, after the Rebellion of 1745, were the last. Wilkes, Horne Tooke and others have, however, since been confined there. Not the least interesting memorials are the quaint and touching inscriptions cut by hapless prisoners on the walls of their dungeons. At present the Tower of London is a great military store-house, in charge of the War Department, containing arms and accoutrements for the complete equipment of a large army.

Trade Dollars.—Previous to the coinage of this dollar, which was brought into existence through the demand on the Pacific coast for a coin to be used in commercial relations, particularly with China and Japan, the old silver dollar of $371\frac{1}{4}$ grains was the only one known. The new dollar contained 420 grains, and eventually was extensively circulated all over the Union, but was retired after the Forty-fourth Congress enacted that it was not a legal tender.

Trade Unions.—In one form or another, combinations have always existed since the employed and employing classes became distinguishable from each other. Trade unions, organized for purposes such as those which contemporary unions contend for, have existed for more than three centuries. So early as 1548 a statute of Edward VI is directed, among other culprits, against certain "artificers, handicraftsmen, and laborers" who had "sworn mutual oaths" to do only certain kinds of work, to regulate how much work should be done in a day, and what hours and times they should work. The usual penalties of fines, pillory and loss of ears were to follow a breach of its enactments. Add the regulation of wages and the employment of union or non-union men to the objects enumerated in this statute, and we have in effect the trades unions of the present day. Many fruitless acts were afterward passed to prevent combinations for raising wages; but since that time the trade unions have increased in numbers and membership, until they include nearly all the laboring classes of England and America. The advocates of the unions insist that they are the only means by which workmen can defend themselves against the aggressions of employers. It is argued that the individual laborer has no chance of resisting the capitalist on equal terms; that starvation treads too closely on his heels to permit his successfully opposing a reduction of his wages, no matter how arbitrary or unjust. It is urged that associations of employers are practically universal, and that their object is mainly to secure for themselves the largest possible share of the profits which are the product of capital and labor united. Yet it cannot be denied that against these uses may be set many serious evils. Strikes are often determined upon by unions at times when the condition of the market renders success impossible, resulting in severe and prolonged suffering. Unions undoubtedly foster an unfortunate spirit of antagonism. Being constantly and consciously on the defensive, they come at last to suspect evil in every movement and to put a sinister interpretation on every action of employers, and in some trades the practice of coercion has grown into systematic terrorism and crime.

Training-Ships, Enlistment on.—A boy seeking admission to the United States training-ship, in order to pass muster, must be fully developed for his age, of good health, and with none of the members or organs of the body impaired. Even the loss or extensive decay of four molar teeth will cause rejection. He must be of good moral character, and able to read distinctly Shellen's twenty-feet test type at a distance of fifteen feet with each eye singly. The shipping-articles or a sworn declaration furnished by the commanding officer must be signed by the father, mother, or guardian. While serving on the training-ship the boys are given an ordinary English education, and receive practical instruction in seamanship. The pay is $9.50 per month and one ration for third-class boys, as they are called when enlisted, $10.50 per month for second-class, and $11.50 per month for first-class. The necessary outfit of clothing is furnished by the Government and charged against their pay, but no allowance is made under any circumstance for traveling expenses to the place of enlistment. No boys under fourteen years or over eighteen can enlist, and they must serve until they are twenty-one years old, unless discharged on the recommendation of a medical survey, or for misconduct. In case of injury while in the service, a pension is granted.

Trajan's Column, a celebrated column at Rome, which was reared A. D. 114, by the Roman Senate and people, in honor of the Emperor Trajan. It is considered not only the greatest work of its architect, Apollodorus, but one of the noblest structures of its kind ever erected. The pedestal is covered with bas-reliefs of warlike instruments, shields and helmets; and a very remarkable series of bas-reliefs, forming a spiral around the shaft, exhibit a continuous history of the military achievements of Trajan. These are in excellent preservation, and independently of their beauty as works of art they are invaluable as records of ancient costumes. A spiral staircase in the interior of the column leads to its summit. The height of the entire column is 132 feet. It stands erect in all its ancient beauty amid the ruins of Trajan's Forum. The summit was originally crowned by a colossal statue of the Emperor, which has been incongruously replaced by one of St. Peter.

Transvaal is a province of South Africa, east of Zululand, which comprises an area of 112,700 square miles, and has a population of some 800,000, not more than 45,000 of which are white. The white inhabitants are of Dutch descent, calling themselves Boers, and were originally emigrants to Cape Colony; but in 1830, getting tired of British rule, the more adventurous of them began exploring for new homes in the wilderness, and eventually settled the entire country now forming the province of Natal and the Orange Free State. The British soon annexed Natal, but the Orange Free State and a settlement beyond the Vaal were allowed to form republics. The Transvaal Republic was not, however, wholly successful in the work of self-government, from the fact that the majority of its population had sought pioneer life to secure freedom from all restraint. Volksraads or general assemblies of the people were held, but the taxes imposed by this body, and the laws it passed, could not be enforced. At last the Cape Government made this the pretext for sending for a British Commissioner, who took possession of and annexed the Transvaal territory. This, however, did not suit the mass of the people, and after two delegations, which had been sent to England to protest against the annexation, failed to obtain any recognition from the English Government, the Volksraad proclaimed the annexation null and void and the republic still in existence. This was in December, 1879, and it was a whole year before these slow-moving people were ready to fight for their liberties. The few engagements which took place between the Boers and the small bodies of British troops sent against them resulted in every instance in a victory for the former, and on about February 26, 1881, an armistice was agreed upon, and a convention held for the formation of a treaty. By this treaty, which was ratified by the Volksraad, a limited suzerainty was secured to the British Government, and the people of the Transvaal were granted full control of their local affairs on their agreeing to abolish slavery and maintain religious toleration. Troubles between the Boers and the natives created a necessity for another convention in 1884, when the British suzerainty was revoked. The Transvaal country, so named because situated beyond the Vaal River, is well watered, and all the districts are thoroughly adapted for the raising of grain and cattle. Gold has been found in paying quantities, but fearing the influx of a mining population, an act was passed in 1883 forbidding the mining of gold and silver. The wonderful discoveries of precious metals, in 1885 and 1886, on the borders of their territory have quite nullified this law, however.

Trappist Monks are a branch of the Cistercian Order of Monks. Their monastery, called La Trappe, is in the French Department of Orne, and was founded in 1140. During the wars that prevailed between the French and English the monastery was repeatedly plundered and the monks dispersed, by which its numbers were so depleted and its religious discipline so utterly destroyed that at the beginning of the reign of Louis XIV there were only seven monks left, whose habits had become so depraved that they were styled "the brigands of La Trappe." In 1664 the Abbot de Rance was put in charge of the monastery and immediately instituted a series of reforms, which in a few years made the Monks of La Trappe noted as one of the most austere orders of Europe. The monastic rule of the order was most severe. The members rose in the morning at 2 o'clock and devoted twelve hours a day to religious exercises and several hours to hard labor. No worldly conversation was allowed; upon meeting, the members were required to salute each other with the solemn words "*Memento mori*" (Remember death). The scanty food of these anchorites consisted of water and vegetables; meat, wine and beer were forbidden. They slept on a board, with a pillow of straw. Their constant effort was to wean the mind from the pleasures of life, and to fix it upon the idea of death. In the latter part of the eighteenth century they had monasteries in Italy and Germany as well as France. During the French Revolution the order was suppressed in France, but was reinstated in its privileges in 1817. In 1870 the order was abolished by law in Italy, and in Germany in 1874. A Trappist colony settled in Pennsylvania, whence they removed to Kentucky, thence to Missouri and to Illinois, and finally in 1813 to Nova Scotia, where they still exist. Since that date two colonies of Trappists have settled in the United States.

Treasury Department, Salaries in.—The salaries of the officials of the Treasury Department of the United States are as follows: Secretary of the Treasury, per annum, $8,000; two Assistant Secretaries, $4,500 each; Comptroller of Currency, $5,-000; Chief Clerk, $2,700; Director of Mint, $4,500; Chief, Bureau of Statistics, $3,000; Chief, Bureau of Engraving and Printing, $4,500; Supervising Architect, $4,500; Superintendent Coast Survey, $6,000; Treasurer of United States, $6,000; Assistant Treasurer, $3,600; Register, $4,000; Solicitor, $4,500; Superintendent Life-Saving Service, $4,000; First Comptroller, $5,000; Second Comptroller, $5,000; First Auditor, $3,600; Second Auditor, $3,-600; Third Auditor, $3,600; Fourth Auditor, $3,600; Fifth Auditor, $3,600; Sixth Auditor, $3,600; Commissioner of Customs, $4,600; Commissioner of Internal Revenue, $6,000; Commissioner of Navigation, $4,000; Chairman of Lighthouse Board, $11,000; Chief, Appointment Division, $2,750; Chief, Warrant Division, $2,750.

Treaty of Ryswick.—By this treaty, which was concluded in 1697, between Louis XIV and Great Britain, the German Empire, Spain and Holland, the long war which followed the League of Augsburg in 1686 was terminated. Louis, by this treaty, acknowledged William of Orange as King of Great Britain and Ireland, restored to Spain his conquests in Catalonia, and a large part of Flanders and Lorraine, and others on the Rhine, to the German Empire. Strasburg and other places in Alsace were definitely ceded to France.

Trial by Jury.—The form of trial by jury is generally conceded to be derived from the institutions of the Greeks and Romans. There was a custom in the ancient city of Athens whereby a certain number of freemen, selected by lot, heard and decided, under the direction of a presiding judge, every case to be tried at law, each case being heard and determined by a different set of men. A similar system was adopted in Rome; and as the Romans always introduced their laws and institutions into all their provinces, it is probable that their mode of judicial procedure was established among the Britains., Another form, called the trial by compurgation, was in use among the Saxons. In this, each party to a suit appeared, with certain of his friends, who swore with him to the truth of his case. As the number of the compurgators was usually six on each side, it is supposed by some that we have here the origin of the number of the modern jury. Witnesses were first brought in to aid the jury during the reign of Edward III, but it was not until the reign of Queen Anne that the law provided that those who had evidence to give could not serve as jurors. In Scotland the jury system was established at a very early date, but was soon after discontinued in civil cases. A jury in that country consists of fifteen, and a majority may render a verdict. The jury in civil cases was re-introduced in the time of George III. In Ireland the jury is substantially the same as in England; but the Repression-of-Crime bill, passed in 1882, provided for the trial of certain cases without juries. In France a jury is only allowed in cases of felony, where a majority of the jurors can render a verdict. In Germany, trial by jury in criminal cases was introduced early in the century. It was established in Prussia in 1819, and again by the Constitution of 1848; but in 1851 political offenses were withdrawn from its operation. The system was adopted by Austria in 1850, by Greece in 1834, and by Portugal in 1837. It has also been introduced in recent times into Italy, into Brazil, and finally into Russia, where the first trial by jury was held August 8, 1886. In each of these last-named countries a verdict can be rendered by the majority. The jury system has existed in Belgium since that country separated from Holland, and includes within its operations political offenses and those of the press. In Switzerland all crimes against the Confederation are tried by jury, and for other crimes each canton has its own machinery. The form of trial by jury was brought from England to America by the colonists, and is protected by mention in the Federal Constitution and in the Constitutions of most of the States. It is also in use in the South American republics. The origin of the institution as found in England is also ascribed by some to the establishment of Norman law there by William the Conqueror, as the Normans had a form of trial by jury much more like that of modern times than any legal usage of the Saxons.

Triple Alliance is the name by which two different treaties are known in history. The first was signed at Hague in 1668 by England, Holland and Sweden, and had for its object the protection of the Spanish Netherlands and the checking of the conquests of Louis XIV of France. The second Alliance was between England, France and Holland, against Spain, in 1717, and provided for the Protestant succession in Great Britain and that of the Duke of Orleans in France; for the retirement of the Pretender from the latter country, and the demolition of Dunkirk, according to the Treaty of Utrecht.

Triumvirate.—"The First Triumvirate" is the name given in Roman history to the private league entered into by Cæsar, Pompey and Crassus—the three most powerful men of their time—to enable them to rule the Roman republic. This compact was not a triumvirate in the proper sense of the term, as it had no legally-constituted existence, but was, in fact, only a treasonable conspiracy of three men against the legitimate authority of the State. "The Second Triumvirate" was the partition of the government between Octavius, Antony and Lepidus immediately after Cæsar's death—an arrangement sanctioned, and therefore legalized, by the Senate. This triumvirate continued for two consecutive terms of five years, soon after which Octavius became supreme, and was thereafter known as Cæsar Augustus.

Trojan War.—The legend regarding the Trojan war has undoubtedly a historical origin in the fact of the actual destruction of Troy by a Grecian military expedition. About 1194–'84 B.C., according to the traditions, Paris, one of the sons of Priam, enticed Helen, the beautiful wife of Menelaus, King of Sparta, away from her husband, and at the call of Menelaus all the heroes of Greece flew to arms to avenge this wrong. The Grecian host numbered 100,000 warriors, among whom were Ulysses, Achilles, Ajax, Diomed and Agamemnon, who, as brother of Menelaus, was chosen to lead the expedition. The siege of the city of Priam lasted ten years. Finally the Greeks, by the device of Ulysses, built an immense wooden horse, in which they concealed a number of their warriors, and left it on the plain in sight of the city, and then retired to their ships as though abandoning the siege. The Trojans, believing that the statue was left as a propitiatory offering to their gods, carried it within their walls, and at night the concealed warriors issued from the horse and opened the gates of the city to their returned comrades, and Troy was sacked and burned. The king and all his sons were killed; in fact, according to the legend, Æneas, and his father Anchises and a few devoted followers were the only ones to escape, and these, after long wanderings by sea and land, finally settled on the shores of Etruria, in Italy. The battles which were fought before the walls of Troy have been immortalized by Homer in the "Iliad."

Trouvere and Troubadour, the names given in Northern and Southern France, respectively, to a class of polished and cultivated bards. At all the courts in Southern France, Northern France, Spain and Italy they were esteemed a brilliant ornament of society. Princes and fair dames (often themselves trouveres or troubadours) were proud of their praise and their service of gallantry, or dreaded the biting raillery of their satiric muse. These poets were usually attended by a jongleur, whose business it was to furnish an instrumental accompaniment to the songs which his master composed and sung. The trouvere and troubadour poetry lasted for about 200 years—1090 to 1290.

Troy and Mycenæ, Sites of.—From 1871 to 1873 Doctor Heinrich Schliemann, a famous eastern traveler and explorer, conducted excavations on the plateau of Hissarlik, which he maintained was the site of ancient Troy. At a depth of fifty feet several layers of ruins were encountered, each of which he considered the remains of a distinct city, one built upon the ruins of another. A vast number of arms, household utensils and ornaments, which bore traces of greater or less skill, besides many curious and valuable vases and various ornaments of gold, amber and silver were discovered. After a long and careful study of the subject, Schliemann came to the conclusion that these belonged to the palace of Priam, the King of Troy, and had been buried for safety on the night when the Greeks entered and burned the city. The ruins . of Mycenæ are for the most part in the neighborhood of Kharvate, and are specimens of Cyclopean architecture. These were also explored by Doctor Schliemann in 1876–'77, and several ancient tombs containing a large quantity of gold and silver ornaments were unearthed.

Trusts.—A "Trust," in its broad sense, is a combination of individuals or corporations for controlling the price of a commodity. It seeks to do this by restricting production or by "cornering" the market, and strives to accomplish its end without incurring the penalties of the law. This endeavor to keep within the law has given rise to many forms of "trust" agreements. The simplest is a mere naked contract between manufacturers or dealers that each shall carry on his business in his own way, but that none shall sell below an agreed minimum price. Examples of this are agreements between the coal producers of Pennsylvania and the trades-union agreements. Another simple form of combination is an agreement that all shall carry on their business independently, but that profits shall all be turned into a common fund and divided in a definitely agreed on ratio, no matter what the profits of each individual may actually have been. Of such a nature are railroad pools. Another kind occurs when a corporation leases the works, or contracts to take all the products of other corporations, or enters into partnership with them. In all of these cases, however, there is a danger of overstepping the bounds of legality. Courts in all parts of the country have repeatedly refused to enforce such contracts if deemed to be injurious to the public; and some authorities have declared them criminal, if dangerous to the common good. This has led to the invention of a subtile and elusive form which we may call the "Trust" proper. In this, the stock of all the stockholders of all the corporations comprising it is placed in the hands of a few men as trustees, thus securing to a dozen or so persons the absolute control of stock representing many millions of dollars and possibly thousands of owners. The Standard Oil Trust and the Sugar Trust illustrate this form, the Standard Oil being probably the pioneer in this line, and now one of the most powerful moneyed institutions in the world. Whether this "Trust" will stand the attacks of its enemies or, in in its turn, will be decided to be illegal it is too soon to judge. In a recent case the New York Supreme Court has declared it illegal and the charters of its constituent corporations liable to forfeiture. As has been said, a "Trust" is not a corporation, nor subject to the restrictions placed by law on incorporated companies. It has no charter to define its powers, nor books which must be subject to inspection by stockholders and Government officials.

Tuesday is so called from *Tuesdag*, Tiw or Tiu being the old Saxon name for the Norse god of war. The day bears a corresponding name in the other Germanic dialects. The French is *Mardi* and the Latin *dies Martis*, from Mars, the Roman god of war.

Tun of Heidelberg.—In 1343 a wine cask, whose capacity was 21 pipes or 2,646 gallons, is said to have been made at Heidelberg, Germany. This, however, was probably destroyed, as a new one was made in its place in 1664, which held 600 hogsheads, or 37,-800 gallons. This the French emptied and knocked to pieces in 1688. But a much larger vessel was made early in the eighteenth century, whose capacity was 50,400 gallons. For many years it was kept full of the best Rhenish wine, which flowed freely during the merry-makings of the electors; but of late years it has not been in use. The Heidleberg tun is interesting simply on account of antiquity and mention in literature, as the modern inventions for the manufacture of liquor on a very large scale have caused the construction of even larger casks to be quite a common thing. The largest vessel of this kind, however, is one made at Konigstein, Germany, in 1725, by Frederick Augustus, King of Poland and Elector of Saxony. This held 233,654½ gallons. The top of this mighty cask is railed in, and affords room for twenty persons to sit and enjoy their cups. All strangers are offered a "welcome cup" of the liquor from this cask; and on its side is engraved a Latin couplet, inviting visitors to drink "to the prosperity of the universe."

Tunnels, Great.—The nine longest tunnels in the world are as follows: Mount St. Gothard, 48,840 feet long; Mont Cenis, 39,840 feet long; Hoosic, 25,080 feet long; Nochistongo, 21.659 feet long; Sutro, 21,120 feet long; Riquivel, 18,623 feet long; Nerthe, 15,153 feet long; Blaizy, 13,455 feet long; Thames and Medway, 11,880 feet long.

Turncoat.—The epithet "turncoat" is supposed to have taken its rise from one of the first dukes of Savoy, whose dominions were open to the contending powers of France and Spain. Being subject to frequent incursions of these rival powers, he was obliged to temporize and favor them as they seemed able or not to injure him. He therefore had a coat made that was blue on one side and white on the other, and might be worn indifferently with either side out. When he was ostensibly on the side of Spain he wore the blue side out, but when the French were to be propitiated he displayed the white side. He therefore became known as Emanuel the Turncoat, and the epithet has therefore come to be applied to those who turn their opinions around to suit their personal interests.

Type-Setting Machines.—The first type-setting machine appears to have been invented by William Church of Connecticut

about 1820. This, after the lapse of twenty years, was followed
by a number of others, scarcely a year passing without one or
more being made the subject of a patent. In 1857 a machine was
invented by Robert Hattersley which is capable of setting from
4,000 to 6,000 types in an hour—about three men's work. This
machine, which occupies a space of about two or three feet, has
a horizontal stage on which is placed a partitioned tray, containing the rows of type running from back to front, each row being,
of course, all the same letter. Descending vertically along the
front of this tray is a series of as many wires with pistons as there
are rows of types, and these pistons are depressed by the keys
acting by bell-cranks, and then return to their positions by means
of India-rubber bands or springs. A propeller kept in a state of
tension by an India-rubber string is placed in the rear of each row
of types, and draws them forward to the piston. When the girl
working the machine presses down, say, an *e* key, it depresses the
e piston, which pulls down with it an *e* type, and drops it into a
tube or channel, which conveys it to what represents the composing-
stick, and so on with every letter, figure, comma or space. Another
successful machine is the Mitchell type-setter. The compositor
has a key-board, each key of which strikes out a type from a brass
slide placed on an incline. The type travels along an endless band
to a spot where it is turned on end and pushed forward by a notched
wheel. The apparatus comprises numerous bands, the lengths and
velocities of which so vary as to enable the types at different distances from the wheel to reach it in the order in which the keys
are struck. The words are built up in rows thirty inches long,
and "justified," as is the case with the Hattersley machine, by
hand.

Type-Writers.—The first type-writing machine, as they are
now known, was invented in 1868 by C. L. Sholes of Wisconsin.
Since that time a great many improvements have been effected in
them by subsequent inventors, the principal advantages gained
being rapidity of execution and legibility. The earliest form of a
type-writer was a rude machine invented in England in 1714, and
in 1855 M. Foucault sent to the Paris Exposition a writing machine
adapted to the uses of the blind.

Tyrian Purple.—From a very early period purple has been one
of the most highly prized of all colors, and came to be the symbol
of royal power. Probably one great reason for this was the enormous cost of the only purple color known to the ancients, the
Tyrian purple, which was obtained in minute quantities only from
a Mediterranean species of molluscous animal or shell-fish. In
the time of Cicero wool double-dyed with this color was called
dibapha, and was so excessively dear that a single pound-weight
cost a thousand denarii, or about $175. Tarentum, the modern
Otranto, was one of the great fisheries of the Romans, and vast
heaps of the shells have been discovered there, the remains of its
former industry. With the decline of the Roman empire the em-

ployment of this purple color ceased, and it was not until a Florentine of the name Orchillini discovered the dyeing properties of the lichen, now called Orchella weed, that a simple purple color was known in Europe. For nearly a century the discovery was kept a secret in Italy, and that country supplied the rest of Europe with the prepared dye, which received the name of Orchil or Archil. Its value, however, was later greatly lessened by the discovery of the beautiful series of purples yielded by coal-tar as the results of the combination of one of its products called aniline with other bodies.

Uhlans.— During the Franco - Prussian war, 1870–'71, the name Uhlan was prominently brought before the world through the bravery and marvelous activity of the Prussian cavalry known by that designation. The Uhlans originally were light cavalry, of Asiatic origin, who were introduced into the north of Europe along with the colonies of Tartars who established themselves in Poland and Lithuania. They were mounted on light, active Tartar horses, and armed with saber, lance (whence the name, which signifies "Lancers"), and, latterly, with pistols. The lance was from five and a half to six and a half feet in length, and was atttached to a stout leather thong or cord, which was fastened to the left shoulder and passed round behind the back, so as to allow the lance to be couched under the right arm. Immediately below its point was attached a strip of gaudy-colored cloth, the fluttering of which was designed to frighten the enemy's horses. The early dress was similar to that of the Turks, and the regiments, or *polks*, were distinguished from each other by the red, green, yellow, or blue color of their uniforms. The Austrians and the Prussians were the first to borrow this species of cavalry from the Poles.

Umbrellas are by no means a modern invention. They are found sculptured on the monuments of Egypt and on the ruins of Nineveh, and their use in China and India is also very ancient. In Greece they had a part in certain religious ceremonies; and there is no doubt, from the paintings on ancient Greek vases, that umbrellas very much like those in use at the present time were known many years before the Christian era. They were also used among the Romans, but only by women. The umbrella also seems to have been a part of an insignia of royalty, as is still the case in parts of Asia and Africa. An English dictionary, published in 1708, defines an umbrella as "a screen commonly used by women to keep off rain." Jonas Hanway is said to have been the first man to have carried an umbrella through the streets of London in rainy weather, about 1750, and he was hooted and jeered at by boys for his fears of a wetting. It is not known, however, when their use began in England, as representations of such articles are found in very ancient manuscripts. Umbrellas were introduced in America in the latter part of the eighteenth century, but their use at first was confined almost exclusively to women, as it was considered very effeminate to carry one.

"**Uncle Sam.**"—The practice of calling the United States Government "Uncle Sam" is believed to have originated in the following manner: During the Revolutionary War a man named Samuel Wilson was a beef inspector at Troy, N. Y., and was very popular with the men in his employ, who always called him Uncle Sam. After the inspection of the beef it was shipped by him to a contractor named Elbert Anderson, and was always marked "E. A. U. S." A joking workman being asked what those letters were the abbreviations of, replied that he did not know unless they were for Elbert Anderson and "Uncle Sam." The joke was kept up and spread, until it became common to refer to all packages marked "U. S." as belonging to "Uncle Sam."

Undines, the name given in the fanciful system of the Paracelsists to the elementary spirits of the waves. They are of the female sex. Among all the different orders of elementary spirits they intermarry most readily with human beings, and the Undine who gives birth to a child under such a union receives with her babe a human soul. But the man who takes an Undine to wife must be careful not to go on the water with her, or at least not to anger her while there, for in that case she will return to her original element. Should this happen, the Undine is not supposed to consider her marriage dissolved; she will rather seek to destroy her husband, should he venture on a second marriage.

Undulatory Theory of Light.—For a long while there were two rival theories to account for the nature of light and optical phenomena, and it is only of late years that the observations and experiments of scientists have fully established the undulatory theory and disproved the corpuscular theory. The former maintains that light is a transference of *energy* to the eye; the latter, that it is a transference of *matter*. The undulatory theory assumes the entire universe and all matter to be pervaded with a highly elastic imponderable fluid, which is called *ether*. Light, then, consists in the propagation of energy by a wave-motion through this fluid—a process exactly analogous to the transmission of sound in air and of waves in water. This theory explains the nature of radiant heat also and its relation to light, considering it is an undulatory motion, in this same *ether*, of similar character but different degree. The now-discarded corpuscular theory, which was supported by no less a man than Sir Isaac Newton, assumed that an infinite number of minute material particles emanated from a luminous body, and, impinging on the eye, gave the sensation of light. Huyghens has the credit of having propounded, developed and illustrated the undulatory theory. His propositions and conclusions were finally and fully substantiated by the successive experiments and demonstrations of Young, Fizeau and Foucault. The velocity of light, or the rate at which this wave-motion is communicated through the *ether*, is 186,000 miles a second.

Unicorn.—Ancient Grecian and Roman authors describe the

unicorn as being the size of a horse, or larger, the body resembling that of a horse, and with one horn a cubit and a half or two cubits long on the forehead, the horn straight, its base white, the middle black, the tip red. The body of the animal was also said to be white, its head red, its eyes blue, and it was said to be so swift that no horse could overtake it. It was supposed to be a native of India, and the oldest author who describes it is Ctesias, who resided for many years as physician at the court of Artaxerxes Mnemon, and who wrote about 400 B. C. His information, however, was all at second-hand. He calls it the wild ass. Although the descriptions of the unicorn given by the ancients are very unlike the Indian rhinoceros, yet probably that animal was the origin of them all. The unicorn is perhaps best known as a heraldic charge or supporter. Two unicorns were borne as supporters of the Scottish royal arms for about a century before the union of the crowns of Scotland and England, and the sinister supporter of the insignia of Great Britain is a unicorn.

Unitarians.—The Unitarians of the present day, like almost all Christian sects, must be divided into two classes—a conservative and a progressive class—or, as they are often called, an old and new school. The former adopt the old rule of the sufficiency of Scripture, though with such qualifications as the scientific criticism of the Bible has rendered indispensable. The most conservative Unitarian, for example, would not contend for the literal truth of the first chapter of Genesis, nor for the doctrine of verbal inspiration in any shape. "The Bible is *not*, but it *contains*, the Word of God," is the form which best expresses their position on this subject. They generally hold the simple humanity of Christ, and even reject the supernatural birth, thinking the part of the Gospels which record that event to be less authentic than the parts referring to the ministry, the death and resurrection of Christ. What, however, chiefly distinguishes the Unitarians of this school from those of the new or progressive school is the place which they give to the miracles as supernatural sanctions of the truth of Christianity. Denying that man has any immediate knowledge of the intuition of spiritual things, they regard Christianity as a system of moral and religious truth external to man's nature, and requiring, in proof of its divine origin, certain evidences beyond its inherent credibility and adaptation to human wants. This evidence they find in the miracles, which they accept as well-attested facts, on the same ground on which all historical facts are accepted. The Unitarians of the progressive school, so far from regarding man as entirely dependent upon his reasoning powers for his knowledge of religion, rather look upon him as standing in a living relationship with the one infinite source of all truth, and as having within his own nature the germs of the highest religious faith. To this view of Christianity the miracles are not felt to be essential as proofs. Generally speaking, the Unitarians of this school are disposed to regard with favor the freest criticism of the Bible. Unitarians of all shades of opinion are agreed in rejecting the entire orthodox scheme—including the doctrines of the Trinity, the vicarious atonement, the Deity of Christ, original sin and everlasting punishment—as both unscriptural and irrational. They celebrate the Lord's Supper in their churches, not as a sacrament, but as a service commemorative of Christ's death and expressive of spiritual communion with him.

United States Bank.—The first United States bank was established by act of Congress, approved July 25, 1791. It was organized at Philadelphia with a capital of $10,000,000, divided into 25,000 shares of $400 each. The act prescribed that any person, copartnership or body politic might subscribe for any number of shares not exceeding 1,000—only the United States could subscribe for more than this number of shares; that with the exception of the United States the subscriptions should be payable one-fourth in gold and silver, and the remaining three-fourths in certain six per cent. bonds of the United States; that the subscribers should be incorporated under the name of "The President, Directors and Company of the Bank of the United States," and the organization should continue until March 4, 1811; that the bank could hold property of all kinds, inclusive of its capital, to the amount of $15,000,000; that twenty-five directors should be chosen, who in turn should choose from their number a President; that as soon as $400,000 in gold and silver was received on subscription the bank could organize, after giving a notice of its intention. The general effect of this institution was very salutary. The credit of the United States became firmly established. The bank-notes stood at par with gold and silver. The large deposits made the money available for the use of the Treasury, and the State bank currency, which had flooded the country with no prospects of redemption, was greatly reduced. But with all its recognized advantages the act to recharter was defeated in 1811 by the casting vote of the Vice-President, George Clinton. Its loss, however, was immediately felt in the sudden and rapid increase of the currency of the State banks. To ward off an impending crisis, a second bank was established by an act approved by President Madison, April 10, 1816, at Philadelphia. A capital of $35,000,000 was required, which was to be equally divided into 350,000 shares, of which the United States took 70,000. The charter extended to March 3, 1836. The bank was prohibited from lending, on account of the United States, more than $500,000, or to any prince or foreign power any sum whatever, without the sanction of law first obtained; and it was also prohibited from issuing bills of less denomination than $5. In time, to facilitate business, branch offices were established in every State. In December, 1829, however, the bank met strenuous opposition in the message of President Jackson, who argued, as did Jefferson when the first bank was started, against the constitutionality of its charter; and when Congress, in 1832, passed a bill to recharter the institution he imposed his veto, and soon after removed from the bank the United States deposits. The bank corporation, however, continued to exist until 1836, when the charter terminated.

United States Commissioners, Duties of.—The President, with the advice and consent of the Senate, has power to appoint Commissioners of Customs, Education, Fisheries, General Land Office, Indian Affairs, Internal Revenue, Patents, Pensions, and also diplomatic commissioners, whose duties are to a great extent explained by the titles of their offices. A Commissioner of a United States Circuit Court, who is appointed under Section 627, Chapter VI, of the Revised Statutes, must enforce observance of the laws concerning or affecting the election of the President and Vice-President of the United States and Congressional Representatives and Delegates; institute prosecutions for violations of civil rights laws; enforce awards of foreign consuls in differences between captains and crews; summon masters of vessels in cases of seamen's wages; imprison or bail offenders against United States laws; apprehend fugitives from justice; grant warrants to internal revenue officers to search premises in certain cases; and discharge poor convicts sentenced by any court of the United States to pay a fine, or fine and costs, upon his taking oath, after he has been confined thirty days, that he is unable to pay.

United States Government Salaries.—The President of the United States, $50,000 per annum; Vice-President, $8,000; Cabinet officers, $8,000 each; United States Senators, $5,000, with mileage; members of Congress, $5,000, with mileage; Chief Justice Supreme Court, $10,500; Associate Justices, $10,000 each; Justices of Circuit Courts, $6,000 each.

United States Mints.—The first building erected in any portion of the United States by authority of the Federal Government was the United States Mint in Philadelphia. This building was of brick, and stood on the east side of Seventh Street, above what is now called Filbert Street. The corner-stone was laid July 31, 1792, by David Rittenhouse, the Director of the Mint. About the year 1831–'32 the Mint was removed to the building at Juniper and Chestnut Streets. In 1835 branch mints were established at New Orleans, La., Charlotte, N. C., and at Dahlonega, Ga.; in 1854 at San Francisco, Cal., and in 1870 at Carson City, Nev., and later at other points.

United States, Oldest Settlements in the.—In 1565 the first permanent settlement in the United States was made at St. Augustine, Fla., by a party of Spaniards under Melendez. Between the years 1540 and 1583 Francisco Vasquez de Coronado, Captain Francisco de Coronado and Don Antonio de Espejo explored New Mexico, and occupied temporarily various points in that region. In the latter year Don Antonio de Espejo took possession of a native pueblo or town, called Tucas or Toas, and named it La

Cindad de Santa Fe, which was identical in site with the present capital of New Mexico. Between 1590 and 1595 forts, colonies and missions were established in New Mexico by Juan de Ouate. In 1607 the first permanent English settlement was planted by the London Company in Virginia at Jamestown, which was so-called in honor of James I. In 1614 the Dutch planted an infant settlement on Manhattan Island, which they called New Amsterdam, and in 1615 a settlement was made at Albany, N. Y., by the same nation.

United States, Seal of the.—The first device for a seal of the United States was prepared under the direction of Benjamin Franklin, John Quincy Adams and Thomas Jefferson, who had been appointed a committee for that purpose July 14, 1776. On one side of the design offered were the Goddesses of Liberty and Justice, and around them were grouped the arms of all the European nations; on the other were: above, the pillar of fire, and, below, Pharaoh and his chariots overthrown in the Red Sea. This design, however, was not approved, and it was not until 1782 that a final decision in regard to the matter was reached. In that year a committee who had been appointed by Congress submitted a design drawn by William Barton of Philadelphia, which on June 20 was approved and finally adopted as the Great Seal of the United States. The obverse of this was the device, familiar to all, of an eagle bearing on his breast the national escutcheon, holding in his right talon an olive-branch, and in his left a bunch of thirteen arrows. Above his head were thirteen stars surrounded by a halo or glory, and a scroll bearing the legend "*E Pluribus Unum.*" The escutcheon was placed upon the breast of the eagle without other support, to show that the United States of America would rely mainly upon their own strength and virtue. The olive-branch and arrows were to indicate that the powers of peace and war were vested in Congress. On the reverse side was an unfinished pyramid; above it an eye and the words "*Annuit Cœptis,*" and beneath it "1776—*Novus Ordo Seculorum.*" The pyramid was used to signify strength and duration, and was left unfinished, to indicate that the great work of building the structure of human liberty was not completed. The motto "*Annuit Cœptis*" and the eye were meant to allude to the many interferences of Providence in favor of the American cause. The date of the Declaration of Independence and the words "*Novus Ordo Seculorum*" ("A new series of ages") allude to the opening of a new era of human progress and freedom. The thirteen bars on the shield typified the States, and the constellation of stars denoted that a new nation was to take its place among the sovereign powers of the world. After the ratification of the Constitution this seal was again formally accepted September 15, 1789, and on March 2, 1799, its custody was transferred to the Secretary of State. In 1841 the old seal was found to be so worn that a new one was made by order of Daniel Webster, in which, for some unknown cause, the number of arrows in the eagle's talon were reduced to six and the regular width of the stripes on the shield were altered. From its adoption half of the seal has done duty for the whole, as the reverse side has never been engraved for the purposes of the Government.

Universalists.—The distinctive peculiarity of the Universalist faith consists in the belief that "evil" will ultimately be eradicated from the world, and that all erring creatures will be brought back to God through the irresistible efficacy of Christ's divine love. They argue that when an infinite, wise, holy and benevolent God resolved to create man, it could only be with a view to his everlasting good; that if he did allow him to be tempted and fall, it must have been because he foresaw that through sorrow and suffering man could rise to higher degrees of perfection; that, therefore, all punishment is of necessity designed as a remedial agent, and not intended to satisfy God's indignation as a sovereign at the disobedience of his subjects; that no other view of the subject is compatible with the Scriptural, and especially the New Testament, representation of God as a "Father," or with the oft-repeated declaration (in various terms) that Jesus Christ was a propitiation for the sins of the whole world. Universalism, as a mode of belief, is of very ancient origin, and its modern adherents, beside urging its congruity with the divine plan of redemption as revealed in Scripture, point to the earliest Christian writings, *e. g.*, the Sibylline Oracles [see *Sibyl*], and cite passages in favor of the doctrine from many of the Church fathers. Universalism was preached in the United States as early as 1741, but the first separate Universalist church was not established until 1780, when the Rev. John Murray started one at Gloucester, Mass. Since his time an important body has sprung up which contains many able, learned and pious divines.

University Fellowships.—In the beginning of the fourteenth century wealthy and benevolent persons had already endowed colleges in the Universities of Oxford and Cambridge, England, for the support of the poorer students, and those receiving these endowments were called *Socii*, or Fellows. The assistance given was originally intended to end at the completion of the course of study; but as the majority of the beneficiaries belonged to the ecclesiastical order and had no other means of support, an understanding gradually arose that the aid granted should be continued until a benefice had been obtained. By the fifteenth century these provisions gradually increased in number and importance, and fellowships were no longer endowed to assist students in going through their course of study, but as a permanent provision for poor young men of the clerical order who showed a taste for learned pursuits, and they could not be held until the first degree of Bachelor of Arts, or student in the civil law, had been taken. Previous to 1854 many of these fellowships were restricted to descendants of kinsmen of the founders, or to the inhabitants of certain dioceses or districts; but that year they were thrown open to all members of the University of requisite standing. The fellowships, which are paid out of the college revenues, vary much in value, the older ones being much the more valuable. They confer on their holders the privilege of occupying apartments in the college, certain perquisites as to meals, and a certain sum in money. Many of them are tenable for life, but in general they are forfeited should the holder attain to certain preferments in the church or at the bar, and sometimes in case of his succeeding to property over a certain amount. In general, also, they are forfeited by marriage, which is a trace of the early monastic form of the University; but a special vote of the college may permit a fellow to marry and still retain his fellowship.

Ursula, Saint.—Maximus, the Roman, being proclaimed Emperor of Britain by his army A. D. 382, went over into Gaul to establish his power against the opposition of the Gallic emperor, Gratian. One of his commanders, Conan, who was a British prince and a Christian, conducted himself so bravely on this expedition that Maximus made him the ruler of Brittany. Conan established his residence at Nantes, and sent embassadors to ask Ursula, a princess of Britain, in marriage from her father, Dunnat, King of Cornwall, with as many young women as were willing to come with her and become the wives of the Britains who had settled with Conan in Brittany. The embassadors were received favorably by King Dunnat, and the Princess and her companions consented, and took ships at London for Brittany. A storm, however, drove them upon the German coast, where they were captured by the Huns, and being exhorted by Ursula to die rather than surrender their virtue, they were all barbarously massacred. The question of the number of slain virgins has never been settled. A historian of the eighth century only says that the number was very great. In the twelfth century we find the assertion that there were 11,000 of them. The ancient record on Saint Ursula's tomb read simply, "Ursula *et* XI. M. V.," which some writers insist meant only "eleven martyred virgins;" but others read the M as a numeral, and translated it 11,000 virgins. There is a church dedicated to the 11,000 virgins in Cologne, near where the massacre took place, where a great pile of skulls and bones is shown as those belonging to the martyred virgins. Saint Ursula, as a saint and martyr of the Roman calendar, is especially honored in Germany, and particularly in Cologne.

Utilitarianism.—The Utilitarian theory, which adopts as the criterion of right the happiness of mankind, has been maintained both in ancient and modern times. Epicurus held it, but in a purely self-regarding form; each person's end was his own happiness exclusively, the happiness of others being instrumental and subordinate. The modern phase of the theory may be said to begin with Hume. He employed, as the leading term of his system, Benevolence, whereby he gave special prominence to the disinterested side of moral actions. He strenuously maintained what must be regarded as the essential feature of the Utilitarian doctrine that no conduct is to be deemed worthy of moral approbation unless, in some way or other, it promotes human happiness, and that actions ought to be visited with disapprobation exactly according as they have the opposite tendency. Among the noted Utilitarians are Jeremy Bentham, Paley, James Mill, Sir James Mackintosh, John Austin, John Stuart Mill, Samuel Bailey and Herbert Spencer.

Utopia, the name of an imaginary island, the scene of Sir Thomas Moore's romance of the "Happy Republic." According to that author the island was discovered by a companion of Amerigo Vespucci. It was the abode of a happy society which, by virtue of its wise organization and legislation, was wholly free from the harassing cares, inordinate and greedy desires and attendant customary miseries of mankind. Passion, malice, envy and hatred were unknown, and all the members of the republic were contented, free from covetousness and ambition. The utmost toleration in religion existed, some members of the republic worshiping the deity and others the sun and stars. All the property of this republic belonged to the Government, and each inhabitant, by his labor, contributed to increase the common store, and drew therefrom what he needed for his own wants; and when his necessities were provided for he desired no more. Merit was the sole ground of promotion in all departments of the society, and wealth was neither sought for nor desired. This ideal picture of society was so different from anything that man, in his natural state, has ever framed, that the name gave a new word to the language, and all projects for the improvement of man's condition which are obviously impracticable have come to be called utopian. The word utopia is from the Greek words *ou*, not, and *topos*, a place; meaning, therefore, nowhere.

Vaccination, as a preventive of small-pox, was discovered by Dr. Edward Jenner, an English physician. His attention was directed to the subject upon casually hearing that persons engaged in milking cows frequently had the cow-pox, a mild disorder of the eruptive kind appearing on the udder of the animal, and communicated in a similar form to their hands, and that the belief was common among the agricultural classes that whoever had taken the disease was secure against the infection of small-pox. After frequent experiments he ascertained that only one form of the eruption on the cow's udder possessed this property, a number of these experiments being made upon his son, a boy six years old. He labored against opposition for many years before the value of his discovery was acknowledged by the medical profession. There are several places in the United States where a business is made of supplying the market with "vaccine points"—small quills, with a coating of the cow-virus on the ends. The name is derived from *vacca*, meaning a cow.

Vacuum.—This word means, literally, empty space, or space wholly devoid of matter. In this sense, the results of modern scientific investigation tend to prove that a vacuum cannot exist, as all space is pervaded by the imponderable elastic fluid called ether, whose existence must be allowed to explain the transmission of light and heat from distant luminous bodies. [See *Undulatory Theory of Light*.] In common language, a vacuum (more or less perfect) is said to be produced when ordinary ponderable matter, as air, has been removed from the interior of a closed vessel. Until the beginning of the present century the most perfect vacuum that could be obtained was what is called the Torricellian vacuum—*i. e.*, the space above the mercury in a carefully-filled barometer-tube. Such a vacuum is, however, almost useless for experimental purposes; and, besides, it contains mercurial vapor. By modern scientific methods and appliances a vacuum may be obtained in which there is left less than 1-135,000 of the original volume of air. An ordinary air-pump in good working order will remove all but about 1-120 of the air in the receiver. The old phrase that "Nature abhors a vacuum" was used to account for various phenomena in the past—among them the rise of water in pumps. Most of these are now well understood, the simple natural laws governing them. Water, for instance, rises in a tube, when the air is exhausted above it, owing to the pressure of the atmosphere on the open surface of the liquid in which the end of the tube is immersed. This pressure or weight of the atmosphere is equal to the weight of a column of water about thirty-two feet high, and, accordingly, will raise the water to this height.

Valentinians, a Gnostic sect or school [see *Gnostics*] founded by Valentinus, who went from Alexandria to Rome about A. D. 140. The distinguishing feature of his system lies, in the first place, in his recognizing heathenism as a preparatory stage of Christianity, and then his dividing the higher spiritual world into fifteen pairs of æons, each consisting of a male and a female. The first pair, or syzygy, is made up of Bythos, or God in himself, and Ennsia, or God as existing in his own thoughts. From these emanated, next, Nous (Intelligence) and Aletheia (Truth), and so on. As the last æon, Sophia, transgressed the bounds that had been laid down by the æon Heros, and a part of her being became lost in Chaos, there was formed a crude being called Achanroth, which, through the Demiurgos that emanated from it, created the corporeal world. Heros now imparted to the souls of men (for all the bodies composing the corporeal world are possessed of souls) a *pneumatic* or spiritual element; but this only attained to full activity when Christ, a collective emanation from all the æons, appeared as a Saviour and united himself with the man Jesus. In the end all that is pneumatic, and even the originally psychic or soul element in as far as it has assimilated itself to the psychic, will return into the Pleroma.

Valley of Death.—On the Island of Java is an oval-shaped hollow, near the summit of a mountain, about thirty-five feet in depth and half a mile wide, which, from the deadly nature of its atmosphere, is known as the "Valley of Death," or the "Poison Valley." This atmosphere is loaded with carbonic-acid gas, and although not at once fatal to human beings, proves so to either dogs or fowls. The valley has seldom been explored much beyond the borders, as from there it is seen that the surface of the ground is strewn with the bones of tigers, pigs, deer and all kinds of birds, and also of human beings. There is also a valley known by a similar name in the county of Inyo, California, between the Paramint Mountains and the Armargosa range. It is forty miles long by about eight miles broad, and its bed in its deepest part lies 150 feet below the level of the sea. Every part of this valley is desert. Its topography and climate have never been accurately observed, for human beings cannot live long enough in its atmosphere to ascertain the needed facts. In the coolest and highest part the thermometer often stands at 125 degrees, so that the deadly quality of the air is perhaps only its intense heat; still it is surmised, as the valley is of volcanic formation, that deadly gases may be emitted from cracks in the rocks.

Valley of the Jordan.—El Huleh (called also the Waters of Merom) is the largest northern body of water which contributes to the Jordan. On the north of the lake is an impenetrable jungle, the wallowing-place of buffaloes. There is a marsh bordering the lake which is ten miles long, and which is covered with reeds and brushes; but on the west there is a fertile plain. From Lake Huleh to the Sea of Galilee (the Lake of Gennesaret) the river passes sluggishly over its bed for a short distance, then over a rocky bed, where it deposits its mud, and then rushes on through a narrow volcanic valley; finally, thirteen miles or so below, it enters Gennesaret. This lake is surrounded by an almost continuous wall of hills, broken or receding occasionally, as at Tiberias, the plain of Gennesaret, and at the Jordan. The river issues from the southern extremity of this lake, and enters a broad valley, or depressed plain or tract, between the mountains. During the spring floods this "lower plain" is inundated; then it plunges over some twenty-seven formidable rapids, and then on to the Dead Sea. The whole distance from the sources of the river to its mouth is not more than 136 miles in a straight line. The cities which in Bible times stood on the lakes and in the valley of the Jordan are generally ruins, and only groups of squalid huts now occupy their sites. In the valley the heat of summer is always great, and sometimes exceedingly oppressive. There are only two seasons—summer and winter—the former, from April to November, rainless or nearly so; the latter, from November to April, rainy. Generally speaking, the country has such products as peas, beans, wheat, barley, grapes, figs, olives, apricots, lemons, oranges and dates. Above the Lake of Tiberias there is a bridge across the Jordan called Jacob's Bridge, over which the road from Damascus to the sea-coast passes.

Vampire.—According to the popular belief of the Slavonic, Romanic and Greek population of the Lower Danube and the Thessalonian Peninsula, the vampire was a blood-sucking ghost. In the mythology of the ancient Greeks, beings of a similar nature existed—the Lamias, beautiful phantom women, who by all sorts of voluptuous delusions allured youths to them in order to feast on their fresh, young and pure blood and flesh. Thessaly, Epirus, and the Wallachians of the Pindus knew another kind of vampire still, which were living men, who by night left their shepherd-dwellings, and, roving about, bit and tore everything they met. Among the Greek Christians there is a belief that the bodies of those who have died in excommunication are kept by the devil in a kind of life; that they go forth from their graves by night and suddenly destroy other men; and also, by other means, procure food. They are called Burkolakka, or Tympanita; and the only way of escaping from their molestation is by digging up their unwashed corpses and burning them, after the removal of the excommunication. According to the popular belief of the Wallachians, every one who is killed by a vampire becomes himself a vampire; and as an outward sign of the vampire-bite usually remains, although not always visible and recognizable by every one, a skilled person, generally a midwife, is called in at the obsequies of every person, of whatever age or sex, to take precautions against the corpse becoming a vampire. These precautions usually consist in driving a long nail through the skull; the body is rubbed in various places with the lard of a pig killed on St. Ignatius'-Day, and a stick made of the stem of a wild rose is laid beside it.

Vampire-Bats.—The vampire-bat is a large South American species of bat whose natural food is insects, but who, when pressed by hunger, will suck blood. In some parts of South America they are very numerous, and domestic animals suffer greatly from their nocturnal attacks. They seem to take advantage of an existing wound, but it is said they can also make one. In parts of Brazil the rearing of calves is impossible, on account of these bats; and there are districts, chiefly those in which limestone-rocks prevail, with numerous caves, in which cattle cannot be profitably kept. They sometimes attack men when sleeping in the open air, but the stories of their fanning their victims with their wings while they suck their blood are fabulous.

Varicose Veins.—When a vein becomes dilated at a certain part of its course, for no apparent physiological object, it is said to be varicose. Certain conditions of the system favor the formation of varices, among which may be noticed an indolent temperament and a debilitated condition of the general system, accompanied by a relaxed state of the walls of the veins; and possibly, also, a congenital predisposition or hereditary tendency. Persons with such a predisposition are more likely to suffer from this affection if their occupation is one which involves much standing or walking; and cooks, washerwomen and foot-soldiers have been selected as specially prone to varicose veins. Varices may occur at almost any period of life, but are chiefly developed during middle age. Their formation is aided by any condition of the system which impedes the circulation, as certain diseases of the heart, lungs and liver, and by continued *high living*, which is especially liable to induce hemorrhoids. Varices occurring in the leg commonly give rise to deep-seated aching pain in the limb, with a sense of weight, fullness and numbness, before there is any external appearance of the affection. In a more advanced stage the ankles swell in the evening, and the feet are always cold. After a time a small tumor of a bluish tint appears, which disappears on pressure, but returns on the removal of the pressure, and is caused by a dilating vein. This dilatation extends, and forms knotty, irregular tumors, soft to the touch, diminishing on pressure or on the patient assuming a horizontal position, and giving a bluish tint to the adjacent skin.

Vaudeville.—The name Vaudeville is a corruption of Vaux de Vire, the name of two picturesque valleys in the Bocage of Normandy, and was originally applied to a song with words relating to some story of the day. These songs were first composed by one Oliver Basselin, a fuller in Vire; they were very popular and spread all over France, and were called by the name of their native place (Les Vaux de Vire). As the origin of the term was soon lost sight of, it at last took its present form. The word is now used to signify a play in which dialogue is interspersed with songs incidentally introduced, but forming an important part of the drama.

Vauxhall Garden was first opened in 1660 and was situated in Lambeth, opposite Millbank, and near the manor called Fulke's Hall, from which it derived its name. For nearly two centuries it was the favorite resort for a large class of London pleasure-seekers; but toward the latter part of the eighteenth century it fell into disrepute through the increasing laxity of the morals of many of its patrons, and on July 25, 1859, it was closed, and shortly afterward its site was laid out into streets and built upon. The garden contained beautiful walks, fountains, booths and buildings, and, according to Pepys, the entertainments there to be had were "mighty devirtising."

Vedas and Puranas, as the great body of the sacred literature of the Hindoos is called, are written in poetry in the most ancient form of the Sanscrit language. The Vedas, which were believed to be inspired, treat of the thirty-three gods of the heavens, of the air and of the earth; of the creation of all things, of the relation of the gods to each other, and the relations and duties of men to each other and to the gods; of surgery, medicine, music, dancing, war, architecture, mechanical arts, astronomy, astrology, grammar, poetry, etc. The Puranas are eighteen in number, and are regarded with great reverence as the production of holy men. They treat of law, theology, including histories of their gods, logic and metaphysics in general, but are filled in the main with superstitions and silly and disgusting narratives.

Veiled Prophet.—Mokanna, the Veiled Prophet, as he was called, was a Moslem impostor whose real name was Haken Ibn Hashem. He was by trade a fuller, and was born near the middle of the eighth century. He pretended to be an embodiment of the living Spirit of God, and being proficient in jugglery, which went for the power of working miracles, soon drew many disciples and followers around him who had implicit faith in his pretensions. He always wore a gilded mask, upon the ground that his countenance was too brilliant to be borne by ordinary mortals, but actually, it is supposed, for the purpose of hiding the deformity of his face. At last the Caliph al Mohdi, finding him growing more and more formidable every day, sent a force against him which finally drove him back into the Castle of Keh, north of the Oxus, where he first poisoned and burned all his family and then threw himself into the flames, which consumed him completely except his hair. He left a message, however, to the effect that he would reappear in the shape of a gray man riding on a gray beast, and many of his followers for many years after expected his reappearance, and they wore as a distinguishing mark nothing but white garments.

Veils.—This familiar article of dress is one of the most ancient in use. Its origin is lost in remoteness, but we find an allusion to the wearing of veils by the Chinese in Ovid, and Juvenal speaks of women as being so delicate as to be overheated by a silken veil. Although generally considered portions of female dress, we read, in the works of Ambrose (A. D. 374), of "silken garments and veils interwoven with gold, with which the body of the rich man is encompassed." Its use is now so extended that it may be found in every part of the civilized world.

Velocity of Sound.—A full human voice speaking in the open air, when it is calm, can be heard at a distance of 460 feet; a powerful human voice, speaking in an observable breeze, with the wind, is audible at a distance of 15,840 feet; the report of a musket, 16,000 feet; a strong brass band, 15,840 feet; a drum, 10,560 feet; very heavy cannonading, 90 miles. Conversation has been maintained over water a distance of 6,696 feet in the arctic regions. The velocity of sound in gases increases with the temperature; in air this increase is about two feet per second for each degree, centigrade. The velocity of sound in fresh water at a temperature of 15 degrees, centigrade, is 4,174 feet per second, as determined by experiments made in the Lake of Geneva in 1827. In air it moves at the rate of about 1,090 feet per second.

Vendetta, the term used to denote the practice, as it prevails in Corsica, of individuals taking private vengeance upon those who have shed the blood of their relatives. The origin of the vendetta has often been referred to the lawlessness which prevailed in many parts of Corsica during the period of the Genoese domination, and to the venality which vitiated the Genoese administration of justice. The women instigate the men to revenge by singing songs of vengeance over the body of the slain, and displaying his blood-stained garments. Often a mother affixes to her son's dress a bloody shred from the dead man's shirt, that he may have a constant reminder of the duty of taking vengeance. If a murderer succeeds in eluding pursuit, the murder may be revenged upon his relatives; and as the vengeance may be taken whenever an opportunity occurs, the relatives of a murderer whose crime is unavenged have to live in a state of incessant precaution. Instances are on record of persons who were, as the phrase is, "suffering the vendetta," having lived shut up in their houses for ten or fifteen years, and being, after all, shot on the first occasion when they ventured out of doors. The duty of taking vengeance lies primarily and especially upon the next of kin. Not to take revenge is deemed in the highest degree dishonorable, and any delay in doing so on the part of the next of kin is made matter of reproach by his relatives.

Venus, Statues of.—The Roman goddess of love and beauty, subsequently identified with the Greek Aphrodite, was a favorite subject of ancient sculptors. The most famous specimen still existing is the Venus de Medici, executed by Cleomenes, the Athenian, about 200 B. C., and generally admitted to be the finest relic of ancient art. It was dug up in several pieces, either at the villa of Hadrian, near Tivoli, or at the Portico of Octavia, in Rome, in the seventeenth century. After remaining for some time in the Medici Palace in Rome (whence its name) it was carried to Florence, by Cosmo III, about 1680, where it is now preserved in the Uffizi Gallery. From the exquisite grace and symmetry of the figure it has become a sort of standard of excellence for the female form. The beautiful Venus de Milo is so called because it was found on the Island of Milo, or Melos, in the Grecian Archipelago. It is now in the Louvre, at Paris. Of modern statues, that by Canova is the most famous.

Vermouth is the name of a French cordial, or *liqueur*, distilled from aromatic herbs.

Veto, from *veto* (Latin), I forbid, signifies the act of one branch of Government in forbidding and preventing the carrying into effect of the vote or resolution of another branch of Government. Every Government with co-ordinate departments has provided that each may put a check upon the acts of the others. In England the Crown has a theoretical right to prohibit any action on the part of Parliament; but this right has not been exercised since 1707. In the United States the President has a right of veto of the Acts of Congress; but in case of such veto Congress may reconsider, and by a vote of two-thirds of each house may pass the bill over the veto. The various States have made similar rules in regard to their State Governments. The Roman veto differed from that of modern times in that it was absolute, and no majority could pass a bill to which it was interposed. A *pocket veto* occurs in case the legislative session ends before the time limited for a veto, without any act of acceptance on the part of the officer or body having the power of veto. In that case it is presumed that such officer or body has not had opportunity for action, and the bill fails.

Vicar.—The word "vicar" (Latin *vicarius*) is formed of a compound of two Latin words, *vicem gerens*, and signifies "acting in the place of another." The word is applied to any ecclesiastic who holds the place and exercises the functions of another person or corporation. In the English Church, a vicar is generally one who holds a parochial office, not in his own right, but as a representative of one of the monastic bodies who own the living, and is different from the *parson*, who holds the office in his own right. The term is also used in the Roman Catholic Church. The vicars of the Pope are called "vicars-apostolic," and are invested with the authority of a bishop, and may act in districts where there is no bishop. Vicars of a bishop may be vicars-general, with the full authority of a bishop throughout a whole diocese, or "vicars-forane," with powers limited to a particular district. A "vicar-capitular" is an officer elected by the chapter of a diocese, during the vacancy of the See, to look after the government of the diocese, but with no power to perform episcopal functions, as ordination and confirmation.

Village Communities.—The village community was the early political unit of the Germanic nations. It consisted of a body of persons united theoretically, at least, by kinship, and living together within certain territorial limits. The village community varied among different peoples and at different periods of history. The German "mark," which takes its name from the boundary surrounding the village and shutting it off from the rest of the world, may be taken as the type. The community comprised a number of families who were supposed to have descended from a common ancestor. Each head of a family owned as his absolute personal property a house and small lot of land, and this descended on his death to one of his sons, although not necessarily the eldest one. These houses were clustered in the center of the mark. The land about was divided into three strips, of value varying according to its fertility and accessibility. These were, in turn, divided into lots. Each householder received as his portion a lot in each of these strips for a term of from one to ten years, at the end of which time a redistribution of the land was made. The government of the mark was largely patriarchal. The heads of families possessed unlimited power, including power of life and death over their children. They met annually in council to decide disputes, redistribute land, admit new-comers and make new laws—thus including all acts of a legislative or judicial nature. Such was the village community in a high stage of perfection. In all portions of its history its nature was essentially the same, its characteristics being (1) a form of common property in land and (2) a patriarchal government. The village community was formerly regarded as peculiar to the Aryan civilization, but this position has now been abandoned. It is common to all peoples in primitive stages. The clan of the Celts was one form. The Greek *Genos* was another. Sparta was formed of a union of village communities. Early Rome had a similar origin. Later, Greece and Rome became illustrations of the city idea, and circumstances cut off the further development of the village communities. In India, Russia and Java the village community reached a thorough development. In parts of England the assembly of the elders extended into the sixteenth century, and the parish vestry still remains as a relic of it. In the Orkney and Shetland Islands, Sir Walter Scott noted the mark system in his own lifetime. In Switzerland, Russia and Java the system exists in a modified form to-day.

Violin.—The origin of the violin can be traced back to a stringed instrument called the ravanastron, invented, it is believed, in 5000 B. C., by Ravana, King of Ceylon. The crwth, which was in use in Wales long before the sixth century, and to which the Anglo-Saxons gave the name of fythel, whence our fiddle, was a similar instrument. The violin of modern form was not made until the fifteenth or sixteenth centuries, and its earliest maker was Gaspard di Salo, of Lombardy; and the Italian school of violin-making was probably founded by him at Brescia. These Brescian instruments—that is to say, those made by Giovanni Paolo Magini, still hold a place among the best ever made. It was not long, however, after the establishment of the Brescian school when the makers of Cremona began to produce instruments which have been objects of wonder and admiration from their time to the present. The three greatest Cremonese makers were Nicholas Amati, Joseph Guarneri del Gesu and Antonius Stradivarius. To those who at the present time willingly pay hundreds and even thousands of dollars for a violin made by one of these great makers, it may be of interest to know that they all were simple, hard-working artisans, who sold their works of genius for a few florins.

Volapuk, or the "universal language," as it is called, is the invention of a German Roman Catholic priest, Johann Martin Schleyer of Constance, in Baden. He published his system in 1870. On account of its extreme simplicity—its grammar contains no artificial genders, a single conjugation, and no irregular verbs—it is very easily acquired. The Volapuk dictionary contains 14,000 words, while any imaginable new word may be easily formed by composition. No sound is employed which is not common the world over, every word is accented on the last syllable, and the orthography is strictly phonetic. The name is from *vola*, of the world, and *puk*, language. It is estimated that over 10,000 persons in Europe have mastered it, and it has been tried to a considerable extent in America also.

Volcanoes.—Volcanoes differ greatly in their dimensions, some being vast mountain masses rising thousands of feet above the sea-level, while others are mere mole-hills. They also exhibit every stage of development and decay, some being in a state of chronic eruption, others only showing activity at long intervals, and yet others having been so long dormant that they can fairly be regarded as extinct. The number of great habitual volcanic vents on the globe still known to be in action is estimated at between 300 and 350. Most of these are marked by mountains of greater or less size. Three of the best known volcanoes of the world—Vesuvius, 3,978 feet; Hecla, 3,970 feet, and Stromboli, 3,000 feet—are of much less elevation than many others altogether unfamiliar. The height, names and locations of twenty-four of the loftiest volcanoes of the world are as follows: Sahama, Peru, 23,000 feet; Llullaillac, Chili, 21,000 feet; Arequipa, Peru, 20,500 feet; Cayambi, Ecuador, 19,813 feet; Cotopaxi, Peru, 19,500 feet; Antisana, Ecuador, 19,200 feet; San Jose, Chili, 18,150 feet; Mount St. Elias, Alaska, 17,900 feet; Popocatepetl, Mexico, 17,884 feet; Orizaba, Mexico, 17,370 feet; Altar, Ecuador, 17,126 feet; Sangai, Ecuador, 17,120 feet; Klintchevskaia, Kamtchatka, 16,512 feet; Iztacihuatl, Mexico, 15,700 feet; Toluco, Mexico, 15,500 feet; Shasta, United States, 14,400 feet; Fujiyama, Japan, 14,000 feet; Mauna Kea, Sandwich Islands, 13,953 feet; Mauna Loa, Sandwich Islands, 13,760 feet; Teneriffe, Canary Islands, 12,236 feet; Mount St. Helens, United States, 12,000 feet; Mount Hood, United States, 11,225 feet; Peak of Tahiti, Friendly Islands, 10,895 feet; Mount Ætna, Sicily, 10,874 feet.

Voluntary Associations.—A voluntary association is an aggregation of individuals organized, without especial authority of the State, to further some business, social, religious or charitable object. Instances of such associations are ordinary social clubs, many church organizations, literary and scientific societies, and political associations. They differ from corporations in that they require no act of the State to perfect their organization. They resemble partnerships in many of their features, but differ from them in that each member is bound by the acts of the others only so far as they were expressly or impliedly authorized by himself. Thus, such a member is not bound by an act of the association to which he did not agree, but voted against and did all in his power to prevent. A voluntary association can and often does hold property, and such property remains with the association through any changes of membership. No member can withdraw and take his portion with him. Voluntary associations are now exceedingly common in all highly-developed societies, and have been formed to carry out almost every conceivable purpose. The name "voluntary association" is also sometimes used to denote corporations formed under a general incorporation law.

Vulgate, The, the Latin translation of the Bible, which is the received version in the Roman Catholic Church. The original

Vulgate was completed in A. D. 405 by Jerome, and between that date and 1546, when it was first declared the authorized version of the Roman Church, it underwent several revisions which completely changed the character of the work. In the latter year the Tridentine Council decreed the preparation of an authentic edition, and the task was undertaken by the Papal Chair; but it was not until 1590 that Sixtus V produced the work. This, however, turned out to be so utterly incorrect and faulty throughout that the copies were speedily suppressed, and another edition, which appeared in 1592, was prepared under Clement VIII, to which, in the next year (1593), that other edition succeeded, which has since remained the normal edition of the Church of Rome, and has been reprinted, unchanged, ever since.

Waits is a name which has at successive periods been given to different classes of musical watchmen. The word, in slightly varied forms, is one common, in the sense of guard or watchman, to all the Germanic languages. It is the German *wacht* or *wache*, Dutch *wagt*, Danigh *vaght*, Swedish *wakt*, Scotch *wate*, and the English *watch*. In the time of Edward IV the waits appear to have formed a distinct class from both the watch and the minstrels. It was their duty to pipe the watch nightly, in the King's court, from Michaelmas to Shrove-Thursday, four times; in the summer-nights, three times; and to make "the *bon gayte*" at every chamber-door and office, for fear of "pycheres and pillars." The waits were not confined to the court, however, for there were musical watchmen at an early period in many provincial towns. The word, in the provinces, was afterward sometimes applied to the town musicians, who may have represented the old waits, but who had no duties to perform. At present the waits are musicians who play during the night or early in the morning at Christmas-time, in expectation of receiving a Christmas-box from those they serenade.

Wake.—The word "wake," which is now used to designate a custom of watching the dead peculiar to the Irish, originally had a different signification. In early times the day was considered as beginning and ending at sunset. Sundays and holidays, in consequence, began not on the morning, but on the previous evening, and worshipers then repaired to the churches for worship. Each church, when consecrated, was dedicated to a saint, and on the anniversary of that day was kept the parish wake, and in many places there was a second wake on the birthday of the saint. On these occasions the floor of the church was strewed with flowers and rushes, and the altar and pulpit were decked with boughs and leaves. In the church-yard, tents were erected to supply cakes and ale for the use of the people on the morrow, which was kept as a holiday. Crowds resorted to the wakes from neighboring parishes, hawkers or merchants were attracted by the crowds, and ultimately they became mere fairs or markets, little under influence of the church, and disgraced by scenes of indulgence

and riot. In 1536, during the reign of Henry VIII, it was ordered
that the day of the dedication of the church be kept in all parishes
on the first Sunday in October, and gradually that festival ceased
to be observed; but the saint's-day festivals are still kept in many
English parishes under the name of "country wakes." The
watching of the dead was known originally as a *lyke-wake*, or
liche-wake, and probably had its origin in a superstitious fear
either of passing the night alone with a dead body or of its being
interfered with by evil spirits.

Walhalla.—According to Scandinavian mythology, those who
fell in battle were transported to a brilliant hall, in front of which
was the beautiful grove Glasur, the trees of which bore golden
fruit. This was called Walhalla. Before the hall, which was so
high that its summit could scarcely be seen, a wolf was hung, as a
symbol of war, over which sat an eagle. The saloon itself, orna-
mated with shields and wainscoted with spears, had 540 doors,
through each of which 800 of the inmates could walk abreast.
Renowned chiefs—especially if they had desolated many countries and wielded the blood-dripping sword far and wide—were
met and welcomed by Bragi and Hermode, as messengers from
Odin. The hall was decorated to honor them, and all the divine
heroes stood up at their reception. All kings came to Walhalla,
even though they did not die on the battle-field. In general, these
joys seem to have been prepared only for those of high rank and
the rich. As it was honorable to come to Walhalla with a great
retinue, and to possess many treasures, the comrades of a leader
who had fallen in battle kill'd themselves of their own free will,
and in his grave were laid, along with his horse and arms, the
treasures won in fight. Every morning the inmates marched out
at the crowing of the cock and fought furiously with one another;
but at midday all wounds healed, and the heroes assembled to
feast with Odin.

Walkyries.—The name "Walkyries" is derived from the old
Norse *val*, which signifies a heap of slaughtered men, and *kjora*,
to choose. In the Scandinavian mythology the Walkyries, also
called battle-maidens, shield-maidens, and wish-maidens, are
beautiful young women who, adorned with golden ornaments, ride
through the air in brilliant armor, order battles and distribute the
death-lots according to Odin's command. Fertilizing dew drops on
the ground from the manes of their horses, light streams from
the points of their lances, and a flickering brightness announces
their arrival in the battle. They rejoice the glazing eye of the
hero with their charming glances, and lead him to Walhalla,
where they act as his cup-bearers. Some of the Walkyries spring
from elves and other superhuman beings; some, also, are the
daughters of princes. They ride generally in companies of three,
or of three times three, or four times three, and have the gift of
changing themselves into swans. Whoever deprives a Walkyrie
of her swan-robe, gets her into his power.

Wandering Jew, The.—There are several versions of the story of "The Wandering Jew." A popular tradition makes the wanderer a member of the tribe of Naphtali, who, some seven or eight years previous to the birth of Christ, left his father to go with the Wise Men of the East, whom the star led to the lowly cot in Bethlehem. It runs, also, that the cause of the killing of the children can be traced to the stories this person related, when he returned to Jerusalem, of the visit of the wise men and the presentation of the gifts they brought to the Divine Infant when He was acknowledged by them to be the King of the Jews. He was lost sight of for a time, when he appeared as a carpenter who was employed in making the cross on which the Saviour was to be lifted up unto the eyes of all men. As Christ walked up the way to Calvary He had to pass the workshop of this man, and when He reached its door, the soldiers, touched by His sufferings, besought the carpenter to allow Him to rest there for a little; but he refused, adding insult to want of charity. Then it is said that Christ pronounced his doom, which was to wander over the earth until the second coming. Since that sentence was uttered he has wandered, courting death but finding it not, and his punishment becoming more unbearable as the generations come and go. He is said to have appeared in the sixteenth, seventeenth, and even as late as the eighteenth century, under the names of Cartaphilus and Ahasuerus, by which the Wandering Jew has been known. One of the legends describes him as a shoemaker of Jerusalem, at whose door Christ desired to rest on the road to Calvary; but the man refused, and the sentence to wander was pronounced. Another version is that he was a servant in the house of Pilate, and gave the Master a blow as He was being dragged out of the palace to go to His death.

War Department, Salaries in.—The salaries of the officials of the War Department of the United States are as follows: Secretary of War, $8,000 per annum; Chief Clerk, $2,500; Adjutant-General, $5,500; Inspector-General, $5,500; Quartermaster-General, $5,500; Commissary-General, $5,500; Surgeon-General, $4,500; Paymaster-General, $5,500; Chief of Engineers, $5,500; Chief of Ordnance, $5,500; Acting Judge-Advocate General, $5,500; Chief Signal Officer, $5,500.

Wars of the United States.—The wars of the United States and the number of United States troops engaged in each have been as follows: War of the Revolution, April 19, 1775, to April 11, 1783, 309,781 men; Northwestern Indian wars, September 19, 1790, to August 3, 1795, 8,983 men; war with France, July 9, 1798, to September 30, 1800, 4,593 men; war with Tripoli, June 10, 1801, to June 4, 1805, 3,330 men; Creek Indian war, July 27, 1813, to August 9, 1814, 13,781 men; war of 1812 with Great Britain, June 18, 1812, to February 17, 1815, 576,662 men; Seminole Indian war, November 20, 1817, to October 21, 1818, 7,911 men; Black Hawk Indian war, April 21, 1831, to September 31, 1832, 6,465 men;

Creek Indian war, May 5, 1836, to September 30, 1837, 13,418 men; Florida Indian war, December 23, 1835, to August 14, 1843, 41,122 men; war with Mexico, April 24, 1846, to July 4, 1848, 112,230 men; Apache, Navajo and Utah war, 1849 to 1855, 2,561 men; Seminole Indian war, 1850 to 1858, 3,687 men; Civil War, 1861 to 1865, 2,772,408 men. The number of troops on the Confederate side, in the Civil War, was about 600,000.

Washington City, Government of.—The government of the city of Washington, D. C., is controlled by a Board of Regents, consisting of three persons, appointed by the President and confirmed by the Senate. This Board exercises the chief executive authority for the District and the city. Its members are appointed for four years, and are removable for good and sufficient cause only. There are a number of bureaus, each controlled by a board of officers under its supervision. These relate to and embrace the entire civil service of the District, except such as falls under the executive departments and the courts, and are known as the Boards of Health, Education, Police, Excise, Public Works, Fire and Buildings. With the exception of the Board of Education, part of whose members are elected by the residents of the District, and the controlling officer of the Board of Public Works, who is appointed by the President from the engineer corps of the army, the members of the several boards are appointed by the Regents. There is also a municipal court which has exclusive civil jurisdiction in matters noncognizable by justices of the peace, and any judge of this court may be designated by the Supreme Court of the District to hold a term and sessions of the police court if necessary. Assessors chosen by the Board of Regents apportion the taxes of the city and District, which are collected by the collector of internal revenue for the District, and are by him paid into the United States Treasury. All other sums collected for fines, etc., are also paid into the United States Treasury, and all disbursements for salaries or for other municipal expenses are made from the United States Treasury. A yearly report, covering all transactions for the year past, is made by the Board of Regents to the President, and in turn submitted to Congress for approval.

Washington Monument.—Notwithstanding the fact that the plan of a monument to General Washington was approved by Congress in the latter part of December, 1799, nothing was done in the matter until 1833, when an association of prominent persons undertook the raising of the needed funds by subscription, and on July 4, 1848, had so far succeeded in their undertaking that the corner-stone of a monument was laid, and during the succeeding eight years the shaft was carried to a height of 156 feet. The work was then suspended, at first for lack of funds, then because of the Civil War, and finally because the foundations were believed to be insecure. In 1876 Congress undertook the completion of the monument. The base was first strengthened, and the work of rebuilding the shaft was resumed in August, 1880, and was finished August 9, 1884. The shaft is 555 feet high, and the entire height of the monument, including the foundations, is 592 feet. The base is 55 feet 1½ inch square. At 500 feet above the ground the monument has four sides, each of which is 35 feet wide. Its area at this point is that of a comfortable six-room house, each room of which might be 12x16 feet. This square forms the base of the pyramidal top which runs from it 55 feet until it terminates in a metallic point. This point is constructed of the largest piece of aluminum ever made. The stones of which the monument is constructed are great blocks of crystal marble from Maryland, and in some cases are 9 feet long, 2 feet thick, and 3 or more feet wide. There are more than 18,000 of them. The foundation is built of Potomac gneiss, and is 81 feet square at the base. One hundred and eighty-one "memorial stones" have from first to last been contributed for use in the monument; but many were considered unworthy of a place, and one sent by Pope Pius IX, in 1855, was stolen during the Know-Nothing agitation, and was broken into pieces and thrown into the Potomac River. The monument was dedicated with imposing ceremonies on February 22, 1885. Its cost was about $1,500,000, which was raised partially by an appropriation by Congress and partially by private subscription. It is 30 feet higher than any other work of man except the great iron Eiffel Tower erected in Paris for the great Exposition of 1889.

Washington's Inauguration, Centennial Celebration of.— There has been considerable discussion as to who is entitled to the credit of having first suggested the idea of the Washington Centennial, but the discussion would appear to be, to a great extent, a very trifling one. On the night of the day when Grover Cleveland was inaugurated President of the United States (March 4, 1885) the New York Historical Society held a stated meeting, and, after resolving that the centennial anniversary of the inauguration of George Washington should be celebrated, a committee was appointed to report a plan for the carrying out of the purpose of the Society in a manner suitable to the occasion—the commemoration of the most important event in the history of the city, the State, and the nation. Nothing practical, however, came of the Historical Society's movement; and nearly two years later the New York Chamber of Commerce went through substantially the same formula, with somewhat more imposing results but nothing of a more practical nature. The Chamber of Commerce resolutions, which were introduced by Nathaniel Niles, declared that the day was "the birthday of the Government of the United States," and asked for the appointment of a committee of five to consider and report appropriate action. The committee of five was accordingly appointed, and made a first report April 1, 1886. This report suggested the appointing of a special committee to prepare a bill to be presented to Congress for the purpose of having April 30, 1889, made a national holiday, and securing an appropriation from

Congress. On May 6, 1886, the President of the Chamber of Commerce appointed a special committee on the Centennial Anniversary; but this terminated the Chamber of Commerce movement. No further attempt toward preparing for the Washington Centennial was made after the Chamber of Commerce meeting in May, 1886, until the fall of 1887. At that time Col. Jesse Enlows Peyton of Haddonfield, N. J., an old Quaker gentleman who has been identified with all the centennial demonstrations from the time of the one in commemoration of the battle of Bunker Hill, came to New York, and in consultation with Algernon Sullivan determined on a call for a meeting of citizens. This call was dated October 10, 1887, and was numerously signed by the leading merchants, lawyers and bankers of New York. In response to it, a meeting was held at the Fifth Avenue Hotel on the evening of November 10, 1887, at which ex-Mayor Hewitt was elected chairman. The result of this meeting was that the Chamber of Commerce and the Historical Society were requested to confer with a committee to be named by the Mayor and organize a general committee, to consist of thirteen members. This committee was afterward consolidated with committees from the Historical Society and a committee of five from the Chamber of Commerce, and a committee, also, from the Society of the Sons of the Revolution— so that its number was increased to fifty-nine members. This was ultimately increased, by the addition of names of prominent citizens, until the committee numbered two hundred. This was known as the General Committee of Two Hundred, the president of which was Hamilton Fish. There were eleven sub-committees at first, but they were ultimately reduced to ten by the consolidation of the Committee on Art and the Committee on Exhibition. The chairmen of the various sub-committees were as follows: Executive, Eldridge T. Gerry; Plan and Scope, Hon. Hugh J. Grant; States, William G. Hamilton; General Government, John A. King; Army, S. Van Rensselaer Cruger; Navy, Asa Bird Gardiner; Entertainment, Stuyvesant Fish; Finance, Brayton Ives; Railroads and Transportation, Orlando B. Potter; Art and Exhibition, Henry G. Marquand; Literary Exercises, Eldridge T. Gerry. The committee held meetings during the summer, but nothing of a practical character was done till late in the fall of 1888; but from that time forward the preparations for the celebration were pushed with untiring energy. The programme as ultimately arranged and carried out provided for three days' celebration. On the morning of the first day—April 29, 1889—President Harrison, accompanied by Vice President Morton, the members of his Cabinet, Judges of the Supreme Court, and other notables, arrived in Elizabeth, N. J., from Washington, where they were received and entertained by Governor Green of New Jersey. At the conclusion of the Elizabeth ceremonies the President and his party, following the route taken by Washington, embarked at Elizabethport, on the United States steamer Despatch, for New York. A line of United States ships of war, yachts and steamboats formed in the upper Bay, and each vessel, after saluting, followed the Presidential steamer. This Naval Parade occupied about two hours' time, and during its continuance the Bay presented a more splendid and attractive appearance than It ever did before in its long and picturesque history. On the arrival of the Despatch in the East River opposite Wall Street ferry slip a barge manned by a crew of ship-masters from the Marine Society of the Port of New York, with Captain Ambrose Snow of the Society as cock-swain, rowed the President to the ferry stairs. The crew of the barge that rowed President Washington from Elizabethport to the foot of Wall Street one hundred years previously were members of the same Society. The President was received, on landing, by the Committee on States. At the conclusion of the cere-monies of reception the President and his suit proceeded, under the escort of United States troops, the Veteran Corps of the Sev-enth Regiment of New York, delegations from the Society of the Cincinnati, the Sons of the Revolution, the Loyal Legion, and Commanders of the Grand Army Posts in New York, up Wall Street to the Equitable Building, where, in the rooms of the Law-yers' Club, a reception was given and luncheon served, by the Committee, to the President and the Commissioners from all the States and Territories. The President then proceeded to the Gov-ernor's Room in the City Hall, where a public reception was held. The day's proceedings closed with a ball, given in honor of the President, in the Metropolitan Opera House. On Tuesday, April 30th, a special service of thanksgiving was held at nine o'clock in St. Paul's Church, in Broadway, which was attended by the Presi-dent and other distinguished guests. This service was conducted by the Right Rev. Henry C. Potter, Bishop of New York. Fol-lowing closely upon the religious ceremonies, the literary exer-cises, commemorative of Washington's Inauguration, took place on the steps of the Sub-Treasury Building in Wall Street, the ex-act locality where Washington took the oath on April 30, 1789. These exercises consisted of an opening prayer by Rev. Richard S. Storrs, D.D., LL. D.; a poem by John Greenleaf Whittier; an oration by Hon. Chauncey M. Depew; an address by President Harrison, and the benediction by Most Rev. Michael A. Corrigan, Archbishop of New York. The Military Parade, which took place at the close of the literary exercises, was the grandest of its kind ever attempted in this country. There were at least 52,000 men in line. These were composed of troops from the regular army, ma-rines, sailors and West Point cadets, militia from nearly every State in the Union, and members of the Grand Army of the Republic. The State troops were arranged in the order in which the States entered the Union; and the Governor of each State, accompanied by his staff, rode at the head of his troops. The proceedings of the second day were brought to a close by a banquet given to the President in the Metropolitan Opera House, where tables were laid for eight hundred guests. The great and only feature of the third day of the celebration—Wednesday, May 1st—was the Industrial and Civic Parade. This procession embraced a succession of floats or mounted tableaux, demonstrating the progress of commerce, the arts and trade within the hundred years of our national life. The colossal pageant included the different industries, appropriately interspersed with organizations of many kinds, civic, industrial, educational, political and charitable. It is estimated that at least 120,000 men participated in this parade. The Centennial Celebration was brought to a close on the evening of the third day by a brilliant exhibition of fireworks in different parts of the city. During the continuance of the Washington Centennial the City of New York presented a most gorgeous appearance. All the public and the majority of the private buildings were profusely decorated. There were four triumphal arches erected—one at the head of Fifth Avenue, two on Madison Square, and one on Wall Street. The principal Madison Square arch was 46 feet high in the clear and 77 feet high altogether; the span was 100 feet. Above the keystone of the arch was a life-sized statute of Washington on horseback, made of *papier-mache*. On either side were immense eagles finished in gold, and soldiers in Continental uniform were placed in niches made in the pillars. The one at the head of Fifth Avenue was built to represent white marble, and was after a design by Stanford White, the architect. It elicited so much admiration that a popular movement is now (1889) on foot to raise $100,000 dollars by private subscription and erect it in marble as a memorial of this, the most notable and elaborate celebration that our country has yet seen.

Watches of the Night.—The Jews, like the Greeks and Romans, says the Rev. Dr. William Smith in his "Bible Dictionary," divided the night into watches instead of hours, each watch representing the period for which sentinels or pickets remained on duty. The proper Jewish reckoning recognized only three such watches, entitled the first or "beginning of the watches" (Lamentations ii, 19), the middle watch (Judges vii, 19), and the morning watch (Exodus xiv, 24; I Samuel xi, 11). These would last, respectively, from sunset to ten o'clock P. M., from ten o'clock P. M. to two o'clock A. M., and from two o'clock A. M. to sunrise. After the establishment of the Roman supremacy the number of the watches was increased to four, which were described either according to their numerical order, as in the case of the "fourth watch" (Matthew xiv, 25), or by the terms "even," "midnight," "cockcrowing," and "morning" (Mark xiii, 35). These terminated, respectively, at nine o'clock P. M., midnight, three o'clock A. M. and six o'clock A. M.

Water-Gas.—Much of the illuminating gas now used is made by the comparatively new process in which the main volume of the gas, consisting of hydrogen, is taken out of water. In the original coal-gas process the illuminating agent is obtained directly from the distillation of soft or bituminous coal; and impurities being removed by washing it with water and then passing it through lime, the gas is ready for burning. The new process is, in outline, as follows: Steam is passed through retorts filled with anthracite coal raised to a white heat by an air-blast. In its passage it is decomposed, and the gas issuing from the pipes at the top consists of a mixture of hydrogen and carbon dioxide. This serves as the *carrier* for the true illuminating agents, which are a comparatively small percentage of the entire volume, and these are combined by mingling with naphtha vapor. This mixture has now about the same composition as the ordinary coal-gas, but must be *fixed*—that is, made a stable compound—by subjecting it to the effect of heat and cold. This is accomplished by conducting it through two series of pipes, surrounded in one case by cold running water, and in the other by steam. It is then purified in the same way as mentioned above. By passing it through a water-tower loosely filled with something, as charcoal, down through which water trickles as the gaseous mixture ascends, the ammonia is dissolved out; then, by passing it through thin layers of lime, the other main impurity, sulphuretted hydrogen, is removed. It is then ready for distribution through the city. Its illuminating power is about the same as, or somewhat greater than, that of coal-gas. The water process produces the gas at a much lower cost; but in the other process there are a number of by-products derived from the distillation of the coal—*e. g.*, coke, coal-tar, and also aqua ammonia, which is present in greater quantities in the coal-gas—which are sold, and thus make the entire cost of manufacture about the same in each case.

Watering Stock.—The credit of having originated the process of watering the stock of railroad companies belongs unquestionably to the late Commodore Vanderbilt. The plan of operation is simple, and consists only in estimating the stock of the road at a figure greatly above its real value. For instance, when Commodore Vanderbilt secured control of the New York Central as well as the Hudson River Railroad in 1868, the combined stock of the two roads was only about $36,000,000. Early in the following year he declared a tremendous dividend of new stock to the stockholders, and raised the estimated value of the two roads to $90,000,000. This action of Vanderbilt's was for the purpose of evading a law of the State of New York which provided that when the dividends of any railroad corporation should reach 10 per cent. the State could declare how the surplus above the 10 per cent. should be applied. This provision, it is plain, was rendered nugatory by Vanderbilt's scheme, as, if a railroad can at any time declare stock dividends with no reference whatever to the costs of construction and repair, a dividend of 10 per cent. may never be declared, though the road may be actually earning 30 or 40 per cent. upon its actual cost.

Water-Spouts are whirlwinds occurring on the sea or on lakes.

When fully formed they appear as tall pillars of cloud stretching from the sea to the sky, whirling round on their axes, and exhibiting the progressive movement of the whole mass precisely as in the case of the dust whirlwind. The sea at the base of the whirling vortex is thrown into the most violent commotion, resembling the surface of water in rapid ebullition. It is a popular idea that the water of the sea is sucked up in a solid mass by water-spouts, but it is in fact only the spray from the broken waves which is carried up. What are sometimes called water-spouts on land are quite distinct from these phenomena. They are merely heavy falls of rain of a very local character, and may or may not be accompanied by whirling winds.

Wealth of Nations.—An approximate idea of the wealth of the principal nations of the world is obtained from an estimate made in 1880. At that time the United States were, as they now are, the richest nation on the globe. The Argentine Republic was worth $1,660,000,000; Austria, $18,065,000,000; Australia, $2,950,000,000; Belgium, $4,030,000,000; Canada, $3,250,000,000; Denmark, $1,830,000,000; France, $40,300,000,000; Germany, $31,615,000,000; Great Britain and Ireland, $43,600,000,000; Greece, $1,055,000,000; Italy, $11,755,000,000; Mexico, $3,190,000,000; Netherlands, $4,935,000,000; Norway, $1,410,000,000; Portugal, $1,855,000,000; Russia, $21,715,000,000; Spain, $7,965,000,000; Sweden, $3,475,000,000; Switzerland, $1,620,000,000; United States, $47,475,000,000.

Wedding Anniversaries.—The custom of celebrating wedding anniversaries with peculiar gifts dates back to the mediæval Germans, among whom, if a married couple lived to celebrate the twenty-fifth anniversary of their wedding, the wife was presented by her friends and neighbors with a silver wreath, partly in congratulation of the good fortune that had prolonged the lives of the couple for so many years, and partly in recognition of the fact that they must have known a fairly harmonious existence, otherwise one or the other would long ago have been worried into the grave. On the celebration of the fiftieth anniversary the wife received a wreath of gold. Thus these anniversaries came to be known as the silver wedding-day and the golden wedding-day. This custom has been enlarged upon until we now have the cotton wedding, which is the first anniversary; the paper wedding, second anniversary; the leather wedding, third anniversary; the wooden wedding, fifth anniversary; the woolen wedding, seventh anniversary; the tin wedding, tenth anniversary; the silk and fine linen wedding, twelfth anniversary; the crystal wedding, fifteenth anniversary; the china wedding, twentieth anniversary; the silver wedding, twenty-fifth anniversary; the pearl wedding, thirtieth anniversary; the ruby wedding, fortieth anniversary; the golden wedding, fiftieth anniversary, and the diamond wedding on the seventy-fifth anniversary.

Wednesday.—The name Wednesday is derived from the

northern mythology, and signifies Woden's or Odin's day. The Anglo-Saxon form was *Wodanes dæg*, the old German *Wuotanes tac*. The Swedish and Danish is Onsday. In the Roman calendar it was *dies Mercurii*.

Weighing, Use of Photography in.—Photography is utilized in the construction of a new balance which has lately been brought before the scientific world. In this novel instrument of precision, after the weight has been roughly approximated, instead of continuing the trials in the usual manner the beam is allowed to come to rest, which it quickly does by means of an ingenious air-buffer, and then the extent of the bending of the beam through the difference of the weights is observed by a microscope, fitted with a network of parallel cross-wires, directed to a small micrometer fixed at the end of the beam. This micrometer is made by a photographic process, and carries figures and lines from one-twentieth to one-fiftieth of a millimeter apart. The introduction of Bunge's short-beam balance—comparatively speaking, only a few years ago—almost revolutionized weighing operations, owing to the dispatch with which they can be carried on. It remains to be seen whether the new instrument, in which photography plays a part, will be an epoch-marking one.

Weights and Measures.—The origin of the British weights and measures, from which the American are derived, is obscure. The first recorded reference to them is that they must be uniform throughout the realm. A statute of 1226 founds the measure of capacity on weight. In 1266 a statute founded measures of weight upon determinate numbers of wheat-corns. Besides, at that time, the units of commercial weight were also units of coin weight. It is related that "an English penny, called a sterling, round and without any clipping, shall weigh thirty-two wheat-corns in the midst of the ear, and twenty pence do make an ounce, and twelve ounces one pound, and eight pounds do make a gallon of wine, and eight gallons of wine do make a London bushel, which is the eighth of a quarter." Down to 1496 the pound thus determined, known as the Tower pound, or the sterling or Easterling pound, continued to regulate the metrological system of England, when it was superseded for this purpose by the troy pound, a pound of fifteen ounces, each ounce being equal to 360 troy grains, or to three-quarters of a troy ounce. The present troy and avoirdupois pounds, containing respectively 12 and 16 ounces, were introduced later, but the exact date is not known. The earliest legislation as to measures of length is found in the British statute-book in 1324, and provides that the inch shall be the length of three barley-corns, round and dry, laid end to end; that twelve inches shall make a foot, and three feet a yard. Previous to the Conquest the British yard had about the length of 39.6 inches, but in 1101 it was reduced by being adjusted to the arm of Henry I. This became untrustworthy, however, and then followed the barleycorn measure. The form of words "round and dry," in the barleycorn measure, was intended to indicate that the seeds should be fully developed, perfect, and well-seasoned. Some antiquarians maintain that the English units are derived from the ancient Egyptians, and that they are found everlastingly preserved in certain measurements in the great Pyramid of Cheops at Gizeh. [See *Pyramids*.]

Were-Wolf, a man transformed into a wolf. The belief in the transformation of men into wolves or other beasts of prey has been .ery widely diffused, and in many of the rural districts of France the *loup-garou* (the latter part of the word is a corruption of the Teutonic *wer-wolf*) is still an object of dread. A man who is thus transformed, or transforms himself, was believed to become possessed of all the powers and appetites of a wolf in addition to his own, and to have a remarkable appetite for human flesh. In the fifteenth and sixteenth centuries the belief in werewolves was, throughout the continent of Europe, as general as was the belief in witches, which it had then come to resemble in many respects. It gave rise to prosecutions almost as frequently as those for witchcraft; and these usually ended in a confession of the accused, and his death by hanging and burning. It was calculated to inspire even greater terror than witchcraft, since it was believed that the were-wolves were constantly lying in wait for solitary travelers, and carrying off and eating little children. In Great Britain, where wolves had early been exterminated, the were-wolf was only known by rumors coming from abroad; but the belief that witches could transform themselves into cats and hares, which did prevail, was precisely analogous to the belief in were-wolves.

Westminster Palace was erected in 1840 on the site of the old houses of Parliament, which were destroyed by fire in 1834. It is 900 feet long by 300 feet wide, is built of limestone from the Yorkshire quarries, and cost about $8,000,000. The palace contains the House of Lords and the House of Commons, which are separated by an octagonal hall with a diameter of 70 feet. The House of Lords is 100 feet long, 45 feet wide and 45 feet high. The room is profusely decorated, and in niches between the windows are statues of barons who signed the Magna Charta—eighteen in number. The gorgeously gilt and canopied throne which is occupied by the Queen when she opens Parliament is in this room, as is also the wool-sack—a large, square bag of wool covered with red cloth—of the Chancellor of Great Britain. The House of Commons is not as handsome as the House of Lords in the matter of decorations, and is not so long, but is the same height and width. The palace also contains a number of other rooms, among which are the Queen's robing-room, the guard-room, the libraries, committee-rooms, etc. In the center of the edifice, above what is known as the Octagon Hall, is a tower 300 feet high. At the southwest corner is the Victoria tower, 346 feet high. At the northwest corner is the clock tower, which is surmounted by a belfry spire 320 feet high. In this tower is a clock with four faces, each 30 feet in diameter, and the hours are struck on a bell called "Big Ben," which weighs nine tons. At the southwestern extremity of the building is the state entrance of the Queen, which communicates directly with what are known as the royal apartments. The entrance to the Octagon Hall is by a passage known as Saint Stephen's Hall, which communicates also with Westminster Hall, a much older building, on the north.

West Point Academy.—Each Congressional District and Territory, also the District of Columbia, is entitled to have one cadet at the United States Military Academy at West Point, the cadet to be named by the Representative in Congress. There are also ten appointments at large, specially conferred by the President of the United States. The number of students is thus limited to 344. The course of instruction, which is quite thorough, requires four years, and is largely mathematical and professional. The discipline is very strict—even more so than in the army—and the enforcement of penalties for offenses is inflexible rather than severe. Academic duties begin September 1st and continue until June 1st. From the middle of June to the end of August cadets live in camps, engaged only in military duties, and receiving practical military instruction. Cadets are allowed but one leave of absence during the four years' course, and this is granted at the expiration of the second year. The pay of a cadet is $540 a year. Upon graduation, cadets are commissioned as second lieutenants in the United States army.

Whalebone.—The whalebone known to commerce is the baleen plates, which take the place of teeth in the mouth of the Baleen whales. They vary in length from a few inches up to ten feet, and even, in rare instances, to twelve feet. They terminate at a point in a number of coarse black fibers of the baleen, which fibers are also found more or less down both sides of the blade, and are much used by brushmakers. Whalebone requires more or less preparation before being fit for use.

Wheat Harvest Calendar.—Wheat ripens in the different sections of the globe as follows: In Australia, New Zealand, Chili and Argentine Republic in January; Upper Egypt and India in February and March; Lower Egypt, India, Syria, Cyprus, Persia, Asia Minor, Mexico and Cuba in April; Texas, Algeria, Central Asia, China, Japan and Morocco in May; California, Oregon, Mississippi, Alabama, Georgia, North Carolina, South Carolina, Tennessee, Virginia, Kentucky, Kansas, Arkansas, Utah, Colorado, Missouri, Turkey, Greece, Italy, Spain, Portugal and South of France in June; New England, New York, Pennsylvania, Ohio, Indiana, Michigan, Illinois, Iowa, Wisconsin, Southern Minnesota, Nebraska, Upper Canada, Roumania, Bulgaria, Austria-Hungary, South of Russia, Germany, Switzerland and South of England in July; Central and Northern Minnesota, Dakota, Manitoba, Lower Canada, Columbia, Belgium, Holland, Great Britain,

Denmark, Poland and Central Russia in August; Scotland, Sweden, Norway and North of Russia in September; Peru and South Africa in November, and Burmah in December.

Wheel, Torture of the, was first used in Germany, it is believed, in the fourteenth century. The criminal was laid on a large cart-wheel, his legs and arms extended and fastened to the spokes, and as the wheel was turned around his limbs were broken with an iron bar. The wheel in France was only used to punish criminals of the most atrocious sort. The victim was first bound to a frame of wood in the form of a St. Andrew's cross—similar to the Roman numeral X. Grooves were cut transversely in the frame above and below the knees and elbows, and the limbs of the wretched victim were broken in these places, and sometimes the executioner struck the criminal two or three blows on the chest or stomach, which usually put an end to his sufferings, and, therefore, were called *coups de grace*, or blows of mercy. If the criminal happened to survive all this, he was then laid upon a small wheel, with his legs and arms doubled under him, to expire. The punishment of the wheel has been occasionally inflicted in Germany during the present century, but was abolished in France at the time of the Revolution.

"Whig" and Tory.—The word "Whig" is believed to be a contraction of "Whigamore," which in some shires of Scotland denotes a drover, and was applied in contempt to those who in 1679 favored the bill for the exclusion of the Duke of York from the line of succession. His partisans were called Tories, and believed that the maintenance of a royal line was the necessary means of a lawful government, and vindicated the divine right of kings. Both terms were used in the United States during the Revolution, the patriots being "Whigs" and the adherents of the crown "Tories." The anti-Jackson party in the presidential election of 1832 took the name of Whig.

Whipping-Post in America.—In 1611 the London Company sent to Jamestown, Va., a code of laws for the colonists, in which whipping was made the penalty for a long list of offenses. In 1654, when the Governor of New Sweden visited Fort Casimir, on the Delaware, part of the entertainment provided for the guests by the Dutch commandant was the whipping of three "jail-birds." In 1669 the Governor and Council of New York ordered an insubordinate citizen—one Konigsmarke—to be publicly flogged, and branded with the letter "R" on his breast. No respect for the sex was allowed to exempt women from a share in the degradation of this punishment until later, and it is certain that women were publicly whipped in New York as late as 1775. In 1785 a man convicted of horse-stealing in Newcastle, Del., was whipped, put in the pillory, and had his ears clipped. In December, 1800, a woman convicted of receiving stolen goods was publicly whipped, receiving twenty-one lashes on the bare back, and was branded on the forehead; and until fifty years later women were occasionally whipped in that State. In 1835 a free negro woman, being guilty of theft, received twenty-one lashes and was sold as a slave for seven years. The whipping of women for larceny and receiving stolen goods ceased to be legal in Delaware in 1855, but it was continued for certain other offenses against morality. The last instance of woman-whipping in the State occurred in 1864. The punishment of the whipping-post for men is still sanctioned by the laws of Delaware, and in 1875 seventeen men were publicly whipped in Newcastle County alone. The history of Ohio tells us that the first punishment decreed for a white man in the State was the whipping of a thief in the Miami settlement, about 1786. From that time until 1815 whipping was the penalty for numerous offenses. Other instances might be given to show how long the statute-books of many States kept these barbarous laws. For instance, when a school for colored girls was opened in Canterbury, Conn., by Miss Prudence Crandall, in 1833, the excitement and opposition of the town was great. A young negro woman who had come to town to attend the school was ordered to leave; and to get rid of her and others an old vagrant law, which had long been a dead letter, was resuscitated. This law required that whipping on the naked body, not exceeding ten stripes, should be inflicted on any person refusing to leave the town after ten days' warning. The girl stayed, however, and the town authorities did not dare to inflict the whipping. Before the year 1860 the whipping-post had been abolished in all of the Northern States. In the Southern States it remained as an incident of slavery, but since the war its use has been rather exceptional than otherwise. In Georgia it has been forbidden by statute, but flogging is still relied upon in some of the States—Virginia, South Carolina and others—to keep in order petty offenders.

Whisky.—The process of distilling liquors from grain is thought to have first been discovered in India, and introduced into Europe by the Moors about 1150. Its use in Ireland dates back to about the same time, but it was not introduced into England until the close of the century. When first made, whisky was used as a medicine; and directions for making usquebaugh, or *aqua vitæ*, are contained in the "Red Book of Ossory," a volume compiled in the fourteenth century, in which it is described as a panacea for all diseases. The name whisky was at first given by the Scotch Highlanders to the liquor which they distilled from barley only, and had not, until later times, its present more general application. Usquebaugh was a Celtic name for the liquor, from which the word whisky is no doubt derived.

White Cross Movement was instituted in England in 1882 by the Right Rev. J. B. Lightfoot, D. D., Bishop of Durham. Branches of the White Cross army have been established in the United States. The obligations which are undertaken by its members are as follows: 1. To treat all women with respect, and endeavor to protect them from wrong and degradation. 2. To endeavor to put down all indecent language and coarse jests. 3. To maintain the law of purity as equally binding upon men and women. 4. To endeavor to spread these principles among my companions and try to help my younger brothers. 5. To use every possible means to fulfill the command "Keep thyself pure." The army originally had a partial connection with the Church of England, but now members of all denominations are included in its membership.

White House Weddings.—The first wedding to occur in the White House was that of Miss Todd, a relative by marriage of President Madison. Then, in their order, came the weddings of Elizabeth Tyler, a daughter of President Tyler; John Quincy Adams, Jr.; Miss Easten and Miss Lewis, both during General Jackson's administration; Martha Monroe; Nellie Grant; Emily Platt, a niece of President Hayes; and last, President Cleveland.

White Lady.—According to popular legend, the White Lady is a being who appears in many of the castles of German princes and nobles upon the eve of any important event, whether joyful or sad, but particularly when the death of any member of the family is imminent. She is regarded as the ancestress of the race, shows herself always in snow-white garments, carries a bunch of keys at her side, and sometimes rocks and watches over the children at night when their nurses sleep. It was long a common belief in Scotland that many of the chiefs had some kind spirit to watch over the fortunes of their houses. Popular tradition has many well-known legends about white ladies, who generally dwell in forts and mountains as enchanted maidens waiting for deliverance. They delight to appear in warm sunshine to poor shepherds or herd-boys. They are either combing their long hair or washing themselves, drying wheat, beating flax or spinning. They also point out treasures and beg for deliverance, offering as reward flowers, corn or chaff, which gifts turn in the instant into silver and gold.

White Lead, largely used as a paint, is the carbonate of lead. The pig-lead is melted and run into molds, forming what are called "buckles," which are shaped like a stove-grate and weigh about a pound each. Iron pots are then taken, which are half-filled with vinegar, and having just above the level of the vinegar projections on the sides, upon which the buckles of lead are placed, not allowing them to touch the liquid. The pots are then stacked up in great numbers in a frame-work which is roofed-in and provided with double walls. They are arranged in layers, with boards and tan between each, and piled up to the height of the building. Beneath them the floor is padded with tanbark, and so are the spaces between the double walls. The whole is then tightly shut in, and the contents of the pots are left to the action of chemical laws. The tan generates heat and makes an oxide of lead, while the carbonic acid which the decomposition of the tan evolves combines with the oxide and gradually reduces the metal to the carbonate—a beautiful, soft and snow-white substance. This result is accomplished after an interval of ten to fourteen weeks. This powder is then taken to long, revolving screens, through the meshes of which it drops into bins, any uncorroded particles of metal being separated by the screens and returned to the caldrons. The sifted lead is then washed, to deprive it of any free acid, stains or impurities, and ground in water, between heavy burr-millstones, into a pulpy mass. This is then gathered and placed upon drying-pans in the kiln-house, and gives the dry white lead of commerce. This dry lead is kneaded with linseed oil, and the mixture is then ground fine in mills.

Wildcat Banks.—The fraudulent institutions known as wildcat banks were started principally in the West and South after the closing up of the United States Bank and the transfer of its deposits to State banks in 1832. The scarcity of capital in these regions made it comparatively easy to put in circulation anything that purported to be money. Hence, any one with a very limited capital—or, in fact, without any capital at all—could open a bank, issue $10,000 or more in small notes, and pass them over in easy loans to land speculators, who, in their turn, paid them out in country villages and among farmers, where the standing of the bank of issue would necessarily be unknown. Hundreds of these banks were started, and immense amounts of so-called money were loaned to build cities in the wilderness, and to contractors anxious to build railroads without material, tools or means of paying wages. In some cases the real place of issue was, for instance, New Orleans or Buffalo, while the bills purported to be issued and payable in, say, Georgia or Illinois. This method of doing business lasted four years, when the panic of 1837, one of the most painful and prolonged crises in the financial history of the United States, overtook the country. Fortunately this led to the adoption in nearly all the States of such banking laws as rendered similar schemes impossible in the future. These institutions were called wildcat banks, owing to their utter lawlessness and because their victims were "most awfully clawed."

Will is an instrument disposing of property after death. The term is properly limited to an instrument disposing of real estate, and differs from a *testament*, which provides for the disposition of personal property. Formerly *non-cupative* or oral wills were allowed, but now they are restricted to the case of soldiers and sailors in emergency. Wills can be made only by persons of "sound and disposing mind," but a liberal rule is applied in determining competency. It is sufficient if the testator has a general idea of what property he has, of what disposition will follow if he makes no will, and of the general effect of the provisions of his will. A monomania in general will not affect his competency. Wills must be written and signed by the testator in the presence of witnesses. The number of witnesses required is regulated by statute, and is generally three or less. No person made a beneficiary under the will may be a witness. The statutory directions for the making of wills must be strictly complied with. Wills are revoked by the marriage of the testator and the birth of issue, by the making of a subsequent inconsistent will, or by physical destruction of the instrument. A *codicil* to a will is an addition made at a later time, and must be executed with the same formalities as the will itself.

William and Mary College was established at Williamsburg, Va., in 1693, and next to Harvard College was the oldest institution of learning in America. At its endowment it was placed under the patronage of the King and Queen of Great Britain. The trustees of the Hon. R. Doyle, the English philosopher, who left his personal estate for " charitable and pious uses," presented a great part of it to this college for the education of Indians. During the Revolutionary War the college lost most of its possessions, and its buildings were used by the French troops as a hospital. Among the noted men who were graduated from William and Mary were Presidents Jefferson, Madison and Monroe, Chief Justice Marshall, and General Scott.

Wilmot Proviso was an amendment to a bill appropriating $2,000,000 for the purchase of certain Mexican territory, and was offered in Congress by Mr. Wilmot, a Democrat, on August 8, 1846. The amendment read "That, as an express and fundamental condition to the acquisition of any territory from the Republic of Mexico by the United States, by virtue of any treaty that may be negotiated between them, and to the use by the Executive of the moneys herein appropriated, neither slavery nor involuntary servitude shall ever exist in any part of said territory except for crime, whereof the party shall be duly convicted." The bill passed the House, but failed in the Senate.

Windsor Castle is situated on the right bank of the Thames, twenty-three miles west of London, near the town of Windsor. The royal residence and the buildings connected with it cover twelve acres of ground, and stand in the midst of a park known as "Little Park," which is four miles in circumference, and is connected by a long avenue of trees, south of the Castle, with the "Great Park," which is eighteen miles in circuit. The Castle was founded by William the Conqueror. The original plans were enlarged upon and completed by Henry I, and the Castle was first used as a royal residence about 1110. The history of the existing edifice, however, begins in the reign of Henry III, but it was not until the time of Edward III that all its portions were completed. The buildings may be said to be grouped in three portions—the middle ward containing the Round Tower, which was built by Edward III, in the eighteenth year of his reign, to receive the Round Table of the Knights of the newly formed Order of the Garter; the lower ward, on the west, containing St. George's Chapel, which was begun by Henry III, completed by Edward III, rebuilt by

Henry VII and added to by Cardinal Wolsey, and the houses of the military knights, cloisters, etc.; and the upper ward, on the east, containing the sovereign's private apartments. Some additions were made to the buildings by Henry VIII, and Queen Elizabeth formed the terraces and built the gate now called by her name. The Star building was erected by Charles II. In 1824–'28 the Castle was repaired and enlarged, but little alteration has since been made. The park and forest immediately adjoining contain many historical trees—such as Elizabeth's Oak; Shakspeare's Oak; the Long Walk, made in the reign of Charles II; and Queen Anne's Ride of Elms, three miles long. Herne's Oak, rendered so famous by Shakspeare, was blown down in September, 1863, and a stone and a young tree now mark the spot. The oldest planted timber in England—that of the reign of Elizabeth—is also in Windsor Park; and there are many oaks of which it is well-established the age must be 1,000 years. In the royal vaults connected with St. George's Chapel a number of kings and queens are buried.

Wine Production of the World.—The average production of wine in the principal vine-growing countries of the world is as follows: France, 765,175,972 imperial gallons; Algeria, 722,000,000 imperial gallons; Italy, 605,000,000 imperial gallons; Spain, 484,-000,000 imperial gallons; Austria-Hungary, 187,000,000 imperial gallons; Portugal, 88,000,000 imperial gallons; Germany, 81,290,-000 imperial gallons; Russia, 77,000,000 imperial gallons; Cyprus, 35,200,000 imperial gallons; Switzerland, 28,600,000 imperial gallons; Greece, 28,600,000 imperial gallons; United States, 18,000,000 imperial gallons; Turkey, 22,000,000 imperial gallons; Cape of Good Hope, 15,400,000 imperial gallons; Roumania, 15,400,000 imperial gallons; Servia, 11,000,000 imperial gallons; Australia, 1,-933,800 imperial gallons; total, 2,485,599,772 imperial gallons.

Witchcraft.—The belief in witchcraft was probably inherited from their pagan forefathers by the early Christians. In 1484 Pope Innocent issued a bull directing the Inquisitors to search out and punish all guilty of such crimes; and in Germany alone, during the following three centuries, more than 10,000 persons were executed in consequence of this bull. Witches were hung in England as late as 1716, and in Scotland until 1722. Thirty thousand persons were sacrificed to this superstition during the 150 years following the reign of Queen Elizabeth. In 1688 four children of John Goodwin, a respectable man in North Boston, were abused by a disreputable Irish woman, and as they immediately afterward began to show strange symptoms, their disorder was attributed to witchcraft, the more so since three Bostonians had already been hung for that offense. It was in Salem, however, where the fanatical excitement attendant upon this superstition was carried to its greatest height in America. The first alleged victims were in the family of Samuel Parris, a clergyman. His daughter, niece and two other girls began to show symptoms like those of the Goodwin children, and accused Tituba, an Indian squaw in the family, of bewitching them, though she stoutly protested her innocence. Soon the number of bewitched increased, and likewise the number of accused. The excitement grew, being constantly fanned by those who should have been foremost in checking it. None were safe from accusation, and many, to save their own lives, accused their dearest friends and relatives. In May, 1692, when Sir William Phipps became Governor of Massachusetts, he appointed a court, consisting of seven judges, for Suffolk, Essex and Middlesex, for the trial of persons accused of witchcraft. These judges were William Stoughton, the Lieutenant-Governor; Jonathan Curwin, John Richards, Bartholomew Gedney, Watt Winthrop, Samuel Sewell and Peter Sergeant, and in the prosecutions that followed Cotton Mather and Samuel Parris were among the chief instigators. Under this tribunal twenty persons were hung, fifty or more tortured into confessions of guilt, the jails were filled, and hundreds more were under suspicion. The means employed to extort confessions were barbarous in the extreme. The lash; the stocks; binding the sufferers in painful postures, as with neck and heels together; starvation and thirst, were among the barbarities resorted to. When the reason of the community awoke to a realization of the injustice of these proceedings, it was confronted with the fact that hundreds of innocent people had been falsely accused, and fanaticism was justly succeeded by most bitter remorse.

Witenagemot, the great national council of England in Anglo-Saxon times, by which the King was guided in all his main acts of government. Each kingdom had its own Witenagemot before the union of the heptarchy in 827, after which there was a general one for the whole country. It was composed of the chief ecclesiastics, the ealdormen of shires, and some of the chief proprietors of land. The powers of the Witenagemot seem to have been very extensive. The King's title, however hereditarily unexceptionable, was not considered complete without its recognition, and it possessed the power of deposing him. It could make new laws and treaties, and along with the King it appointed prelates, regulated military and ecclesiastical affairs, and levied taxes. Without its consent the King had no power to raise forces by sea or land. It was also the supreme court of justice, civil and criminal. The Witenagemot was abolished by William the Conqueror.

Woman Suffrage.—The Constitution of the Colony of New Jersey granted suffrage to all inhabitants, under certain qualifications, irrespective of sex. This act was repealed, however, in 1807. The first Woman's Rights Convention was held July 19, 1848, at Seneca Falls, N. Y., and its claims for women were based upon the Declaration of Independence. On October 23, 1850, a National Woman's Rights Convention was held at Worcester, Mass. From that time until 1866 the subject was agitated in America and England, but no decisive action was taken. In the latter year the American Equal Rights Association presented the first petition for woman suffrage to Congress. Two years later (1868) the New England Woman Suffrage Association was formed, and the work of memorializing Legislatures and Congress, holding conventions and circulating documents began in earnest. By 1870 the agitation had assumed such proportions that the Republican Convention in Massachusetts, held October 5th of that year, admitted Lucy Stone and Mary A. Livermore as regularly accredited delegates. Since then several State conventions have indorsed woman suffrage. December 10, 1869, the Legislature of the Territory of Wyoming granted the right of suffrage to women. The same right was granted in 1883 in the Territory of Washington, but has since been declared unconstitutional. Woman suffrage, limited to school elections or school meetings, has been conferred in the States of Kansas, Washington, Nebraska, New Hampshire, Texas, Vermont, Arizona, the Dakotas, Montana, Colorado, Minnesota, Wisconsin, Massachusetts, New Jersey, Michigan and New York. In the two latter States the law requires that they be tax-payers. Widows and unmarried women may vote as to special district taxes in Idaho Territory if they hold taxable property. In Kentucky any white widow having a child of school age is a qualified school voter; if she has no child, but is a tax-payer, she may vote on the question of taxes. In Oregon widows having children and taxable property may vote at school meetings. Widows, or unmarried women not minors who pay taxes and are listed as parents, guardians or heads of families, may vote at school meetings in Indiana. They have full municipal suffrage in Kansas, and vote on the sale of liquor in Arkansas and Mississippi. In England, Scotland and Wales women (unless married) vote for all elective officers, except member of Parliament, on like terms with men. In Ireland women vote everywhere for poor-law guardians; in Dundalk and other seaports, for harbor boards; in Belfast, for all municipal officers. In Sweden their suffrage is about the same as in England, except that they vote indirectly for members of the House of Lords. In Russia women (heads of households) vote for all elective officers and on all local questions. In Austria-Hungary they vote (by proxy) at all elections. In Italy widows vote for members of Parliament. In all the countries of Russian Asia women vote wherever a Russian colony settles. Municipal woman suffrage exists in New Zealand, Victoria, New South Wales, Queensland and South America. Iceland, the Isle of Man and Pitcairn Island have full woman suffrage. Tasmania, Sicily, Sardinia, and a host of islands elsewhere, have partial woman suffrage.

Women, Myths of the Origin of.—Woman's first appearance has been a fruitful subject of legends. The Phœnician myth of creation is found in the story of Pygmalion and Galatea. There the first woman was carved by the first man out of ivory, and then endowed with life by Aphrodite. The Greek theory of the creation of woman, according to Hesiod, was that Zeus, as a cruel jest, ordered Vulcan to make woman out of clay, and then induced the various gods and goddesses to invest the clay doll with all their worst qualities, the result being a lovely thing, with a witchery of mien, refined craft, eager passion, love of dress, treacherous manners and shameless mind. The Scandinavians say that as Odin, Vill and Ve, the three sons of Bor, were walking along the sea-beach they found two sticks of wood, one of ash and one of elm. Sitting down, the gods shaped man and woman out of these sticks, whittling the woman from the elm and calling her Ernia. One of the strangest stories touching the origin of woman is told by the Madagascarenes. In so far as the creation of man goes, the legend is not unlike that related by Moses, only that the fall came before Eve arrived. After the man had eaten the forbidden fruit he became affected with a boil on the leg, out of which, when it burst, came a beautiful girl. The man's first thought was to throw her to the pigs; but he was commanded by a messenger from heaven to let her play among the grass and flowers until she was of marriageable age, then to make her his wife. He did so, called her Baboura, and she became the mother of all races of men. The American Indian myths relative to Adam and Eve are numerous and entertaining. Some traditions trace back our first parents to white and red maize; another is that man, searching for a wife, was given the daughter of the king of muskrats, who on being dipped into the waters of a neighboring lake became a woman.

Wool-Sack, the name given to the seat of the Lord Chancellor of England in the House of Lords, which is composed of a large square bag of wool without either back or arms, and covered with a red cloth. It was first introduced in the House of Lords as the Chancellor's seat in the time of Elizabeth as a memento of an act which was passed against the exportation of wool, that commodity being then the main source of the national wealth of England.

World's Fairs.—The first exhibition of the industries of all nations was held in the Crystal Palace, a magnificent structure of glass and iron especially built for the purpose, in London, England, in 1851. The fair opened May 1st, and lasted until October 15th. The idea of holding such an exhibition was suggested by Mr. Whishaw, Secretary of the Society of Arts, London, in 1844; but the first direct movement toward its accomplishment was made by the Prince Consort in 1849, when he called a meeting of the Society of Arts, of which he was president, and proposed that it should take the initiative in getting up a world's fair. A formal commission, with Prince Albert at its head, was appointed by the Society early in 1850, and in a short time a subscribed guarantee fund of £200,000 was obtained and the project was fairly begun. This exhibition was a great success, and was followed by a similar fair, which opened at New York, July 14,

1853. This fair continued open for four months, and was even more complete and magnificent than that of Great Britain, as no civilized country failed to exhibit samples of its best work in art and manufacture. The fair was held, like its predecessor in London, in a building especially constructed for the purpose out of glass and iron, and also called the Crystal Palace. In 1862 a second fair was held at London, to which Prince Albert subscribed £10,000. He died, however, before it was opened. Similar exhibitions were held in London in 1871-'72-'73-'74, but not proving financially successful they were then given up. World's fairs have also been held at Paris in 1855, 1867, 1878 and 1889; in Vienna, in 1873; at Berlin, in 1881; at Philadelphia (the Centennial Exposition), in 1876; and at New Orleans in 1885. Annual exhibitions, open to the whole world's contributions, are held at Philadelphia, Chicago, Cincinnati and Louisville; but these are necessarily of much less pretentious character than those mentioned above. These great exhibitions, although they have perhaps not accomplished all that was expected of them at their inauguration, have certainly served as a powerful stimulus to the world's industry, and have also added much toward the general progress of civilization and education in both hemispheres.

Writing, History of.—The very first origin of the art of writing has been a matter of speculation from the earliest times. The myths of antiquity ascribe it to Thoth, or to Cadmus, which only denotes their belief in its being brought from the East, or being, perhaps, primeval. The Talmud ascribes it to a special revelation. Unquestionably the first step toward writing was rude pictorial representations of objects, the next the application of a symbolic meaning to some of these pictures, and gradually all pictures became symbolic, and for convenience were abbreviated. Later they became conventional signs, and in time they were made to stand for the sounds of spoken language. The various systems of writing of the ancient world had probably at least three sources— the Egyptian, the Assyrian and the Chinese systems—all of which were originally hieroglyphics, or made up of pictures. The Egyptians had four distinct styles of writing—the hieroglyphics, hieratic, enchorial and Coptic. The hieroglyphic was probably in use before 4,000 B. C., and at first was made up entirely of pictures; but about 2,000 B. C. the hieratic form was introduced, in which the hieroglyphs were greatly simplified and developed into purely linear forms. The enchorial form of writing was in use from 700 B. C. to A. D. 200, and was a still further simplification of the earlier forms, finally developing into the alphabetic form known as the Coptic. The cuneiform writing of the Assyrian empire disputes the honors of antiquity with the Egyptian early forms. This was probably hieroglyphic in its origin, but became modified by the different nations occupying the Assyrian empire until it assumed the form of the inscriptions as now known to archæologists. The name of this writing is from a Latin word meaning a wedge, and it is so called because all the characters used are made up of different arrangements of a single pointed figure resembling a wedge in form. There were three classes of cuneiform characters used in the period of development of this form of writing; first, the Assyrian or Babylonian, which was very complicated, containing from six hundred to seven hundred symbols; the Scythian or Median, having about one hundred characters only; and the third the Persian, which is purely alphabetic. The Chinese gives an example of a written language which was arrested in an early period of its development before the alphabetic stage had been reached. The people of China still use a written character for a word, as they did thousands of years ago. The Egyptian is the most important of those early systems, as from it was probably derived the Phœnician alphabet, which became the parent of all the graphic systems of the modern world. The Egyptians never fully separated the hieroglyphic and phonetic symbols, but the Phœnicians adopted the latter only, and thus originated the first purely alphabetic plan of writing. The Phœnician alphabet was the parent of five principal branches of graphic forms, the most important of which is the Greek, which was the parent of the Roman alphabet, from which sprung the alphabets of all modern European nations and those taken from them by the people who now inhabit the Western hemisphere.

Wyandotte Cave is situated in Jennings Township, Crawford County, Ind., near the Ohio River, and is a rival of the Mammoth Cave of Kentucky in grandeur and size. It excels the latter cave in the number and varieties of its stalagmites and stalactites, and in the size of several of its chambers. One of these chambers is 350 feet in length, 245 feet in height, and contains a hill 175 feet high, on which are three fine stalagmites. Epsom salts, niter and alum have been obtained from the earth of the cave.

Wycliffe.—This celebrated Reformer was born, it is supposed, in the village of Wycliffe, near Richmond, Yorkshire, England, about the year 1324, and was educated, it is believed, at Queen's and Merton Colleges, Oxford. In 1372 he took the degree of Doctor of Theology, and lectured in the University as a professor of theology. In 1374 he was one of an embassy sent by Edward III to negotiate at Bruges with the delegates of Gregory XI concerning the papal reservation of benefices in England, and became obnoxious to the Pope for his action at that time; and, in consequence, letters were sent to Oxford and Canterbury, to the Bishop of London, and to the King, in 1377, demanding inquiry regarding the doctrines imputed to him, and that he should be at once put into custody. Previous to this, however, Wycliffe had been summoned before an English convocation in St. Paul's on a charge of heresy, but the meeting was dissolved through an altercation between the Duke of Lancaster and Lord Percy, and he withdrew under the protection of powerful friends. In 1378 he was summoned to appear before a synod of the clergy in Lambeth; but the synod were prohibited by the Queen-mother from taking any action injurious to him, and he was released with an admonition. In 1381 he gave the greatest offense by lecturing at Oxford against the doctrine of transubstantiation and another synod was called, and ten of the opinions which he had publicly preached were declared to be heretical. In 1382 he was debarred from teaching in the University by the King. He died at Lutterworth, December 31, 1384. In 1428 his remains were exhumed and burned, and the ashes were cast into the Swift by order of Clement VIII, in conformity with the decree of the Council of Constance, who, May 5, 1415, condemned as heretical, false and erroneous forty-five articles maintained by Wycliffe, and ordered that his bones should be dug out of consecrated ground and cast on a dunghill. His greatest work was the first complete translation of the Scriptures into English and their circulation among the people. He was unquestionably a man of vigorous intellect, of simple faith, and earnest and manly courage. He had a great retinue of poor preachers and a large following among all classes in the country, who later came to be known as Lollards. [See *Lollards.*] He made a strong impression in his age, and his influence was felt even to the time of the Reformation in the sixteenth century.

Xebec was formerly an armed vessel of great speed used by the Algerine corsairs. It carried three masts, on which square or lateen sails could be set. The bow and stern were remarkable for the small angle they made with the water. The sides were low, and the upper deck of great convexity, that the water might readily flow off through the scuppers. They carried from 16 to 24 guns. A few of these vessels—unarmed—still sail the Mediterranean as carriers of perishable goods.

Yale College was founded in 1700 under the trusteeship of the ten principal ministers of the Colony of Connecticut, who each contributed a gift of books. It was first established at Saybrook, but in 1716 was removed to New Haven. Among its early patrons were Governor Yale, after whom it was named, and Bishop Berkeley. Of its four faculties, the medical was organized in 1812, the theological in 1822, the legal in 1824, and the philosophical in 1847.

Yankee-Doodle.—The air known as "Yankee-Doodle" was originally "Nankee-Doodle," and is as old as the time of Cromwell. It was known in New England before the Revolution, and is said to have been played by the English troops in derisive allusion to the then popular nick-name of the New Englanders; and afterward the New Englanders, saying that the British troops had been made to dance to "Yankee-Doodle," adopted the air.

Yankee, Origin of the Name.—The theories which have been advanced as to the origin of this name are numerous. According to Thierry it was a corruption of Jankin, a diminutive of John, which was a nickname given by the Dutch colonists of New York to their neighbors in the Connecticut settlements. In a history of the American war, written by Dr. William Gordon, and published in 1789, was another theory. Dr. Gordon said that it was a cant word in Cambridge, Mass., as early as 1713, used to denote especial excellence—as a Yankee good horse, Yankee good cider, etc. He supposed that it was originally a by-word in the college, and being taken by the students into parts of the country, gradually obtained general currency in New England, and at length came to be taken up in other parts of the country, and applied to New Englanders as a term of slight reproach. Aubury, an English writer, says that it is derived from a Cherokee word — *eankke* — which signifies coward and slave. This epithet was bestowed on the inhabitants of New England by the Virginians for not assisting them in a war with the Cherokees. The most probable theory, however, is that advanced by Mr. Heckewelder, that the Indians, in endeavoring to pronounce the word English, or Anglais, made it Yengees or Yangees; and this originated the term.

Yellowstone Park is situated, the greater part, in Wyoming Territory, and the remainder in Montana and partly in Idaho, and comprises 3,575 square miles. The adaptability of this section of the country to the purposes of a national park was first brought prominently before the public by a company of surveyors who visited the region in the year 1869. In 1870 and 1871 the territory was again explored by scientific expeditions, and the reports of the first visitors were confirmed The expedition of 1871 was headed by Professor Hayden, and upon his representations an act was passed by Congress, and approved March 1, 1872, by which what is now known as the Yellowstone National Park was " reserved and withdrawn from settlement, occupancy, or sale, and dedicated and set apart as a public park or pleasure-ground for the benefit and enjoyment of the people." This great park contains the most striking of all the mountains, gorges, falls, rivers and lakes in the whole Yellowstone region. The mountain ranges rise to the height of 10,000 to 12,000 feet, and are always covered with snow. The banks of the Yellowstone River abound with ravines and canyons, which are carved out of the heart of the mountains through the hardest rocks. The most remarkable of these is the canyon of Tower Creek and Column Mountain, which is about ten miles in length, and is so deep and gloomy that it is called "The Devil's Den." The Grand Canyon, which begins where Tower Creek ends, is twenty miles in length, is impassable throughout, and is inaccessible at the water's edge except at a few points, and its depth is so profound that no sound ever reaches the ear from the bottom. The Park contains a great multitude of hot springs of sulphur, sulphate of copper, alum, etc. There are at least 50 geysers that throw columns of water to the height of from 50 to 200 feet, and the falls of this wonderland are considered marvelous. The altitude of the entire Park is 6,000 feet or more above the sea-level.

Yosemite Valley, or, as it is also called, Yohamite, is situated in the eastern portion of California, and is from 8 to 10 miles long, and a little more than a mile wide. In some places the valley is filled with noble oaks; in others it opens out into broad, grassy fields. The natural beauties of this region are of world-wide report. It has pine-covered mountains, towering, with very steep slopes, to the height of 3,500 feet, a precipice, or bluff, in one place rising perpendicularly 3,089 feet above the valley; in another, a rock, almost perpendicular, 3,270 feet high; waterfalls pouring over its sides from heights of 700 to almost 1,000 feet; and one great waterfall broken into three laps, but of which the whole height is 2,550 feet. Of the other waterfalls on the sides of the valley, the Pohono, or Bridal Veil Waterfall, is particularly to be remarked for its beauty, as well as for its height, which is 940 feet, and almost unbroken. The Yosemite Valley was first entered by white men in 1855, but now, like the valleys of Switzerland, has its hotels and guides, and is yearly visited by American and foreign tourists.

Zenana, or Zanana, a Persian word which signifies "belonging to women." In Bengal a native gentleman's house consists of an outer and inner part. Each of these is in the form of a quadrangle. The former, well furnished, with fine rooms and windows looking out upon the public street, is for the use of men; the latter, of a mean and even squalid appearance, is devoted to the women, and is known as the Zenana, or Zanana. From 50 to 100 Hindoo women are sometimes gathered together in these houses. They may go into each other's rooms, or take an airing in the courtyard, but must not be seen in public. Till about twenty-five years ago no Christian woman was permitted to enter a Bengal Zenana, but since then the lives of the inhabitants of these prison-houses have been materially brightened and enlarged through the efforts of European and American female missionaries.

Zodiacal Light is the name given to a singular appearance seen after sunset or before sunrise at all seasons of the year in low latitudes, and is obviously due to illuminated matter surrounding the sun in a very flat, lenticular form, nearly coinciding with the plane of the ecliptic, or, rather, with the sun's equator, and extending to a distance from the sun greater than that of the earth. It was first called to the attention of astronomers by Cassini about 1683, and was long regarded as the sun's atmosphere. This idea, however, has been found to be incorrect, and it is now generally believed that the explanation of the phenomenon is to be found in supposing it to consist (like the rings of Saturn) of an immense assemblage of small cosmical masses, rocks, stones and pieces of metal, such as are continually encountering the earth in the form of aerolites or meteorites. For the dynamical stability of such a system it is only necessary that each fragment should separately describe its elliptic orbit about the sun.

Zodiac, The, is the name given by the ancients to an imaginary band extending around the celestial sphere, having as its mesial line the ecliptic or apparent path of the sun. The signs of the zodiac embrace the twelve important constellations which, owing to the motions of the earth, appear to revolve through the heavens within a belt extending nine degrees on each side of the sun's apparent annual path, and within or near which all the planets revolve. Since the sun appears successively in each of these constellations during the year, the zodiac was divided into twelve equal parts, corresponding to the months. These signs and their subdivisions were used in measuring time, and as a basis of astronomical and astrological calculations and predictions. Astronomers now, for convenience, use these signs, giving to each constellation an extent of thirty degrees, although the constellations vary in size. These signs are Aries, representing the ram; Taurus, the bull; Gemini, the twins; Cancer, the crab; Leo, the lion; Virgo, the virgin; Libra, the balance; Scorpio, the scorpion; Sagittarius, the archer; Capricornus, the goat; Aquarius, the water-bearer, and Pisces, the fishes. On the 20th of March the sun enters Aries, and at midnight Virgo, the opposite constellation, will be overhead. During the month of April the sun will pass into Taurus, and at midnight Libra will be overhead. The early astronomers were astrologers, and claimed to be able to predict the future careers of individuals and nations by observing the positions and movements of the planets and the condition of the weather at the most important periods of men's lives. A man born when the sun was in the constellation Scorpio was believed to be naturally bent toward excessive indulgence of the animal passions; one born when the sun was in Aries was destined to be a great scholar or ruler; one born when the sun was in Pisces was predestined to grovel or be a servant, and so on. The porticoes of the temples of Denderah and Esne, in Egypt, have representations of the zodiacal constellations which are of great antiquity and have formed a fruitful theme of discussion; but the truth seems to be that nothing is as yet known respecting these ancient representations, for the manner in which the investigations have been mixed up with the Biblical question of the antiquity of man has prevented any truly scientific research. The Greeks would seem to have borrowed their constellations from the Egyptians and Babylonians, and this is corroborated to some extent by occasional remarks of Greek writers as to the positions of various constellations at certain times, which positions are inconsistent with the supposition of the observer being in Greece. The zodiacal figures of the Hindus, ancient Persians, Chinese and Japanese have such a remarkable resemblance to those of the Egyptians that there can be little doubt as to their common origin.

Zoological Gardens.—The greatest Zoological Garden in the world is that in London, being situated in the very heart of the city, and a public street running through it which divides it into two sections. Walls are erected along the street, and visitors go from one section to another by means of a tunnel passing under the street. The grounds comprise about sixty acres, and are well filled with buildings, ponds, etc. There are real beaver ponds, aviaries, bear pits, monkey houses—in short, a place for everything in the animal line. This park was opened in 1828, and during the last five years the annual number of visitors has averaged about 700,000, while in 1886 there were added to the collection of animals 1,338. The Berlin Park is ranked by naturalists next to that of London; and the two in Paris, if combined, would make one as extensive as any in the world. In the United States the Philadelphia "Zoo" is the most extensive so far as buildings and collections go, and the enclosure comprises thirty-three acres of Fairmount Park. The Cincinnati Zoological Park embraces sixty-five acres of suburban land, and was opened in 1875. The Chicago gardens are in the central part of the city, and have one of the finest herds of buffalo to be seen. In New York the collection of animals are kept in Central Park. There are in all forty-eight zoological gardens in the world, six of them being in the United States.

Zululand is situated on the eastern coast of Africa, north of Natal. Its area is about 10,000 square miles, and its population before the war with England in 1879 was about 250,000. This war, which brought the Zulus and their King, Cetewayo, into prominent notice, was forced upon them by the representatives of the British Government in Natal, who had long been anxious to annex the country. In order to have some pretense for a forcible occupation of the land, Sir Bartle Frere demanded of Cetewayo that large fines in cattle should be paid for offenses of the Zulus on the border; that he should disband his army, and not attempt to form it again; and that he should allow a British officer to live in Zululand and assist him in administering the government. This naturally brought about the desired war. At first the Zulu army, which numbered about 42,000 men, was successful in every battle, and had Cetewayo desired to push his advantage after the battle at Isandlwana he could have crossed the border and completely annihilated the English; but from the first he insisted that he was fighting on the defensive only, and his soldiers were under strict orders not to go over into Natal to fight. The final battle in the war was fought on July 4, 1879, resulting in a total defeat of the Zulu army, and on August 13th Cetewayo was taken to Cape Town as a prisoner. Subsequently he was taken to England, but in December, 1882, he was reinstated King of Zululand, to rule it as a vassal of England. In 1883 he was wounded in a battle with one of the subordinate chiefs, who had been left in possession of a large tract of country at the north, and died in Natal in March, 1884. It was in the Zulu War that the young Prince Imperial of France was killed, he having joined the English army in search of renown.

MEDICAL DICTIONARY.

A **BATEMENT.** Decrease of fever.

Abdomen. The belly.

Abnormal. Unnatural, irregular.

Abscess. A collection of purulent matter.

Absorption, absorptive. Taking up or soaking up.

Acephalous. Without a head.

Acid. Sour ; a substance which neutralizes alkalies.

Adhesive strips, adhesive plaster. Cloth or other material coated on one side with sticking composition.

Afterbirth. A body attached to the womb and by a cord to the child, supplying blood and nourishment before birth.

Albumen, albuminous. One of the elements of the body that hardens with heat. The white of an egg.

Aliment, alimentary. Food. The alimentary canal begins with the mouth and ends with the rectum.

Alkali. Caustic ; a substance which neutralizes acids.

Alterative Altering or purifying the blood.

Alternating. One medicine following another after an interval.

Altruism. Regard for another.

Alveoli. The bony sockets to the teeth.

Alvine. Pertaining to the intestines.

Anæmia. Deficiency in blood. The want of red corpuscles gives the pallid appearance to the skin.

Anæsthesia. Deprived of sensation.

Anaphrodisiac. An agent to blunt sexual appetite.

Anastomosis. Communication between blood-vessels.

Anatomy. A description of the organs of the body.

Anodyne. Relieving pain.

Antacid. Neutralizing acid.

Antibilious. A term applied to active cathartics.

Antidote. Medicines counteracting poisons and rendering them inert.

Anti-malarial. Preventing an attack of malaria.

Antiperiodic. Breaking up periodicity or appearance at regular intervals.

Antiperistaltic. Forcing the contents of the bowels backward into the stomach.

Antiseptic. Destroying poison.

Antispasmodic. Stopping spasms.

Antrum. See page 403.

Anus. The lower opening of the bowel.

Aörta. A large artery arising from the heart.

Aperient. A gentle laxative or purge.

Aphonia. Loss of voice.

Aphthous. Affected with aphthæ ; a curd-like covered sore.

Areola, areolar. The connecting tissue between fibres and vessels. Pertaining to areolæ.

Artery. A blood-vessel which (with one exception) carries the red blood.

Asphyxia. Suspended animation.

Aspirator. A pumping apparatus with a long, fine, sharp-pointed tube for removing fluids from internal parts.

Assimilation. The act of transforming the food into the various parts of the body.

Asthenic. Debilitated.

Atrophy, atrophied. Wasting away. Withered.

Auscultation. Discovering chest diseases by listening.

Axillary. Arising from a depression between the stem and leaf-stock.

BANDAGE. A long piece of cloth. of variable width, used for binding.
    Beaumb. To deprive of sensibility.
Bicuspid teeth. The fourth and fifth teeth from the centre of the lips.
Bile, bilious. A fluid secreted by the liver· Pertaining to bile : a peculiar temperament.
Blastema. A germ.
Bloodletting. Opening a vein in the arm to let out blood.
Bolus. A large pill or anything of its size·
Bougie. A flexible instrument for dilating the urethra.
Bronchial tubes. Vessels carrying air to the lungs. Bronchi.
Bronchus, bronchi. The lower air-passage.
Buccal walls. Inner surface of the cheeks.

CACOPLASM. Bad or low form of organization.
    Cœcum. A part of the intestines emptying into the colon ; the blind gut.
Calcareous. Of the nature of lime.
Calculus, calculous. A stony formation. Pertaining to calculus.
Capillary. Blood-vessels, hair-like in size.
Capsule. A covering or case.
Carbon. One of the elementary bodies or metalloids.
Cardiac. Pertaining to the heart.
Carnivora. Flesh-eating animals.
Cartilage, cartilaginous. A white, elastic, solid part of the body. Gristle. Gristly.
Caseous. Like cheese.
Castration. Removing the testicles.
Catamenial. Relating to the monthly flow.
Cathartics. Agents that produce evacuation of the bowels.
Catheter. A tube with an eyelet near its end, used for conveying fluids. See illustrations,
    pages 529 and 531.
Caustics. Corrosive or burning substances.
Celibate. A bachelor.
Cell. The smallest particle of living matter. The body and all of its parts are made up
    of cells.
Cellular tissue. The tissue uniting all parts of the body.
Cerebellum. The small or lower brain.
Cerebrum. The great or upper brain.
Cerumen, ceruminous. Ear-wax. Waxy.
Cholesterine. A crystallizable substance formed in the bile.
Chronic. Long-standing, seated.
Chyle. The milky fluid formed from digested food, and which is emptied directly into
    the blood-vessels.
Chyme. See page 38.
Cicatrix, cicatrices. The scar from a wound. Scars.
Circulation. The flow of blood from the heart to the extremities and back again.
Circumcision.
Clonic. Rigid, with occasional relaxation of the muscles.
Coagulate. To harden, as the white of an egg, by boiling.
Coitus. Sexual connection.
Collapse. Complete prostration or inaction.
Colliquative. Exhaustive.
Coma. Comatose, profound sleep.
Conception. Being with child in the womb.
Congenital. Dating from birth.
Congestion. The flow of blood to a part. Stagnant circulation.
Conjunctiva. The membrane covering the ball of the eye and inner surface of the eye-
    lids.
Contagion. Communication of disease from one to another by touch, food, drink, or
    the atmosphere.
Continence. Abstinence from sexual congress.
Convalesce, convalescence. To recover health and strength. Period of recovery.
Convulsions. Spasms.
Cornea. The tough transparent membrane in the front of the eyeball.
Corpuscle. A minute body. A particle.
Corroborant. A remedy which gives strength ; tonic.
Corrosive. Burning.

Cortical. The bark or external portion.

Costiveness. Irregular and delayed motion of the bowels. Constipation.

Counter-irritation. Irritating one part to relieve irritation in another.

Cramps. Sudden and painful contractions of muscles.

Cranial. Belonging to the skull.

Crisis. The period of change; it may be to worse or to better.

Cul-de-sac. A pouch.

Cupping. Drawing blood by lancing, and the application of a heated cup.

DECUSSATE. To cross each other.

Defecation. Evacuation of the bowels.

Dejections. Matter voided from the bowel.

Delirium. Mental aberration.

Deltoid muscle. A muscle passing over the shoulder and terminating at the centre and outer part of the upper arm.

Depurative. Purifying. Removing impurities.

Dextrine. A substance obtained from starch.

Diagnosis. Discovery of a disease by its symptoms; discriminating between a disease and others with which it may be confounded.

Diaphoretic. Inducing perspiration: sweating.

Diaphragm. The muscle separating the chest and its contents from the abdomen and its contents.

Diastaltic. Reflex action induced by the spinal marrow.

Diathesis. Tendency of the constitution to a particular disease.

Diathetic. Relating to predisposition to disease.

Dietic, dietetic. Relating to the food and drink.

Digestion. Conversion of the food into form suitable for nourishment and into refuse or excrement.

Disinfectant. Purifying or cleansing from infection.

Diuretic. Increasing by secretion the quantity of urine.

Dram. One-eighth of an ounce, or a teaspoonful of fluid.

Drastic. Very powerful cathartic action.

Duct. Canal.

Duodenum. The first part of the intestines.

Dysmenorrhœa. Painful menstruation.

Dyspnœa. Difficult breathing.

ECONOMY. The parts constituting the body or the laws governing them.

Effete. Worn out: useless.

Effusion. Escape of a fluid.

Elimination. Ejection by stimulating the secreting organs.

Eliminatives. Agents which expel substances from the body, as by the skin, kidneys, etc.

Emaciation. Loss of flesh.

Embryo. The animal in its earliest existence in the uterus.

Emesis. Vomiting.

Emission.

Emulsion. A pharmacal compound of oil and water.

Emunctory. Any organ of the body acting as the outlet of effete and worn-out matter.

Enceinte. Pregnant.

Encephalon. The head; all within the head.

Encysted. Covered with a membrane or sac.

Endosmosis. Fluids passing through membranes into structures.

Enema. Liquid injections into the bowel.

Enervation. Weakness.

Enteric. Intestinal.

Entozoa. Worms.

Epidemic. A disease attacking many individuals in a locality at the same time.

Epithelial. Relating to the thin covering to the eyes, lips, mouth, intestines, and the like.

Erosion. Corrosion; eating away.

Erosis. Amatory passion.

Eructations. Wind or gases raised from the stomach with some noise.

Essence, essential. The active principle of plants. A diluted oil.

Eustachian tube. A canal about two inches in length connecting the ear and back of the mouth (pharynx).

Exacerbation. Increase in fever.
Exanthematous. Attended with fever and skin eruption.
Excito-motory. Reflex nervous action.
Excito-nutrient. Affecting nutrition by reflex nervous action.
Excito-secretory. Affecting secretion by reflex nervous action.
Excrement, excrementitious. Matter ejected from the bowel.
Excretion, excretive. The faculty of selecting and discharging from the system fluids, as in sweating and in urine, useless matter as in feces, and impurities by either.
Exhaling. Breathing out; throwing off vapor.
Expectorant. Remedies which loosen phlegm in the air-passages, and hence facilitate its discharge and relieve oppressed breathing.
Expectorate. To discharge mucosities by coughing and spitting.
Expiration. Exhaling air by the lungs.
Extravasate. To escape from the containing vessel and permeate the surrounding textures.
Exudation. Escaping or discharging through pores.

FARINACEOUS. Containing farina or flour.
Fascicles. Little bundles of fibres.
Fauces. The back of the mouth and upper part of the throat.
Feces, fecal. That part of the food remaining after digestion and which is ejected at intervals from the bowels.
Feculent. Foul.
Fermentation. Chemical action and combination by which new substances are formed.
Fibre, fibrous. The hard, elastic, organic particle which, aggregated, forms muscle and other tissues.
Fibrine. An organic substance, fluid, coagulable, found in the blood, lymph, etc.
Filaments. A thready fibre.
Flagellation. Flapping the body with the corner of a wet towel or the snap of a whip.
Flatulence. Wind in the stomach and bowels.
Fœtus, fœtal. The young of any animal during uterine existence. Pertaining to the unborn.
Follicle. A little depression throwing off moisture to keep the contiguous part soft and supple.
Foreskin. The prolonged skin of the penis, which covers the glans or head.
Fumigation. Disinfection by gas, smoke, or vapor.
Function. The normal or healthy action of an organ.
Fundament. The seat; anus.
Fungus. Parasitical plant.

GANGLION. Masses of nerves resembling brain.
Ganglionic. Composed of ganglia.
Gangrene. Mortification; local death.
Gastric juice. The digestive fluid secreted by the stomach.
Generative. Productive.
Genetic. Pertaining to the genital organs.
Genitals. The generative organs.
Germ theory. The theory of the propagation of disease by germs floating in the atmosphere.
Gestation. The period of carrying the young in the womb.
Glands, glandular. Organs of the body, each possessing vital properties peculiar to itself, as secretion of tears, milk, saliva, urine, excretion, etc.
Glans. The conical end of the penis, covered by the foreskin.
Gluten. The ingredient in flour (farinæ) which gives it adhesiveness.
Grain. One-sixtieth of a dram.
Graminivora. Grain-eating animals.
Granular. Consisting of little grains.
Granules. Little grains.
Griping. The pains of colic.
Gullet. The canal for food leading from the throat to the stomach.
Gynæcology. That part of the science of medicine devoted to the diseases of women.

HECTIC. Debilitated; exhausted.
    Hereditary. Transmitted from parent to child.
Hibernate, hibernation. A partial suspension of animation. Animals that sleep through the winter, hibernate.
Histogenetic. Tissue-forming.
Hydragogues. Medicines producing copious, watery, alvine discharges.
Hydrocarbons. Starch, sugar, and oils.
Hydrogen. A light, inflammable gas, forming, by chemical combination, water and animal and vegetable matter.
Hygiene, hygienic. The science of the preservation of health.
Hymen. A fold of membrane at the outer orifice of the vagina, found sometimes, but not always, in virgins.
Hypertrophy. Increased nutrition and consequent growth.
Hypnotic. Producing sleep.
Hypochondriasis. Belief in the possession of an imaginary disease.
Hypodermic. Under the skin.
Hypodermic syringe. An instrument for injecting liquid remedies under the skin.

ILEUM. The convoluted portion of the intestines.
    Impotence. Loss of sexual power; inability to copulate.
Indications. The symptoms or conditions needing medication.
Infection, infecting. The communication of disease by touch, food, drink, or the breath.
Infecundity. Unfruitfulness.
Infiltrate. To penetrate the pores of a part.
Inflammation. A condition attended with heat, pain, redness, and swelling.
Injection. Passing a liquid into a cavity of the body, through and by means of a syringe.
Innocuous. Harmless.
Inoculation. Taking a disease by contact with an abraded surface.
Insolation. Sunstroke.
Insomnia. Inability to sleep.
Inspiration. Inhaling air by the lungs.
Inspissated. Thickened by evaporation.
Instinct. An inborn principle directing to health and self-preservation.
Intercostal. Between the ribs.
Intestine, intestinal. The canal from the stomach to the anus; the bowels. Relating to the intestines.
Invermination. Infested with worms.
Iris. The colored membrane seen in the eyeball; it is blue in blue eyes, gray in gray eyes, etc.
Irritation. Local excitement, or excess of vital action.

KIDNEYS. Two organs, one on each side of the spine, internally and above the small of the back, which secrete the urine from the blood.

LACHRYMAL gland. Organ for forming tears.
    Lachrymation. Weeping.
Lacteal. Milky. Vessels containing chyle.
Larynx. The Adam's apple of the neck; the upper part of the windpipe which contains the organs of voice.
Lancinating. A deep and sudden pain, compared to the stab of a lancet.
Leeching. Removing blood by the application of a leech.
Lesion. A diseased change.
Leucocytes. White corpuscles of the blood.
Leucorrhœa. Whites.
Liquor sanguinis. The fluid part of the blood, holding in solution fibrine, albumen, etc.
Liver. The great assimilating gland of the body. It is situated below the diaphragm or midriff, and above the stomach, bowels, and kidney, and extends from the base of the chest to the spine, and from side to side.
Lobe. A rounded, projecting part.
Loins. The small of the back, between the ribs and pelvis.
Lungs. Two organs situated in the chest, one on each side, with the heart between; the organs of respiration.

Lymph, lymphatic. The fluid secretion of the lymphatic glands, which is emptied into the circulation.

MACKINTOSH. Cloth covered with waterproof material.
    Malaria. Poisoning emanations in the air, producing disease.
Mammary gland. The female breast.
Mastication. Chewing the food.
Masturbation. Personal excitement of the sexual organs.
Median line. An imaginary line dividing the body into the right and left side.
Medulla oblongata. An organ, marrow-like, lying at the base of the skull.
Medullary. Pertaining to the marrow.
Membrane, membranous. A thin, web-like structure covering parts and organs, and lining cavities.
Meninges. Coverings of the brain and spinal cord.
Mensis, menses. The monthly uterine flow during the middle age of women.
Menstrual. Pertaining to the monthly flow.
Mesentery. The folds of the peritoneum which hold the intestines in place.
Metamorphosis. Transformation.
Metastasis. Change in the seat of a disease.
Miasm, miasmatic. The germs of disease floating in the air, which produce infection.
Microscope. An instrument for magnifying minute objects.
Micturate. To evacuate the bladder.
Molar teeth. The sixth, seventh, and eighth teeth from the centre of the lips.
Molecule. A little portion of any body.
Morbid. Diseased.
Motor. Moving.
Mucilages. The gummy principle of plants.
Mucoid. Like mucus.
Mucus, mucous. A viscid fluid, which in health keeps the membranes in their proper condition.
Myopic. Near-sighted.

NARCOTIC. A stupefying remedy; in large doses destroying life.
    Nausea. Sickness at the stomach; ineffectual effort to vomit.
Navel. The round scar at the centre of the abdomen, marking the place of attachment of the cord previous to and at birth.
Neuralgia. Nerve-pain.
Neurine. The substance of which the brain is composed.
Nitrogen, nitrogenous. The gas constituting four-fifths of the volume of the atmosphere.
Noxious. Poisonous; harmful.
Nucleus, nuclei. The germinal point in a cell: kernel.
Nutrition. Increasing in growth, or supplying the materials for growth.

OBCORDATE. Half egg-shape and half heart-shape.
    Obesity. Excessively fat.
Œsophagus. The food-passage from the throat to the stomach.
Œstruation. Periodical sexual desire; heat.
Oleaginous. Oily.
Ophthalmoscope. An instrument for examining the interior of the eye by concentrated and reflected light.
Optic nerve. The nerve conveying visual impressions from the eye to the brain.
Osmosis. Attraction of fluids for each other through moist membranes and their motion.
Ossicles. Little bones.
Ounce. One-sixteenth of a pound: in fluids, eight drams or teaspoonfuls.
Oxygen. The gas constituting one-fifth the volume of the atmosphere. It supports combustion.

PAD. A folded cloth used as a support.
    Palate. Roof of the mouth.
Palatine arch. The arch, in the rear of the mouth, formed by the palate bone.
Palsy. Loss of sensation or motion, or both; paralysis.

Pancreas, pancreatic juice. A large gland in the abdomen, beneath and behind the stomach. Its secretion.

Papillæ. Little raised points upon the surface; they can be seen upon the tongue.

Papulose, papular. With dry pimples.

Paralysis. To lose the power of motion in a part, or sensation, or both.

Parasites. Animals or plants that subsist upon others.

Parenchyma. The texture of organs like the liver, kidneys, etc.

Parotid gland. A gland at the angle of the lower jaw, which secretes saliva and discharges it by a short tube upon the cheek near an upper molar (back) tooth.

Paroxysm. The period of more aggravated symptoms, following an interval of comparative freedom.

Parturition. Childbirth.

Pathology. That department of medical science whose object is the knowledge of disease.

Pelvis. The bony structure at the termination of the spine, enveloping and protecting the lower intestines, bladder, genitals, etc.

Pentandria Monogynia. A name given to a class of plants having five stamens and one style.

Percussion. Striking with the finger-tips to discover by the resonance the condition of internal parts.

Perineum. The part between the genitals and the anus or tip of the spine.

Periodicity. Occurring at regular periods, as a chill every other day, etc.

Periosteum. The tough membrane covering all bones.

Peristaltic. The peculiar motion of the intestines which propels its contents forward, somewhat like the crawling of a worm.

Peritoneum. The membrane lining the abdominal walls and covering the intestines.

Petaloid. Resembling a leaf-stock.

Petals. The colored leaves of a flower.

Pharmacist, pharmaceutist. One who manufactures drugs.

Pharmacy. The manufacture of drugs.

Pharynx. The posterior portion of the cavity of the mouth, behind the palate, above the wind-pipe and gullet. The breath and food pass through it.

Phosphorus, phosphates. A substance familiar to us in matches. It is a constituent of the brain and nerves.

Phrenic nerve. The respiratory nerve. It arises in the neck, passes through it and the chest, and is mainly distributed to the diaphragm.

Physiology. The functions of the organs of the body; the phenomena of life.

Pile-compressor. An instrument supporting the rectum and anus.

Placenta. A fleshy body attached to the womb and by a cord to the child, supplying blood and nourishment before birth.

Plasma. The fluid portion of the blood holding in solution fibrine, albumen, etc.

Plastic. Formative.

Plethora. Abounding in blood; full-blooded.

Pleura. A wetted membrane lining the walls of the chest and covering the outer surface of the lung. There are two.

Plexus. A net-work of blood-vessels or nerves.

Pneumogastric nerve. The great nerve distributed to the chest and stomach.

Polypus. A kind of tumor.

Post-mortem. After death.

Prepuce. The prolonged skin of the penis which covers the glans or head.

Probang. A whalebone rod with a sponge on one end.

Probe. A wire for examining wounds, canals, etc.

Prophylactic. Preventive.

Prostate gland. A gland at the upper portion of the urethra surrounding it and touching the bladder.

Psoas muscle. The great muscle which draws the thigh up to the abdomen.

Puberty. That period of life, about the age of 13, when the procreative organs most rapidly develop; hair grows about them and upon the face of the male, the breasts of the female enlarge, and, in fact, the period of youth has passed and that of manhood or womanhood arrived.

Pubic bone. A bone in the lower abdomen immediately under that part of the surface covered with hair.

Pulse.

Pupil. The circular opening in the colored part of the eye (iris).

Purgative. A medicine causing free alvine discharges.

Pus. Matter discharged from inflamed tissue.
Pustules. Mattery pimples.

RECEPTACULUM CHYLI. A hollow organ for holding chyle.
    Rectum, rectal. That portion of the bowels nearest the outlet.
Recuperate. To regain health and strength.
Regurgitate. To flow backward.
Remission. Decrease in fever.
Renal. Pertaining to the kidney.
Respiration. Breathing.
Retching. Ineffectual effort to vomit.
Retina. The lining to the eye.
Revulsive. Agents which create diseased action on the surface to relieve internal disorder.
Roborant. Strengthening; tonic.
℞, recipe. Take the articles following.

SACCHARINE. Of the nature of sugar.
    Saliva. One of the digestive fluids which is mixed with the food during mastication.
Sanitarium. A remedial institute.
Schneiderian membrane. The lining of the nasal cavity.
Scrofulous. Of the nature of scrofula.
Scrotum. The skin covering the testicles.
Sebaceous. A name given to the oil-glands of the skin.
Secernent. Secreting.
Secrete, secretion. Drawing out fluids from the blood; each gland absorbs material peculiar to itself.
Sedatives. Remedies which control or depress excessive vital action.
Self-pollution. Personal excitement of the sexual organs.
Semen. The fecundating fluid of the male which is secreted by the testicles.
Seminal. Pertaining to semen or sperm.
Sensorium. The centre of sensations.
Sepals. The leaves of the envelope of a flower.
Serum, serous. The watery portion of animal fluids.
Sigmoid flexure. A bend in the intestines just above the rectum.
Sinapism. An irritating plaster.
Sound. A solid rod, catheter shape.
Spasms. Violent and involuntary muscular movements.
Specific disease. Syphilitic diseases; private diseases.
Speculum. An instrument for dilating the orifice to internal canals or cavities.
Spermatic. Pertaining to sperm or the organs of generation.
Spermatic cord. A cord consisting of blood-vessels, nerves, and the canal of the sperm, which supports the testicle.
Spermatozoa. The formative agents in generation found in the semen of the male.
Sphincter. A round muscle closing an outlet.
Spicula. A splinter of bone.
Spleen. A spongy organ situated deep in the upper abdomen, between the kidney and stomach.
Sputa. Expectorated matter.
Squamous. Scaly.
Stercoraceous. Excrementitious.
Sternutatives. Remedies which provoke sneezing.
Stethoscope.
Sthenic. Possessing excessive strength.
Stun. Unconsciousness produced by a blow or fall.
Stupor. Diminished sensibility or exercise of the intellectual faculties.
Styptic. Arresting hemorrhage; astringent.
Sublingual gland. A salivary gland under the tongue.
Sudoriferous. A name given to the sweat-glands of the skin.
Suppository. A semi-solid medicine deposited in the rectum.
Suppurate. To discharge matter or pus.
Suspensory bandage.
Sympathetic nerves. The nervous system of the automatic functions.
Symptom. A sign of disease.
Syncope. Fainting.

TAMPON. A plug made of lint or cotton.

Tapping. Drawing off fluids in cavities by puncturing the surface.

Tenesmus. Violent contractions.

Testes. The male organs contained in the scrotum.

Testicles. Testes.

Tetanus. Permanent contraction of muscles.

Therapeutics. The department of medical science concerned the treatment of disease.

Thoracic. Pertaining to the chest.

Thyroid glands. Throat-glands.

Tissues. The anatomical elements of organs.

Tonics. Remedies which improve the health and strength.

Tonsil. A gland at the side of the throat near the soft palate.

Toxic. Poisonous.

Trachea. That part of the windpipe between the larynx or vocal organs and the bronchial tubes.

Traumatic. Pertaining to a wound.

Tubercle. Concretions of degenerated matter.

Tubule. A little tube or canal.

Tympanitic. Having a drum-like sound from the accumulation of air.

Tympanum. The drum of the ear.

ULCER, ulceration. A chronic sore situated in the soft parts. A diseased action resulting in ulcer.

Umbilicus. The navel.

Urænic. Pertaining to urine.

Urea. A constituent of urine.

Ureters. The canals, two in number, carrying the urine from the kidneys to the bladder.

Urethra. The canal or pipe leading from the bladder for the conveyance of urine from the body.

Uric acid. A constituent of urine; in excess it forms combinations, producing calculus or stone.

Urine. The secretion of the kidneys which collects in the bladder and is discharged through the urethra.

Uterus. An organ situated between the bladder and rectum and above the vagina, which holds the fœtus during gestation.

Uvula. A fleshy organ hanging from the centre of the soft palate.

VACCINE. Pertaining to small-pox.

Vagina. The canal, five or six inches in length, leading to the uterus or womb.

Varicose. Pertaining to a dilated vein.

Vascular. Full of blood-vessels.

Vaso-motor. Affecting vessels by reflex nervous action.

Vein. A blood-vessel which, with one exception, carries the blue or venous blood.

Ventricle. A chamber in the heart.

Vertigo. Dizziness.

Vesicle. A bladder-like sac.

Vesicular. Full of little vessels.

Vicarious. In place of another; a function performed through other than the natural channels.

Virus. The poison transmitting infectious disease.

Viscus, viscera. An organ of the body. Organs.

Vitality. The vital principle.

Void. To evacuate.

Vomiting. Emptying the stomach upward.

WATER-BRASH. A profuse flow of saliva.

Womb. An organ situated between the bladder and rectum and above the vagina, which holds the fœtus during gestation.

ZÖON, zoä. Animal. Animals.

Zymotic. Epidemic and contagious.

MYTHOLOGICAL DICTIONARY.

ACHATES. A friend of Æneas, whose fidelity was so exemplary that *Fidus Achates* has become a proverb.

ACHILLES, the son of Peleus and Thetis, was the bravest of all the Greeks in the Trojan war. During his infancy, Thetis plunged him in the Styx, thus making every part of his body invulnerable except the heel by which she held him.

ACTÆON. A famous huntsman, son of Aristæus and Autonoe, daughter of Cadmus. He saw Diana and her attendants bathing, for which he was changed into a stag and devoured by his own dogs.

ADONIS, son of Cinyras and Myrrha, was the favorite of Venus. He was fond of hunting, and was often cautioned not to hunt wild beasts. This advice he slighted, and at last was mortally wounded by a wild boar.

ÆGIS. The shield of Jupiter. He gave it to Pallas, who placed Medusa's head on it, which turned into stones all those who gazed at it.

ÆNEAS. A Trojan prince, son of Anchises and Venus. He married Creusa, the daughter of Priam, and they had a son named Ascanius. During the Trojan war Æneas behaved with great valor in defense of Troy.

ÆOLUS, the ruler of storms and winds, was the son of Hippotas. He reigned over Æolia. He was the inventor of sails, and a great astronomer, from which the poets have called him the god of wind.

ÆSCULAPIUS, son of Apollo and Coronis, or as some say of Apollo and Larissa, daughter of Phlegias, was the god of medicine.

AJAX, son of Telamon and Peribœa, or Eribœa, was one of the bravest of the Greeks in the Trojan war.

ALBION, son of Neptune and Amphitrite, came into Britain, where he established a kingdom and introduced astrology and the art of building ships. Great Britain is called "Albion" after him.

ALECTO. One of the furies. She is represented with her head covered with serpents, and breathing vengeance, war and pestilence.

AMPHION, son of Jupiter and Antiope. He cultivated poetry, and made such progress in music that he is said to have been the inventor of it, and to have built the walls of Thebes by the sound of his lyre.

AMPHITRITE. A daughter of Oceanus and Tethys, who married Neptune. She is sometimes called Salatia. She was mother of Triton, a sea deity.

ANDROMEDA. A daughter of Cepheus, king of Æthiopia, and Cassiope. She was promised in marriage to Phineus when Neptune drowned the kingdom and sent a sea monster to ravage the country, because Cassiope had boasted that she was fairer than

Juno and the Nereides. The oracle of Jupiter Ammon was consulted, but nothing could stop the resentment of Neptune except the exposure of Andromeda to the sea monster. She was accordingly tied to a rock, but at the moment the monster was about to devour her, Perseus, returning from the conquest of the Gorgons, saw her, and was captivated with her beauty. He changed the monster into a rock by showing Medusa's head, and released Andromeda and married her.

ANTIOPE, daughter of Nycteus, king of Thebes, and Polyxo, was beloved by Jupiter. Amphion and Tethus were her offspring.

APHRODITE. The Grecian name for Venus, because Venus is said to have been born from the froth of the ocean.

APIS. A god of the Egyptians, worshipped under the form of an ox. Some say that Isis and Osiris are the deities worshipped under this name, because they taught the Egyptians agriculture.

APOLLO. Son of Jupiter and Latona; called also Phœbus. He was the god of the fine arts and the reputed originator of music, poetry and eloquence. He had received from Jupiter the power of knowing futurity, and his oracles were in repute everywhere.

ARETHUSA, a nymph of Elis, daughter of Oceanus, and one of Diana's attendants. As she returned one day from hunting she bathed in the Alpheus stream. The god of the river was enamored of her, and pursued her over the mountains, till Arethusa, ready to sink from fatigue, implored Diana to change her into a fountain, wich the goddess did.

ARGUS. A son of Arestor, whence he is sometimes called Arestorides. He had a hundred eyes, of which only two were asleep at one time. Juno set him to watch Io, whom Jupiter had changed into a heifer, but Mercury, by order of Jupiter, slew him, by lulling all his eyes to sleep with the notes of the lyre. Juno put the eyes of Argus in the tail of the peacock, a bird sacred to her.

ARIADNE, daughter of Minos, second king of Crete, and Pasiphæ, fell in love with Theseus, who was shut up in the labyrinth to be devoured by the Minotaur. She gave Theseus a clue of thread by which he extricated himself from the windings of the labyrinth. After he had conquered the Minotaur he married her, but after a time forsook her. On this, according to some authorities, she hanged herself.

ATE. Daughter of Jupiter and goddess of all evil. She raised such discord among the gods that Jupiter banished her from heaven and sent her to dwell on earth, where she incited mankind to evil thoughts and actions.

BACCHUS was son of Jupiter and Semele, the daughter of Cadmus. He was the god of wine, and is generally represented crowned with vine leaves.

BOREAS. The name of the north wind blowing from the Hyperborean mountains. According to the poets, he was son of Astræus and Aurora. He was passionately fond of Hyacinthus.

BRIAREUS. A famous giant, son of Cœlus and Terra. He had a hundred hands and fifty heads, and was called by men by the name of Ægeon.

CACUS, a famous robber, son of Vulcan and Medusa, represented as a three-headed monster vomiting flames. He resided in Italy, and the avenues of his cave were covered with human bones.

CADUCEUS. A rod entwined at one end with two serpents. It was the attribute of Mercury, and was given to him by Apollo in exchange for the lyre.

CALLIOPE. One of the Muses, daughter of Jupiter and Mnemosyne, who presided over eloquence and heroic poetry.

CASSANDRA, daughter of Priam and Hecuba, was passionately loved by Apollo, who promised to grant her whatever she might require, and she obtained from him the power of seeing into futurity.

CASTOR and **POLLUX** were twin brothers, sons of Jupiter and Leda. Mercury carried them to Pallena, where they were educated. As soon as they arrived at manhood they embarked with Jason in quest of the Golden Fleece. In this expedition they evinced great courage. Pollux defeated and slew Amycus in the combat of the Cestus, and was afterwards considered to be the god and patron of boxing and wrestling. Castor distinguished himself in the management of horses.

CERBERUS. A dog of Pluto. According to Hesiod he had fifty heads, but according to other mythologists he had three only. He was placed at the entrance to the infernal regions to prevent the living from entering, and the inhabitants of the place from escaping.

CERES, the goddess of corn and harvests, was daughter of Saturn and Vesta. She was the mother of Prosperpine, who was carried away by Pluto while she was gathering flowers.

CHARON. A god of the infernal regions, son of Nox and Erebus, who conducted the souls of the dead in a boat over the rivers Styx and Acheron.

CHIMÆRA. A celebrated monster which continually vomited flames. It was destroyed by Bellerophon.

CHIRON. A centaur, half a man and half a horse, son of Philyra and Saturn. He was famous for his knowledge of music, medicine and shooting, and taught mankind the use of plants and medicinal herbs.

CIRCE. A daughter of Sol and Perseis, celebrated for her knowledge of magic and venomous herbs.

CLIO. The first of the Muses, daughter of Jupiter and Mnemosyne. She presided over history.

CLOACINA. A goddess at Rome who presided over the Cloaæ, which were large receptacles for the filth of the whole city.

CLOTHO, the youngest of the three Parcæ, who were daughters of Jupiter and Themis, were supposed to preside over the moment of birth. She held the distaff in her hand and spun the thread of life.

CLYTIA or **CLYTIE.** A daughter of Oceanus and Tethys, beloved by Apollo. She was changed into a sunflower.

COMUS. The god of revelry, feasting and nocturnal amusements. He is represented as a drunken young man with a torch in his hand.

CYBELE. A goddess, daughter of Cœlus and Terra, and wife of Saturn.

CYCLOPES. A race of men of gigantic stature, supposed to be the sons of Cœlus and Terra. They had only one eye, which was in the center of the forehead. According to Hesiod they were three in number, named Arges, Brontes and Steropes.

DAPHNE. A daughter of the River Peneus, or of the Ladon, and the goddess Terra, of whom Apollo became enamored. Daphne fled to avoid the addresses of this god, and was changed into a laurel.

DEJANIRA. A daughter of Œneus, king of Ætolia. Her beauty procured her many admirers, and her father promised to give her in marriage to him who should excel in a competition of strength. Hercules obtained the prize, and married Dejanira.

DIANA. The goddess of hunting. According to Cicero there were three of the name, viz., a daughter of Jupiter and Proserpine, a daughter of Jupiter and Latona, and a daughter of Upis and Glauce. The second is the most celebrated, and all mention of Diana by ancient writers refers to her. To shun the society of men she devoted herself to hunting, and was always accompanied by a number of young women who, like herself, abjured marriage. She is represented with a quiver and attended by dogs. The most famous of her temples was that at Ephesus, which was one of the wonders of the world.

DIOMEDES, a son of Tydeus and Deiphyle, was king of Ætolia, and one of the bravest of the Grecian chiefs in the Trojan war. He often engaged Hector and Æneas, and obtained much military glory.

DRYADES. Nymphs that presided over the woods. Oblations of milk, oil and honey were offered to them. Sometimes the votaries of the Dryads sacrificed a goat to them.

ECHO. A daughter of the Air and Tellus, who was one of Juno's attendants. She was deprived of speech by Juno, but was allowed to reply to questions put to her.

ELYSIUM. The Elysian Fields, a place in the infernal regions, where, according to the ancients, the souls of the virtuous existed after death.

ENDYMION. A shepherd, son of Æthlius and Calyce. He is said to have required of Jupiter that he might always be young. Diana saw him as he slept on Mount Latmus, and was so struck with his beauty that she came down from heaven every night to visit him.

EOS. The name of Aurora among the Greeks.

ERATO. One of the muses. She presided over lyric poetry, and is represented as crowned with roses and myrtle and holding a lyre in her hand.

EREBUS. A deity of the infernal regions, son of Chaos and Darkness. The poets often use the word to signify the infernal regions.

EUROPA. A daughter of Agenor, king of Phœnicia, and Telaphassa. Her beauty attracted Jupiter, and to become possessed of her he assumed the shape of a handsome bull, and mingled with the herds of Agenor while Europa was gathering flowers in the meadows. She caressed the animal and mounted on his back. The god crossed the sea with her and arrived in Crete, where he assumed his proper form and declared his love. She became mother of Minos, Sarpedon and Rhadamanthus.

EUTERPE. One of the Muses, daughter of Jupiter and Mnemosyne. She presided over music.

FAUNI. Rural deities represented as having the legs, feet and ears of goats, and the rest of the body human.

FLORA. The goddess of flowers and gardens among the Romans. She was the same as the Chloris among the Greeks.

FORTUNA. A powerful deity among the ancients, daughter of Oceanus according to Homer, or one of the Parcæ according to Pindar. She was the goddess of Fortune, and bestowed riches or poverty on mankind.

GALATÆ. A sea nymph, daughter of Nereus and Doris. She was loved by Polyphemus, the Cyclops, whom she treated with disdain, while she was in love with Acis, a shepherd.

GANYMEDES. A beautiful youth of Phrygia. He was taken to heaven by Jupiter while tending flocks on Mount Ida, and he became the cup bearer of the gods in place of Hebe.

GIGANTES. The sons of Cœlus and Terra, who, according to Hesiod, sprang from the blood of a wound inflicted on Cœlus by his son Saturn. They were represented as huge giants with strength in accordance with their size.

GLAUCUS. A fisherman of Bœotia. He observed that the fishes which he caught and laid on the grass became invigorated and leaped into the sea. He tasted the grass, and suddenly felt a desire to live in the sea. He was made a sea deity by Oceanus and Tethys.

HARPYLÆ. The Harpies, winged monsters who had the face of a woman, the body of a vulture, and feet and fingers armed with claws. They were three in number—Aello, Ocypete and Celeno. They were daughters of Neptune and Terra.

HEBE. A daughter of Jupiter and Juno. She was made cupbearer to the gods, but was dismissed from the office by Jupiter because she fell down in a clumsy posture as she was pouring out nectar at a festival, and Ganymedes succeeded her as cupbearer.

HELENA. One of the most beautiful women in the age in which she lived. Her beauty was so universally admired, even in her infancy, that Theseus, with his friend Pirithous, carried her away when she was ten years of age and concealed her with his mother, but she was recovered by Castor and Pollux, and restored to her native country.

HERCULES. A celebrated hero who, after death, was ranked among the gods.

HESIONE. A daughter of Laodemon, king of Troy. It was her fate to be exposed to a sea monster, to whom the Trojans presented yearly a young girl to appease the resentment of Apollo and Neptune, whom Laodemon had offended. Hercules undertook to rescue her, and attacking the monster just as he was about to devour her, killed him with his club.

HYACINTHUS. A son of Amyclas and Diomede, greatly beloved by Apollo and Zephyrus. He was accidentally killed by Apollo, who changed his blood into a flower which bore his name.

HYGEIA. The goddess of health, daughter of Æsculapius. She was held in great veneration among the ancients.

ICARUS. A son of Daedalus who, with his father, took a winged flight from Crete to escape the anger of Minos. His flight was too high, and thus the sun melted the wax which cemented his wings, and he fell into the sea and was drowned.

Io, a daughter of Inachus, was a priestess of Juno at Argos. Jupiter changed her into a beautiful heifer, and eventually restored her to her own form. She was greatly persecuted by Juno.

ISIS. A celebrated deity of the Egyptians, daughter of Saturn and Rhea, according to Diodorus of Sicily.

JANUS. An ancient king who reigned in Italy. He was a native of Thessaly, and, according to some writers, a son of Apollo.

JUNO. A celebrated deity among the ancients, daughter of Saturn and Ops. Jupiter married her, and the nuptials were celebrated with the greatest solemnity in the presence of all the gods. By her marriage with Jupiter, Juno became the queen of all the gods, and mistress of heaven and earth. She presided over marriage, and patronized those of her sex who were distinguished for virtuous conduct.

JUPITER. The chief of all the gods of the ancients.

LAOCON. A priest of Apollo who in the Trojan war was opposed to the admission of the wooden horse to the city.

LARES. Gods of inferior power at Rome, who presided over houses and families.

LEMURES. The manes of the dead. The ancients supposed that after death the departed souls wandered over the world and disturbed the peace of its inhabitants.

LETHE. One of the rivers of hell, whose waters were imbibed by the souls of the dead which had been for a certain time confined in Tartarus. Those who drank of this river forgot whatever they had previously known.

LUCIFER. The name of the planet Venus or morning star.

LUCINA. Daughter of Jupiter and Juno. She was the goddess who presided over the birth of children.

MEDUSA. One of the three Gorgons, daughter of Phorcys and Ceto. She was the only one of the Gorgons subject to mortality. She was celebrated for her personal charms and the beauty of her hair, which Minerva changed into serpents.

MARS, the god of war, was the son of Jupiter and Juno. The loves of Mars and Venus are greatly celebrated. On one occasion, while in each other's company, Vulcan spread a net round them, from which they could not escape without assistance. They were thus exposed to the ridicule of the gods till Neptune induced Vulcan to set them at liberty.

MELPOMENE. One of the Muses, daughter of Jupiter and Mnemosyne. She presided over tragedy. She is generally represented as a young woman wearing a buskin and holding a dagger in her hand.

MERCURIUS. A celebrated god of antiquity, called Hermes by the Greeks. He was the messenger of the gods, and conducted the souls of the dead into the infernal regions.

MINERVA, the goddess of wisdom, war and all the liberal arts, sprang, full grown and armed, from the head of Jupiter, and was immediately admitted to the assembly of the gods, and became one of the most faithful counsellors of her father. Her power in heaven was so great, she could hurl the thunders of Jupiter, prolong the life of men, and bestow the gift of prophecy.

MINOTAURUS. A celebrated monster, half a man and half a bull, for which a number of young Athenian men and maidens were yearly exacted to be devoured.

MNEMOSYNE. A daughter of Cœlus and Terra, mother of the nine Muses. Jupiter assumed the form of a shepherd in order to enjoy her company.

MOMUS, the god of mirth among the ancients, according to Hesiod, was the son of Nox. He amused himself by satirising the gods by turning into ridicule whatever they did.

MORPHEUS. A minister of the god Somnus, who imitated very naturally the gestures, words and manners of mankind. He is sometimes called the god of sleep. He is generally represented as a sleeping child, of great corpulence, with wings.

NAIADES. Inferior deities who presided over rivers, springs, wells and fountains.

NEMESIS. One of the infernal deities, daughter of Nox. She was the goddess of vengeance.

NEPTUNUS. One of the gods, son of Saturn and Ops, and brother to Jupiter and Pluto. He was devoured by his father as soon as he was born, and restored to life again by a potion given to Saturn by Metis, the first wife of Jupiter.

NEREIDES. Nymphs of the sea, daughters of Nereus and Doris. According to most of the mythologists, they were fifty in number. They are represented as young and handsome girls, sitting on dolphins and armed with tridents.

NESSUS. A celebrated Centaur killed by Hercules for insulting Dejanira.

NOX. One of the most ancient deities among the heathens, daughter of Chaos. She gave birth to the Day and the Light, and was mother of the Parcæ, Hesperides, Dreams, Death, etc.

NARCISSUS, a beautiful youth, son of Cephisus and the nymph Liriope, was born at Thespis in Bœotia. He saw his image reflected in a fountain and became in love with it, thinking it to be the nymph of the place. His fruitless attempts to reach this beautiful object so provoked him, that he killed himself. His blood was then changed into a flower which still bears his name.

OCEANIDES and OCEANITIDES. Sea nymphs, daughters of Oceanus, from whom they received their name. According to Apollodorus they were 3,000 in number.

OCEANUS. A powerful deity of the sea, son of Cœlus and Terra. He married Tethys, the Oceanides being their children.

OPS. A daughter of Cœlus and Terra, the same as the Rhea of the Greeks, who married Saturn and became mother of Jupiter.

ORPHEUS. A son of Œger and the Muse Calliope. He received a lyre from Apollo, or, according to some, from Mercury, on which he played in so masterly a manner that the melodious sounds caused rivers to cease to flow, and savage beasts to forget their wildness.

OSIRIS. A great deity of the Egyptians, husband of Isis. The ancients differ in opinion concerning this celebrated god, but they all agree that as ruler of Egypt he took care to civilize his subjects, to improve their morals, to give them good and salutary laws, and to teach them agriculture.

PÆAN. A surname of Apollo derived from the word *Pæan*, a hymn which was sung in his honor for killing the serpent Python.

PALLAS. A name of Minerva. She is said to have received the name because she killed a noted giant bearing that name.

PAN. The god of shepherds, huntsmen, and the inhabitants of the country. He was in appearance a monster; he had two small horns on his head, and his legs, thighs, tail and feet were like those of the goat.

PANDORA. A celebrated woman; the first mortal female that ever lived, according to Hesiod.

PASIPHAE. A daughter of the Sun and of Perseis, who married Minos, king of Crete. She became the mother of the Minotaur which was killed by Theseus.

PENATES. Certain inferior deities among the Romans, who presided over the domestic affairs of families.

PHAON. A boatman of Mitylene, in Lesbos. He received a box of ointment from Venus, who presented herself to him in the form of an old woman. When he had rubbed himself with the unguent he became beautiful, and Sappho, the celebrated poetess, became enamored with him. For a short time he devoted himself to her, but soon treated her with coldness, upon which she threw herself into the sea and was drowned.

PHILOCTETES was one of the Argonauts. He received from Hercules the arrows which had been dipped in the gall of the Hydra.

PARCÆ. The Fates, powerful goddesses who presided over the birth and life of mankind.

PEGASUS. A winged horse sprung from the blood of Medusa. According to Ovid he fixed his abode on Mount Helicon, where, by striking the earth with his foot, he raised a fountain which has been called Hippocrene.

PHLEGETHON. A river in the infernal regions, between the banks of which flames of fire flowed instead of water.

PHYLLIS. A daughter of Sithon. She received Demophoon, who landed on her coasts on his return from the Trojan war, and fell in love with him, and he reciprocated her affection; but afterwards proving faithless, Phyllis hanged herself, and according to an old tradition was changed into an almond tree.

PIDUS. King of Latium, son of Saturn, who married Venilia. As he was hunting he was met by Circe, who became enamored with him. She changed him into a woodpecker.

PLEIADES. A name given to seven daughters of Atlas and Pleione. They were placed after death in the heavens and formed a constellation.

PLUTO, son of Saturn and Ops, inherited his father's kingdom with his brothers, Jupiter and Neptune. He received as his portion the kingdom of the infernal regions, of death, and funerals. He seized Proserpine as she was gathering flowers, and carrying her away on his chariot, she became his wife and queen of the infernal regions.

PLUTUS, the god of riches, was the son of Jason, or Jasius, and Ceres.

POLYHYMNIA. One of the Muses, daughter of Jupiter and Mnemosyne. She presided over singing and rhetoric.

POMONA. A nymph at Rome, who was supposed to preside over gardens and to be the goddess of fruit trees.

PROSERPINA, a daughter of Ceres and Jupiter, called by the Greeks Persephone. As she was gathering flowers Pluto carried her off to the infernal regions, where he married her. Ceres, having learnt that her daughter had been carried away by Pluto, demanded of Jupiter that Pluto should be punished. As queen of hell, Proserpine presided over the death of mankind.

PSYCHE. A nymph who married Cupid. Venus put her to death because of this, but Jupiter, at the request of Cupid, granted immortality to her.

PYTHON. A celebrated serpent sprung from the mud and stagnated waters which remained on the surface of the earth after the deluge of Deucalion. Apollo killed the monster.

SIRENES. The Sirens. They lured to destruction those who listened to their songs. When Ulysses sailed past their island he stopped the ears of his companions with wax, and had himself tied to the mast of his ship. Thus he passed with safety, and the Sirens, disappointed of their prey, drowned themselves.

SATURNUS. The son of Cœlus, or Uranus, by Terra. It was customary to offer human victims on his altars till this custom was abolished by Hercules. He is generally represented as an old man bent with age, and holding a scythe in his right hand.

SILENUS. A demigod, who is represented generally as a fat old man riding on an ass, with flowers crowning his head.

SISYPHUS. Son of Æolus and Enaretta. After death he was condemned, in the infernal regions, to roll a stone to the summit of a hill, which always rolled back, and rendered his punishment eternal.

SOMNUS, son of Nox and Erebus, was one of the infernal deities, and presided over sleep.

SPHINX. A monster, having the head and breasts of a woman, the body of a dog, the tail of a serpent, the wings of a bird, and the paws of a lion.

STYX. A celebrated river of the infernal regions. The gods held it in such veneration that they always swore by it, the oath being inviolable.

TARTARUS. One of the regions of hell, where, according to Virgil, the souls of those who were exceptionally depraved were punished.

TERPSICHORE. One of the Muses, daughter of Jupiter and Mnemosyne. She presided over dancing.

THALIA. One of the Muses. She presided over festivals and comic poetry.

THETIS. A sea deity, daughter of Nereus and Doris. She married Peleus, their son being Achilles, whom she plunged into the Styx, thus rendering him invulnerable in every part of the body except the heel by which she held him.

TITANES. The Titans. A name given to the gigantic sons of Cœlus and Terra.

TRITON. A sea deity, son of Neptune and Amphitrite. He was very powerful, and could calm the sea and abate storms at his pleasure.

TYPHŒUS, or TYPHON. A famous giant, son of Tartarus and Terra, who had a hundred heads. He made war against the gods, and was put to flight by the thunderbolts of Jupiter, who crushed him under Mount Ætna.

URANIA. One of the Muses, daughter of Jupiter and Mnemosyne. She presided over astronomy.

VENUS. One of the most celebrated deities of the ancients; the goddess of beauty and mother of love. She sprang from the foam of the sea, and was carried to heaven, where all the gods admired her beauty.

VESTA. A goddess, daughter of Rhea and Saturn. The Palladium, a celebrated statue of Pallas, was supposed to be preserved within her sanctuary, where a fire was kept continually burning.

VULCANUS. The god who presided over fire, and who was the patron of those who worked in iron.

BUSINESS VOCABULARY.

Acceptance. A draft drawn on a party and by him indorsed on the face with his agreement to pay it when due.

Account. A statement of indebtedness, etc.

Acquittance. A discharge in full.

Ad valorem. In proportion to value.

Annul. To cancel.

Assets. Funds or effects.

Assignment. A transfer of property on certain conditions for stated purposes.

Assignee. A person to whom anything is assigned.

Assignor. The person who assigns.

Balance. Difference between two statements or accounts.

Bankrupt. A person unable to pay his debts.

Bill of Exchange. An order for money to be paid.

Bill of Sale. A contract signed and sealed for the sale of personal property.

Bills Payable. Name given to notes made and to be paid by a party.

Bills Receivable. Notes made and to be paid to a party.

Bond. An instrument or deed providing a money security.

Capital. The amount of assets on which a business is carried on.

Check. An order on a bank for the payment of money.

Capitation. A tax on every male who is of age.

Commission. The amount or proportion charged by an agent in a business transaction.

Company. An association for transacting business.

Consideration. The sum of money or thing for which a transaction is made.

Consign. To send goods, etc., to a party.

Consignee. One to whom goods are consigned.

Consignor. One who consigns goods.

Contract. A bargain or agreement.

Conveyance. A document transferring property.

Days of Grace. Three days legally allowed beyond the date for payment.

Debit. To make debtor in an account or books.

Default. Failure to pay.

Discount. A sum taken from a bill or note.

Dividend. Interest on stock investments, etc.

Draft. An order for the payment of a certain sum

Drawer. One who draws a draft, etc.

Drawee. The person on whom the draft is drawn.

Effects. Property of every description.

Entry. A record made in books of account.

Executor. One appointed to carry out the provisions of a will.

Exhibit. A writing or official statement.

Face. The sum named in a note, etc.

Failure. A bankruptcy.

Firm. The style or name of a company under which it transacts business.

Foreclose. To deprive a mortgagor by legal process of his right of redemption.

Goods. A term applied generally to merchandise, etc.

Gross. Entire, as gross receipts. Twelve dozen.

Guarantee. A security.

Honor. To accept and pay a note, draft, etc.

Hypothecate. To make a security of.

Indorsement. A signature on the back of a bill, note, etc.

Insolvent. Unable to pay all debts.

Interest. A certain proportion of a sum as profit; a share.

Inventory. A catalogue, or list.

Joint Stock. Stock held by more than one person, or in company.

Judgment. Decree of court to pay in a suit.

Lease. A usually written contract for hiring of land or buildings.

Legal Tender. Money decreed by the Government to be legal and a proper means of payment.

Letter of Credit. A letter giving a certain credit to a person named therein.

Letters Patent. A written instrument granting certain rights and powers.

Letters of Administration. The instrument granting authority to administrators.

Lien. A valid claim by reason of some debt.

Liquidation. The settling and adjustment of accounts.

Maturity. The time when a payment is due.

Mortgage. A conditional conveyance of property giving a right of redemption.

Mortgagor. One giving such a conveyance.

Mortgagee. One to whom such a conveyance is given.

Net. The amount remaining after making all deductions.

Partnership. An association of two or more persons for the transaction of business.

Par Value. The face value.

Payee. The person to whom a payment is due.

Protest. A notary's official notice of non-payment of a note, draft, or check.

Rebate. A reduction in consideration of prompt payment.

Receipt. A written acknowledgment of payment.

Salvage. Compensation for assistance in saving a vessel.

Schedule. An inventory.

Set-off. A claim off-setting a debt.

Sight. The time when a draft is presented.

Suspend. To stop payment.

Silent Partner. One who furnishes capital but whose name does not appear in a firm.

Sterling. The British standard of coinage.

Scrip. A certificate of joint stock.

Staple. A standard commodity or production.

Teller. A bank official who pays out and receives money.

Transfer. A conveyance of right, property or title.

Voucher. A document proving a receipt or other fact.

NAUTICAL VOCABULARY.

Abaft. Toward the stern.

About. To take the opposite tack.

Anchor. The heavy piece of iron which holds the ship at rest.

Alee. On the side away from the wind.

Astern. In the direction of the stern.

Athwart. In a line across the ship.

Beating. Sailing against the wind by tacking.

Bow. The front of a vessel.

Bend. To fasten; as, to bend on a rope.

Berth. A ship's anchorage, or a narrow shelf for sleeping on.

Block. A pulley.

Bolt Rope. The rope surrounding the sail to which it is sewed.

Brace. A rope attached to a boom or yard by which they are moved.

Boom. The spar at the bottom of a sail by which it is extended.

Bulkhead. A partition within the hull.

Bulwarks. The sides of a vessel surrounding and extending above the deck.

Cable. A strong rope or chain.

Caboose. A kitchen on deck.

Camel. An arrangement for assisting a ship over shoals.

Carry Away. To break or lose a rope or spar.

Cat Block. The tackle block for hoisting the anchor.

Cat's Paw. A light puff of wind.

Caulk. To make tight the seams of a vessel.

Clew. To bind up.

Clew Lines. Ropes for clewing.

Combings. The raised edges around the hatches.

Cock Pit. A room for wounded men in a war vessel.

Companionway. The cabin stairway.

Compass. An instrument showing the vessel's course

Coxswain. The steerer of a small boat.

Deadlight. An iron shutter covering a port hole.

Dead Reckoning. The keeping the course of a vessel with the use of log line and compass.

Deck. The covering or floor to a ship.

Draught. The depth of water required to float a vessel.

Fathom. Six feet.

Fender. A piece of wood or other material to prevent the contact of two vessels.

Footrope. A rope extending along and under a yard on which the seamen stand.

Fore and Aft. From bow to stern.

Forecastle. That part forward of the foremast.

Foremast. The mast nearest the bow.

Forge. To move slowly ahead

Founder. To sink.

Furl. To roll up.

Gaff. The upper spar holding up a fore and aft sail.

Galley. The kitchen.

Gangway. An entrance to a ship.

Grapnel. A small anchor.

Halyards. Ropes for hoisting sails.

Hatch, or Hatchway. An opening in the deck.

Heave to. To stop by bringing a ships bow to the wind.

Hold. The interior of a vessel.

Hull. The body only of a vessel.

Jaw. The mast end of a boom or gaff.

Jib. A triangular sail at a ship's bow.

Jurymast. A temporary mast.

Jibe. To shift a sail from one side to the other.

Keel. The lowest timber in a ship.

Knot. A nautical mile.

Larbord. The left hand of a ship looking toward the bow.

Launch. To let a ship slide into the water.

Lead. A mass of lead used in sounding.

Lee. Away from the wind.

Leeway. The lee motion or space of water.

Locker. A chest or box.

Log or Logline. A rope used for measuring the speed of a vessel.

Log or Logbook. The ship's record or diary.

Luff. To bring a ship nearer to the wind.

Manrope. A rope used in going up or down the ship's side.

Mast. An upright piece of timber set in a ship for supporting sails, rigging, etc.

Masthead. The head or top of a mast.

Mess. A number of men eating together.

Midships. The middle, or widest part of a ship.

Mizzenmast; Mizzensail. The hindmost when there are three.

Moor. To secure a ship in any position.

Nip. A short turn, as in a rope.

Painter. A rope used to secure a boat to anything.

Pay Out. To slacken or give out, as to pay out a rope.

Peak. The upper and outer corner of a boom sail.

Pintle. The bolt on which a rudder is hung.

Port. The same as larbord.

Port or Porthole. An opening in a ship's side to admit light and air.

Quarter. The stern portion of a ship's side.

Rake. The inclination of a mast.

Reef. A portion of the sail which is clewed up when the wind is too high to expose the whole.

Reef. To take up such a portion.

Reeve. To pass the end of a rope through a pully, etc.

Rigging. A term applied generally to a vessel's ropes, etc.

Road. An open space of water where ships may anchor.

Rowlock. Arrangement for giving purchase to an oar in rowing.

Rudder. The contrivance which steers a vessel.

Scud. To sail before a heavy wind or gale.

Sail. The sheet of canvas which is exposed to the wind and gives motion to the vessel.

Seams.   Where the ship's planks join.
Sheet.   A rope for controlling and moving a sail.
Shore.   A prop under a beam.
Skipper.   The name given generally to the master of a small vessel.
Sloop.   A vessel with but one mast.
Sound.   To ascertain the depth of the water.
Spar.   A name applied to a mast, boom, gaff, yard, etc.
Stern.   The rear portion of a vessel.
Stay.   A rope supporting or keeping in place a mast.
Tack.   To go against the wind in a zig-zag course, and to change a
    ship's course by shifting her rudder and sails.
Taut.   Tight.
Thwarts.   A boat's seats.
Tiller.   A bar for moving a rudder.
Trick.   A sailor's duration of time in steering.
Warp.   To move a vessel by a line fastened at the end to an anchor.
Watch.   A certain portion of time for duty.
Wake.   The track left in the water by a moving vessel.
Weather.   Toward the wind.
Weigh Anchor.   To raise the anchor.
Waist.   That portion of the deck between the quarter-deck and
    forecastle.
Windlass.   A machine for raising the anchor or cargo.
Windward.   The point from whence the wind blows.
Yacht.   A sailing vessel used for pleasure.
Yard.   A spar supporting and extending a sail.
Yardarm.   Either half of a yard.
Yaw.   A movement causing a temporary change of course.

DICTIONARY OF MUSICAL TERMS.

Accompaniment.   A secondary part added to the principal for the
    improvement of the general effect.
Adagio.   A slow movement.
Ad libitum.   Implies that the time of the movement is left to
    the discretion of the performer.
Allegretto.   With cheerful quickness.
Andante.   Somewhat sedate; slowly.
Animato, Animaso, or Con Anima.   Animated; with spirit.
Assai.   Very; used as an adverb with another word.
A temp.   In regular time.
Beat.   An indication of a certain duration of time.
Ben.   Implying well as Ben marcato.
Calando.   A gradual diminution in speed and tone.
Chromatic.   Proceeding or formed by semi-tones.
Con.   With; as Con expressione.
Crescndo.   A gradual increase in tone.
Da.   By.   *Delicato.*   With delicacy.
Dales, or Dal.   In a soft, quiet manner.
Doloroso.   In a melancholy, sad style.

Espressioo, or *Con esspressione.* With expression.

Fine. The end. *Fork,* or *For.* Strong, loud.

Furioso. With great animation. *Giusto.* In perfect time.

Grave. The slowest time or movement.

Gusto, Con gusto. With style; taste. *Il.* The.

Impetuoso. Impetuously. *In.* In; as in tempo.

Intrado, or *Introduzione.* An introduction to a piece of music.

Largo. A slow and solemn degree of time.

Legato. In a smooth, even manner. *Leggiando.* Lightly.

Marcato. In a marked manner. *Meme.* The same.

Mezzo. In a medium degree; as Mezzo forte.

Moderato. Moderately. *Malto.* Very; as Malto forte

Movimento. Movement; time. *Nobile.* Grandly; impressively.

Obligato. An essential portion of a composition.

Ottava, or *8va.* An octave.

Pedale, or *Ped.* Signifies that performer must press down pedal

Pen. A little. *Piano,* or *P.* Soft.

Pianissimo, or *PP.* Very soft. *Plus.* More.

Poco a poco. Gradually; by a regular gradation.

Pomposo. Pompously. *Precipitato.* Very quickly; hurriedly.

Premiere. First; as Premiere fois; first time.

Presto. Very quick. *Primo.* As Violino primo, first violin.

Quasi. In the manner of; like *Quieto.* With repose, quietly

Rapido. Rapidly. *Rinforzando.* Rinf. or Rf. with increase.

Ritenente, Ritenato. Decreasing in speed.

Segno. Sign, as al segno, go back to sign.

Sempre. Always, as Sempre piano. *Serioso.* Seriously.

Solo, Sola. Alone. A composition rendered by one person.

Sostenuto or *Sost.* Prolonged, sustained.

Spirito. With spirit.

Staccato. Each note to be distinctly marked.

Stesso. The same.

Syncopation. Connecting the last note of a bar with the first note
of the following, thus forming one prolonged note with a
duration equal to the two.

Syncopate. In a syncopated style. *Tanto or Ton.* Not so much.

Tardo. Slowly. *Tempo Comodo.* Conveniently.

Theme. A subject. *Tranquillo.* Tranquilly.

Tremendi. With terrific expression.

Tremando, Tremolo. The rapid striking of a note so as to produce
a tremulous effect.

Trille, or *Trillo.* A trill or shake.

Trio. A composition for three performers.

Triplet. A group of three notes equal in duration of time to two
notes of the same value.

Un A. As un poco, a little.

Veloce. Rapidly.

Velocissimo. With great rapidity.

Vigoroso. With vigor.

Vivace. Vivamented; briskly.

Volti Subito. Turn over quickly.